Springer Series in Design and Innovation 39

Springer Series in Design and Innovation (SSDI) publishes books on innovation and the latest developments in the fields of Product Design, Interior Design and Communication Design, with particular emphasis on technological and formal innovation, and on the application of digital technologies and new materials. The series explores all aspects of design, e.g. Human-Centered Design/User Experience, Service Design, and Design Thinking, which provide transversal and innovative approaches oriented on the involvement of people throughout the design development process. In addition, it covers emerging areas of research that may represent essential opportunities for economic and social development.

In fields ranging from the humanities to engineering and architecture, design is increasingly being recognized as a key means of bringing ideas to the market by transforming them into user-friendly and appealing products or services. Moreover, it provides a variety of methodologies, tools and techniques that can be used at different stages of the innovation process to enhance the value of new products and services.

The series' scope includes monographs, professional books, advanced textbooks, selected contributions from specialized conferences and workshops, and outstanding Ph.D. theses.

The volumes of the series are single-blind peer-reviewed.

Keywords: Product and System Innovation; Product design; Interior design; Communication Design; Human-Centered Design/User Experience; Service Design; Design Thinking; Digital Innovation; Innovation of Materials.

How to submit proposals

Proposals must include: title, keywords, presentation (max 10,000 characters), table of contents, chapter abstracts, editors'/authors' CV.

In case of proceedings, chairmen/editors are requested to submit the link to conference website (incl. relevant information such as committee members, topics, key dates, keynote speakers, information about the reviewing process, etc.), and approx. number of papers.

Proposals must be sent to publishing editor Mr. Pierpaolo Riva (pierpaolo.riva@springer.com).

Sangeun Jin · Jeong Ho Kim · Yong-Ku Kong ·
Jaehyun Park · Myung Hwan Yun
Editors

Proceedings of the 22nd Congress of the International Ergonomics Association, Volume 1

Better Life Ergonomics for Future Humans (IEA 2024)

Springer

Editors
Sangeun Jin
Industrial Engineering
Pusan National University
Busan, Korea (Republic of)

Yong-Ku Kong
Industrial Engineering
Sungkyunkwan University
Jangan-Gu, Suwon-Si, Kyonggi-do, Korea (Republic of)

Myung Hwan Yun
Department of Industrial Engineering
Seoul National University
Gwanak-Gu, Soul-t'ukpyolsi, Korea (Republic of)

Jeong Ho Kim
Oregon State University
Corvallis, OR, USA

Jaehyun Park
Department of Industrial and Management Engineering
Incheon National University
Incheon, Korea (Republic of)

ISSN 2661-8184 ISSN 2661-8192 (electronic)
Springer Series in Design and Innovation
ISBN 978-981-95-0210-3 ISBN 978-981-95-0211-0 (eBook)
https://doi.org/10.1007/978-981-95-0211-0

This Springer imprint is published by the registered company Springer Nature Singapore Pte Ltd.
The registered company address is: 152 Beach Road, #21-01/04 Gateway East, Singapore 189721, Singapore

Preface

This proceedings book is a publication of selected excellent papers presented at the World Congress on Ergonomics, the International Ergonomics Association 2024 (IEA 2024), held in Jeju Island, Republic of Korea, in August 2024. Representatives from over 50 countries, totaling approximately 1,600 ergonomics professionals, attended the event to present their outstanding research findings in the field of ergonomics and share their insights. About 1100 abstracts and full papers were presented, and all were subjected to a stringent peer review process that ensured both anonymity and double-blinding. Only submissions meeting the established standards were selected for inclusion in the conference proceedings.

The proceedings aim to encompass a broad spectrum of theories and applications within human factors and ergonomics (HFE). This multidisciplinary field is dedicated to understanding the interactions between humans and various systems, products, environments, and technologies. The volume covers a diverse range of scientific areas, including engineering, design, human biology, psychology, and so forth. It explores the application of human factors and ergonomics across various domains such as healthcare, medicine, transportation, aviation, automotive, construction, mining, manufacturing, agricultural engineering, education, and sustainable development.

The themes of the IEA 2024 conference and the structure of the papers included in each volume of the proceedings are as follows:

IEA 2024 Conference Theme: "**Better Life Ergonomics for Future Humans**"

Volume I: Affective Design (I), Aging (I), Agriculture (I), AI (I), Anthropometry (I), ATWAD (I), Aviation (I), Bio-signal (I), Building and Construction (I).

Volume II: Building and Construction (I), Design (I), DHM (I), Gender (I), Healthcare (I), HMI (I), Macro-ergonomics (I), Manufacturing (I).

Volume III: Manufacturing (I), Musculoskeletal (I), Product (I), Resilience (I), Robotics (I), Safety and Health (I), Slips (I), Sustainable Development (I), Training Education (I).

Volume IV: Training Education (I), Transport (I), UI/UX (I), Visual (I), VR/AR Metaverse (I), Others (I).

Volume V: Others (I), Affective Design (II), Aging (II), Agriculture (II), AI (II), Anthropometry (II), ATWAD (II), Bio-signal (II), Design (II), DHM (II), Healthcare (II), HMI (II), Macro-ergonomics (II), Manufacturing (II), Musculoskeletal (II), Product (II), Resilience (II), Safety and Health (II).

Volume VI: Safety and Health (II), Slips (II), Sustainable Development (II), Training Education (II), Transport (II), UI/UX (II), Visual (II), VR/AR Metaverse (II), Others (II), Affective Design (III), AI (III), Anthropometry (III), ATWAD (III), Bio-signal (III), Building and Construction (III), Design (III), DHM (III), Healthcare (III), Macro-ergonomics (III), Manufacturing (III), Musculoskeletal (III), Product (III), Robotics (III) Safety and Health (III), Space (III), Sustainable Development (III), Training Education (III), Transport (III), UI/UX (III), Visual (III), Others (III).

Organization

Editor-in-Chief of the Proceeding Book (Volumes I–V)

Name & Title	Address	Email & URL
Yong-Ku Kong Professor, Ph.D., CPE.	2066, Seobu-ro, Jangan-gu, Suwon-si, Gyeonggi-do, 16419, Republic of Korea Dept. of Industrial Engineering, Sungkyunkwan University	ykong@skku.edu https://sites.google.com/site/skkuergospace/

Editors of the Proceeding Book (Volumes I–V)

Name & Title	Address	Email & URL
Myung Hwan Yun Professor, Ph.D.	Building #39, 1 Gwanak-ro, Gwanak-gu, Seoul, 08826, Republic of Korea. Dept. of Industrial Engineering, Seoul National University	mhy@snu.ac.kr https://his.snu.ac.kr/
Jaehyun Park Professor, Ph.D.	120 Neungdon-ro, Gwangjin-gu, Seoul 05029, Republic of Korea Dept. of Industrial Engineering, Kunkuk University	jaehpark@inu.ac.kr https://sites.google.com/site/uvlabinu/
Sangeun Jin Associate Professor, Ph.D.	2, Busandaehak-ro 63beon-gil, Geumjeong-gu, Busan, 46241, Republic of Korea Dept. of Industrial Engineering, Pusan National University	sangeunjin@pusan.ac.kr https://hse.pusan.ac.kr/hse/index.do
Jeong Ho Kim Associate Professor, PhD.	212 Adriance Lab Rd., College Station, TX 77843-1266, USA. Environmental and Occupational Health, Texas A&M University	Jay.kim@oregonstate.edu https://health.oregonstate.edu/labs/oeb

Contents

Affective Design (I)

Affective Design (I)

Affective Design of Shopping Bags to Promote Recycling

Jenna Cristina B. Balasbas, Leanne Jessica O. Co, Rosemary R. Seva(✉), and Svettlana Marie S. Vera

Industrial and Systems Engineering, De La Salle University, Manila, Philippines
rosemary.seva@dlsu.edu.ph

Abstract. This study investigates how design manipulations, specifically in color, pattern, and shape, affect behavioral responses in the context of recycling. The experiment involved three independent variables, each at two levels: color, pattern, and shape of a bag. Eight different bags were evaluated using a between-subjects design. Ninety-six participants took part in a masked experiment that required them to evaluate fabric and scissors. Each participant was provided with an experimental bag containing all the necessary materials. After the experiment, participants were asked to dispose of the waste generated, with a trash bin placed at the exit of the room to facilitate disposal. One week later, participants were interviewed about their recycling behavior to determine what they had done with the bag. Recycling behavior was rated on a 4-point scale. The study validated that affective design features, such as color and pattern, significantly influence consumers' recycling decisions. Additionally, the interaction between color and pattern on the shopping paper bag was found to be significant, indicating that the presence of both features enhances recycling behavior.

Keywords: sustainability · affective design · recycling

1 Introduction

With the rapid growth of the global apparel industry [1], an increase in packaging consumption is inevitable. Aside from providing protection for the product, it is also a factor that influences the consumer at the point of sale [2]. It is also a critical component to building a brand's identity and image by supporting the brand's strategy of expressing its identity to different markets and engage customers [3]. Among the different types of packaging, the one in direct contact with the product and with the customer is the primary packaging which is the shopping paper bag in the context of the fast fashion industry. Aside from the packaging function, companies hope that customers will continue to use the bags they provided to promote their brand name.

Shopping paper bag is one of the most sought-after types of shopping bag along with plastic shopping bag [4]. Given the extensive usage of shopping paper bags, especially since the Total Plastic Bag Ban Act has been passed into law in the Philippines [5] the recyclability of shopping paper bags is an opportunity to minimize the overall waste being

S. Jin et al. (Eds.): IEA 2024, SSDI 39, pp. 3–8, 2025.
https://doi.org/10.1007/978-981-95-0211-0_1

thrown into landfills. It was found that by partaking in social behaviors such as recycling, individual consumers can positively bring about large-scale environmental changes [6]. The success of any recycling program is predominantly dependent on the participation of consumers; thus, it is crucial to understand what drives consumers' disposal decisions. A significant portion of what ends up in landfills is recyclable material indicating the necessity for understanding the underlying psychological processes behind recycling behavior [7].

Past studies showed that environmental issues can be addressed by integrating aesthetics into the product. Aesthetics contribute to the recyclability of a product because of consumer attachment [8]. Affective design is a methodology that incorporates the customer's feelings into the design process by translating feelings into design elements that can elicit positive emotional responses from the consumers [9]. The positive emotional response affects consumer behavior such as keeping the product for longer periods of time.

In the study of consumer perception, it was revealed that packaging design elements, such as graphics, color, and product information, are profoundly involved in the decision-making of consumers. Thus, the preferences and behavior of consumers are the prime issues that must be considered when designing a new package since the customers' choices and desires drive the marketing process.

Previous studies have not determined the influence of a paper bag's affective properties such as color, shape, and pattern on the consumer's disposal decision. Montazeri et al., [10] studied the variations in different levels of saliency for color while Trudel et al. [7] and Trudel et al. [6] considered the effect of size and distortion from its original shape, of piece of paper and aluminum can, respectively. Ruumpol [11] studied the influence of packaging shape and color on the product's perceived healthfulness, and not its recyclability. Therefore, this study investigated how manipulations in design, particularly in these three features, can affect people's behavioral responses in the context of recycling.

2 Method

2.1 Participants

The required number of samples computed considering a confidence level of 90% and an assigned margin of error of 0.25 is 73. However, the experimental design required 96 participants, so this number of participants was recruited. The number of males and females was equal in the sample.

2.2 Independent Variables

The independent variables were the configurations of the shopping paper bag: color, pattern, and shape. The setting of the factors was chosen based on a previous survey conducted to determine the most preferred color and pattern of existing shoppers in the Philippines. Participants chose between the five primary hues from the Munsell Color System which are: Red, Blue, Yellow, Purple, and Green while pattern options included

5 different patterns that are already existing in the market which are: Checkered, Polka Dots, Gingham, Chevron, and Stripes. As for the shape, wide bottom, and wide top were the only options. The most preferred color and pattern were compared to the kraft paper bag (brown). Samples of the paper bags can be seen in Fig. 1.

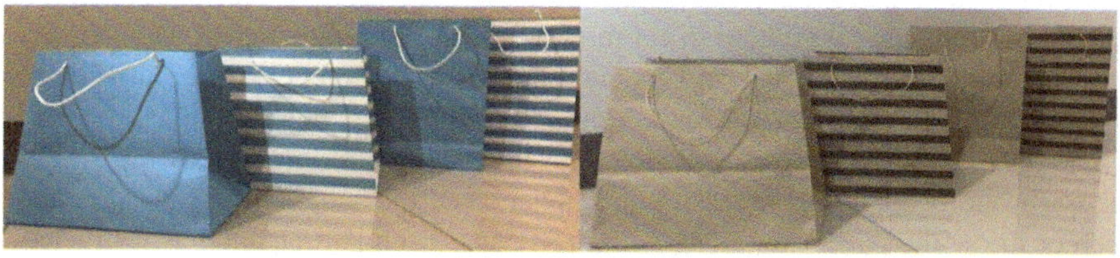

Fig. 1. Sample shopping paper bags

2.3 Dependent Variables

The dependent variable was the subject's recycling decision rated as follows: 1-threw the bag outside the room or on the floor; 2-threw the bag in the school; 3-brought the bag home; 4-brought the bag home and reused; and 5-brought the bag home, reused, and kept.

2.4 Experimental Design

Eight types of shopping paper bags with unique configurations in terms of color, pattern, and shape were used corresponding to a two-level full factorial design. The setting of the independent variables is summarized in Table 1.

Table 1. Setting of independent variables

Factor	Level 1	Level 2
Color	Kraft	Blue
Pattern	Plain	Stripes
Shape	Straight bottom	Wide bottom

2.5 Procedure

The experiment was conducted in a laboratory room at a University. Once inside the room, the participants were not allowed to leave until they have finished the experiment or informed the researchers that they do not want to continue with the experiment. Participants encoded their personal information and answered the post-experiment questions on a computer in the venue. Each participant was asked to sign a written consent form for the experiment. Only fast fashion shoppers were included in the experiment through a screening process.

In the experiment, the participants were given a shopping paper bag, a pair of scissors, 3 different types of cloth: Nylon, Acrylic, and Polyester, each having a different color (Pink for Nylon, Green for Acrylic, and White for Polyester), a piece of paper, and a piece of plastic. They were told to cut the fabric using a certain pattern and choose the material that is easiest to cut and evaluate the scissors used. The recycling behavior assessment was assessed after they left the room. By instructing the subjects to cut all 5 materials using the scissors provided, they were forced to throw away the scraps in the trash bin located outside the room. This allowed the subject to decide whether to keep or throw the paper bag along with the scraps. Each participant was instructed to leave the room after the experiment and leave nothing on the table except the scissors placed inside the box. Placed beside the exit is a trash bin where the subject may throw away the scraps, and the shopping paper bag. The participant's recycling was assessed by determining how the bag was disposed of and when. After a week, the participants were contacted to know what they have done with the paper bag.

2.6 Statistical Analysis

Analysis of Variance (ANOVA) was used to determine the significant main effects and interactions affecting recycling behavior. Data were analyzed using SPSS 21.0. The significance level considered was 0.05.

3 Results

A 3-way between groups ANOVA was used to examine the main effects and interactions of color, shape, and pattern as they relate to the recycling behavior of participants. There are two significant main effects: color ($F(1, 89) = 7.66$, $p < 0.01$) and pattern ($F(1, 89) = 5.92$, $p = 0.02$). The interaction between color and pattern is also significant ($F(1, 89) = 4.4$, $p = 0.04$).

The interaction plot for the ratings in Fig. 2 shows the mean rating of recycling behavior for every pairwise comparison of the factors. It can be seen that the interaction between color and pattern has the highest interaction as evidenced by the slope of the lines. The mean recyclability rating for blue, paired with any pattern or shape, is always higher than that of kraft.

The outcome of the study was consistent with Ksenia's [12] where color was the most noticeable design packaging element that influenced consumer behavior. The blue paper bag had a higher average recyclability rating than kraft paper bags with means of 3.685 and 3, respectively. In a related study, Montazeri et al. [10] found a significant difference in people's recycling behavior depending on the color of the trash bin. Recycling was higher for green bins compared to grey bins probably because of its salience and perceived meaning. It was apparent that the meaning of color has an effect on a person's decision to throw trash or keep it. In the case of the shopping bag in this study, participants during the debriefing expressed that the kraft shopping paper bags

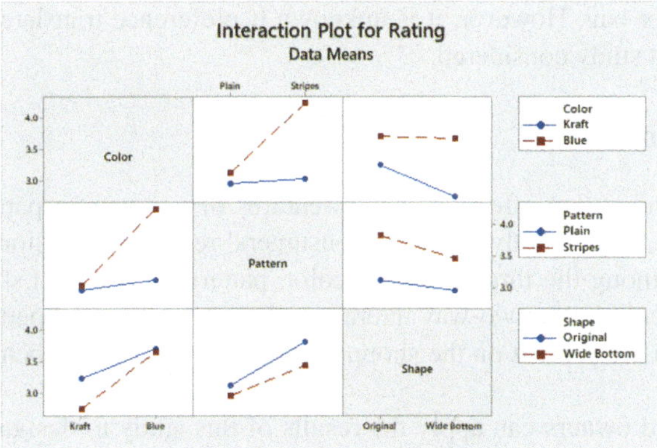

Fig. 2. Interaction Plot for Rating

are viewed to have a lower quality, diminishing their intention to recycle. This kind of paper bag is also commonly compared to the blue paper bag. When asked if another color of a paper bag will also prompt them to recycle, the intention had been contingent on the color of the paper bag. They preferred a bag of their favorite color or neutral. The significance of color can also be explained by Jonauskaite et al's [13] findings that blue is the most common favorite color for both males and females and that there was no significant difference in the percentages of males and females who chose blue as their favorite color.

This study is the first one to consider the effect of shape on the recycling behavior of paper bags. Packaging shape was previously studied by Ruumpol [11] which found that it affects the consumer's perception of a product's healthiness. Hassan et al. [14] also discovered that the packaging shape has a positive influence on consumers' purchasing decisions. The paper bags used in the experiment came in two shapes: one was the typical shape of a paper bag where the width of the bottom is of the same size as the width of the top; the other shape has a wider width at the bottom than at the top and thus has a trapezoidal face. Some respondents who were given wide bottom paper bags in the experiment mentioned that they prefer the normal paper bag as this was less difficult to store and because with its narrow bottom, the contents of the bag would move less and be steadier and more firmly fixed in position, unlike in the wide bottom paper bag, where the contents would be more likely to move and scatter around inside. In the end, however, they still chose to keep the wide bottom paper bag, passing the threshold of recycling, which is 3. There were also some respondents who favored the wide-bottom shopping paper bag as it allowed them to carry more items and because of its uniqueness in shape. These observations align with Ksenia's [12] argument that shape is an important attribute of packaging from a logistics point of view. However, there was no significant difference between the two shapes in relation to the dependent variable.

Another significant factor in the experiment is the pattern. This result validates the findings of Park & John [15] where respondents prefer to carry around a Victoria's Secret shopping paper bag with pink and red undertones with vertical stripes compared to using a plain pink paper bag. However, it is unknown if preference translates into recycling which the current study considered.

4 Conclusion

The study confirmed that affective design features of a shopping paper bag, such as color and pattern, significantly influence consumers' recycling decisions. Additionally, the interaction among the three features (color, pattern, and shape) showed a significant effect, particularly the two-way interaction between color and pattern. When both color and pattern are present on the shopping paper bag, recycling behavior is notably enhanced.

Fashion brand owners can apply the results of this study to design their bags in a way that promotes recycling. They should consider using colors other than kraft, as it is common and often perceived as low quality. Although well-designed shopping bags may be more expensive, they can enhance the brand's image and serve as an effective marketing tool.

References

1. Singh, G.: Fast fashion has changed the industry and the economy - foundation for economic education. City (2017)
2. Kuvykaite, R., Navickiene, L.: Impact of package elements on consumer's purchase decision. Econ. Manag. **14**, 441–447 (2009)
3. Ghodeswar, B.M.: Building brand identity in competitive markets: a conceptual model. J. Product Brand Manag. **17**(1), 4–12 (2008)
4. Muthu, S.S., Li, Y., Hu, J., Mok, T., Ding, X.: Eco-Impact of Plastic and Paper Shopping Bags. J. Eng. Fibers Fabrics. **7**, 26–37 (2012)
5. Biona, J. B. M. M., Gonzaga, J. A., Ubando, A. T., Tan, H. C.: A comparative life cycle analysis of plastic and paper packaging bags in the Philippines. City
6. Trudel, R., Arg, J.J., Meng, M.D.: The recycled self: Consumers' disposal decisions of identity-linked products. J. Consum. Res. **43**(2), 246–264 (2016)
7. Trudel, R., Argo, J.J., Meng, M.D.: Trash or recycle? How product distortion leads to categorization error during disposal. Environ. Behav. **48**(7), 966–985 (2015)
8. Walker, S.: Experiments in sustainable product design. J. Sustain. Prod. Des. **7**, 41–50 (1998)
9. Jiao, J., Zhang, Y., Helander, M.: A Kansei mining system for affective design. Expert Syst. Appl. **30**(4), 658–673 (2006)
10. Montazeri, S., Gonzalez, R. D., Yoon, C., Papalambros, P. Y.: Color, cognition, and recycling: how the design of everyday objects prompt behavior change. Dubrovnik-Croatia (2012)
11. Ruumpol, I.: In the eye of the consumer: the influence of package shape and package color on perceived product healthfulness (2014)
12. Ksenia, P.: Packaging design as a marketing tool and desire to purchase (2013)
13. Jonauskaite, D., Dael, N., Chèvre, L., Althaus, B., Tremea, A., Charalambides, L., Mohr, C.: Pink for girls, red for boys, and blue for both genders : colour preferences in children and adults. Sex Roles. **80**(9), 630–642 (2018)
14. Hassan, S.H., Lee, W.L., Peng, W.W.: The influence of food product packaging attributes in purchase decision: a study among consumers in Penang, Malaysia. J. Agribusiness Market. **5**, 14–28 (2012)
15. Park, J.K., John, D.R.: Got to get you into my life: Do brand personalities rub off on consumers? J. Consum. Res. **37**(4), 655–669 (2010)

Exploring the Dynamics of Affect and Cognitive Assessment in Trust and Reliance on Decision Support Systems in Healthcare

Ezekiel Bernardo[1(✉)], Rosemary Seva[1], Angelimarie Miguel[1], Karen Sagun[2,3], Adrian Joseph Estrella[2], and John James Jovellano[2]

[1] Industrial and Systems Engineering Department, Gokongwei College of Engineering, De La Salle University, Manila, Philippines
ezekiel.bernardo@dlsu.edu.ph
[2] Quezon City Center for Children with Disabilities, Quezon City, Philippines
[3] College of Rehabilitation Sciences, University of Santo Tomas, Manila, Philippines

Abstract. In the convergence of healthcare and technology, Decision Support Systems (DSS) hold promise for enhancing accessibility and efficiency, particularly in underserved regions like the Philippines. This study explores the impact of cognitive (perceived usefulness) and affective (emotional responses) components on trust and reliance in DSS among 219 Filipino parents. Findings reveal that while cognitive factors foster trust, it is the affective dimension that primarily drives reliance. Moderating effects of trust disposition and technological anxiety were also examined, highlighting the importance of emotional engagement and clear communication. The results emphasize the need for user-centric DSS designs that evoke positive emotions and provide transparent information to build trust and reliance.

Keywords: Privacy policies · trust · comprehension · digital privacy · user-centric design

1 Background of the Study

In an era marked by rapid technological advancements, the convergence of healthcare and technology has emerged as a pivotal frontier, aimed at bridging gaps in accessibility and efficiency. The integration of Artificial Intelligence (AI) into healthcare systems exemplifies this synergy, offering the potential to revolutionize how medical professionals diagnose, treat, and manage patient care (Maghsoudi et al. 2020). One of the most significant benefits of this technological convergence is the harnessing of AI's computational power to facilitate complex decision-making processes, a critical necessity in the healthcare domain.

A prime example of AI's transformative potential in healthcare is the Decision Support System (DSS). These systems provide healthcare professionals with enhanced analytical tools, enabling more informed and accurate decision-making (Biller-Andorno

S. Jin et al. (Eds.): IEA 2024, SSDI 39, pp. 9–14, 2025.
https://doi.org/10.1007/978-981-95-0211-0_2

et al. 2021). Particularly in regions like the Philippines, where the ratio of patients to healthcare professionals is disproportionately high, DSS can offer valuable support by supplementing the efforts of overburdened medical staff.

The primary metric for evaluating the efficacy of DSS has traditionally been its accuracy (Matteo et al. 2021). Higher predictive capabilities are often equated with greater utility and reliability. However, despite significant advancements in algorithmic development and the availability of sophisticated hardware, a critical issue persists: the adoption of these systems. This issue is often measured through the levels of trust in the system and the overall reliance on it by healthcare professionals (Deley and Dubois 2020).

Delving deeper into the problem, it becomes apparent that the high accuracy of DSS alone does not guarantee widespread adoption. Beyond cognitive aspects of trust, such as logical evaluation of system performance, there is a need to consider the affective components—emotions and feelings that influence user behavior. In this context, cognitive trust is often measured through perceived usefulness, while affective trust is gauged by the emotions felt by users. The foundational studies of human-computer interaction reveal that these irrational or affective components play a significant role in shaping user behavior and system adoption (Onnasch and Laudine 2021).

Emotional responses have been shown to be powerful determinants of behavior change across various fields of study. In the context of e-commerce, for instance, positive emotions drive the adoption of online shopping platforms and social media applications (Li et al. 2024). Conversely, negative emotions can lead to dissatisfaction with other systems. The importance of the affective component extends to AI and DSS, where the emotional experiences of users can significantly impact their trust and reliance on these technologies.

Design elements and the superficial components of a system often evoke emotional responses, a concept rooted in Kansei engineering (Ismail and Lokman 2020). Unlike human interactions, where trust is cultivated through interpersonal dynamics, interactions with DSS involve patients and healthcare professionals responding to algorithms, which lack traditional cues for trust evaluation. This unique dynamic raises a crucial question: *Is the affective component, or the emotional response, important for fostering trust and reliance necessary for the adoption of DSS in healthcare?* To supplement answering this, paper aims to address by:

- Examining the role of affect and relative importance of cognitive in trust building and reliance
- Unraveling the different aspect of DSS that is important to trigger affect
- Understanding the moderating impact of user characteristics in the adoption

This research aims to address this question by exploring the impact of affective components on trust and reliance in DSS within the healthcare sector. By examining the interplay between emotional responses and system adoption including the user's characteristics, this study seeks to uncover insights that can guide the design of more effective and trustworthy DSS. Ultimately, this research endeavors to contribute to the ongoing discourse on how to enhance the adoption of AI-driven technologies in healthcare, ensuring they fulfill their potential to improve patient care and healthcare outcomes.

2 Review of Related Literature

2.1 Cognitive Evaluation and Affective Assessment

In human-computer interaction (HCI), cognitive factors like perceived usefulness are critical predictors of trust and reliance. Derived from previous technology adoption model, perceived usefulness indicates that users' belief in a system's effectiveness significantly influences their willingness to trust and depend on it. Numerous studies support this, showing that when users find a system useful, they are more likely to trust and rely on it for essential tasks (Venkatesh et al. 2011; Abbad 2021). For example, in healthcare, the perceived usefulness of Decision Support Systems (DSS) is linked to increased trust among professionals, leading to greater reliance on these systems for diagnostic and treatment recommendations (Bussone et al. 2015).

While cognitive assessments are essential, the impact of affective factors, particularly emotions, is increasingly recognized in HCI research. Emotional responses to technology significantly influence users' trust and reliance. Positive emotions, such as joy and satisfaction, enhance trust and reliance by fostering safety and confidence (Dirin et al. 2023). Conversely, negative emotions, like frustration and anxiety, reduce trust and deter system engagement. In DSS, emotional engagement is vital; users often rely on intuitive feelings rather than solely rational evaluations, especially when lacking technical expertise (Antoniadi et al. 2021).

2.2 User Characteristics

Trust disposition, defined as an individual's general tendency to trust others, plays a critical moderating role in the relationship between cognitive and affective predictors and trust in HCI. Individuals with a high trust disposition are more likely to extend trust to technology based on perceived usefulness and positive emotional experiences (McKnight et al. 2020). This propensity can amplify the effects of both cognitive and affective factors, leading to higher trust and reliance on the system. On the other hand, technological anxiety—an individual's apprehension or fear regarding the use of technology—can significantly dampen these relationships. High levels of technological anxiety can undermine the positive effects of perceived usefulness and emotional engagement, resulting in lower trust and reliance (Müller et al. 2024). Studies indicate that addressing technological anxiety through user education and supportive design can mitigate its negative impact, thereby enhancing overall trust and reliance.

3 Methodology

Anchored by the conceptual framework for this study as shown in Fig. 1, the methodology employed in this study comprised a controlled synchronous experiment designed to gather affect- and cognitive-based assessments from Filipino parents directly overseeing their children's medical history, specifically those categorized as indigent and proficient in Filipino. Utilizing convenience sampling, the study aimed to recruit 100 participants, aligning with the minimum target recommended by Westland (2010) for detecting significant effects. Ethical considerations were addressed through consent forms, clearly outlining the experimental nature and non-medical nature of the study. Participants were introduced to Decision Support System (DSS) concepts and exposed to a sample video from the CDC's Milestone Tracker Application, followed by questions assessing perceived usefulness and emotional responses. The methodology, drawing inspiration from prior research conducted by the research group (Bernardo and Seva 2023), employed covariance-based structural equation modeling to analyze the dynamic relationships among demographic data, disposition stance, perceived usefulness, integral emotion, trust, and reliance.

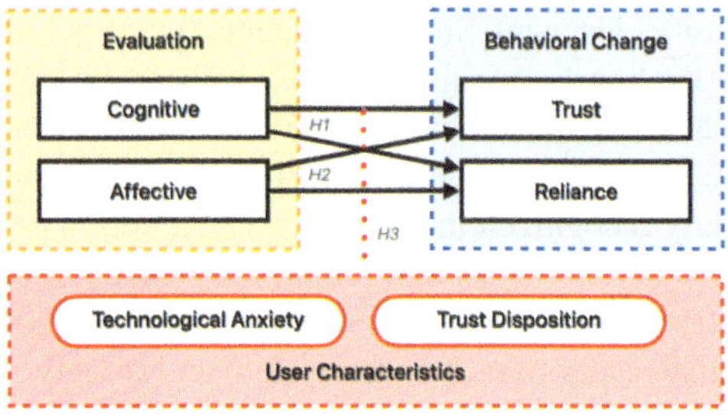

Fig. 1. Healthcare Decision Support System Trust and Reliance Adoption (HDSS-Tram) Model

4 Results and Analysis

The study encompassed a total of 233 participants, of which 219 provided usable data, resulting from 14 participants not completing the interview process. Data gathering spanned a period of 30 days, during which all sessions adhered successfully to the planned methodology, maintaining a cumulative duration of 20 min per participant. No issues were raised during the preliminary stages, and ethical concerns were effectively addressed during the onboarding process. Exploratory factor analysis revealed that the questionnaire measuring trust loaded significantly, without encountering any reliability, consistency, or validity issues. Furthermore, through 1000 bootstrapped structural equation model runs, a good model fit was achieved.

The findings from participants underscored the significant influence of both affective and cognitive components on trust in Decision Support Systems (DSS). While cognitive factors contributed to trust formation, it was the affective dimension that predominantly drove reliance on the system. This observation highlights the multifaceted nature of trust formation in DSS, where cognitive understanding and emotional responses intertwine to shape users' reliance on the system.

Participants emphasized the pivotal role of clear and comprehensive explanations in fostering cognitive trust, emphasizing the importance of transparent communication in building confidence in DSS recommendations. Moreover, the study highlighted the significance of emotional resonance in driving reliance, particularly in contexts where users lacked medical expertise. The reliance on positive emotions, akin to intuitive gut feelings, suggested that users might prioritize subjective feelings of confidence over objective cognitive assessments when entrusting critical healthcare decisions to DSS (Table 1).

Table 1. Structural equation model results

	From	To	Std. Est.	*p*-Value	Supported?	Moderated?	
						TD	*TA*
H1a	Cognitive	Trust	0.523	<0.001	Yes	Yes	Yes
H1b	Cognitive	Reliance	0.031	0.349	No	Yes	Yes
H2a	Affective	Trust	0.665	0.003	Yes	Yes	Yes
H2a	Affective	Reliance	0.816	<0.001	Yes	Yes	Yes

Notes: TD - trust disposition, *TA* - technological anxiety

Importantly, participants expressed a willingness to extend trust beyond traditional healthcare professionals to non-medical individuals if positive emotional responses were evoked, underscoring the profound impact of emotional engagement on trust formation. Participants suggested that making the DSS less robot-like and incorporating human-like interaction methods, along with providing discussions on the rationale behind decisions based on user benefits and drawbacks, could enhance user trust and reliance. Additionally, incorporating designs similar to current social media applications in DSS workflow could evoke more positive affect, enhancing user engagement and trust.

The moderation test further elucidated the importance of trust disposition and technological anxiety in shaping users' trust and reliance tendencies. Individuals with high trust disposition amplified the effect of positive emotions, while those with high technological anxiety exhibited dampened trust and reliance tendencies. Participants suggested that proper introduction of the system, including showcasing its scope, accuracy, and testimonials from other users, could mitigate negative moderations to trust and reliance.

These insights underscore the imperative of designing DSS that not only provide accurate information but also evoke positive emotional responses, thereby fostering a deeper sense of trust and reliance among users. Ultimately, participants indicated that they would rely on DSS if they perceived an emotional connection and a nuanced understanding of their needs.

5 Conclusion and Recommendation

In conclusion, this study highlights the importance of designing healthcare Decision Support Systems (DSS) that elicit positive emotional responses and provide accurate information to foster trust and reliance. The findings emphasize the interplay between affect and cognition in shaping trust in DSS recommendations. By advocating for holistic user experiences, including transparent communication and emotional engagement, the research addresses the complexities of healthcare decision-making in resource-constrained settings like the Philippines. Integrating user-centric design principles that balance cognitive and emotional factors will be essential for enhancing DSS acceptance and adoption, ultimately improving healthcare delivery and outcomes.

References

Abbad, M.M.: Using the UTAUT model to understand students' usage of e-learning systems in developing countries. Educ. Inf. Technol. **26**(6), 7205–7224 (2021)

Antoniadi, A.M., Du, Y., Guendouz, Y., Wei, L., Mazo, C., Becker, B.A., Mooney, C.: Current challenges and future opportunities for XAI in machine learning-based clinical decision support systems: a systematic review. Appl. Sci. **11**(11), 5088 (2021)

Bernardo, E., Seva, R.: Affective analysis of explainable artificial intelligence in the development of trust in AI systems. Intelligent Human Systems Integration (IHSI 2023): Integrating People and Intelligent Systems. **69**(69) (2023)

Biller-Andorno, N., Ferrario, A., Jöbges, S., Krones, T., Massini, F., Barth, P., et al.: AI support for ethical decision-making around resuscitation: proceed with care. J. Med. Ethics. **48**(3), 175–183 (2021). https://doi.org/10.1136/medethics-2020-106786

Bussone, A., Stumpf, S., O'Sullivan, D.: The role of explanations on trust and reliance in clinical decision support systems. In: In 2015 International Conference on Healthcare Informatics, pp. 160–169. IEEE (2015, October)

Deley, T., Dubois, E.: Assessing trust versus reliance for technology platforms by systematic literature review. Soc. Media Soc. **6**(2), 2056305120913883 (2020)

Dirin, A., Nieminen, M., Laine, T.H.: Feelings of being for mobile user experience design. Int. J. Hum. Comp. Interact. **39**(20), 4059–4079 (2023)

Ismail, N.N.N.N., Lokman, A.M.: Kansei engineering implementation in web-based systems: a review study. In: International Conference on Kansei Engineering & Emotion Research, pp. 66–76. Springer Singapore, Singapore (2020, August)

Li, L., Chen, X., Zhu, P.: How do e-commerce anchors' characteristics influence consumers' impulse buying? An emotional contagion perspective. J. Retail. Consum. Serv. **76**, 103587 (2024)

Maghsoudi, T., Cascón-Pereira, R., Hernández-Lara, A.: The role of collaborative healthcare in improving social sustainability: a conceptual framework. Sustainability. **12**(8), 3195 (2020). https://doi.org/10.3390/su12083195

Matteo, E., Roma, P., Zafonte, S., Panniello, U., Abbate, L.: Development of a decision support system framework for cultural heritage management. Sustainability. **13**(13), 7070 (2021). https://doi.org/10.3390/su13137070

McKnight, D.H., Liu, P., Pentland, B.T.: Trust change in information technology products. J. Manag. Inf. Syst. **37**(4), 1015–1046 (2020)

Müller, L.S., Nohe, C., Reiners, S., Becker, J., Hertel, G.: Adopting information systems at work: a longitudinal examination of trust dynamics, antecedents, and outcomes. Behav. Inform. Technol. **43**(6), 1096–1128 (2024)

Onnasch, L., Laudine, H.: Impact of anthropomorphic robot design on trust and attention in industrial human-robot interaction. ACM Trans. Hum. Robot Interact. **11**(1), 1–24 (2021). https://doi.org/10.1145/3472224

Venkatesh, V., Thong, J.Y., Chan, F.K., Hu, P.J.H., Brown, S.A.: Extending the two-stage information systems continuance model: incorporating UTAUT predictors and the role of context. Inf. Syst. J. **21**(6), 527–555 (2011)

Westland, C.: Lower bounds on sample size in structural equation modeling. Electron. Commer. Res. Appl. **9**(6), 476–487 (2010). https://doi.org/10.1016/j.elerap.2010.07.003

Evaluating Visual Flow Effectiveness in Layout Design Through the Lens Of Yi Graphic

Bo Yuan(✉) and Sakol Teeravarunyou

King Mongkut's University of Technology, 126 Pracha Uthit Rd., Thonburi, Thailand
{bo.yuan,sakol.tee}@kmutt.ac.th

Abstract. The integration of Yi ethnic graphics with contemporary artistic styles has emerged as a significant area of study. However, current research tends to focus on traditional art forms or general modern design techniques, overlooking the fusion of these distinct areas. This study seeks to evaluate the efficacy of layout design guidelines that incorporate the concept of visual flow. Thirty participants took part in an eye-tracking experiment, where eight pairs of images were tested following the guidelines outlined in a graphic design book. The findings revealed that only one pair of images aligned with the guideline. Notably, various graphic components, including figures, faces, and background images, significantly influenced visual flow. This conclusion underscores the importance of designers considering the complex interplay between attention-grabbing elements and visual strategies that may regulate viewers' gazing behavior.

Keywords: Layout · Visual flow · Eye tracking · Graphic elements · Perception

1 Introduction

China, a multi-ethnic country, is home to approximately 8.71 million Yi (Nuosu) people in southern regions. Yi packaging is pivotal in the international market, yet Yi products often lack distinctive cultural characteristics and innovation [1].There is a notable absence of integration between Yi elements and contemporary design [2]. Historically, Yi graphics were tied to religious and shamanistic themes, depicting deities, natural forces, and ancestral spirits, and serving ritualistic purposes for protection [3].These traditional motifs and symbols have evolved into modern mediums, merging ancient traditions with contemporary art forms [4].This evolution underscores the adaptive resilience of Yi cultural expressions, preserving their essence while engaging with evolving artistic landscapes.

Visual flow, a key concept in design, describes the journey of the viewer's eye through a layout. Eye tracking has been utilized to analyze visual patterns and user attention [5]. Numerous studies have employed eye tracking in the examination of composition [6],specifically applied to layout design in comic books, websites, and packaging. Research indicates that artists and designers use visual strategies like leading lines, familiar-unfamiliar shapes, bright-dull colors, perspectives, and size variation [7].

S. Jin et al. (Eds.): IEA 2024, SSDI 39, pp. 15–20, 2025.
https://doi.org/10.1007/978-981-95-0211-0_3

Another aspect investigated is the differing perspectives of experts and novices in graphic education [8].

Research on reading comics reveals participants often deviate from the traditional Z-pattern, favoring hierarchical panel organization. However, this finding is debated, as participants numbered panels in sequence, potentially not reflecting authentic reading behavior [9].

This study evaluates the effectiveness of current layout design guidelines incorporating visual flow, focusing on how Yi graphics influence viewers' visual trajectories and attention distribution. The research questions are:

1. Which direction, left-to-right or right-to-left, captures the most attention in horizontal visual flow?
2. What is the impact of reversing the N-pattern by positioning the photo on the left side instead of the right?
3. Do participants consistently follow the text leading direction when presented with both meaningful and non-meaningful text?
4. How does horizontal visual flow across columns differ between monochrome and color images in the right-to-left direction?
5. How can graphic components be controlled and distributed throughout the layout using format?
6. How does bottom-up visual flow compare between photo and symbolic images?
7. How do bottom-up visual flows differ between photo and symbolic images?
8. How does vertical visual flow from top to bottom compare between linear repetition rhythm and a figure image?

2 Method

2.1 Participants and Tasks

The study involved 30 office workers (18 males, 12 females, mean age 43, SD = 10 years). Each participant underwent a 10-min A/B eye tracking test, looking at eight pairs of images representing redesigned layouts based on good design principles [10]. The images were randomly chosen to prevent transitive learning. To avoid continuous fixation on the center of the image, the presentation of the fixation point was placed outside the image area for approximately 400 ms (see Fig. 1), after which the stimulus was displayed for around 450 ms. A new presentation of the fixation point followed each image.

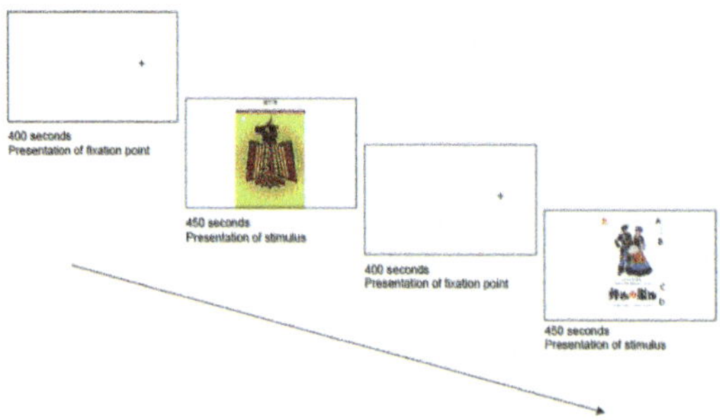

Fig. 1. Diagram of the study procedure. The fixation cross locates outside the stimulus.

2.2 Apparatus and Software

Participants' eye movements were tracked using the SMI iView X RED4, equipped with a 9-point automatic calibration grid and a chin rest, to measure visual flow. These measurements were compared through A/B testing against established design guidelines using eight pairs of images (see Fig. 2). Each visual layout facilitated scan path tracking, with cells designated by letter sequences from A to Z. The Levenshtein ratio was used to compute similarity scores for the text analysis task, with higher scores indicating greater similarity [11]. Calculations were done using python-Levenshtein 0.23.0 from PyPI.

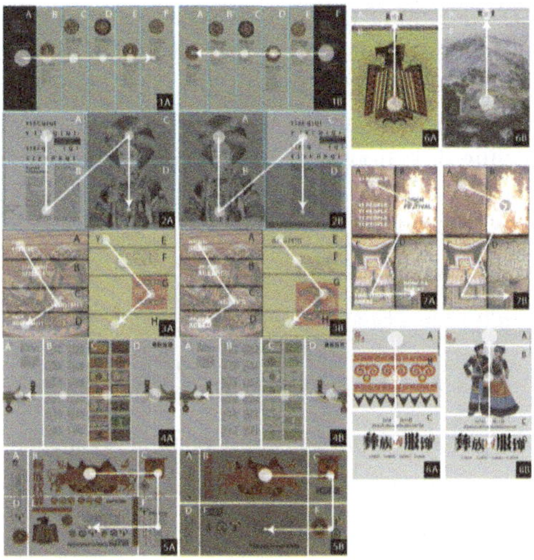

Fig. 2. Stimulus of A/B testing (1A) horizontal visual flow from left to right and (1B) horizontal visual flow from right to left, (2A) text content and (2B) background photo content, (3A) text leading direction, (3B) non-meaningful text leading direction, (4A) horizontal visual flow across column (4B) monochrome across column ,(5A) spreading graphic, (5B) grid layout (6A) guiding symbolic image and (6B) guiding photo image, (7A) Z pattern with font, (7B) Z pattern with non-font, (8A) top-down guide symbol, (8B) top-down guide figure.

3 Result

The result of 8 paired show as follows:

1. Comparing horizontal visual flow from left to right and right to left.

   Interestingly, most subjects initially fixated on the center of the objects and then shifted their gaze from left to right. A paired-samples t-test revealed a significant difference in the ratio of left-to-right (M = 60.77, SD = 17.72) and right-to-left (M = 49.93, SD = 14.24); t(29) = 2.85, p = 0.008. His suggests the column bar was not a preferred starting point and could be placed on either side. Participants showed a significantly higher preference for the left-to-right direction over right-to-left (Fig. 3).

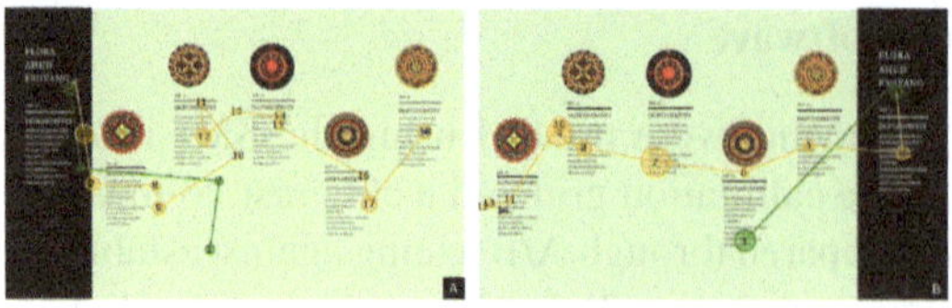

Fig. 3. Scan path from left to right (a) and right to left (b)

2. Reversal of the N-pattern between left side and right side.

   Around 50% of participants followed the N reverse visual flow pattern (M = 58.47, SD = 115.4), indicating the Yi lady's background photo attracted attention (see Fig. 4). When the photo was on the left, over 50% of participants began their gaze from that side (M = 60.97, SD = 14.28). The attention map shows the face consistently attracts the most attention, whether on the left or right side of the page.
3. Contrasting text leading direction with non-meaningful text leading direction.

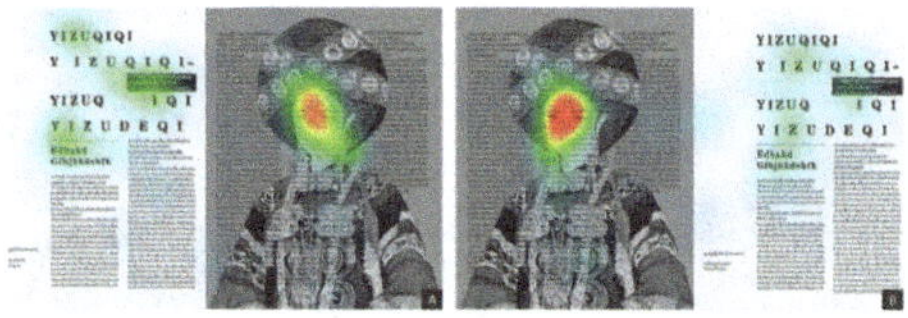

Fig. 4. Attention map of two images on right (a) and left side(b)

   Around 50% of participants followed both the text leading direction (M = 50.50, SD = 16.46) and the non-meaningful text leading direction (M = 50.53, SD = 15.33). These two pictures exhibited a similar ratio. Participants reported focusing more on the image background than the text.
4. Examining horizontal visual flow across columns, around 50% of participants followed the left-to-right pattern (M = 49.33, SD = 10.22) despite guidelines suggesting right to left. No significant difference was observed between color and monochrome images (M = 48.10, SD = 11.64) for Yi symbols.
5. Contrasting graphic components throughout the layout, most participants initially fixated on the two bull symbols but did not follow the book's visual flow guidelines. Around 50% adhered to the visual flow with distributed graphic components (M = 50.37, SD = 48.63). Despite a clear layout format with a border, participants did not follow the guidelines (M = 48.63, SD = 18.68). The correlation between both stimuli was moderately positive and statistically significant (r(30) = 0.52, p = 0.003).
6. Comparing the bottom-up visual flow between a photo and symbolic images (Fig. 5).

   This image aims to focus attention on the top logo, with around 90% of participants following the guidelines (refer to Fig. 2 of 6B). The image presented effectively attracts attention (M = 91.73, SD = 15.52). Changing the image to a bird symbol resulted in similar results (M = 87.90, SD = 16.17). Therefore, no significant differences were observed when changing the image.

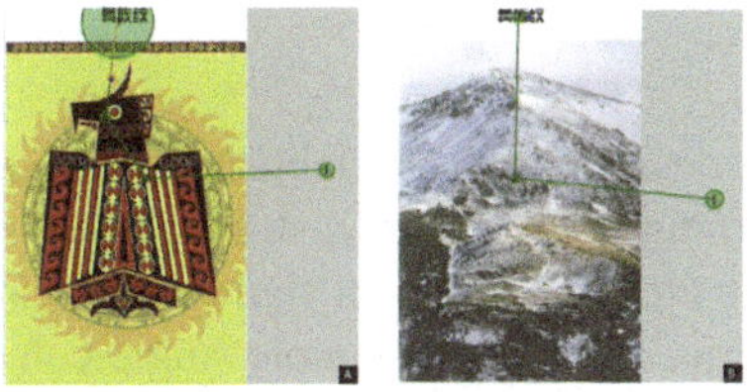

Fig. 5. The bottom up visual following the book guideline.

7. Investigating the Z-pattern visual flow, around 60% of participants followed the guideline. Typeface elements with a background image (M = 61.93, SD = 13.39) showed no significant difference compared to the image alone (M = 65.13, SD = 13.82). With typeface, attention spread across the image; without typeface, attention focused on the image center.
8. Analyzing vertical visual flow, around 70% of participants followed the top-to-bottom pattern. No significant difference was observed between linear repetition rhythm (M = 69.63, SD = 14.19) and figure image (M = 69.10, SD = 16.42). The correlation between both stimuli was moderately strong and statistically significant (r(30) = 0.612, p = 0.000). Most participants focused on the center of core images or rhythm symbols rather than starting at the top, as evident in the attention map.

4 Discussion

Visual flow patterns vary among individuals, often exhibiting a left-to-right orientation. In cultures like Chinese, reading may involve a right-to-left vertical orientation. The impact of cultural differences on visual flow is a significant research avenue. Faces, such as those of the Yi hill tribe, capture attention regardless of placement, engaging brain regions like the fusiform face area (FFA) and occipital face area (OFA) [9],which may benefit marketing of Yi hill tribe products. However, placing a face might disrupt a reversed N-pattern reading flow.

A limitation of this study is the layout text, which is not designed for reading comprehension but rather to examine visual flow. Creating an N-pattern reading experience akin to a magazine column poses challenges. Text direction is less effective with a background containing semantic content, as images like a sheep horn draw more attention than text, suggesting a plain background might enhance text leading effectiveness.

Participants deviated from the intended visual flow when graphic components were dispersed throughout the layout, with the Yi symbol drawing attention in multiple locations. Redirecting visual flow might be achieved by emphasizing text columns over standalone images or using lines to guide the gaze from start to endpoint. Investigating visual strategies such as familiar-unfamiliar shapes, bright-dull colors, perspectives, leading lines, and object size variations can regulate viewers' gaze behavior [6, 7].

5 Conclusions

Our testing reveals notable deviations from established book guidelines in various layout designs, especially concerning N reverse or Z-shaped visual flow patterns. A/B testing shows that altering graphic elements does not significantly change visual flow between versions. Successful patterns are found in simple single-column vertical layouts, with both bottom-up and top-down flows. Yi graphic elements, such as objects and figures, are particularly attention-grabbing, creating both opportunities and pitfalls in design. Designers must balance attention-grabbing elements with visual flow for effective and culturally sensitive design. The forthcoming research direction involves a comprehensive exploration of Yi graphic elements in conjunction with effective visual strategies that align with traditional Yi graphic aesthetics.

References

1. Bujimo, Azlin, P.K.A., Siow, M.L., Lama, Z.Q.F.V.A.R.: Integration of Chinese Yi traditional cultural elements in contemporary designs: a scoping review. J Legal Ethical & Regul Isses. **25**, 1 (2022)
2. Zhao, H., Gao, J.: Never abandon the essence: study on Yi nationality pattern innovation and inheritance method. Art Des. **305**, 130–131 (2018)
3. Harrell, S., Yongxiang, L.: The history of the history of the Yi, Part II. Mod China. **29**, 362–396 (2003). https://doi.org/10.1177/0097700403029003004
4. Chen, F., Qinling, D., Yang, K.: A study on the extraction of texture from ethnic minorities by shape grammar. In: 5th International Conference on Modern Education and Social Science. Guangzhou, China (2019) https://www.researchgate.net/publication/338869838
5. Kirtley, C.: How images draw the eye: an eye-tracking study of composition. Empir. Stud. Arts. **36**, 41–70 (2017). https://doi.org/10.1177/0276237417693564
6. Torabi, F., Teeravarunyou, S.: How experts and novices perceive the photographic image composition: an eye-tracking study on composition. In: International Conference on Applied Human Factors and Ergonomics, pp. 750–758. Springer (2021)
7. Gayen, P., Banerjee, A., Borgohain, J., Banik, G., Patnaik, P.: In: Martins, N., Brandão, D. (eds.) Can Visual Artists Regulate Designs to Manipulate Viewers' Gaze Patterns? An Exploration with Eye-Tracker BT - Advances in Design and Digital Communication III, pp. 507–522. Springer Nature Switzerland, Cham (2023)
8. Cohn, N.: Navigating comics: an empirical and theoretical approach to strategies of Reading comic page layouts. Front. Psychol. **4** (2013)
9. Kanwisher, N., Yovel, G.: The fusiform face area: a cortical region specialized for the perception of faces. Philos. Trans. R. Soc. B Biol. Sci. **361**, 2109–2128 (2006). https://doi.org/10.1098/rstb.2006
10. SendPoints: Principles for Good Layout Design: Commercial Design. SendPoints Publishing Co., Ltd., Hong Kong (2020)
11. Levenshtein, V.I.: Binary codes capable of correcting deletions, insertions, and reversals. In: Soviet Physics Doklady, pp. 707–710. Soviet Union (1966)

Exploring How Horror Design Elements Impact the Perception of Game Difficulty

Panasit Chaiyanan(✉) and Sakol Teeravarunyou

School of Architecture and Design, King Mongkut's University of Technology, Thonburi, Bangkok 10140, Thailand

panasitchy@au.edu, sakol.tee@kmutt.ac.th

Abstract. Conventional video game design increases the difficulty by asking for faster physical reflexes and precision from the player. This research explores an alternative method of changing the player's perception of a video game's difficulty using horror elements. Three games were developed for the experiment, each sharing the same layout and objective. Game A (Non-Horror/Easy) featured a brightly lit environment and a slow-moving robot enemy. Game B (Non-Horror/Difficult) retained the visual style of Game A but was designed to be more difficult in a conventional way by having a faster robot that instantly kills the player. Game C (Horror/Easy) had the same slow-moving robot enemy from Game A but with added horror elements: dim lighting, audio cue, and the robot was replaced with a generic horror-themed creature. The study surveyed thirty experienced video game players using a modified NASA TLX test. The survey's results confirmed that the participants felt Game B (Non-Horror/Difficult) demanded faster reflexes than Game A and C. Despite the enemy having the same slow movement and damage input, participants felt that Game C demanded faster reflexes than Game A. Participants also reported an increased level of stress with Game C, even slightly more than Game B. Lastly, Game C gave participants the same feeling of having just finished something difficult, higher than Game A and slightly higher than B.

Keywords: Video Game · Emotional Engagement · Horror · Difficulty

1 Introduction

The video game industry has been moving towards inclusivity with customizable control layouts, text-to-speech, and even one-handed custom controls to accommodate as many players as possible [1]. Inclusivity does not just mean catering to players with impairment; game developers also attract new players who may not be as skilled in physical maneuvering [2].

Despite the trend of inclusivity in video games, games must still be challenging. Uncomfortable interactions are necessary to entertain and educate the user [3]. Even when players experienced negative emotions after losing, [4] showed that they still appreciated the unique experience being offered. According to Mihaly Csikszentmihalyi's flow theory, staying in the space between boredom and anxiousness toward losing

S. Jin et al. (Eds.): IEA 2024, SSDI 39, pp. 21–27, 2025.
https://doi.org/10.1007/978-981-95-0211-0_4

is crucial to keeping a user engaged [5]. As developers aim to cater to players of all skill levels, an alternate way to increase difficulty should be explored.

Horror games have always been designed to have simplistic puzzles and forgiving penalties for dying. In [6], Phillipe Morine, co-founder of Red Barrels Game, stated that challenges may disrupt the player's immersion because the player might be too focused on accomplishing the objective. This observation suggests that the horror game's narrative and atmosphere somehow made up for the lack of challenge and sufficiently satisfied the players. This study aims to test whether increasing the difficulty mentally rather than physically by adding horror elements can provide the same satisfaction of finishing something difficult.

2 Theoretical Background

Emotional states have been shown to significantly impact a person's cognitive performance, particularly in tasks requiring spatial cognition and rapid decision-making. When a negative emotional state affects a person's cognitive performance, it can lead to undesired outcomes [7]. However, extreme negative emotions do not equate to horror, which is a distinct emotional experience that can be viewed as positive.

Ziwen Zhang's study, [8], revealed that players' reception of a horror video game is heavily influenced by their perception of its difficulty. Moderate difficulty levels that allow for simple trial and error without excessive challenge can enhance player satisfaction [8]. Another study, [9], found that the lower the game's conventional difficulty, the more players claimed to have enjoyed the game.

In a book by Bernard Perron, [10], which focused on the emotional impact of horror games' design elements, it was stated that fear is a deliberate part of the design, strategically used to evoke both emotional and physical reactions from players.

In [11], the effectiveness of using light to elicit a response in the horror video game Amnesia: The Dark Descent was examined. By enabling the player to manipulate light through the game's mechanics, the game successfully evoked emotional responses. Regarding audio cues, [12] concluded that sound elements are crucial in stimulating stress, anxiety, and tension in players who were playing horror games.

3 Method

Preliminary research was conducted by interviewing five people who had played a 2023 horror video game: Fears to Fathom - Ironbark Lookout. The interview subjects' feedback in the preliminary research was used to help develop the three games for testing.

3.1 Participants

The participants' ages ranged from 15 to 41. There are 22 males and 8 females. All of them have at least 1 year of experience playing video games which helps them understand common video game terminologies and commonly shared mechanics, such as instinctively using WASD on the keyboard to navigate.

3.2 Apparatus and Software

The three games being used for testing were developed specifically for this research.

All three games require the player to navigate a hallway to find a key and then return to the starting point and unlock the locked door.

Game A (Non-Horror/Easy) featured a brightly lit hallway (see Fig. 1a), a slow-moving robot enemy who needs to hit the player several times before the player loses.

Fig. 1. The screen snapshot of Game A, B, and C with subjects.

Game B (Non-Horror/Difficult) had the same brightly lit hallway (see Fig. 1b). The robot enemy was faster and was designed to chase after the player. It can kill the player's character with only one hit.

Game C (Horror/Easy) was designed very similarly to Game A, but with added audio-visual horror elements. The hallway was dark (see Fig. 1c). There was a stock audio sound of a scream. The enemy's appearance changed from a robot to a creature, but it still has the same slow movement and low damage output from Game A.

The survey used in this research is an adaptation of the NASA Task Load Index (NASA-TLX). Participants were asked to complete the survey, which was divided into three parts for each of the three games. The questions in each part were identical.

The data were analyzed using One-way ANOVA. Before starting, participants were informed that the survey would ask about their mental awareness as well as stress level, but they were not made aware of the objective of the research or the expected result from the hypothesis. Each time the participants completed one of the games, they were asked to complete the session corresponding to that game.

4 Result

A one-way analysis of variance (ANOVA) was conducted to examine the differences in temporal demand, mental demand, emotion, frustration, and performance across three games (A, B, and C). Table 1 summarizes the ANOVA results.

Table 1. Analysis of variance for temporal demand, mental demand, emotion, frustration, and performance across three games.

	Source of variation	Sum of Squares	df	Mean Sq.	F	Sig
Temporal Demand (reflex)	Between groups	76.20	2	38.10	9.69*	0.000
	Within Groups	342.20	87	3.93		
	Total	418.40	89			
Mental Demand	Between groups	49.36	2	24.68	4.97*	0.009
	Within Groups	432.03	87	4.97		
	Total	481.39	89			
Emotion	Between groups	160.69	2	80.34	16.20*	0.000
	Within Groups	431.53	87	4.96		
	Total	592.22	89			
Frustration i.e., stress	Between groups	147.80	2	73.90	14.61*	0.000
	Within Groups	440.20	87	5.06		
	Total	588.00	89			
Performance	Between groups	99.62	2	49.81	12.21*	0.000
	Within Groups	354.87	87	4.08		
	Total	454.49	89			

The mean differences in temporal demand for both Game B (Non-Horror/Difficult) and Game C (Horror/Easy) is significantly higher than for Game A (Non-Horror/Easy) at the $p < 0.05$ level [$F(2, 87) = 9.69$, $p = 0.000$]. Participants reported feeling rushed in both Game B and Game C. They did not report feeling rushed in Game A.

The mean mental demand score for Game C (Horror/Easy) was the highest, with a significant difference observed compared to both Game A and Game B at the $p < 0.05$ level [$F(2, 87) = 4.97$, $p = 0.009$]. Participants reported experiencing a high level of mental demand while playing Game C (Table 2).

The mean emotion score for Game C (Horror/Easy) was the highest, with a significant difference observed compared to both Game A and Game B at the $p < 0.05$ level [F(2,

Table 2. Mean differences in temporal demand, mental demand, emotion, frustration, and performance between three games.

	Group of position	Mean	1.A	2. B	3. C
Temporal Demand (reflex)	1. Game A (Non-horror/Easy)	5.23	–	−2.00*	−1.90*
	2. Game B (Non-horror/Difficult)	7.23		–	.10
	3. Game C (Horror/Easy)	7.13			–
Mental Demand	1. Game A (Non-horror/Easy)	4.93	–	0.13	−1.50*
	2. Game B (Non-horror/Difficult)	4.80		–	−1.63*
	3. Game C (Horror/Easy)	6.43			–
Emotion	1. Game A (Non-horror/Easy)	4.43	–	−0.37	−3.00*
	2. Game B (Non-horror/Difficult)	4.83		–	−2.63*
	3. Game C (Horror/Easy)	7.43			–
Frustration i.e., stress	1. Game A (Non-horror/Easy)	4.10	–	−0.70	−3.00*
	2. Game B (Non-horror/Difficult)	4.80		–	−2.30*
	3. Game C (Horror/Easy)	7.10			–
Performance	1. Game A (Non-horror/Easy)	5.40	–	−3.0	−2.37*
	2. Game B (Non-horror/Difficult)	5.70		–	−2.07
	3. Game C (Horror/Easy)	7.77			–

87) = 16.20, p = 0.000]. Participants reported feeling excitement while playing Game C.

The mean frustration score for Game C (Horror/Easy) was the highest, with a significant difference observed compared to both Game A and Game B at the $p < 0.05$ level [$F(2, 87) = 14.61$, $p = 0.000$]. Participants reported feeling stressed while playing Game C the most.

The mean performance score for Game C (Horror/Easy) was the highest, with a significant difference observed compared to both Game A and Game B at the $p < 0.05$ level [$F(2, 87) = 12.21$, $p = 0.000$].

5 Discussion

The temporal demand, which measured the sense of urgency a player feels, was significantly higher for Game B (Non-Horror/Difficult) and Game C (Horror/Easy) compared to Game A (Non-Horror/Easy). This indicates that the participants felt more pressed for time in a similar way, despite Game C not demanding faster reflexes.

The mental demand was significantly greater for Game C (Horror/Easy) compared to the other two games. This suggests that the horror elements in Game C imposed a higher cognitive load on the participants.

The emotion and frustration scores were also higher for Game C (Horror/Easy) than the other two games, much higher than Game A and slightly higher than Game B. The experiment yields a similar outcome to [10].

Finally, the performance scores, which measured the sense of accomplishment, were significantly greater for Game C (Horror/Easy) compared to Game A (Non-Horror/Easy). This implies that the horror elements in Game C provided a similar sense of achievement as the conventionally more difficult Game B.

Future studies may include a more diverse sample of participants, such as individuals with various physical and cognitive disabilities. Additionally, studies could explore the long-term effects of these alternative difficulty-increasing approaches on player retention, satisfaction, and overall gaming experience.

Outside of gaming, horror elements can be incorporated into various other fields, where giving the user a sense of accomplishment after finishing a difficult task is appreciated. This may include education, safety training, and simulation exercises.

6 Conclusion

The findings of this study explored the relationship between horror elements, perceived difficulty, and player experiences in video games. A significant number of participants indicated that the simple mechanic but with the horror-elements-infused game (Game C) felt more difficult than the non-horror but the difficult game (Game B), challenging traditional assumptions about how to increase difficulty in game design. These results highlighted the many ways players can experience challenges while playing a game.

Moving forward, game designers can leverage these insights to create more engaging and immersive gaming experiences that cater to a diverse range of player preferences. Future studies can explore how each type of horror element affects players' perception of the game's difficulty and the satisfaction they experience by overcoming challenges.

References

1. Brown, M., Anderson, S.: Designing for disability: evaluating the state of accessibility design in video games. Games Cult. **16**(6), 702–718 (2020)

2. Cairns, P., et al.: Video Gaming Accessibility. IEEE Conference Publication (2015)
3. Benford, S., Greenhalgh, C., Giannachi, G., Walker, B., Marshall, J., Rodden, T.: Uncomfortable interactions. In: Proceedings of the SIGCHI Conference on Human Factors in Computing Systems 2005–2014 (2012). https://doi.org/10.1145/2207676.2208347
4. Gowler, C.P.R., Iacovides, I.: "Horror, guilt and shame" – Uncomfortable experiences in digital games. In: Proceedings of the Annual Symposium on Computer-Human Interaction in Play (2019). https://doi.org/10.1145/3311350.3347179
5. Csikszentmihalyi, M.: Flow: The Psychology of Optimal Experience. Harper & Row, New York, NY (1990)
6. Maiberg, E.: Why horror games are more fun to watch than play. VICE (2015). https://www.vice.com/en/article/z43eb9/why-horror-games-are-more-fun-to-watch-than-play
7. Fouché, M.: Player experience of minimalist video game design: case study of indie horror iron lung. Games Cult. (2024). https://doi.org/10.1177/15554120241235437
8. Zhang, Z.: Analysis of the design aesthetics and player emotions of horror games: Take 'Little Nightmares' as a case (Degree project). University of Skövde, School of Informatics (2022)
9. Dardis, F., Schmierbach, M., Sherrick, B., Luckman, B.: How game difficulty and ad framing influence memory of in-game advertisements. J. Consum. Mark. **36**(1), 1–11 (2019)
10. Perron, B.: Horror Video Games: Essays on the Fusion of Fear and Play. McFarland & Co. (2009)
11. Hellgren, R., Sokolov, A.: The effectiveness of using light to elicit a response in Amnesia: The Dark Descent. Independent thesis Basic level (degree of Bachelor) (2023). http://uu.diva-portal.org/smash/get/diva2:1765469/FULLTEXT01.pdf
12. Graja, S., Lopes, P., Chanel, G.: Impact of visual and sound orchestration on physiological arousal and tension in a horror game. IEEE Trans. Games. **13**(1), 287–299 (2020)

The Impact of Streamer's Commentary on the Emotional Engagement of Horror Game Playthroughs

Panasit Chaiyanan(✉) and Sakol Teeravarunyou

School of Architecture and Design, King Mongkut's University of Technology, Thonburi, Bangkok 10140, Thailand

panasitchy@au.edu, sakol.tee@kmutt.ac.th

Abstract. This research aimed to explore the impact of streamer commentary on the playthrough viewer's emotional experience in single-player narrative-driven games. This study used quantitative and qualitative approaches by surveying and interviewing 34 people who regularly watch playthroughs. They were asked to watch three different playthroughs of "No Snake Hotel," a 2022 horror game chosen for its brevity and simplicity, with several visual and audio cues containing lore and foreshadowing. The playthroughs were categorized as no commentary, casual commentary, and thorough commentary. The study identified 15 key commentary opportunity points in the game, 6 of which were narrative foreshadowing that can help build suspense. The casual commentary playthrough interacted with 5 out of 15 commentary opportunity points and none of the foreshadowing, while the thorough commentary playthrough interacted with 13 out of 15 commentary opportunity points and all the foreshadowing. No commentary playthrough was deemed scarier by 73.5% of participants. However, 94.1% of participants preferred the two playthroughs with commentary. The minority of participants, 5.9%, who preferred no commentary, wanted to preserve the tone. In contrast, 70.6% of participants who preferred thorough commentary stated that this playthrough provided them with suspense-related emotions such as excitement, apprehension, and anxiety.

Keywords: Video Game · Streaming · Playthrough · Suspense

1 Introduction

The idea of thousands of fans watching competitive video games as esports can be equated to traditional sports fans watching physical sports [1]. However, the reasons behind people watching single-player narrative-driven video games remain largely unexplored. Even so, playthrough viewers have turned streamers of story-based games into millionaires [2]. Horror game-focused YouTube channels are among the highest-subscribed streamers of any genre, suggesting a substantial audience for specifically this genre of games [3]. For developers, horror games featured in the playthroughs received a significant boost in sales, with the most noticeable impact seen in games produced by small independent studios, which most horror games are [4].

S. Jin et al. (Eds.): IEA 2024, SSDI 39, pp. 28–33, 2025.
https://doi.org/10.1007/978-981-95-0211-0_5

Millions of playthrough viewers may not watch horror game playthroughs primarily to experience horror emotions directly. Research suggests that horror games often appear less scary when streamers play them while making jokes and screaming hysterically to entertain their viewers [5]. While humor may be one factor that draws viewers, it does not explain why horror games saw increased sales, as the streamer's humor was not found within the game [6]. Some elements within the playthrough suddenly made the game attractive to the viewers.

This research suspects that the streamers may unknowingly enhance the suspense in their playthroughs through their commentary. They pointed out lore, foreshadowing, and other narrative elements that the viewers might have missed on their own [7]. In this way, streamers can take what the video game provides, such as subtle hints of danger, and expand upon them to make the game appear more challenging and the stakes seem higher to their viewers, even if the consequences for failure are not severe [8]. This research suspects that maybe instead of sheer horror, it is the emotions of anxiety and excitement that are the reason viewers choose to watch horror game playthroughs [9].

If game developers understand why people watch these streamers, and if it is indeed for the emotional excitement through suspense, they can craft their game's narrative with streamers and their audiences in mind [10]. By collaborating with the streamers indirectly through design, especially streamers who may not be as skilled at spotting foreshadowing points and narrating, game developers can create more suspenseful narratives for the millions of viewers who watch playthroughs, potentially increasing engagement with the game.

2 Literature Review

Studies have investigated the influence of streamer commentary on viewer engagement during gameplay experiences, particularly in the horror genre. Chen highlights the importance of sound design and audio cues in creating immersive and suspenseful horror game experiences. This study emphasizes the crucial role of streamer commentary in guiding viewer attention and interpreting the narrative, suggesting that streamers' reactions can heighten fear and anticipation [11].

Grimshaw suggests that streamers play a critical role in adding suspense and enhancing engagement, potentially outweighing the reduction in fear caused by humorous or light-hearted commentary. Through their performance, streamers can foreshadow upcoming events, build suspense, and alter the story's perception [12].

Both studies acknowledge the potential of streamers to enhance viewer engagement, but they do not go into detail about how different types of streamers can impact engagement differently. This research will argue that a streamer's ability to effectively narrate and point out foreshadowing elements can be a deciding factor in enhancing viewer engagement compared to other streamers.

3 Method

The study employed a within-subjects experimental design to investigate the impact of streamer commentary on viewers' emotional engagement during a horror game playthrough.

3.1 Participants

A total of 34 participants were recruited for the study, consisting of 25 males, 6 females, and 3 of unspecified gender. Their ages ranged from 18–45, with 58.8% being below 25 years old.

3.2 Apparatus

The study utilized the independent horror game "No Snake Hotel" (2022) developed by Two Star Game. The game was chosen for its minimal design, absence of enemies, and no possibility of the player dying until the end. No Snake Hotel's barebone design and lack of difficulty allowed for a greater focus on the commentary opportunity points without shifting the focus to the difficulty of the gameplay or its mechanics.

Participants watched three separate playthroughs of "No Snake Hotel" under different commentary conditions in this order: no commentary, casual commentary, and thorough commentary.

Commentary opportunity points are visual and audio cues that have the potential to initiate a verbal response or reaction from the streamer. The commentary opportunity points range from posters on the wall, written notes left on tables, doors that were barricaded with objects, horror-themed audio cues, and a blood stain on the carpet.

The researcher identified a total of 15 commentary opportunity points throughout the game, with 6 of these points considered foreshadowing, a literary device known to lead to emotions associated with suspense, such as apprehension.

In the no commentary condition, participants watched a playthrough of the game without any narration or reaction from the streamer. In the casual commentary condition, the streamer narrated about 5 out of the 15 identified commentary opportunity points and reacted to only 2 out of the 6 foreshadowing moments (see Fig. 1a). In contrast, the thorough commentary condition featured a streamer who reacted to and narrated 13 out of the 15 commentary opportunity points, while also reacting to and narrating all 6 foreshadowing moments (see Fig. 1b).

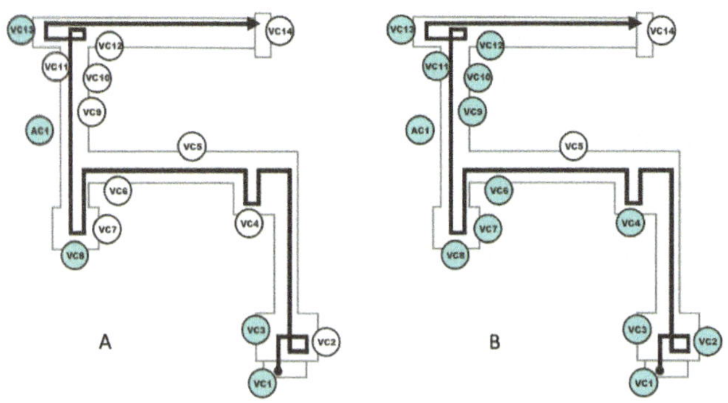

Fig. 1. Commentary opportunity points utilized by each playthrough with commentary

4 Result

Table 1. Results from the survey asking the participants about the 3 playthroughs

Description	Result (%)		
	No commentary	Casual commentary	Thorough commentary
Playthrough preference	5.9	23.5	70.6
Continue watching	5.9	26.5	67.6
	No commentary	With commentary	
Scare factor	94.1	5.9	
		Before thorough commentary	During thorough commentary
Green snake sighting		41.2	58.8

The data collected from the survey was analyzed using a combination of quantitative and qualitative methods. The analysis focused on identifying patterns and trends in the participants' responses, with particular attention paid to their preferences for different types of playthroughs and their emotional reactions.

When asked which commentary condition made them feel more scared, 94.1% of participants reported feeling more scared during the no commentary playthrough (see Table 1). However, 70.6% of participants still preferred the thorough commentary. When given a choice to continue watching one of the playthroughs for enjoyment, 67.6% of participants chose the thorough commentary condition.

Interviews with participants revealed that they preferred the thorough commentary because it provided more information and increased their excitement and engagement with the game.

During the thorough commentary playthrough, a small snake made a sudden appearance in the game. Participants watched the playthrough in order: no commentary, casual commentary, and then thorough commentary. This was set up because thorough commentary revealed more information. 58.8% of participants reported that they had missed the snake in the first two playthroughs, and only saw it during the thorough commentary playthrough.

The interview with the participants took place at the end of the survey, asking for a rationale behind their choice of playthrough. The participants were grouped according to their responses to the question of which playthrough they prefer the most. Two people were in Group A for no commentary, nine were in Group B for casual commentary, and twenty-three people were in Group C for thorough commentary.

Participants in Group A mentioned that their choices were based on wanting to experience the emotions they believed the game's developer intended. One participant noted that the thorough commentary disrupted their immersion. Another participant stated that the tone of the game's horror should have been preserved.

Among the nine participants in Group B who chose casual commentary, four believed that the casual commentary better preserved the horror tone of the game compared to the thorough commentary. One participant mentioned that they were not interested in the full story of the game and just wanted to feel like they were sitting next to a friend playing the game.

Group C consisted of twenty-three participants. Five participants in this group stated that they felt more suspenseful while watching the thorough commentary. Three participants chose the thorough commentary because they valued the detailed information provided, which led to feeling more immersed. Three others mentioned that the primary reason for their preference was that the thorough commentary made the game less scary. A notable response from one participant indicated that when the knowledgeable streamer providing thorough commentary got scared, it made the participant feel anxious.

5 Discussion

The preference for the commentary playthroughs over no commentary, despite the latter being confirmed by participants as scarier, suggests that some viewers of horror game playthroughs prioritize something else over direct fear. This aligns with [8] which indicates that streamers' commentary can guide viewer attention throughout the game, which can lead to heightened anticipation.

The preference for thorough commentary indicates that varying levels of streamer performance and narration skills can impact viewer enjoyment. The fact that many participants did not notice the small snake, illustrates the significant role of a streamer's commentating ability. Narrative details of the game can be overlooked when playing casually. Game developers should ensure that even streamers who might rush through the game do not miss crucial narrative elements that enhance the storyline's suspense. By helping the streamer guide their viewers through the game's narrative more easily, they can increase the appeal of their playthroughs and attract a larger audience for the game's story and characters.

For the interview, Groups A and B seemed to care about preserving the game's tone when choosing which type of commentary to watch. In contrast, Group C's viewers were primarily interested in obtaining as much information as possible from the game, which some claimed made them feel more suspenseful. If a streamer can be as knowledgeable as those preferred by Group C while maintaining the horror tone, it might be possible to convert Group B viewers to watch thorough commentary as well.

Further research should explore how extensively game developers should consider streamers in their design process. Streamers could be viewed not merely as a marketing tool but as a primary source of exposure to game narratives for millions of viewers. Additionally, investigating which elements, such as lore, foreshadowing, and Easter eggs, are most likely to elicit reactions from streamers could provide valuable insights for game design.

6 Conclusion

Streamers can play a crucial role in enhancing the gaming experience by highlighting important details and guiding viewers' attention, as evidenced by the participants' strong preference for thorough commentary playthroughs. However, not all streamers have the same skill level in narrating and performance. By understanding the importance of thorough commentary from streamers to the viewer's engagement of a playthrough, game developers may decide to design their games with the streamers in mind to deliver their stories to millions of viewers experiencing the game in this format. Future studies can further explore the relationship between game developers and streamers to optimize this relationship for mutual benefit.

References

1. Seo, Y.: Electronic sports: a new marketing landscape of the experience economy. J. Mark. Manag. **32**(1–2), 1–13 (2016)
2. Taylor, T.L.: Watch me play: twitch and the rise of game live streaming. Princeton University Press, Princeton, NJ (2018)
3. Smith, S., Obrist, M., Wright, P.: Live-streaming changes the (video) game. Int. J. Hum. Comput. Interact. **36**(13), 1185–1201 (2020)
4. Jiao, Y., Sarigöllü, E., Lou, L., Huang, B.: How streamers foster consumer stickiness in live streaming sales. J. Theor. Appl. Electron. Commer. Res. **18**(3), 1196–1216 (2023). https://doi.org/10.3390/jtaer18030061
5. Perron, B.: Horror Video Games: Essays on the Fusion of Fear and Play. McFarland (2009)
6. Consalvo, M.: When paratexts become texts: de-centering the game-as-text. Crit. Stud. Media Commun. **34**(2), 177–183 (2017)
7. Sjöblom, M., Hamari, J.: Why do people watch others play video games? An empirical study on the motivations of twitch users. Comput. Hum. Behav. **75**, 985–996 (2017)
8. Chen, C.: Hardcore viewer engagement and social exchange with streamers and their digital live streaming communities. Qual. Market Res. **26**(1), 37–57 (2023)
9. Grimshaw, M.: The audio aesthetics of horror games. In: Perron, B. (ed.) Horror Video Games: Essays on the Fusion of Fear and Play, pp. 137–157 (2009)
10. Liao, S., Humphreys, L.: Lifestreaming: Living a Connected Life. The MIT Press (2016)
11. Chen, J.: Exploring the impact of streamer commentary on viewer engagement in horror game playthroughs. J. Gaming Virt. Worlds. **12**(2), 145–160 (2020)
12. Grimshaw, M., Schott, G.: A conceptual framework for the study of visual and auditory horror elements in games. In: Proceedings of DiGRA 2017. Digital Games Research Association (2017)

Emotion and Gaze Movement Analysis in Preference Evaluation of Steering Wheel Design

Yejin Lee(✉) and Kwang Tae Jung

KOREATECH, Cheonan, Chungnam 31253, South Korea
Yejin3210@koreatech.ac.kr

Abstract. The steering wheel is one of the interface components drivers see most when driving a car. Therefore, studies from various perspectives are necessary to increase drivers' preference for steering wheel design. This study was conducted for two purposes. The first was to derive emotional factors important to preference through emotion analysis of the steering wheel. The second was to investigate the possibility of using gaze movements to evaluate steering wheel preference. Twenty samples were used to assess preferences and emotions about steering wheel design. Subjects evaluated for their design preferences and emotions after viewing the steering wheel image displayed on the monitor for 10 s while wearing an eye tracker. A 5-point Likert scale was used to evaluate preference, and the Semantic Differential method was used to assess emotion. Eight subjects participated in the experiment, and twenty emotional vocabularies were used for emotion evaluation. Factor analysis was performed to derive emotional factors. Heat map entropy for gaze movement was calculated to analyze the relationship between gaze movement and preference. The analysis revealed that the most significant emotional factor in preference was "familiarity." Furthermore, a positive correlation was found between preference and heat map entropy. This suggests that as preference for the steering wheel design increases, subjects tend to look at the various components more evenly. These findings have practical implications as they can guide emotional design strategies to increase steering wheel preference and provide a novel evaluation method.

Keywords: Steering wheel · Preference · Emotion · Heat map entropy

1 Introduction

In the modern automotive industry, systematically reflecting consumers' emotional requirements in car design is crucial for achieving higher competitiveness [9, 12]. Since drivers spend most of their time inside the car, design focusing on emotions gradually shifts from exterior to interior elements [3].

In particular, the steering wheel is the interface element that the driver has the most tactile contact with and where the driver's gaze rests the most as it is the part with the most

S. Jin et al. (Eds.): IEA 2024, SSDI 39, pp. 34–39, 2025.
https://doi.org/10.1007/978-981-95-0211-0_6

interaction not only for driving the car but also for receiving or controlling information on car-related systems [9, 10, 13].

Automobile manufacturers are investing significant effort into the design of steering wheels to enhance drivers' emotional satisfaction by considering their preferences and tastes [2, 9]. Recently, steering wheels have been designed in various shapes that deviate from the typical round shape, taking drivers' preferences into account. This phenomenon is becoming more evident with the spread of electric vehicles and the addition of various interface control devices to steering wheels. Drivers' preferences for steering wheels are closely related to emotions, which refer to users' feelings and images toward interactive objects [1, 6]. Since emotion is one of the critical factors affecting user experience, which has become an issue recently, the importance of emotion in products and interfaces is becoming more prominent [4, 8].

Numerous studies have been conducted on the design and emotions related to steering wheels. Park and Choi [9] proposed a new evaluation model for steering wheel design elements and customer emotional assessment. You et al. [13] studied the grip of steering wheels, identifying that material, shape, and initial impressions contribute to the grip. Jin et al. [2] highlighted vital design elements of steering wheels and argued that differences in these elements affect drivers' emotional satisfaction. Kim and Lee [3] researched customer evaluations of car interiors, identifying factors contributing to a sense of luxury. Park and Ahn [7] studied modifying steering wheel designs based on the drivers' gripping postures. They extracted physical interface parts from the conventional round steering wheel and proposed a new design.

As mentioned above, research has continued to improve driver satisfaction with steering wheels through a design that considers emotions. However, it is challenging to find research on analyzing emotional factors that significantly impact steering wheel preference and methods to evaluate preference objectively. Suppose we know how preference for a specific product or interface relates to emotion. In that case, designing a product or interface that can increase user preference will be possible. If preference can be evaluated objectively, it can also be used to assess design preference [11].

Therefore, this study was conducted for two purposes. The first was to identify the emotional factors that affect preference for steering wheel design, and the second was to find out how to use gaze movement as a measure to evaluate preference for steering wheel design objectively.

2 Experiment

2.1 Emotional Vocabulary and Steering Wheels for Experiment

This study used the semantic differential (SD) method to evaluate a subject's emotion toward the steering wheel. To this end, vocabulary that expresses emotions about steering wheels was collected. First, 108 emotional vocabularies were collected through literature survey and Internet search. And next, vocabularies with low relevance were removed and vocabularies with similar meanings were integrated through a review by three emotion experts. Finally, 20 emotional vocabularies were ultimately selected for emotion evaluation. The 20 vocabulary words are as follows: light-heavy, unique-common, strong-weak, sleek-blunt, curvy-straight, neat-messy, masculine-feminine, symmetrical-asymmetrical, simple-complex, attractive-unattractive, modern-classic, soft-hard, sophisticated-unsophisticated, natural-artificial, elaborate-rough, organized-unorganized, harmonious-disharmonious, familiar-unfamiliar, convenient-inconvenient, and innovative-conservative.

Twenty steering wheel designs were selected for the emotional evaluation. The samples used for emotional measurement were chosen based on their diverse design forms rather than market share or brand considerations to capture a wide range of emotional responses. To minimize the influence of existing brand images on the participants' emotions, logos were removed from the photos, and all designs were presented in black and white.

2.2 Experimental Method

Eight participants (four men and four women) took part in the experiment to evaluate preferences and emotional responses to steering wheels. The average age was 22.1 for men and 20.8 for women. None of the subjects had any driving experience. While wearing an eye tracker, the subjects viewed a steering wheel image randomly presented on the front monitor for 10 s, and their preference and emotion for the design were evaluated (see Fig. 1).

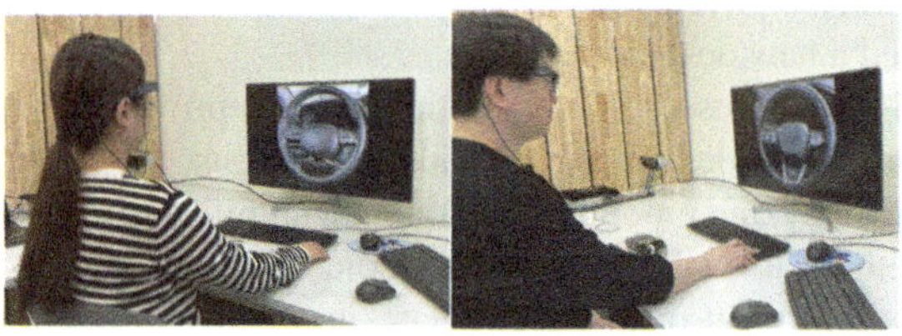

Fig. 1. Experiment scene

3 Results

3.1 Preference and Emotional Analysis of Steering Wheel

Factor analysis was performed to derive emotional factors from the emotional vocabularies of steering wheels. Looking at the results, the first group included the vocabulary of "messy, asymmetrical, complex, disorganized, and disharmonious." Considering the included vocabulary's characteristics, the first group's emotional factor was defined as "harmony." The second group included vocabulary such as "common, unattractive, classic, natural, familiar, convenient, and conservative." The emotional factor of the second group was defined as "familiarity." The third group included vocabulary such as "heavy, strong, blunt, straight, masculine, and hard," and the emotional factor of the third group was defined as "robustness." The fourth group included vocabulary such as "unsophisticated and rough." The emotional factor of the fourth group was described as "sophistication."

Through factor analysis, the scores of each steering wheel for emotional factors were obtained, and cluster analysis was performed on the steering wheels using the emotional scores to classify the steering wheels into three groups as follows:

Group 1: 1,4,7,9,11,14,18
Group 2: 2,3,5,10,12,13,15,16,17
Group 3: 6,8,19,20

Correlation analysis was performed to determine the relationship between steering wheel preference and emotional factors. Looking at the results, preference showed a fairly high correlation with familiarity at $r = 0.588$, and the correlation coefficient was statistically significant at the significance level of 0.01 ($p = 0.006$). In addition, there was a weak correlation with harmony, having a correlation coefficient of $r = 0.405$, with the value being statistically significant at the significance level of 0.1. However, robustness and sophistication did not show a significant correlation with preference. From the correlation analysis results, it can be seen that subjects tended to prefer the steering wheel design with which they are more familiar.

3.2 Gaze Movement Analysis in Preference Evaluation

The concept of entropy was used to express gaze movements in evaluating steering wheel preference as a single quantitative value. Gaze entropy measures the degree of disorder in gaze movement. The subjects' gaze movements during the preference evaluation process were expressed as a heat map (see Fig. 2), and entropy was calculated from the heat map.

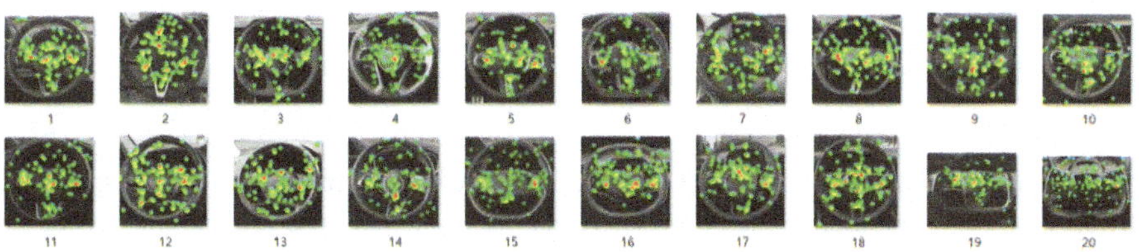

Fig. 2. Steering wheels and the heat map of gaze movement

Assuming the heat map of the gaze distribution follows a Gaussian distribution, from the point with the longest to shortest gaze duration, the Gaussian distribution can be applied to calculate the heat map entropy. The heat map entropy is calculated as $H = -\sum_{xy} \tilde{f}(x, y) \cdot \log \tilde{f}(x, y)$, where $\tilde{f}(x, y)$ is the combined probability distribution of the heat maps X and Y [5]. A Python program was developed and used to obtain heat map entropy.

A correlation analysis determined the correlation between preference and heat map entropy. As a result, it was found that there was a correlation between preference and heat map entropy, having a correlation coefficient of $r = 0.522$. This value was statistically significant at the significance level of 0.05 ($p = 0.026$). Therefore, it can be seen that there is a relatively high degree of correlation between preference and heat map entropy and that the value of heat map entropy tends to increase as preference increases. Additionally, as preference for the steering wheel increases, subjects tend to look at various components rather than just paying attention to specific parts of the steering wheel.

The correlation between preference and gaze entropy can also be confirmed through a significance analysis of heat map entropy and preference among the three groups of steering wheels classified according to emotional scores. The average preference between steering wheel groups was found to have a statistically significant difference at the significance level of 0.05 ($F = 6.921$, $p = 0.006$), and the average heat map entropy was found to have a statistically significant difference ($F = 4.461$, $p = 0.028$) (see Fig. 3). In detail, a post hoc analysis (Duncan test) was performed to determine whether there were substantial differences between steering wheel groups regarding preference and heat map entropy. As a result, there was no significant difference between Group 1 and Group 2 in both preference and heat map entropy. Group 3 was found to be significantly different from the two groups.

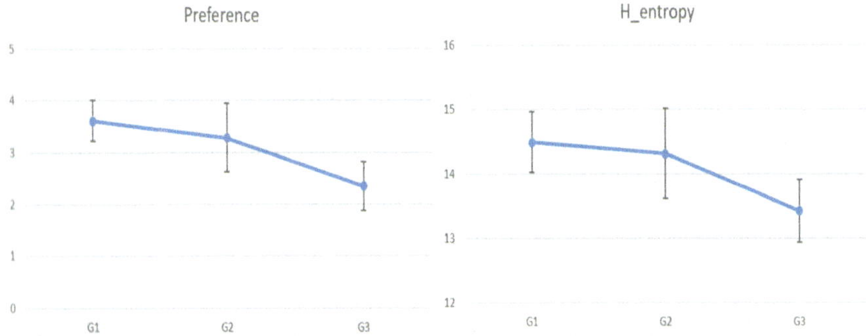

Fig. 3. Preference and heat map entropy according to the steering wheel group

Looking at the average of each group, the heat map entropy was also high in the group with high preference (see Fig. 3). Thus, the higher the preference, the higher the heat map entropy.

4 Conclusion

This study was conducted to identify emotional factors important to steering wheel preference and provide a basis for evaluating preference through gaze movements. As a result of the survey, preference closely correlated with the emotional factor "familiarity." Additionally, it was confirmed that gaze movements appear differently depending on steering wheel preference. In other words, as preference increases, the gaze movement does not stay on a specific component for a long time, but the gaze tends to remain evenly on various elements. From the results of this study, it was found that to increase the preference for steering wheel design, it is necessary to design the steering wheel to give drivers a familiar feeling. It was also found that heat map entropy can be used as a valuable measure to evaluate steering wheel preference. This study was conducted as a primary study to find out the design direction from an emotional aspect to increase the preference for a steering wheel and use gaze movements to evaluate the preference for a steering wheel. Although the experiment was conducted with a relatively small number of subjects, the results of this study are significant as they suggest an emotional design direction to increase preference for steering wheels and provide a basis for objectively evaluating preference.

Acknowledgement. This research was supported by "Regional Innovation Strategy (RIS)" through the National Research Foundation of Korea(NRF) funded by the Ministry of Education(MOE)(2021RIS-004).

This paper was supported by the new professor research program of KOREATECH in 2024.

References

1. Han, S.H., Yun, M.H., Kim, K., Kwahk, J.: Evaluation of product usability: development and validation of usability dimensions and design elements based on empirical models. Int. J. Ind. Ergon. **26**, 477–488 (2000)
2. Jin, B., Choi, J., Hwangbo, H., Ji, Y.: A study about emotional grip-stability evaluation model of steering wheel design. In: The Proceeding of 2010 Conference of HCI (2010)
3. Kim, K., Lee, E.: A study on the materials of automotive interior design. J. Basic Des. Art. **12**(6), 26–36 (2011)
4. Law, E.L.-C., Van Schaik, P.: Modelling user experience - an agenda for research and practice. Interact. Comput. **22**(5), 313–322 (2010)
5. Lee, Y., Jung, K.T., Lee, H.C.: A basic study on the use of eye movement entropy in the emotional satisfaction evaluation of design. J. Ergon. Soc. Korea. **39**(5), 487–500 (2020)
6. Nagamachi, M.: A new ergonomic consumer-oriented technology for product development. Kansei Eng. **15**, 3–11 (1995)
7. Park, H., Ahn, S.: Transformative steering wheel UX design for autonomous car. In: Proceedings of HCIK 2022, South Korea, pp. 116–121 (2022)
8. Park, J., Han, S.H., Kim, H.K., Park, J., Kim, H.: Developing affect model through literature review. In: Fall Conference of Ergonomics Society of Korea, South Korea (2011)
9. Park, P., Choi, M.: A proposal of the study about element design and customer emotional evaluation for steering wheel. In: Spring Conference of Ergonomics Society of Korea, South Korea (2015)
10. Steele, M., Gillespie, B.: Shared control between human and machine: using a haptic steering wheel to aid in land vehicle guidance. In: Proceedings of the Human Factors and Ergonomics Society 45th annual meeting (2001)
11. Suh, S., Lee, C.: The emotional sensibility estimation system for front-load washer. J. Korea Acad. Ind. Coop. Soc. **11**(3), 821–826 (2010)
12. White, G.L.: Car makers battle inferiors in hopes of earning buyer's respect. Wall Street J. (2001)
13. You, H.S., Jo, H.S., Park, W.C., Kim, T.H.: Analysis of the feeling of grip for steering wheel. In: Proceeding of the 2012 Conference of the Korean Society of Automotive Engineers, pp. 1885–1891 (2012)

Assessing Divergent Thinking through the Color Queue Creation Task: Effect of Randomly Moving Background Dots

Effect of Randomly Moving Background Dots

Taiki Matsunaga(✉), Ryunosuke Fukada, Kimi Ueda, Hirotake Ishii, and Hiroshi Shimoda

Graduate School of Energy Science, Kyoto University, Kyoto, Japan
matsunaga.taiki.84r@st.kyoto-u.ac.jp

Abstract. With the advent of the information society in recent years, creativity is becoming increasingly important, and divergent thinking is gaining prominence. The Alternative Uses Test (AUT) is the most used test using language for evaluating divergent thinking. However, its result is affected by differences in native language and the evaluation is dependent on the person conducting the assessment. To solve these problems, we developed the Color Queue Creation Task (CQCT) as a new task. The purpose of this study is to demonstrate the validity of flexibility measured with CQCT. The experiment to validate CQCT was conducted with the participation of six university students. We asked them to perform the CQCT under three conditions: presenting color dot background, gray-scale dot background, and non-presenting. The position and color of the dots change over time. As a result, flexibility measured under the presenting condition was higher than under the non-presenting condition. This suggests that CQCT can be useful as a divergent thinking test. Future study should be conducted with a larger number of participants.

Keywords: Creative Thinking · Divergent Thinking · Flexibility · CQCT

1 Introduction

With the advent of the information society in recent years, creative thinking has become increasingly important. Creative thinking can be classified into divergent and convergent thinking (Guilford 1967). Divergent thinking is thinking that generates many ideas, while convergent thinking is thinking that leads conclusion from many ideas. Divergent thinking is more important because the quality and quantity of ideas generated is crucial for leading good conclusion.

To discuss how divergent thinking can be improved, evaluation tasks measuring divergent thinking are needed. A typical example of an existing evaluation task is the Alternative Uses Test (AUT) (Guilford 1967). However, as the task requires verbal responses to ideas and the ideas are evaluated by people, the evaluation is subjective,

S. Jin et al. (Eds.): IEA 2024, SSDI 39, pp. 40–45, 2025.
https://doi.org/10.1007/978-981-95-0211-0_7

time-consuming and the difficulty level varies depending on the language. In previous study, to solve the problems, a Color Queue Creation Task (CQCT) was developed and an index of flexibility F, one of the aspects of divergent thinking, was proposed (Matsunaga et al. 2024). An experiment with cognitive load was conducted to demonstrate the validity of this CQCT as evaluation task, but it failed to show validity. Therefore, it is necessary to modify the experimental conditions and conduct another experiment to validate the flexibility score measured with the CQCT. In addition, it is also necessary to examine the characteristics and validity of the flexibility measured by CQCT based on a comparison with the flexibility measured by the AUT, an existing test.

The objective of this study was to demonstrate the validity of flexibility score measured with CQCT by comparing the results of the CQCT in three conditions: presenting color dot background, gray-scale dot background, and non-presenting. The AUT also was performed after the CQCT, and the results were compared. Approval was obtained from the Institutional Ethics Committee of Graduate School of Energy Sciences, Kyoto University.

2 Methods

2.1 Influence of External Random Stimuli on Divergent Thinking

Previous studies have suggested that external random stimuli can improve divergent thinking by affecting a person's internal randomness (Finke et al. 1996; Proctor 1993). Random stimuli from outside can cause new idea associations by influencing each person's biased thought patterns. One of the first theories of creativity proposed that creativity results from the selection of the best of randomly generated ideas within humans (Campbell 1960). Therefore, external random stimuli may stimulate randomness in humans and increase the range of ideas that can be selected. Based on the above, we thought that providing external random stimuli is effective in influencing people's latent randomness and enhancing the performance of divergent thinking.

If the flexibility F is higher when an external random stimulus is given, compared to non-presenting random stimulus, then the validity of the CQCT may be demonstrated. Figure 1 shows the CQCT interface under each condition. The gray-scale dot background is a random stimulus, as the dot's position changes randomly over time. In the color dot background condition, in addition to the random stimulus, dots are displayed that randomly changes color over time, from which color selection is possible. Therefore, the flexibility score F is expected to be larger in the color dot condition than in the gray-scale dot condition.

2.2 Procedure

To verify the validity of whether the flexibility score F assessed by the CQCT can measure a person's divergent thinking, an experiment was conducted where participants performed the CQCT under two conditions with and without visual random stimuli presented in the background of the CQCT and evaluated the flexibility of divergent thinking. They were also asked to perform the AUT to test the correlation between the

CQCT flexibility score and the AUT flexibility score F_{AUT}. To evaluate F_{AUT}, we used an index calculated from the cosine similarity based on the variance representation obtained from the ideas (Fukada et al. 2023). In this experiment, 6 participants, undergraduate and graduate students aged 18 or older enrolled at Kyoto University, performed the CQCT and the AUT.

Figure 2 shows experimental environment of participants during experiment. During the CQCT, participants used tablet devices (Apple 10.2-inch iPad, Wi-Fi, 64 GB, Space Grey). They changed colors by swiping the color change area displayed in the center of the screen, and then tapped the selection button displayed at the bottom of the screen to determine the colors they selected one by one. During AUT, participants used a display (EX-LDH271DB-B 27-inch) and a keyboard to enter their ideas in the column in the center of the screen and sent their ideas one by one using the Send button.

Figure 3 shows the experimental protocol for CQCT. The experiment consisted of a practice task to familiarize the participants with the interface and the main task as an evaluation task. The CQCT was performed under the conditions with and without color or gray-scale dot in the background of the task as a visual random stimulus, and the effects of the presence or absence of the visual random stimulus were examined. After completing the CQCT, participants performed AUT on two subjects. Figure 4 shows the experimental protocol for AUT. The first subject (cardboard) was used as a practice task, while the second (PET bottles) was used for analysis.

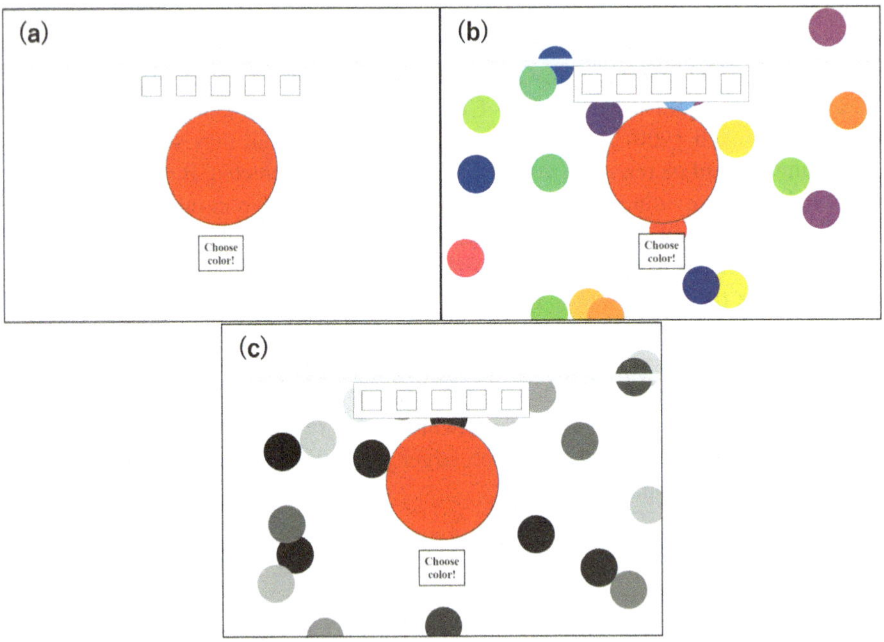

Fig. 1. CQCT interfaces in non-presenting (a), color dot background (b) and grey-scale dot background (c) conditions.

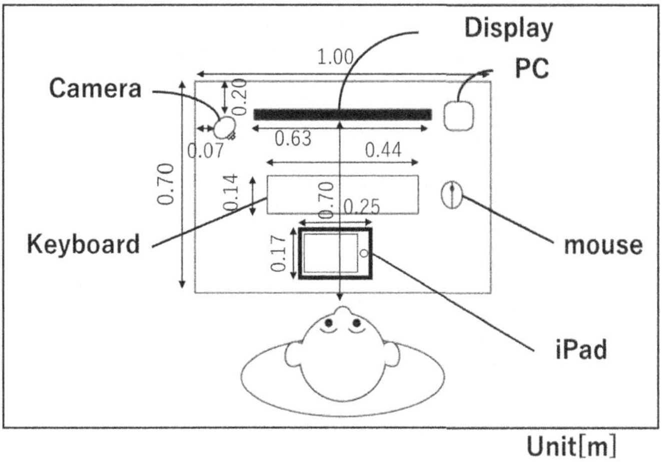

Fig. 2. Experimental environment of the participants during the experiment.

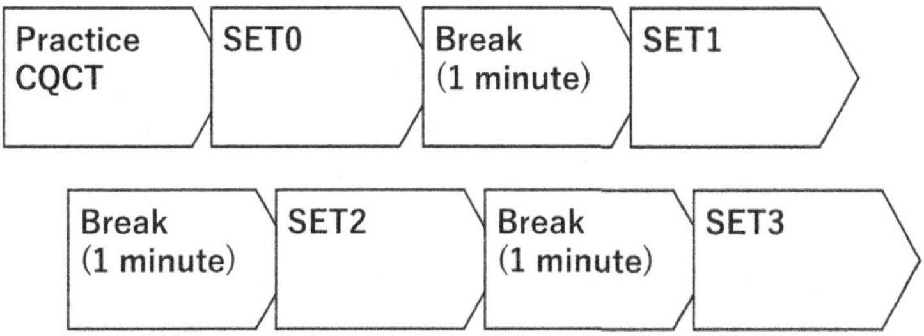

Fig. 3. Experimental protocol in the CQCT.

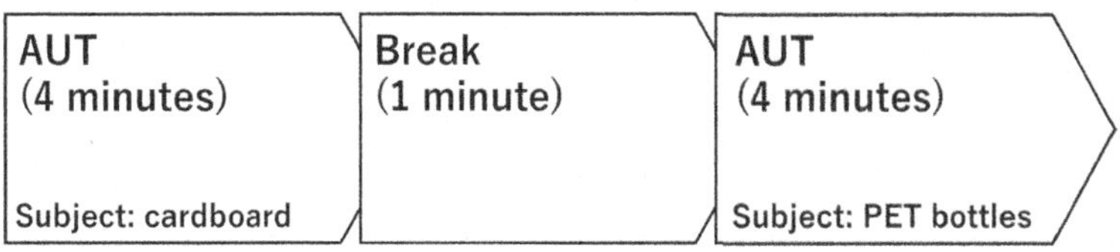

Fig. 4. Experimental protocol in the AUT.

3 Results and Discussion

Figure 5 shows the results of the CQCT under three conditions: non-presenting, color dot background, and gray-scale dot background conditions. For the mean value of the CQCT flexibility score in each condition, it was 19.67 in the non-presenting condition, 28.33 in the color dot background condition, and 27.17 in the gray-scale dot background condition, respectively. The flexibility score for the color dot background condition was higher than that for the non-presenting condition. Similarly, that for the gray-scale dot background condition was higher than that for the non-presenting condition. Fig. 6 shows correlation between the flexibility score for the CQCT in non-presenting condition and the flexibility score F_{AUT} for the AUT. Pearson's correlation coefficient r was 0.163, showing little correlation.

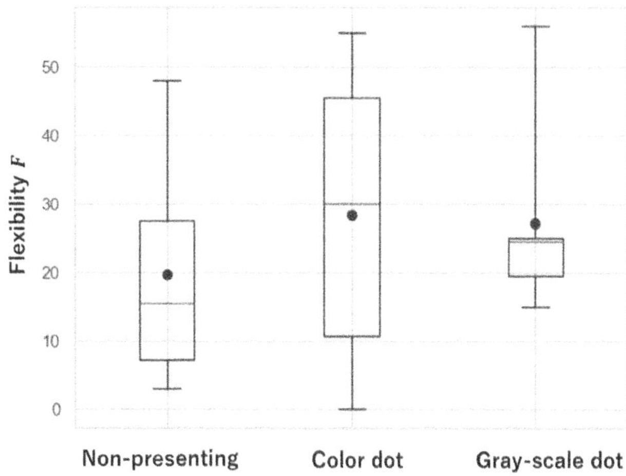

Fig. 5. Flexibility F results for each condition.

The higher flexibility score in the presenting conditions compared to the non-presenting condition suggests the validity of the CQCT. However, the sample size was 6, which makes the results unreliable. We expected the color dot condition to have larger mean values of flexibility than the gray-scale dot condition because the color dot condition gives respondents a choice of colors in addition to the random stimuli. However, the results showed the opposite. This could indicate a mechanism at work that was not initially anticipated but may also be due to the unreliability of the numbers due to the small sample size. Regarding the correlation between the CQCT and AUT flexibility scores, the reasons for the small correlation may be that the order of experimental conditions for the CQCT affected the flexibility score and that the sample size was small. Therefore, it is necessary to conduct the experiment again with a larger sample size.

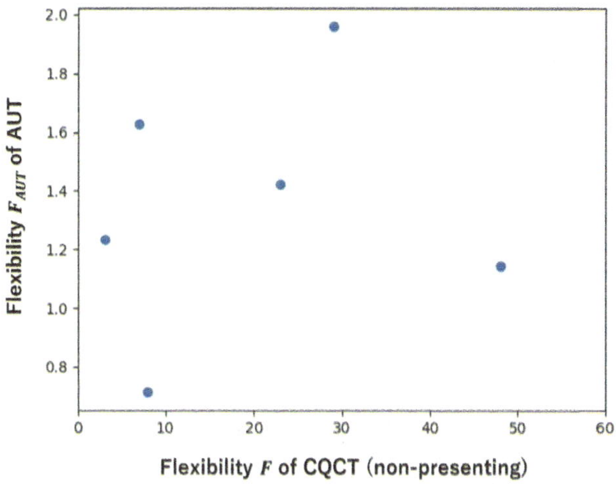

Fig. 6. Correlation between flexibility F of CQCT in non-presenting condition and flexibility F_{AUT} of AUT.

4 Conclusion

Flexibility score was higher in the color dot and gray-scale dot background conditions than in the non-presenting condition. These results suggest that the proposed task, CQCT and its evaluation index of flexibility score , which is calculated based on responses to the developed CQCT, is appropriate.

References

Campbell, D.T.: Blind variation and selective retention in creative thought as in other knowledge processes. Psychol. Rev. **67**(6), 380–400 (1960)

Finke, R.A., Ward, T.B., Smith, S.M.: Creative Cognition. Theory, Research, and Applications. MIT Press (1996)

Guilford, J.P.: The Nature of Human Intelligence. McGraw-Hill, New York, NY (1967)

Young, J.W.: A Technique for Producing Ideas. McGraw-Hill (2003)

Proctor, R.A.: Computer stimulated associations. Creat. Res. J. **6**, 391–400 (1993)

Fukada, R., Ueda, K., Ishii, H., Shimoda, H., Obayashi, F.: A study on a method for automated evaluation of flexibility of alternative uses test. In: The 85th National Convention of IPSJ, vol. 4, pp. 129–130 (2023)

Sequeira, S.: Randomness and creativity. Trends Neurosci. **24**, 694 (2001)

Matsunaga, T., Fukada, R., Ueda, K., Ishii, H., Shimoda, H.: Proposal of color queue creation task for automatic divergent thinking evaluation. AHFE Int. Creat. Innovat. Entrepren. **125**, 1–8 (2024)

Deciphering Eye Fixation Patterns Across Varied Multiple Choice Question Types and Difficulty Levels

Sia Moon[1], Sujin Seong[2], Byungkyu Choi[2], Hyun K. Kim[3], and Jaehyun Park[2](✉)

[1] Department of Industrial and Management Engineering, Incheon National University, Incheon, South Korea

[2] Department of Industrial Engineering, Konkuk University, Seoul, South Korea
jaehpark@konkuk.ac.kr

[3] Department of Artificial Intelligence Convergence, Kwangwoon University, Seoul, South Korea

Abstract. This study aims to identify learners' behavioral characteristics by analyzing eye movements during multiple-choice questions (MCQs). Three types of MCQs were set to analyze eye movements: history, mathematics, and shopping. Each of the three types of questions has a different cognitive process. Regions of interest (AOIs) were set to examine eye movements during question-solving in different cognitive processes. From an analytical point of view, the AOIs were classified into questions and four multiple-choice areas. The questions were presented on PPT slides. Eighteen participants participated in the experiment, with an average age of 22.6 years. We measured eye fixation metrics (Fixation count, Fixation duration) while participants solved a question. We found different fixation patterns depending on the type of questionnaire item. For the three question types, eye fixation on the view the participant chose was high. Also, the percentage of correct answers was the same for the 1, 2, 3, and 4 multiple-choice views. However, eye fixations were higher in views 2 and 3 in the multiple-choice view, as participants sometimes guessed the question. This study can contribute to investigating eye movement patterns in multiple-choice questions.

Keywords: Multiple Choice Questions · Fixation Pattern · Areas of Interest

1 Introduction

With the recent development of online education, online learning utilizing computers and tablet PCs has been actively practiced [1]. Existing studies have attempted to identify learners' behavioral characteristics using non-verbal real-time communication tools such as eye gaze and physical behavior [2]. There are many different kinds of human cognitive processes, such as solving math problems [3], memorizing [4], and wanting to buy something [5]. Since these different cognitive processes occur in the brain, we compared and analyzed users' eye movements while computing MCQs. We wanted to understand perception and attention through learners' eye movements. In particular, eye movements

S. Jin et al. (Eds.): IEA 2024, SSDI 39, pp. 46–51, 2025.
https://doi.org/10.1007/978-981-95-0211-0_8

are one of the most efficient non-verbal communication tools, playing an important role in providing information and regulating interactions [6]. Eye movements can be used to determine perception, attention, and intention [7]. Therefore, in this study, eye movements were measured through multiple-choice questions, MCQs, and different types of problem-solving. Eye fixations during problem-solving were considered a good indicator of the characteristics of each problem type. Therefore, we used the number of fixations and fixation time as indicators in this study. The results of this study will serve as a basis for further research on basic cognitive processes.

2 Method

2.1 Participants

The participants in this study consisted of 18 undergraduate students (10 males and 8 females). The average age of the participants is 22.6 (± 1.41) years old. 14 of the 18 participants had a visual acuity of 0.7 or better, and 4 wore clear contact lenses. All 18 participants had no problems completing the experiment, and only two of the 18 participants had previous experience with eye trackers.

2.2 Experimental Design

In this study, we used Tobii Pro glasses 3 to observe eye movements. For question-solving, we set up AOIs by dividing the question and view areas within a task. Eye fixation metrics (i.e. fixation duration, fixation count) were extracted from each AOIs. The distance between the participant and the question screen monitor was set to 40 cm. In the preparation phase of the experiment, participants wore the eye tracker and adjusted the calibration. In this experiment phase, three types of questions (i.e. History, Math, and Shopping) were solved. There were 10 questions for each type, for a total of 30 questions. Participants were asked to answer all questions verbally. There was no time limit for solving the questions. At the end of the experiment, the data was extracted using Tobii pro lab by Tobii. We organized the data according to each factor. One-way ANOVA and LSD were used to analyze the results. The overall experimental process is shown in Fig. 1; an AOI is shown in Fig. 2.

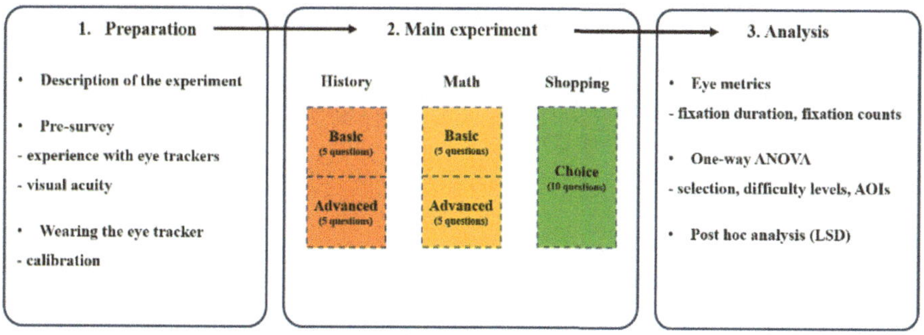

Fig. 1. Experiment procedure

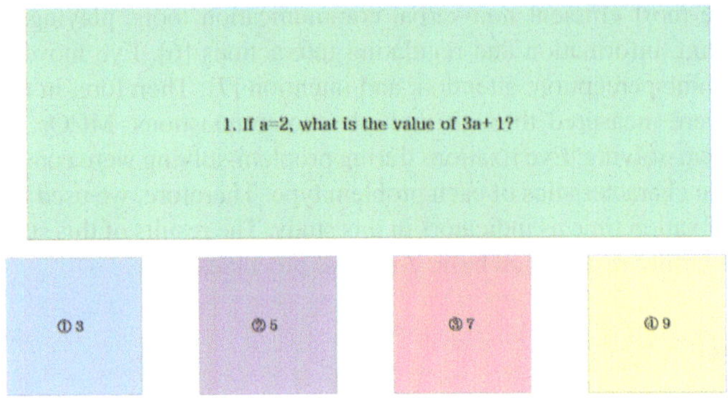

Fig. 2. Set up AOI areas (e.g., mathematics). * Green, blue, purple, pink, and yellow indicate question, 1,2,3, and 4, respectively.

3 Result

3.1 Comparison According to Selection

When solving the MCQs, we predicted that participants' gaze would be directed to the view they thought was the correct answer. To confirm this, we analyzed the views participants selected as the correct answer and those they did not choose. The analysis showed that the view selected as the correct answer had a higher fixation duration, with the math type having the lowest fixation duration. In contrast, the shopping type had the highest fixation duration. The fixation count results showed a similar pattern (Fig. 3).

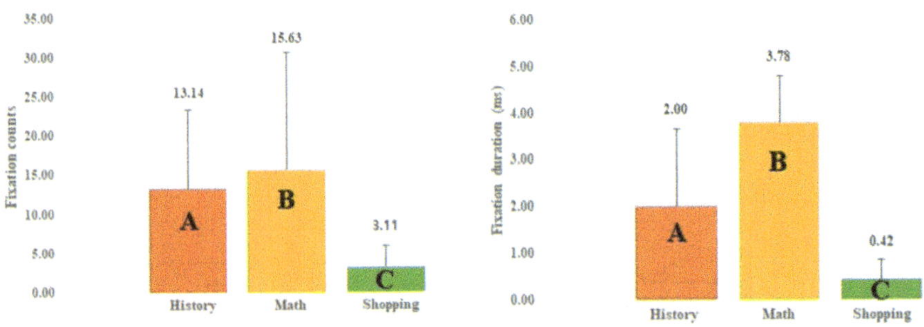

Fig. 3. Fixation metrics comparison of selections by question. * Different alphabets indicate statistically significant differences ($p < 0.05$)

3.2 Comparison According to Selection by Four Views

After identifying that fixations were higher in the selected view, check the distribution of fixations in each of the four views. In addition, the percentage of correct answers was set to be the same for each of the four views in the history and math types (20 questions in total). However, fixation duration and fixation counts were higher in views 2 and 3. The difference between views 2 and 3 was not statistically significant. But, compared to views 1 and 4, we can see a higher fixation pattern. Shopping also had a relatively even distribution of fixations compared to the other two areas, with no bias toward any particular view. Participants' fixations were generally lowest in view 4 and highest in view 2 (Fig. 4).

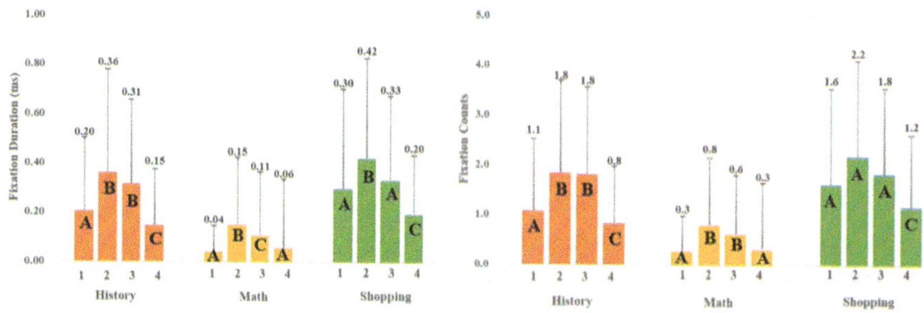

Fig. 4. Fixation metrics comparison of selections by 4 views (each type). * Different alphabets indicate statistically significant differences ($p < 0.05$). * History stands for Korean history. 1,2,3,4 represents views 1 to 4.

4 Discussion

In this study, we analyzed eye fixation movements across MCQs that require different cognitive processes. Fixations were identified by segmenting the task's AOI into question and view areas.

4.1 Comparison According to Selection

In the view area, fixation was highest for the view selected as the correct answer. In this regard, users typically increase their eye gaze intensity on keywords they are interested in [8]. We also observed that history and shopping had the highest fixations and math had the lowest, suggesting that users' eye gaze is directed to the area where the correct answer exists. We also observed that math had the highest fixations in the question area rather than the view area because math tends to focus on numbers rather than text [9]. Furthermore, shopping selects items to purchase in the view area, so we can assume that eye fixations are evenly distributed across the view area. Solving questions that require these different cognitive processes is characterized by the eye fixation movements of each.

4.2 Comparison According to Selection by 4 Views

To compare gaze fixation behavior in the four views, we set the number of correct answers to be the same for all questions. However, in views 1 and 4, gaze fixation was low. The highest gaze fixation in views 2 and 3 suggests that users' behavior while answering questions in MCQs is psychologically influenced. Sometimes, all participants know the correct answer and solve the question. However, some of the 18 participants might tend to guess for questions they do not know. When participants faced a question they did not realize, eye fixations were higher in views 2 and 3 when choosing one of the four views. We did not inform participants before the experiment that the number of all answer views was the same. Therefore, we think eye fixation movements in specific views are higher when solving questions they do not know. In addition, a previous study has investigated the psychological basis of participants' guessing for MCQs [10]. We think that the psychological foundations of the results of this study on views 2 and 3 can also be applied to future studies.

5 Conclusion

This study analyzed eye fixations during MCQs of different cognitive processes. Three question types (i.e., History, Math, Shopping) were used to divide AOI settings within the task slides. By extracting and evaluating eye fixation metrics (fixation count and duration), we could distinguish patterns in eye movements according to the type of question. Each question type feature had a different interpretation of fixations. The findings of this study provide basic cognitive science findings. The results of this study can serve as a framework for future research on eye movement patterns to improve educational performance. While this study provides valuable insights, it is important to acknowledge its limitations, such as the homogeneity of the problem types and the uniform age of the participants.

Appendix

The GitHub repository at https://github.com/sia-0/MCQ-Questions-Full-.git contains full question slide (ppt) in this study.

References

1. Oliveira, G.: 2(5), 99–110 (2016)
2. Kuang, Z., Wang, F., Andrasik, F., Hu, X.: Instructor's direct gaze not body orientation affects learning. J. Comput. Assist. Learn. (2023)
3. Kleinke, C.L.: Gaze and eye contact: a research review. Psychol. Bull. **100**(1), 78–100 (1986)
4. Rosch, J.L., Vogel-Walcutt, J.J.: A review of eye-tracking applications as tools for training. Cogn. Tech. Work. **15**, 313–327 (2013)
5. Musso, M.F., Boekaerts, M., Segers, M., Cascallar, E.C.: Individual differences in basic cognitive processes and self-regulated learning: their interaction effects on math performance. Learn. Individid. Differ. **71**, 58–70 (2019)

6. Wang, Y.: Formal description of the cognitive process of memorization. In: Transactions on Computational Science V: Special Issue on Cognitive Knowledge Representation, pp. 81–98 (2009)
7. Chen, A., Lu, Y., Wang, B.: Customers' purchase decision-making process in social commerce: A social learning perspective. Int. J. Inf. Manag. **37**(6), 627–638 (2017)
8. Gunawan, F.E., Wijaya, O., Soewito, B., Candra, S., Suharyanto, C.E., Sekishita, N.: An analysis of concentration region on powerpoint slides using eye tracking. In: 2017 4th International Conference on Electrical Engineering, Computer Science and Informatics (EECSI), pp. 1–5. IEEE (2017, September)
9. Spagnolo, C., Capone, R., Gambini, A.: Where do students focus their attention on solving mathematical tasks? An eye tracker explorative study. In: Proceedings of the 44th Conference of the International Group for the Psychology of Mathematics Education, vol. 4, pp. 89–96, Khon Kaen, Thailand (2021)
10. Kubinger, K. D., & Gottschall, C. H. (2007). Item difficulty of multiple choice tests dependant on different item response formats--An experiment in fundamental research on psychological assessment. Psychol. Sci., 49(4), 361
11. Oliveira, G., Grenha Teixeira, J., Torres, A., Morais, C.: An exploratory study on the emergency remote education experience of higher education students and teachers during the COVID-19 pandemic. Br. J. Educ. Technol. **52**(4), 1357–1376 (2021)

Predicting the Factors that Affect M-commerce Application "Stickiness"

Adrianne Ong(✉) and Rosemary Seva

De La Salle University, Manila, Philippines
{adie_ong,rosemary.seva}@dlsu.edu.ph

Abstract. The expanding mobile commerce landscape gives companies a unique avenue to connect with consumers. With most existing studies focusing on long-term user behavior, such as loyalty and continued use, research on app stickiness has yet to be explored in-depth. App stickiness refers to the short-term user behavior categorized by the number of daily average users and the duration of engagement with the application in one session. This study investigates the relationships between cognitive experience, affective experience, trust, satisfaction, and app stickiness in m-commerce applications. Partial Least Squares Structural Equation Modeling was used to analyze data collected from m-commerce application users. The findings support positive relationships between cognitive experience, affective experience, satisfaction, and app stickiness however, the connection between trust and app stickiness was inversely related. This result is attributed to potential demographic influences, suggesting the need for further research to explore the potential moderating effects of user characteristics on the trust-app stickiness relationship in m-commerce contexts.

Keywords: App Stickiness · Affective Experience · Cognitive Experience

1 Introduction

1.1 Background of the Study

The digital revolution transformed the retail environment, with e-commerce booming at an estimated value of $6.3 trillion in 2024 [1]. Mobile commerce (m-commerce), an e-commerce subcategory that involves mobile app usage, has become more popular, accounting for 65.7% of global e-commerce sales in 2022 (valued at $3.744 billion) [2]. Increased mobile adoption due to its functionality and convenience has driven this shift, with more users who favor mobile apps over traditional websites [3].

The growing m-commerce landscape presents a unique opportunity for businesses to reach consumers. Designers have been developing ways to keep users engaged by observing cognitive and affective experiences. Cognitive experience refers to how the mind processes information during navigation (e.g., knowing, exploring, and understanding). Affective experience refers to the collective emotional responses, preferences, and perceptions experienced during encounters. Salvendy [4] proposed a two-way interaction between the affective and cognitive experience when a stimulus triggers. Another

S. Jin et al. (Eds.): IEA 2024, SSDI 39, pp. 52–58, 2025.
https://doi.org/10.1007/978-981-95-0211-0_9

way designers keep customers in an app is through continued use [5] and loyalty [6], which are long-term user behaviors that refer to a user's willingness to use an app again in the future. On the other hand, app stickiness refers to a user's current short-term behavior (e.g., duration of stay, involvement, and daily engagement). App stickiness can be measured in two ways, either through the number of daily active users and average session duration [7]. For example, an app with many daily users but a short average session time could imply numerous clicks to open the app but little interest in actual usage. In contrast, an app with fewer daily users but a higher average session duration and conversion rate may indicate more engaged users but relatively fewer users overall. Molinillo et al. [6] explored the relationship of cognitive and affective experience to loyalty and found a higher significance of the connection between loyalty and affective experience. The same finding was observed by Alnawas et al. [7], who used retail app stickiness as a factor related to cognitive and affective factors instead of loyalty.

Trust and satisfaction are important predictors of user behavior due to their connection to perceived app performance [8]. Zhou et al. [9] confirmed the significant relationship between cognitive (identified as perceived utility, hedonic value, and privacy risk) and affective (identified as trust and satisfaction) factors with app stickiness.

Given the extent of existing literature on app stickiness, this study aims to observe the relationship between cognitive experience, affective experience, trust, and satisfaction with m-commerce app stickiness. Previous research on m-commerce apps failed to consider trust and satisfaction in determining the relationship between cognitive and affective experience with app stickiness. This paper proposes that basic emotions are more appropriate affective factors because they arise directly from interface stimuli and allow a better understanding of user reactions. Existing literature on m-commerce app stickiness is also rare. Moreover, studies have focused on long-term behavior (continued use and loyalty) but failed to explore short-term behavior (app stickiness). App stickiness goes beyond usage intentions and focuses on actual user behavior. This study addresses these gaps and highlights the need to improve existing app stickiness models for m-commerce apps to drive higher engagement.

1.2 Hypotheses

To determine the factors that affect the stickiness of m-commerce apps, this study aims to answer the following hypotheses:

H1: Cognitive experience positively influences trust in m-commerce apps.
H2: Cognitive experience positively influences satisfaction in m-commerce apps.
H3: Affective experience positively influences trust in m-commerce apps.
H4: Affective experience positively influences satisfaction in m-commerce apps.
H5: Trust in m-commerce apps positively influences app stickiness.
H6: Satisfaction in m-commerce apps positively influences app stickiness.

1.3 Proposed Model

The model by Alnawas et al. [7] was used as a base model for this study, with trust and satisfaction as direct connections to app stickiness, as Zhou et al. [9] suggested. Cognitive and affective experiences were considered as user dimensions, trust and satisfaction as outcomes of user dimensions, and app stickiness as user response (Fig. 1).

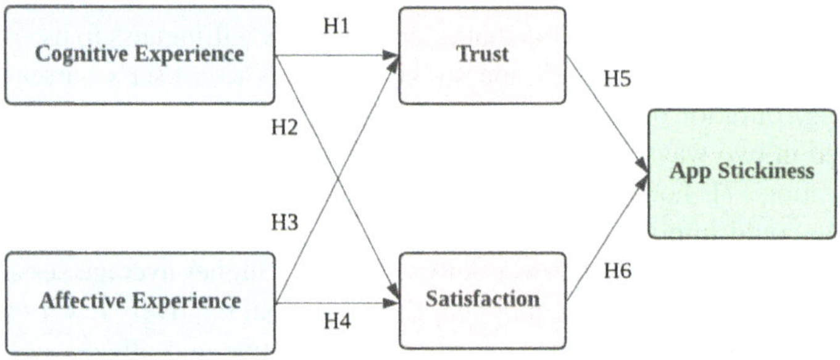

Fig. 1. Proposed m-commerce app stickiness model

2 Methodology

2.1 Data Collection and Analysis

Data was collected using a convenience sampling method through Google Forms. Participants must have used m-commerce platforms at least once. All measures were gathered from existing literature and were evaluated using a 7-point Likert scale. The Minimum Sample Size Estimation method proposed by Kock and Hadaya [10] was used to ensure adequate participants. Collected data was analyzed through Partial Least Squares Structural Equation Modeling (PLS-SEM) using SmartPLS version 4 [11]. PLS-SEM generates statistically sound inferences on the relationships observed and extends the inferences to apply to a larger population [12, 13].

2.2 Data Screening

161 responses were collected, including four non-users of m-commerce platforms. These four responses were removed, resulting in a new total of 157 respondents with a mean age of 29.8. Majority of the respondents were female (67.52%) and part of Gen Z (68.15%). Most participants were students (63.06%) who have an iOS operating system (68.79%). Unlike the previous categories, the frequency of usage was spread out, with more than half using m-commerce platforms at least once a week (Table 1).

A significance level of 0.5 and a minimum beta-coefficient of 0.2 are applied, as Chin [14] proposed that beta-coefficients must be between 0.2 and 0.3 to be valid. Applying 0.2 to the formula by Kock and Hadaya [10] and using the sum of the z-scores at 95% and 80% confidence intervals (1.645 and 0.841, respectively), the minimum sample size needed is 155. Thus, this study meets the required sample size.

$$
\begin{aligned}
&|\beta|_{min}\sqrt{\hat{N}} > Z_{0.95} + Z_{0.8} \rightarrow \\
&\hat{N} > \left(\frac{Z_{0.95}+Z_{0.8}}{|\beta|_{min}}\right)^2 \rightarrow \\
&\qquad\qquad n_{min} > \left(\frac{2.486}{0.2}\right)^2 \\
&\hat{N} > \left(\frac{2.486}{|\beta|_{min}}\right)^2 \cdot \quad n_{min} > 154.505 \cong 155\ \textit{respondents}
\end{aligned}
\tag{1}
$$

Table 1. Demographics of participants (N = 157).

Characteristics	Category	N	%	Characteristics	Category	N	%
Age	Gen Z (18-27)	107	68.15%	Occupation	Student	99	63.06%
	Young Millennial (28-35)	9	5.73%		Employee	38	24.20%
	Old Millennial (36-43)	8	5.10%		Self-employed	8	5.10%
	Young Gen X (44-51)	16	10.19%		Household wife/husband	10	6.37%
	Old Gen X (52-59)	14	8.92%		Unemployed	2	1.27%
	Young Boomers (60-69)	3	1.91%		Other	0	0.00%
Sex	Female	106	67.52%	Frequency of Usage of M-Commerce Platforms	Daily	11	7.01%
	Male	49	31.21%		4-6 times a week	24	15.29%
	Prefer not to say	2	1.27%		2-3 times a week	34	21.66%
Operating System	iOS	108	68.79%		Once a week	24	15.29%
	Android	49	31.21%		Once every two weeks	31	19.75%
	Other	0	0.00%		Once a month	33	21.02%

3 Results and Discussion

3.1 Data and Hypothesis Validation

The model fit indices provided by the software are within the corresponding threshold values. Thus, the model is deemed fit to represent the data and can explain a significant portion of the observed variation. The minimum required beta coefficient of 0.2 was seen in all paths except for H5, which signifies that all paths are deemed valid except for H5. Additionally, all p-values are below 0.05, which makes the connections significant. Despite the significance of the p-value of H5, this hypothesis was still rejected because it failed to meet the minimum value for the beta coefficient (Table 2).

Table 2. Model fit indices and hypothesis validation

Model Fit	Model Value	Recommended Value	Fit?
SRMR	0.073	< 0.08	Yes
NFI	0.938	> 0.90	Yes

Standardized Root Mean Square Residual (SRMR) and Normed Fit Index (NFI)

Hypothesis	Model Paths		Values		Remarks
	From	To	Beta-coefficient	p-value	
H1	Cognitive Experience	Trust	0.200	0.008 < 0.05	Accepted
H2		Satisfaction	0.265	0.005 < 0.05	Accepted
H3	Affective Experience	Trust	0.560	0.000 < 0.05	Accepted
H4		Satisfaction	0.420	0.000 < 0.05	Accepted
H5	Trust	App Stickiness	-0.023	0.037 < 0.05	Rejected
H6	Satisfaction		0.683	0.000 < 0.05	Accepted

With the study successfully assessing the proposed App Stickiness model, below is a further discussion of the hypotheses:

(Accepted) H1. A positive cognitive experience allows a sense of immersion within the m-commerce app, where users feel absorbed in the app's content and functionalities. This finding is consistent with Molinillo et al. [6] and Zhou et al. [9], who also observed a direct relationship between the two variables. Clear app design, immersive experiences, and smooth navigation through a well-structured interface can create a perception of reliability, leading users to trust the app's security for transactions.

(Accepted) H2. The direct relationship between cognitive experience and satisfaction is also observed in the studies by Molinillo et al. [6] and Zhou et al. [9]. Being immersed in an m-commerce application can be brought about by clear and concise information, allowing users to stay in the app because they understand its features. Clear product information, smooth app performance, immersive experiences, and consistent information flow enhance satisfaction by creating a sense of presence and simplifying decision-making. User-friendly interfaces and efficient search functions minimize effort and frustration, leading to a more positive experience.
(Accepted) H3. Affective experience creates trust by building emotional connections between the application and the user. An enjoyable experience through engaging design and seamless interactions evokes positive emotions in users. This emotional connection cultivates a sense of familiarity and comfort, leading users to perceive the application as reliable. The positive relationship between affective experience and trust is supported by the studies conducted by Molinillo et al. [6] and Putra et al. [5].
(Accepted) H4. Users interacting with an m-commerce app that evokes positive emotions tend to perceive the experience as fulfilling. This emotional response can be triggered by an interface design with aesthetic elements that evoke joy and ease of use. Like the previous hypothesis, a positive relationship between affective experience and satisfaction aligns with research by Molinillo et al. [6] and Putra et al. [5].
(Accepted) H6. User satisfaction with an m-commerce application can contribute to app stickiness because users with a sense of fulfillment would engage with the app more [9]. Satisfied users would be more encouraged to revisit the app for future needs, which translates to increased session frequency. This can be through utilizing loyalty programs, leaving product reviews, and engaging with other users.
(Rejected) H5. The negative relationship between trust and app stickiness was due to the relatively low trust but high app stickiness ratings. This may be attributed to users who continue to use m-commerce apps despite privacy concerns. The majority of the participants are students from Generation Z (ages 21–28). Compared to other generations, Gen Z is less concerned about how apps use their personal data [15]. In fact, more than 40% of Gen Z individuals agree to exchange their personal information for discounts and freebies from stores [16]. Thus, perceived trust in an m-commerce app may not particularly play a significant role for the participants of this study. If the features of the m-commerce app meet their needs, then Gen Z individuals will engage with the app, even with a low perceived trust [17]. Nonetheless, this finding should prompt app designers to win back users' trust through enhanced privacy measures.

4 Conclusion and Recommendations

In the competitive m-commerce environment, stakeholders must also assess an application's short-term performance through app stickiness to better determine the current reach of an application. To assess the role of user experience in app stickiness, cognitive and affective experience, trust, and satisfaction were integrated. The validated model showed a positive connection between all factors except trust and app stickiness, which may be attributed to the participant's demographics, who do not perceive trust as a significant factor as much as the other generations. Overall, the proposed app stickiness model of m-commerce applications is still able to confirm the relationship between cognitive and affective experience, trust, satisfaction, and app stickiness, which is a valuable finding given the rarity of studies on app stickiness.

Despite contributing to the relatively new concept of app stickiness and addressing the gap in the effect of cognitive and affective experience, trust, and satisfaction with app stickiness, model testing to a wider demographic is suggested to further observe the negative impact of trust on app stickiness. A positive impact on a diverse sample size could infer the significant impact of demographics on the proposed model. Moreover, research extensions could include connections between app stickiness with loyalty and continued use. In this way, stakeholders could confirm if long-term behavior (continued use and loyalty) depends on short-term behavior (app stickiness).

References

1. van Gelder, K.: E-commerce worldwide - statistics & facts, Statista. https://www.statista.com/topics/871/online-shopping/. Last accessed 11 March 2024
2. Chevalier, S.: M-commerce as share of total online retail by region 2022, Statista. https://www.statista.com/statistics/806323. Last accessed 11 March 2024
3. Harrison, R., Flood, D., Duce, D.: Usability of mobile applications: literature review and rationale for a new usability model. J. Interact. Sci. **1**, 1 (2013)
4. Salvendy, G.: Handbook of Human Factors and Ergonomics. (1990)
5. Putra, P., Dewi, R., Budi, I.: Usability factors that drive continued intention to use and loyalty of mobile travel application. Heliyon. **8**(9), e10620 (2022)
6. Molinillo, S., Navarro-García, A., Anaya-Sánchez, R., Japutra, A.: The impact of affective and cognitive app experiences on loyalty towards retailers. J. Retail. Consum. Serv. **54**, 101948 (2020)
7. Alnawas, I., Al Khateeb, A., El Hedhli, K.: The effects of app-related factors on app stickiness: the role of cognitive and emotional app relationship quality. J. Retail. Consum. Serv. **75**, 103412 (2023)
8. Rose, S., Clark, M., Samouel, P., Hair, N.: Online customer experience in e-retailing: an empirical model of antecedents and outcomes. J. Retail. **88**(2), 308–322 (2012)
9. Zhou, X., Rau, P., Jie, Z.: Stickiness formation among mobile apps of different social levels: multigroup analysis using the cognitive–affective–conative framework. Inf. Technol. People. **37**(3), 1208–1228 (2023)
10. Kock, N., Hadaya, P.: Minimum sample size estimation in PLS-SEM. Inf. Syst. J. **28**, 227–261 (2018)
11. Ringle, C., Wende, S., Becker, J.: SmartPLS 4. Bönningstedt: SmartPLS (2024). https://www.smartpls.com
12. Nandi, S., Nandi, M.L., Khandker, V.: Impact of perceived interactivity and perceived value on mobile app stickiness: an emerging economy perspective. J. Consum. Market. **38**, 721–737 (2021)
13. Hair, J., Risher, J., Sarstedt, M., Ringle, C.: When to use and how to report the results of PLS-SEM. Eur. Bus. Rev. **31**(1), 2–24 (2019)
14. Chin, W.W.: Commentary: issues and opinion on structural equation modeling. MIS Q. **22**(1), 7–16 (1998)
15. Ashcraft, L.: There's a generational divide on privacy. https://www.emarketer.com/content/privacy-concerns-dont-get-in-way-of-gen-z-enthusiasm-about-ai-enabled-banking. Last accessed 28 March 2024

16. Skinner, S.: Mind the Gap: Are Gen Zers too trusting with their data online? https://www.mckinsey.com/~/media/mckinsey/email/genz/2022/09/27/2022-09-27b.html. Last accessed 28 March 2024
17. Piacenza, J.: Most Trusted Brands Report 2023. https://pro-assets.morningconsult.com/wp-uploads/2023/05/Most-Trusted-Brands-2023.pdf. Last accessed 28 March 2024

Evaluation of Usability and Arousal Levels in Electric Vehicles Using In-Vehicle Physiological Signals: A Focus on Motion Sickness

Jiyeon Shin[1], Yein Song[1], Cai Wang[1], Jungyeon Park[1], Jaehoo Bae[1], Jae Sik Yang[2], Seonghyeon Kim[2], Sangwoo Bahn[3], and Myung Hwan Yun[4](✉)

[1] Department of Industrial Engineering, Seoul National University, Seoul, South Korea
[2] Hyundai Motor Group, Seoul, South Korea
[3] Department of Industrial Engineering, Kyung Hee University, Seoul, South Korea
[4] Institute for Industrial System Innovation, Seoul National University, Seoul, South Korea
mhy@snu.ac.kr

Abstract. Managing vehicle stress and arousal is essential for safe and satisfying driving experiences. However, unexpected movements and degraded driving experience quality can cause rapid changes in arousal levels during driving. One of the important factors affecting the quality of the user experience is motion sickness. This study uses various biometric indicators to understand the impact of motion sickness severity and arousal levels. Specifically, this research investigates the relationship between biometric signals, particularly electrocardiogram (ECG) indicators, and motion sickness in real driving environments. By analyzing ECG-derived metrics, we aim to identify patterns associated with increased arousal and stress levels, potentially leading to the development of personalized driver support systems.

Keywords: Electric Vehicle · Motion Sickness · Electrocardiogram · Real Vehicle Test

1 Introduction

Electric vehicles (EVs) offer a different driving experience than traditional internal combustion engines. Specifically, unlike conventional vehicles, EVs employ a mech-anism known as regenerative braking, which can lead to rapid deceleration and ac-celeration, potentially causing motion sickness [1]. This phenomenon can also be explained by existing theories of motion sickness [2, 3]. Addressing this issue is crucial for the usability and comfort of EVs and the overall user experience [4]. Understand-ing these reactions by measuring biometric signals, such as electrocardiogram (ECG) indicators, can provide valuable insights into effective mitigation strategies for EV-induced motion sickness.

S. Jin et al. (Eds.): IEA 2024, SSDI 39, pp. 59–63, 2025.
https://doi.org/10.1007/978-981-95-0211-0_10

Previous studies have demonstrated the utility of ECG and other biometric signals in monitoring driver stress and fatigue. However, the analysis of the relationship between ECG indicators and motion sickness during actual driving has yet to be fully explored. Therefore, this study aims to investigate this unexplored area by analyzing ECG-derived metrics in the context of EV-induced motion sickness through multiple regression analysis.

2 Method

Thirteen participants were selected based on gender, age, and motion sickness susceptibility, as determined by the Motion Sickness Susceptibility Questionnaire (MSSQ) [5]. Participants with MSSQ scores in the top 50–95% were included to make a representative sample of individuals prone to motion sickness.

The vehicle used in this study was a Kia EV6. Motion sickness severity was measured using surveys on a Samsung Galaxy Table S7 (11-inch), and ECG data was recorded with a Laxtha PolyG-A device. The driving route consisted of a 10 km loop within the University, chosen for its minimal traffic and lack of traffic signals. Participants were seated in the rear seat, with the experimenter in the left rear seat and the driver in the front seat. Visual occlusion was achieved using white felt curtains on the windows and between the front and rear seats to minimize external visual stimuli. The ECG equipment was secured with sponges to reduce movement artifacts.

The procedure involved briefing participants on the experiment, obtaining consent, and fitting them with ECG electrodes. Baseline measurements and practice surveys were conducted prior to the driving session. During the 30-min driving session, participants completed surveys every 2 min, prompted by a beep sound, and ECG data was continuously recorded at a sampling frequency of 128 Hz. Primary measures included heart rate (BPM), HRV metrics (HRV Triangular Index, pNN50, RMSSD, SDNN), and subjective motion sickness severity (MISC [6], MSSS [7]) (Table 1).

Table 1. Metrics Considered in Time-Domain Analysis

Index	Definition	Unit
mHR	Average Heart Rate	bpm
SDNN	Standard Deviation of NN Intervals	ms
RMSSD	Root Mean Square of RR Intervals	ms
HRV Triangular	Geometric Distribution of RR Intervals	N/A
pNN50	Proportion of Heartbeat Intervals Differing by More Than 50 ms	%

3 Result

Multiple regression analysis was used to examine the impact of various ECG met-rics on the motion sickness indicators MISC and MSSS. For the MISC results, the model explained a significant proportion of the variance, 2 = 0.717, adjust-ed 2 = 0.702, (7103)

= 47.77, <0.001. The analysis revealed that several predictors significantly contributed to the model. BPM (b = 0.0493, SE = 0.029, t = 1.696, p = 0.093) showed a positive trend but was not statistically significant. However, pNN50 (b = 0.076, SE = 0.031, t = 2.478, p = 0.015) was a significant positive predictor of MISC, indicating that higher pNN50 values were associated with increased motion sickness severity. In contrast, HRV Triangular (b = −0.1265, SE = 0.048, t = −2.649, p = 0.009), RMSSD (b = −0.033, SE = 0.012, t = −2.844, p = 0.005), and SDNN (b = −0.1321, SE = 0.084, t = −1.568, p = 0.119) were negative predictors, although SDNN was not statistically significant. Time (b = 0.0037, SE = 0.001, t = 11.104, p < 0.001) was also a significant positive predictor, indicating that motion sickness severity in-creased over time.

For the MSSS results, the model similarly explained a significant proportion of the variance, 2 = 0.781, adjusted 2 = 0.716, (7103) = 51.08, < 0.001. BPM (b = 0.0564, SE = 0.016, t = 3.533, p = 0.001) and pNN50 (b = 0.0564, SE = 0.017, t = 3.345, p = 0.002) were significant positive predictors of MSSS, suggesting that higher values of these metrics were associated with increased susceptibility to motion sickness. HRV Triangular (b = −0.0229, SE = 0.006, t = −3.811, p < 0.001), RMSSD (b = −0.0334, SE = 0.006, t = −5.24, p < 0.001), and SDNN (b = −0.3321, SE = 0.038, t = −8.74, p < 0.001) were significant negative predictors, indicating that lower values of these metrics were associated with higher motion sickness susceptibility. Time (b = 0.002, SE = 0.000, t = 12.816, p < 0.001) was a significant positive predictor, showing that motion sickness susceptibility increased over time. Below is a plot that visualizes the results of the multiple regression analysis (see Fig. 1).

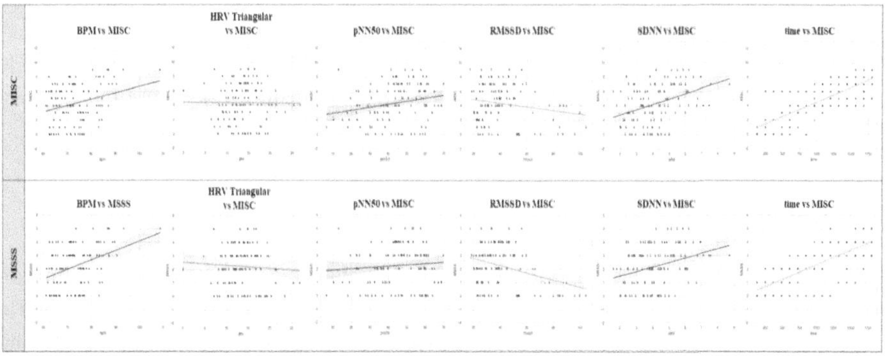

Fig. 1. Relationships between ECG Metrics and Motion Sickness Indicators (MISC and MSSS)

Results indicated that BPM and pNN50 positively correlated with increased motion sickness severity, while HRV Triangular, RMSSD, and SDNN negatively correlated. Additionally, time was positively correlated with motion sickness severity, suggesting a gradual increase over time.

4 Discussion

Increased BPM (beats per minute), a measure of heart rate, signifies a heightened heart rate, often linked to elevated arousal and stress, which can contribute to motion sickness. Lower HRV Triangular Index values, a measure of heart rate variability, also indicate reduced heart rate variability and poor autonomic regulation, making individuals more susceptible to motion sickness.

Understanding the role of different HRV metrics is a complex but crucial aspect of our research. Higher pNN50 values, reflecting increased parasympathetic activity, can indicate a different pattern of motion sickness or the body's effort to recover from stress. This contrasts with RMSSD and SDNN values, which decrease with re-duced parasympathetic activity, indicating poorer stress resilience and autonomic imbalance, thereby worsening motion sickness. The difference in patterns between pNN50 and other metrics like RMSSD and SDNN can be attributed to the former considering the ratio of successive heartbeats, while the latter focuses on specific intervals. This nuanced understanding of HRV metrics is key to our research and can help us develop more effective strategies to combat motion sickness.

Prolonged exposure to motion accumulates autonomic stress, exacerbating motion sickness symptoms. These findings suggest that ECG-derived metrics can predict and mitigate motion sickness in electric vehicles (EVs). By integrating these indicators into a personalized driver support system, real-time feedback and adjustments can en-hance comfort and safety, potentially revolutionizing the way we design and use EVs.

Such a system could monitor the driver's ECG, analyze key HRV metrics, adjust vehicle settings such as seat position, temperature, or cabin lighting, or provide bio-feedback to manage physiological responses, thus reducing distractions caused by motion sickness and improving driving experience and road safety. The system could also provide alerts or warnings when the driver's HRV metrics indicate a high risk of motion sickness, allowing for proactive measures to be taken.

5 Conclusion

This study not only reveals significant relationships between ECG metrics and motion sickness in EVs but also provides practical implications for the automotive and biometric technology industries. The link between increased heart rate and decreased heart rate variability with higher motion sickness severity offers valuable insights for the development of personalized driver support systems and adaptive vehicle technologies. These innovations, when implemented, can significantly reduce motion sickness and enhance the overall user experience in EVs. Moving forward, future research should refine these models and explore additional biometric signals, thereby improving predictive accuracy and intervention strategies, and directly impacting the practical applications of this research.

Acknowledgments. This work was supported by the BK21 FOUR Program (Education and Research Center for Industrial Innovation Analytics) funded by the Ministry of Education, Korea.

References

1. Kuiper, O.X., Bos, J.E., Schmidt, E.A., Diels, C., Wolter, S.: Knowing what's coming: unpredictable motion causes more motion sickness. Hum. Factors. **62**(8), 1339–1348 (2020)
2. Bos, J.E., Bles, W., Groen, E.L.: A theory on visually induced motion sickness. Displays. **29**(2), 47–57 (2008)
3. Diels, C., Bos, J.E., Hottelart, K., Reilhac, P.: Motion sickness in automated vehicles: the elephant in the room. Road Veh. Automat. **3**, 121–129 (2016)
4. Diels, C., Bos, J.E.: Self-driving carsickness. Appl. Ergon. **53**, 374–382 (2016)
5. Golding, J.F.: Motion sickness susceptibility questionnaire revised and its relationship to other forms of sickness. Brain Res. Bull. **47**(5), 507–516 (1998)
6. Bos, J.E., MacKinnon, S.N., Patterson, A.: Motion sickness symptoms in a ship motion simulator: effects of inside, outside, and no view. Aviat. Space Environ. Med. **76**(12), 1111–1118 (2005)
7. Czeisler, M.É., Pruski, J.M., Wang, P., Wang, J., Xiao, C., Polymeropoulos, M.H., Polymeropoulos, V.M.: Validation of the motion sickness severity scale: secondary analysis of a randomized, double-blind, placebo-controlled study of a treatment for motion sickness. PLoS One. **18**(1), e0280058 (2023)

Retail UX: An Anthology of Sensory Experience in Physical Retail from the Perspective of User Centered Design

Paulo Eduardo Hauqui Tonin(✉), Giselle Schmidt Alves Dias Merino, Elton Moura Nickel, and Flavio Anthero Nunes Vianna dos Santos

Universidade do Estado de Santa Catarina, Florianópolis, SC 88035-901, Brazil
paulotonin@gmail.com

Abstract. The article highlights the relevance of User-Centered Design in the context of physical retail, exploring the importance of sensory stimuli in the customer experience. With a multidisciplinary approach that unites different disciplines, the study seeks to understand how these stimuli can benefit brands and companies in attracting and retaining customers. Faced with the growing migration of consumers to digital platforms, the survival of physical stores, especially those of small and medium-sized enterprises (SMEs), requires distinctive actions. These actions involve, for instance, the creation of meaning and value through sensory-oriented experience design. The study, exploratory in nature, aims to formulate a problem and collect information about the phenomenon, bringing together a variety of concepts and methodological approaches from different eras. The anthology presented provides an integrated view of the theme, helping professionals and SMEs better understand the evolution of thinking about the sensory experience in physical retail from the perspective of User-Centered Design and its intrinsic relationship with Human Factors.

Keywords: User-Centered Design · Sensory Stimuli · Experience Design · Physical Retail · Human Factors

1 Introduction

1.1 Problem Statement

User-Centered Design integrates insights from Semiotics, Environmental Psychology, Design Theory, Management, and Marketing to explore sensorial experiences in physical retail. This approach focuses on enhancing user experience through cognitive and behavioral responses, aiding brands in customer attraction and retention. Amidst a rising preference for online shopping accelerated by COVID-19, physical stores leverage sensory stimuli to maintain relevance [1–3]. Design plays a pivotal role in creating and managing these sensory experiences, supported by literature highlighting their branding benefits through cohesive messaging [4, 5]. For SMEs, lacking in Design Experience practices, integrating sensorial strategies aligned with brand identity is crucial for effective customer engagement [5, 6]. This holistic perspective benefits both professionals and smaller enterprises seeking to innovate in retail environments.

S. Jin et al. (Eds.): IEA 2024, SSDI 39, pp. 64–69, 2025.
https://doi.org/10.1007/978-981-95-0211-0_11

1.2 Objective/Question

The main objective of this study is to understand the evolution of sensory experience in physical retail through User-Centered Design. Despite extensive work on sensory stimulation in stores, many solutions fail due to ineffective brand-user communication [4, 5]. Focusing on the user, this exploratory research asks: *How can an integrated perspective, combining various concepts, help professionals and SMEs rethink the application of sensoriality in physical stores?*

1.3 Methodology

This exploratory research aims to gather information and identify problems related to the sensory experience in physical retail through a User-Centered Design approach. Using bibliographical research, it seeks to provide a multidisciplinary understanding of this phenomenon. The study integrates models and theories from *Peirce* (1931–1958), *Mehrabian and Russell* (1974), *Krippendorf* (1984), *Malnar and Vodvarka* (2004), *Brown* (2009), *Lindstrom* (2011), *Manzano* et al. (2012), *Hulten* (2017), and *Matsumura* (2020). These references cover Semiotics, Environmental Psychology, Design Theory and Management, Sensory Design, and Marketing (see Fig. 1).

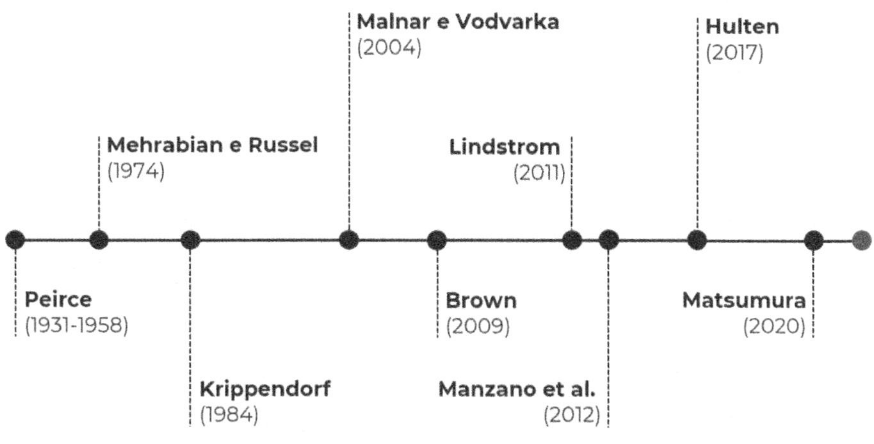

Fig. 1. An Anthology on Retail UX. Source: Author (2024).

2 Literature Review

2.1 *Peircean* Semiotics and the Creation of Signs

Peirce's semiotic study, grounded in phenomenology, explores the perception of conscious phenomena, ranging from basic sensory experiences to complex abstractions. His triadic model of signs integrates internal properties, meanings, and their effects on receivers, elucidating communication dynamics such as reference, applicability, and recipient responses. Peirce identifies three foundational elements—firstness (chance and quality), secondness (dependence and action), and thirdness (generality and intelligence)—which underlie all phenomena [7]. Central to his theory is the sign, which connects what is presented to the mind, its significance, and the interpretative outcomes it engenders. This interplay shapes theories on signification, denotation, reality, reference, and interpretation, highlighting how signs externalize internal thoughts and emotions into external symbols, emphasizing their formal properties and governing principles [7, 8].

2.2 The Stimulus-Organism-Response from Environmental Psychology

Mehrabian and Russell's environmental psychology model elucidates how retail environments shape consumer purchasing intentions through a cognitivist perspective. This approach examines the interactions between humans and environmental stimuli, emphasizing how factors like lighting can evoke emotional responses such as frustration or satisfaction, influencing whether consumers choose to make purchases or leave without buying [9]. The model categorizes consumer experiences based on pleasure/displeasure and arousal/non-arousal dimensions, which dictate cognitive responses of approach or withdrawal and significantly impact consumer behavior and repeat visits. Understanding these dynamics helps companies optimize their physical environments to foster positive consumer experiences and maximize sales potential [9].

2.3 The Role of Attribution in Design

Language functions as a system of signs and symbols that reference the non-linguistic world and express individual meanings. The theory of artifact meaning in language highlights how artifacts gain significance in narratives, impacting human behavior and various aspects of society. In retail, storytelling is vital, using figures of speech like analogy, metaphor, and simile to enhance narratives. Language coordinates human interaction, directs attention, frames perception, creates facts, and is both relational and embodied. Attributes, defined as characteristics or essential properties, reveal sensory qualities and emotions, influencing cognitive and behavioral responses. In the sensory-perceptual realm, attributes include aesthetic, symbolic, and style aspects, with colors playing a fundamental role in conveying these attributes [10].

2.4 Sensory Design

Good design practices should activate multiple senses—vision, touch, sound, smell, taste, and bodily awareness—allowing everyone to receive information, explore, experience the world, and make social connections, regardless of sensory abilities or limitations. Sensory design is inherently inclusive. Malnar and Vodvarka's sensory slider is a tool for analyzing and measuring sensory experiences in physical stores, showing existing and expected levels of perception for each sense. The model's extremes, deprivation and overload, indicate whether sensory stimuli are too mild or too intense, potentially leading to difficulty in perception and mental confusion due to information overload [11, 12].

2.5 The User-Centered Design Process

User-Centered Design (UCD) and Human Factors are intertwined disciplines focused on optimizing interactions between people and systems. Design Thinking, as articulated by Brown, promotes a multiperspective approach where diverse viewpoints align with user objectives. This iterative framework helps organizations deeply understand and effectively address customer needs, fostering sustainable growth and profitability. By prioritizing authentic user requirements, products and services become intuitive and accessible, crucial for brands integrating seamlessly into users' daily lives. Brown's three-phase project evolution—Inspiration, Ideation, and Implementation—balances convergent decision-making with divergent exploration, ensuring comprehensive problem-solving [13, 14].

2.6 Sensory Branding

Sensory branding in retail aims to create immersive shopping environments that engage consumers through their senses, fostering emotional connections with brands and boosting sales. This strategy integrates global sensory elements into store design and product presentation to shape consumer perceptions, enhance brand loyalty, and increase satisfaction. Research underscores the impact of multi-sensory experiences in enriching product interactions and strengthening brand affinity [4, 5]. Leading brands like Tiffany & Co., Apple, and Mercedes effectively utilize sensory cues to enhance consumer experiences, aligning sensory stimuli with brand identity to ensure consistency and quality. As consumer preferences lean towards memorable experiences, these strategies not only entertain and prolong customer visits but also enhance and brand value. Implementing sensory branding strategies involves aligning sensory cues with brand identity, strategically deploying them in retail settings, and prioritizing consistency, differentiation, and quality [5].

2.7 Sensoriality and Behavior

The human brain processes sensory information intricately through cognitive functions, influencing our perception and responses to the environment. Sensory perception involves data gathering, processed across various brain systems. Cognitive processes such as attention, interpretation, and memory filter and give meaning to sensory inputs, shaping preferences and behaviors. Emotional responses, influenced by sensory stimuli and cognitive interpretation, determine the intensity and nature of emotions. In retail, effective experience design integrates sensory elements to create engaging environments aligned with customer preferences, enhancing loyalty and competitive advantage. By incorporating cognitive processes and sensory strategies, brands can optimize emotional responses, purchasing decisions, and long-term profitability, shaping sustainable brand identities [15, 16]. Congruent sensory stimuli play crucial roles: they influence perception by grouping similar objects and interpreting context, direct attention toward relevant aspects, form the initial repository of information for memory storage, and impact intuition and subconscious processes, thus influencing decision-making [17].

3 Conclusion

The anthology presents an integrated view of Sensory Experience Design, illustrated in Fig. 2. The sensory experience can be built in four sequential steps: (1) *Attribution:* defining attributes that represent the brand by considering its identity, cultural context, target audience, products, and location; (2) *Sensory Designation:* creating actions for each sense based on these attributes; (3) *Adjustment:* regulating stimulus intensity and prioritizing implementable solutions based on resources; and (4) *Effects:* creating value and recognition for the company, influencing cognitive and behavioral processes, and enhancing customer satisfaction and loyalty.

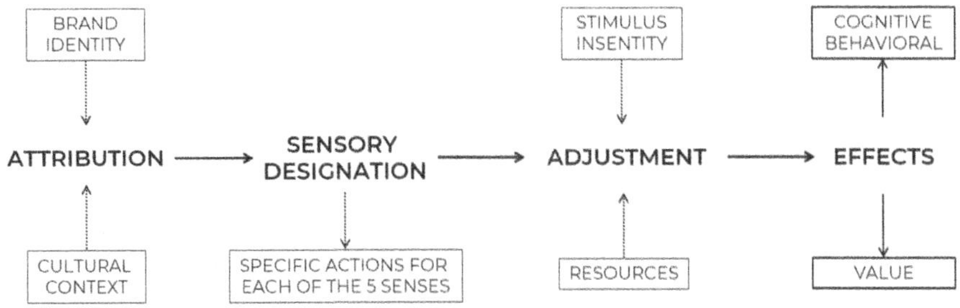

Fig. 2. An Integrated view on Sensory Experience. Source: Author (2024).

In retail, language serves as the guiding force behind storytelling, creating narratives that resonate with consumers. Techniques like analogy and metaphor enrich these narratives, bridging gaps in understanding and ensuring swift comprehension of concepts. Establishing brand identity goes beyond visual representation; it hinges on attributes that define value and identity in the eyes of customers. Integrating sensory elements within physical stores poses challenges, blending architectural features, layout, and product-related sensory cues across diverse categories. While sensory branding thrives among large corporations, SMEs often struggle to implement these strategies effectively without adequate support. Alignment of sensory stimuli with brand attributes is crucial, ensuring messages resonate appropriately without overwhelming or underwhelming consumers.

Attributes form the cornerstone of effective communication in retail, shaping how brands connect with individuals. They dictate a brand's essence, influencing store perception and enhancing overall customer experience. Harmonizing sensory stimuli with brand attributes, products, and target audience preferences is essential for reinforcing emotional bonds and creating memorable consumer experiences. Each SME requires a tailored approach to integrate sensory elements into physical retail environments, aligning with specific language attributes to foster meaningful brand-consumer relationships and meet evolving consumer expectations.

References

1. Brown, T.: Design thinking. Harv. Bus. Rev. **86**, 84–92 (2008)
2. Ferrara, M., Lecce, C.: Design for enterprises: developing European SMEs capabilities for design-driven innovation. Markets Global. Dev. Rev. **4**(2), Article 7 (2019)
3. Hauqui Tonin, P.E.: Behavioral and cognitive methods to assess users and assist physical point of sale experience design. In: Black, N.L., Neumann, W.P., Noy, I. (eds.) Proceedings of the 21st Congress of the International Ergonomics Association - IEA 2021 Lecture Notes in Networks and Systems, vol. 223, p. 2022. Springer, Cham
4. Hulten, B.: Branding by the five senses: a sensory branding framework. J. Brand Strat. **6**, 1–12 (2017)
5. Krippendorf, K.: The Semantic Turn: A New Foundation for Design. Taylor & Francis, Boca Raton, FL (1984)
6. Lindstrom, M.: Brand Sense: Sensory Secrets Behind the Stuff we Buy. Free Press, New York, NY (2010)
7. Lipps, A., Lupton, E.: Senses: Design Beyond Vision. Princeton Architetural Press, New York, NY (2018)
8. Lowdermilk, T.: User-Centered Design: a Developer's Guide to Building User-Friendly Applications. O'Reilly & Associates, Sebastopol (2013)
9. Malnar, J.M., Vodvarka, F.: Sensory Design. University of Minnesota Press, Minneapolis (2004)
10. Manzano, A.R.: Marketing sensorial: comunicar con los sentidos en el punto de venta. Pearson, Madrid (2012)
11. Matsumura, N.: Shikake: the Japanese Art of Shaping Behavior through Design. Liveright Publishing Corporation, New York, NY (2020)
12. Mehrabian, A., Russell, J.A.: An Approach to Environmental Psychology. The MIT Press, Cambridge (1974)
13. Peirce, C.S.: In: Hartshorne, C., Weiss, P., Burks, A.W. (eds.) Collected Papers, vol. 8. Harvard University Press, Cambridge (1931–1958)
14. Santaella, L.: O que é semiótica. Brasiliense, São Paulo (1986)
15. Solanki, A., Nelson, A., Saunders, N.: As Shopping Behaviors Evolve, the Retail Experience Must Follow Best Practices for Shifting to An Experience-Per-Square-Foot Business Strategy. Colliers International & Global Data, Toronto (2017)
16. Solanki, A., Nelson, A., Saunders, N.: Why Online Isn't the End of the Physical Retail Store: Myths, Misconceptions and Opportunities. Colliers International & Global Data, Toronto (2017)
17. Tonin, P., Santos, C., Mager, G., Nickel, E.: Sensory-perceptual attributes in the creation of the store's image: how they act on user behavior and improve physical retail experience. In: Ahram, T., Taiar, R. (eds.) Human Interaction & Emerging Technologies (IHIET-AI 2022): Artificial Intelligence & Future Applications. AHFE (2022) International Conference. AHFE Open Access, vol. 23. AHFE International, USA (2022)

Fake Feedback for Increasing Self-perceptions of Altruism and Sympathy to Promoting Pro-environmental Behavior

Preliminary Experiment for Designing Intervention

Kimi Ueda(✉), Kazuto Hashimoto, Hirotake Ishii, and Hiroshi Shimoda

Kyoto University, Kyoto , Kyoto 6068501, Japan
ueda@energy.kyoto-u.ac.jp

Abstract. It is believed that people need to implement more pro-environmental behaviors (PEB) to protect the global environment. However, it is also known that even if people are aware of the necessity and importance of addressing environmental issues, it is difficult for them to implement PEB. Therefore, it is important to promote people's PEB through interventions. In this study, for promoting PEB, we proposed an intervention to increase self-perceptions of sympathy and altruism by using fake feedback and conducted an evaluation experiment. Intervention designed in this study includes two types of personality-check style questionnaire: one using personality ratings from a close friend, and the other using a behavior choice quiz designed to make people naturally choose kinder behavior. The results indicated the intervention method needs further improvement, especially for empathy, because the participants were not sufficiently convinced of the evaluation, but the method of using false feedback itself is considered feasible.

Keywords: Fake feedback · Pro-environmental behavior · Altruism · Sympathy

1 Introduction

It is believed that people need to implement more pro-environmental behaviors (PEB) to protect the global environment. However, it is also known that even if people are aware of the necessity and importance of addressing environmental issues, it is difficult for them to implement PEB. Therefore, it is important to promote people's PEB through interventions.

It has been reported that not only external factors but also internal factors such as individual personality, values, and knowledge influence the implementation of PEB [1], and that "Agreeableness" of a Big Five scale that indicates cooperativeness toward others, is correlated with PEB [2]. Furthermore, among the sub-scales of Agreeableness, "Sympathy" and "Altruism" were found to be significantly related to PEB [3]. Based on these findings, we hypothesized that increasing one's self-perception of one's own altruism and sympathy may promote PEB. In this study at first, we designed and examined the intervention to increase self-perception of altruism and sympathy.

S. Jin et al. (Eds.): IEA 2024, SSDI 39, pp. 70–74, 2025.
https://doi.org/10.1007/978-981-95-0211-0_12

The objective of this study is to examine the effectiveness of the designed intervention method on increasing one's own awareness of altruism and sympathy by conducting an experiment.

2 Method

Interventions were designed referring to studies about applying fake feedback [4, 5]. Table 1 shows the experimental procedures. We recruited pairs of friends, and each was asked to conduct tasks in a separate room. In this experiment, two fake feedback were applied to participants.

First, participants were asked to answer questions about their own and their friends' personalities and were given fake feedback that they were rated as kind also by their friends. Feedback was same sentence for all participants such that "the test examines which trait is most dominant among passion, stability, curiosity, kindness and seriousness. The results showed that kindness was judged to be the most dominant". The personality test consisted of a total of 80 items from the NEO-PI-R in Japanese [6], including eight items on a factor "altruism", eight items on a factor "tender-mindedness", which is chosen as "sympathy", and 16 randomly selected items each from four other factors. For the items assessing the friend's personality, the subject of all 80 items was replaced by 'your friend' which indicates who participated with them. To assess the original personality traits of the participants, the altruism and sympathy scores of the NEO-PI-R when rating themselves are reported as results. Including the ratings from a friend, it is expected to prevent discomfort or invalidity with fake feedback caused by discrepancies with their own responses.

Second, they were asked to answer some quizzes that ask to choose behavior in specific daily situations. Quiz was designed to make them easily choose the kind behavior. For example, "Question: You have one friend whom you have recently become friends with. Today is the first time you have visited your friend's lodgings. The friend has prepared a home-cooked meal for you. However, the food is bad and not tasty for you. Answer: (a) Simply tell your friend "It is bad" and stop eating, (b) Eat it patiently and lie that it tastes good, (c) Tell your friend honestly about the taste and apologize you are not able to eat any more." In this example, (a) is a particularly unfriendly choice, designed to make it harder for participants to choose than (b) and (c). Fake feedback was also provided after completing 20 quizzes such that "your kindness score was 94" for all participants. By designing that makes it easier for people to avoid the not-kind choice and to choose the kind options, it is expected that they will be more likely to accept the rating themselves as kind person even if it's fake.

At the end of the experiment, 4 questionnaires were conducted to assess the effectiveness of the fake feedback. Details are shown at the bottom of Table 2. PEBT [7], a test for measuring the degree of PEB was conducted before and after the personalities test, behavior quiz and their feedback, but the results will not be reported as this was a trial run to examine the conditions of the PEBT.

Table 1. Experimental Procedures.

Procedure	Approximate Time (min.)
Explanation of participation, Informed consent	15
Explanation of PEBT[a]	10
PEBT set1[a]	15
Own personality check (80 items from NEO-PI-R)	45
Friend's personality check (80 items from NEO-PI-R)	
Feedback (Fake feedback)	
Quiz "for people of kind personalities"	
Feedback (Fake feedback)	
PEBT set2[a]	15
Questionnaires, Interviews	10
Explanation about this experiment, Informed consent	5
Delivering rewards	5
Total	120 (around 2 h)

[a] PEBT was trial run to adjust its settings and its results were not analyzed in this experiment.

The experiment was conducted with the approval of the ethics review committee of the authors' affiliation, and informed consent was obtained at the beginning of the experiment and obtained again after explaining the actual objective and intervention of the experiment, such as that the feedback was fake.

3 Results

Pairs of two close friends were recruited, with a total of four pairs of eight participants.

The mean age of the participants was 20.5 years (SD = 1.4), with six males and two females. The mean sympathy (tender-mindedness) score of the NEO-PI-R for all participants was 18.6 (S.D. = 8.0) and the mean altruism score was 14.6 (S.D. = 3.1). Table 2 shows all scores obtained from each participant and average scores. (1) Sense of validity of the tests (1–5) was 3.8 (SD = 0.9) and (2) acceptance with the ratings (1–5) was 2.5 (SD = 0.9). The average scores of self-perception of (3) sympathy and (4) altruism (rated from 1 to 5) following personality tests were 3.0 (SD = 1.2) and 3.3 (SD = 1.5) respectively.

Table 2. Experimental result: Scores obtained from each participant.

ID	NEO-PI-R Sympathy (0–32)	NEO-PI-R Altruism (0–32)	(1) Validity (1–5)	(2) Acceptance (1–5)	(3) Sympathy (1–5)	(4) Altruism (1–5)
1	20	16	5	4	4	4
2	31	19	4	3	5	5
3	22	13	4	1	2	5
4	20	12	4	2	2	2
5	3	10	4	3	2	1
6	19	18	3	3	3	4
7	21	16	4	2	2	2
8	13	13	2	2	4	3
Average (S.D.)	18.6 (8.0)	14.6 (3.1)	3.8 (0.9)	2.5 (0.9)	3.0 (1.2)	3.3 (1.5)

[a] Questionnaire details:
NEO-PI-R for Japanese: each factor is calculated as the sum of 8 questions (rated from 0: disagree to 4: agree).

(1) Test validity: "Did you think the personality test was valid and based on appropriate evidence?" (rated from 1: disagree to 5: agree)
(2) Test acceptance "Did you accept the results of your personality test?" (rated from 1: not accepted to 5: accepted)
(3) Sympathy: "Based on the results of the personality test, do you think you are capable of understanding the feelings and circumstances of others?" (rated from 1: disagree to 5: agree)
(4) Altruism: "Based on the results of the personality test, do you think yourself to be a person who acts for the benefit of others?" (rated from 1: disagree to 5: agree)

4 Discussions

Three out of eight participants: less than half participants gave a score of 4 or more to their (3) self-perception of sympathy after fake feedback. On the other hand, four out of eight participants gave (4) altruism a score of 4 or more, and the mean score was also better than sympathy. However, one participant (ID5) gave a score of 1 in (4) altruism, suggesting that the impact may vary depending on one's original personality characteristics.

Regarding the validity of the personality check format, seven out of eight participants scored 3 or more points, suggesting that most participants felt the format was valid. The format of the test using actual personality test items and the behavior choice quiz was considered to be natural. On the other hand, only four participants gave a score of 3 or more for the acceptability of the personality test results, and the average score was also below 3. Participant ID3 who gave the lowest score of 1 in (2) acceptance said in the interview that "it was difficult to accept the feedback because when I experienced a similar personality test before, my personality check results tended to show a predominance of passion and seriousness, which differed from the results of this test." It was suggested that in such cases the sense of acceptance tends to be low, diminishing the effect of the fake feedback. In addition, participant ID5, who scored particularly low on the self-assessment of sympathy and altruism using the NEO-PI-R, gave scores of 2 and 1 to (3) and (4) respectively, suggesting that feedback with content that deviates extremely from the original personality is also unlikely to be accepted. To address these concerns, measures such as adjusting the content of feedback based on the results of the original empathy and altruism assessment, or using a more ambiguous form of test content, could be considered.

Also, participant ID8 stated, "I gave a high score to (3) Sympathy because I have always done well in reading classes, and I think I have a high level of empathy." The questionnaire asked what they thought of their personality after the feedback, with the sentence starting with "Based on the results of the personality test," in questionnaire (3) and (4). However, there was concern that participants answered considering just about their usual personality. Therefore, improvements are needed, such as conducting questionnaires before and after the feedback and analyzing the difference or changing the questionnaire sentence to be clearer.

As a next step, improving the intervention methods and evaluation questionnaires, it is necessary to assess PEB and to investigate the effects of the improvement of self-perceived sympathy and altruism obtained through the intervention on PEB using PEBT adjusted in this experiment.

5 Conclusions

In this study, we proposed an intervention to increase self-perception of empathy and altruism by using fake feedback and evaluated its effectiveness. The results showed that the intervention method needs further improvement, especially for empathy, because the participants were not sufficiently convinced of the evaluation, but the method of using false feedback itself is considered feasible.

References

1. Kollmuss, A., Agyeman, J.: Mind the gap: why do people act environmentally and what are the barriers to pro-environmental behavior? Environ. Educ. Res. **8**, 239–260 (2002)
2. Hirsh, J.B.: Environmental sustainability and national personality. J. Environ. Psychol. **38**, 233–240 (2014)
3. Soutter, A.R.B., Mõttus, R.: Big Five facets' associations with pro-environmental attitudes and behaviors. J. Pers. **89**, 203–215 (2021)
4. Kappes, A., Oettingen, G., Pak, H.: Mental contrasting and the self-regulation of responding to negative feedback. Personal. Soc. Psychol. Bull. **38**, 845–857 (2012)
5. Rigoni, D., Braem, S., Pourtois, G., Brass, M.: Fake feedback on pain tolerance impacts proactive versus reactive control strategies. Conscious. Cogn. **42**, 366–373 (2016)
6. Shimonaka, Y., Nakazato, K., Gondo, Y., Takayama, M.: Construction and factorial validity of the Japanese NEO-PI-R. Jpn. J. Pers. **6**, 138–147 (1998)
7. Lange, F., Steinke, A., Dewitte, S.: The pro-environmental behavior task: a laboratory measure of actual pro-environmental behavior. J. Environ. Psychol. **56**, 46–54 (2018)

Emotion Recognition Through Smartphone-Based Gait Analysis with Dimensional Theory

Lu Wang, Xiaojun Lai, and Pei-Luen Patrick Rau(✉)

Department of Industrial Engineering, Tsinghua University, Beijing, China
rpl@tsinghua.edu.cn

Abstract. Gait is an important indicator that reflects an individual's physical or mental health status. This study employed smartphones to measure participants' gait across various emotional states to develop gait-based emotion recognition. We also assessed emotion recognition based on real-world gait and the impact of emotion feedback to validate long-term emotion motoring. Results indicated that when the emotion deviated from the neutral state, the gait parameters also deviated and the manifestation in gait was related to both the valence and arousal of the emotion. Among positive emotions, high and low arousal emotions showed significant differences in gait parameters. No significant changes were observed in gait parameters after emotional feedback. The recognition accuracy of the gait-based emotion recognition model was higher for high-arousal emotions, but not sufficient for low-arousal emotions. Based on the dimensional theory of emotion, this study focused on the healthy adult population, established a gait-based emotion prediction model, and further validated it in daily life.

Keywords: Gait · Emotion recognition · Dimensional theory · Smartphone

1 Introduction

Gait studies typically focus on older adults and special medical populations. However, recognizing emotions in the daily lives of healthy adults offers many benefits, including enhancing self-management, improving interactive system design, and reducing professional accidents. Traditional emotion recognition relies on multimodal features such as facial expressions, speech, and physiological signals [1, 2], complicating continuous daily monitoring. Smartphones equipped with accelerometers and gyroscopes can continuously monitor gait, an indicator of emotional state, thus facilitating daily emotion recognition. Gait measured by a smartphone placed in a front pocket aligned well with gait speed, cadence, and step length measured in the laboratory, suggesting that smartphones offer a portable and user-friendly method for gait measurement [3].

Previous research has predicted specific emotions like anger, sadness, and happiness through gait analysis, ignoring emotional intensity [4]. According to the dimensional theory of emotions, emotions can be categorized by valence (negative or positive) and

S. Jin et al. (Eds.): IEA 2024, SSDI 39, pp. 75–82, 2025.
https://doi.org/10.1007/978-981-95-0211-0_13

arousal (low or high) [5]. Neuroscience evidence indicates that valence and arousal affect cognitive processes and human behavior through distinct neural mechanisms. Gait serves as a relevant behavioral indicator. Prior research has explored emotional states' effects on gait initiation based on valence and arousal [6], warranting further exploration. Furthermore, emotion regulation occurs during emotion onset, with common management strategies including cognitive reappraisal and expressive suppression [7]. Providing individuals with emotional feedback may enhance cognitive reappraisal, aiding emotional recognition and regulation.

This study explored the gait-emotion relationship in healthy adults using smartphones to measure sensor-based gait parameters based on dimensional theory. The research questions proposed are:

RQ1: In laboratory scenarios, which gait parameters distinguish emotional states during normal walking? Do these parameters differ during dual-task walking?

RQ2: In real-life scenarios, can gait effectively recognize emotions? How does emotional feedback affect subsequent gait?

We conducted a pilot study to validate the gait-monitoring application and confirm the wearing position of smartphones. We then conducted a two-phase experiment. Phase I elicited specific emotions in participants through video clips, assessed participants' emotional valence and arousal using the Self-Assessment Manikin (SAM) [8] scale, and collected their gait data during normal walking and dual-task walking. Phase II collected gait data of participants when they were in different emotions in real-life environments to verify the gait-based emotion recognition model established using the Phase I data.

2 Method

2.1 Experimental Design

The pilot study conducted a 4 (wearing position) × 2 (walking task) within-subject design. Participants wore a smartphone on different body parts: the L3 region of the lower back, right upper arm, right wrist, and right hand held. The walking tasks included normal walking and dual-task walking. The order of independent variables was balanced using a Latin square design. The Phase I study employed a 5 (emotion category) × 2 (walking task) within-subject design. Emotions were evoked via videos: positive high-arousal, negative high-arousal, positive low-arousal, negative low-arousal, and neutral. Emotion induction was assessed using a 9-point SAM scale, with a score of 1–4 for positive valence, low arousal; a score of 6–9 for negative valence, high arousal; and a score of 5 for neutral emotion. The Phase II study was similar to Phase I, except that the five emotional states occurred naturally in real life. Additionally, gait data during normal walking were collected before and after emotional feedback.

2.2 Participants

The pilot study included 16 participants (8 males, mean age 23.5 ± 3.8 years). Phase I recruited 70 participants, 42 of whom successfully experienced the five categories of emotions (19 males, mean age 22.9 ± 3.4 years). Phase II recruited 45 participants

(18 males, mean age 22.6 ± 2.6 years) to validate the Phase I emotion recognition model using real-life emotional state and gait data. An additional 20 participants (17 trusting the emotional feedback, 7 males, mean age 23.8 ± 3.6 years) were recruited for gait measurements before and after emotional feedback. Participants were able to walk freely without assistive devices and were free of conditions affecting gait such as pain symptoms in the back, leg, or foot. They were screened for depression and anxiety using the State-Trait Anxiety Inventory scale. The study was approved by the Ethics Committee of the author's institution. All participants signed an informed consent form.

2.3 Procedures

The pilot study and Phase I were conducted in a 60-meter-long and 3-meter-wide corridor. Participants were briefed on the experiment and signed a consent form. In the pilot study, participants wore smartphones on different body parts and performed normal walking (at a comfortable daily speed) and dual-task walking (subtracting 1, 2, 3, …, from a given three-digit number) randomly. In Phase I, participants watched neutral, positive, and negative video clips (counterbalanced by Latin Square) and reported their emotional valence and arousal using the SAM scale. Then, participants wore a smartphone on their right wrist based on the pilot study results and performed walking tasks randomly. They rested for 30 seconds between videos to minimize carryover effects. Phase II was conducted in real-life settings like playgrounds and the downstairs of dormitories to maintain real-life emotional contexts. Phase II was similar to Phase I and participants' gait data was collected in several times without emotion induction. Furthermore, participants performed normal walking and were informed that their emotional state was negative, rested for 30 s, and then performed a second normal walking.

2.4 Dependent Variables and Measurements

Gait parameters were collected using a revised gait-monitoring application originally designed by Zhong and Rau [9]. Android smartphones equipped with inertial measurement units, such as accelerometers and gyroscopes, were used. The pilot study employed OnePlus 9R, while the formal experiments used Honor Magic 4, with a sampling frequency of approximately 30 Hz. The application collected participants' walking data for 30 s, with voice prompts initiating and terminating the gait assessment. MATLAB algorithms were developed to calculate step frequency, acceleration root mean square (RMS), RMS ratio (RMSR), average step time, step variability, step regularity, step symmetry, and smoothness. Detailed information is shown in Table 1.

2.5 Data Analysis

In the pilot study, step frequency derived from the y-axis acceleration data in the L3 region served as the gold standard. Pearson correlation analysis was conducted with other positions to determine the smartphone-wearing position for the formal experiment. In Phase I, based on the results of normality and homogeneity of variance, one-way repeated-measures ANOVA or Friedman tests were used to explore differences in gait parameters

Table 1. Calculation and meaning of dependent variables.

Dependent variables	Calculation
Step frequency (Hz): the number of gait cycles are completed per second	Process the acceleration signal using a Fast Fourier Transform
Acceleration root mean square (RMS): higher RMS value indicating lower gait stability	$\sqrt{\frac{\int_{t_1}^{t_n} a(t)^2 dt}{t_n - t_1}}$
Ratio of acceleration root mean square (RMSR): normalized RMS	$\frac{RMS_x}{\sqrt{RMS_x^2 + RMS_y^2 + RMS_z^2}}$
Average step time (s)	t_{MEAN}
Step variability: a value closer to 0 indicating higher gait stability	$\frac{t_{SD}}{t_{MEAN}}$
Step regularity: a value closer to 1 indicating higher regularity	$\frac{1}{n-1}\sum_{i=1}^{n-k} x_{t_i} x_{t_{i+k}}$, where $x(t) = \frac{a(t) - a_{MEAN}}{a_{SD}}$
Step symmetry: a value closer to 1 indicating higher symmetry	$\frac{A_{d1}}{A_{d2}}$, A_{di} is the autocorrelation coefficient of the ith dominant periods of the acceleration signal
Smoothness: a smaller value indicates smoother movement	$\sqrt{\frac{1}{t_2 - t_1}\int_{t_1}^{t_2} x(t)^2 dt}$

across different emotional categories and between non-neutral and neutral emotions. Post-hoc multiple comparisons tested detailed differences in each gait parameter across emotions during different walking tasks. Paired t-tests or Wilcoxon signed-rank tests examined differences in gait parameters between normal walking and dual-task walking under different emotional types. Ordinal logistic regression models, built on valid Phase I data, were validated with Phase II gait data for emotion recognition. Finally, paired t-tests or Wilcoxon signed-rank tests were performed on gait data before and after emotional feedback to explore its effects on gait parameters.

3 Results

Results of the pilot study revealed that, for step frequency, the correlation of the L3 region in lower back was highest with hand-held ($r = 0.95$, $p < 0.001$), followed by wrist ($r = 0.93$, $p < 0.001$), and upper arm ($r = 0.87$, $p < 0.001$) during normal walking. For dual-task walking, the order was hand-held ($r = 0.76$, $p < 0.01$), wrist ($r = 0.51$, $p = 0.07$), and upper arm ($r = -0.19$, $p = 0.54$). Considering experiment stability (individuals may hold phones differently) and application value (simulating bracelets), the wrist position was chosen for the formal experiment.

Results of Phase I indicated that emotional types significantly affected gait parameters (all $p < 0.05$) regardless of walking task type, except step variability during dual-task walking ($\chi^2 = 7.73$, $p = 0.10$). Post-hoc comparisons in Table 2 suggested that no gait parameters could individually distinguish between negative high-arousal and negative low-arousal emotions. For example, as shown in Fig. 1, during normal walking, positive high-arousal emotion exhibited the fastest step frequency (1.89 steps/s), followed by positive low-arousal emotion (1.84 steps/s), and then negative low-arousal emotion (1.77 steps/s), negative high-arousal emotion (1.75 steps/s), and neutral emotion (1.80 steps/s). A similar tendency appeared during dual-task walking, despite no significant difference in step frequency between neutral and positive low-arousal emotions. In summary, gait parameters were more effective in recognizing emotions during normal walking (9/10) than dual-task walking (6/10).

Table 2. Differentiation of emotions by gait parameters.

Comparisons		Step frequency	RMS	RMSR	Average step time	Step variability	Step regularity	Step symmetry	Smoothness
Negative high-arousal vs. negative low-arousal	T1								
	T2								
Negative high-arousal vs. neutral	T1				*				
	T2								
Negative high-arousal vs. positive high-arousal	T1	***	***	***	***				***
	T2	***	***	***	***				***
Negative high-arousal vs. positive low-arousal	T1	***		***	***	*			
	T2								
Negative low-arousal vs. neutral	T1				*	*			
	T2	*							
Negative low-arousal vs. positive high-arousal	T1	***	***	***	***	**		*	***
	T2	***	***	***	***				***
Negative low-arousal vs. positive low-arousal	T1	***	*	***	***	***			*
	T2	*	*						
Neutral vs. positive high-arousal	T1	***	**	***	**			*	**

(*continued*)

Table 2. (*continued*)

Comparisons		Step frequency	RMS	RMSR	Average step time	Step variability	Step regularity	Step symmetry	Smoothness
	T2	***	*	***	***		**	*	*
Neutral vs. positive low-arousal	T1	*		**			*	*	
	T2								
Positive high-arousal vs. positive low-arousal	T1	***			*				
	T2	***		*	***				*

Note: *** $p < 0.001$; ** $p < 0.01$; * $p < 0.05$; T1: normal walking task, T2: dual-task walking task.

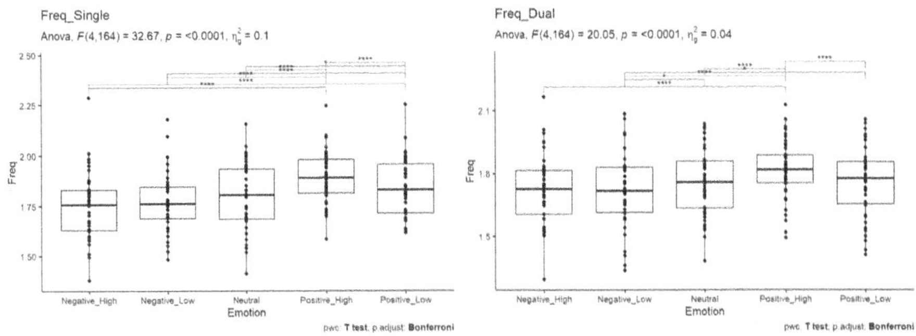

Fig. 1. Step frequency in normal and dual-task walking task.

Further analysis of gait parameters differences between neutral and non-neutral emotions revealed no significant differences in step regularity during both normal ($\chi^2 = 7.49$, $p = 0.06$) and dual-task walking ($\chi^2 = 4.89$, $p = 0.18$), as did step variability ($\chi^2 = 6.54$, $p = 0.09$) and step symmetry ($\chi^2 = 6.54$, $p = 0.09$) during dual-task walking. Post-hoc comparisons showed that compared to the neutral emotion, pleasant emotions were correlated with a shorter average step time, increased instability (larger RMS and reduced step variability), and higher smoothness. Conversely, unpleasant emotions were associated with a longer average step time, smaller RMS, increased step variability, and lower smoothness. Regarding emotional arousal, significant differences were observed in step frequency, RMS, RMSR, average step time, between high- and low-arousal emotions in the context of pleasant emotions, but not in the case of unpleasant emotions. Dual-task walking led to smaller gait changes in response to emotions compared to normal walking.

In Phase II, regression models for emotion recognition of the two walking tasks were developed based on Phase I results. The coefficients of height, step frequency, and RMSR were significant in the normal walking task model, indicating that step frequency and RMSR were effective in recognizing different emotions, suggesting recognizing emotions by gait parameters alone was more challenging. The normal walking model showed higher accuracy (66.67%) in recognizing positive high-arousal emotion in daily life in Phase II, but lower accuracy for low-arousal emotions. No significant changes in gait parameters were observed after emotional feedback (all $p > 0.05$).

4 Discussion

This study simplified gait measurements using a smartphone placed on the wrist to simulate a wearable device, investigated the relationship between dimensional emotions and gait parameters, and established and validated gait-based emotion recognition models for daily life. Deviations from a neutral emotional state were associated with changes in gait parameters, influenced by both the valence and the arousal of emotions. The gait-based emotion recognition models successfully identified high-arousal pleasant emotions in daily life. Dual-task walking, which required cognitive resources, appeared to reduce the impact of emotion on gait changes. Real-life scenarios, involving dual tasks that provoke emotional responses, might exert a more pronounced impact on gait patterns. Previous studies on emotion and gait analysis primarily focused on a few discrete categories of emotions such as happiness, angry, and sadness. This study conducted gait analysis using continuous emotional states based on valence and arousal, providing useful insights into ambiguous emotions.

However, limitations include the use of emotionally stimulating videos with relatively few types of emotions and short durations, affecting emotion induction and leading to a small effective sample size for establishing emotion recognition models. Additionally, this study only explored the feedback regulation of unpleasant emotions, subsequent research can further explore the impact of pleasant emotion feedback.

References

1. Poria, S., Cambria, E., Bajpai, R., Hussain, A.: A review of affective computing: from unimodal analysis to multimodal fusion. Inform. Fus. **37**, 98–125 (2017). https://doi.org/10.1016/j.inffus.2017.02.003
2. Dzedzickis, A., Kaklauskas, A., Bucinskas, V.: Human emotion recognition: review of sensors and methods. Sensors. **20**(3), Article 3 (2020). https://doi.org/10.3390/s20030592
3. Shahar, R.T., Agmon, M.: Gait analysis using accelerometry data from a single smartphone: agreement and consistency between a smartphone application and gold-standard gait analysis system. Sensors. **21**(22), Article 22 (2021). https://doi.org/10.3390/s21227497
4. Kang, G.E., Gross, M.M.: The effect of emotion on movement smoothness during gait in healthy young adults. J. Biomech. **49**(16), 4022–4027 (2016). https://doi.org/10.1016/j.jbiomech.2016.10.044
5. Russell, J.A.: A circumplex model of affect. J. Pers. Soc. Psychol. **39**(6), 1161–1178 (1980). https://doi.org/10.1037/h0077714
6. Gélat, T., Chapus, C.F.: Reaction time in gait initiation depends on the time available for affective processing. Neurosci. Lett. **609**, 69–73 (2015). https://doi.org/10.1016/j.neulet.2015.10.003
7. McRae, K., Gross, J.J.: Emotion regulation. Emotion. **20**(1), 1–9 (2020). https://doi.org/10.1037/emo0000703

8. Bradley, M.M., Lang, P.J.: Measuring emotion: the self-assessment manikin and the semantic differential. J. Behav. Ther. Exp. Psychiatry. **25**(1), 49–59 (1994). https://doi.org/10.1016/0005-7916(94)90063-9
9. Zhong, R., Rau, P.-L.P.: A mobile phone–based gait assessment app for the elderly: development and evaluation. JMIR Mhealth Uhealth. **8**(5), e14453 (2020). https://doi.org/10.2196/14453

Native and Foreign Language Effects in Human-AI Teams

Dian Yu, Pei-Luen Patrick Rau(✉), and Liang Ma

Department of Industrial Engineering, Tsinghua University, Beijing, China
rpl@tsinghua.edu.cn

Abstract. This research investigated the effect of native and foreign languages and responsibility attribution to self and AI during collaboration. The study performed a 2 (language: Chinese, English) × 2 (outcome: success, failure) mixed-design experiment, with Chinese as their native language and English as their foreign language. During the experiment, changes in blood flow within the prefrontal cortex were monitored using a functional Near-Infrared Spectroscopy (fNIRS). Tasks conducted in native tongue were approached with greater ease and confidence, which was reflected in their decision-making patterns; individuals were less likely to be swayed by different opinions or choices. In native language scenarios, there was a tendency to attribute success to oneself, stemming from a sense of confidence and control, supported by the self-serving bias. The case was opposite in a foreign language context, possibly due to reduced self-confidence in language proficiency. Failures were more readily attributed to AI when operating in a native language, possibly as a means of deflecting personal blame, whereas in a foreign language, the attribution of failure swung back towards oneself, reflecting uncertainties in handling the language effectively.

Keywords: Foreign Language Effect · Bilingual · Responsibility attribution · fNIRs · Human-AI team

1 Introduction

With nearly half of the world's population being bilingual or multilingual, it raised the concern of focus on how bilingualism affect human-AI teams [1]. When humans collaborate with AI systems, the language used for communication and decision-making can significantly impact the effectiveness of the interaction. In native language settings, individuals are likely to experience a higher level of comfort and fluency, enabling more efficient and confident decision-making processes [2]. Conversely, operating in a foreign language may introduce additional cognitive load, potentially affecting the quality of decision-making [3]. AI has been perceived as social actors according to the Computers Are Social Actors (CASA) paradigm [4]. Most research identified the level of robot autonomy to be an important factor of influencing human responsibility attribution [5, 6]. This paper aimed to identify the responsibility attribution under human-AI teams with neurological support.

S. Jin et al. (Eds.): IEA 2024, SSDI 39, pp. 83–88, 2025.
https://doi.org/10.1007/978-981-95-0211-0_14

2 Literature Review and Hypotheses

Foreign Language Effect (FLE) highlights how the use of a foreign language can significantly influence decision-making processes, emotional responses, and moral judgments [7, 8]. Attribution is the process through which individuals deduce the causes behind behaviors, events, or outcomes [9]. People typically attribute successes to internal factors like skills or effort, and failures to external circumstances such as luck or difficulty [10]. This tendency, known as self-serving bias, has been supported by research across various contexts [11, 12]. Language can influence self-serving bias through its impact on cognitive and emotional processing. Students who processed feedback in a non-native language exhibited a greater self-serving bias compared to those who processed feedback in their native language [13].

- H1.1a: Success attributed to self is higher than to the AI agent when participant collaborates with AI using native language.
- H1.1b: Success attributed to the AI agent is higher than to self when participant collaborates with AI using foreign language.
- H1.2a: Failure attributed to the AI agent is higher than to self when participant collaborates with AI using native language.
- H1.2b: Failure attributed to self is higher than to the AI agent when participant collaborates with AI using foreign language.

FLE has been a subject of interest in how it influences emotional bias and decision-making. A functional Magnetic Resonance Imaging (fMRI) study revealed that bilingual individuals exhibited less emotional response and loss aversion in their second language, which influenced their decision-making process [14]. In this study, the prefrontal cortex (PFC) was selected to be the key area of focus for functional Near-Infrared Spectroscopy (fNIRS) measurement. The PFC can be divided into left and right regions, where the left is often associated with language production and processing, logical reasoning and analytical thinking, as well as decision-making. While in the right region of the PFC, it is more frequently associated with global processing of information in a more holistic manner, and involved in creative thinking, intuition, and processing abstract concepts [15].

- H2.1: Activation in the left side of the PFC is higher than in the right side when participant collaborates with AI using foreign language, due to greater language processing needs.
- H2.2: Activation in the right side of the PFC is higher than in the left side when participant collaborates with AI using native language, due to greater emotional response.

3 Methodology

3.1 Experiment Design and Participants

The study performed a 2 (language: Chinese, English) x 2 (outcome: success, failure) mixed-design experiment. A total of nine university students (male: 4, female: 5), aged 20 to 29, from varying disciplines were recruited. All participants were Chinese students with Chinese as their native language and completed at least 10 years of English lessons in school. The age at which participants started learning Chinese ($M = 0.67$, $SD = 0.87$) was significantly younger than when they started learning English ($M = 7.11$, $SD = 2.62$).

Dependent variables included in the experiment were attribution to self and attribution to the AI agent [6]. Based on the ratings, we evaluated their allocation of causal responsibility between self and the AI partner. A higher mean value indicated higher attribution of either success or failure to self and AI. During the experiment, changes in blood flow within the PFC were monitored using an fNIRS device. The average change in oxyhemoglobin (Oxy-Hb) over a certain time frame was used to gauge neural activity levels [16]. During each language, there were three phases: (1) thought initiation phase, an active thinking process by the participants; (2) guided conversation phase, where participants read and responded to AI's text; (3) questionnaire phase, where participants had to read and answer the questions based on the task outcome.

3.2 Task and Procedure

After arrival, participant was briefed on the experiment and signed the consent form if they agree to take part in the actual experiment. The participant was first asked to fill in the pre-experiment questionnaire which included demographic information and language background information. The experimenter then proceeded to assist them in wearing the fNIRS equipment to collect the blood oxygen level in the brain. Once they are ready to start, the AI agent sends out a message to guide them on the subsequent steps.

There was a total of six dessert and six beverage tasks, each participant had twelve sets of selections to make, each set contains three images. Out of the twelve sets, half of which was decided through conversing in Chinese, native language of the participants, and the other six were presented in English, foreign language of the participants. Participants communicated with the AI agent through a chatting area. The experiment adopted the Wizard of Oz method, where all the messages sent out by the AI are actually manipulated by the human experimenter on the other side of the screen, using scripted sentences. The AI agent first introduced itself and instructed the participants to present their own choice for each new set of images, after which the AI agent commented on each image and stated its choice. After every three sets of selections, the experimenter tabulated the number of likes and presented the final outcome to the participant.

Data analysis on performance and questionnaires were performed using R Studio and excel. As the data did not fulfill normality, non-parametric Wilcoxon signed-rank test was used to compare means between the different groups. fNIRS data of each participant was preprocessed using Homer3 in Matlab, and subsequent data was also analyzed using Wilcoxon signed-rank test.

4 Results

4.1 Responsibility Attribution

Participants attributed more success and failure to self than to AI under all conditions according to the mean values. Based on the results of Wilcoxon signed-rank test, when the task succeeded, significantly higher attribution of success ($V = 0$, $p = 0.027$) was made to AI under English condition ($M = 4.04$, $SD = 1.46$) than Chinese condition ($M = 3.15$, $SD = 0.94$). No significant difference in attribution of success and failure to self under both languages. However, we noticed that greater attribution of success to self was made under Chinese condition than English condition, while greater attribution of failure was made to self under English condition than Chinese condition. Therefore, it can be concluded that under native language, participant tends to attribute greater success to self and greater failure to AI, and the opposite under foreign language condition. This finding partially supported Hypotheses 1.

4.2 Neuro Activities

Effect of Native and Foreign Languages

The mean HbO concentration (mM x mm) of all nineteen channels were computed. Based on the results, thought initiation processes required higher brain activity ($V = 4978$, $p < 0.001$) in Chinese events ($M = 5.40 * 10^{-8}$) compared to English ($M = -4.07 * 10^{-8}$). There was no significant difference between brain activities between Chinese and English tasks during each phase, but different from thought initiation phase, the English tasks led to an increase in HbO concentration as compared to Chinese tasks during conversation phase and questionnaire phase. Overall, English tasks ($M = 6.56 * 10^{-9}$) resulted in a marginally significantly higher brain activity ($V = 53{,}945$, $p = 0.092$) than Chinese tasks ($M = -5.56 * 10^{-8}$). Thus, we can conclude that changes in the PFC varied depending on the language and nature of the task, suggesting different cognitive processes in native versus foreign language settings.

Effect of Brain Region

Since different sides of the PFC correspond to different functionalities of brain activities, we analyzed the difference between these two regions with respect to each phase of the tasks. Based on the Wilcoxon signed-rank test results, only during the thought initiation phase is there a significant difference in HbO concentration between the different languages in both left ($V = 1560$, $p = 0.05$) and right ($V = 1228$, $p < 0.001$) sides of the brain. Under Chinese language, there is greater brain activation in the PFC during thought initiation process. Although the other comparisons were all insignificant, it is still interesting to note that for Chinese tasks, all phases observed greater changes in left PFC, whereas for English tasks, all phases observed greater changes in the right PFC. We can therefore associate this finding with our previously identified brain region functionalities, where native language induced language processing, logical reasoning, and decision-making, while foreign language tasks were associated with global processing and creativity. Hypotheses 2 are partially supported in this case.

5 Discussion

In this study, we examined the influence of native and foreign language on the cognitive process during collaboration with AI partner and the human decision-making process. Several key findings were identified and elaborations are provided below.

Language plays a pivotal role in cognitive effort and decision-making in human-AI teams. When engaging in tasks in a foreign language, individuals typically exert more cognitive effort due to the added complexity of processing a non-native language. Specifically, during thought initiation processes, higher cognitive activity is observed when participants used their native language. This implies that tasks conducted in one's native tongue are approached with greater ease and confidence, which is reflected in their decision-making patterns. The left PFC, known for its involvement in language processing, logical reasoning, and decision-making, shows greater neural changes during these tasks, suggesting a linguistic and logical engagement.

When tasks are performed in a foreign language, individuals appear more susceptible to external influences. This could be attributed to the additional cognitive resources required for language translation and comprehension, leaving less capacity for critical assessment of external inputs. Interestingly, greater neural changes are observed in the right PFC, which is associated with global processing, creativity, and intuition, potentially indicating a more holistic approach to problem-solving in a non-native language. Individuals paid less attention to language wording detail but approached them at a whole to get the meaning out of it.

Success and failure attributions also vary with language context. In native language scenarios, there is a tendency to attribute success to oneself, stemming from a sense of confidence and control. However, in a foreign language context, there is a shift, with success more often attributed to AI assistance, possibly due to reduced self-confidence in language proficiency. Conversely, failures are more readily attributed to AI when operating in a native language, possibly as a means of deflecting personal blame, whereas in a foreign language, the attribution of failure swings back towards oneself, reflecting uncertainties in handling the language effectively.

6 Conclusion

This study dived deeper into understanding how the native and foreign language affected bilingual decision-making process with evidence from neuro measurements. This nuanced interplay between language, cognition, and attribution in human-AI collaboration underscores the importance of considering linguistic factors when designing AI systems and interfaces for multicultural and multilingual user bases. This research was limited by the small sample size and manual control of fixed responses. Future research can consider further exploration on AI-related factor (e.g., interactive modality) and human-related factor (e.g., culture).

Acknowledgements. This work was supported by the National Natural Science Foundation of China (71942005).

References

1. Eberhard, D.M., Simons, G.F., Fenning, C.D.: Ethnologue: Languages of the Americas and the Pacific, 25th edn. SIL International (2022)
2. Circi, R., Gatti, D., Russo, V., Vecchi, T.: The foreign language effect on decision-making: a meta-analysis. Psychon. Bull. Rev. **28**(4), 1131–1141 (2021)
3. Maschio, N.D., Crespi, F., Peressotti, F., Abutalebi, J., Sulpizio, S.: Decision-making depends on language: a meta-analysis of the foreign language effect. Biling. Lang. Congn. **25**(4), 617–630 (2022)
4. Nass, C., Steuer, J., Tauber, E.R.: Computers are social actors. In: Proceedings of the SIGCHI Conference on Human Factors in Computing Systems, pp. 72–78 (1994)
5. Furlough, C., Stokes, T., Gillan, D.J.: Attributing blame to robots: I. The influence of robot autonomy. Hum. Factors. **63**(4), 592–602 (2021)
6. Lei, X., Rau, P.-L.P.: Should I blame the human or the robot? Attribution within a human–robot group. Int. J. Soc. Robot. **13**(2), 363–377 (2021)
7. Costa, A., Vives, M., Corey, J.D.: On language processing shaping decision making. Curr. Dir. Psychol. Sci. **26**(2), 146–151 (2017)
8. Hayakawa, S., Costa, A., Foucart, A., Keysar, B.: Using a foreign language changes our choices. Trends Cogn. Sci. **20**(11), 791–793 (2016)
9. Kelley, H.H., Michela, J.L.: Attribution theory and research. Annu. Rev. Psychol. **31**(1), 457–501 (1980)
10. Miller, D.T., Ross, M.: Self-serving biases in the attribution of causality: fact or fiction? Psychol. Bull. **82**(2), 213–225 (1975)
11. Allen, M.S., Robson, D.A., Martin, L.J., Laborde, S.: Systematic review and meta-analysis of self-serving attribution biases in the competitive context of organized sport. Personal. Soc. Psychol. Bull. **46**(7), 1027–1043 (2020)
12. Deffains, B., Espinosa, R., Thöni, C.: Political self-serving bias and redistribution. J. Public Econ. **134**, 67–74 (2016)
13. van Hugten, J., van Witteloostuijn, A.: The foreign language effect on the self-serving bias: a field experiment in the high school classroom. PLoS One. **13**(2) (2018)
14. He, Y., Margoni, F., Wu, Y., Liu, H.: fMRI evidence reveals emotional biases in bilingual decision making. Brain Struct. Funct. **226**(5), 1405–1421 (2021)
15. Cheng, S., Qiu, X., Li, S., Mo, L., Xu, F., Zhang, D.: Different roles of the left and right ventrolateral prefrontal cortex in cognitive reappraisal: an online transcranial magnetic stimulation study. Front. Hum. Neurosci. **16**, 928077 (2022)
16. Strangman, G., Boas, D.A., Sutton, J.P.: Non-invasive neuroimaging using near-infrared light. Biol. Psychiatry. **52**(7), 679–693 (2002)

Aging (I)

Evaluation of Indian Kitchen Design for Ageing in Place Using Space Syntax Theory

Sukesha Ghosh(✉) and Swati Pal

Industrial Design Center, Indian Institute of Technology, Bombay, India
{sukeshaghosh,swatipal}@iitb.ac.in

Abstract. The trend of Ageing in Place is on the rise in Indian urban cities, driven by challenges such as limited dwelling spaces with increase in smaller apartment sizes. The older adults are compelled to adapt to the space constraints, mostly in terms of smaller kitchen sizes and functionality. This research aims to identify the parameters that contribute to kitchen design for older adults and assess the impact of physical and cognitive behavioural factors with the spatial organisation on their quality of life and well-being. The study incorporates mixed method investigation on various kitchen typologies through field study employing controlled observation followed by interviews and analysing individual behaviour through the lens of space syntax theory using depthMapX v0.8.0. The study identified the depth value of reaching out spaces such as platform, top and bottom shelves, addressing significant correlation between kitchen spatial layout and task efficiency. The findings of this investigation will help propose novel design principles for kitchen spaces in compact living scenarios ageing in place.

Keywords: Ageing in place · Kitchen Design · Space Syntax · Spatial optimization

1 Introduction

Urban India is witnessing extensive development of high-density housing blocks that offer compact homes, with a compound annual growth rate of 2.8%, leading to an increase in the urbanization rate from 27.8% to 31.2% over the period 2001–2011 (Gaurav and Karan 2016; MoHUA 2023). The trend among the ageing population to opt for these compact residences despite physical constraints is high, as older adults (aged 65 and above) aim to maintain independence and perform daily tasks on their own (Mnea and Zairul 2023; MoHUA 2016; Vaishnav et al. 2022). The kitchen, an integral space in any household, poses specific challenges for older adults due to safety and security issues, as cognitive and motor skills tend to decline with age, making kitchen activities more complex and potentially hazardous for ageing population (Bhatia and Singla 2019; Singh et al. 2023). Therefore, ensuring user-centric and flexible residential design for older adults aids in the sense of security and helps improve their ability to age in place, enhancing the quality of life and enabling them to perform daily tasks safely and efficiently in their homes (Hrovatin et al. 2012). However, the current design of residential facilities often fails to consider the issues and conditions of the elderly population, highlighting the urgent need for more age-appropriate design solutions.

S. Jin et al. (Eds.): IEA 2024, SSDI 39, pp. 91–97, 2025.
https://doi.org/10.1007/978-981-95-0211-0_15

Many studies in gerontology, sociology, and behavioural sciences have highlighted the significance of the behaviour of ageing adults and spatial organizations (Al-wabil et al. 2007; Zhang et al. 2023). Various researchers have claimed that spatial configuration and designed spaces influence spatial behaviour, promoting better physical and mental experience for individuals (Kim 1999; Mariana et al. 2018). This in turn, contributes to a higher quality of life that closely aligns with WHO norms of health and well-being (Kim 1999; Vahedi 2010; WHO 1992). However, changing and modifying residential built space for ageing people involves critical factors addressing physical and cognitive issues of ageing individuals (Hwang et al. 2011; Qian et al. 2022). Qualitative interviews and fieldwork have been conducted to evaluate how physical factors such as posture, movement, and the usability of space, as well as cognitive parameters like memory, attention, speed, and intensity of task difficulties, can help analyze kitchen design and associated problems (Mariana et al. 2018; Tarboush and Erçin 2021). However, these studies lack quantitative support and require more robust and analytical approaches to validate the findings regarding spatial configurations and behavioural changes.

Several quantitative studies exploring older adults and spatial design have rigorously used space syntax as a tool for analysis, employing it to study the association between spatial arrangements, whether built or unbuilt, and human behaviour (Haq and Luo 2012; Omer and Goldblatt 2017; Wang et al. 2022). To date, this tool has largely focused on public domains such as health and social environments, with researchers mainly using this analysis technique to produce data through graphical representations (Zhang et al. 2023). For example, one study documents the physical activity assessment of older Japanese adults, highlighting the association between cognitive functions and street network (Koohsari et al. 2019). Another research focuses on the intersection of social behaviour and public spaces to improve social interaction among the elderly in Beijing city (Omer and Goldblatt 2017). There are studies found in the health care domain investigating nursing homes and the circulation within structures with daily living activities. In the interior residential domain, researchers using space syntax theory have explored the daily activities of older adults and spatial planned layouts (Song et al. 2020). For example, a study on elderly housing in Jakarta, Indonesia, examines the connection between activity, mobility, and space, noting that spaces such as the lobby and reception area have a high degree of integration and connectivity (Mariana et al. 2018). Another study on the indoor built environment, specifically the kitchen environment, compares task efficiency among cognitive impaired adults and measures aspects for promoting age-appropriate retrofitting of family residential spaces (Y. Wang et al. 2022). However, very few studies have emphasized the importance of spatial layouts and spatial behaviour that examine the physical and cognitive functions of older adults to augment spatial design using space syntax. Moreover, there is no empirical examination that caters to Indian older adults and spatial behavioural analysis in the interior residential domain, necessitating thorough exploration to study older individuals in the Indian context.

Traditionally, Indian kitchens have been designed to accommodate multiple meals, prioritizing efficiency in tasks like grinding, chopping, and cooking, which influence layout and tool placement (Bhatia et al. 2023). Design elements such as low platforms for sitting while cooking and storage for large vessels reflect cultural practices and ergonomic considerations (Archana and Kumar 2021). However, compact housing trends promoting modular kitchens and cabinet systems, which offer more storage space and efficient workspace, have largely been influenced by Western standards (Khandelwal 2024). These designs have deviated from Indian norms of traditional cooking environments, affecting older people by replacing tasks that were traditionally done sitting or squatting now require prolonged standing and bending that causes illnesses with posture deformities and musculoskeletal disorders (Abdelsalam et al. 2023; Bhatia and Singla 2019). Water handling tasks occasionally lead to excessive spillage in the kitchen, resulting in severe accidents due to falls for older people living independently (Ibrahim and Davies 2012). Hence, prioritizing cultural significance in design and emphasizing comfort and safety, in conjunction with the behavioural aspects of ageing in place, becomes crucial when examining kitchen layouts, circulation, and spatial organizations.

This research aims to identify the parameters that contribute to kitchen design for older adults and assess the impact of physical and cognitive behavioural factors with the spatial organization on their quality of life and well-being. The objective of this exploratory research is to study three common typologies of kitchen designs layouts in urban Indian context, by selecting ageing in place of older adult users. This research incorporates mixed method investigation through field study employing controlled observation followed by interviews and analysing behaviour with space through the lens of space syntax theory using depthMapX v0.8.0. The findings of this investigation will help propose novel design principles for kitchen spaces in compact living scenarios ageing in place.

2 Methodology

Employing exploratory research, this study focuses on a user group of older adults aged 65 to 85 years, who reside in urban India and use kitchens as their primary daily activity areas. Before the study commenced, permissions were obtained from the Institute Review Board (IRB), and written consent forms were provided to the participants. The research categorizes compact kitchen units into three design typologies, (1) single platform, (2) double platform and (3) L-shape type (see Fig. 1) and uses controlled and structured observations to gauge the behaviour of older adults during their regular kitchen task. This is followed by surveys and questionnaires to facilitate qualitative findings through thematic analysis (Low et al. 2023).

Next the study analyzes space usage patterns, spatial organization, and layout prioritization by studying individual kitchens through the lens of space syntax theory using DepthMapX v0.8.0 tool. Space syntax theory, introduced by Professor Bill Hillier, utilizes statistical analyses to demonstrate how the design of horizontal or vertical circulation influences user behaviour, such as interaction with workspace, circulation and movement patterns, and choices of space prioritization (Hillier and Tzortzi 2007).

3 Results

The research recruited 30 older adults for a controlled observational study. The average age of the sample was 70 (SD = 5.3) years and primarily comprised women (22/30, 73%) those who spent more than 5–6 h in the kitchen on an average. Using space syntax the

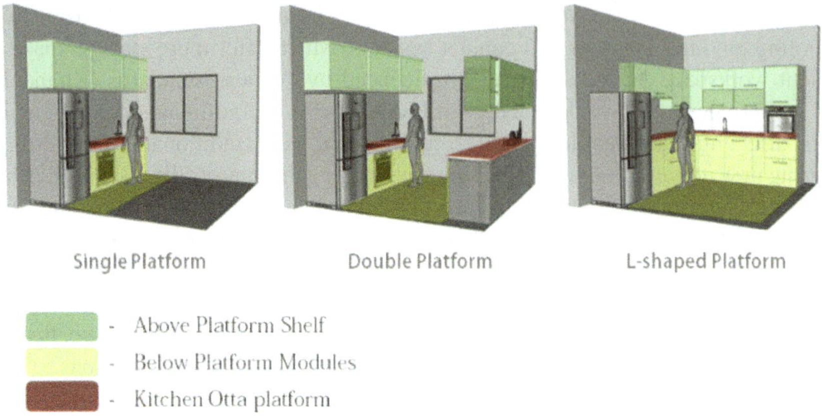

Fig. 1. Kitchen platform typologies, (1) Single platform, (2) Double platform and (3) L-Shaped platform

study identified the depth value of reaching out spaces such as platform, top and bottom shelves. Depth value refers to the minimum number of connections a space must use to reach out to other networked spaces, the higher the depth value the lower is the degree of integration and vice versa. The study sample shows that depth value with ageing and typologies is (1.89 and 1.70) in L-shaped, (1.2 and 0.5) in double platform and (0.76 and 1.6) in single platform respectively (see Fig. 2). Followed by observations during the kitchen task about 50% of the participants preferred L-shaped kitchen typologies, citing that this layout significantly increased their quality of life ($p = 0.010$) due to sufficient workspace and improved efficiency in working. The observations showed that layouts lacking sitting areas posed greater challenges for task performance, with chronic musculoskeletal issues predominantly observed in women (75%).

4 Discussion

Concentrating on the characterization of spatial configuration as an evolving process that links the physical environment to human spatial behaviour and experiences as defined by Professor Hillier (1996) (Hasgül 2015), this study highlights a significant correlation between kitchen spatial layout and task efficiency. It reveals evidence of ageing with physical and cognitive impairments affecting kitchen activities, emphasizing the significant importance of modifying designs to meet individual needs. Cultural influences and festivities were found to increase the workload in kitchen activities, with older individuals spending more than 7 h preparing traditional delicacies.

Previous research demonstrates studies of spatial configuration that provide better understanding of human behavioural experiences considering factors such as the area, sizes, characteristics and perception of space (Kim 1999). The majority of spatial research on built environment studies have focused on experiences and perceptual factors such as light, noise, colour, and materials, and have further experimented with interior spaces by manipulating walls and materials concentrating on visual elements

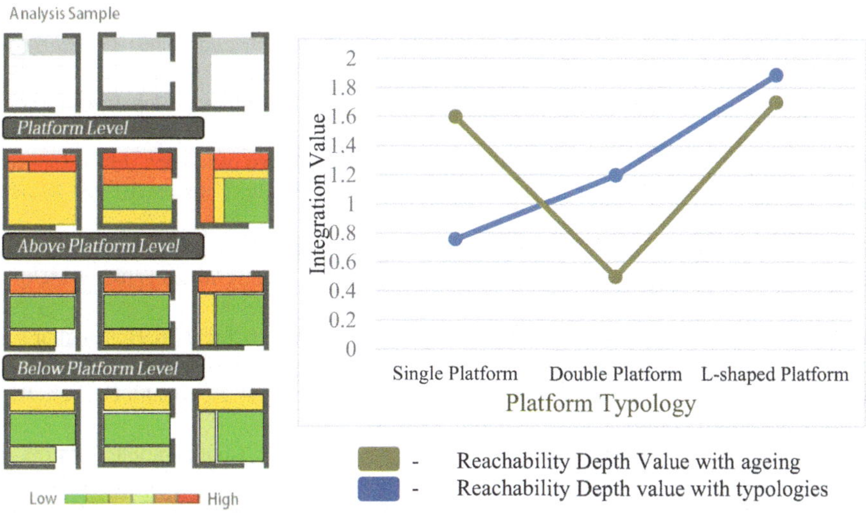

Fig. 2. Sample indicating the reachability depth value of three kitchen typologies during task performance

(Wang et al. 2021). However, our study focused more on exploring human spatial behavior considering furniture arrangement, spatial organization, and modifications of space in line with spatial configuration and behavioural studies (Wang et al. 2022).

5 Conclusions

In conclusion, the study emphasizes the need for age-appropriate design interventions and retrofitting in kitchen areas. Temporal space manipulation can aid spatial optimization, a correlation was established between kitchen spatial layout and task efficiency amongst older individuals. The observations revealed that spatial typologies significantly reduce the impact of musculoskeletal issues among the ageing population. By optimizing kitchen layouts to reduce reaching distances and facilitate movement, these changes can assist practitioners, architects, and interior designers in creating spaces that prioritize the comfort and safety of older adults. The contribution of this study is determining that space syntax theory can be used to study interior spatial layouts and organizations. Further research needs to be conducted to design and built kitchen layouts for task efficiency for ageing in place.

References

Abdelsalam, A., Wassif, G.O., Eldin, W.S., Hamid, M.A.A., Damaty, S.I.: Frequency and risk factors of musculoskeletal disorders among kitchen workers. J. Egypt. Public Health Assoc. **6**, 3 (2023). https://doi.org/10.1186/s42506-023-00128-6

Al-wabil, A., Zaphiris, P., Wilson, S.: Methodologies for involving older adults in the design process. Universal Access HCI. **4554**(2005), 593–602 (2007). https://doi.org/10.1007/978-3-540-73279-2

Archana, Kumar, D.: Analysis of traditional Indian kitchen Compatible anthropometric design implications. October (2021)

Bhatia, A., Singla, S.: Ergonomic evaluation and customized design of kitchen. Int. J. Innovat. Technol. Explor. Eng. **8**(9 Special Issue), 1033–1039 (2019). https://doi.org/10.35940/ijitee.I1166.0789S19

Bhatia, A., Singla, S. K., Bansal, A.: Ergonomics Design: A Smart Concept of Indian Kitchen. Lecture Notes in Networks and Systems. (2023, January 1). https://doi.org/10.1007/978-3-031-50151-7_38

Gaurav, W., Karan, S.: Affordable Housing in India: Key Initiatives for Inclusive Housing for All. Jones Lang Lasalle, Indian Chamber of Commerce, February, 3–5 (2016)

Haq, S., Luo, Y.: Space syntax in health-care facilities research: a review. Health Environ. Res. Des. J. **5**(4), 98–117 (2012)

Hasgül, E.: Space as Configuration Patterns of Space. Space as Configuration: Patterns of Space and Culture. Theory and History of Architecture Conference Proceedings, November 2015. (2015). https://www.researchgate.net/publication/335910605_Space_As_Configuration_Patterns_of_Space

Hillier, B., Tzortzi, K.: Space syntax. In: A Companion to Museum Studies, vol. 3, pp. 282–301 (2007). https://doi.org/10.1002/9780470996836.ch17

Hrovatin, J., Širok, K., Jevšnik, S., Oblak, L., Berginc, J.: Adaptability of kitchen furniture for elderly people in terms of safety. Drvna Industrija. **63**(2), 113–120 (2012). https://doi.org/10.5552/drind.2012.1128

Hwang, E., Cummings, L., Sixsmith, A., Sixsmith, J.: Impacts of home modifications on aging-in-place. J. Hous. Elder. **25**(3), 246–257 (2011). https://doi.org/10.1080/02763893.2011.595611

Khandelwal, N.R.: The Evolution of Kitchen Design: A Comprehensive Guide to Modular Kitchens. The Times of India. (2024, February 12) https://timesofindia.indiatimes.com/hot-picks/the-evolution-of-kitchen-design-a-comprehensive-guide-to-modular-kitchens/articleshow/107630137.cms

Kim, Y. O.: Spatial configuration, spatial cognitionand spatial behaviour: the role of architectural intelligibility inshaping spatial experience. Doctoral Thesis, University of London (1999).

Koohsari, M.J., Nakaya, T., McCormack, G.R., Shibata, A., Ishii, K., Yasunaga, A., Oka, K.: Cognitive function of elderly persons in Japanese neighborhoods: the role of street layout. Am. J. Alzheimers Dis. Other Dement. **34**(6), 381–389 (2019). https://doi.org/10.1177/1533317519844046

Ibrahim, N.I., Davies, S.: Aging: physical difficulties and safety in cooking tasks. Work-a J. Prevent. Assess. Rehab. **41**, 5152–5159 (2012, January 1). https://doi.org/10.3233/wor-2012-0804-5152

Low, S.K., Cheng, M.Y., Pheh, K.S.: A thematic analysis of older adult's perspective of successful ageing. Curr. Psychol. **42**(13), 10999–11008 (2023). https://doi.org/10.1007/s12144-021-02371-6

Mariana, Y., Triwardhani, A.J., Djimantoro, M.I.: The study of a space configuration using space syntax analysis case study: an elderly housing. IOP Conf. Ser. Earth Environ. Sci. **109**(1), 012048 (2018). https://doi.org/10.1088/1755-1315/109/1/012048

Mnea, A., Zairul, M.: Evaluating the impact of housing interior design on elderly independence and activity: a thematic review. Buildings. **13**(4), 1–20 (2023). https://doi.org/10.3390/buildings13041099

MoHUA: Development and regulations of retirement homes. **4**(1), 1–23 (2016)

MoHUA: Ministry of Housing and Urban Affairs Annual Report 2022–23 (2023)

Omer, I., Goldblatt, R.: Using space syntax and Q-analysis for investigating movement patterns in buildings: the case of shopping malls. Environ. Plann. B Urban Analyt. City Sci. **44**(3), 504–530 (2017). https://doi.org/10.1177/0265813516647061

Qian, Q.K., Ho, W.K.O., Jayantha, W.M., Chan, E.H.W.: Aging-in-place and home modifications for urban regeneration. Land. **11**, 1–15 (2022) https://www.mdpi.com/2073-445X/11/11/1956

Singh, C., Martinez, C.M.J., Jayadas, A.: Assessment of perceived discomfort in older women with and without osteoarthritis and young women when reaching for items on different Shelf Heights. J. Aging Environ. **37**(4), 442–459 (2023). https://doi.org/10.1080/26892618.2022.2109791

Song, S., Wang, D., Zhu, W., Wang, C.: Study on the spatial configuration of nursing homes for the elderly people in Shanghai: based on their choice preference. Technol. Forecast. Soc. Chang. **152**, 119859 (2020). https://doi.org/10.1016/j.techfore.2019.119859

Tarboush, R.M., Erçin, Ç.: User's need in architectural spaces development, existing kitchen design in Northern Cyprus. Eur. J. Sustain. Dev. **10**(2), 13–32 (2021). https://doi.org/10.14207/ejsd.2021.v10n2p13

Vahedi, S.: World health organization quality-of-life scale (WHOQOL-BREF): analyses of their item response theory properties based on the graded responses model. Iran. J. Psychiatry. **5**(4), 140–153 (2010) http://www.ncbi.nlm.nih.gov/pubmed/22952508

Vaishnav, L.M., Joshi, S.H., Joshi, A.U., Mehendale, A.M.: The national programme for health care of the elderly: a review of its achievements and challenges in India. Ann. Geriatr. Med. Res. **26**(3), 183–195 (2022). https://doi.org/10.4235/agmr.22.0062

Wang, C., Zhang, F., Wang, J., Doyle, J.K., Hancock, P.A., Mak, C.M., Liu, S.: How indoor environmental quality affects occupants' cognitive functions: a systematic review. Build. Environ. **193**, 107647 (2021). https://doi.org/10.1016/j.buildenv.2021.107647

Wang, Y., Lin, D., Huang, Z.: Research on the aging-friendly kitchen based on space syntax theory. Int. J. Environ. Res. Public Health. **19**(9), 5393 (2022). https://doi.org/10.3390/ijerph19095393

WHO: Programme on Mental Health-WHOQOL User Manual. Report. (1992). https://doi.org/10.1371/journal.pone.0262833

Zhang, Y., Wu, Z., Wu, Z., Liu, Y., Yang, Z.: Using space syntax in close interaction analysis between the elderly: towards a healthier urban environment. Buildings. **13**(6), 1456 (2023). https://doi.org/10.3390/buildings13061456

The Construction of Community Service Facilities System on Age-Friendly

Xiaoman Jiang[1], Xiaoli Wu[1](✉), Xilu Tang[1], and Chengqi Xue[2]

[1] Nanjing University of Science and Technology, Nanjing, NJ 210094, China
wuxlhhu@163.com
[2] Southeast University, Nanjing, NJ 210096,, China

Abstract. With the acceleration of the aging process and the increase of the elderly population, the construction of age-friendly communities has become an important link in the development of elderly care services. Literature collection and collation are conducted to analyze the progress of community service facility system construction on age-friendly community and community service facility system construction, to elaborate on the relevant research results. It summaries the current status and hot issues of age-friendly communities, analyzes and summarizes the related research on the construction of the age-friendly community service facility system from four dimensions: the configuration of community facilities for age-friendly, the spatial layout of facilities for age-friendly, the transformation ideas of facilities for age-friendly, and the evaluation of age-friendly community. The overall ergo-nomic design of community service provides an interactive community service map design scheme that can adapt to the characteristics and needs of the daily behavior and activities of the elderly. In the future, more attention should be paid to the high-level needs of the elderly and the construction of guiding principles and evaluation indicators for the age-community.

Keywords: Age-friendly · Community service · Service facility · System construction

1 Research on Age-Friendly Communities

Please note that the first paragraph of a section or subsection is not indented. The first paragraphs that follows a table, figure, equation etc. does not have an indent, either.

With the increase of the elderly population, the pension model combining community and home care has gradually become the mainstream, and the construction of age-friendly communities has become one of the important contents of the research. Plouffe et al. (2010) [2] proposed that physical accessibility, proximity, safety, affordability and inclusion are important characteristics of age-friendly cities, providing reference for evaluation of age-friendly communities. Pedell et al. (2021) [3]. A case study found that considering the digital, physical and social dimensions of age-friendly urban components "communication and information", "outdoor space and architecture" and "social engagement" better contribute to the social participation and long-term health of older

S. Jin et al. (Eds.): IEA 2024, SSDI 39, pp. 98–107, 2025.
https://doi.org/10.1007/978-981-95-0211-0_16

persons. Daven et al. (2020) [4] provides a quantifiable framework of spatial indicators to assess the local living environment according to the Guidelines for Building an age-friendly city. Wallhagen et al. (2021) [5] through qualitative and quantitative analysis, Factors such as outdoor space, built homes, community support and health services were found to be significantly related to life satisfaction of the elderly. Liddle et al. (2020) [6] proposes the development of digital connectivity in age-friendly communities to optimize the social connections of older persons within the community. Ide et al. (2022) [7]. The study found that the higher the degree of social participation in addition to the neighborhood contact, the higher the happiness of the elderly, so the social participation can be used as an indicator of suitable aging community assessment.

In recent years, scholars in China have also studied the construction of age-friendly communities from various aspects. Guo Shijie et al. (2016) [8] proposed "Small homogeneity, large mix, construction of mixed communities" and "Inhabitant suitable for old, facilities for old. Activity is old "macro level suitable for aging com-munity transformation strategy. Zhang Qian (2017) [9]. Put forward the concept of "community darning" to build an active aging existing community living space shared by all through transformation, implant, link, copy and other methods. Chen Xiaoyu et al. (2020) [10]. A multi-level spatial excavation of "Development goal-Potential Assessment - renewal guidance" was constructed three types of space updating and its guidance are proposed. Tang Jichun et al. (2021) [11] constructed an aging com-munity public space with street space renewal, public life activation and service system construction Space micro update framework. Huang Wenwei et al. (2021) [12] constructed an index system for the degree of age-friendly of existing communities in Yichang City and a structural equation model for the evaluation of age-friendly transformation of existing communities.

Search "Age-friendly Community" in "Web of Science" and count the top 20 keywords with co-occurrence frequency (see Table 1) for reference. CiteSpace software was used to perform cluster analysis on the results. TF*IDF weighted algorithm was adopted in this clustering, and the result was $S = 0.7462$ and $Q = 0.4221$. In cluster analysis, it is generally believed that when $Q > 0.3$, the cluster structure is significant. When $S > 0.5$, the clustering is reasonable. When $S > 0.7$, the cluster structure can be convincing. To sum up, the clustering structure can be convincing. The cluster structure is shown in Fig. 1. It can be seen that the nine hot issues in the research field of age-friendly communities abroad are living alone, peer education, residential areas, dementia, social participation, systematic evaluation, disability, hip, and human-centered design.

Based on the co-occurrence frequency of keywords and the results of cluster analysis, it can be seen that the current foreign studies on the aging community are more from the perspective of senile diseases and health of the elderly, such as senile dementia, disability and hip rehabilitation, and emphasize the people-oriented design concept. There are few researches on the public space and service facilities for the aged in the aging community. The possible reason is that foreign communities have been built for more than a century, the construction of public service facilities has been relatively complete and the level of social welfare is relatively high, so there are few studies on the construction of service facilities system from the perspective of aging. However, the construction of public service facilities in our country is still lagging behind. In recent years, the research

Table 1. Distribution of top 20 co-occurrence frequencies of "Age-friendly Community" keywords in Web of Science.

Number	Frequency	Centrality	Earliest Year	Keyword	Number	Frequency	Centrality	Earliest Year	Keyword
1	63	0.27	2008	Health	11	14	0.09	2010	Program
2	41	0.20	2009	Older Adult	12	14	0.06	2014	Association
3	39	0.20	2011	Community	13	13	0.06	2014	Built Environment
4	27	0.05	2014	Physical Activity	14	12	0.08	2014	Quality of Life
5	26	0.24	2015	People	15	10	0.05	2015	Risk
6	21	0.07	2017	City	16	10	0.04	2014	Older People
7	19	0.07	2014	Care	17	10	0.04	2014	Disability
8	18	0.11	2014	Adult	18	10	0.09	2015	Intervention
9	18	0.07	2014	Environment	19	10	0.03	2011	Prevalence
10	16	0.16	2015	Dementia	20	9	0.05	2010	Life

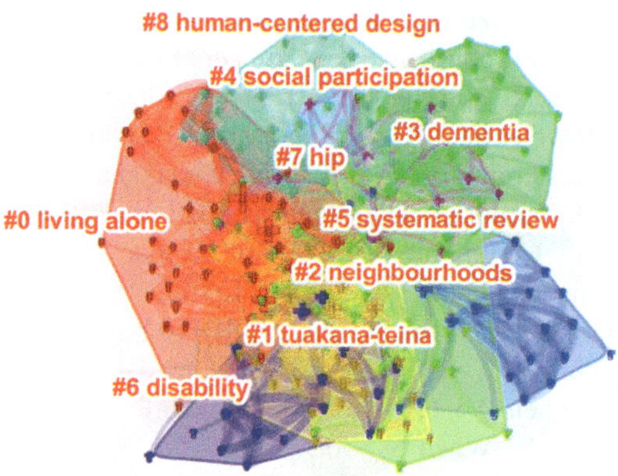

Fig. 1. Results of CiteSpace cluster analysis in the field of age-friendly in foreign communities.

hotspots and centers on aging communities mostly focused on the transformation and renovation of aging service facilities in old communities and existing communities.

2 Research on Community Aging Service Design

By consulting relevant literature, summarizing relevant studies, and using field visits, questionnaire interviews and other research methods, this paper mainly designs and researches community age-appropriate services from two aspects: the current situation of community age-friendly services and the age-friendly behavior model. The basic information of the investigation is as follows: A total of 10 elderly people were interviewed, 200 questionnaires were sent out, and 162 questionnaires were collected in total, of which 114 were valid.

2.1 A Subsection Sample

By consulting the construction data of age-appropriate communities and related literature research, this paper summarizes and collates some successful cases of age-appropriate community construction in China's market at present. This paper selects three cases of Taikang Home elderly care community, Vanke all-age elderly care community and Shanghai Qinheyuan Elderly Apartment for description (see Table 2).

Table 2. Nursing community case summary.

<table>
<tr><th>Community Name</th><th>Spatial Arrangement</th><th>Similarity</th></tr>
<tr><td>Taikang Home elderly care community</td><td>The semi-enclosed courtyard is divided into north and south areas. In the transitional zone between the north and the south, there is a commercial street for the elderly, an activity center and a university for the elderly</td><td rowspan="3">They are equipped with basic places and facilities for the daily activities of the elderly, such as the vitality center for the daily leisure and sports of the elderly, and the university for the elderly to study</td></tr>
<tr><td>Vanke all-age elderly care community</td><td>Central Park is the core of the space, and other Spaces are distributed around it in a U-shaped shape. The second floor U-shaped belt is an activity belt, and the third floor is built with public service facilities</td></tr>
<tr><td>Shanghai Qinheyuan Elderly Apartment</td><td>The overall structure is an outer ring type, and there is a commercial street for the elderly distributed on the right side, which has sports and fitness places, life necessities places, education and learning places, etc.</td></tr>
</table>

2.2 Research on Adaptive Aging Behavior Model

1. **Characteristics of the elderly.** In terms of physiological characteristics, with the growth of age, the physical function of the elderly will have a relatively large decline, such as the decline of the motor system is prone to fatigue, the degradation of the sensory system, the weakening of the sensory ability, and the aging reaction speed of the nervous system, so its activity ability is restricted to a certain extent. In the planning of the 15-min community life circle, Shanghai proposed that a 5-min walk could reach a distance of 200 to 300 meters, a 10-min walk of 500 m, and a 15-min walk of 800–1000 m [13]. Based on the activity ability of the urban elderly of about 40 m per min, the daily activity circle of the elderly is defined, as shown in Table **3** below.

Table 3. Activity circle and characteristics of daily behavior of the elderly.

Daily Activity Circle	Travel Time	Activity Radius	Motion Frequency
Basic mobile circle	5 min	200-250 m	High
Neighborhood circle	10 min	450 m	Relatively high
Daily activity circle	15 min	600-700 m	Medium
Widen activity circle	More than 15 min	More than 700 m	Relatively low

In terms of psychological characteristics, the social role of the elderly has changed, and their leisure time has increased greatly, which will also change their psychology. Because the elderly have more free time after retirement, but the social participation is low, and the frequency of communication with people is reduced, which is easy to make them feel lonely. At the same time, retirement also reduces the social status and economic income of the elderly, which is easy to produce feelings of inferiority and anxiety, and they are eager to find their own value in the old life. Ac-cording to Maslow's hierarchy of needs theory, we should not only pay attention to the physiological and safety needs of the elderly, but also pay more attention to the needs of social interaction, respect and self-realization of the elderly in the construction of age-appropriate communities in the future.

In terms of behavioral characteristics, based on the influence of physiological and psychological factors, the daily behavior of the elderly has the characteristics of gathering, and they are more inclined to participate in some collective activities and social activities. They like to chat together in parks or squares, watch other people's activities, or carry out activities with some elderly people who have common interests. In addition, regionality is also an important feature of their daily behavior. The elderly are more accustomed to carrying out activities in their own familiar space places, such as walking and chatting in the community green space, dancing and playing tai chi in the park square, playing chess and playing cards under the canopy and pavilion.

2. **Contents of daily behaviors and activities of the elderly**. According to the survey on the daily behaviors and activities of the elderly in the community, 103 respondents need to buy food on a daily basis, more than 70% of respondents take a walk or bask in the sun in the park or on the walking path, 64 respondents choose daily medical treatment and 46 respondents choose regular physical examination. In the community sports equipment, chess and cards, the proportion of choice is relatively high. It can be seen that buying vegetables, taking a walk in the park or walking path or basking in the sun are the main contents of the daily activities of most elderly people; Sports and fitness activities such as community sports equipment and leisure and entertainment activities such as chatting, chess and cards are also important contents of the daily behavior activities of the elderly; At the same time, because of the physiological factors of the elderly, daily medical treatment and regular physical examination are also an indispensable part of their daily life.

According to the survey on the daily behaviors and activities of the elderly out-side the community, 91 respondents would go to the outside of the community for medical treatment, 52 respondents would have regular physical examination, 72 respondents would go to other people's homes and 54 respondents would attend par-ties outside the community. Sixty-nine respondents said they regularly go to large supermarkets or shopping malls outside their communities to shop. It can be seen that the daily activities of the elderly outside the community are mainly medical and health; This is followed by social activities such as going to other people's homes and parties. At the same time, going to large supermarkets or shopping malls is also an important part of the daily behavior of the elderly.

3. **Daily behavior and activity needs of the elderly**. According to the survey of the elderly's demand for community services, from the six service types, the use of safe and clean living environment services reached 213 times, while the use of other five services was relatively small. In terms of the types of new services needed, the demand for publicity and education increased 329 times, and the demand for life support and care increased 247 times. A comprehensive analysis of the services used by the elderly and the services they hope to add can be obtained: the elderly have a strong demand for publicity and education activities in the community, followed by safe and clean living environment and life support and care services; At present, the community service type used by the elderly more is the safe and clean living environment, while the use of other types of services is low, which may be due to the lack of such services in the community. It is expected that the service of publicity and education and life support and care need to be added, so we should pay attention to the construction and development of these services.

   In terms of specific service content, it is stratified according to the use and need to increase the service content for the elderly. The first level is more than 80% of the respondents' needs, and the second level is more than 70% of the respondents' needs. In the construction of age-appropriate community services, we should focus on the first and second level of service content, and other service content should also be built according to the actual situation. The service contents of Tier 1 and Tier 2 are shown in Table 4 below.

In summary, combined with the results of field investigation and interview, it can be concluded that the following contents should be constructed in the construction of space places suitable for aging communities: community square, park or green space; Shelters and pavilions; Community clinics or health centers; Activity room (such as chess room, painting room, library, etc.) In the construction of facilities and equipment suitable for aging communities, the following contents should be constructed: community sports equipment, walking paths, seats, and public toilets. In the construction of age-appropriate community services, the following contents should be constructed: regular landscaping and remediation of the community environment, daily cleaning of domestic waste, providing psychological counseling and other services, regularly carrying out knowledge lectures and publicity and education, regularly organizing elderly people to participate in public welfare activities, providing intelligent products and technical training.

Table 4. Hierarchy of community service needs.

Hierarchy of Needs	Type of Service	Service Content
First level (over 80%)	Safe and clean living environment	Regular greening, beautification and remediation of the community environment
		Community household garbage should be cleaned up in a timely manner
	Medical and health	Provide chat, psychological counseling, emotional comfort, relationship adjustment and social integration services
	Publicity and education	Regular health, safety and fraud prevention, rights and interests protection, law and other knowledge lectures and publicity education
	Social participation	Organize the elderly to participate in public welfare activities, such as community service, environmental protection, knowledge dissemination, social security, etc.
	Technology for the elderly	Provide smart products and technical training assistance
Second level (over 70%)	Life support care class	Elderly supplies, such as canes, wheelchairs, walkers, anti-slip bracelets, badges, etc.
		Organize volunteers or social workers to visit the elderly living alone and empty-nesters regularly
	Publicity and education	Education and learning activities for the elderly should be carried out regularly
		Carry out neighborhood help activities to encourage the neighborhood to provide life care and love for the elderly in need
	Technology for the elderly	The tradition of manual service and cash charges is maintained in some establishments

3 Design Practice of Community Aging Service Map

3.1 Design Goal

In the previous investigation, it was found that the place of daily behavior and activities of the elderly was relatively limited, usually only a single park or green space, and the activity content was single. The main reasons are: first, the memory ability and learning ability of the elderly decline, it is difficult to recognize too complex road system, so dare not go to strange places to carry out activities, fearing that they can not find the way back; Second, the channels for the elderly to obtain information are relatively simple, and they do not know other activity places in the community except the activity places they often go to; Third, at present, there are few activities and elderly care service organizations in the community, and the publicity is not in place, so that most elderly people miss the opportunity to participate. Therefore, this paper attempts to present the intelligent age-appropriate community in the form of an interactive community service map, so that it can be perceived and used by the elderly, so as to effectively facilitate the behavior activities of the elderly in the community, enrich the daily behavior activities of the elderly, and promote the improvement of the community service system for the elderly.

3.2 Color Map Design

Different colors are used to represent different functional space places or facility types (as shown in Fig. 2). For the colors of building space types, pale gray is mainly used to represent residential buildings, purple for commercial buildings, bright blue for medical and healthcare buildings, dark orange for senior activity facilities or buildings, dark pink for care service buildings, yellow-green for other types of buildings in the community, yellow for kindergartens, light orange for activity plazas, light yellow for open blocks, dark green for public toilets, and pink for community walkways. In terms of the color of the community landscape environment, green is mainly used to represent wooded green space, grass green for grassy green space, light pink for floral green space, and light blue for lake water system. At the same time, when shaping the color of buildings or facilities, the same hue of lower brightness color is used for tracing to enhance the outer contour; and three degrees of the same hue, deep, medium and light, are used for shaping the surface, so that the building appears to be more three-dimensional in the sense of view. And in the color shaping of the building's surrounding environmental information, it chooses a flat language to represent, and the building to form a more distinctive contrast.

The use of different colors to represent the types of building facilities and environmental information in the map can enable the elderly to quickly obtain the approximate location of the same or similar Spaces or facilities in the community, have a preliminary understanding and understanding of the community environment, simplify the complexity of the map, and reduce the cognitive difficulty of the elderly.

Fig. 2. Map visualization color design.

3.3 Features and Application Scenarios

Based on application requirements, a total of three kinds of community service maps are designed, which are community color map, community 3D model map and community AR reality map, as shown in Fig. 3. The three community service maps have their own characteristics and application scenarios. Community color map mainly uses different colors to represent the building facilities and environmental information in the community, simplifying the complexity of the map and reducing the difficulty of cognition. It is mainly used to display the overall information of spatial facilities in the community, simplify the process for the elderly to find similar spatial facilities, and quickly search for similar spatial facilities through colors. The 3D model map of the community matches the real environment, showing the real 3D community model to the user, which is more three-dimensional and intuitive. It is mainly used in route search and navigation, which is more authentic than the color map, and can quickly obtain the real environment and road conditions of the whole community, and the route display is more intuitive. Community AR reality map presents the community map and environment in the form of AR, in which community information and services leap to the front of your eyes, mainly used to query nearby activities and information, the space and buildings in the community are no longer cold, but more humane, convenient for the elderly's daily travel, so that community elderly care services can be seen everywhere.

Fig. 3. Three kinds of community service map description.

References

1. Opinions of the General Office of the State Council on Promoting the Development of Elderly Care Services (No. 5, 2019)
2. Plouffe, L., Kalache, A.: Towards global age-friendly cities: determining urban features that promote active aging[J]. J. Urban Health Bull. N.Y. Acad. Med. **87**(5), 733–739 (2010)
3. Pedell, S., Borda, A., Keirnan, A., Aimers, N.: Combining the digital, social and physical layer to create age-friendly cities and communities. Int. J. Environ. Res. Public Health. **18**(1), 325 (2021)
4. Davern, M., Winterton, R., Brasher, K., Woolcock, G.: How can the lived environment support healthy ageing? A spatial indicators framework for the assessment of age-friendly communities. Int. J. Environ. Res. Public Health. **17**(20), 7685 (2020)
5. Wallhagen, M.I., Strawbridge, W.J., Tremblay, K.: Leveraging the age friendly healthcare system initiative to achieve comprehensive, hearing healthcare across the spectrum of healthcare settings: an interprofessional perspective. Int. J. Audiol. **60**, 80–85 (2021)
6. Liddle, J., Pitcher, N., Montague, K., Hanratty, B., Standing, H., Scharf, T.: Connecting at local level: exploring opportunities for future design of technology to support social connections in age-friendly communities. Int. J. Environ. Res. Public Health. **17**(15), 5544 (2020)
7. Ide, K., Jeong, S., Tsuji, T., Watanabe, R., Miyaguni, Y., Nakamura, H., Kimura, M., Kondo, K.: Suggesting indicators of age-Friendly City: social participation and happiness, an ecological study from the JAGES. Int. J. Environ. Res. Public Health. **19**(9), 5096 (2022)
8. Guo, S., Jinfu, C.: Aging transformation of old communities under the guidance of differentiated needs: a case study of Qingshan district community in Wuhan [C]. In: Shenyang :2016 China Urban Planning Annual Conference (2016)
9. Qian, Z.: Community darning, Intergenerational mutual aid – Building an existing community living space shared by all [J]. New Archit. **40**(01), 14–18 (2017)
10. Xiaoyu, C., Hongqing, J., Shiying, Z.: Research on evaluation and renewal guidance of aging renovation potential of stock space [C]. In: Chengdu :2020/2021 China Urban Planning Annual Conference and 2021 China Urban Planning Academic Season (2021)
11. Jichun, T., Xin, C.: Aging renovation of public space in old communities under the concept of micro-renewal [C]. In: Chengdu: 2020/2021 China Urban Planning Annual Conference and 2021 China Urban Planning Academic Season (2021)
12. Wenwei, H., Han, W., Zixi, W.: Research on the adaptive retrofit of existing residential areas based on structural equation model [J]. South. Archit. **42**(04), 138–144 (2021)
13. Shanghai Municipal Administration of Planning and Land Resources: Shanghai 15-minute community living circle planning guidelines (for trial implementation) [R] (2016)

How Can the Built Environment of the Home Enable Aging-in-Place? Insights from a Multi-Sited Ethnography of Elderly Living at Home in India

Gourab Kar(✉), Mohd Sahil Khan, Sidharth Sonowal, Sanket Subhas Naik, S. Aswin, and Sabyasachi Paldas

Department of Design, Indian Institute of Technology Delhi, New Delhi 110016, India
gourab@iitd.ac.in

Abstract. India is projected to age rapidly in the coming decades. The proportion of people aged 60 years and above is estimated to rise from 10.5% of the population in 2022 to 20.8% in 2050 and to 36% by the turn of the century. While the country is in early stages of a transition to an older society, little is known about how the built environment of home enables or hinders the elderly in performing activities-of-daily-living. Therefore, this study used ethnographic methods to investigate the degree of person–environment fit for the elderly who are aging-in-place. A multi-sited ethnography of elderly living at home was conducted in Dibrugarh, Panaji and New Delhi, India. Using environmental traces, participant observation and semi-structured user interviews, researchers documented human-environment interactions of sixty-four elderly in their homes. User interviews were transcribed into English and analysed using qualitative data analysis software. Thematic analysis of research data revealed the need for environmental accommodations to compensate for the lack-of-fit between the elderly person's abilities and demands of the built environment. Functional challenges for the elderly can be classified into - postural transitions, reduced reach envelopes, lack of independent mobility, culturally-rooted behaviours and need to address the latent fear of falls. Findings from study offer insights on how redesign of the built environment of home can enhance safety, independence and assistance for elderly who are aging-in-place. Future research needs to build the evidence base and develop theoretical foundations linking the ecology of aging with the enabling role of the built environment.

Keywords: person-environment fit · ethnography · environmental gerontology · aging-in-place · environmental accommodations · inclusive design

1 Introduction

Over the next few decades, India is projected to age rapidly. The proportion of people aged 60 years and above is estimated to rise from 10.5% of the total population in 2022 to 20.8% in 2050 and to 36% by the turn of the century [1]. A distinguishing feature of

S. Jin et al. (Eds.): IEA 2024, SSDI 39, pp. 108–114, 2025.
https://doi.org/10.1007/978-981-95-0211-0_17

aging in India is the significant interstate variation in growth of the elderly population. This may be due to varying stages and pace of the demographic transition across states. States in the north such as Bihar and Uttar Pradesh, and in the east such as Assam have elderly populations lower than the Indian average, while states in the south such as Goa, Tamil Nadu and Kerala have significantly higher proportion of the elderly [2].

As people age, changes in the body and mind result in decreased strength, range of motion and balance, leading to decline in functional abilities. Elderly in India report challenges in performing activities-of-daily-living such as bathing, dressing, walking across the room, eating, getting in or out of bed, and using the toilet [3]. The two most difficult activities reported by the elderly were getting in or out of bed and use of toilets. With India in the early stages of a transition to an older society, little is known about how the built environment of the home enables or hinders the elderly in performing activities-of-daily-living. Therefore, there is a crucial need to investigate the *degree of person-environment fit* for the elderly who are aging-in-place [4–6]. This is especially relevant as empirical research at the intersection of environmental gerontology and inclusive design is at a nascent stage in India [7]. Findings from this multi-sited ethnography would inform the inclusive design of built environments for the elderly that enhance safety, independence and functional performance [8]. Therefore, this ethnographic research investigated how the built environment of the home enables or hinders the experience of aging-in-place for elderly in India. Research questions focused on: *What are challenges of functional reach and mobility for the elderly at home? What are compensatory strategies adopted by the elderly to perform activities-of-daily-living? How can the design of the built environment enhance safety and independence for the elderly at home?*

2 Methodology

A multi-sited ethnography of the elderly aging-in-place was conducted in three cities located in the east (Dibrugarh, Assam), south (Panaji, Goa) and north (New Delhi) of the country. The choice of the cities was based on familiarity of researchers with the location and ability to speak the language of the elderly residents. Sixty-four elderly residents, aged 55–85 years old, were observed at home performing activities-of-daily-living. Informed consent was obtained prior to the study and the elderly were not compensated for participation. Rather than start with a predefined hypothesis, researchers focused on observing human-environment interactions of the elderly in their homes to develop a comprehensive understanding of the *degree of person-environment fit* [4–6]. Using environmental traces, participant observation and user interviews, researchers documented human-environment interactions of the elderly in their homes [9, 10]. Research data included sketches, floor layouts, field notes, video recordings, photographs and interview transcripts.

Data from environmental traces and ethnographic observations helped the research team to develop a questionnaire which was used for semi-structured interviews with the elderly. These interviews with the elderly were conducted in their homes and lasted for about 45–60 min. The language of conversation in the interviews was Assamese in Dibrugarh, Konkani in Panaji and a combination of Hindi and Malayalam in New Delhi.

In a few instances, a family member or caregiver assisted the elderly in communicating with the interviewer. These interviews enabled the researcher to triangulate data gathered from environmental traces and observations with responses from the interviews. The logic of using three research tools in sequence was to enable the research team to delve deeper into the unique experiences of the elderly, especially highlighting how changes in their body and mind due to the process of aging impacted their ability to independently perform activities-of-daily-living.

To facilitate the conversation with the elderly residents, researchers used photo elicitation techniques such as showing photographs and sketches from the environmental traces and participant observations. The use of these conversation aids enabled the researchers to collect additional information, clarify points, move the conversation forward, or change the subject [10]. Each interview was transcribed into English and the interview script was analysed into themes using qualitative data analysis software [11]. Thematic analysis is an inductive data analysis process that involves generating themes from the data. It begins with a data extraction process and culminates in the development of themes that effectively address the research questions [12]. Salient themes emerging from the study are discussed in the following section.

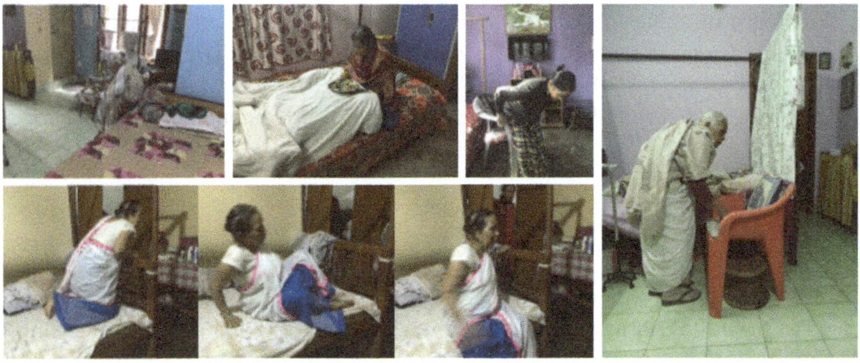

Fig. 1. Observations of elderly getting in or out of the bed.

3 Results

Analysis of research data helped identify five themes which are elaborated below:

Postural transitions - such as getting up from bed, rising up from a chair or a toilet seat is difficult for the elderly. Such changes in posture may be accompanied by feeling dizzy in the head (postural hypotension) with increased risks of falls. Designs of enabling home environments for the elderly should consider ways to enhance safety in postural transitions. These could be achieved by provision of grab rails on walls adjacent to circulation areas, grab bars in the toilet and bathrooms, use of chairs with armrests and the beds with supports such as bed rails to enable ingress and egress (see Fig. 1).

Functional Reach - The functional reach envelope for elderly is significantly reduced because of decline in physical strength, range of motion and sense of balance. Consequently, the elderly find it difficult to bend down and/or reach forward to pick up things near the floor level, or reach upwards to pick up things above shoulder height (see Fig. 2). Worksurfaces and storage areas, especially in the kitchen and toilets, should be designed to be near the waist-height of the elderly to reduce need for them to bend down or reach above the shoulder. Likewise, objects such as door handles and switches that need to be touched or grasped should be near the elbow height of the elderly.

Fig. 2. Observations of elderly augmenting their functional reach with aids

Independent Mobility - Safe and independent mobility inside homes and surrounding spaces is negatively impacted by changes in the floor level. Many elderly residents were afraid of using stairs inside the house due to a fear of falls. Stairs rarely had handrails at appropriate height, the tread and riser for stairs was not optimized for the movement of the elderly and illumination levels in stairwells was inadequate (see Fig. 3). Most staircase configurations could not be retrofitted with a stair-lift. There is a need for empirical research to develop evidence-based designs of internal and external staircases which offer safe and independent mobility for elderly.
Culturally-rooted behaviours - Practices such as floor-sitting, especially in the *prayer room* and use of squat toilets, need to be relooked due to reduced functional capabilities of the elderly (see Fig. 4). A few elderly residents expressed regret in not being able to sit on the floor, especially in the *prayer room*. Rather than eliminate the practice of floor-sitting or use of a squat toilets by the elderly, there is need for culturally responsive environmental accommodations such as grab bars integrated with wall and/or furniture to enable the elderly to safely transition between floor-seated and standing postures.
Fear of falling - Aging is both a physical as well as psychological phenomenon. Many elderly are afraid of falls. Once an elderly person experiences a fall, he or she loses the confidence to independently perform activities-of-daily-living such as bathing or use of the toilet. As a consequence, the elderly need assistance from a family member or caregiver. Therefore, designing an enabling environment for the home must not only cater to functional and spatial needs of the elderly when they are independently able,

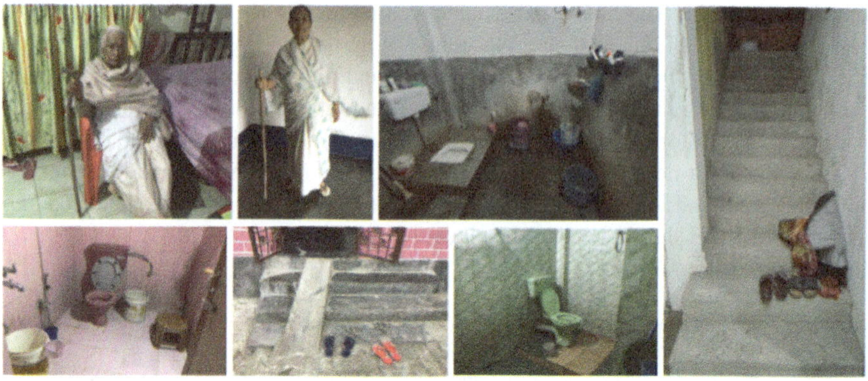

Fig. 3. Challenges for independent mobility at home for the elderly

but also when they need assistance from a family member or caregiver. Design data such as the width of toilet doors, space for bathing and changing clothes etc. have to be reconsidered based on the need for independence as well as assistance for the elderly.

Fig. 4. Observations of culturally-rooted behaviours inside and outside the home

4 Discussion

This study used multi-sited ethnography to document challenges encountered by elderly in performing activities-of-daily-living. Thematic analysis of research data revealed that environmental accommodations to support aging-in-place could potentially bridge the gap between elderly person's abilities and demands of the built environment. Findings not only offer insights on challenges of functional reach and independent mobility for elderly but also suggest how redesign of the built environment can enhance safety, independence and assistance for elderly at home.

The findings should be considered in context of the strengths and limitations of the study. The strengths of the study include - first, the relatively large sample size of sixty-four elderly; second, the geographical distribution of elderly in three distinct locations in the north (New Delhi), east (Dibrugarh) and south (Panaji) of the country; third, the use of environment-behaviour research tools such as environmental traces, participant observations and user interviews [10]; fourth, the focus on identifying the role of the built environment in hindering or enabling aging-in-place [6, 7]. The limitations of the study are—first, physical abilities of the elderly participants were not assessed; second, memory and cognition relating to aging-in-place were not delved into; third, topics related to mental health and emotional wellbeing of elderly emerged during interviews—however, since research was limited to environmental accommodations, these facets were not discussed in detail; and finally, the social environment which plays a crucial role in lives of the elderly was not discussed since it was not the core focus of the study.

In future, research studies on environmental gerontology for India's rapidly aging population should focus on the physical, cognitive, emotional and social experience of aging. Insights from empirical studies should translate into designs of environmental accommodations that need to be tested and validated through full-scale simulations. The home is central to healthy aging and well-being in old age. The study of home environments has long been an important area of research for environmental gerontology. Future research needs to build the evidence base and develop theoretical foundations linking ecology of aging with the enabling role of the built environment.

References

1. International Institute for Population Sciences & United Nations Population Fund 2023. India Ageing Report 2023, Caring for Our Elders: Institutional Responses. United Nations Population Fund, New Delhi (2023) https://india.unfpa.org/sites/default/files/pub-pdf/20230926_india_ageing_report_2023_web_version_.pdf, last assessed on 28 Nov 2024
2. Ministry of Health and Family Welfare, Population Projections for India and States 2011–36: Report on the Technical Group of Population Projections. https://mohfw.gov.in/sites/default/files/Population%20Projection%20Report%202011-2036%20-%20upload_compressed_0.pdf, last assessed on 28 Nov 2024
3. Longitudinal Ageing Study in India (LASI) Wave 1, 2017–18, India Report. https://iipsindia.ac.in/sites/default/files/LASI_India_Report_2020_compressed.pdf, last assessed on 28 Nov 2024
4. Lawton, M.P.: Environment and Aging. Brooks/Cole, Los Angeles, CA (1980)
5. Chaudhury, H., Oswald, F.: Advancing understanding of person-environment interaction in later life: one step further. J. Aging Stud. **51**, 100821 (2019)
6. Danford, G.S., Steinfeld, E.: Measuring the influences of physical environments on the behaviors of people with impairments. In: Enabling Environments: Measuring the Impact of Environment on Disability and Rehabilitation, pp. 111–137. Springer US (1999)
7. Iwarsson, S.: Assessing the fit between older people and their home environments—An occupational therapy research perspective. In: Wahl, H.-W., Scheidt, R., Windley, P. (eds.) Focus on Aging in Context: Socio- Physical Environments. Annual Review of the Gerontological Society of America 2003, pp. 85–109. Springer, New York, NY (2004)
8. Steinfeld, E., Maisel, J.: Universal Design: Creating Inclusive Environments. John Wiley & Sons (2012)

9. Cranz, G.: Ethnography for Designers. Routledge (2016)
10. Zeisel, J.: Inquiry by Design: Environment/Behavior/Neuroscience in Architecture, Interiors, Landscape and Planning. WW Norton & Co., New York, NY (2006)
11. NVivo Qualitative Data Analysis. Version 12 [Software]. QSR International Pty Ltd. (2018). Available from: https://support.qsrinternational.com/nvivo/s/
12. Adu, P.: A Step-by-Step Guide to Qualitative Data Coding. Routledge (2019)

Exploring Energy Expenditure Patterns for Walking among Guangzhou Elderly

Zhelin Li(✉), Zhipeng Zhang, Xiang Liang, Danqi Wang, and Lijun Jiang

School of Design, South China University of Technology, Guangzhou 510000, China
202221055695@mail.scut.edu.cn, zhelinli@scut.edu.cn

Abstract. *Objective*: The aim of this study is to explore the energy expenditure patterns of elderly during walking activities within the community and to analyze the association between physical characteristics and walking energy expenditure.
Methods: A cross-sectional study was conducted in two communities in Guangzhou, collecting walking activity data from 70 elderly. Using questionnaires, travel diaries, and map drawings, we recorded participants' daily walking frequency, duration, and walking trajectories. The Pandolf equation was utilized to calculate the energy expenditure for a single walking trip. Pearson correlation analysis and ANOVA were employed to analyze the relationship between walking energy expenditure and physical characteristics as well as walking attributes.
Results: The results showed that among elderly, walking energy expenditure was significantly associated not only with age ($r = -0.919$; $p < 0.001$), but also with the objective category of the activity ($p = 0.007$).
Conclusion: The findings indicate that elderly with higher age have lower energy expenditure during walking. Additionally, the objective significantly affects walking energy expenditure. Future interventions in communities can promote an active and healthy lifestyle among elderly through various ways.

Keywords: Elderly · Walking · Energy Expenditure

1 Introduction

In recent years, the degree of aging in China has intensified. As age increases, health declines, and individual family structures evolve, the daily activity range of elderly gradually diminishes, making walking the primary form of physical activity [1]. Walking promotes metabolic circulation, enhances cardiopulmonary function [2], and maintains joint flexibility, providing elderly with a low-intensity but highly effective form of physical activity.

Currently, most studies on energy expenditure patterns either focus on adolescents [3] and healthy adults [4], or measure the overall energy expenditure encompassing various activity types [5]. These studies often use costly methods such as the doubly labelled water method [6]. Research specifically addressing the energy expenditure of walking activities within community settings for elderly remains scarce.

Therefore, the aim of this study is to explore the energy expenditure patterns of walking activities among elderly in the community and to analyze the potential association

S. Jin et al. (Eds.): IEA 2024, SSDI 39, pp. 115–120, 2025.
https://doi.org/10.1007/978-981-95-0211-0_18

between physical characteristics and walking energy expenditure, thereby providing a basis for community aging-friendly infrastructure.

2 Methods and Data

2.1 Study Design and Participants

A cross-sectional study was conducted from August to September 2023 in two communities in Guangzhou (WS: Wu Shan Community East Residential Area in Tianhe District and KY: Ke Yuan Community Residential Area in Yuexiu District. The study aimed to analyze the walking behavior of elderly, recruiting participants aged 60 years and above who maintain a certain level of daily activity and have no severe physical disabilities or internal diseases. Physiological and behavioral data of the elderly participants were collected.

2.2 Data Collection Procedures

Data collection was conducted over a week in both WS and KY communities. The project collected demographic information through questionnaires, including age, gender, years of education, and medical history, and measured height, weight, and maximum grip strength on site. Regarding walking activity data collection, daily activity frequency was gathered through questionnaires, and a travel diary was used to record the objective category, timing, and duration of daily walking activities. Additionally, maps were drawn to track the walking routes of residents.

Both communities are built on hilly terrain, and grade is a significant factor influencing walking energy expenditure. We obtained vector maps with elevation information and used digital levels to accurately measure the grade of the main roads to gather community topographic information.

2.3 Measures

This study calculated the energy expenditure of a single walking trip, i.e., the energy consumed from the starting point to the destination of the activity (excluding short stops en route). The Pandolf equation [7], which incorporates walking speed and road grade as critical parameters, was used for energy calculation. The average walking speed of elderly in different age groups was referenced from the CHARLES 2015 dataset [8].

Calculating road grade was an essential part. During community surveys, daily walking routes were collected using travel diaries, which were then converted into GPX format geographic files through map redrawing. The tracks were stored as latitude and longitude sequences, and the best way to obtain the grade of each segment of the route was by calculating the ratio of elevation difference to distance difference between two adjacent track points. The main road grades were measured in the community, setting a lowest point and using the Depth-First Search (DFS) algorithm to obtain the height of other path points relative to this point. After obtaining the community's elevation data, the Radial Basis Function (RBF) interpolation method was used to derive the community's interpolation model, allowing the prediction of elevation based on latitude and longitude within the community. Thus, for each track, the grade of the segments could be calculated, resulting in more accurate energy expenditure data.

2.4 Statistical Analysis

A database was established and data statistical analyses were conducted using MATLAB R2024a. To provide an overall summary of the data, descriptive statistics such as mean and standard deviation were performed on physical characteristics and walking energy expenditure in MET (metabolic equivalent of task), hereafter referred to as EEM(energy expenditure in MET). Pearson correlation coefficients were then used to explore the relationships between walking distance, walking duration, EEM, and physical characteristics. Additionally, ANOVA was used to analyze whether the objective category of activities impacts energy expenditure.

3 Results

3.1 Characteristics of Walking Activities

A total of 144 elderly participated in this data collection round. Valid data were obtained from 70 participants (WS community:30; KY community:40). Among them, 18 was male and 52 was female. A total of 177 records of daily walking activities were collected, with 40 records was male and 137 records was female. Data on walking distance, duration, and EEM are shown in Table 1. Table 1 indicates that although males had shorter average walking distances and durations than females, the average walking energy expenditure for both males and females was 1.89 METs.

Table 1. Characteristics of daily walking activities

Variable	Male (n = 18)	Female (n = 52)	Total (n = 70)
Walking distance(m)	345.92 ± 223.35	368.01 ± 249.28	363.02 ± 243.22
Walking duration(s)	510.71 ± 313.66	561.71 ± 402.85	550.18 ± 384.27
EEM(MET)	1.89 ± 0.17	1.89 ± 0.16	1.89 ± 0.16

3.2 Energy Expenditure of Walking Activities

The 177 walking activity records were categorized into nine objective categories: A1. Shopping for groceries; A2. Physical exercise; A3. Playing chess or mahjong; A4. Escorting grandchildren; A5. Singing and dancing; A6. Leisure walking (e.g., strolling, visiting parks, walking dogs); A7. Running errands (e.g., taking out the trash, picking up packages, collecting meals for seniors); A8. Group activities (e.g., classes, work, volunteer activities); and A9. Others. As shown in Table 2, some objective categories, such as A1, A2, and A6, had higher frequencies of walking activities compared to other categories.

Table 2. Average walking energy expenditure by objective category

Objective	A1	A2	A3	A4	A5	A6	A7	A8	A9
WS	1.85 ± 0.16 (n = 24)	1.83 ± 0.14 (n = 20)	1.72 ± 0.15 (n = 4)	2.08 ± 0.01 (n = 2)	1.76 ± 0.12 (n = 7)	1.9 ± 0.1 (n = 7)	1.8 ± 0.16 (n = 7)	1.99 ± 0.12 (n = 5)	1.9 ± 0.23 (n = 4)
KY	1.91 ± 0.17 (n = 40)	1.91 ± 0.17 (n = 15)	2.02 ± 0.12 (n = 4)	2.09 ± 0.05 (n = 6)	1.83 ± 0.33 (n = 2)	1.89 ± 0.12 (n = 12)	1.89 ± 0.2 (n = 10)	1.94 ± 0.15 (n = 6)	1.95 ± 0.16 (n = 2)
Combined	1.89 ± 0.16 (n = 64)	1.87 ± 0.16 (n = 35)	1.87 ± 0.2 (n = 8)	2.09 ± 0.04 (n = 8)	1.78 ± 0.16 (n = 9)	1.9 ± 0.11 (n = 19)	1.85 ± 0.18 (n = 17)	1.96 ± 0.13 (n = 11)	1.92 ± 0.19 (n = 6)

3.3 Energy Expenditure Analysis

Pearson correlation was used to analyze association between walking data and physical characteristics. It shows that EEM was significantly positively correlated with weight ($r = 0.216$; $p = 0.004$), BMI ($r = 0.193$; $p = 0.01$), but strongly negatively correlated with age ($r = -0.919$; $p < 0.001$). Walking duration was also significantly positively correlated with age ($r = 0.217$; $p = 0.004$).

ANOVA was used to analyze the relationship between activity objective category and EEM. The results shown in Table 3 indicated that for the WS data, objective categories had significant relationships with EEM ($p = 0.043$, $\eta^2 = 0.193$). Meanwhile, these relationships in the KY data were not significant. Overall, across both communities, the relationship was statistically significant ($p = 0.007$, $\eta^2 = 0.116$). Post hoc comparisons using the Tukey HSD indicated that A4 had significant differences with A1 ($p = 0.016$), A2 ($p = 0.008$), A5 ($p = 0.001$), and A7 ($p = 0.011$).

Table 3. p-values between activity objective category and walking distance, duration, and EEM

Variable	WS	KY	Combined
Walking distance(m)	0.001**	0.178	0.466
Walking duration(s)	0.002**	0.296	0.476
EEM(MET)	0.043*	0.250	0.007**

4 Discussion

The results indicate that walking energy expenditure among the elderly is associated not only with physical characteristics but also with the objective category of walking. Regarding average walking energy expenditure, there is no significant difference between males and females, but the average value of 1.89 METs is lower than the slow walking energy expenditure reference value (2.50 METs) for healthy Chinese adults (18–64 years old) [9]. This can be attributed to age, as the average age of participants in this study was 73.8 years, older than in Qiu's study. The correlation analysis shows that increasing age significantly reduces walking energy expenditure, consistent with previous studies on age and overall energy expenditure [6, 11].

Another notable finding is the relationship between the objective category of activities and walking distance, duration, and energy expenditure. This relationship is more pronounced in the WS community but not in the KY community. We speculate that this is due to the WS community's comprehensive facilities, such as senior universities and fitness squares, promoting internal walking activity. In contrast, the KY community is smaller and more enclosed, requiring residents to go outside for exercise, socialization, or shopping, making it difficult to show differences in walking activities within the community. However, when combining data from both communities, the objective category of activities still significantly correlates with energy expenditure. For example, the elderly expend less energy on grocery shopping (A1), likely because they choose nearby markets. Conversely, they spend more energy on activities like picking up and dropping off grandchildren (A4), possibly because these activities involve longer distances and durations.

Finally, the limitations of this study should be acknowledged. Since all walking activity data were derived from interviews, questionnaires, and hand-drawn routes, the inherent accuracy of the data is challenged by methodological limitations. Additionally, during data collection, female volunteers participated more actively than males, resulting in a higher female sample size. Combined with the overall sample size limitation, these factors may bias the results. Moreover, given the cross-sectional design of this study, we cannot infer clear causal relationships from the current findings.

5 Conclusion

This study provides valuable insights into the daily walking energy expenditure patterns of elderly living in community settings. The results identified that physical characteristics are associated with walking energy expenditure, and the category of walking activities is also a significant factor. Future research can expand the sample size, adopt more objective data collection methods, and conduct longitudinal studies to gain deeper insights. This study offers a method for assessing the daily walking energy expenditure of elderly and can inform various community interventions aimed at promoting proactive and healthy lifestyles among this population.

Acknowledgements. Supported by the National Key Research and Development Program of China (No. 2022YFF0607000):Research and Application of Ergonomics Key Technical Standards for Elderly-oriented Community.

References

1. Gu, Z.L., Chai, Y.W.: Change of mobility of urban elderly and effects on their daily life: a narrative analysis of the life of a retired couple living in an urban community. Prog. Geogr. **34**, 1617–1627 (2015)
2. Smith, T.C., Wingard, D.L., Smith, B., Kritz-Silverstein, D., Barrett-Connor, E.: Walking decreased risk of cardiovascular disease mortality in elderly with diabetes. J. Clin. Epidemiol. **60**, 309–317 (2007)

3. Dan, Y., Guo, Z., Ming, L., Deqian, M.: Energy expenditure at physical activities of young . middle-aged adults in southern China. J. Hyg. Res. **39**, 715–718 (2010)
4. Marquet, O., Floyd, M.F., James, P., Glanz, K., Jennings, V., Jankowska, M.M., Kerr, J., Hipp, J.A.: Associations between worksite walkability, greenness, and physical activity around work. Environ. Behav. **52**, 139–163 (2020)
5. Ramalho, J.R.D.O., Lima-Costa, M.F., Firmo, J.O.A., Peixoto, S.V.: Energy expenditure through physical activity in a population of community-dwelling Brazilian elderly: cross-sectional evidences from the Bambuí cohort study of aging. Cad. Saude Publica. **27**, s399–s408 (2011)
6. Lopes De Pontes, T., Pessanha, F.P.A.D.S., Junior, R.C.F., Pfrimer, K., Alves, N.M.D.C., Fassini, P.G., Almeida, O.L.S., Moriguti, J.C., Lima, N.K.D.C., Santos, J.L.F., Ferriolli, E.: Total energy expenditure and functional status in elderly: a doubly labelled water study. J. Nutr. Health Aging. **25**, 201–208 (2021)
7. Pandolf, K.B., Givoni, B., Goldman, R.F.: Predicting energy expenditure with loads while standing or walking very slowly. J. Appl. Physiol. **43**, 577–581 (1977)
8. Jing, Y., Ziying, W., Yilun, W., et al.: Research on the status of gait speed and determinants of slow gait speed in Chinese elderly population. Chin. J. Health Statist. **39**, 494–498 (2022)
9. Junqiang, Q., Junchao, Y., Mingyue, L., et al.: Compilation of physical activities of healthy Chinese adults: reference values for energy expenditure, Chin. J. Sports Med. **41**, 335–349 (2022)
10. Abadi, F.H., Muhamad, T.A., Salamuddin, N.: Energy expenditure through walking: meta analysis on gender and age. Procedia. Soc. Behav. Sci. **7**, 512–521 (2010)
11. Cruz-Jentoft, A.J., Bahat, G., Bauer, J., Boirie, Y.: Writing Group for the European Working Group on Sarcopenia in Older People 2 (EWGSOP2), and the Extended Group for EWGSOP2, Sarcopenia: revised European consensus on definition and diagnosis. Age Ageing. **48**, 16–31 (2019)

Ergonomics Data Measurement Service Design for the Elderly in the Urban Community

Zhelin Li, Jiayi Su, Xinyue Cao, Yuting Bai, Shutong Zhao, and Lijun Jiang(✉)

South China University of Technology, Guangzhou, China
ljjiang@scut.edu.cn

Abstract. The design of aging-friendly communities relies on the collection and analysis of ergonomics data among the elderly. This study analyzes the characteristics and problems of measuring elderly ergonomics data in different communities in Guangzhou, China. From the perspective of service design, it analyses pain points encountered during these measurements, and discusses the needs and expectations of the stakeholders involved in the activities. Focusing on optimizing user experience, the study proposes service strategies in terms of stakeholders, measurement items, measurement processes, and incentives. It also constructs a generalized process for gathering ergonomics data from the elderly in the urban community, serving as a valuable resource for conducting participatory scientific research with the elderly in the urban community and the design of ageing in place.

Keywords: Elderly · Ergonomics Data · Community Aging · Service Design

1 Introduction

The gathering of elderly ergonomics data is essential for scientific community aging construction [1], and large-scale measurements of elderly ergonomics data are necessary in the community. Factors such as older adults' own physical strength, cognition, and the measurement process can impact the measurement experience [2]. Therefore, establishing a scientific and reasonable process of large-scale ergonomics data measurement in the community can not only enhance the sense of social engagement and worth, but also provide a reference for elderly to participate in designing research activities.

2 Background and Methodology

2.1 Background

The Chinese national standard GB/T 10000–2023, Human Body Dimensions of Chinese Adults, lacks ergonomic data for individuals over the age of 70 [3], limiting the design of age-appropriate products. The comprehensive collection of ergonomic data, including sensory capabilities and physiological dimensions, is crucial to meet the multifaceted needs of older adults [4].

S. Jin et al. (Eds.): IEA 2024, SSDI 39, pp. 121–127, 2025.
https://doi.org/10.1007/978-981-95-0211-0_19

Currently, about 90% of Chinese older adults in China use the home-based aging model, but have low participation in social activities and low self-efficacy [5]. A study by Yuanyuan Liu et al. pointed out the need to focus on specific elements when recruiting older users to participate in research [6], while Longfei Gong suggested promoting older adults' community participation from multiple perspectives [7].

Existing studies have focused on ergonomics data collection methods for older adults [8], but there are fewer studies measuring the experience of the activities, and there is an urgent need to optimize the poor sense of participation experience in related data measurement activities.

2.2 Methodology

In this study, a multi-session ergonomics data measurement for the elderly was conducted in the communities in Guangzhou for 37 days, and multidimensional ergonomics data were collected from 841 older adults, including vision, hearing, touch, smell, body size, gait, and psychological and mobility. We constructed user experience maps to gain a deeper understanding of the needs and experiences of older adults. The characteristics of stakeholders involved in the activities were analyzed and key service touchpoints were identified to create useful, good, and desirable services for older adults and effective, efficient, and unique services for the organization [9].

3 User Requirements Analysis

3.1 User Experience Maps

During the five measurement campaigns conducted in several communities in Guangzhou, we identified some common problems and drew a user experience map accordingly (see Fig. 1). The data measurement process was divided into three stages: process of obtaining event information, the measurement process, and the report collection stage. By analyzing the actions and emotional responses of older users during these stages, we identified deficiencies in the experience and potential opportunities for improvement.

The analyses revealed that the main pain points for most of the elderly including unclear processes, lack of understanding of measurement methods, difficulty in filling in information, challenges in using the facilities, confusing sequences, and inconvenience in getting reports. For the elderly with limited mobility, it was more difficult to stand for long time and go up and down the steps, and they were prone to lose balance when taking off their shoes to take measurements. Meanwhile, the staff suffered from fatigue due to repetitive teaching of the instruments and when dealing with larger numbers of people. Key opportunity points to address these issues are to optimise the measurement process, improve information transmission. As well as providing user-friendly instruments and equipment will help to improve the participation experience for older people.

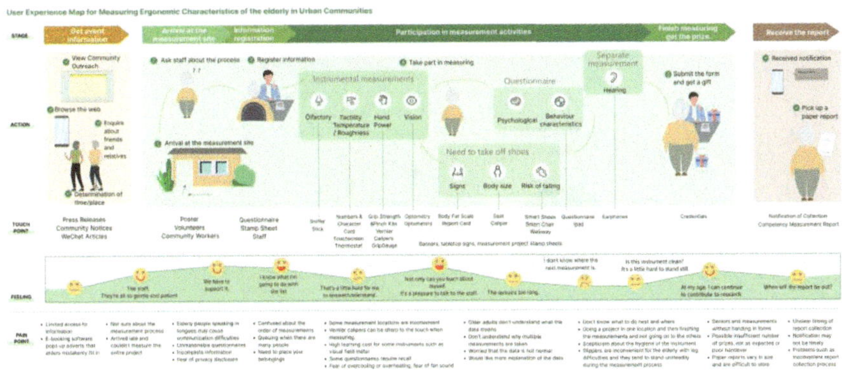

Fig. 1. User Experience Map for Measuring Ergonomic Characteristics of the elderly in Urban Communities

3.2 Community Disparity Analysis

Community variability influences the implementation of measurement activities, including scale, process, outreach, and incentives. Space restrictions and the size of the older adult population dictate the scale of measurement activities, and when measurements are conducted in several spaces, this can cause confusion among participants and reduce the quality of the experience. Therefore, it is important to consider the impact of spatial layout and movement on older people's willingness to participate in order to optimize the efficiency of the activity and the experience.

Different types of communities require differentiated promotional and motivational strategies. Communities with more intellectuals, such as those around universities, are more likely to have older people willing to participate in research activities, while older people in neighbourhood-type communities may be more interested in health information and practical gifts. Therefore, promotions and incentives need to be tailored to the specific needs and interests of older people.

3.3 Stakeholder Analysis

During measurement activities, stakeholders were categorized as core and peripheral (see Fig. 2). The core stakeholders included the project measurement team, community street offices, senior living organizations, and friends and relatives of the elderly. The project measurement team was responsible for the design of the equipment and the implementation of the activities, while the neighbourhood committee and the senior living organizations assisted in the recruitment of participants and the provision of venues. External stakeholders include equipment suppliers, government agencies, healthcare providers, and other organizations. Through collaboration with the project team, these groups aim to obtain data on older adults, promote product sales, or enhance community services.

The project team pursues efficient data collection, the elderly seek self-body knowledge and a sense of community belonging, government organizations intend to enhance

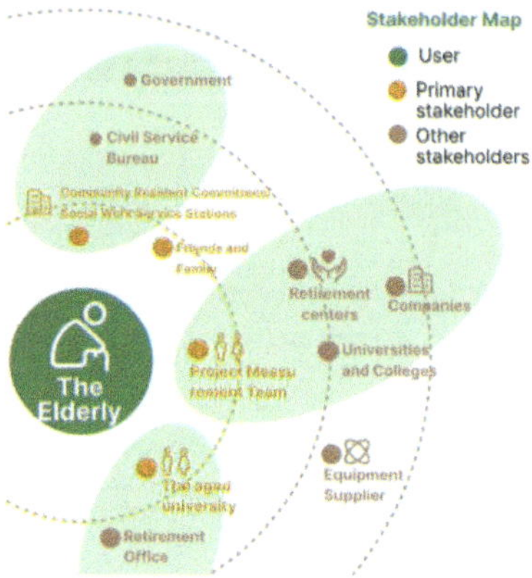

Fig. 2. Stakeholder Map

service quality and public image, senior living organizations are committed to improving the quality of life of older adults, and vendors and others are concerned with market opportunities and the value of data. In order to achieve a win-win situation, the needs and expectations of these stakeholders must be effectively coordinated.

4 Design and Implementation

4.1 Strategies for Service Design

Facilitate collaboration among stakeholders. Work together to advertise measurement activities using multiple information channels. Identify trustworthy and easily accessible venues for the elderly, such as community centers and senior universities.

Construct a special program by combining ergonomic features. Develop measurement programs related to the health needs and interests of the elderly, such as visual acuity and body fat measurement. Utilize characteristic measurement items, such as hand strength, tactile olfactory test, etc., to stimulate the interest of the elderly groups.

Optimize information communication and processes from the perspective of the elderly. As far as the process is concerned, the distribution of measurement items and the elderly movement path should be planned according to the measurement site, and the navigation and marking system should be clearly defined. Information communication should be detailed, comprehensive, concise and effective. Provide handrails, resting facilities, and volunteer assistance for elderly individuals with mobility issues.

Implement incentives that cater to the diverse expectations of the elderly population.

4.2 Service Blueprint

By identifying the key processes of ergonomic data measurement activities for the elderly, we have optimized the contact points related to ergonomic data measurement for the elderly in the community and developed a blueprint for expandable and repeatable services from the perspective of the elderly users (see Fig. 3). Prior to measurement, collaborate with stakeholders to publicize through multiple channels, select suitable measurement sites, and reasonably plan and set up measurement projects. During the measurement, optimize information communication, standardize the measurement process, assign responsibility for the measurement project, arrange the measurement sequence and guide the measurement in an orderly manner. After the measurement, appropriate incentives were given and measurement results and explanations were provided to the elderly as soon as possible.

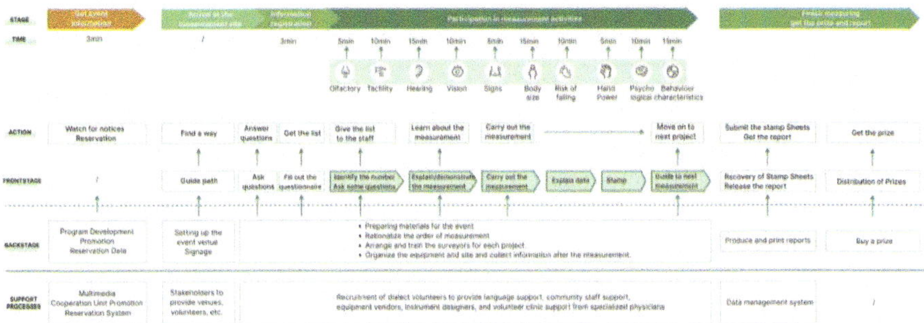

Fig. 3. Service Blueprint

4.3 Service Design Implementation

To verify the rationality and feasibility of the service blueprint and service process planning, we plan to conduct a data measurement activity for the elderly in collaboration with the China Academy of Building Research Ltd.

During the implementation, we presented the service blueprint and the notes to ensure that the partner had a clear understanding of each step during the measurement activity. Based on the dimensions of the measurement site and requirements provided by the partner, we carried out spatial planning for the measurement project and designed a suitable moving line (see Fig. 4).

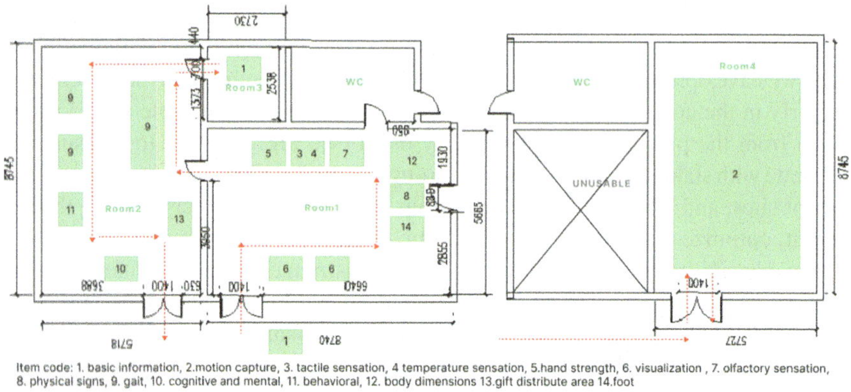

Fig. 4. Measurement project spatial distribution

5 Conclusion

This study constructs a set of ergonomics data measurement process applicable to the elderly in Chinese urban communities. The characteristics of the elderly group, the scale of measurement activities, the measurement environment and facilities are the main factors affecting the service strategy.

The service process is not only applicable to the Guangzhou area, but also provides a model for other areas to follow. Cultural differences and resource conditions in different regions need to be fully considered in the implementation process to ensure the universality and effectiveness of the service design.

References

1. Pamuk, D., Faezi, S.A., Başıbüyük, G.Ö.: Ergonomics and aging: a bibliometric analysis. Work. **72**(3), 853–864 (2022)
2. Tangchonlatip, K., Chamratrithirong, A., Lucktong, A.: The potential for civic engagement of older persons in the ageing society of Thailand. J. Health Res. **33**(5), 386–397 (2019)
3. Zhang, R.Y.: Interpretation of the national standard of "Chinese adult body size" — Interview with Zhang Xin, Deputy Director of the National Technical Committee on Human Factors Standardization and Deputy Director of the Human Factors Research Room, Basic Research Institute, China Standardization Research Institute. China Standardiz. **20**, 6–11 (2023)
4. Zhou, H., Wang, Q., Ouyang, W., Zhang, S.: Research on application of ergonomics and digital technology in community elderly-oriented adaptations. Chin. J. Dig. Med. **18**(12), 19–25 (2023)
5. Wang, G.: Analysis on Influencing Factors of Social Participationof the Elderly in China. Master's thesis. Jilin University (2022). https://doi.org/10.27162/d.cnki.gjlin.2022.001269
6. Liu, Y., Sun, T., Zheng, Z.: Research on the recruitment methods of "recruiting older users": a case study about exploring how to recruit older users in Beijing to participate in product design research. Zhuangshi. **11**, 76–81 (2022)
7. Gong, L.: A Study on Optimizing Community Participate on of Urban Elderly People through Group Work from the Perspective of Active Aging. Master's thesis,. Shandong University (2023). https://doi.org/10.27272/d.cnki.gshdu.2023.005403.005

8. Hu, H.: Anthropometric Measurement of the Elderly. Master's thesis, Tsinghua University (2005). https://kns-cnki-net-s.webvpn.scut.edu.cn/kcms2/article/abstract?v=axnrJTP8flxT6HB5U9Cjm114PGRfCKmWYicS7-sHJaVDqC5yJllmZIxDsEauXVYmB1BXL0D3OdnfvvKg7VtFT6rzglD4m_fGMCHr17gLjNvuMOC2la-F70yw4Szl6bN6EwW7PKrtDiz1afmuajFVlg==uniplatform=NZKPTlanguage=CHS
9. Johnston, R.: Service design. In: Cooper, C.L. (ed.) Wiley Encyclopedia of Management, 1st edn, pp. 1–2. Wiley (2015). https://doi.org/10.1002/9781118785317.weom100215

Multi-Dimensional Elderly User Portraits Based on South China Region

Zhelin Li(✉), Yuting Bai, Lijun Jiang, Jiayi Su, and Yulin Tan

South China University of Technology, Guangzhou, Guangdong Province, China
zhelinli@scut.edu.cn

Abstract. In the era of aging in China, in order to accurately provide age-appropriate services and design products for the elderly, this paper conducts a study on user portraits of the elderly in the community. The group carried out five ergonomics measurements of the elderly in Guangzhou City, established a data set containing high-dimensional ergonomics characteristics data of 841 elderly people, retained the complete measurements of 210 elderly people's data including 6 aspects with a total of 12 items, after the principal component analysis (PCA) to reduce the dimension. Two-step clustering algorithm was then used to analyze the total of 6 dimensions (Age, Sex, Hand Strength, Mental State, Cognitive Level, Behavioral Activities) of characteristics of the variables, to constructing six categories of user portraits of elderly people in South China, which show differences in physiology, psychology, cognitive ability and behavioral activities, the study can pro-vide a basis for accurate promotion of products and services for the elderly.

Keywords: User Portraits · Elderly · Ergonomics · Aging Adaptation · Outdoor Behavior

1 Introduction

In China, the problem of aging is becoming more and more serious. As of 2020, the number of elderly people aged 60 years and above in China reached 264.02 million, accounting for 18.7% of the total population, and it is expected that the proportion of elderly people will reach 25% by 2030 [1]. The lack of personalized services and precise products for the elderly has become increasingly prominent [2]. Ergonomics data show the current situation of physiological, psychological and cognitive abilities of the elderly in a scientific and objective way, and assist in the design of products and services that better meet the real needs of the elderly [3]. Elderly user portraits can not only categorize hundreds of millions of elderly people and give them labels to accurately describe their characteristics, but also capture the pain points and needs of different elderly people, and provide them with accurate recommendation to promote the overall health and well-being of the elderly [4].

S. Jin et al. (Eds.): IEA 2024, SSDI 39, pp. 128–133, 2025.
https://doi.org/10.1007/978-981-95-0211-0_20

2 Literature Review

Existing user portraits of elderly people usually categorize elderly by age, ignoring the influence of physical and psychological aspects on elderly people' performance (Chen, Wang and Jiang, 2023 [3]; Li and Yang, 2009 [5]). In addition, the characteristics of elderly are subjectively summarized from interviews, without scientific validity (Yu, Chen and Wang, 2023 [6]). Some articles focus on some specific behaviors of the elderly according to their own research topics (He, Zhu and Bai, 2021 [7]; Kuang, 2022 [8]). Some studies have pointed out that muscle mass and cognitive function have obvious correlation [9, 10]. Meanwhile, the psychological dimension should also be considered [4]. Therefore, this paper considers 6 dimensions of elderly (age, gender, physical, psychological, cognitive and behavioral characteristics).

3 Methodology

3.1 Literature Research and Field Research

Find, read and summarize the relevant literature in the field of user portraits to pro-vide a literature base for the research route of this paper. From August to December 2023, five measurement activities were conducted within Guangzhou City, Guang-dong Province, to measure and obtain high-dimensional ergonomic characteristics data from 841 elderly.

3.2 Data Processing and Statistical Analysis

Filtering Complete Data and Processing Hand Strength Data
Screening yielded data from 82 males and 128 females, totaling 210 elderly individuals (mean age 71.7, with a minimum age of 52 and a maximum age of 93). Each participant provided complete data on all 12 items (gender, age, right hand grip strength, two-finger pinch strength, right wrist torque, stress level scores, anxiety level scores, depression level scores, cognitive level scores, physical activity scores, social activity scores, and cognitive activity scores), resulting in a total of 2520 data points. Subsequent data process and analysis used SPSS24.0. Since hand strength varies greatly between male and female genders, a direct comparison of the strength value is inaccurate. The strength value is converted into a level in the male and female population, such as the grip strength level formula as below. The smaller the resultant value, the lower the grip strength level of the elderly person proved to be.

$$The\ male's\ strength\ level = \frac{Number\ of\ men\ with\ strength\ less\ than\ this\ person + 1}{Total\ number\ of\ males} \tag{1}$$

Principal Component Analysis (PCA)
Three items of hand strength (right hand grip strength level, two-finger pinch strength level, and right wrist torque level), three items of mental state (stress level score, anxiety level score, and depression level score), and three items of behavioral activity [11]

(physical activity score, social activity score, and cognitive activity score) were subjected to principal component analysis. The KMO sampling aptitude quantities for all three sets of principal component analysis >0.6, and the significance of the Bartlett's test of sphericity <0.05. This proves that the use of principal component analysis is correct and reasonable. Choose the components with feature value >1 and the cumulative variance explained ≥85%. Calculate the composite score, and simplify the raw data of 12 dimensions into 6 dimensions as shown in Fig. 1.

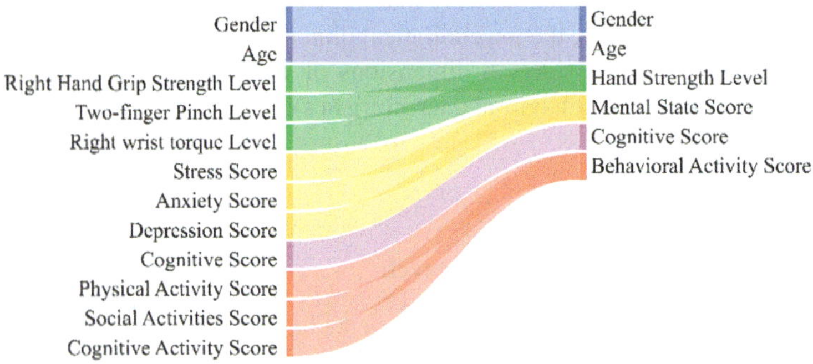

Fig. 1. Schematic diagram of simplified dimensions of principal component analysis

Two-Step Clustering

Two-step clustering method is suitable, because gender is a categorical variable and the remaining 5 dimensions are continuous variables. The clustering results were 6 categories and the silhouette coefficient is 0.4. Reordering them according to the importance of the predictor variables. The values of the center of mass of each cluster are shown in Table 1. The cluster center of mass scatter plot is shown in Fig. 2.

Table 1. Clustered center of mass mean

Tips	Gender	Age	Mental State	Hand Power	Cognitive Level	Behavioral Activities
	\	\	Lower values mean better	Higher values mean better	Higher values mean better	Higher values mean better
Group 1	All female	66	12.34	0.68	25.52	90.12
Group 2	All female	78	3.85	0.37	26.62	88.78
Group 3	All male	81	4.04	0.41	23.44	82.66
Group 4	Male (75%)	75	20.28	0.36	24.13	63.47
Group 5	All male	68	3.93	0.78	27.29	89.71
Group 6	All female	65	2.84	0.81	27.97	98.18

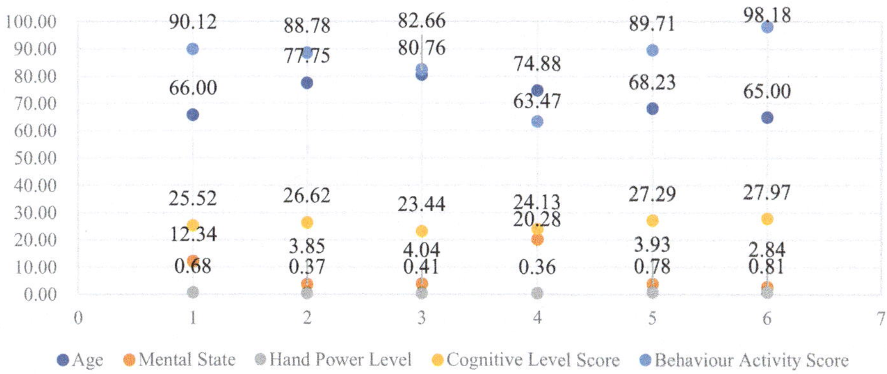

Fig. 2. Scatterplot of center of mass (mean) of clustered groups in five dimensions.

4 Results

In the same dimension, the center of gravity is normalized into a value between 0 and 1, with "0" represents the worst in 6 groups and "1" represents the best. A heat map as shown in Fig. 3.

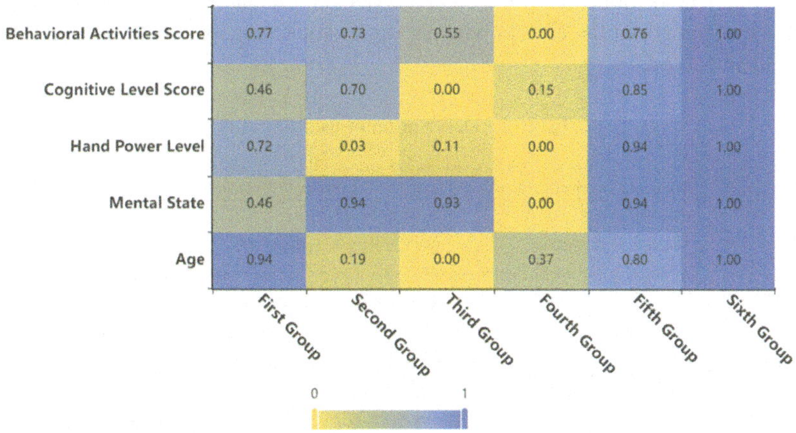

Fig. 3. Heat map of clustered centers of mass (normalized into a value between 0 and 1)

The six categories of elderly people have distinctive features so obviously in hand strength, mental state, cognitive level and behavioral activities in line with the initial concepts. They are: Younger Elders with Cognition Declining but Physical Fitness (10.5% of total), Approaching Senior-aged Elderly with Weakness of Strength but Positive Mindset (24.3% of total), Octogenarian with Optimistic mindset but Inactive Exercise (15.7% of total), Elderly with Declining Functions and Repressed Minds (3.8% of total), Balanced and stable elderly living on their own (20.5% of total), Mentally agile and active young elders (25.2% of total). The labels of characteristic differences in the performance of six groups shown as Table 2.

5 Discussion and Conclusion

In today's aging world, most of the existing papers on the classification of the elderly are classified directly according to age, or subjectively conclude based on questionnaire interviews, while this paper highlights the importance of scientific data, which can scientifically and reliably provide the basis of targeting recommendations for product design and services for the elderly. However, there are still shortcomings in this paper, such as: the hand strength is used as one of the physical function measures in this study, and more factors should be examined in the subsequent study to ensure that the overall physical condition of the elderly is accurately summarized. Generalize the overall physical condition of the elderly. The results of this study are expected to promote comprehensive and personalized health care for the elderly. For example, indoor recreational equipment should be designed for the elderly who are optimistic to accept new things but reluctant to go out and so on.

Table 2. Description of user portraits

Group 1	Younger Elders with Cognition Declining but Physical Fitness (10.5% of total)		
	Relatively young	Some emotional distress	Willing to exercise
	Muscle in good condition	Body younger than mind	High level independence
Group 2	Approaching Senior-aged Elderly with Weakness of Strength but Positive Mindset (24.3% of total)		
	Women predominant	Cheerful attitude	Active in social
	Strength deteriorated	Clear mindset	Near Octogenarian
Group 3	Octogenarian with Optimistic mindset but Inactive Exercise (15.7% of total)		
	Loss of hand strength	Cognitive deteriorated	Avoids own exertion
	Mental state is good	Reluctant social	Mean age 81
Group 4	Elderly with Declining Functions and Repressed Minds (3.8% of total)		
	Physical serious decline	Decline in memory	Tendency to depression
	Under heavy stress	Reduce independence	Near senior-aged
Group 5	Balanced and stable elderly living on their own (20.5% of total)		
	Strength maintained well	Optimistic outlook	Good cognition
	Various manual activities	Balanced and stable state	Middle age
Group 6	Mentally agile and active young elders (25.2% of total)		
	Strong muscle	Stable mental state	Engage in social
	Excellent thinking ability	Keen to exercise	Young elderly

References

1. Council, Office of the Leading Group of the Seventh National Population Census of the State: Major Figures on 2020 Population Census of China, p. 7. China Statistics Press, Beijing (2021)
2. Wei, Y.: Exploration of product design strategies for the elderly from a caring perspective. **21**, 7–9 (2022). https://doi.org/10.14013/j.cnki.scxdh.2022.21.028
3. Chen, X., Wang, Y., Jiang, Y.: Research on home-based caring lifestyle of urban elderly groups in Zhejiang Province. Ind. Des. **09**, 25–30 (2023)
4. Liu, F., Lu, Y., Sui, Y., Qi, Z., Tian, Z.: Empty nesters research on the status quo and optimization of community home care model for urban. **8**, 101–105 (2021)
5. Li, B., Yang, H.: Analysis of the elderly lifestyle and user model. Pack. Eng. **30**(05), 120–122 (2009). https://doi.org/10.19554/j.cnki.1001-3563.2009.05.044
6. Yu, W., Chen, C., Wang, H.: A Study on building a precision push system of community-based sports services for older adults based on user profiles. China Sport Sci. **43**(04), 38–48 (2023). https://doi.org/10.16469/j.css.202304004
7. He, Z., Zhu, Q., Bai, M.: The construction of urban elderly user portrait from the perspective of pension service. J. Intell. **40**(09), 154–160 (2021)
8. Kuang, Y.: Barriers to digital integration of the elderly group: influencing factors, user portraits and policy responses. J. Huazhong Univ. Sci. Technol. (Soc. Sci. Ed.). **36**(01), 46–53 (2022). https://doi.org/10.19648/j.cnki.jhustss1980.2022.01.06
9. Kohara, K., Okada, Y., Ochi, M., Ohara, M., Nagai, T., Tabara, Y., Igase, M.: Muscle mass decline, arterial stiffness, white matter hyperintensity, and cognitive impairment: Japan Shimanami health promoting program study. J. Cachexia Sarcopenia Muscle. **8**(4), 557–566 (2017). https://doi.org/10.1002/jcsm.12195
10. Chen, F., Li, W.: Advances in the correlation between sarcopenia and cognitive impairment. Neural Injury Funct. Reconstr. **15**(11), 641–44+51 (2020). https://doi.org/10.16780/j.cnki.sjssgncj.20200101
11. Zhang, Y., Yang, X., Guo, L., Li, Y.: Study on development and evaluation of a questionnaire on leisure activities of the elderly in China. Tianjin J. Nurs. **30**(01), 18–22 (2022)

Bridge Employment's Effects on Retirees' Mental Health

Bouhafs Mebarki[1(✉)] and Mohamed Mokdad[2]

[1] Laboratory of Ergonomics, University of Oran 2 Mohamed Ben Ahmed, Oran, Algeria
mebarki.bouhafs@univ-oran2.dz

[2] College of Arts, University of Bahrain, Zallaq, Bahrain

Abstract. Many retirees pick up their careers again for a variety of reasons. Some of them have to do with escaping the loneliness they developed after retiring. It also includes finding another financial resource that aids in starting a business or living a respectable life. Bridge employment is the term for this new endeavor. The fact that the new work enables employees to meet unmet demands is crucial.

The objective of this research is to study the effects of bridge employment on retirees' mental health. In addition, this research aims to answer the following questions:

1. Is there a difference in mental health between retirees who started a bridge work and retirees who did not start?
2. Does the mental health differ according to the nature of the work (full-time/part-time)?

A semi-experimental approach was used to answer these questions among a sample of retirees (males and females) from the education sector, which were split into experimental and control group (18 subject each).

Results showed that employees who have started a bridgework have much better mental health than retired employees who don't do any bridge employment at all, and the mental health of part-time workers is higher than that of full-time workers.

The mental health of the elderly is affected by a variety of issues (physical, psychological, and health-related). This research has shown that engaging in part-time work contributes to increasing the mental health of retired elderly.

Keywords: Life Expectancy · Industrially Developing Countries · Retirees · Bridge Employment · GHQ-28

1 Introduction

In the twentieth and twenty-first centuries, mankind has witnessed an increase in life expectancy. Despite the fact that the increase in life expectancy occurred first in the industrially developed countries, in the last decades of the twenty-first century the increase in life expectancy also occurred in the industrially developing countries as well. In some countries such as South Korea [1], the progress was faster than that of some industrial

S. Jin et al. (Eds.): IEA 2024, SSDI 39, pp. 134–139, 2025.
https://doi.org/10.1007/978-981-95-0211-0_21

countries including the UK [2]. The reasons may be the development of a culture of healthy eating among people, reduction in smoking rates as well as the development of health care services provided to individuals [3]. These measures not only eliminated infectious diseases (Malaria, Cholera, Tuberculosis, AIDS, COVID-19, etc.), but also contributed to increasing the human lifespan to unprecedented levels [4].

As a result, many retirees who retire at the Legal (legislative) age of retirement (the age of sixty to sixty-five), suffer from a kind of emptiness, because they leave work while they still enjoy good physical and psychological health. They can also still work and contribute to community development [5]. In addition, the elderly literature indicates that old age is often associated with psychological problems (depression, anxiety, emptiness, etc.) [6].

This unwanted condition has led many retirees to pursue other jobs after the work from which they retired. This is called bridge work. It may be an extension of their first work or it may be different from it. The working time period may be full or shorter, depending on the status of each retiree and the institution in which he/she works [7].

In fact, there are types of bridge employment. Based on what is done, we have career (similar to previous work) and non-career bridge employment (different from previous work). Also, based on the working hours spent by the workers at work, we have part-time and full-time bridge work [8].

Old age might be accompanied by several physical, mental and psychological health problems [9]. However, do retirees who engage in work after retirement suffer from mental problems?

This is the focus of this research, which aims to answer the following questions:

1. Is there a difference in mental health between retirees who started additional work and retirees who did not start any additional work?
2. Does the mental health differ according to the nature of the work (full-time/ part-time)?

2 Methodology

2.1 Method

This research takes the semi-experimental approach as a way to answer its questions.

2.2 Sample

The emphasis will be on those in the education sector because to their accessibility and familiarity with responding to the questionnaire's questions. Two groups (males and females) served as the basis for the study; one was experimental and consisted of eighteen people who worked extra hours. Regarding the second, it consists of a control group of eighteen people who continued to live in retirement and did not start working after that. The experimental group's average age was 63.19 (SD: 2.30). On the other hand, the control group's average age was 64.39 (SD: 3.30).

2.3 Tools

For data collection, researchers used the General Health Questionnaire (GHQ-28). This questionnaire was developed in 1978 to identify common mental conditions [10]. It is used in various fields with different generations. The questionnaire consists of a number of items, each with a four-point Likert scale of responses. There are versions with 12, 28, 30 and 60 items. Among these versions, the one that consists of 28 items (GHQ-28), is the most truthful, widespread and used in health studies. It has been translated from English into 38 languages in the world [11], including the Arabic spoken in Algeria [12]. As for its psychometric properties, a number of researchers have indicated that the GHQ has very good levels of validity and reliability [12].

The questions are broken down into the following four axes:

Items 1, 2, 3, 5, 6, and 7 are on the first axis. They quantify physical complaints. Items 8, 9 through 14 are on the second axis. They quantify insomnia and anxiety problems. 15, 16, 17, 18, 19, 20, and 21 are on the third axis. They gauge the social dysfunction. 22, 23, 24, 25, 26, 27, and 28 are on the fourth axis. They gauge extreme depression. A score is assigned to each item based on the selected option throughout the questionnaire correction process, as follows: There is a total possible score range of 0 to 84, with (0) for "Better than usual," (1) for "Same as usual," (2) for "Worse than usual," and (3) for "Much worse than usual." Therefore, lower scores denote psychological health at a high level while higher values suggest psychological health at a low level.

3 Results

This research answers the following questions:

First, is there a difference in mental health between retirees who started additional work and retirees who did not start any additional work?

Table 1. Shows the level of mental health between the two groups.

Indicators	Bridge work sample	Non-bridge work sample
Mean	1.22	2.67
SD	0.81	0.84
N	18	18
T test	5.256	
df	34	

It is noted from Table 1, that there is a significant difference between the average scores of the group that started working after retirement (1.22), and the average scores of the group that did not start any work after retirement (2.67). This means that working after retirement contributed to improving the level of mental health among retirees involved in bridgework compared to the level of mental health among retirees who did not begin any work after retirement.

Second, does the mental health differ according to the nature of the work (full-time/ part-time)? Results are depicted in Table 2.

Table 2. The difference between the two groups of retired people who started full-time bridgework, and those who started partial part-time bridge work.

Indicators	Full-time bridge work sample	Part-time bridge work sample
Mean	1.20	1.00
SD	0.92	1.07
N	10	08
U-Value	34	
Conclusion	The critical value of U at $p < 0.05$ is 17 Therefore, the result is not significant at $p < 0.05$	

Despite the fact that the Mann-Whitney non-parametric statistical test result indicates that the difference between the two groups (full-time bridge work group and part-time bridge work group) is not statistically significant, the average of the first group is equal to (1.2) and the average of the second group is equal to (1.00). This shows that the level of mental health of the part-time group appears higher than that of the full-time group.

4 Discussion

Can work be a factor that helps increase the mental health of retirees who start working again after their official retirement? The results obtained show that work helps increase the psychological health of individuals. Many previous researchers have confirmed this result. Belloni et al. [13] pointed out that work is a crucial factor in workers' health, including mental health. Marmot et al. [14] also pointed out that work plays a prominent role in increasing the psychological, mental and physical health of workers. The work is not like that, unless it is suitable for people who feel happy while doing it. In addition to these researchers, we may cite many other researchers who arrived to the same conclusions [15]. Furthermore, they pointed out that the harm of not been active on the mental health of individuals during retirement is similar to the harm of unemployment.

In addition to this, a number of retirees receive only a small financial return that is not sufficient to satisfy the requirements of the retirees and their families. Accordingly, whoever begins another job after retirement benefits from the return it provides to them to satisfy other needs (Investment loss, running out of money, major health event, inflation impact, etc.). Bridgework can also be one of the outlets that can save retirees from what is called "retirement boredom" [16]. In addition to the above, bridge work contributes to family stability in that it may address the problem of the "Retired Husband Syndrome" which can afflict the lives of at least some families [17].

The results show that the level of mental health among retirees who engaged in part-time bridgework was relatively higher than the level of mental health among retirees who engaged in full-time bridgework. These results lead us to say that engaging in work is beneficial for retirees, provided that this work is not full-time because this type of work takes a lot of time from them and is also more stressful, both physically and mentally to the elderly. Engaging in partial bridge keeps retirees busy and makes them feel that they are still able to serve society. It also enables them to obtain a financial return that satisfies the needs of themselves and the families they support. These results may differ from the findings of Rosenthal et al. [18] which indicates that full-time work provides greater psychological health compared to part-time work and full unemployment. The reason for the differences may be that Rosenthal et al' research focused on regular workers and not on retirees who engaged in bridgework.

5 Conclusion

This research has highlighted the issue of mental health among retirees who engage in bridge work. Through the quasi-experimental approach, it was found that the psychological health of those who engage in overtime work is higher than the psychological health of those who do not engage. It has also been shown that the mental health of those who engage in additional part-time work is better than that of those who engage in full-time work. Therefore, urging retirees to engage in additional part-time work is desirable. This behavior is not only beneficial to retirees, but to society as a whole, because these individuals possess a lot of expertise and experience that not only benefits those who are employed, but also benefits the entire community.

References

1. Yang, S., Khang, Y.H., Harper, S., Davey Smith, G., Leon, D.A., Lynch, J.: Understanding the rapid increase in life expectancy in South Korea. Am. J. Public Health. **100**(5), 896–903 (2010)
2. Riley, J.C.: Estimates of regional and global life expectancy, 1800–2001. Popul. Dev. Rev. **31**(3), 537–543 (2005)
3. Mathers, C.D., Stevens, G.A., Boerma, T., White, R.A., Tobias, M.I.: Causes of international increases in older age life expectancy. Lancet. **385**(9967), 540–548 (2015)
4. Roser, M., Ortiz-Ospina, E., Ritchie, H.: Life expectancy. Our world in data (2013.) Available: https://ourworldindata.org/life-expectancy. Last accessed 16 July 2023
5. Das, B., Rainey, D.V.: Is Attracting Retirees a Sustainable Rural Economic Development Policy? In: A paper prepared for presentation at the Southern Agricultural Economics Association Annual Meetings Mobile, Alabama, February 4–7, 2007 (2007)
6. Courtin, E., Knapp, M.: Social isolation, loneliness and health in old age: a scoping review. Health Soc. Care Community. **25**(3), 799–812 (2017)
7. Beehr, T.A., Bennett, M.M.: Working after retirement: features of bridge employment and research directions. Work Aging Retire. **1**(1), 112–128 (2015)
8. Gobeski, K.T., Beehr, T.A.: How retirees work: predictors of different types of bridge employment. J. Organ. Behav. **30**(3), 401–425 (2009)
9. Wilkinson, P., Ruane, C., Tempest, K.: Depression in older adults. Br. Med. J. **363**, k4922 (2018)
10. Goldberg, D.: Manual of the General Health Questionnaire. NFER-Nelson, Windsor (1978)
11. Sterling, M.: General health questionnaire–28 (GHQ-28). J. Physiother. **57**(4), 259 (2011)

12. Borji Shaker, A.D.: Evaluating the psychometric properties of the general health questionnaire (GHQ-28) on a sample of healthy subjects. J. Stud. Health Psychol. **2**(4), 08–24 (2017)
13. Belloni, M., Meschi, E., Pasini, G.: The effect on mental health of retiring during the economic crisis. Health Econ. **25**, 126–140 (2016)
14. Marmot, M., Friel, S., Bell, R., Houweling, T.A., Taylor, S., Health C.O.S.D.O: Closing the gap in a generation: health equity through action on the social determinants of health. Lancet. **372**(9650), 1661–1669 (2008)
15. Harvey, S.B., Modini, M., Joyce, S., Milligan-Saville, J.S., Tan, L., Mykletun, A., Bryant, R.A., Christensen, H., Mitchell, P.B.: Can work make you mentally ill? A systematic meta-review of work-related risk factors for common mental health problems. Occup. Environ. Med. **74**(4), 301–310 (2017)
16. Weiss, R.: The Experience of Retirement. Cornell University Press, New York, NY (2018)
17. Ciani, E.: Retirement, pension eligibility and home production. Labour Econ. **38**, 106–120 (2016)
18. Rosenthal, L., Carroll-Scott, A., Earnshaw, V.A., Santilli, A., Ickovics, J.R.: The importance of full-time work for urban adults' mental and physical health. Soc. Sci. Med. **75**(9), 1692–1696 (2012)

SwAge-Model – A Theoretical Model, Tool and Action Proposals for Dialogue and Discussion on Employee Work Situation and Career Development

Kerstin Nilsson[1,2](✉)

[1] Division of Occupational and Environmental Medicine, Lund University, Medicon Village, Scheelevägen 8, By 402A, 223 81 Lund, Sweden
kerstin.nilsson@med.lu.se, kerstin.nilsson@hkr.se
[2] Division of Public Health, Kristianstad University, 291 88 Kristianstad, Sweden

Abstract. Introduction: The average life expectancy is above 80 years of age in more than one in three countries on Earth. As well, the proportion of the population active in the labor force is ageing in many countries. It is important that individuals maintain good employability until an older age to make it possible and effective to extend working life and postpone the pension age as a measure to promote a sound social economy and to support welfare systems in different countries.
Objective: The aim of this study was to investigate organizational measures and suggestions to promote and make improvements for a healthy and sustainable working life for all ages in an extended working life.
Method: The data were collected through both focus group interviews and individual interviews that included 145 participants in different sex, different positions, and professions. All the interviews were analyzed together by deductive content analysis.
Result: The study identified several suggestions for measures and actions to increase employability sorted in the themes:

A. to promote a good physical and mental work environment;
B. to promote personal financial and social security;
C. to promote relations, social inclusion and social support in the work situation;
D. to promote creativity, knowledge development and intrinsic work motivation.

Conclusion: This study identified several suggestions for measures and actions based on the spheres of determination in the theoretical SwAge-model (sustainable working life for all ages). Out of the result the SwAge-model could be used to identify the need and as a tool for dialogue and discussion on employees´ work situation and to implement different suggested measures for practical use in organizations and enterprises to perform a Healthy and Sustainable working life for employees in all ages.

Keywords: Sustainable working life · Ageing · Work environment · SwAge-model · Demography · Employability

S. Jin et al. (Eds.): IEA 2024, SSDI 39, pp. 140–147, 2025.
https://doi.org/10.1007/978-981-95-0211-0_22

1 Introduction

The population of the labor force in the OECD countries (the Organization for Economic Co-operation and Development) is estimated to decrease by an average of 10% in 2060 [1]. However, this varies between countries; in Greece, Japan, Korea, Latvia, Lithuania, and Poland the proportion of working age population is estimated to decrease by 35% or more. Due to the global demographic change many more people will need to work until an older age, and organizations and enterprises need to implement measures to facilitate an extended working life. The challenge is how to enable and incentivize people to remain in working life until an older age [1–3]. The knowledge that has been developed for sustainable working life for all ages is important to use in the development of measures and tools in organizations and in workplaces so that more people can, want and have the strength to work to an older age [4–10]. However, based on prior knowledge and reviewing literature on the subject there is a limited number of studies and information on how organizations and enterprises can and wish to implement measures and strategies to promote a healthy and sustainable extended working life.

Due to global demographic change, the proportion of working-age population is decreasing while the proportion of older people is increasing, affecting the economic situation in several countries [1]. By 2060, the workforce is expected to decline by an average of 10% in OECD countries (Organization for Economic Co-operation and Development) [1]. However, the age distribution differs between countries. Japan, Korea, Latvia, Poland, Greece and Lithuania appear to be particularly affected, as the proportion of the working-age population there is expected to decline by >35% in 2060. Old-age pensions are being postponed as many more people need to work into old age. Organizations and companies therefore need to take measures that enable and stimulate people to remain in work into old age and to facilitate and promote a healthy and sustainably extended working life [1–3]. It is important that knowledge, measures and tools developed for a sustainable working life for all ages are used by organizations and workplaces so that more people can, want and have the strength to work into old age [4–10].

1.1 Objective

The objective of this study was to identify and develop measures and proposals for organizations and enterprises to promote and stimulate improvements towards a healthy and sustainable extended working life.

2 Method and Material

2.1 Participants and Data Collection

The study population included 145 participants (73 women and 72 men) in different positions: first line managers (n = 45), senior employees (55–72 years of age) (n = 87) from both blue- and white-collar professions, trade union workers (n = 6), and human resources (HR) personnel (n = 7). The participants work in different domains from the public as well as the private sector and in both female- and male-dominated workplaces. The senior employee occupations were concrete worker, salesperson, administrator, mechanic, engineer, technician, construction worker, farmer, installer, carpenter, electrician, social worker, nurse assistant, nurse and physician.

The data were collected through both focus group interviews and individual interviews using a semi-structured interview guide to invite the respondents to reflect on proposals to promote and stimulate improvements to be able and willing to work until an older age and towards a healthy and sustainable extended working life for all in the workplace. Some of the data has previously been analyzed for other purposes, i.e., the attitude between managers and employees in relation to an extended working life, the transfer of knowledge between generations, why some had left working life early and others worked until older age, and work motivation. The participants were recruited in different ways. A total of 105 informants (65 employees 55–72 years of age, 7 human resource personnel and 33 first line managers) were recruited through a snowball selection at organizations and enterprises after the researchers invited the respective workplace to participate in the study and the organization and the enterprise had accepted. Twenty-two individuals responded, received further information and participated in the interview study. Additionally, twelve participants from an ongoing intervention study with managers were asked to participate and received further information on the study by phone and were asked to participate. Of those all accepted and gave consent to participate in the interview study. The six participants from trade unions were invited in another way. The researcher e-mailed written information about the study directly to the trade union with an announcement and invitation for interested participants to volunteer for the study.

2.2 Analysis

All the transcribed interview data was put together and analyzed by deductive content analysis, to crystallize the relevant parts. Deduction can be said to constitute a conclusion from the general to the individual. Deductive content analysis is a suitable choice when an existing theory involves the application of conceptual categories in the analysis of a new context [11]. The analysis in this study was performed in several steps, and started by constructing a formative categorization matrix with four pre-set categories based on theories and the determinant spheres in the SwAge-model[1] [4–10] (Fig. 1).

[1] The SwAge model is a theoretical model, but also used as a practical tool, consisting of nine different influence areas that are significant to a sustainable working life for all ages [4–10]. Those nine areas relate to the four spheres of determination regarding employability, the possibility of being able to and willing to be part of working life. Those nine areas, as well as the four spheres of determination regarding employability, also relate to different ways of defining and concept age and ageing. All those parts are included and visualized in the SwAge-model. The four spheres of employability, sorting in the nine determining and areas for sustainable working life and the way of concept age, are:

A. The health effects of the work environment, which relate to biological age and ageing, and include the following areas of determination: (1) Self-rated health, diagnoses and functional diversity, (2) physical work environment with unilateral movements, heavy lifting, risk of accidents, climate, chemical exposure and risk of contagion, (3) mental work environment

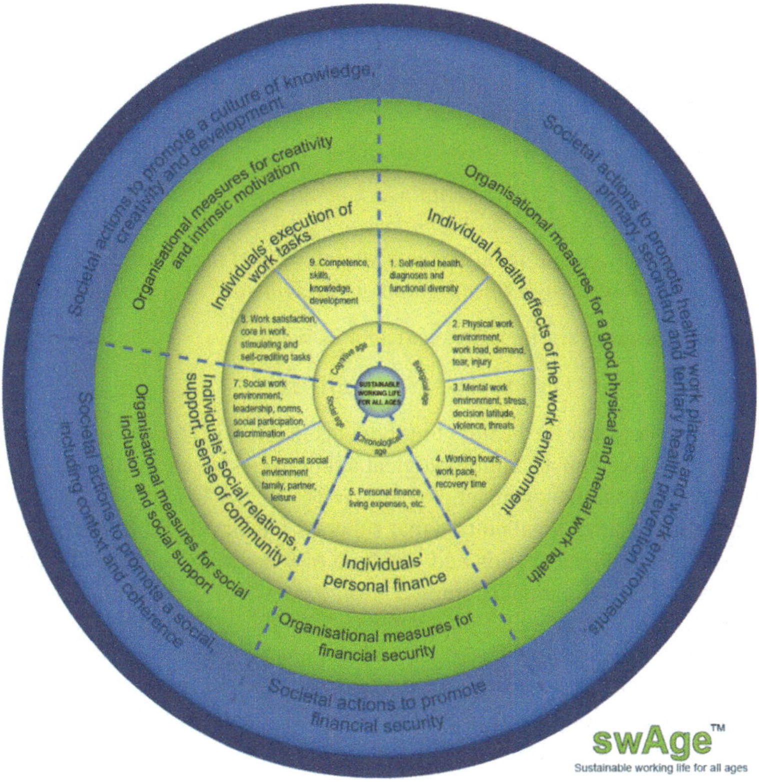

Fig. 1. The SwAge-model – a theoretical model with practical implication of the total complexity of working life and determinants of a healthy and sustainable working life at all ages

---

with risk of stress and fatigue syndrome, threats and violence, and (4) working hours, work pace and the possibility of recuperation during and between work shifts for the employee.

B. Economics and financial incentives, which relate to chronological ages and association to society's control of various financial carrots and sticks, for example, through the pension system and social insurance system. Economics and financial incentives include the following determinant area: (5) The personal financial situation's effects on individuals' needs and willingness to work.

C. Relationships, social support and participation, i.e., attitudes in the social context in which the individual finds himself/herself, are considered as well as whether the individual feels included or excluded in the group and receives sufficient social support from the environment when needed, relate to social age and ageing during the life cycle and include the areas of determination: (6) The effects of the personal social environment, with family, friends and leisure context, and (7) the social work environment with leadership, discrimination and the significance of the employment relationship context for individuals' work.

D. Execution of tasks and activities relate to cognitive age and ageing, intelligence ability, memory, learning and instrumental support, and include the following areas of determination: (8) Motivation, satisfaction, and stimulation in the execution of work tasks, and (9) knowledge,

3 Results

The study identified several suggestions for measures and actions based on the spheres of determination in the theoretical SwAge-model (sustainable working life for all ages) to increase employability in the themes:

A. *to promote a good physical and mental work environment;*
B. *to promote personal financial and social security;*
C. *to promote relations, social inclusion and social support in the work situation;*
D. *to promote creativity, knowledge development and intrinsic work motivation*

The identified suggestions for measures and actions were:

A. *Measures for the Work Environments Health Effects*

- Measures to consider the health of individuals in relation to their biological aging
- Measures to take into account biological aging in risk assessments in systematic work environment management
- Promote an organizational culture that supports the use of ergonomic aids
- Measures for change, rotation and variation of work tasks in order to reduce the risk of physical and mental strain
- Measures with increased communication, information and participation to reduce work stress
- Measures to reduce the risk of violence and threats in the work situation
- Support groups to jointly reflect and discuss experiences of risk of injuries, illness, and threats and violence at work
- Develop good work schedules
- Measures for a reasonable work pace, and provide opportunities for recovery after work peaks
- Measures that promote employees' self-care for healthy (occupational) health
- Measures that promote the possibility of exercise and physical activity, i.e. promote "maintenance of functions", to maintain and improve mental and physical health
- Access to occupational health care and expert support to prevent work environment problems and increase good occupational health

B. *Measures for Personal Financial Security*

- Measures for a sustainable personal financial situation, e.g. through a sustainable salary, financial benefits and insurance
- Joint reflection in the workplace on preventive organizational measures to support continuous employability into older age

---

competence, and the importance of competence development for the individual's work. Working life is constantly changing and employees must be and remain employable in relation to the requirements of knowledge and skills to execute the activities and tasks that their work entails.

- Measures to promote and increase employees' use of measures, tools, safety equipment and aids in the workplace with the aim of preventing and reducing the risk of occupational injury, occupational disease and sick leave

C. *Measures to Promote Relations, Social Support and Inclusion*

- Measures to reduce negative attitudes and (age) discrimination
- Measures to support good social integration in the work group to increase participation and community
- Measures to promote community, social support and increase participation in working life
- Take measures for attitudes and norms that promote the status of senior employees in a profession and a work team
- Social support to promote and increase the self-esteem of senior employees in the organization
- Measures to promote and increase the attitude of employees as an investment in productivity
- Measures to promote the norm in the workplace about the need for a good work-life balance

D. *Measures for Execution of Work Tasks*

- Measures to increase employees' work motivation and job satisfaction from their tasks and activities at work
- Measures to highlight and take advantage of employees' unique abilities
- Measures to change work tasks and job rotation with the aim of developing skills, as well as stimulating and increasing job satisfaction
- Measures to enable participation in knowledge and skills development to maintain continued employability into older age
- Pedagogical measures to adapt skills development to the employee's cognitive aging
- Development of an organizational culture that recognizes and uses the experience and knowledge of (senior) employees.

4 Discussion

The demographic shift challenges and opportunities are of special interest to many countries and societies [1–3], and require the implementation of policies and actions in organizations and enterprises to help people stay healthy, active, and employable until an older age [1–15]. The findings in this study represent different sectors of work domains, different occupational groups, and professions, and occupations from different hierarchical positions within the organizations. Therefore, the results from this study are of great interest. Because most organizations and enterprises in the OECD countries need to act and implement sustainable measures and strategies at the workplaces to make an extended working life possible for a greater number of individuals [1]. The analysis in this study identifies the need of regular conversations, communication and close dialogue to manage employees, to develop good working conditions and develop the organizations to be more ageing friendly. Additionally, the analysis developed action proposals to increase employability based on the spheres of determination in the theoretical SwAge-model (sustainable working life for all ages). Those measures and action proposals were sorted into four themes: A. to promote a good physical and mental work environment; B. to promote personal financial and social security; C. to promote relations, social inclusion and social support in the work situation; and D. to promote creativity, knowledge development and intrinsic work motivation. In related studies in the research group a tool for dialogue and discussion on employee work situation and career development which can be used for the implementation of the identified action proposals [6]. As earlier research stated, it is of great importance to use available evidence-based tools, as the SwAge-model theory and tool, with the intent to implement a sustainable working life for all ages, of supporting employability and enabling people to participate in working life longer [4–10].

A limitation in the study design is that findings from qualitative studies are not transferable to all other cultural contexts. However, regarding the transferability of the findings, it could be said that the developed themes are relevant to many others in similar workplaces. The findings were also well-aligned with earlier studies about employability and senior employees' problems and possibilities regarding whether they can and want to participate in an extended working life. The results thereby add to the accumulation of knowledge regarding measures for senior employees' possibility of working in an extended working life.

5 Conclusion

Proposals for measures to make working life sustainable so that more people can work longer are urgently needed in many countries due to ongoing demographic developments. Regular conversations, communication and close dialogue are needed and are a prerequisite for good working conditions and a sustainable working environment, as well as to be able to manage employees and develop the organization further. The action proposals from this study, the theories of SwAge-model, and the tools for workplace analysis, dialogue and discussion developed out of the SwAge-model, could be used to identify specific measure needs and actions. This tool needs to be revisited regularly throughout the employees' entire working life to enable a healthy and sustainable working life in and for all ages, and for an extended working life.

References

1. OECD: Pensions at a Glance OECD and G20 Indicators. OECD Publishing, Paris (2019)
2. WHO: UN Decade of Healthy Ageing 2021–2030. UN Decade of Healthy Ageing
3. EU: Ageing workforce. European Foundation for the Improvement of Living and Working Conditions. https://www.eurofound.europa.eu/topic/ageing-workforce
4. Nilsson, K.: A sustainable working life for all ages—the SwAge-model. Appl. Ergon. **86**, 103082 (2020)
5. Nilsson, K.: Designing Sustainable Working Lives and Environments: Work, Health and Leadership in Theory and Practice, 1st edn, pp. 1–334. CRC Press (2024). https://doi.org/10.1201/9781032616681

6. Nilsson, K.: When is work a cause of early retirement and are there any effective organisational measures to combat this? A population-based study of perceived work environment and work-related disorders in Sweden. BMC Public Health. **20**, 1–15 (2020)
7. Nilsson, K., Nilsson, E.: Organisational measures and strategies for a healthy and sustainable extended working life and employability—a deductive content analysis with data including employees, first line managers, trade union representatives and HR-practitioners. IJERPH. **18**, 5626 (2021)
8. Nilsson, K., Nilsson, E.: Can they stay or will they go? A cross sectional study of managers' attitudes towards their senior employees. IJERPH. **19**, 1057 (2022)
9. Nilsson, K.: Conceptualization of ageing in relation to factors of importance for extending working life. Scand. J. Public Health. **44**, 490–505 (2016)
10. Nilsson, K.: Why work beyond 65? Discourse on the decision to continue working or retire early. Nordic J. Work. Life Stud. **2**, 7–28 (2012)
11. Hsieh, H.-F., Shannon, S.E.: Three approaches to qualitative content analysis. Qual. Health Res. **15**, 1277–1288 (2005)
12. de Wind, A., et al.: The role of ability, motivation, and opportunity to work in the transition from work to early retirement—testing and optimizing the early retirement model. Scand. J. Work Environ. Health. **41**, 24–35 (2015)
13. Van der Klink, J.J.L., et al.: Sustainable employability—definition, conceptualization, and implications. Scand. J. Work Environ. Health. **42**, 71–79 (2016)
14. Fleuren, B.P.I., et al.: Time takes us all? A two-wave observational study of age and time effects on sustainable employability. Scand. J. Work Environ. Health. **44**, 475–484 (2018)
15. Fleuren, B.P., et al.: Unshrouding the sphere from clouds: towards a comprehensive conceptual framework for sustainable employability. Sustainability. **12**, 6366 (2020)

Are Italian Older Adults Ready for Gerontechnologies? Results from a Survey for Active and Healthy Ageing

Mattia Pistolesi(✉), Claudia Becchimanzi, and Francesca Tosi

Department of Architecture DIDA, University of Florence, Ergonomics and Design Lab, S. Pertini 93 street, Calenzano, Florence, Italy
mattia.pistolesi@unifi.it

Abstract. This study aims to investigate the use of modern health technologies (personal computers, tablets, smartwatches, smart TVs, digital assistants, Artificial intelligence, Apps for wellness, nutrition and sport, smart clothing, subcutaneous devices, glucometer, pulse oximeter, ECG and spirometer), which can be used even without specific medical knowledge, by Italian citizens, the promotion and monitoring of health and wellness. The national study required the submission of a questionnaire, disseminated online using the Google Forms platform. 209 Italian citizens participated in the study, of whom only 190 were eligible, considering the inclusion criteria of the research programme. Based on the Active Ageing Index (AAI) programmed by the United Nations Economic Commission for Europe (UNECE), the study involved people aged 55 and over. The results that emerged will be discussed in the article and will enable the research team to plan and draft the project matrix guidelines as envisaged by the research programme "Age-It Ageing well in ageing society" (Spoke 9, Work Package 1, Task 1.1), an extended partner-ship funded within the framework of the National Recovery and Resilience Plan, whose objective is the study of advanced gerontechnologies for active and healthy ageing with low TRL.

Keywords: Design for health · Human-Centred Design · Gerontecnology · Active ageing · Healty ageing · Gray Digital Divide

1 Introduction

In recent years, many technologies addressed the ageing problem, offering solutions aimed at active and healthy ageing. It is well known that technology will impact individual ageing and may revolutionise older people's quality of life and healthcare delivery [1].

Scientific literature draws attention to the generation gap because older adults have fewer opportunities to access new health technologies. The existence of the Gray Digital Divide, i.e. the difference in access and use of ICT between the older adults and the young population, has been documented in numerous international studies [2–4].

S. Jin et al. (Eds.): IEA 2024, SSDI 39, pp. 148–154, 2025.
https://doi.org/10.1007/978-981-95-0211-0_23

The mistrust of older adults towards the use of new technologies, the still low technological literacy, the aseptic nature of the human-computer relationship and, in general, with digital devices constitute some of the main obstacles to the full realisation of the potential offered by new technologies, in terms of greater social inclusion of the older adults. On the other hand, one of the elements that will characterise the new generation of older adults in the future is the progressive, or possible, rapprochement with new technologies. This factor can significantly expand the possibilities of communication, sociability, information and access to services. Moreover, in recent years, we assisted to a fundamental shift, also involving the research in Design, in which the elderly are no longer considered as a problem to be solved with new, high-performance technologies [5, 6] but rather are seen as technologically able users [7] who must be involved in the development and design processes of gerontechnologies by focusing on their daily lives and concerns [6, 8, 9].

This motivation led the article's authors to conduct a national survey, whose aim is to understand the use of technologies by Italian citizens, in relation to the activities for promoting and monitoring their health and wellbeing.

2 Methodology

As part of the research programme "Age-It Ageing well in ageing society" [10], it was appropriate to develop an exploratory questionnaire, divided into three parts: (i) respondent's biographical data; (ii) health status concerning technology, consisting of general questions that aim to understand the respondents' health status and what activities they carry out for the monitoring and promotion of health status and wellbeing; and finally, (iii) acceptability and experience in the use of technology, consisting of questions that aim to investigate what technologies, which are used today for the monitoring and promotion of health status and wellbeing, what difficulties respondents experience and what possible new ways of interacting with the proposed technologies.

First of all, there is no universally accepted classification of gerontechnology in the scientific literature. Halicka & Surel [11] divide gerontechnology into nine domains: health, education, interpersonal communication, safety, mobility, care, leisure care, housing and, Digital Accessibility. Van Bronswijk et al. [12] divide gerontechnology into four intervention domains: enrichment and satisfaction, prevention and engagement, compensation and substitution, care support, and care organisation. Other authors [13, 14] categorise gerontechnology as assistive technologies intended for the support of daily activities, facilitation of social ties, communication, mobility, personal health, physical and cognitive activity and finally, safety. Ultimately, gerontechnology encompasses the field of products and services applied to human beings, insofar as they aim to increase the quality of life in the most advanced segments.

For this reason, common technologies, usable even without specific medical knowledge, suitable for the promotion and monitoring of a person's state of health and wellbeing were considered as the object of study, including: personal computers, tablets, smartwatches, smartphones, smart TVs, digital assistants, artificial intelligence, apps for wellbeing, nutrition and sport, smart clothing, subcutaneous devices, glucometer, pulse oximeter, ECG and spirometer.

The following aspects were evaluated for each product: experience, emotional aspects, interaction, element of preference, usefulness, comprehension, reliability and difficulty of use. According to the Active Ageing Index [15], the study described in this article focuses on people aged 55 and over who are residents in Italy. The recruitment criteria are the following: to be an Italian citizen residing in one of the Italian provinces and to be at least 55 years old without distinction of age, gender, education or religion. The questionnaire was disseminated online using the common social networks LinkedIn and Facebook. A 5-point Likert rating scale was used, where 1 corresponds to 'completely agree', 3 neither agree nor disagree, and 5 completely disagree.

3 Results

3.1 Biographical Data

209 Italian citizens took part in the study, of whom only 190 are eligible considering the inclusion criteria of the research programme (n = 83 male, n = 107 female). A large part of the sample involved in the study are still employed (n = 107), while the others are retired (n = 72), unemployed (n = 6) and other.

Many participants are resident in Tuscany (n = 120), while the remainder reside in Campania (n = 23), Emilia Romagna (n = 11), Veneto (n = 11), Calabria (n = 6), Umbria (n = 4), Sicily (n = 4), Lazio (n = 3), Marche (n = 2), Liguria (n = 2) Abruzzo (n = 1), Apulia (n = 1), Lombardy (n = 1) and Piedmont (n = 1).

3.2 Health Status and Technology

The health status of the respondents is positive (n = 162). Only a small proportion of the respondents declare a passable (n = 25) and poor (n = 3) state of health.

Although the results are encouraging, 42 out of 190 respondents declare that they are well and do not suffer from any health complaints of concern, while the remaining part (n = 148) declares that they have one or more health complaints (e.g. complaints of the feet, legs, pelvic area, arms and hands, abdomen, shoulders, head and neck, eyes, chest and heart, musculoskeletal complaints and, finally, cancer, hypertension, osteoporosis and thrombosis).

In order to understand the relationship between the health status of the respondents and the use of the potential offered by modern technologies, two questions were asked to find out how the participants behave about their health status. Regarding the question "*What do you do when you have an unknown symptom?*" the prevalence of the respondents prefer to go to a general practitioner (n = 125), while another overwhelming proportion prefer to use the web to find an answer (n = 57).

As for the question "*how do you prefer to access the services of the healthcare system?*", the results indicate a preference for going to a healthcare location (n = 114) and for human interaction with medical staff (n = 91). Other answers indicate the possibility of using the telephone or instant messaging (n = 24), the possibility of meeting the medical staff virtually (n = 8) and the possibility of communicating via e-mail (n = 16).

3.3 Acceptability, Experience and Technology

As mentioned in Sect. 2, this study considers several technologies that can also be used by end-users for health management and consequently for activities promoting active and healthy ageing.

About the use of the *personal computer*, the results indicate that 43 out of 174 users use it for the promotion and monitoring of health and wellbeing. More than half of the respondents consider using the tool to promote and monitor health status helpful, trusting and understanding the data shown (e.g., biometric data, health parameters, statistics, medical records, etc.). As for the use of the *tablet*, only 11 out of 74 users use it to promote and monitor their health and wellbeing. Again, the results regarding the use of the tool, the confidence in the data collected and the understanding of the data shown are positive. The results regarding using the *smartwatch* tell us that 21 out of 30 users use it to promote and monitor health and wellbeing. The results regarding the use of the tool, the confidence of the data collected and the understanding of the data shown are very favourable. The same applies to the *smartphone*. Although 55 out of 183 users also use it to promote and monitor their health and wellbeing, the results regarding the use of the tool, the confidence of the data collected, and the understanding of the data shown are very encouraging and, therefore, positive. The results change regarding the use of technologies that are still little used, such as the case of the *smart TV*. Only one user also uses it for health management and monitoring. The respondent states that it is helpful and that he trusts and understands the data shown. As for the use of the *digital assistant*, only 2 out of 21 users use it to promote and monitor health and wellbeing. Again, the results regarding the use of the tool, the trust in the data collected and the understanding of the data shown are, on average, favourable. Only 1 in 21 users use *artificial intelligence* for health management and monitoring. This user states that it is useful, that they trust the data collected and that they understand the data shown. For further details, see Fig. 1.

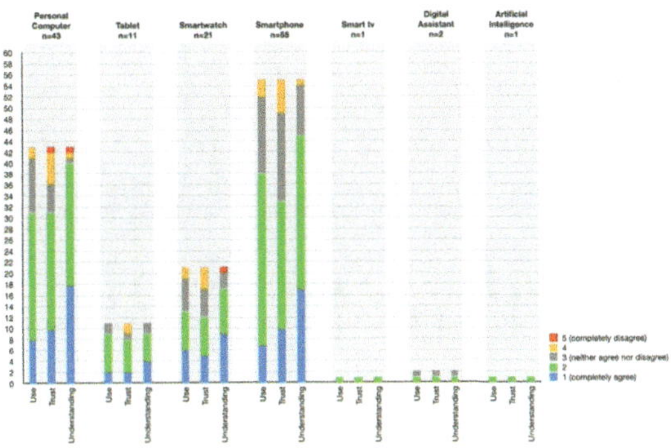

Fig. 1. Results of technologies that can also be used for health management.

If we refer to technologies developed exclusively for the management of people's health status, 27 out of 190 users use *health apps*. The results are, on average, positive, with 12 respondents considering the use of the tool for promoting and monitoring their state of health to be useful, trusting and understanding the data shown, while 13 users answered the question neutrally. As for the *food/nutrition apps*, 7 users state that they use them. About half of the respondents state that they experience some difficulty in recognising the usefulness of the apps, trusting the data collected, and understanding the data shown. With regard to *sports apps*, 27 out of 190 users state that they use them. The results are, on average, positive; in fact, more than half of the respondents finds the use of apps useful, trusts the data collected and understands the data shown. With regard to the use of *smart clothes*, only a small part of the sample involved in the study claims to use them (n = 6). This result may be caused by the low diffusion and knowledge of this technology. Although use is limited, the results indicate average positive values. More than half of the respondents states that smart clothing are useful and trusted and understood the data shown. Regarding the *subcutaneous devices*, only 1 user also uses them for health management and monitoring. This user states that it is actually useful and that he trusts the data collected and understands the data shown. 3 users use the *glucometer* for the promotion and monitoring of health and wellbeing. The results regarding the use of the instrument, trusting the data collected and understanding the data shown are very favourable. 24 users use the *pulse oximeter*. The results are, on average, positive; in fact, more than half of the respondents find the use of this tool useful for the promotion and monitoring of health, trust the data collected and understand the data shown. 10 users also stated that they use the *ECG* for their own health management. Also in this case, the findings follow the trend of the results described above and are, therefore, positive. Finally, with regard to the use of the *spirometer*, no answers were given. For further details, see Fig. 2.

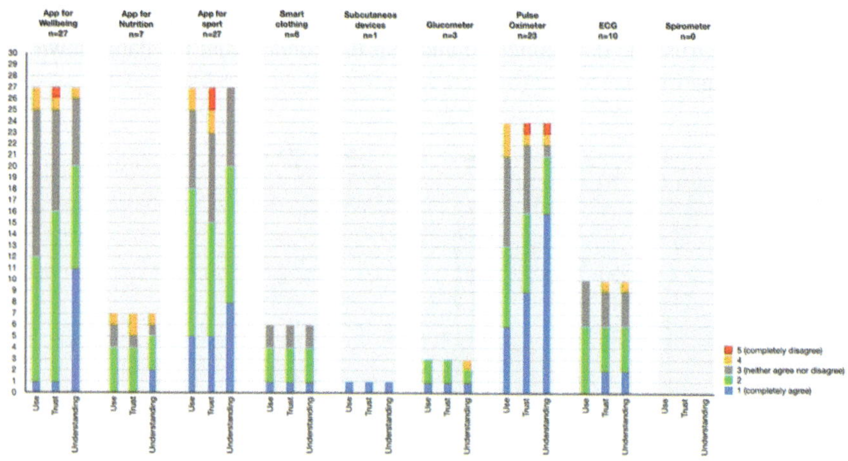

Fig. 2. Results of technologies that can only be used for health management.

4 Discussion and Conclusion

This study shows an overall positive reliability and applicability of the method used, in particular to bring out data from the sample involved. The results, although on average encouraging and positive, provide concrete indications as to how the technologies proposed in the study are used, now and in the future, by people also for the promotion of active ageing and health.

Furthermore, accepting the hypothesis that scientific progress and technological innovation are unstoppable processes that can have a fundamental impact on both the health system and citizens, an important finding to emerge from our study is the willingness on the part of the sample involved to keep human relationships alive, more so when it comes to health management. This may be the cause of little or no preference to digitalise human health and difficulty in using technology.

The results also shows limitations. First of all, some of the proposed technologies are more widely used than others, so it is conceivable that the results that emerge are reliable, while for the others (smart TV, digital assistant, artificial intelligence, smart clothing, subcutaneos devices, glucometer, ECG and spirometer), the results that emerge are not scientifically valid and therefore further studies are required. This may be the cause of a limited or sporadic use of health management technologies. For this reason, further studies are necessary.

Finally, in order to meet the objectives of the Age-it research programme, further research activities are programmed, with the aim to deeply investigate the collected data, within focus group sessions with a group of citizens over 55 and workshop sessions with young designers. These new activities will be described and discussed in further scientific articles.

References

1. Lee, C.: Technology and aging: the jigsaw puzzle of design, development and distribution. Nat. Aging. **2**, 1077–1079 (2022). https://doi.org/10.1038/s43587-022-00325-6
2. van Dijk, J.A., Hacker, K.: The digital divide as a complex and dynamic phenomenon. Inf. Soc. **19**(4), 315–326 (2003)
3. van Dijk, J.A.: Digital divide research, achievements and shortcomings. Poetics. **34**(4–5), 221–235 (2006)
4. Manchester, H., Jarke, J.: Considering the role of material gerontology in reimaging technology design for ageing populations. Int. J. Ageing Later Life. **15**(2), 181–213 (2022). https://doi.org/10.3384/ijal.1652-8670.3531
5. Peine, A., Neven, L.: The co-constitution of ageing and technology—a model and agenda. Ageing Soc. **41**(12), 2845–2866 (2020). https://doi.org/10.1017/S0144686X20000641
6. Vines, J., Pritchard, G., Wright, P., Olivier, P., Brittain, K.: An age-old problem: examining the discourses of ageing in HCI and strategies for future research. ACM Trans. Comput. Hum. Interact. **22**(1), 1–27 (2015)
7. Mitzner, T.L., Boron, J.B., Fausset, C.B., Adams, A.E., Charness, N., Czaja, S.J., Dijkstra, K., Fisk, A.D., Rogers, W.A., Sharit, J.: Older adults talk technology: technology usage and attitudes. Comput. Hum. Behav. **26**(6), 1710–1721 (2010). https://doi.org/10.1016/j.chb.2010.06.020

8. Baker, S., Waycott, J., Carrasco, R., Hoang, T., Vetere, F.: Exploring the design of social VR experiences with older adults. In: Proceedings of the 2019 on Designing Interactive Systems Conference, pp. 303–315 (2019). https://doi.org/10.1145/3322276.3322361
9. Wallace, J., Duncan, T., Lawson, S., Trueman, J., Montague, K., Carvalho, L., Groot, L., Craig, C., Fisher, H., Koulidou, N.: Design research to support ongoingness. Bereavem. Care. **39**(2), 88–92 (2020). https://doi.org/10.1080/02682621.2020.1771969
10. AGE-IT, http://www.ageit.eu
11. Halicka, K., Surel, D.: Gerontechnology — new opportunities in the service of older adults. Eng. Manag. Product. Services. **13**(3), 114–126 (2021). https://doi.org/10.2478/emj-2021-0025
12. van Bronswijk, J.E.M.H., Bouma, H., Fozard, J.L., Kearns, W.D., Davison, G.C., Tuan, P.-C.: Defining gerontechnology for R&D purposes. Geron. **8**(1), 3–10 (2009). https://doi.org/10.4017/gt.2009.08.01.002.00
13. Peek, S.T.M., Wouters, E.J.M., van Hoof, J., Luijkx, K.G., Boeije, H.R., Vrijhoef, H.J.M.: Factors influencing acceptance of technology for aging in place: a systematic review. Int. J. Med. Inform. **83**, 235–248 (2014). https://doi.org/10.1016/j.ijmedinf.2014.01.004
14. Haufe, M., Peek, S.T.M., Luijkx, K.G.: Matching gerontechnologies to independent-living seniors' individual needs: development of the GTM tool'. BMC Health Serv. Res. **19**(26) (2019). https://doi.org/10.1186/s12913-018-3848-5
15. United Nations Economic Commission for Europe: Fact Sheet on Active Ageing. UNECE, Geneva (2012)

Research on the Demand and Product Design of Long-Term Care Services for the Disabled Elderly in the Community

Yuhan Wu[1], Xiaoli Wu[1](✉), Xilu Tang[1], and Chengqi Xue[2]

[1] Nanjing University of Science and Technology, Nanjing 210094, Jiangsu, China
wuxlhhu@163.com
[2] Southeast University, Nanjing 214135, Jiangsu, China

Abstract. The aging of the population is accelerating, the burden of social care is increasing, the incapacity rate of the elderly is rising, and solving the problem of caring for the disabled elderly has become an important part of social care, so it is very important to explore the real needs and preferences of the disabled elderly in the community. Using interviews and questionnaires to conduct research on the community's disabled elderly, establish a typical user profile based on the results of the research, analyze the pain points and needs of the disabled elderly home care, and design a product for the home health management of the disabled elderly, including hardware and software interface design, to maintain the health and safety of the community's disabled elderly at home, and to provide a design case for the construction of the elderly elderly care service system for the disabled.

Keywords: Disabled Elderly · Community Services · Needs Research

1 Introduction

1.1 Research Background

According to data from the National Bureau of Statistics of China, the elderly population aged 65 and above in China is 190.64 million, accounting for 13.50%. The results of a sample survey on the situation of the elderly in urban and rural areas in China show that more than 40 million elderly people in China are in a state of incapacity or semi-incapacity" [1]. Ageing at home, ageing in the community and ageing in institutions" is how the Chinese government has positioned the three modes of ageing at home, ageing in the community and ageing in institutions in recent years.

In recent years, researchers and scholars have conducted numerous studies on the current needs of the disabled elderly and found that the phenomenon of unmet needs of the disabled elderly is relatively common [2–4].

National Key Research and Development Program "Research and Application of Key Technology Standards for Age-Friendly Ergonomics in Communities" Key Project (2022YFF0607003,2022.9–2025.9).

S. Jin et al. (Eds.): IEA 2024, SSDI 39, pp. 155–162, 2025.
https://doi.org/10.1007/978-981-95-0211-0_24

At present, China is actively carrying out the construction of community care for the elderly, but due to the complexity of the health and care issues involved. Therefore, it is particularly important to explore in depth the real needs and preferences of the elderly in terms of community care.

1.2 Research Methods

Combined with Maslow's Hierarchy of Needs Theory to explore the needs of the disabled elderly in depth [5], caring for the disabled elderly should not only satisfy their most basic physiological needs, but also pay attention to their socialization, self-worth, self-esteem and respect and other needs, to create a healthier living environment for them [6]. Through interviews and questionnaires, we fully investigated the living status and needs of the disabled elderly to form a typical portrait of the disabled elderly. By analyzing the collected data, the priority of the needs of the disabled elderly for community elderly services is derived, providing reference and guidance for designing products and services that meet the needs of the disabled elderly.

2 Research and Study

2.1 Interviews

In this paper, the interview method was used in the pre-survey stage to get a preliminary grasp of the basic situation of the elderly with disabilities and the community in which they live. The interviews involved a total of 15 mildly, moderately and severely disabled elderly people, of which the ratio of men to women was 6:9, and the characteristics of the interviewed community groups are shown in Table 1.

Table 1. Interviews on the characteristics of the community group of disabled elderly

Community Name	Characteristics of the Disabled Elderly Group
Nanjing University of Science and Technology	The interviews involved the disabled elderly in the first and sixth districts of Nanjing University of Science and Technology, which are characterized by higher education, higher incomes, and more long-term caregivers for the elderly
Gulou District, Nanjing	The nursing homes are mainly for the disabled elderly, characterized by higher levels of disability, more comprehensive care services, higher service costs, and a combination of medical and nursing care

(continued)

Table 1. *(continued)*

Community Name	Characteristics of the Disabled Elderly Group
Shecun, Jiangning District, Nanjing	Shecun is a model village for the elderly, with an assisted living center for the elderly. The characteristics of the elderly in Shecun include lower income, more left-behind elderly, lack of care services, inconvenient transportation, and difficulties in accessing medical care for the disabled

2.2 Questionnaire Construction

Based on the content of the preliminary survey, the needs of the disabled elderly were firstly extracted and categorized and summarized in Table 2.Secondly, the questionnaire structure was built. After several discussions, the project team finally determined that the questionnaire structure is composed of five parts, namely, "1. basic information", "2. assessment of daily living ability (ADL) [7]", "3. mental state and social participation", "4. daily behavioral activities and space", "5. assessment of daily life", and "6. assessment of daily life". Assessment", "4. Daily Behavioral Activities and Space", and "5. Satisfaction and Needs of Facilities and Services".

Table 2. Summary Table of Requirements

Classification of Requirements	Content of Needs
Demand for daily life care services	Meal assistance service, hygiene service, mobility service, escort service, companion care service, safety confirmation service
Demand for medical care services	Regular medical checkups, vital signs testing, care for common symptoms, medication guidance and treatment, specialized care, emergency care, post-surgery recovery care
Health guidance service needs	Rehabilitation training/rehabilitation guidance, behavioral safety guidance, guidance on the use of assistive devices, guidance on the prevention of common diseases, guidance on the prevention of chronic diseases, guidance on healthy diet, guidance on emergency self-help methods
Rehabilitation Service Needs	Exercise therapy, physical therapy, occupational therapy, speech training, psychological therapy

(continued)

Table 2. (*continued*)

Classification of Requirements	Content of Needs
Demand for community safety protection	Aging-adapted home renovation, public space service facilities, public space access facilities, installation of emergency caller, emergency rescue
Spiritual and psychological needs	Companion services, holiday greetings/celebrations, regular visits, psychological counseling and guidance
Demand for social participation services	Participation in learning activities, recreational and leisure activities, and social activities

3 Typical User Profiles

The results of the questionnaire were sorted out and analyzed and summarized into nine typical user profiles of the disabled elderly, namely, mobility impaired, long-term bedridden, perceptual failure, cognitive impairment, chronic illness, multiple diseases, mental depression, social isolation, and unstable security, considering four aspects: physiological characteristics, psychological characteristics, disease conditions, and life care, and the results were as shown in Fig. 1.

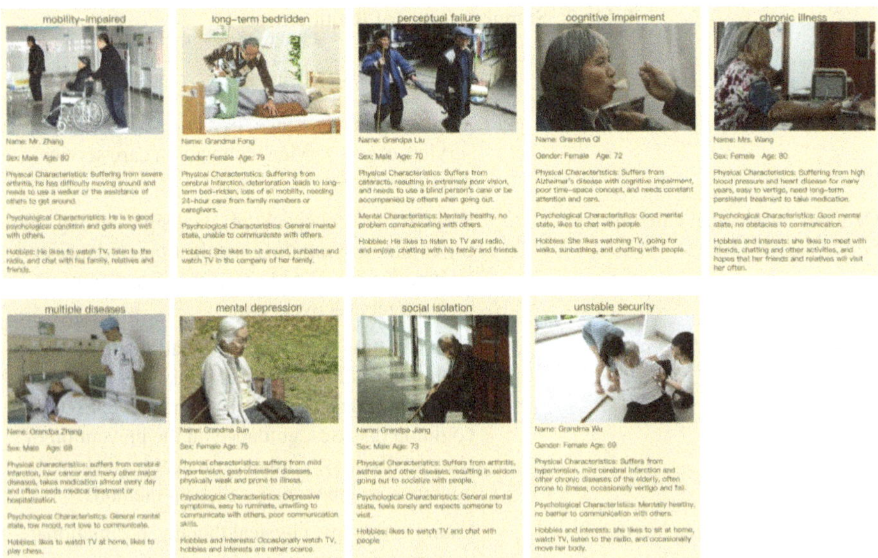

Fig. 1. Typical User Profile

4 Demand Weighting Analysis Based on AHP Hierarchical Analysis Method

Based on the results of the data collected from the questionnaire survey, the weights of the demand types were analyzed in combination with the assignment method, and the AHP matrix was calculated using the sum and product method, and the weight values of the indicators were 13. 920%, 22.491%, 2.927%, 4.455%, 26.962%, 12.101%, and 17.144%, respectively, as shown in Table 3.

Table 3. Requirement weighting

Item	Eigenvector	Weight value	Maximum eigenvalue	CI value
Demand for daily life care services	0.974	13.920%	7.445	0.074
Demand for medical care services	1.574	22.491%		
Health guidance service needs	0.205	2.927%		
Rehabilitation Service Needs	0.312	4.455%		
Demand for community safety protection	1.887	26.962%		
Spiritual and psychological needs	0.847	12.101%		
Demand for social participation services	1.200	17.144%		

The prioritization of needs is based on the weights, in which community safety protection and medical care services have the highest weight values.

From the prioritization of needs, it can be seen that the product design of the disabled elderly tends to take life safety as the main consideration. Among them, community safety and protection needs and medical care needs are ranked first and second, indicating that the disabled elderly are more concerned about safety and physical health issues. The design of product systems for the disabled elderly should be centered on the two aspects of health and safety in order to improve the quality of life of the disabled elderly and protect their physical and mental health.

5 Product Design

5.1 Product Positioning

The product proposes a home medical health management program for the disabled elderly who have limited mobility and difficulty in seeking medical treatment. The product effect diagram of the health and safety management system for the disabled elderly is shown in the Fig. 2. The system adopts modularized design and is mainly divided into product host, safety call module, routine detection module, blood collection and detection module and work.

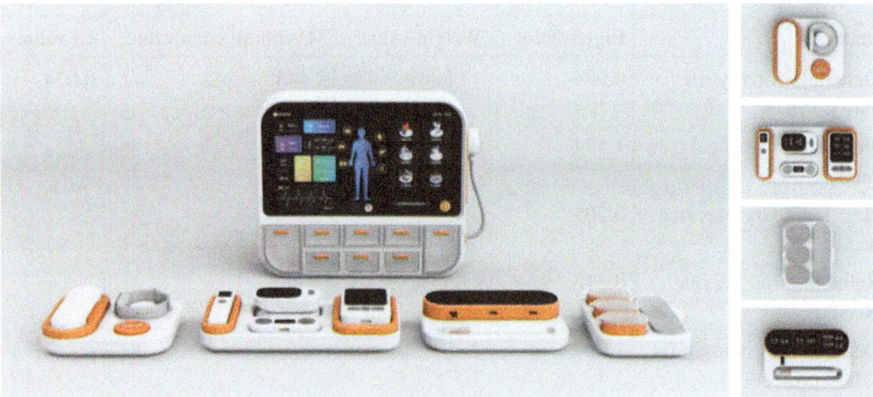

Fig. 2. Product Effect Diagram

To establish a set of home health management system for the disabled elderly, called AGCARE, for the disabled elderly real-time monitoring of the physical condition, suggesting which indicators are not at the normal level, and give assessment recommendations; can detect eight basic physical indicators; provide remote diagnosis of disease management, provide management programs, matching doctors; medication management, record all prescriptions, prompting the disabled elderly to take the appropriate medication on time; to provide psychological counseling services, but also self-testing of the state of mind (Fig. 3).

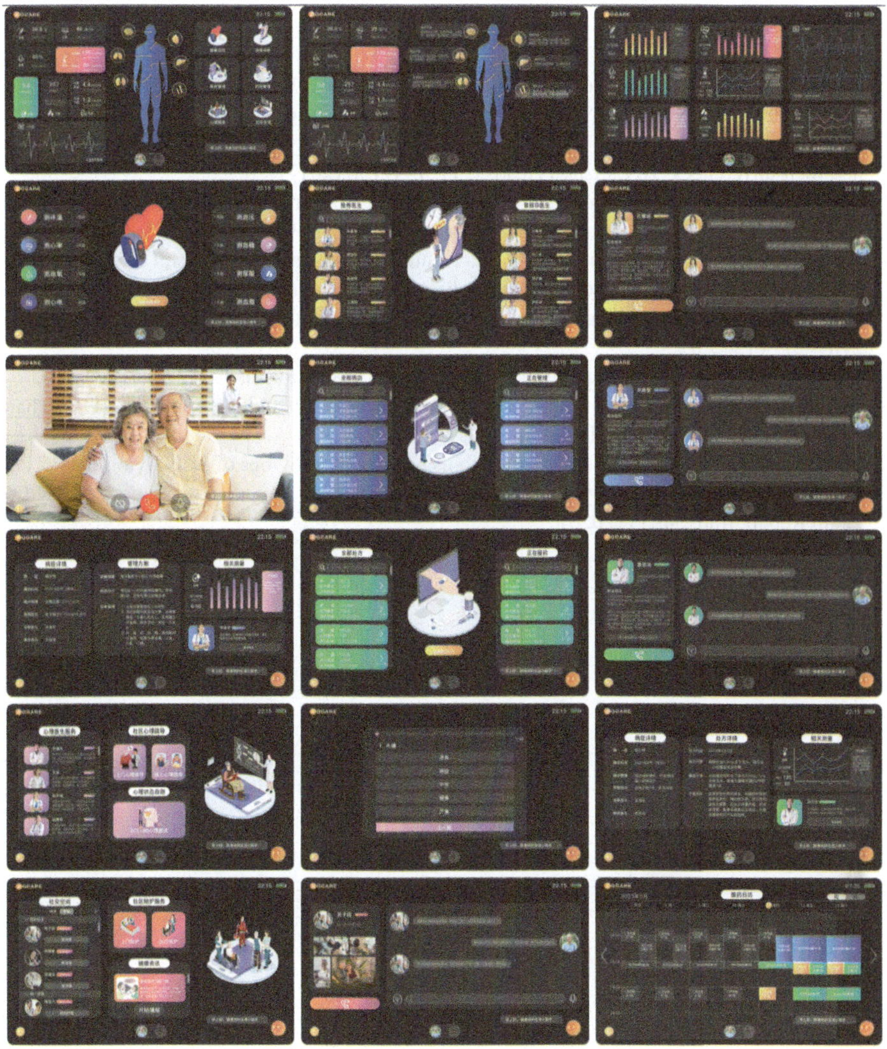

Fig. 3. Part of the product interface show

6 Conclusions

Firstly, Maslow's hierarchy of needs theory was introduced to analyze the physiological and psychological needs of the disabled elderly, and seven types of needs were summarized. Second, a questionnaire is designed to analyze the priority of needs. Finally, product system design is carried out around the community safety protection and medical care needs with higher weight in the priority ranking, outputting the design of AGCARE community health and safety management system for the disabled elderly, which provides a design case reference for the construction of ageing-adapted community service system.

References

1. Ping, G.: Analysis of data from the 2006 China Urban and Rural Elderly Population Status Tracking Survey [M]. China Social Publishing House, Beijing (2009)
2. Yang, C., Vincent, M.O.R.: The care needs of disabled elderly people: degree of unmet needs and their differences [J]. Lanzhou Acad. J. **11**, 144–156 (2017)
3. Danxian, W., Xiaolu, G.: Analysis of unsatisfied needs for home disabled elderly care: a perspective based on spatial resource linking [J]. Int. Urban Plann. **35**(01), 55–62 (2020)
4. Zongzhuang, L., Lijia, J., Xin, W., et al.: A study on the satisfaction level and influencing factors of daily life care needs of elderly disabled individuals living at home in rural areas of China from the perspective of family resource endowment [J]. Modern Prev. Med. **49**(15), 2789–2794 (2022)
5. Maslow, A.H.: A theory of human motivation. Psychol. Rev. **50**(4), 370–396 (1943)
6. Mustofa, A.Z.: Hierarchy of human needs: a humanistic psychology approach of Abraham Maslow. Kawanua Int. J. Multicult. Stud. **3**(2), 30–35 (2022)
7. Pashmdarfard, M., Azad, A.: Assessment tools to evaluate activities of daily living (ADL) and instrumental activities of daily living (IADL) in older adults: A systematic review[J]. Med. J. Islam Repub. Iran. **34**, 33 (2020)

Agriculture (I)

Empowering Farmers: Ergonomics in Pesticide Risks Prevention and Health at Work

Goutille Fabienne[1,2](✉)

[1] Epicene, Bordeaux Population Health Center, INSERM (U1219), Université de Bordeaux - ISPED Case 11, 146 rue Léo Saignat, 33076 Bordeaux Cedex, France
Fabienne.goutille@uca.fr
[2] Laboratoire ACTé (EA 4281), Université Clermont Auvergne, 3, rue de la Chébarde, BP60104, 63178 Aubière Cedex, France

Abstract. This study explores integrating farmers' expertise into occupational health policies to manage pesticide risks. Using the Prevexpo intervention-research project, it highlights the benefits of collaborative prevention strategies. Combining ergonomic and anthropological methods, it demonstrates that involving farmers enhances their capacity for innovation and improves health outcomes, ultimately fostering more sustainable agricultural practices.

Keywords: Pesticide Risk Management · Collaborative research · Occupational Health · Farmers work activity · Sustainable Agriculture

1 Introduction

Current policies for managing pesticide-related risks pose a significant challenge: reconciling formal exposure assessment models with the complex realities of agricultural practices. These policies often overlook the expertise and participation of farmers in developing effective preventive measures. This gap raises a crucial question: how can farmers' experience and knowledge be fully integrated into occupational health policies, particularly in the context of pesticide risk prevention?

To address this inquiry and provide support to workers engaged, we initiated collaborative research (Myers 2018). In a continuation of the work of Quandt et al. (2001) on pesticide prevention, farmers and researchers came together, forming an Expanded Community of Research-Intervention (ECRI) (Oddone et al. 2020; Goutille 2022). This article explores this question by examining how farmers' involvement can be integrated into occupational health policies through ECRI. Drawing on data collected during the Prevexpo intervention-research project and its accompanying film (Girardot-Pennors 2022), this study analyzes vineyard treatment practices from the perspectives of both researchers and winegrowers. By intertwining these viewpoints, it aims to foster a mutual understanding of this activity.

The analysis highlights the challenges faced by the CERI in understanding and transforming work practices to reduce pesticide-related risks and to improve health of farmers. Balancing the toxic perception of plant protection products and their role in

S. Jin et al. (Eds.): IEA 2024, SSDI 39, pp. 165–168, 2025.
https://doi.org/10.1007/978-981-95-0211-0_25

productivity, winegrowers navigate complex compromises between plant health and human well-being. Through an ergonomic lens, this study proposes prevention strategies developed in collaboration with farmers based on their practices, with the goal of enhancing their capacity for action, innovation, and ultimately, their health. Incorporating a developmental ergotoxicology perspective, this study examines the integration of farmers into pesticide risk prevention policies. Ergonomic and anthropological methods reveal complex exposures, empowering farmers to develop context-specific preventive measures. Collective action fosters transformative practices, emphasizing human, plant, and environmental health. This approach decentralizes risk management, promoting sustainability in agriculture.

2 Method

The Prevexpo intervention-research project adopted an ergotoxicological approach (Sznelwar 1992; Garrigou 2011; Galey et al. 2019) focusing on personal and collective agency. Farmers acted as participants in the intervention research, engaging according to their values and aspirations. Ergonomic and anthropological methods were combined to understand the determinants of exposure. The system for characterizing and transforming pesticide-related risk conditions was designed to support farmers' agency, enabling them to develop effective regulations balancing production outcomes and self-protection (Mollo 2022).

As intervening researchers, we assumed a third-party role, collaborating with wine professionals in toxic environments to identify critical conditions and transform them into safe ones. We sought to support farmers in managing competing objectives, repairing damage, avoiding threats, and implementing contextually adapted plans. By participating in collective activities mobilizing subjectivity and addressing real work challenges, we provided farmers with ergotoxicological methods to facilitate the transformation of their work-related issues.

The transformative intervention-research of Prevexpo involved the pooling and sometimes confronting of general and local knowledge among members of the CERI. This community, formed during the research, included farmers, their associates, and researchers from various disciplines. It leveraged professional experience and scientific knowledge to identify and resolve nuisances.

The study is based on 5 years of involvement in the French wine industry, including 70 interviews on the use of plant protection products and pesticide exposure. Winegrowers and researchers compared their perspectives on the "Grand Narrative" through their "small stories." Quantitative and qualitative methods were combined to produce occupational health knowledge, with winegrowers involved at all stages of the research.

Filmed observations of treatment activities and pesticide metrology were recorded over two to three full days in five research enterprises. Various pesticide tracers were used to measure exposure. The CERI selected three sampling techniques: surface sampling, patch sampling, and atmospheric sampling. Documentation of pesticide exposure was developed based on the winegrowers' questions and concerns, with metrology taking the form of "constructed" or "popular" metrology. Winegrowers chose sampling points, conducted observations, and developed new practices to mitigate exposure.

The proposed method for risk prevention and occupational health promotion involved six steps: (1) Engage professionals in action against exposure. (2) Initiate dialogue beyond targeted risks. (3) Support contextualization of risk conditions. (4) Involve professionals in reflexive activities. (5) Support collective action in creation. (6) Encourage professionals to share and promote their activities.

3 Main Results

Ergotoxicological tools revealed exposure to multiple chemical agents and decomposition products in workspaces and agricultural operations. Pesticide residues were found on equipment, personal protective equipment, and in living spaces. Collective analysis showed that winegrowers are constantly in contact with polluted environments, with exposure occurring during and beyond the handling of products and preparation of treatments.

Farmers, at the core of the approach, explored ways to transform critical conditions at the intersection of contradictory demands. Shared analysis invited the CERI to address dysfunctions in the production system and regulatory issues. Workshops highlighted the complexity of treatment activities and identified determinants limiting pesticide risk prevention in real work, such as product container design, safety data sheets, equipment ergonomics, and personal protective equipment limitations.

Prescriptions designed and regulated in social, political, and scientific spheres induce measures that restrict the use of plant protection products without promoting occupational health in the wine industry. Innovations in production rules, safety equipment, and treatment technologies often prioritize economic performance over human capacity to modify norms and life projects. Multi-scale analysis demonstrated that technological advances, territorial constraints, and environmental obligations contribute to pesticide-related risk conditions. Changing the representation of exposure encourages the analysis of systemic factors without denying farmers' responsibility in producing exposure.

The developmental ergotoxicological approach allowed winegrowers to discuss individual challenges related to balancing productivity and self-preservation. Their meetings fostered the sharing of strategies to reduce critical situations caused by regulated production and prevention systems. Practical workshops facilitated concrete transformations in treatment and protection materials, combining performance and health.

4 Discussion and Conclusion

In conclusion, to understand and prevent real exposures to pesticides, it is necessary to decentralize risk assessment and prevention. Users of plant protection products must become co-authors of prevention measures and be include to design health at work programs. Our work shows that the involvement of stakeholders in the analysis of risk situations allows them (and) us to take ownership and develop prevention approaches. Collaborative actions on the field helps farmers to objectify and address risks, transforming their "vehicle body" of pesticides (Mohammed-Brahim 2009) into an "acting body" (for health). An active body that builds work and prevention practices for human, plant and environmental health.

The ergonomic approach with a developmental aim proposed in this study contributes significantly to occupational risk prevention by producing specific and situated data on exposures and by supporting professionals in the development of new prevention and protection practices at work along the career along. It encourages farmers to intervene in technical and preventive systems, promoting their capacity for innovation at different spatial, temporal and political scales.

Thus, this active and collaborative research demonstrates that integrating farmers into the process of preventing risks not only improves the health and well-being of agricultural workers, but also strengthens the sustainability of agricultural practices.

References

Galey, L., Judon, N., Jolly, C., Goutille, F., Morelot, S., Albert, M., Lhospital, O., Martin, P., Noel-Suberville, C., Pasquereau, P., Aublet-Cuvelier, A., Mohammed-Brahim, B., Garrigou, A.: Proposition méthodologique en ergotoxicologie pour révéler les expositions à des produits chimiques. Activités. **16**(1) (2019). https://doi.org/10.4000/activites.4103

Garrigou, A.: Le développement de l'ergotoxicologie. In: Une contribution de l'ergonomie à la santé au travail. Habilitation à diriger des recherches. Université de Bordeaux, Bordeaux (2011)

Girardot-Pennors, H.: Rémanences. Construction d'une communauté de recherche élargie. [Film documentaire]. 63 min. Université de Bordeaux (2022). https://www.youtube.com/watch?v=mvmYLDz-RbE

Goutille F.: Ne plus ignorer les agriculteurs : une contribution de l'ergonomie à la prévention du risque pesticides en milieu viticole. [PHD thesis]. Université de Bordeaux (2022). http://www.theses.fr/2022BORD0079/document

Mohammed-Brahim, B.: Travailler en présence de substances toxiques : un corps à corps au quotidien. Corps. **6**, 53–59 (2009). https://doi.org/10.3917/corp.006.0053

Mollo, V.: Cultiver la diversité pour développer l'agentivité. La réflexivité dans la démarche ergonomique" Activités [En ligne], 20-1 | 2023, mis en ligne le 15 avril 2023 (2022). http://journals.openedition.org/activites/8476

Myers, K.: Collaborative research: history from below. In: Facer, K., Dunleavy, K. (eds.) Connected Communities Foundation Series, pp. 1–49. University of Bristol (2018)

Oddone I, Marri G, Gloria S, Briante, G, Chiatella, M, Re, A. Ambiente de trabalho: a luta dos trabalhadores pela saúde., 2.ª ed. rev. ampl. Hucitec; 1981 (2020)

Quandt, S.A., Arcury, T.A., Pell, A.I.: Something for everyone? A community and academic partnership to address farmworker pesticide exposure in North Carolina. Environ. Health Perspect. **109 Suppl 3**(Suppl 3), 435–441 (2001). https://doi.org/10.1289/ehp.01109s3435. PMID: 11427393; PMCID: PMC1240562

Sznelwar, L.I.: Analyse ergonomique de l'exposition de travailleurs agricoles aux pesticides : essai ergotoxicologique. Thèse de doctorat en ergonomie, CNAM de Paris, Paris (1992)

Analysis of Musculoskeletal Pain Among Colombian - Flower Growers

Yordán Rodríguez[1](✉), Jonathan Osorio-Vasco[2], and Elizabeth Pérez[3]

[1] National School of Public Health, Universidad de Antioquia, Medellin, Colombia
yordan.rodriguez@udea.edu.co

[2] Politécnico Colombiano Jaime Isaza Cadavid, Medellin, Colombia

[3] Grupo de Investigación y Desarrollo en Ergonomía, Ergoyes: Comunidad de Ergonomía, Medellín, Colombia
elizabeth.perez@ergoyes.com

Abstract. Colombia is one of the world's leading flower-producing and exporting countries. As a result, many people, including small farmers, work in flower production, contributing significantly to local communities' economic stability. This study focused on analyzing the development of musculoskeletal pain in 37 Colombian flower growers at the beginning and end of a typical workday. This cross-sectional study used a body map to record pain in 21 body parts and a visual analog scale to measure pain intensity. The Wilcoxon signed-rank test analyzed changes in musculoskeletal pain intensity between the beginning and end of the workday, categorizing pain as mild (≤10 mm), moderate (>10 mm and ≤20 mm), or severe (>20 mm). Additionally, changes were further classified based on the percentage increase in pain, with mild (≤25%), moderate (>25% and ≤50%), and severe (>50%) levels. Significant increases in musculoskeletal pain were observed in 17 body parts, with the highest increases reported in the right hand-wrist, right ankle-foot, lower back, and right shoulder. The intensity of musculoskeletal pain at the end of the workday was moderate for 15 body parts, while for six body parts, it was mild. The average percentage change of musculoskeletal pain was severe in 20 body parts, while in the left elbow, it was moderate. The study underscores the importance of implementing ergonomic improvements in work practices to prevent musculoskeletal disorders, thereby enhancing the health and productivity of workers in this key export industry.

Keywords: Musculoskeletal Disorders · Physical Workload · Work Fatigue · Standing Work · Future of Work

1 Introduction

Colombia is the second largest flower producer in the world after Holland, with a 17% share of the global market [1]. During 2022, the Colombian flower industry exported US$ 2052 million and 317,000 tons of flowers [1], with the United States being the main destination for Colombian flowers (79% of exports [2]. This industry generates 200,000 direct and indirect jobs, 60–70% of which women hold [1, 2]. Antioquia, a department of Colombia, accounts for 27% of domestic flower production [2].

S. Jin et al. (Eds.): IEA 2024, SSDI 39, pp. 169–174, 2025.
https://doi.org/10.1007/978-981-95-0211-0_26

Despite the encouraging economic scenario for flower production in Colombia, there are reports of exposure to risk factors such as work activities with high demand for repetitive movements, grips with force requirements, forced postures of upper and lower limbs for prolonged periods, and high demand in the pace of work resulting in musculoskeletal symptoms and musculoskeletal disorders of occupational origin [3–5].

The objective of this study was to analyze the development of musculoskeletal pain reported by 37 Colombian flower growers in the department of Antioquia between the beginning and the end of an 8-h typical workday.

2 Methodology

A cross-sectional study was conducted in two flower companies in the Antioquia department, Colombia. The sample of 37 workers (n = 20 for company 1, n = 17 for company 2) was selected at convenience. The evaluation was conducted at the beginning and end of an 8-h workday, and the information collection lasted 3 days for each company. The workers participated voluntarily and signed an informed consent.

The body map proposed in ISO/TS 2064628 [6] was applied at the beginning and end of the workday to record pain perception. Twenty-one body parts were evaluated: neck, upper back, lower back, and the right and left of the shoulder, arm, elbow, forearm, hand-wrist, thigh-hip, knee, leg, and ankle-foot.

For the statistical report on the sociodemographic variables, such as sex, age, height, weight, and length of service, descriptive statistics such as mean and standard deviation were used. The Body Mass Index (BMI) was categorized according to the ranges established by the World Health Organization [7].

A visual analog scale (VAS) was used to evaluate the intensity of musculoskeletal pain (0 mm: no pain and 100 mm: maximum pain) [8]. The average was used to analyze musculoskeletal pain intensity, and the difference between the beginning and end of the workday was calculated for each body part. Also, the percentage change between the averages was calculated (see Eq. 1).

$$\Delta D\% = ((D2--D1)/D1) \times 100 \quad (1)$$

Where: D1 is musculoskeletal pain at the beginning of the working day, and D2 is at the end.

The Wilcoxon signed-rank test was used to analyze the differences in pain intensity between the beginning and end of the workday. Three ranges were established to show pain intensity levels by body zone: mild pain $\leq$10 mm (green), moderate pain >10 mm and $\leq$20 mm (yellow), and severe pain >20 mm (red).

Based on the percentage change in musculoskeletal pain, three ranges were established: mild pain $\leq$25% (green), moderate pain >25% and $\leq$50% (yellow), and severe pain >50% (red).

For the graphic representation of musculoskeletal pain and generation of figures of the body map, the Ergonomic Evaluation Platform developed by Ergoyes (www.ergoyes.com) was used.

3 Results

A total of 37 workers (23 men and 14 women) participated in the study, with an average of 33.46 years (SD = 8.99), average height of 163.18 cm (SD = 8.23), average weight of 63.25 kg (SD = 9.43), average length of service at the time of the study was 48.32 months (SD = 66) and the BMI report was: normal or healthy weight 67.6%, overweight 27% and obese 5.4%.

The difference in the average musculoskeletal pain intensity for the 21 body parts was positive, reflecting the increase in pain at the end of the workday (see Table 1).

Table 1. Average change, intensity, level, percentage increase, and difference in musculoskeletal pain between the beginning and end of the day (n = 37, *P < 0.05).

Body part		Pain intensity (beginning)	Pain intensity (end)	Difference	% Difference	Wilcoxon test	
						Z	P
Neck	–	4.1892	10.5405	6.351	151.611	–3.266	0.001*
Upper back	–	7.0270	11.3784	4.351	61.924	–1.871	0.061
Low back	–	4.4054	17.1892	12.784	290.185	–4.544	0.000*
Shoulder	Right	3.6757	16.9189	13.243	360.291	–3.308	0.000*
	Left	2.6757	10.9189	8.243	308.076	–2.712	0.007*
Upper arm	Right	3.1351	11.3514	8.216	262.075	–2.384	0.017*
	Left	4.1622	9.0541	4.892	117.532	–1.788	0.074
Elbow	Right	0.7351	6.2703	5.535	752.986	–3.726	0.000*
	Left	2.7568	4.0270	1.270	46.075	–0.705	0.481
Forearm	Right	2.1892	9.5135	7.324	334.565	–2.837	0.005*
	Left	2.8919	7.2432	4.351	150.465	–1.579	0.114
Hand-wrist	Right	1.9730	19.7568	17.784	901.358	–3.963	0.000*
	Left	5.7027	15.1351	9.432	165.402	–2.891	0.004*
Thigh-hip	Right	2.6486	12.5946	9.946	375.519	–2.985	0.003*
	Left	2.6216	11.1892	8.568	326.808	–3.127	0.002*
Knee	Right	5.5946	10.6000	5.005	89.468	–2.055	0.040*
	Left	4.2703	9.9459	5.676	132.909	–2.018	0.044*
Leg	Right	2.9459	14.7568	11.811	400.927	–4.088	0.000*
	Left	4.6757	12.2432	7.568	161.847	–3.470	0.001*
Ankle-foot	Right	3.0270	17.8108	14.784	488.398	–3.990	0.000*
	Left	4.6486	14.1892	9.541	205.236	–2.558	0.011*

Significant differences in musculoskeletal pain were found between the beginning and end of the workday in 17 body segments (see Table 1). The body segments that changed significantly were the neck, lower back, and on the right side of the body: shoulder, arm, elbow, forearm, hand-wrist, thigh-hip, knee, leg, ankle-foot; and the left side of the body: shoulder, hand-wrist, thigh-hip, knee, leg, ankle-foot.

The intensity of musculoskeletal pain at the end of the workday was moderate for 15 body parts, while for six body parts, it was mild (see Table 1). The body parts with the highest intensity of musculoskeletal pain at the end of the workday were the right-hand wrist (19,756), right ankle-foot (17,818), lower back (17,189), and right shoulder (16,918). In Fig. 1, the level of pain intensity is represented with colors.

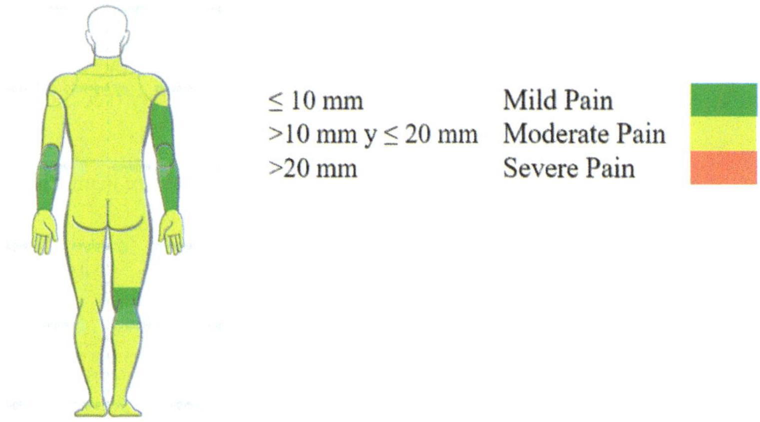

Fig. 1. Average level of musculoskeletal pain recorded at the end of the workday (n = 37). Source: Developed using the Ergoyes ergonomic evaluation platform. (www.ergoyes.com).

The average percentage change in musculoskeletal pain was positive in all 21 body parts analyzed (see Table 1). The average percentage change of musculoskeletal pain was severe in 20 body parts, while in the left elbow, it was moderate (see Fig. 2).

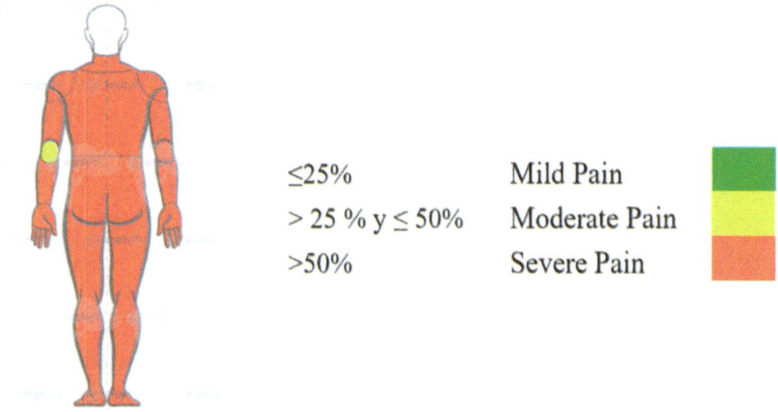

Fig. 2. Average percentage change in musculoskeletal pain. (n = 37). Source: Developed using the Ergoyes ergonomic evaluation platform. (www.ergoyes.com).

4 Discussion

This study shows that the flower grower population analyzed presented symptoms of musculoskeletal pain in several body parts and that the increase in pain between the beginning and the end of the workday was significant.

It should be noted that the body parts with the greatest intensity of pain reported were the shoulder, ankle-foot, and lower back on the right side. These results correspond to the awkward postures that workers must adopt during their work (see Fig. 3). Similar results in the Colombian floricultural population have been reported previously [4].

Fig. 3. Flower growers at work.

A limitation of this study is that the sample size of the population of flower growers studied is not significant. Therefore, further studies should expand the sample size and consider other types of sampling that include other flower-producing geographic areas of the country.

Finally, the results indicate the need to carry out more in-depth ergonomic analyses to improve flower growers' working and health conditions.

5 Conclusions

This research illustrates the increased musculoskeletal pain throughout a typical workday among Colombian flower growers, particularly in regions like the hand-wrist, shoulder, ankle-foot, and lower back. The study underscores the importance of implementing ergonomic improvements in work practices to prevent musculoskeletal disorders, thereby enhancing the health and productivity of workers in this key export industry. Significant increases in musculoskeletal pain were observed in 17 body parts, with the highest increases reported in the right hand-wrist, right ankle-foot, lower back, and right shoulder.

References

1. Ministerio de Agricultura y Desarrollo Rural: Las flores del ‘ País de la Belleza ’ conquistan el mundo con calidad [Internet]. 2023 [citado el 31 de mayo de 2024]. Recuperado a partir de: https://shorturl.at/9s8h4
2. Instituto Colombiano Agropecuario – ICA: Con 700 millones de tallos, Colombia aporta variedad, color y belleza a la celebración de San Valentín [Internet]. 2024 [citado el 31 de mayo de 2024]. Recuperado a partir de: https://www.ica.gov.co/noticias/ica-colombia-exporta-flores-san-valentin-2024
3. Hernández, D., Wilder, A., Orjuela R, M.E.: Factores laborales y extralaborales de floricultores con Síndrome del Túnel del Carpo. Cundinamarca-Colombia 2013. Med. Segur. Trab (Madr). **62**, 199–211 (2016)
4. Orozco Vásquez, M.M., Zuluaga Ramírez, Y.C., Campos Guzmán, N.R.: Sintomatología musculoesquelética entrabajadores de postcosecha de un cultivo deflores de Cundinamarca. Rev. Asoc. Esp. Med. Trab. **31**, 127–246 (2022)
5. Kong, Y.K., Lee, S.J., Lee, K.S., Kim, G.R., Kim, D.M.: Development of an ergonomics checklist for investigation of work-related whole-body disorders in farming - AWBA: agricultural whole-body assessment. J. Agric. Saf. Health. **21**, 207–215 (2015)
6. ISO: TECHNICAL SPECIFICATION ISO / TS Ergonomics guidelines for the optimization of musculoskeletal workload (2014)
7. Organización Mundial de la Salud: Obesidad y sobrepeso. 2020 [Internet]. Nota Descr. N°311. 2021 [citado el 7 de febrero de 2023]. Recuperado a partir de: https://www.who.int/es/news-room/fact-sheets/detail/obesity-and-overweight#:~:text=En el caso de los,igual o superior a 30
8. Price, D.D., McGrath, P.A., Rafii, A., Buckingham, B.: The validation of visual analogue scales as ratio scale measures for chronic and experimental pain. Pain. **17**, 45–56 (1983)

AI (I)

Improving Surgical Safety by Deep Learning Approaches for Enhanced Gauze Detection in Laparoscopic Procedures: A Case Study

Benkun Chen[1,2], Lichen Wang[1], Beiming Song[1], Di Liu[1,2(✉)], Rong Yin[1,2(✉)], and Kang Li[1,2(✉)]

[1] Industrial Engineering, Pittsburgh Institute, Sichuan University, Chengdu, China
{di.liu,rong.yin}@scupi.cn, likang@wchscu.cn

[2] West China Biomedical Big Data Center, Sichuan University, Chengdu, China

Abstract. Laparoscopic surgery is a minimally invasive surgical procedure that is commonly used with several advantages over traditional open surgery for a variety of medical procedures. However, in some cases, gauze is left in the abdominal cavity and may lead to serious inflammatory reactions caused by foreign bodies and intestinal obstruction by intraluminal migration, which will have catastrophic repercussions. Since laparoscopes use lenses to enter and illuminate the view inside the patient's body, the images and videos could be analyzed by using Computer Vision Technology (CVT) to identify and track surgical instruments. This study focuses on reducing medical errors by enhancing gauze detection during laparoscopic surgery using three deep learning models, which are U-Net, U-Net++, and Trans-U-Net models, designed for image segmentation tasks. The performance of these models is evaluated using four metrics to compare the effectiveness of these three semantic recognition techniques. The results indicate that U-Net++ and Trans-U-Net have better overall performance and higher precision compared to U-Net, which is likely due to their improved feature extraction capabilities and ability to capture more complex patterns within surgical imagery. In addition, the Trans-U-Net model has the best performance according to the comprehensive evaluations. The findings of this research are expected to assist in reducing the mental workload of surgeons in monitoring and memorizing the location of gauze and enabling the surgeons to focus more on the surgical procedures, thus reducing the risk of adverse events and enhancing patient safety in laparoscopic surgery within clinical practice.

Keywords: Computer Vision Technology (CVT) · Laparoscopic Surgery · Machine Learning · Medical Errors · Gauze Detection

1 Introduction

Laparoscopic surgery is a minimally invasive surgical procedure that is commonly used for a variety of medical procedures, including appendectomy, adrenal tumor removal, differential diagnosis of liver disease, ovarian cyst removal, hysterectomy, and so on [1].

S. Jin et al. (Eds.): IEA 2024, SSDI 39, pp. 177–182, 2025.
https://doi.org/10.1007/978-981-95-0211-0_27

Typically, laparoscopes use 10 mm or smaller lenses that enter the patient's body and emit light on the lenses by fiber optics to illuminate the view inside human body. The images collected from the lenses are then projected on an external screen through various microsensors [2]. Through three to five tiny incisions in the patient's abdomen or one incision in the navel, the surgeon operates the surgical instruments and delivers drugs and surgical equipment to the patient's body, such as specialized surgical tools and a camera. These surgical tools differ from standard surgical tools in that they are typically configured specifically for laparoscopic surgery, enabling the surgeon to manipulate them inside the body using just a thin rod [3]. The camera provides a high-definition view of the surgical site, allowing the surgeon to perform the procedure with precision and accuracy. During laparoscopic surgery, the surgeon has to use the laparoscope to assess the position of surgical sites and maneuver the surgical tools in a small area to complete the procedure and guarantee the patient's safety.

Laparoscopic surgery offers several advantages over traditional open surgery, including less scarring, reduced pain and bleeding, shorter hospital stays, and faster recovery times [4]. However, in some cases, adverse events such as medication administrations errors exist [5]; as well as gauzes being left in the abdominal cavity and may lead to serious inflammatory reactions caused by foreign bodies and intestinal obstruction by intraluminal migration [6], which will have catastrophic repercussions. Thus, this study focuses on reducing medical errors by enhancing gauze detection during laparoscopic surgery. Since the lenses are used during the surgery to illuminate the view inside the patient's body, the images and videos could be analyzed by using Computer Vision Technology (CVT) to identify and track surgical instruments, thereby reducing the risk of adverse events occurring due to gauze being unintentionally left in patient's body. This study aims to evaluate the efficacy of several machine learning methods in gauze detection during laparoscopic surgery using CVT.

CVT is a field of artificial intelligence (AI) that uses machine learning and neural networks to teach computers to process videos and images to identify and extract information [7], which has been extensively studied by researchers aimed to apply in the medical field. A study proposed an approach that uses a multimodal convolutional neural network to detect the surgical tools in the videos of minimally invasive surgery [8], marking an exploratory instance of using deep neural networks (DNNs) for detecting surgical instruments. In the meantime, fully convolutional networks (FCNs) and weakly supervised learning could be used to detect and localize the surgical tools without explicit spatial annotations. However, these methods are restricted to surgical tools with fixed morphologies and are not suitable for detecting those with changeable morphologies, such as gauze. For detecting gauzes, several researchers used some popular medical imaging algorithms, such as YOLOv3 [9], YOLOv5x6 [10], and U-Net [11], and the results indicated that the U-Net algorithm had better performance. Thus, in this study, the algorithm U-Net and its variations U-Net++ [11] and Trans-U-Net are evaluated to identify gauze from the dataset. The trained models were applied to the testing dataset for evaluating their performance based on the following metrics: mean Intersection over Union (IoU), mean precision, mean recall, and mean F1-Score, which are commonly used to evaluate the accuracy of the semantic segmentation algorithm in different aspects. The findings of this research are expected to assist in reducing the risk of adverse events and enhancing patient safety in laparoscopic surgery within clinical practice. The results are anticipated to aid surgeons in locating gauze during minimally invasive laparoscopic surgeries, reducing the mental workload of surgeons in monitoring and memorizing the location of gauze, and enabling the surgeons to focus more on the surgical procedures.

2 Methods

In this study, we used the video frames from a publicly available dataset provided in 2022, which consists of 42 video files (30 with gauze presence, and 12 without gauze presence) collected in different settings [9]. The segmentation dataset was designed to simulate various surgical scenarios in laparoscopic surgery, which included absence of gauze, absence of gauze with tools presence, presence of a unique clean gauze and tools, presence of a unique stained gauze and tools, and presence of multiple gauzes in different states (see Fig. 1) [9].

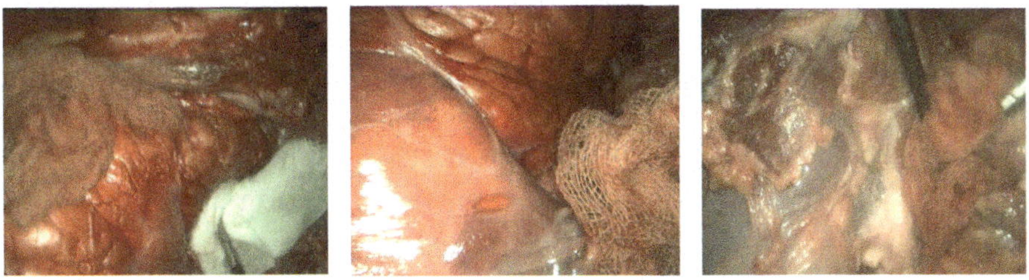

Fig. 1. Examples of video frames from the dataset

The gauze shown in the video frame was manually labeled with a binary mask to represent the gauze (in white) and background (in black) using LabelMe. Among the 2000 labeled images in the dataset, 850 images were discarded due to poor labeling or poor performance. For the remaining 1150 images, 1000 were randomly selected for model training, and 150 were used for model testing. Three semantic segmentation algorithms (i.e., U-Net, U-Net++, and Trans-U-Net) were used to forecast images with white and black format (see Fig. 2) since these models are capable of learning from a relatively small training set. Thus, the contrast between the labeled and predicted images can show the performance of these algorithms.

The trained models were applied to the testing dataset for evaluating the performance based on the following metrics: mean Intersection over Union (IoU), mean precision, mean recall, and mean F1-Score, which are commonly used to evaluate the accuracy of the semantic segmentation algorithm in different aspects.

3 Results

Table 1 summarizes the evaluation results of the three deep learning models. The legend "gauze" refers to the detection of either the areas that were labeled as gauze or the area that the algorithm automatically recognized as gauze; "background" refers to the detection of the area in the image other than the gauze; "mean" represents the average accuracy of "gauze" and "background" detection.

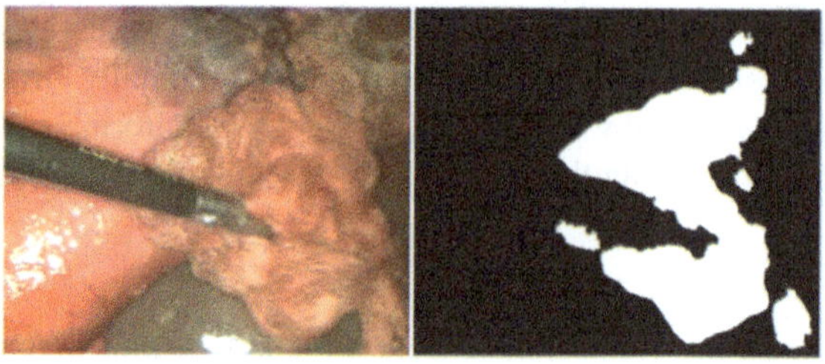

Fig. 2. An example of the application with U-Net model

Table 1. Results of deep learning methods

Model	Object	IoU	Recall	Precision	F1-score
U-Net	Gauze	68.74%	**91.27%**	73.59%	81.48%
	Background	90.15%	92.06%	**97.75%**	94.82%
	Mean	79.44%	91.66%	85.67%	88.56%
U-Net++	Gauze	81.63%	87.85%	**93.15%**	90.42%
	Background	**93.39%**	**97.44%**	94.91%	96.16%
	Mean	87.51%	92.57%	**94.03%**	93.29%
Trans-U-Net	Gauze	**82.93%**	89.58%	91.64%	**90.60%**
	Background	92.79%	96.94%	96.12%	**96.53%**
	Mean	**87.86%**	**93.16%**	93.78%	**93.47%**

Overall, among the four metrics, the Trans-U-Net model performs the best in three metrics, with results of 87.86%, 93.16%, and 93.47% for mean IoU, mean recall, and mean F1-Score, respectively. For mean precision, the U-Net++ model performs the best, achieving a result of 94.03%.

Meanwhile, since one of the main objectives of this study is recognizing the gauze rather than the background, the results of IoU, precision, recall, and F1-Score for recognizing gauze are also compared for the three models. The IoU for gauze indicates that the Trans-U-Net model performs the best with a value of 82.93%, while the results for the U-Net model and the U-Net++ model are 68.74% and 81.63%, respectively. The recall for gauze shows that the U-Net model has the highest value of 91.27%; however, the performance of the U-Net++ model and the Trans-U-Net model are close to the U-Net model, which are 87.85% and 89.58%, respectively. The U-Net++ model has the highest precision for gauze at 93.15%, followed by the Trans-U-Net model at 91.64% and the U-Net model at 73.59%. The Trans-U-Net model has the highest F1-Score for gauze 90.60%, while the U-Net model and the U-Net++ model have values of 81.48% and 90.42%, respectively.

4 Discussion

In this study, three machine learning (ML) methods for gauze detection during laparoscopic surgery were compared and evaluated using four indices. As the primary performance indicator, the Intersection over Union (IoU) value provides a comprehensive assessment of the semantic segmentation algorithm. Traditionally, target detection is considered accurate when the IoU value exceeds or equals 0.5. Although for the detection of gauze in laparoscopic surgeries, an IoU threshold of 0.5 alone may not sufficiently mitigate risks and safeguard patients. A previous study of Sanchez-Brizuela et al. (2022) obtained an IoU value of more than 85% in their experiments by using the U-Net model [9]. The results of our study reached a relatively good IoU of 87.51% and 87.86% for the U-Net++ model and the Trans-U-Net model, respectively, indicating that these two models could be considered for detecting gauze in routine minimally invasive laparoscopic surgeries.

For most of the evaluation metrics, the results of the Trans-U-Net model and the U-Net++ model are close to each other; however, the U-Net model did not perform as well as the other two models. This finding is likely due to the Trans-U-Net model and the U-Net++ model improved feature extraction capabilities and ability to capture more complex patterns within laparoscopic surgical imagery. Meantime, the Trans-U-Net model has the best performance for the recognition of gauze alone and overall detection of both gauze and background in laparoscopic surgery. Therefore, the results suggest that the Trans-U-Net model has the best effectiveness and performance based on the comprehensive evaluations.

Using Computer Vision Technology (CVT) to identify and track surgical instruments based on the images and videos during the surgery has drawn broad attention from other researchers [7–11]. This study is considered an application example for research on the use of ML in the medical field and introduces a methodology for improving surgical safety with automatic gauze detection in laparoscopic procedures. Even though the accuracy rates for correctly detecting the gauze in the images are relatively high for the three ML methods in this study, we did not discuss if the methods could be used for real-time monitoring of the laparoscopic surgical process. Future studies should examine how the object detection speed of those deep learning models impacts their feasibility for use during surgeries. The detection speed may also be a critical factor that impacts patients' safety, particularly under emergent scenarios requiring swift decisions such as massive bleeding during the operation.

Another potential limitation of this study is that the surgery videos we applied were sourced from one dataset designed for testing the gauze detection algorithm under different conditions [9]. Thus, the videos were recreated in a laparoscopic simulator using animal organs instead of surgical operations on real patients. Future studies may verify the model performance across other laparoscopic datasets. Meanwhile, the performance of other deep learning models, such as the recently proposed YOLOv10 [12], may be evaluated, particularly regarding the model's effectiveness and efficiency.

5 Conclusion

This study examined the effectiveness and performance of three semantic recognition techniques for gauze detection in laparoscopic surgery. The outcomes of this study are expected to provide insights for (i) enhancing patient safety during laparoscopic surgery, (ii) reducing the mental workload of surgeons in monitoring and memorizing the location of gauze, and (iii) enabling the surgeons to focus more on the surgical procedures.

Acknowledgements. This research is partially supported by funding from the 1-3-5 project for disciplines of excellence at West China Hospital, Sichuan University.

References

1. Longmore, S.K., Naik, G., Gargiulo, G.D.: Laparoscopic robotic surgery: current perspective and future directions. Robotics. **9**(2), 42 (2020)
2. Limb, C., Rockall, T.: Principles of laparoscopic surgery. Surgery (Oxford). **41**(2), 106–116 (2023)
3. Ahmed, I., Paraskeva, P.: A clinical review of single-incision laparoscopic surgery. Surgeon. **9**(6), 341–351 (2011)
4. Madad Zadeh, S., Francois, T., Calvet, L., Chauvet, P., Canis, M., Bartoli, A., Bourdel, N.: SurgAI: deep learning for computerized laparoscopic image understanding in gynaecology. Surg. Endosc. **34**, 5377–5383 (2020)
5. Neyens, D.M., Yin, R., Abernathy III, J.H., Tobin, C., Jaruzel, C., Catchpole, K.: The movement of syringes and medication during anesthesiology delivery: an observational study in laparoscopic surgeries. Appl. Ergon. **118**, 104263 (2024)
6. Kalliakmanis, V., Pikoulis, E., Hitos, A., Karavokyros, I.G., Gougoudi, E., Leppaniemi, A.: A retained foreign body in the peritoneal cavity causing intestinal obstruction by intraluminal migration. Zentralblatt fur Chirurgie. **132**(1), 70–72 (2007)
7. Kitaguchi, D., Takeshita, N., Hasegawa, H., Ito, M.: Artificial intelligence-based computer vision in surgery: recent advances and future perspectives. Ann. Gastroenterol. Surg. **6**(1), 29–36 (2022)
8. Sarikaya, D., Corso, J.J., Guru, K.A.: Detection and localization of robotic tools in robot-assisted surgery videos using deep neural networks for region proposal and detection. IEEE Trans. Med. Imaging. **36**(7), 1542–1549 (2017)
9. Sánchez-Brizuela, G., Santos-Criado, F.J., Sanz-Gobernado, D., de la Fuente-López, E., Fraile, J.C., Pérez-Turiel, J., Cisnal, A.: Gauze detection and segmentation in minimally invasive surgery video using convolutional neural networks. Sensors. **22**(14), 5180 (2022)
10. Lai, S.L., Chen, C.S., Lin, B.R., Chang, R.F.: Intraoperative detection of surgical gauze using deep convolutional neural network. Ann. Biomed. Eng. **51**(2), 352–362 (2023)
11. Dangoury, S., Sadik, M., Alali, A., Fail, A.: V-net performances for 2D ultrasound image segmentation. In: In 2022 IEEE 18th International Colloquium on Signal Processing & Applications (CSPA), pp. 96–100. IEEE (2022)
12. Wang, A., Chen, H., Liu, L., Chen, K., Lin, Z., Han, J., Ding, G.: YOLOv10: real-time end-to-end object detection. arXiv preprint arXiv:2405.14458. (2024)

Methodological Exploration to Evaluate the Role of AI in Animation Production Efficiency: Application of Network Data Envelopment Analysis (NDEA) Model

Yihui Chen(✉), Tao Yu, and Younghwan Pan

Kookmin University, Seoul 02707, South Korea
17787105270@kookmin.ac.kr

Abstract. This study methodically investigates the applicability of the Network Data Envelopment Analysis (NDEA) model to assess the efficiency impacts of integrating Artificial Intelligence (AI) into animation production, emphasizing the model's adaptability and its potential as groundwork for future research in this innovative intersection. As AI integration in animation production promises significant efficiency improvements, the industry faces challenges in quantitatively assessing these impacts due to the complexity and multifaceted nature of animation workflows. This research aims to bridge this methodological gap by precisely locating and adopting the most appropriate NDEA model, providing the animation production space with a tailored efficiency assessment framework to evaluate the efficiency impact of AI. Through literature review, model selection and adaptation, and empirical evaluation, this study confirms the suitability of the NDEA model, especially after specific adjustments, for examining the efficiency impacts of AI in animation production. The research not only enriches the academic discourse on efficiency measurement in creative industries but also lays a foundational stone for future investigations, offering a clearer path toward integrating AI in creative processes.

Keywords: Artificial intelligence · NDEA · Animation production

1 Introduction

In recent years, artificial intelligence (AI) technology has garnered significant attention in the field of animation production, with its applications experiencing explosive growth. The continuous development of AI technology and the increasing sophistication of algorithms have enabled AI to play important roles in various stages of animation production, including character design, animation creation, and scene construction [1–4]. These technologies not only reduce the workload of animators but also enhance the liveliness and realism of animated characters. For instance, by improving rendering queue management methods and applying intelligent algorithms, 3D graphics engine animation design has achieved ideal animation effects [5].

S. Jin et al. (Eds.): IEA 2024, SSDI 39, pp. 183–188, 2025.
https://doi.org/10.1007/978-981-95-0211-0_28

In this context, it is crucial to study the impact of AI on animation production efficiency. Improving production efficiency can reduce the time and cost of animation production while enhancing the quality and creative freedom of animated works. However, evaluating this efficiency improvement requires scientific methods and models. Data Envelopment Analysis (DEA), as a non-parametric method, has been widely used in efficiency evaluation. Since its introduction by Charnes et al. [6] in 1978, DEA models have been applied to efficiency evaluations in various fields such as schools, banks, and hospitals. Traditional DEA models consider the internal structure of Decision Making Units (DMUs) as a "black box," making it difficult to analyze the internal efficiencies of complex systems. Therefore, NDEA models have emerged, aiming to analyze the internal interactions and multi-stage processes within systems [7, 8].

This study aims to explore the applicability of the NDEA model in evaluating the impact of AI on animation production efficiency. By comprehensively applying the NDEA model, we hope to provide more accurate and comprehensive efficiency evaluations, thereby supporting the further application of AI technology in animation production. Specifically, we will interview industry experts to analyze factors affecting production efficiency and select the most suitable model based on these factors, discussing its adaptability and potential improvements.

2 Methodology

2.1 Theoretical Discussion of NDEA Model

Network Data Envelopment Analysis NDEA is developed from DEA which is a widely used non-parametric method for evaluating the efficiency of decision-making units (DMUs) introduction by Charnes et al. [6] The main reason for choosing NDEA model is that it can deal with the internal structure and multi-stage process of complex system. The traditional DEA model regards the internal structure of DMU as a "black box", and only focuses on the relationship between inputs and outputs. Although this method is effective in many applications, the traditional DEA model is insufficient for complex systems containing multiple continuous stages and internal interactions [9].

The NDEA model provides a more detailed and comprehensive evaluation of efficiency by considering the interactions between the internal components of the system. For example, An et al. proposed an NDEA model for evaluating the efficiency of interactive systems, It shows its advantages in dealing with complex system structures [7]. In addition, Ratner et al. reviewed the application of NDEA models in different domains between 2017 and 2022, Its effectiveness in dealing with complex system structures is emphasized [8].

The basic NDEA model is suitable for systems with a single phase but containing multiple internal processes. This type of model provides a more detailed efficiency assessment by analyzing the individual processes inside the system. For example, in the education system, the efficiency performance of various departments can be assessed [9].

The application of NDEA to animation production involves evaluating the efficiency of different stages and processes influenced by AI. By adapting NDEA models to fit the unique characteristics of animation production, researchers can obtain a more nuanced understanding of how AI technologies impact production efficiency. This theoretical framework allows for the identification of key metrics and indicators to measure efficiency, providing valuable insights for both animation studios and AI developers.

The multi-stage NDEA model is suitable for systems with multiple continuous production stages. For example, in the manufacturing industry, product production often needs to go through multiple links, and the efficiency of each link will affect the final production efficiency [10]. The parallel NDEA model is suitable for complex systems with parallel subprocesses. In the banking system, different branches may operate in parallel, and their respective efficiency will affect the overall operational efficiency of the bank. The dynamic NDEA model is suitable for dynamic systems that change with time [11]. The two-layer NDEA model is suitable for systems with a two-layer structure, such as upstream and downstream in the supply chain. In supply chain management, it is necessary to evaluate the efficiency performance of upstream suppliers and downstream customers [12].

2.2 Expert Interview

The interviewees include a CG animation director from a renowned game company and a senior 3D animator. The CG animation director mentioned that AI tools have already been integrated into the early stages of the production process, particularly in concept design and illustration. Currently, AI is mainly used as a reference tool, but he believes that AI tools will be incorporated into more stages of animation production in the future. He pointed out that AI technology has great potential to improve production efficiency by significantly reducing repetitive tasks, allowing creators to focus on more creative tasks. The senior 3D animator is more conservative. He acknowledges the advantages of AI technology but remains cautious about its practical application in the production process.

The CG animation director believes that AI technology can improve production efficiency in the following ways: 1. Accelerating Concept Design: AI can quickly generate multiple design options for designers to choose and modify. 2. Enhancing Illustration Quality: AI-assisted tools can improve the details and realism of illustrations. 3. Reducing Repetitive Tasks: AI tools can automate repetitive tasks, such as transitions between animation frames. The senior 3D animator pointed out that AI mainly impacts auxiliary functions of tools, but he is cautious about over-relying on these tools, as it may limit creative expression.

The senior 3D animator believes that overly fragmented processes can reduce efficiency, as animators often need to wait for the previous person's layout work to be completed before starting their keyframe work.

Challenges in AI animation production include technology maturity and workflow integration. Stability and reliability of AI tools also need improvement. Key factors affecting efficiency are team coordination, experience, funding, timeline, pipeline maturity, and leadership expertise, guiding the selection of NDEA models.

3 Model Selection and Modification Direction

This study focuses specifically on the production process of 3D animated short films. 3D animation production involves multiple continuous stages. Considering these stages and the interactions between them, the multi-stage NDEA model is the most suitable for evaluating AI's impact on each stage's efficiency. This model can effectively assess the efficiency of individual stages while considering the overall production process.

If the existing model cannot fully address the research requirements, modifications will be proposed to enhance its applicability. The modifications may include Incorporating Parallel Sub-processes: Considering the possibility of parallel workflows in animation production, the model should be capable of handling multiple concurrent processes. This addition will reflect real-world production scenarios more accurately. Dynamic Changes Consideration: Given the long-term and phase-specific nature of animation projects, the model should account for dynamic changes over time. Integrating dynamic NDEA elements will allow for a more comprehensive evaluation of efficiency throughout different project stages.

These modifications aim to create a more robust and adaptable NDEA model that can accurately evaluate AI's impact on 3D animation production efficiency.

Below is a proposed structure of the modified NDEA model for 3D animation production, which reflects the stages and quantifiable parameters discussed (see Fig. 1).

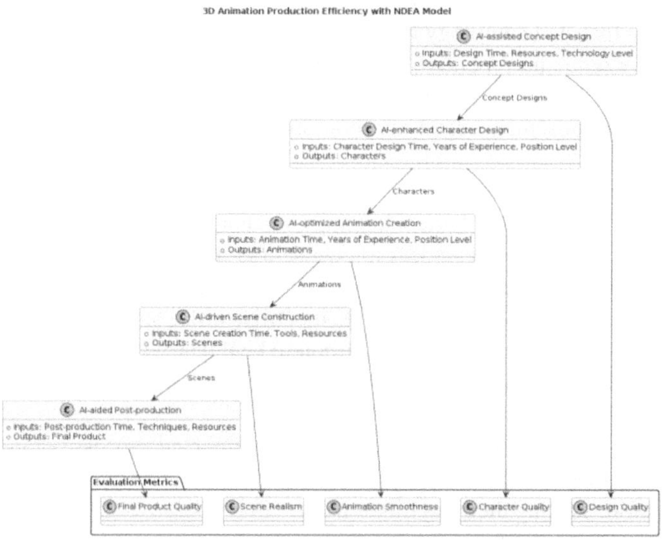

Fig. 1. NDEA model structure diagram designed for 3D animation flow.

The multi-stage NDEA model, potentially enhanced with considerations for parallel sub-processes and dynamic changes, is the most appropriate for this study. This model will enable a detailed analysis of AI's impact on the efficiency of various stages in the 3D animation production process, with quantifiable and practical parameters.

4 Discussion and Conclusion

The multi-stage NDEA model demonstrates its applicability and effectiveness in evaluating the impact of AI on the efficiency of 3D animation production. Through expert interviews and literature review, the key factors affecting the efficiency of 3D animation production are identified and integrated. The expert feedback provides valuable insights into the practical use of AI in animation production, showing that AI tools can significantly reduce repetitive tasks, improve design quality, and boost overall production efficiency. The model effectively captures the complex interactions between different stages of the animation production process, provides a comprehensive efficiency assessment of each stage by quantifying inputs and outputs, and its adaptability enables it to be modified to incorporate parallel subprocesses and dynamic changes, making it highly applicable in real-world scenarios.

The research concludes that AI has a significant positive impact on the efficiency of 3D animation production. The multi-stage NDEA model is a robust and adaptable tool for evaluating this impact, providing detailed insights into each stage of the production process.

This study providing the animation industry with a practical framework for assessing and improving production efficiency through AI integration and extending the application of the NDEA model to new domains, demonstrating its flexibility and robustness. However, the complexity of the data collection process poses challenges, and future research should focus on optimizing these measurements and exploring more factors that affect efficiency, as well as longitudinal studies to gain insight into the long-term impact of AI on animation production. In addition, future research can explore the integration and impact of more advanced AI techniques in the animation process and extend the model to more diverse animation projects and production environments to verify its applicability and enhance its practicality.

References

1. Cavazza, M., Charles, F., Mead, S.J.: AI-based animation for interactive storytelling. In: Proceedings Computer Animation 2001. Fourteenth Conference on Computer Animation (Cat. No. 01TH8596), pp. 113–120. IEEE (2001) Accessed 12 Apr 2024
2. Shu, Z., Xiao, B.: Computer animation based on artificial intelligence and artificial life. Comput. Sci. (2007) Accessed 27 Mar. 2024
3. Femenia-Serra, F., Neuhofer, B., Ivars-Baidal, J.A.: Towards a conceptualisation of smart tourists and their role within the smart destination scenario. Serv. Ind. J. **39**(2), 109–133 (2019)
4. Bao, W.: The application of intelligent algorithms in the animation design of 3D graphics engines. Int. J. Gaming Comput.-Mediat. Simul. **13**(2), 1–12 (2021)
5. Gao, X.R.: 3D animation technologies and efficiency. Appl. Mech. Mater. **421**, 681–684 (2013)
6. Charnes, A., Cooper, W.W., Rhodes, E.: Measuring the efficiency of decision making units. Eur. J. Oper. Res. **2**(6), 429–444 (1978)
7. An, Q., Yang, M., Chu, J., Wu, J., Zhu, Q.: Efficiency evaluation of an interactive system by data envelopment analysis approach. Comput. Ind. Eng. **103**, 17–25 (2017)

8. Ratner, S.V., Shaposhnikov, A.M., Lychev, A.V.: Network DEA and its applications (2017–2022): a systematic literature review. Mathematics. **11**(9), Art. no. 9 (2023)
9. Kao, C.: Network data envelopment analysis: a review. Eur. J. Oper. Res. **239**(1), 1–16 (2014)
10. Yang, F., Sun, Y., Wang, D., Ang, S.: Network data envelopment analysis with two-level maximin strategy. RAIRO-Oper. Res. **56**(4), 2543–2556 (2022)
11. Omrani, H., Soltanzadeh, E.: Dynamic DEA models with network structure: an application for Iranian airlines. J. Air Transp. Manag. **57**, 52–61 (2016)
12. Fathi, A., Saen, R.F.: A novel bidirectional network data envelopment analysis model for evaluating sustainability of distributive supply chains of transport companies. J. Clean. Prod. **184**, 696–708 (2018)

User Acceptance of Large Language Model-Powered Conversation Agents for Mental Health Support

Nuo Cheng, Ruifeng Yu(✉), and Xuanzhi Wang

Department of Industrial Engineering, Tsinghua University, Beijing, China
yurf@mail.tsinghua.edu.cn

Abstract. The emergence of Large Language Models (LLMs) like GPT-4 revolutionizes mental health care, enhancing counseling and therapy. This study investigates the factors influencing user acceptance of Large Language Model (LLM)-powered conversational agents in mental health support, utilizing frameworks that integrating Technology Acceptance Model (TAM) and the Unified Theory of Acceptance and Use of Technology (UTAUT). It examines how perceived benefits, perceived risks, trust, and perceived anthropomorphism shape acceptance, with attention to gender differences and familiarity with LLMs. A questionnaire-based study of 202 participants assessed these factors, and multiple linear regression analysis and structural model identified performance expectations and social influence as significant predictors of acceptance, supporting TAM's core concepts. The study concludes that perceived benefits are crucial for acceptance, with trust also playing a key role. Enhancing performance expectations can mitigate technological concerns. These insights are vital for designing effective LLM-powered mental health support systems, aiming to improve user satisfaction and overall mental health outcomes.

Keywords: Large Language Models · Technology Acceptance · Mental Health Support

1 Introduction

The emergence of Large Language Models (LLMs) such as GPT-4 heralds a new era in mental health care, offering groundbreaking solutions in counseling and therapy. These models address the global mental health crisis, marked by an urgent need for services and a shortage of mental health professionals [1, 2]. They hold significant promise in enhancing mental health diagnostics and treatment, indicating a paradigm shift in healthcare practices [1, 3, 4].

Our study aligns with Technology Acceptance Model (TAM) and the Unified Theory of Acceptance and Use of Technology (UTAUT), investigating the multifaceted aspects of user acceptance of LLM-powered agents in mental health support. We explore how perceived benefit, perceived risk, trust, and perceived anthropomorphism shape user acceptance. The study also acknowledges the significance of demographic factors like

S. Jin et al. (Eds.): IEA 2024, SSDI 39, pp. 189–195, 2025.
https://doi.org/10.1007/978-981-95-0211-0_29

gender in technology adoption, reflecting broader trends in mental health awareness [5–7].

In conclusion, this research aims to provide a nuanced understanding of the factors influencing user acceptance of LLM-powered conversational agents in mental health support.

2 Methods

In this study, we conceptualize the acceptance of Large Language Model-powered intelligent conversation agents within a theoretical framework that categorizes the determinants of acceptance into four distinct domains: perceived benefit, perceived risk, trust, and perceived anthropomorphism.

In this study, we consider three dimensions for perceived benefits: performance expectancy, social influence, and hedonic motivation. Perceived risk comprises technological concerns, ethical concerns, and regulation concerns. Trust in technology acceptance is the confidence users have in the reliability, safety, and effectiveness of a system [8, 9], which in this context, refers to LLM-powered conversation agents. Perceived anthropomorphism involves the extent to which users attribute human-like qualities, such as empathy, intelligence, or emotional understanding, to non-human entities like AI systems [10].

Based on the literature review, the constructs and questionnaire items were developed, containing questions about basic personal information, measures of perceived benefit [11], risk [12], trust [9], and perceived anthropomorphism [10].

3 Results

The study's participant cohort (N = 202) consisted of a gender distribution with males representing 57.92% and females accounting for 42.08%. In evaluating the internal structure validity of our factors, items with factor loadings below 0.5 were excluded to ensure robustness within each construct. On the level of individual factors, a threshold of Cronbach's Alpha greater than 0.7 was established as a criterion for retention. The reliability and validity of the questionnaire are confirmed to be satisfactory.

3.1 Multiple Linear Regression (MLR)

Eleven variables (gender, familiarity with LLMs, willingness to receive psychological counseling, performance expectation, social influence, hedonic motivation, technological concerns, ethical concerns, regulation concerns, trust, and perceived anthropomorphism) were utilized as independent variables in the regression model with acceptance as the dependent variable. The results are in Table 1.

The stepwise regression analysis initially revealed an unexpected positive coefficient for technological concerns. This prompted an investigation into potential interaction effects, leading to a subsequent stepwise regression incorporating second-order interaction terms. The refined analysis, as depicted in Table 2 demonstrates several key findings.

Table 1. Results of multiple linear regression.

Factors	Coef		p
Gender (Female)	0.16*		0.03
Psychological Counseling Willingness (No)	−0.20**		<0.01
Performance Expectation	0.40***		<0.01
Social Influence	0.11*		0.03
Hedonic Motivation	0.29***		<0.01
Technological Concerns	0.11*		0.04
R^2		0.66	
Adjusted R^2		0.64	

Table 2. Results of multiple linear regression with interaction terms.

Factors	Coef		p
Gender-Female (Gender)	0.95**		<0.01
Psychological Counseling Willingness-No (LPCW)	−0.74*		0.05
Social Influence (SI)	0.11*		0.03
Technological Concerns (TC)	−0.52*		0.01
Regulation Concerns (RC)	−0.17**		0.01
Trust (TR)	0.60***		<0.01
TC*PE	0.17**		<0.01
Gender*HM	−0.21*		0.02
FAM*HM	0.10*		0.05
FAM*TR	−0.15**		<0.01
R^2		0.69	
Adjusted R^2		0.67	

The model's overall predictive strength was solid, as indicated by an R-squared value of 0.69 and an adjusted R-squared of 0.67, suggesting that a significant proportion of the variance in acceptance could be explained by the model, which now included the complexity of interaction effects among the considered factors.

3.2 Structural Model

Considering the interplay between factors and their categorization into four distinct classes (benefit, risk, trust, and perceived anthropomorphism), a structural model (PLS-SEM) was constructed based on the regression results.

The path coefficients and their corresponding p-values are presented in Fig. 1, which graphically summarizes the relationships and strengths between the constructs within the structural model. The estimated model demonstrated a satisfactory level of fit in predicting acceptance, with an R-squared of 0.62 and an adjusted R-squared of 0.61.

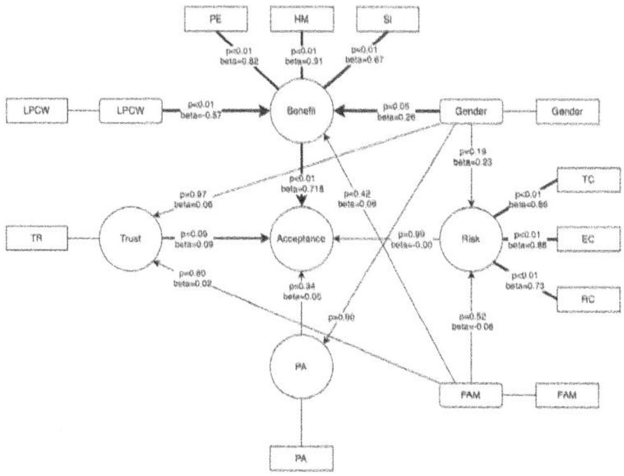

Fig. 1. Structural model.

In this research, we refined our structural model by eliminating factors that showed no significant impact on user acceptance (Fig. 2). The model exhibits good explanatory power, with an R-squared value of 0.62 and an adjusted R-squared of 0.61.

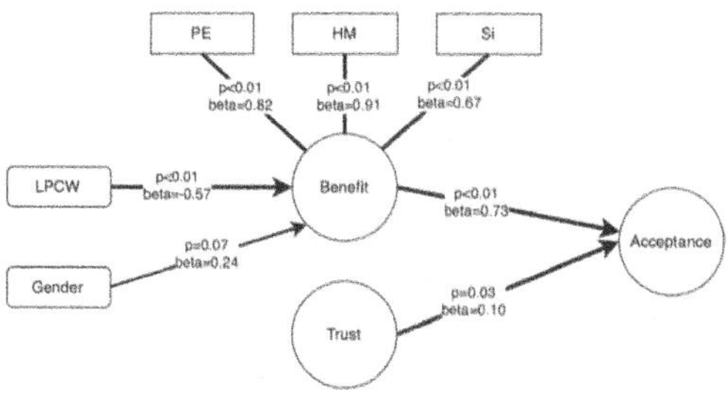

Fig. 2. Streamlined structural model.

4 Discussion

The study's comprehensive analysis, incorporating multiple linear regression and a structural model, reveals a nuanced understanding of user acceptance of LLM-powered conversational agents, particularly in the mental health domain. The prominence of perceived benefits (performance expectations, social influence and hedonic motivation) in our findings echoes the central tenet of Davis's Technology Acceptance Model [13], emphasizing the importance of performance expectations and social influences in the context of mental health support technologies. Gender differences, with females showing higher acceptance, may reflect broader trends in mental health awareness and help-seeking behavior. The reluctance to engage in psychological counseling negatively impacted acceptance, highlighting individual predispositions' role.

The interaction between technological concerns and performance expectations implies that users' performance expectations can mitigate the apprehensions associated with technological risks. In the mental health context, performance expectations could potentially offset apprehensions about technological risks.

The regression and structural models both highlight the nuanced relationship between familiarity with LLM technology, trust, and acceptance. As users become more familiar with these technologies, their trust-related concerns might evolve, influencing their acceptance and willingness to use these tools for mental health support.

The structural model's findings provide a robust framework for understanding acceptance. The substantial positive effect of benefits on acceptance (beta $= 0.718$, $p < 0.01$) aligns with the established understanding that performance expectations and social influences are pivotal in the decision to embrace new technologies. Similar to the regression results, the structural model results indicating that females tend to perceive higher benefits from LLM-powered conversational agents, while individuals without a willingness to receive psychological counseling perceive significantly lower benefits, align with existing theories on technology acceptance. The positive yet slight influence of trust on acceptance echoes the sentiments of Gefen, Karahanna, and Straub, who emphasized trust's integral role in the adoption of online technologies [14].

Interestingly, the model did not find a significant negative impact of risk factors on acceptance. This observation parallels Pavlou's assertion that perceived risks do not always inhibit technology adoption, particularly when the benefits are perceived as substantial [15]. It suggests that when users perceive substantial benefits, such as effective mental health support, they may be more willing to overlook potential risks.

The lack of a significant influence of perceived anthropomorphism on acceptance provides a novel perspective in the context of mental health, which is different from the three-factor theory posits varying effects on user engagement with technology [16]. While anthropomorphic features are not statistically significant predictors of acceptance, they are still highly valued by users (average rating of 4 on a 5-point scale). This suggests a consistent user attitude favoring these features.

5 Conclusion

This study's comprehensive exploration into the factors influencing user acceptance of LLM-powered conversational agents for mental health support has yielded significant insights. It is evident that perceived benefits, particularly performance expectations and social influence, are critical drivers of acceptance. Gender differences also play a significant role, with females showing higher acceptance rates, possibly due to varying perceptions and expectations of technology.

The study also highlighted the complex interplay between technological concerns and performance expectations, suggesting that enhancing users' performance expectations could effectively mitigate apprehensions about technological risks. Trust, while slightly less impactful than perceived benefits, remains a crucial factor in the acceptance of online mental health support technologies, emphasizing trust's vital role in the adoption of online technologies [14]. The study also reveals that while users highly value anthropomorphic features such as empathy and emotional support in mental health conversational agents, these aspects do not significantly drive acceptance.

The acceptance is a complex phenomenon, heavily swayed by perceived benefits, trust, and the interactions between various factors. Integrating these insights into the design and promotion of LLM-powered agents can significantly enhance their effectiveness and acceptance in mental health support, ultimately leading to improved user satisfaction and well-being.

References

1. Xu, X., Yao, B., Dong, Y., Yu, H., Hendler, J., Dey, A.K., Wang, D.: Leveraging Large Language Models for Mental Health Prediction via Online Text Data. arXiv preprint arXiv:2307.14385 (2023)
2. Zhong, Y., Chen, Y.-J., Zhou, Y., Yin, J.-J., Gao, Y.-J.: The Artificial intelligence large language models and neuropsychiatry practice and research ethic. Asian J. Psychiatr. **84**, 103577 (2023)
3. van Heerden, A.C., Pozuelo, J.R., Kohrt, B.A.: Global mental health services and the impact of artificial intelligence–powered large language models. JAMA Psychiatry. **80**, 662–664 (2023)
4. Wang, X., Li, X., Yin, Z., Wu, Y., Liu, J.: Emotional intelligence of large language models. J. Pac. Rim Psychol. **17**, 18344909231213958 (2023)
5. Williams, M.D., Rana, N.P., Dwivedi, Y.K.: The unified theory of acceptance and use of technology (UTAUT): a literature review. J. Enterp. Inf. Manag. **28**, 443–488 (2015)
6. Or, C.: The role of attitude in the unified theory of acceptance and use of technology: a meta-analytic structural equation modelling study. Int. J. Technol. Educ. Sci. **7**, 552 (2023)
7. Ayaz, A., Yanartaş, M.: An analysis on the unified theory of acceptance and use of technology theory (UTAUT): Acceptance of electronic document management system (EDMS). Comput. Hum. Behav. Rep. **2**, 100032 (2020)
8. Wu, K., Zhao, Y., Zhu, Q., Tan, X., Zheng, H.: A meta-analysis of the impact of trust on technology acceptance model: investigation of moderating influence of subject and context type. Int. J. Inf. Manag. **31**, 572–581 (2011)
9. Körber, M.: Theoretical considerations and development of a questionnaire to measure trust in automation. In: Proceedings of the 20th Congress of the International Ergonomics Association (IEA 2018) Volume VI: Transport Ergonomics and Human Factors (TEHF), Aerospace Human Factors and Ergonomics, vol. 20, pp. 13–30. Springer (2018)
10. Prakash, A.V., Das, S.: Intelligent conversational agents in mental healthcare services: a thematic analysis of user perceptions. Pac. Asia J. Assoc. Inf. Syst. **12**, 1 (2020)
11. Schomakers, E.-M., Lidynia, C., Vervier, L.S., Calero Valdez, A., Ziefle, M.: Applying an extended UTAUT2 model to explain user acceptance of lifestyle and therapy mobile health apps: survey study. JMIR Mhealth Uhealth. **10**, e27095 (2022)
12. Esmaeilzadeh, P.: Use of AI-based tools for healthcare purposes: a survey study from consumers' perspectives. BMC Med. Inform. Decis. Mak. **20**, 170 (2020)
13. Davis, F.D.: Perceived usefulness, perceived ease of use, and user acceptance of information technology. MIS Q., 319–340 (1989)
14. Gefen, D., Karahanna, E., Straub, D.W.: Trust and TAM in online shopping: an integrated model. MIS Q. **27**, 51–90 (2003)

15. Pavlou, P.A., Fygenson, M.: Understanding and predicting electronic commerce adoption: an extension of the theory of planned behavior. MIS Q., 115–143 (2006)
16. Epley, N., Waytz, A., Cacioppo, J.T.: On seeing human: a three-factor theory of anthropomorphism. Psychol. Rev. **114**, 864 (2007)

A Pilot Study Exploring User Needs and Expectations for AI-Based Academic Search Tools

Hanbyeol Choi and Lin Wang(✉)

Department of Library and Information Science, Incheon National University, Incheon 22012, Republic of Korea
wanglin@inu.ac.kr

Abstract. With the rapid advancement of artificial intelligence (AI) technology, academic search processes are being significantly transformed. Traditional academic search methods are often time-consuming and labor-intensive, requiring substantial effort from researchers for background research and literature reviews. AI technology offers a solution by enhancing the efficiency and accuracy of literature retrieval through natural language processing, machine learning, and deep learning. This study aims to understand user needs and expectations for AI-based academic search tools through a survey. The results indicate that users highly value features such as summary and content extraction for papers/theses, automatic translation, and text-data metadata analysis. Factor analysis categorizes essential features into four primary factors: non-text material analysis, customized searching, text material analysis, and advanced features. These findings highlight the potential of AI to revolutionize academic search, making it more efficient and comprehensive, and provide insights for the development of user-centered AI academic search tools.

Keywords: Academic Research · Information Retrieval · Artificial Intelligence · User Needs

1 Introduction

With the rapid development of artificial intelligence (AI) technology, the field of academic search is undergoing profound changes. The traditional academic search process is often time-consuming and labor-intensive, requiring scholars to spend considerable time on background research and literature reviews. This process involves searching for relevant literature, filtering important information, and synthesizing data, all of which directly impact the progress and quality of research. However, the introduction of AI technology offers new possibilities for this field.

The application of AI in academic search can significantly reduce the time scholars need for preliminary preparation and greatly enhance the accuracy and comprehensiveness of literature retrieval [1]. Through technologies such as natural language processing, machine learning, and deep learning, AI can quickly process vast amounts of academic

S. Jin et al. (Eds.): IEA 2024, SSDI 39, pp. 196–200, 2025.
https://doi.org/10.1007/978-981-95-0211-0_30

literature, automatically identifying and recommending articles and books that are highly relevant to the research topic. This not only helps researchers efficiently complete background research and preliminary studies but also allows them to build a comprehensive and accurate knowledge base in a shorter time. Currently, AI-based academic search systems are gradually shifting from keyword matching to semantic understanding, enabling a better grasp of the intent behind user queries and providing more relevant and in-depth search results [2].

To better apply AI in academic search, it is crucial to understand the actual user needs. Therefore, this study aims to explore the specific needs and expectations of users when using AI technology for academic searches through a survey. This research will not only aid in the development of AI academic search tools that better meet user needs but also provide valuable insights for the improvement and promotion of related technologies.

2 Literature Review

The application of artificial intelligence (AI) technology in academic search and literature review is bringing revolutionary changes for researchers. Mendoza and Aguilar [3] evaluated the impact of AI tools on literature reviews in the social sciences, providing empirical data on efficiency gains. Their study found that AI tools significantly reduce the time required for literature reviews and improve the coverage and depth of analysis, thereby offering researchers a more comprehensive research background.

Extance [4] discussed how AI, by synthesizing and summarizing vast amounts of research data, overcomes the limitations of traditional databases, thereby transforming the way literature reviews are conducted. By utilizing natural language processing (NLP) technology, AI can quickly generate summaries and comprehensive reports of relevant literature based on the user's research topic. Additionally, AI can provide highly relevant literature recommendations and trend analysis through network and machine learning technologies. The Nature Publishing Group [5] discussed the effectiveness of the latest AI-driven literature search tools in managing and retrieving academic literature. Their research indicated that these tools not only significantly reduce the preparation time for researchers but also help in quickly establishing a comprehensive knowledge base by providing highly relevant search results.

Overall, the application of AI technology in academic search and literature review has shown significant advantages. By leveraging NLP, machine learning, and generative AI technologies, AI tools can greatly enhance the efficiency and accuracy of literature retrieval [6]. However, despite the notable improvements in efficiency and precision, the widespread adoption of AI still faces challenges in terms of technology and user acceptance. Researchers need to develop more user-friendly and accessible AI tools to improve user experience and acceptance [7]. Therefore, this study will employ a questionnaire survey method to investigate the target population who frequently use academic search tools. The aim is to gather their functional and interaction design requirements for AI-based academic search tools.

3 Method

This study utilized an online survey as the research method to investigate the primary needs of users requiring academic search services, specifically in relation to AI-based academic search systems.

3.1 Research Questions

There are two research questions in total:

Research question 1: What are the most importance features of AI-based academic search tools perceived by the participants?
Research question 2: What are the main features that AI-based academic search tools need to have?

3.2 Participants

Participants in this survey were required to have experience using academic search tools and AI-based search tools. A total of 24 respondents participated in this study, including 18 women and 6 men. Their average age was 26.0 years, with a standard deviation of 4.65 years. Among them, 11 were current undergraduates or graduates, 11 were current master's students or graduates, and 2 were current doctoral students or graduates.

3.3 Survey Design and Procedure

The survey questionnaire consisted of two main parts. The first part collected basic demographic information and the participants' experience with AI and academic search tools. The second part constituted the main body of the survey, focusing on the participants' functional and interactive needs for AI-based search systems. In this part, the participants need to rate the importance of all AI-based academic search features by 7-likert scales.

4 Result

First, this study conducted descriptive statistical analysis to obtain basic demographic information of the respondents and their experiences with AI and academic search tools. Then, factor analysis was performed on all variables related to academic search functionalities and interaction needs, extracting several important factors.

First, for the first research question what the most importance features of AI-based academic search tools perceived by the participants are, the respondents rated the importance of all AI-based academic search features included in the questionnaire. The scoring results are shown in the Table 1.

The respondents considered all AI-based features in the questionnaire to be important. Based on the scores, the three most important features are: summary and content extraction functions of papers/theses, automatic translation and text-data metadata analysis.

Table 1. Descriptive data analysis of the features.

Features	Mean	SD
Research Topic Recommendation	5.13	1.39
Visualize Search Results	6.04	0.91
Customized based on Search History	5.75	1.07
Customized based on Reading History	5.92	0.93
Customized based on Published Papers	5.29	1.55
Automatic Translation	6.13	0.99
Paper/theses Summary	6.25	0.74
Book Summary	5.92	1.14
Video/Audio Summary	5.25	1.39
Text-data Metadata Analysis	6.13	0.85
Figure Metadata Analysis	5.29	1.43
Image/Audio Metadata Analysis	5.38	1.31

Table 2. Data analysis result.

Features	Factor 1	Factor 2	Factor 3	Factor 4
Figure Metadata Analysis	**0.916**	0.286	0.058	−0.096
Image/Audio Metadata Analysis	**0.898**	0.252	0.165	−0.068
Video/Audio Summary	**0.876**	−0.058	0.172	0.191
Customized based on Search History	0.338	**0.872**	−0.004	−0.061
Customized based on Reading History	0.032	**0.801**	0.359	−0.065
Research Topic Recommendation	0.095	**0.764**	0.302	0.071
Text-data Metadata Analysis	0.142	0.146	**0.839**	−0.044
Paper/theses Summary	0.161	0.393	**0.743**	0.030
Book Summary	0.627	0.156	**0.638**	−0.031
Visualize Search Results	0.129	0.238	0.236	**−0.812**
Customized based on Published Papers	0.227	0.598	0.172	**0.670**
Automatic Translation	0.082	0.171	0.581	**0.658**

Second, for the second research question what the main features that AI-based academic search tools need to have, factor analysis was used to investigate the main factors. The result is shown in Table 2.

The KMO and Bartlett's test result was $p < 0.001$. All the AI searching features in this study can be categorized into four main factors, which are named based on their primary features as follows: Factor 1: non-text material analysis; Factor 2: customized searching; Factor 3: text material analysis; Factor 4: advanced features.

5 Conclusion

The findings of this study underscore the significant potential and current user expectations of AI-based academic search tools. The descriptive analysis revealed that users highly value features such as the summary and content extraction functions for papers/theses, automatic translation, and text-data metadata analysis. These features were consistently rated as the most important, indicating that users prioritize functionalities that enhance the efficiency and depth of their literature review process.

Factor analysis further categorized the essential features into four primary factors: non-text material analysis, customized searching, text material analysis, and advanced features. These factors highlight the diverse needs of users, ranging from the ability to analyze multimedia content to the necessity for personalized search experiences based on individual research histories.

The study's results emphasize the critical role of AI in transforming academic search by offering more accurate and comprehensive retrieval of relevant literature. By addressing user preferences for specific functionalities, developers can create more effective AI-based tools that streamline the research process, making it more efficient and less time-consuming. Furthermore, the identification of key features and their categorization into distinct factors provide a clear roadmap for future enhancements in AI-based academic search tools.

References

1. Dönmez, İ., Idin, S., Gülen, S.: Conducting academic research with the AI interface ChatGPT: Challenges and opportunities. J. STEAM Educ. **6**(2), 101–118 (2023)
2. Razack, H.I.A., Mathew, S.T., Saad, F.F.A., Alqahtani, S.A.: Artificial intelligence-assisted tools for redefining the communication landscape of the scholarly world. Sci. Edit. **8**(2), 134–144 (2021)
3. Mendoza, M., Aguilar, L.: Evaluating the impact of AI on literature review processes in the social sciences. Nature. **608**, 464–466 (2022)
4. Extance, A.: How AI technology can tame the scientific literature. Nature. **563**, 397–398 (2018)
5. Nature Publishing Group: Artificial-intelligence search engines wrangle academic literature. Nature. **614**, 10–12 (2023)
6. Al Naqbi, H., Bahroun, Z., Ahmed, V.: Enhancing work productivity through generative artificial intelligence: a comprehensive literature review. Sustainability. **16**(3), 1166 (2024)
7. Lu, W., Liu, J.: AI in academic search and retrieval: opportunities and challenges. Nature. **579**, 25–27 (2020)

Embodied Experience of Drag Persona Using AI: A Gender-Based Methodology for Ergonomics

Alejandro Daniel Murga González(✉)

Universidad Autónoma de Baja California, Tijuana, Baja California 22260, Mexico
alejandro.murga@uabc.edu.mx

Abstract. This work aims to establish a participative design methodology with a queer perspective for human representation using AI. The empirical approach centers on the drag performance community in Tijuana, Mexico, specifically focusing on the embodied experience of the drag persona as it negotiates meanings between *representation* and its *mise-en-scène*. This exploration serves as a means to challenge traditional representations and broaden the understanding of *wellbeing* in the fields of Ergonomics and Design. The project is an integral part of an ongoing doctoral research and was carried out during the Tijuana Design Week 2024. The workshop consisted of a group reflection about the queer perspective in Design and Ergonomics; a performance carried out by the local drag performers *Astrid Búk Kake* and *La Alanina*; and the collaborative production of images to illustrate a situated image of the drag persona. The production of images was done with the aid of Microsoft Copilot, a language model that helped translate specific categories within the social group into images, which were debated in terms of representational coherence. In this sense, the performance is proposed in theoretical terms as a conscious design action on the individual and social body that allows new performativities beyond the binaries.

Keywords: human representation using AI · Ergonomics and Design · persona design · gender performativity · drag performance · embodiment

1 Problem Statement and Theoretical Framework

In the field of social and cultural studies, *gender* is conceptualized as a socially constructed and as a performative relational category that impacts social systems in terms of norms, discourses, and materiality [1]. In contrast, in fields such as Ergonomics and Design, this category is historically naturalized through the understanding of the body with fixed designations, such as *human*, seen as an information processing system [2]; and *user*, referring to labor divisions [3]. This perspective, grounded in the ideological goal of "maximum efficiency, productivity, and job satisfaction" [4], neglects the consideration of *self-representation* [5]. Consequently, the design and ergonomics problem is historically perceived as a *labor* problem [6], which is in itself a gender-biased concept -in terms of sexual division-, contributing to the perpetuation of the gender binary and power dynamics through *statistical human bodies* [7], and thus rendering sex-gender

S. Jin et al. (Eds.): IEA 2024, SSDI 39, pp. 201–206, 2025.
https://doi.org/10.1007/978-981-95-0211-0_31

dissidence invisible. With this in mind, the naturalization of hegemonic human representations leaves the concept of *embodiment and performativity* in terms of gender perspective, as a theoretical vacancy in the field of Ergonomics and Design.

In this line of thought, it is worth problematizing in Ergonomics and Design the social notion of the *standard* as a social necessity, as Walter Gropius stated: "The living conditions of the majority of *men* are essentially the same" [8] [translation and italics by the author]. This would be later reflected in the need to systematize the understanding of the *man*-product and *man*-machine relationships [9], where, in words of Tomás Maldonado, rational decisions do not regard "consumer tastes and even less on interpreting their preferences" [translation by the author] [9]. Therefore, the *standard* revolved around the uncontested notion of the *Modern Man* [10] and its derivative concepts. For that matter, Cooper and Bowers [11] problematize the concept of the *user* as a discursive structure that can deviate from the *reality* of individuals. Later on, Suchman [12] exposed this structure as representation strategies such as *user-scenarios* and *personas*. Godden [13] extended this perspective to *Universal Design* -one of the approaches in Ergonomics- arguing that it sets unattainable, problematic, and inadequate goals due to the constantly changing landscape of body inclusion within the *standard*.

It is worth noting that previously in the feminist field, Monique Wittig's critical thought on language stated [14] that the very term *human* refers to a minority of people: the dominant group that owns the means of production which tend to universalize - or *standardize*- its own concepts; and that those concepts have a shaping action on materiality. During that period, Judith Butler [15, 16] asserted that *concepts* possess the power to both produce that which they name and distinguish between what is considered *human* and what is perceived as *less-than-human*. This similarly applies in the field of Ergonomics, where distinctions are drawn between bodies and experiences considered *normal* and those that are not. This can be observed in the notions of anthropometric tables, percentiles, and the design guides for modern Design and Ergonomics done by authors such as Henry Dreyfuss with *The measure of man: human factors in design* [18].

In a productive and material line, Ian Hacking [18] had already interpreted objects as extensions of ideas. This aligns with Corona-Martínez's earlier suggestion in the field of Design: "the designer invents the object in the very act of *representing* it" [19] [translation and italics by the author], posing a "tension between the one who appears and the one who *performs*" [20] [italics by the author]. With this perspective in mind, it can be asserted that Ergonomics and Design possesses the *performative* power not only to produce objects but also *embody* what is defined as *human*, often overlooking queer body representations. To overcome this, Romero-Caballero [21] and Amao-Ceniceros [22] regard the concept of performance as a *counter-visualization* and *counter-narrative* that disrupts the notion of -*standard*- representation implanted by the colonial gaze of gender. For that matter, Drag performance can be seen as a design strategy to visualize LGBTTTQA+ rights [23].

2 Theoretical Proposal, Research Question and Methodology

The tension between *representation*, *performativity*, and *embodiment* within the fields of Ergonomics, Design, and Queer Studies leads to proposing the notion of *drag persona* as a counter-representation strategy embodied through performance; and a conscious design action on the individual/social body that allows new performativities beyond the binaries. Nevertheless, it is important to clarify its operation within the methodology of design, which conduces to the research question: How does the drag persona embody a queer perspective through design? The objective of this work is to analyze the embodied experience of the drag persona through an ergonomic and a design approach. This is done to propose a participative design methodology for *personas* in design using AI representations that encompasses two aspects: unveiling the dominant thinking about hegemonic representations and generating counter-representations.

The methodology is based on Frayling's paradigm of *research through design* [24], which consists in generating knowledge through design practices. In this sense, the *persona design* [25, 26], regarded as performative a design strategy, was scrutinized under a queer perspective during a collaborative workshop within the events of the Tijuana Design Week 2024. The location selected was *Enclave Rabia Caracol*, a safe space run by a social organization focused on migrant, diverse, and homeless communities. Participant selection involved groups formed through convenience sampling and through an open call for the workshop. The selection criteria included being part of the diverse community and contributing to the production of the Tijuana's Drag, within fields of arts and design.

The workshop dynamic began with a group reflection about queer perspective in Design and Ergonomics; a performance carried out by the local drag performers *Astrid Búk Kake* and *La Alanina*; and the collaborative production of images to illustrate a situated image of the *drag persona*. The production of images was done with the aid of Microsoft Copilot, a language model that helped to "translate" specific categories within the social group into images which were debated in terms of representational coherence. The visualization dynamic was based on *fotohistorias*, a participative method of generating categories through visualizations [27–29]. The main focus was to collectively break down jargon related to the LGBTTTQA+ community and Drag performance in order to "translate" into prompts for the AI to illustrate. This was specifically done by creating thesaurus to render visible the consensus and dissents through the persona design process. In this research, fotohistorias are proposed using AI images as opposed to the traditional photography approach in order to have consistency with the fictional aspect of *personas* and unveiling dominant thinking [30]. It is worth noting that the exposition of *Astrid Búk Kake's* and *La Alanina's* performance helped participants to contextualize and be guided by them.

3 Early Results, Discussion and Future Research

As a result of the workshop, specific cultural categories emerged, such as *VIHchota*, a compound neologism combining *bichota* (associated with feminine empowerment within specific *Latinx* communities) and being HIV proud. Another, more general term, *orgullo sidoso*, emerged as complementary. This was translated into design principles and elements that included incorporating red in attire and exaggerations in makeup, body, and messages. It is worth pointing out that even though the term is situated in terms of class, gender and cultural background, and has material impact that can illustrate the meaning of the *VIHchota*, the group highlighted controversies regarding whether the representation was consistent with Tijuana's context, or if it simply represents a hegemonic body (Fig. 1).

Fig. 1. AI result.

With this in mind, one limitation in the use of AI is its difficulty in comprehending culturally situated terms that circulate exclusively within Latin LGBTTTQA+ Spanish-speaking communities, and the capacity to break them down. Further steps include processing the data following the Grounded Theory methodology in order to describe, systematize and arrive to a theoretical saturation about embodiment of queer perspective through drag performance, with aims of stablishing a definition of the drag persona as a counter-representation strategy for design. A preliminary operationalization of variables is shown in Table 1, which illustrates the persona's *linguist dimension* of gender performativity with the emergency of situated terms; the moderate *disruptive dimension* of feminine representation, and the *normative dimension* of hegemonic embodiment. This allows the designers to be aware of biases in the process of defining personas and be capable of carrying out situated and collaborative iterations. This exploration highlights the promising aspect of persona design with the critical lens of gender perspective to allow self-representation in the design methodology.

As a final remark, it is worth highlighting that images produced took on a performative and bodily dimension due to their participative production and level of acceptance. The synergy between AI image production and participant observation enabled the community to self-represent specific queer *Latinx* categories, which can subsequently inform design decisions. This collective effort contributes to understanding queer representation in the field, embodying notions such as pride and legitimacy. The methodology employed challenges the notion of the standard and statistical human bodies by offering

Table 1. Operationalization of variables.

Variables	Preliminary values
1. Type: queer jargon 2. Prompt attributes: gender, class, HIV status 3. Level of acceptation 4. Binary disruption	1. *VIHchota,* empowered woman, HIV proud 2. *Prompt*: redhead woman with curly hair with gothic style form 90's. Glam dark makeup. Wearing a blanket with a message: *orgullo sidoso* 3. With reservations 4. Hegemonic representation of white femininity

a participative alternative, emphasizing that human representations have an impact on realty and can be addressed through the design process with a queer perspective.

References

1. Butler, J.: Gender Trouble: Feminism and the Subversion of Identity. Routledge, New York (1990)
2. Kling, R.: Towards a person-centered computer technology. In: Proceedings of the ACM Annual Conference, pp. 387–391. ACM (1973). https://doi.org/10.1145/800192.805740
3. Kelly, J., Matthews, B.: Displacing use: exploring alternative relationships in a human-centred design process. Des. Stud. **35**(4), 353–373 (2014). https://doi.org/10.1016/j.destud.2014.02.001
4. Schneider, M., Arble, F., Olson, N., Wolff, D.: An overview of ergonomic considerations in computer systems. In: Proceedings of the Seventeenth Annual Computer Personnel Research Conference, p. 116 (1980). https://doi.org/10.1145/800085.802735
5. Wang, A., Barocas, S., Laird, K., Wallach, H.: Measuring representational harms in image captioning. In: Proceedings of the 2022 ACM Conference on Fairness, Accountability, and Transparency, pp. 324–335 (2022). https://doi.org/10.1145/800085.802735
6. Hendrick, H.: The IEA and International ergonomics: past, present and future. In: Ergonomics in Russia, the other Independent States, and Around the World, vol. 2, pp. 1–12 (1993)
7. Brulé, E., Kazi-Tani, T.: Disputing Ergonomics, Deconstructing Users. A Queer Perspective on Design. Design History Society (2015)
8. Conrads, U.: Programas y Manifiestos de la Arquitectura del Siglo XX, pp. 144–145. Editorial Lumen, Barcelona (1973)
9. Betts, M.: Divergencias en torno al concepto de funcionalismo en la historia del Diseño. In: Primera Escuela de Chicago, Bauhaus y HfG Hochschule für Gestaltung. Cuadernos del Centro de Estudios de Diseño y Comunicación, p. 134 (2021). https://doi.org/10.18682/cdc.vi139.5095
10. Wright, F.: A Testament. Horizon Press, New York (1957)
11. Cooper, G., Bowers, J.: Representing the user: notes on the disciplinary rhetoric of human-computer interaction. In: The Social and Interactional Dimensions of Human-Computer Interfaces, pp. 48–66 (1995)
12. Suchman, L.A.: Human-Machine Reconfigurations: Plans and Situated Actions, 2nd edn. Cambridge University Press, Cambridge (2007)

13. Godden, R., Hsy, J.: Universal design and its discontents. In: Kim, D., Stommel, J. (eds.) Disrupting the Digital Humanities, 1st edn, p. 111 (2016)
14. Wittig, M.: El pensamiento heterosexual. El pensamiento heterosexual y otros ensayos, Egales, Editorial, 3rd edn, pp. 45–57, Barcelona, España (2006)
15. Butler, J.: Bodies That Matter: On the Discursive Limits of Sex. Routledge, New York (1993)
16. Butler, J.: Undoing gender. Psychology Press (2004)
17. Dreyfuss, H.: The Measure of Man: Human Factors in Design. Whitney Library of Design (1967)
18. Hacking, I.: ¿La construcción social de qué? Paidós, Barcelona (2001)
19. Corona-Martinez, A.: Ensayo sobre el Proyecto, p. 10. Editorial CP67, Buenos Aires (1990)
20. Bell, V.: Performative knowledge. Theory Cult. Soc. **23**(2–3), 214–217 (2006)
21. Romero-Caballero, B.: La colonialidad de la naturaleza. Visualizaciones y "contra-visualizaciones" decoloniales para sostener la vida. Extravío: revista electrónica de literatura comparada. **8**, 1–22 (2015)
22. Amao, M.: De las narrativas dominantes a las contranarrativas: diseñar para dislocar los estereotipos de género. In: Repensar los diseños: de lo binario a lo queer, pp. 169–192 (2021)
23. Contreras, G.: El diseño activista y el drag: Activist design and drag. Inventio. **17**(42), 1–12 (2022). https://doi.org/10.30973/inventio/2021.17.42/8
24. Frayling, C.: Research into Art & Design. Royal College of Art, London (1993)
25. Nielsen, L.: Scenarier som udviklingsværktøj. Designværkstedet. (1998)
26. Nielsen, L.: Personas-user focused design, vol. 1373. Springer, London (2013)
27. Quirós, C.: Una propuesta para el estudio de la fotohistoria: el método iconográfico (2005)
28. Yefimova, K., Neils, M., Newell, B., Gomez, R.: Fotohistorias: participatory photography as a methodology to elicit the life experiences of migrants. In: 2015 48th Hawaii International Conference on System Sciences, pp. 3672–3681. IEEE (2015). https://doi.org/10.1109/HICSS.2015.443
29. Pérez, A.: "Fotos y Recuerdos": Latinx Early Childhood Teachers Counter-Story Through FotoHistorias. Teachers College, Columbia University (2021)
30. Murga-González, A.D., Guardia-Manzur, A., Hall-Fernández, W.: Las mediaciones en las representaciones identitarias de género y etnicidad a través del lenguaje visual y escrito desde el Diseño y el Arte. In: Cuadernos del Centro de Estudios de Diseño y Comunicación (No. 191.), pp. 97–107 (2023)

Conceptualization of Demonstrators for Human-Technology Interaction with a Three-Layer Model

Adjan Hansen-Ampah[1(✉)], Andrea Altepost[1], Farah Elaroussi[1], Linda Hirsch[2], Wolfgang Merx[1], Leif Oppermann[2], Astrid Rosenthal-von der Pütten[3], Anna Milena Rothermel[3], and Stefan Schiffer[3,4]

[1] Institut für Textiltechnik of RWTH Aachen University, Otto-Blumenthal-Straße 1, 52074 Aachen, Germany
{adjan.hansen-ampah,andrea.altepost,farah.elaroussi, wolfgang.merx}@ita.rwth-aachen.de

[2] Fraunhofer Institute for Applied Information Technology FIT, Schloss Birlinghoven, 53757 Sankt Augustin, Germany
{linda.hirsch,leif.oppermann}@fit.fraunhofer.de

[3] Individual and Technology at RWTH Aachen University, Theaterplatz 14, 52062 Aachen, Germany
{arvdp,milena.rothermel,stefan.schiffer}@itec.rwth-aachen.de

[4] MASCOR Institute, FH Aachen University of Applied Sciences, Eupener Straße 70, 52066 Aachen, Germany
s.schiffer@fh-aachen.de

Abstract. We present a three-layer model of stakeholder involvement, developed as part of the ongoing WIRKsam project. WIRKsam uses artificial intelligence (AI) to create or modify socio-technical work systems in a participatory fashion and in such a way that all stakeholders benefit from better conditions of labor. While the technological elements of these changes are easy to highlight to others, it is difficult to convey the human-related and organizational changes and their benefits. Therefore, we aim to develop demonstrators in the field of human factors which should showcase the transformation of work and not just technology, using extended reality (XR) in an transdisciplinary setting.

Keywords: Human Factors · Demonstrators · Socio-technical System · XR · HMI · HCI · KI · AI

1 Introduction

Technology seems to be the easiest part of a new socio-technical work system in production environments to speak about with interested parties – be it company representatives, civil society, or others – while social factors are difficult to grasp. This holds true for a technology as complex as AI. The technical parts can be demonstrated rather easily, for example, how algorithms are employed to maximize production planning effectiveness and efficiency.

S. Jin et al. (Eds.): IEA 2024, SSDI 39, pp. 207–214, 2025.
https://doi.org/10.1007/978-981-95-0211-0_32

However, demonstrating how integrating AI into a work system shapes the way employees work and how this new way of working can improve work processes and job satisfaction, is an entirely different story. How do you illustrate the "old-fashioned" way of working, for instance, the monotony of manually doing visual quality control tasks for eight hours a day? How do you show how their everyday work improved after introducing AI systems and reshaping the entire work system according to the HTO concept [11, 16]? These and other questions are the focus of the WIRKsam Competence Center, a joint human factors project set out to investigate how work systems and processes can be altered with the help of AI in such a way that all stakeholders, especially shopfloor employees, benefit from better conditions of labor. This research is conducted with the help of 11 companies which provide 12 socio-technical use cases. Moreover, demonstrators shall be developed which ideally show both the current and new ways of working and how stakeholders benefit from participatory socio-technical design processes in these use cases. In our project, we use demonstrator as a synonym for "experience prototypes" [14] that allow scenario- and context-based experience of AI-enhanced work systems through XR technologies. The development of demonstrators is both part of the individual use cases and the focus of a dedicated work package inside of the overall project structure.

The aim of this paper is to outline a first concept for creating such a demonstrator which combines approaches from human factors, sociology of technology, social psychology, informatics and XR interaction.

2 Stakeholder Participation in the WIRKsam Competence Center

The goal of WIRKsam is to participatively design socio-technical work systems which use AI to benefit all stakeholders. To do so, WIRKsam created an iterative procedure model which operates on the basis of the above mentioned HTO concept and therefore assumes "that technical, organizational and human-related aspects of work system design" [10] have to be taken into account simultaneously [9]. This WIRKsam Procedure Model (WPM) [10] is set up as a circular phase model with distinct but closely coupled and overlapping technological (CRISP-DM) and work-scientific (APRODI and SozioTex) processes.

In each phase, different participatory methods are employed. In the Orientation Phase, a viable use case is identified and selected in our Innovation Workshop with the help of different – albeit predominantly managerial – corporate roles.

In the Focusing Phase, social network analysis methods can be used to identify stakeholders relevant for the actual use case – on the level of both individuals and groups/roles [7]. Using this information, the HTO Workshop [2, 8, 9] gathers the relevant stakeholders and lets them develop and discuss work system designs which become part of socio-technical requirement specifications [15].

These requirements are then implemented in the Realization Phase. To ensure that all HTO aspects and stakeholders' needs are considered, the work system design is carried out iteratively. A multistage workshop concept based on Domain-Driven Design (DDD), developed by MASCOR Institute at FH Aachen University of Applied Science, is used to transfer the different domains and stakeholders found in a company to the new AI-assisted work system. Drawing on the results of the HTO and DDD workshops, HMI mockups and first software versions are developed and tested in subsequent work system tests. The goal of these tests, which are carried out with direct involvement of employees, is to not only assess the technical ("T") side of the solution, i.e. aspects such as usability, digital stress, and adherence to work design principles [5, 6]. Also aspects belonging to "H" and "O", such as opportunities for qualification, integration of the new system into the operational structure, and employees' freedom of action, are taken into account. Furthermore, suggestions for improvement for the next iterations are gathered.

Once the work system has been deemed sufficiently optimized, it is set up as a pilot facility inside the company (Stabilization Phase). In this phase, the work system prototype is embedded into the organizational framework and can be tested and assessed by stakeholders in a less controlled environment.

3 The Role of Demonstrators in WIRKsam

The WPM is primarily intended to shape and guide research in the 12 use cases in which prototypes of AI tools are being developed and their influence on the socio-technical work system is being explored and evaluated. In addition to this main task, the development of demonstrators is a cornerstone of WIRKsam. The vision of WIRKsam is to be a self-sustained competence center after the funding term, offering its service of AI-related socio-technical research and development to companies. Demonstrators can not only showcase the positive outcomes of participative work system design to prospective clients, but can fulfill additional purposes, such as describing the contexts of some of the work system prototypes, explicating participation concepts, or acting as an experimentation environment for the research of human-technology interaction (HTI).

3.1 Low- and High-Fidelity Demonstrators

Demonstrators are crucial throughout the project phases and beyond by providing implemented or crafted system versions that allow testing the concept through experience with users (a.k.a. workers in WIRKsam). Earlier versions can be integrated with low-fidelity and made of, e.g., cardboard or Wizard-of-Oz setups (WoZ) that allow simulating, enacting, or envisioning the interaction with a system to detect potential issues [3, 4]. Studies in social psychology often make use of the WoZ principle [12] for experiments. WoZ setups can be used as a method for testing and evaluating systems or prototypes that are not yet fully functional. Participants interact with an allegedly intelligent and autonomous system which indeed is operated by an experimenter. In the context of demonstrators WoZ setups can be used to test different versions of AI-systems even when they are not fully implemented or working properly yet.

In comparison, high-fidelity demonstrators can demonstrate AI solutions embedded into a scenario and help companies to learn about the potential of AI solutions for the presented interaction and their own businesses through experience. Technologies such as XR serve this purpose well as they enable 3D digital, spatial replicas of work environments or mobile, and flexible augmentation of stationary and existing machines [13]. Thus, XR provides the scenario and context-relations in which the AI and workers are supposed to collaborate. Such demonstrators enable users to explore and further develop these solutions. Another advantage of demonstrators applied throughout the project is that they foster shared understanding and communication. Thus, our approach to participation regarding demonstrators is twofold. On the one hand, participation means developing demonstrators in a participatory fashion. Different methods are utilized to do so. For instance, we conducted workshops in the context of biannual project meetings. In these, all project partners (academic and industrial) and especially the company representatives gather requirements and design implications. Similarly, university courses are used to convey the importance of demonstrators in specific use cases such as scrap minimization and predictive maintenance and to gather insights from students as to how they should be designed [1]. On the other hand, we conceptualize demonstrators as a means to participatively test and enhance work system designs and human-technology interaction with regard to different stakeholders.

3.2 Social Psychological Factors

From a social psychology perspective, having demonstrators opens up a new ground for gaining insights into how humans interact with technology and how affected they feel by the new technology regarding their self-efficacy and self-concept as skilled workers. With demonstrators, we can explore the middle ground between studies in the laboratory and in the field (Living Lab). Many studies can only be conducted in the laboratory because conducting a study in the field would interfere with the regular productive environment too much. However, with demonstrators and with immersive ones even more so, we could replicate the real situation very closely and thus evaluate human behavior in interactions with technology in more realistic scenarios. Additionally, potential confounding variables that could interfere in field studies can be controlled, while simultaneously ensuring that the setting maintains a high degree of naturalism, thereby increasing validity. Especially the last point, high degree of naturalism, is important as study participants will more directly 'experience' the new work situation and thus will also experience how the new work system differs from the old one and what this means for their self-concept; insights that are very hard to achieve in focus groups or prospective interviews in which users merely imagine future scenarios.

3.3 The Three-Layer Concept of Stakeholder Involvement

Since the initial purpose of demonstrators in WIRKsam was to promote the Competence Center, the envisioned main audience was company representatives, especially persons in managerial positions. The extension of purposes therefore coincides with an expansion of the target group: different stakeholders with varying levels of involvement have to be addressed. To do so adequately, we developed the three-layer concept of stakeholder involvement which categorizes different purposes, stakeholders and their involvement.

The first layer of involvement encompasses stakeholders who are directly affected by changes made to the socio-technical work system. In most of our cases, these are first and foremost shopfloor employees entrusted with carrying out industrial processes such as melt spinning, quality control or surface treatment. However, also employees tasked with production planning or R&D are directly affected in some of our use cases.

The second layer is comprised of indirectly or not yet involved stakeholders. Indirectly involved stakeholders can be part of the organization, or they can be external actors. The former group consists of corporate roles or functions such as human resources and employees from preceding or subsequent processes. The latter group includes indirectly involved stakeholders such as business clients who are affected by changes to products, e.g. concerning quality.

The third layer consists of societal stakeholders who are not affected by changes to the concrete work system in itself. Rather, they are affected on a societal level, e.g. via aggregated / emergent effects of such workplace innovations. Examples of societal stakeholders include other researchers and university students, actors in ministries and politics, company representatives and chambers of industry, commerce and crafts, economic development agencies, and the general population.

All three involvement levels have to be addressed by demonstrators, albeit differently. Regarding the first level, demonstrators are conceptualized as an experimentation environment. For example, they could be used to figure out differences in how employees perceive the quality of AI systems stemming from training data which have allegedly been labeled by coworkers with varying degrees of expertise (trainee vs. foreperson). Regarding the second level, demonstrators could be used to show clients how changing the way employees work positively affects product quality or other operational targets. Lastly, demonstrators could act as a tool to inform and educate the wider population on the transformation of work, e.g. in schools.

4 Expected Results

We plan to iteratively and participatively create demonstrators which appeal to all three layers of stakeholders. In what follows, we refer to a use case to roughly sketch out how a demonstrator could look like and which outcomes we expect.

4.1 Our Use Case: Forming and Tempering

Our exemplary use case focuses on the forming and tempering process as part of the manufacturing of shearing spiral blades. At the moment, manufacturing a new lot involves the following steps (amongst others):

- getting a bundle of semi-finished spirals which were pre-formed in a previous, fairly manual process,
- manually pre-adjusting the machinery using experiential knowledge,
- forming and tempering the first blade, and
- checking the form and testing the hardness of this blade.

If both hardness and form are satisfactory, the whole lot can be produced using the setup. However, if either one of the two variables is out of specification, the blade has to be scrapped and further adjustments have to be made. This can result in a rather lengthy, stressful and frustrating trial-and-error process since there are many adjustment screws, and adjusting for hardness can negatively impact the form and vice versa. Our goal is to replace the manual machinery with robots which position the forming and tempering tools, and an AI system which makes suggestions on the aforementioned positioning parameters. With help of these suggestions, which can be modified or completely ignored by the employees, who retain full control over production, we hope to reduce the extent of trial and error and the stress and scrap caused by it.

4.2 Demonstrating the Work Systems

A first low-fidelity version of a demonstrator could capture the visual differences between the two production systems, e.g. with help of cardboard models or simple digital models. However, this first version would not adequately convey the actual changes in everyday work and how employees benefit from them. Since a more realistic setting is important from a social psychological perspective (cf. 3.2), additional interactive elements could be added in the XR environment. For example, gamification could be utilized: In a first scenario, "players" could be tasked with trying to set up the "old" production system via various manual adjustment screws and could get feedback on hardness and accuracy of fit as well as number of faulty blades and time spent until successful setup or giving up. In a subsequent scenario, players would use a modern AI assisted HMI to set up the robots' positions and, as before, would receive feedback on their performance.

Regarding the first layer of stakeholders, we plan to use the high-fidelity demonstrator for preliminary work system tests, e.g. in order to gain insights on employees' acceptance of the new work system and to gather suggestions for improvement. To do so, they would skip the demonstration of the old system and would directly start the second scenario. For shopfloor employees who work at other stations and nonetheless know how difficult the forming and tempering process is (layer 2), the second scenario could be used to promote the work system. This might make more employees consider changing positions. Similarly, the XR demonstrator could be used at events such as trade fairs to attract potential apprentices and young job applicants (layer 2). Regarding the third layer of stakeholders, the demonstrator could convey the importance and benefits of the participatory design of work systems, the achieved difference in job satisfaction, and the possibilities of digitalization in general and AI in particular.

5 Summary

Our paper presents a three-layer model for creating demonstrators that showcase the participatory transformation of socio-technical work systems using AI. Developed as part of the WIRKsam project, the model engages stakeholders at different levels of involvement using XR to convey human, technological, and organizational impacts and benefits. Low- and high-fidelity demonstrators enable concept testing, shared understanding, and experimentation for HTI research. The model combines approaches from human factors, sociology, psychology, informatics, and XR interaction to guide the development of demonstrators that allow users to experience and shape AI-enhanced work systems.

Acknowledgments. WIRKsam Competence Center receives funding from the Federal Ministry of Education and Research (BMBF) in the program "Regionale Kompetenzzentren der Arbeitsforschung" (grant numbers 02L19C600ff.) administered by Project Management Agency Karlsruhe (PTKA).

References

1. Altepost, A., Berlin, F., Ferrein, A., Harlacher, M.: Demonstrativ-aktiv-iterativ: Arbeitssysteme mit Künstlicher Intelligenz an Demonstratoren im Reallabor vermitteln, erproben und weiterentwickeln. In: Dokumentation des 69. Arbeitswissenschaftlichen Kongresses Hannover 01.03. - 03.03.2023. Nachhaltig Arbeiten und Lernen - Analyse und Gestaltung lernförderlicher und nachhaltiger Arbeitssysteme und Arbeits- und Lernprozesse, Hannover (2023)
2. Bau, M., Altepost, A.: MTO und PBA als integraler Transformationsansatz. Tech. Rep. 3. ILAG Institut Leistung Arbeit Gesundheit, Plön (2023)
3. Ehn, P., Kyng, M.: Cardboard computers: mocking-it-up or hands-on the future. In: Greenbaum, J., Kyng, M. (eds.) Design at Work: Cooperative Design of Computer Systems, pp. 170–195. Lawrence Erlbaum Associates (1991)
4. Feng, K.J.K., Coppock, M.J., McDonald, D.W.: How do UX Practitioners Communicate AI as a Design Material? Artifacts, conceptions, and propositions. In: Proceedings of the 2023 ACM Designing Interactive Systems Conference, pp. 2263–2280. DIS '23, Association for Computing Machinery, Pittsburgh, PA (2023). https://doi.org/10.1145/3563657.3596101
5. Grote, G., Ryser, C., Wäfler, T., Windischer, A., Weik, S.: KOMPASS: a method for complementary function allocation in automated work systems. Int. J. Hum. Comput. Stud. **52**(2), 267–287 (2000)
6. Hacker, W., Sachse, P.: Allgemeine Arbeitspsychologie, 4th edn. Psychische Regulation von Arbeitstätigkeiten. vdf Hochschulverlag, Zürich (2023)
7. Hansen-Ampah, A.: Gemeinsam scheitern. Entwicklung eines netzwerkbasierten Innovationsmodells zur prognostizierenden (Nachhaltigkeits-)Analyse soziotechnischer Neuerungen. PhD, Rheinisch-Westfälische Technische Hochschule Aachen, Aachen (2023). https://doi.org/10.18154/RWTH-2023-03546., https://publications.rwth-aachen.de/record/955533
8. Hansen-Ampah, A., Altepost, A., Elaroussi, F., Berlin, F.: Expertise aus allen Richtungen: Partizipative Arbeitssystemgestaltung mit dem MTO-Workshop (2024)
9. Hansen-Ampah, A., Altepost, A., Merx, W., Berlin, F., Elaroussi, F.: There Is More to the Picture Than Meets the AI: Using MTO to Shape and Implement AI in Textile Production, Dresden (2023)
10. Harlacher, M., Altepost, A., Elsen, I., Ferrein, A., Hansen-Ampah, A., Merx, W., Niehues, S., Schiffer, S., Nasim, F.: Approach for the Identification of requirements on the design of AI-supported work systems (in problem based projects). In: EPEAI Conference AI in Business and Economics. Mülheim A.D.R
11. Karltun, A., Karltun, J., Berglund, M., Eklund, J.: HTO—a complementary ergonomics approach. Appl. Ergon. **59**, 182–190 (2017)
12. Kelley, J.F.: An iterative design methodology for user-friendly natural language office information applications. ACM Trans. Inf. Syst. **2**(1), 26–41 (1984). https://doi.org/10.1145/357417.357420
13. Oppermann, L., Uzun, Y., Buchholz, F., Riedlinger, U., Fuchs, S., Stenzel, H., Odenthal, L., Altepost, A., Bau, M.: Industrial Metaverse? Human-Centred Design for Collaborative Remote Maintenance and Training Using XR-Technologies. In: XR Meets the Metaverse - Proceedings of the 8th International Augmented and Virtual Reality Conference 2023, Las Vegas, USA. Springer Proceedings in Business and Economics (2023)
14. Rico, J., Brewster, S.: Gesture and voice prototyping for early evaluations of social acceptability in multimodal interfaces. In: International Conference on Multimodal Interfaces and the Workshop on Machine Learning for Multimodal Interaction. ICMI-MLMI '10. Association for Computing Machinery, New York, NY (2010). https://doi.org/10.1145/1891903.1891925

15. Roth, S., Kötter, W.: Soziotechnisches Lastenheft: Herangehensweise bei der Anforderungsermittlung an digitale Assistenzsysteme am Beispiel eines mittelständisch geprägten Industrieunternehmens. In: Bericht zum 66. Arbeitswissenschaftlichen Kongress vom 16–18. März 2020. Berlin (2020)
16. Strohm, O., Ulich, E.: Unternehmen arbeitspsychologisch bewerten. vdf Hochschulverlag AG, Zürich (1997)

How to Optimize Design Creative Performance Using Generative AI?

Jeongyun Kang(✉) and Dongwook Hwang

Kwangwoon University, Seoul 01897, South Korea
jh.joyce.k@gmail.com, dongwookkr@kw.ac.kr

Abstract. With a growing interest in Generative AI, this study investigates the impact of different prompting approaches, including base, zero-shot, and few-shot learning, and the role of human intervention in generating creative design solutions using GPT-4. Specifically, it distinguishes exemplary ideas that are superior in terms of creativity from those that are not, and investigates how different inputs in training influence the resulting creative performance. The study results revealed that zero-shot prompts, especially those emphasizing diversity, produced the most varied solutions. Few-shot prompts, using high-quality (top) and low-quality (bottom) examples, demonstrated that top examples resulted in greater diversity compared to bottom examples. The findings highlight the crucial role of human judgment in input training, noting that high-quality examples broaden the space in few-shot learning. Therefore, this research suggests insights into the necessity of integrating Gen-AI with human intervention by demonstrating how human-AI collaboration can be fine-tuned to maximize benefits in creative endeavors.

Keywords: Generative AI · Creativity · Human-AI Collaboration

1 Introduction

While computational evaluation methods like cosine similarity and convex hull volume have facilitated the analysis of creative output performance in the domain of ideation and design, previous studies evaluating the creative potential of Generative AI (Gen-AI), such as GPTs, have encountered limitations. These limitations stem from the use of randomly selected examples for training input, leading to phenomena like hallucination and irrelevant/infeasible solutions [1, 2]. To overcome these shortcomings, this study focuses on leveraging GPT-4 for creative design solutions by examining the impact of different prompting approaches and emphasizes human intervention, specifically by categorizing prompts into 'top' and 'bottom' groups, to analyze variations in creative outputs.

This study aims to explore the necessity of human intervention in the process of generating creative ideas by GPT-4. The study proposes to analyze and compare creative performance based on the nature of the input training. Specifically, it distinguishes exemplary ideas that are superior in terms of creativity from those that are not, and investigates how different inputs in training influence the resulting creative performance.

S. Jin et al. (Eds.): IEA 2024, SSDI 39, pp. 215–220, 2025.
https://doi.org/10.1007/978-981-95-0211-0_33

2 Related Work

2.1 Zero-Shot Learning

Zero-shot learning, recognized in Natural Language Processing (NLP), enables immediate application of a Large Language Model (LLM)'s capabilities to unfamiliar tasks by tapping into its broad linguistic and contextual knowledge base [3]. It allows LLMs to generate responses that are intuitively aligned with the task, drawing on its vast training across various text corpora [4]. Zero-shot learning thus represents a significant stride in Gen-AI, particularly LLMs like GPT-4, showcasing the ability of models to generalize their learning to new contexts. This method is particularly beneficial in creative tasks, where the requirement is often for original and out-of-the-box thinking, without the constraints of specific training data.

2.2 Few-Shot Learning

Few-shot learning, another NLP technique applied in LLMs, is particularly effective when dealing with specialized tasks that require a degree of contextual understanding beyond the model's standard training [5]. By providing Gen-AIs with a handful of relevant examples, few-shot learning effectively fine-tunes the model's responses to align more closely with the specific requirements of the task.

There is currently an active discourse surrounding Gen-AI and its capacity for creativity. Numerous studies have concentrated on assessing the relative creativity of humans compared to Gen-AI. However, there is a gap in research regarding the collaborative potential between humans and Gen-AI to generate superior ideas, as well as the methods by which human intervention can enhance this collaborative process. To address this gap, we propose the following research question:

RQ1. How do different prompt engineering strategies affect the variability of design solutions generated by GPT-4, and what role does human intervention play in optimizing these outcomes?

3 Method

3.1 Selection of Design Solution Prompts

The process of selecting and adapting design prompts for this study involved sourcing from a previous study [2] that compared human-generated solutions with those produced by LLMs in various problem domains. These prompts share a common theme: they all require innovative design solutions to address everyday challenges. Their applicability extends across diverse user groups, emphasizing practicality and usability in daily life. The design prompts used for the study are listed in Table 1.

Table 1. Design Solution Prompts.

No.	Prompt
1	Generate 100 design solutions for a lightweight exercise device that can collect energy from human motion
2	Generate 100 design solutions for a device that disperses a light coating of a powdered substance over a surface
3	Generate 100 design solutions for a device that allows people to get a book that is out of reach
4	Generate 100 design solutions for a measuring cup for the blind

3.2 Implementation of Zero-Shot and Few-Shot Learning

The standard input for the zero-shot learning model is identified as the base prompt. To create zero-shot prompts, these base prompts were modified by adding adjectives like *diverse* and *novel*. The aim was for GPT-4 to directly generate solutions that differ from those elicited by the base prompts. This approach was intended to uncover the model's capacity to interpret and integrate new directives, thereby producing a broader range of innovative design solutions.

For the few-shot examples, two design experts analyzed responses to base prompts, selecting five highly creative (top) and five less creative (bottom) responses per prompt, totaling ten examples. Inter-rater reliability using Cohen's Kappa coefficient showed substantial agreement of 0.79, indicating substantial agreement between them [6]. In each few-shot learning iteration, one example from the top five and one from the bottom five was used to refine the prompt. Figure 1 illustrates the workflow of different prompting approaches in this study.

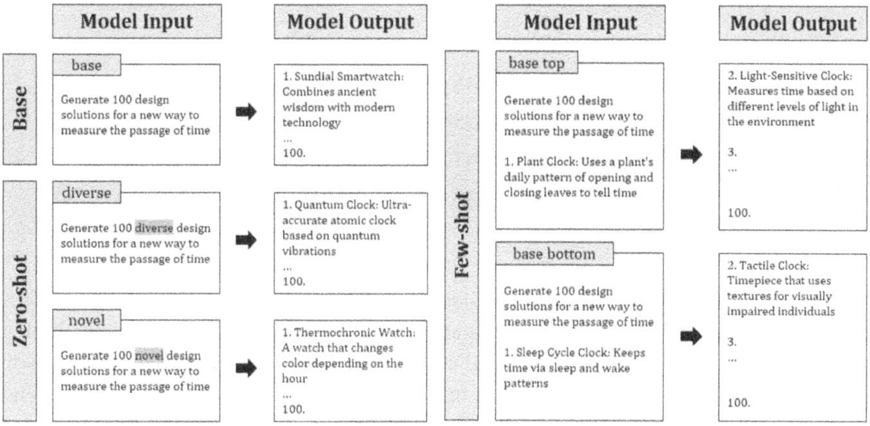

Fig. 1. Workflow of base, zero-shot, and few-shot learning for design solutions.

3.3 Evaluation

In this study, the evaluation of outputs generated from GPT-4 using base, zero-shot, and few-shot prompts was conducted using two computational metrics. Cosine distance was initially employed to measure the similarity between vectorized design solutions, providing a quantitative assessment of how closely or distinctively each solution related to the others [7]. Each design solution was transformed into a 384-dimensional vector using SentenceBERT from SentenceTransformers, specifically the *all-MiniLM-L6-v2* model for its optimal balance of speed, size, and quality.

Following the cosine distance analysis, the convex hull volume was calculated using Principal Component Analysis (PCA) to project the high-dimensional vectors into a lower-dimensional space. This metric quantified the overall diversity of the GPT-4 generated solutions. This sequential approach allowed for a comprehensive examination of the data, exploring individual similarities and differences, and assessing their collective variance and spread within the conceptual design space.

4 Results

4.1 Cosine Distance

The similarity between a set of solution ideas was calculated with cosine distances, using base prompts as a reference point, against zero-shot (diverse, novel) and few-shot base (top, bottom) categories. Notably, the result showed significant differences between zero-shot diverse and few-shot bottom, as detailed in Table 2.

Table 2. Results of Cosine Distance.

Prompt	Zero-shot		Few-shot	
	Diverse	Novel	Top	Bottom
1	0.792	0.601	0.591	0.569
2	0.586	0.645	0.531	0.542
3	0.681	0.655	0.667	0.658
4	0.735	0.647	0.688	0.604
M	0.698	0.637	0.619	0.594

Within the zero-shot learning analysis, the zero-shot diverse category, representing solution ideas generated in a *diverse* manner without any prior examples, had the highest mean cosine distance of 0.698. This indicates that these ideas exhibit the lowest similarity to the base prompts, reflecting a broader range of variation and less adherence to the initial prompts. Conversely, the zero-shot novel category, which includes ideas generated through novel approaches without prior examples, had a mean cosine distance of 0.637. Although these ideas are still quite varied, they maintain a slightly higher level of adherence to the base prompts compared to the diverse category.

In the few-shot learning analysis, the results demonstrate that providing examples significantly impacts the similarity of generated ideas to the base prompts. The few-shot top category, consisting of solution ideas generated from the most creative responses to the base prompts, had a mean cosine distance of 0.619. This indicates that despite using highly creative examples, the solutions still show a relatively high level of adherence to the base prompts. The few-shot bottom category had the lowest mean cosine distance of 0.594.

4.2 Convex Hull Volume

The analysis of Convex Hull Volume across different prompt types reveals notable variations in response diversity. These variations highlight the impact of prompt design and the use of examples on the range of responses generated by GPT-4.

In the zero-shot categories, diverse prompts achieved the highest average volume (0.279), indicating a broad range of responses when the word *diverse* is explicitly emphasized. This suggests that prompts designed to encourage diversity effectively enhance the variability in generated content. On the other hand, novel prompts, with an average of 0.248, showed a narrower range. This indicates that while novelty-focused prompts aim to produce unique responses, they do not significantly increase the overall diversity compared to diverse prompts (Table 3).

Table 3. Results of Convex Hull Volume.

Prompt	Base	Zero-shot		Few-shot	
		Diverse	Novel	Top	Bottom
1	0.212	0.161	0.207	0.246	0.219
2	0.227	0.276	0.275	0.181	0.201
3	0.313	0.294	0.279	0.300	0.248
4	0.336	0.383	0.233	0.330	0.236
M	0.272	0.279	0.248	0.264	0.226
SD	0.061	0.091	0.035	0.066	0.021

Within the few-shot categories, the top prompts exhibited an average of 0.264. This is higher than the 0.226 average of the bottom prompts. This comparison illustrates that high-quality examples can more effectively broaden the range of responses. However, both few-shot conditions demonstrated lower volumes compared to the zero-shot diverse and base prompts. This reduction in diversity may be attributed to design fixation, where the provided examples limit the variability of responses.

5 Discussion

The results of this study illuminate the nuanced impact of human intervention in categorizing inputs as 'top' and 'bottom' quality on GPT-4's creative outputs under both zero-shot and few-shot learning frameworks. In few-shot learning, 'top' inputs, representing higher-quality examples, led to an expanded novelty space compared to 'bottom' inputs. This distinction underlines the critical role of human judgment in shaping the AI's creative process, as the model's responses varied in quality based on the categorization of the prompts.

The findings also emphasize the differential capabilities of GPT-4 across various prompting strategies. Zero-shot learning with 'diverse' prompts produced the most noticeably diverse range of responses and this effect was more pronounced than in the few-shot top scenario. The few-shot categories, although benefiting from high-quality examples, showed lower convex hull volumes compared to zero-shot diverse and base prompts, indicating a trade-off between guidance and diversity.

In summary, this research not only demonstrates the potential of LLMs like GPT-4 in the creative design process but also emphasizes the importance of human intervention in optimizing the model's performance. The strategic selection and categorization of prompts play a pivotal role in enhancing the novelty and diversity of GPT-4's outputs. These findings offer valuable insights for integrating Gen-AIs into creative workflows, highlighting how human-AI collaboration can be fine-tuned to maximize the benefits of Gen-AIs in creative endeavors. This study contributes to the growing understanding of balancing AI capabilities and human guidance to optimize creative outputs.

Acknowledgments. The present research has been conducted by the Excellent researcher support project of Kwangwoon University in 2024.

References

1. Liu, J., Shen, D., Zhang, Y., Dolan, B., Carin, L., Chen, W.: What Makes Good In-Context Examples for GPT-3? arXiv preprint, arXiv:2101.06804 (2021)
2. Ma, K., Grandi, D., McComb, C., Goucher-Lambert, K.: Conceptual Design Generation Using Large Language Models. arXiv preprint, arXiv:2306.01779 (2023)
3. Palatucci, M., Pomerleau, D., Hinton, G.E., Mitchell, T.M.: Zero-shot learning with semantic output codes. In: Bengio, Y., Schuurmans, D., Lafferty, J., Williams, C., Culotta, A. (eds.) NIPS 2009, vol. 22. NIPS, Vancouver (2009)
4. Espejel, J.L., Ettifouri, E.H., Alassan, M.S.Y., Chouham, E.M., Dahhane, W.: GPT-3.5, GPT-4, or BARD? Evaluating LLMs reasoning ability in zero-shot setting and performance boosting through prompts. Nat. Lang. Process. J. **5**, 100032 (2023)
5. Lake, B., Salakhutdinov, R., Gross, J., Tenenbaum, J.: One shot learning of simple visual concepts. In: Carlson, L. (ed.) Proceedings of the Annual Meeting of the Cognitive Science Society, vol. 33, pp. 2568–2573. Cognitive Science Society, Boston (2011)
6. McHugh, M.L.: Interrater reliability: the kappa statistic. Biochem. Med. **22**(3), 276–282 (2012)
7. Zhang, J., Wang, F., Ma, F., Song, G.: Text similarity calculation method based on optimized cosine distance. In: O'Conner, L. (ed.) 2022 International Conference on Electronics and Devices, Computational Science (ICEDCS), vol. 1, pp. 37–39. IEEE, Marseille (2022)

Analyzing the AI Kiosk User Experience to Improve Accessibility for the Elderly

Gayoung Kim and Hyun K. Kim(✉)

Kwangwoon University, Seoul 01897, South Korea
hyunkkim@kw.ac.kr

Abstract. In this study, we developed a kiosk with AI technology to provide voice guidance, enhancing the accessibility of kiosks for the elderly. We analyzed the user experience of the elderly compared to a kiosk without AI technology. According to the results of the experiments on 20 elderly people over the age of 60, there was a statistically significant difference between the two kiosks, with the AI kiosks achieving higher average scores. This suggests that the elderly perceive higher satisfaction, ease of use, usefulness, and fun when using AI kiosks than General kiosks. Additionally, the voice guidance provided when difficulties are detected helps reduce difficulties and psychological anxiety during use. The findings of this study can be used to utilize AI technology and improve accessibility when designing kiosks for the elderly.

Keywords: Kiosk · Artificial intelligence · Accessibility · Elderly · User experience

1 Introduction

Kiosk devices are becoming more widely utilized in the marketplace owing to continuous technological advances [1], but their accessibility has not been considered. Elderly people unfamiliar with digital technology struggle to use kiosks [2]. According to a survey by the Seoul Digital Foundation, only 45.8% of seniors aged 55 and older have used a kiosk. Their digital competency scores, including information literacy, digital citizenship, and attitudes toward digital technologies, are significantly lower than those of users under 55 [3]. Majority of the elderly struggle with using kiosks independently, and with the rise of unmanned stores, the chances of getting help are decreasing. There is a need for assistive devices to help individuals use them independently. Most studies addressing the difficulties of kiosk use among the elderly focused on improving UI design [4–7]. However, these studies are limited as they did not consider low digital literacy and technology acceptance of elderly. Along with UI improvements, user guidance features, such as voice or video guides, are needed [8], but there is a lack of research in this area.

In this study, we aim to improve the accessibility of kiosks by using AI to identify the difficulties of the elderly and provide voice guidance. We developed a kiosk with difficulty detection AI (AI Kiosk) and voice guidance. We analyzed the user experience of the elderly compared to a kiosk without these features (General kiosk).

In this study, we tried to answer the following research question:

S. Jin et al. (Eds.): IEA 2024, SSDI 39, pp. 221–226, 2025.
https://doi.org/10.1007/978-981-95-0211-0_34

RQ: How much more positive user experience does an AI kiosk with difficulty detection and voice guidance provide for the elderly compared to a General kiosk?

2 Prototype

As shown in Fig. 1, the AI kiosk provides a "Sequential Step Guide" and "Difficulty Detection Guide." The "Sequential Step Guide" delivers clear voice instructions for each step with minimal required actions, feedback, and input. "Difficulty Detection Guidance" offers audio and video guidance for input and interface positions on each screen when identifying challenges for the elderly. These features are delivered through a kiosk assistant called "Kio" at the top of the interface, which displays facial expressions and animations with subtitles and voice guidance. The prototype was developed in a web browser. Kio utilized a 3D model of the robot with Mixamo animations in three.js. Text-to-speech technology provided voice guidance using the Web Speech API. To detect the difficulties experienced by the user, two webcams captured user images in real-time. We used Media Pipe to recognize faces and body gestures and face-api.js to detect facial expressions. The criteria for judging the difficulty faced by the elderly included facial expressions, emotions, gestures, and latency. Facial expressions and emotions can be detected through eye frowns, mouth openings, and negative emotions, such as sadness, anger, fear, disgust, and surprise. Body gestures, such as hand raising, pointing, and touch latency of 8 seconds, were also included in the criteria. After detecting difficulties of the elderly, the kiosk provided the option for choosing guidance through the "Yes" and "No" buttons. After selecting "yes," it provides a video and voice guidance on its usage, as shown in Fig. 1.

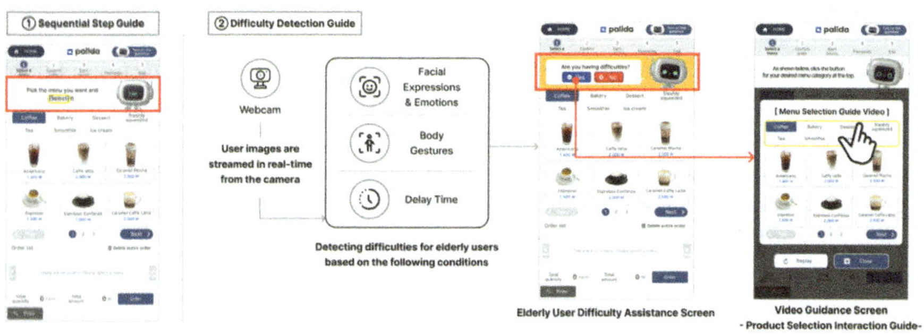

Fig. 1. AI kiosk screens and system processes.

3 Methods

We experimented with 20 elderly people aged 60 or more (9 males, 11 females, mean age: 66 (SD = 3.05)). There were two kiosks: General Kiosk, a kiosk without AI features and voice guidance, and AI Kiosk, a kiosk with AI features and voice guidance. We designed a within-subjects design with two different scenarios for both kiosks, in a balanced order.

Participants completed a survey and a post-interview after using a 21-inch kiosk to order a menu. The questionnaire consisted of 22 questions on an 11-point Likert scale (0 = strongly disagree to 10 = strongly agree) for perceived ease of use, perceived usefulness, enjoyment, customization, and user satisfaction, as shown in Table 1. The post-interview includes questions on AI kiosk and General kiosk preferences, satisfaction with AI features, etc.

Table 1. Questionnaire to evaluate the user experience of the kiosks.

Factor	Questionnaire	Reference
Perceived ease of use	1. Learning to operate the kiosk would be easy for me	[9]
	2. I would find it easy to get the kiosk to do what I want it to do	
	3. My interaction with the kiosk would be clear and understandable	
	4. I would find the kiosk to be flexible to interact with	
	5. It would be easy for me to become skillful at using a kiosk	
	6. I would find the kiosk easy to use	
Perceived usefulness	7. Using kiosk in my job would enable me to accomplish tasks more quickly	
	8. Using kiosk would improve my job performance	
	9. Using kiosk in my job would increase my productivity	
	10. Using a kiosk would enhance my effectiveness on the job	
	11. Using a kiosk would make it easier to do my job	
	12. I would find a kiosk useful in my job	
Enjoyment	13. The operation of the firm's kiosk is interesting	[10]
	14. I feel good being able to use the kiosk	
	15. The firm's kiosk has interesting additional functions	
	16. The firm's kiosk provides me with all relevant information	
Customization	17. The firm's kiosk understands my specific needs	
	18. The firm's kiosk has my best interests at heart	
	19. The firm's kiosk has features that are personalized for me	
User satisfaction	20. Overall, I am satisfied with the kiosk by the firm	[11]
	21. The kiosk offered by the firm exceeded my expectations	
	22. The kiosk offered by the firm are close to my idea	

4 Results

To analyze the user experience factors between kiosks, we conducted a one-way repeated measure analysis of variance (ANOVA) analysis using R studio. The results showed that there were significant differences between the General Kiosk and AI Kiosk in all factors, as shown in Table 2. The AI Kiosk scored higher than the General Kiosk across all factors, with the highest score for Enjoyment and the lowest score for Perceived ease of use, as shown in Fig. 2.

Table 2. Results from a one-way repeated measures ANOVA analysis of elderly kiosk user experience factors by condition.

Factor	Questionnaire	
	F	*p*
Perceived ease of use	7.958	0.011*
Perceived usefulness	9.267	0.007**
Enjoyment	10.59	0.004**
Customization	12.82	0.002**
User satisfaction	10.9	0.004**

Participants 17 out of 20 preferred the AI Kiosk, which provided voice guidance and clear instructions. Participants reported that the AI kiosk was good at identifying difficulties and providing appropriate help. The voice guidance made them feel like they were being guided directly and helped them resolve their difficulties by correcting their mistakes. A few participants familiar with using kiosks regularly tended to prefer General Kiosk as the voice guidance confused them. Some people had difficulty with the instructions, adding and deleting menus, knowing where to touch, etc. During the interviews, the AI kiosks scored 8.4 (SD = 1.56) for AI functionality and 8.8 (SD = 1.17) for the amount of voice guidance. Most participants indicated that the AI performed well in identifying when they were in trouble and that the amount of information in the voice guidance was appropriate.

5 Discussions

The elderly feel more satisfied, at perceived ease of use, perceived usefulness, and have more fun when using AI kiosks, when using AI kiosks, compared to when using general kiosks. The survey revealed that AI kiosks scored higher on average. This demonstrates that AI-based difficulty detection and voice guidance improve kiosk usability for the elderly and enhance order efficiency. Particularly, the enjoyment factor has the highest average in AI kiosk, suggesting that the elderly perceived AI technology, voice guidance, and kiosk assistants as new and fun experiences. *"It was comfortable because the kiosk recognized when I did not know and guided me (P1)."* They had a personalized experience

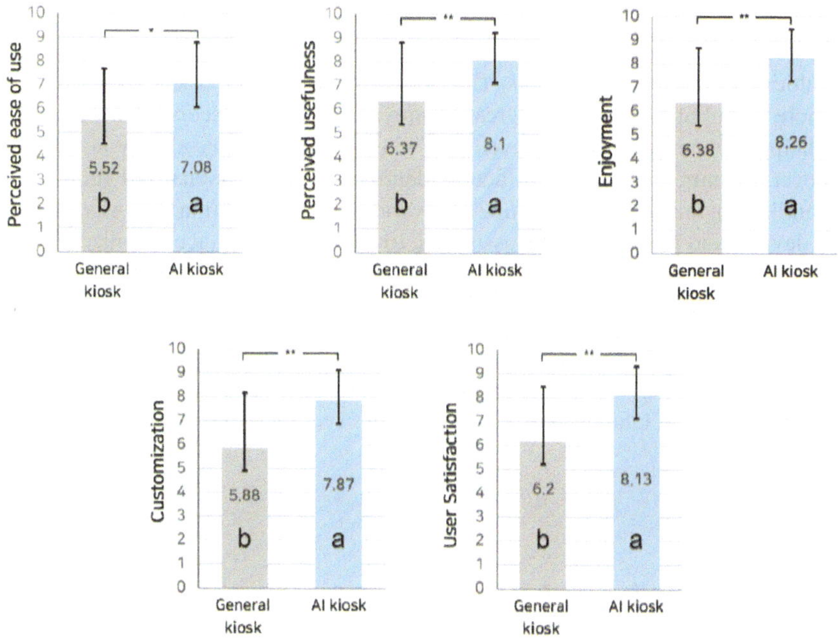

Fig. 2. Graph of results from a one-way repeated measures ANOVA analysis of kiosk user experience factors for the elderly (different alphabets indicate statistically significant differences).

because the AI identified their behavior to provide customized guidance and feedback. This suggests that the elderly is more satisfied with AI-enabled kiosks and are more receptive to new AI technologies.

Voice guidance that detects difficulties can relieve the elderly of anxiety and improve their confidence in using the kiosk. *"When I got lost, the voice guided me, it was like having a human beside me (P6)."* In interviews, most participants said that when they got frustrated, they were given timely guidance, which was like having a human there to help them. When they pressed the wrong button, the guidance helped them identify exactly how to interact with it so they could recognize and correct it. Prior study has addressed that web voice assistants can improve task confidence in older adults [12]. Voice guidance could be an opportunity to improve technology acceptance by relieving psychological anxiety and increasing confidence in technology for the elderly.

However, there were comments that the video guidance component of the AI kiosk was fast and thus the position of the interface to select was difficult to identify. In the future, we need to consider the speed of the video and the visibility of the design and apply an affordance design that invites users to touch.

6 Conclusions

In this study, we analyzed the user experience of the elderly with AI features for detecting difficulties and voice-guided kiosks. The elderly found the AI kiosks to be easier to use and more useful and experienced greater enjoyment and satisfaction. This is expected to be helpful when designing or developing kiosk systems for the elderly in the future. Moreover, we anticipate that the difficulty identification and personalized guidance features outlined in this study will be utilized in various areas in addition to kiosks, including smart devices and personal digital assistants, to enhance elderly accessibility.

Acknowledgement. This work was supported by the National Research Foundation of Korea (NRF) grant funded by the Korea government (MSIT) (No. RS-2023-00253917). And this research was also supported by the MSIT(Ministry of Science and ICT), Korea, under the ICAN(ICT Challenge and Advanced Network of HRD) program (IITP-2022-RS-2022-00156215) supervised by the IITP(Institute of Information & Communications Technology Planning & Evaluation).

References

1. Hilton, T., Hughes, T., Little, E., Marandi, E.: Adopting self-service technology to do more with less. J. Serv. Mark. **27**(1), 3–12 (2013)
2. Shin, Y., Kim, H.K., Kim, G., Kang, M., Ryou, K., Park, T.: A Study on the eye tracking to improve the usability of Kiosks for Seniors. J. Ergonom. Soc. Korea. **42**(3), 269–287 (2023)
3. Seoul Digital Foundation: A Survey on the Digital Competency of Seoul Citizens. (2021)
4. Jeon, S.Y., Song, J.S.: A study on the Usability Evaluation for UI Design of the Kiosk in General Hospital Setting for Senior Generation-Focus on UI Design of the Kiosk in 'H' University Hospital in Seoul. J. Kor. Soc. Des. Cult. **26**(1), 411–421 (2020)
5. Kim, Y.B., Nam, Y.H.: A study on the elderly-friendly UX Design for Accessibility Improvement of Fast Food Kiosks-Focusing on KFC. J. Integr. Des. Res. **20**(4), 39–58 (2021)
6. Sin, E.J., Lim, S.B.: Development of evaluation indicators and usability evaluation of Kiosk for the elderly—the Case of KORAIL's Kiosk for Ticketing. J. Kor. Content Assoc. **22**(1), 188–196 (2022)
7. Ha, J.H., Kim, S.I.: A study on the increase of kiosk user experience in non-face-to-face era for the elderly-focused on the McDonald Kiosk. J. Digit. Converg. **19**(8), 285–292 (2021)
8. Sengpiel, M.: Teach or design? how older adults' use of ticket vending machines could be more effective. ACM Trans. Access. Comput. (TACCESS). **9**(1), 1–27 (2016)
9. Davis, F.D.: Perceived usefulness, perceived ease of use, and user acceptance of information technology. MIS Q. **13**(3), 319–340 (1989)
10. Lin, J.-S.C., Hsieh, P.-L.: Assessing the self-service technology encounters: development and validation of SSTQUAL scale. J. Retail. **87**(2), 194–206 (2011)
11. Iqbal, M.S., Ul Hassan, M., Habibah, U.: Impact of self-service technology (SST) service quality on customer loyalty and behavioral intention: the mediating role of customer satisfaction. Cogent Bus Manag. **5**(1), 1 (2018)
12. Sato, D., Kobayashi, M., Takagi, H., Asakawa, C., Tanaka, J.: How voice augmentation supports elderly web users. In: Proceedings of the 13th International ACM SIGACCESS Conference on Computers and Accessibility, pp. 155–162 (2011)

Research on Image Processing-Based Control System to Increase Vehicle Interior Space Efficiency

Hui-Jun Kim[1] and Sung-Hee Kim[2(✉)]

[1] Department of IT Convergence, Dong-eui University, Busan, South Korea
[2] Department of ICT Industrial Engineering, Dong-eui University, Busan, South Korea
sh.kim@deu.ac.kr

Abstract. This study introduces a computer vision-based control system that removes traditional components such as steering wheels and pedals in level 3+ autonomous vehicles to maximize interior space. The system mimics conventional driving for easy adoption by current drivers. We set up a remote-controlled test vehicle environment with six detailed tracks and conducted experiments comparing this new system with traditional methods, assessing usability among twenty licensed drivers. Results indicated comparable ease of use, satisfaction, and learning ease, prompting future research directions. This study's significance lies in its enhancement of space efficiency and the ease of learning the interaction method for existing drivers.

Keywords: Human-Computer Interaction · Computer-Vision · Future Driving Control System

1 Introduction

As autonomous driving technology advances, autonomous vehicles are transitioning from level 2 to level 3 [1]. With the commercialization of higher-level autonomous vehicles on the horizon, vehicles are evolving from mere transport into mobile living spaces [2]. Thus, maximizing vehicle interior space is becoming essential [3], leading automakers like Volvo, Audi, and Hyundai to propose concept vehicles with interiors that double as bedrooms or offices by eliminating traditional control systems. However, these concept vehicles are currently impractical with existing technology and remain highly futuristic. Additionally, the trust issues drivers [4] have with current autonomous vehicles necessitate research into automotive control methods suitable for level 3 to level 4 vehicles. We have developed an image processing-based motion recognition control system that requires no physical space and enables existing drivers to adopt this method effortlessly by mimicking traditional driving actions.

S. Jin et al. (Eds.): IEA 2024, SSDI 39, pp. 227–232, 2025.
https://doi.org/10.1007/978-981-95-0211-0_35

2 Related Works

Gesture recognition technology is extensively used in human-computer interaction as it provides a natural and intuitive way to communicate [5]. Current gesture recognition technologies are divided into wearable device usage and computer vision-based methods [6, 7]. Initial computer vision-based approaches faced challenges in recognizing a rich array of gestures with few markers [8], but recent advancements in computer vision technology have resolved these issues. Devices with high degrees of freedom, such as robots and drones [9, 10], are increasingly using this technology, and APIs such as MediaPipe [11] and Openpose [12] are being employed in many control systems [10]. However, there is a lack of research on control systems and interaction methods suitable for futuristic vehicles utilizing gesture recognition. Thus, this study proposes a motion recognition control system and verifies its applicability.

3 Methods

3.1 Selection of Control Motions

In this study, the control motions of the motion recognition control system (MRCS) were recognized based on the upper limbs of users, direction control motions (DCM), and speed control motions (SCM). We designed these motions to allow existing drivers to acquire operational methods quickly without additional training, by mimicking the physical movements associated with traditional control systems. Firstly, DCM involved mimicking the arm movements of a driver turning a steering wheel (see Fig. 1(a). Next, SCM mimicked the foot movement when using an accelerator pedal (see Fig. 1(b). Additionally, gear changes were configured as keyboard presses (i.e., drive, reverse, and park). To prevent unintended motion recognition situations, motion recognition was stopped in the park state.

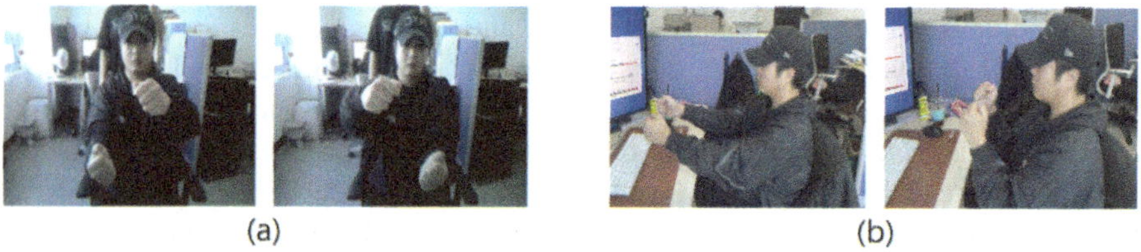

Fig. 1. Control Motion Examples: (a) direction control; (b) left acceleration, right deceleration.

3.2 Motion Recognition Method

The DCM and SCM were identified using a markerless technique that calculates angles and directions between hand positions in an image. We started with the hand recognition phase using the MediaPipe Hand Model, which detects 21 landmarks (LMs) in 3D coordinates (x, y, z) [11]. In data preprocessing, we defined representative vectors for recognizing the DCM and SCM. For the DCM, we used a vector from LM 0 on both hands in the xy-plane to show hand tilt. We also set a normal vector through LM 0's midpoint on both hands as the reference vector for angle and direction calculations. For the SCM, which works in depth, we chose a vector on the yz-plane from LM 0 to 9 as the representative vector, with a normal vector to the z-axis as the reference from LM 0's midpoint on both hands. The motion recognition and analysis followed, calculating angles and rotational directions between these vectors for both DCM and SCM, and interpreting the motions from these results. The angle calculation utilized Eq. (1).

$$\theta = \cos^{-1}\left(\frac{\mathrm{v1}\cdot\mathrm{v2}}{(\|\mathrm{v1}\|\,\|\mathrm{v2}\|)}\right) \tag{1}$$

The rotational direction between the two representative vectors and the reference vector was calculated using Eq. (2). DCM recognized left turns if the result was positive and right turns if negative, with the heading angle recognized similarly. SCM recognized deceleration if the result was positive and acceleration if negative, and equally recognized change in speed.

$$\theta = \sin^{-1}\left(\frac{\mathrm{v1.xv2.y} - \mathrm{v1.yv2.x}}{(\|\mathrm{v1}\|\,\|\mathrm{v2}\|)}\right) \tag{2}$$

3.3 Experimental Environment Setup

Development of the Control Group. The traditional control system (TCS) was developed to compare with our proposed control system in the same experimental environment, using a driving simulation device (Thrustmaster, T150) to implement the traditional control method.

Fabrication of the Test Vehicle and Remote Driving GUI. The test vehicle served as the control subject for the MRCS and TCS. For the safety of the participants, we fabricated the test vehicle. We selected it as the control subject, equipping the vehicle with front and rear cameras to provide participants with a first-person driving perspective, allowing them to drive based on real-time video with GUI. Also, GUI provided speed, gear status, and vehicle direction (Fig. 2).

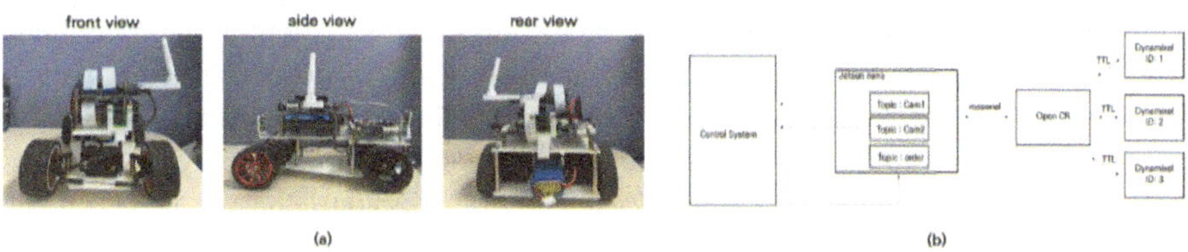

Fig. 2. Test Vehicle and Software Architecture: (a) test vehicle, (b) software architecture.

Construction of the Test-Driving Track To create various driving scenarios and allow for objective comparisons, we constructed a test-driving track measuring 42 square meters. The driving track was modeled after the South Korean driver's license test site and consisted of six detailed tracks (i.e., 1. Incline course, 2. U-turn course, 3. Right turn course, 4. T-junction course, 5. Left turn course, 6. Acceleration course).

4 Experiment

This experiment aimed to verify the applicability of the interaction method through MRCS proposed in this study. We conducted a usability comparison experiment with 20 male licensed drivers, using a within-subject design where the same participant group operated the MRCS (experimental group, EG) and the TCS (control group, CG). For safety, participants remotely drove the test vehicle, using the provided GUI to navigate the test-driving track. The control systems operated in a computer environment with NVIDIA GeForce RTX 3090 and ABKO QHD 1944P webcam. The research protocol was reviewed and approved by the Institutional Review Board of Dong-eui University (DIRB-202310-HR-R-31), approved on October 17, 2023.

4.1 Usability Evaluation Survey and Evaluation Indicators

To compare the usability between control systems, we conducted a questionnaire based on the USE model [13], structured with 19 items centered around ease of use, satisfaction, and learning ease, scored on a 7-point Likert scale. The latter part of the survey allowed free responses regarding ease of use, satisfaction, learning ease, and areas for improvement. Additionally, we used quantitative evaluation indicators such as driving time for each detailed track (seconds), total driving time (seconds), and the number of collisions recorded by an assistant examiner. Finally, a post-survey for statistical analysis included demographic analysis, asking about gender, age, average weekly driving frequency, trust level in autonomous driving technology, and the necessity of a control system in autonomous vehicles.

4.2 Experiment Procedure

We distributed pre-explanatory documents to participants regarding the operation methods of the MRCS and the TCS, as well as the test-driving track. To prevent order effects and carry-over effects, we applied counterbalancing. Participants performed a practice drive using each control system. They were shown a third-person perspective video in the practice session to facilitate adaptation to remote driving. After using each control system, participants completed a usability evaluation survey consisting of ease of use, satisfaction, and learning ease. Participants were allowed breaks according to their feedback before and after the driving experiment. Upon completion of all driving experiments, demographic analysis was conducted using a post-evaluation form.

5 Results

5.1 Qualitative Results

In this study, the significance level α was set at 0.05, and the Mann-Whitney U test was conducted using SPSS 22.0 for Windows. Firstly, the usability comparison between the CG and EG showed no statistically significant differences in the 7 items stating, "driving was as desired". However, the item "operation was easy" showed a significant difference ($z = 68.0$, $p < 0.001$), with the CG ranking higher than the EG. Next, the satisfaction comparison between the two groups showed no significant differences in the 6 items of "satisfaction with driving on each detailed track". However, "overall driving satisfaction" ($z = 77.5$, $p = 0.001$), "willingness to use" ($z = 90.0$, $p = 0.002$), and "willingness to recommend" ($z = 119.5$, $p = 0.024$) showed statistically significant differences, with all three items ranking the CG higher than the EG. Lastly, the comparison of learning ease between the two groups showed no statistically significant differences in the items "Ease of learning" and " Ease of remembering".

Furthermore, the qualitative questionnaire at the bottom of the questionnaire was analyzed for frequency, showing that most participants generally expressed high satisfaction with the CG, citing familiarity with the traditional method as a reason. Most participants also showed high satisfaction with the EG although a few participants expressed low satisfaction due to reasons such as "delays in recognition due to image processing time" and "difficulty in getting a feel due to the lack of a physical interface".

5.2 Quantitative Evaluation Indicators

The homogeneity test between the MRCS and the TCS was conducted using an independent samples T-test. The test variables included "driving time for each course," "total track driving time," and "number of collisions." The results showed no statistical differences in "5th course driving time" ($t = 0.109$) and "number of collisions" ($t = 0.240$), with the TCS showing shorter driving times and fewer collisions across all test variables on average.

6 Discussion

This study introduced an MRCS to enhance interior space efficiency in Level 3 to Level 4 autonomous vehicles before they become common. Through experiments, we validated this method by comparing it with traditional control systems. Although ease of use, satisfaction, and learning ease were generally higher with the TCS, similar scores across detailed metrics suggest that the motion recognition method matches the usability of traditional methods. All items scored above average (4 points), highlighting the MRCS's potential. However, further research must tackle issues like reliable motion recognition, rapid image processing, extensive safety verification, and ensuring comfortable control for sustainable driving.

7 Conclusion

This work was supported by Innovative Human Resource Development for Local Intellectualization program through the Institute of Information & Communications Technology Planning & Evaluation (IITP) grant funded by the Korea government (MSIT)(IITP-2024-RS-2020-II201791), Following are results of a study on the "Leaders in INdustry-university Cooperation 3.0" Project, supported by the Ministry of Education and National Research Foundation of Korea.

References

1. Zanchin, B.C., Adamshuk, R., Santos, M.M., Collazos, K.S.: On the instrumentation and classification of autonomous cars. In: 2017 IEEE International Conference on Systems, Man, and Cybernetics (SMC), pp. 2631–2636 (2017)
2. Clark, B., Parkhurst, G., Ricci, M.: Understanding the Socioeconomic Adoption Scenarios for Autonomous Vehicles: A Literature Review (2016)
3. Koo, S.: An Observation on Alterations of Usability in Automobile Interior Design with Autonomous Driving Technology Escalation (2019)
4. American Automobile Association (AAA): https://newsroom.aaa.com/2024/03/aaa-fear-of-self-driving-cars-persists-as-industry-faces-an-uncertain-future/. Accessed 14 Mar 2024
5. Oudah, M., Al-Naji, A., Chahl, J.: Hand gesture recognition based on computer vision: a review of techniques. J. Imaging. **6**(8), 73 (2020)
6. Bhowmick, S., Talukdar, A.K., Sarma, K.K.: Continuous hand gesture recognition for English alphabets. In: 2015 2nd International Conference on Signal Processing and Integrated Networks (SPIN), pp. 443–446 (2015)
7. Tang, D., Chang, H.J., Tejani, A., Kim, T.K.: Latent regression forest: structured estimation of 3D hand poses. IEEE Trans. Pattern Anal. Mach. Intell. **39**(7), 1374–1387 (2016)
8. Wang, R.Y., Popović, J.: Real-time hand-tracking with a color glove. ACM Trans. Graph. **28**(3), 1–8 (2009)
9. Gourob, J.H., Raxit, S., Hasan, A.: A robotic hand: Controlled with vision based hand gesture recognition system. In: 2021 International Conference on Automation, Control and Mechatronics for Industry 4.0 (ACMI), pp. 1–4. IEEE (2021)
10. Yeh, Y.P., Cheng, S.J., Shen, C.H.: Research on intuitive gesture recognition control and navigation system of UAV. In: 2022 IEEE 5th International Conference on Knowledge Innovation and Invention (ICKII), pp. 5–8. IEEE (2022)
11. Zhang, F., Bazarevsky, V., Vakunov, A., Tkachenka, A., Sung, G., Chang, C. L., Grundmann, M.: Mediapipe Hands: On-Device Real-Time Hand Tracking. arXiv preprint arXiv:2006.10214 (2020)
12. Cao, Z., Simon, T., Wei, S.E., Sheikh, Y.: Realtime multi-person 2D pose estimation using part affinity fields. In: Proceedings of the IEEE Conference on Computer Vision and Pattern Recognition, pp. 7291–7299 (2017)
13. Lund, A.M.: Measuring usability with the use questionnaire12. Usabil. Interface. **8**(2), 3–6 (2001)

Evaluating the Application of ChatGPT in Outpatient Triage Guidance: A Comparative Study

Dou Liu[1,2], Ying Han[3], Xiandi Wang[3], Xiaomei Tan[1], Di Liu[1,2], Guangwu Qian[2,4], Kang Li[1,2], Dan Pu[3], and Rong Yin[1,2](✉)

[1] Industrial Engineering, Pittsburgh Institute, Sichuan University, Chengdu, China
rong.yin@scupi.cn

[2] West China Biomedical Big Data Center, Sichuan University, Chengdu, China

[3] Department of Medical Simulation Center, West China Hospital, Chengdu, China

[4] Department of Computer Science, Pittsburgh Institute, Sichuan University, Chengdu, China

Abstract. The integration of Artificial Intelligence (AI) in healthcare presents a transformative potential for enhancing operational efficiency and health outcomes. Large Language Models (LLMs), such as ChatGPT, have shown their capabilities in supporting medical decision-making. Limited studies have explored the application of ChatGPT in outpatient departments. With a focus on streamlining workflows and enhancing efficiency for outpatient triage, this study specifically aims to evaluate the consistency of responses provided by ChatGPT in outpatient guidance, including both within-version response analysis and between-version comparisons. For within-version, the results indicate that the internal response consistency for ChatGPT-4.0 is significantly higher than ChatGPT-3.5 ($p = 0.03$) and both have a moderate consistency (71.2% for 4.0 and 59.6% for 3.5) in their top recommendation. However, the between-version consistency is relatively low (mean consistency score = 1.43/3), indicating few recommendations match between the two versions. Interestingly, ChatGPT-3.5 responses are more likely to be complete than those from ChatGPT-4.0 ($p = 0.02$), suggesting possible differences in information processing and response generation between the two versions. The findings offer insights into AI-assisted outpatient operations, facilitating the exploration of potentials and limitations of LLMs in healthcare utilization. Future research may focus on carefully optimizing LLMs and AI integration in healthcare systems based on ergonomic and human factors principles, precisely aligning with the specific needs of effective outpatient triage.

Keywords: Digital Health Tools · Large Language Models (LLMs) · AI-Assisted Outpatient triage · Healthcare Innovation

1 Introduction

In recent years, the rapid evolution of Large Language Models (LLMs) has significantly advanced ability in understanding and generating human language texts. Among these, ChatGPT has emerged as a particularly notable model [1], attracting widespread attention

S. Jin et al. (Eds.): IEA 2024, SSDI 39, pp. 233–238, 2025.
https://doi.org/10.1007/978-981-95-0211-0_36

upon its release. Attributed to its profound capabilities in handling text-based problems, chatbot has been extensively integrated across various domains, especially in healthcare [2–4]. Exploring the integration of Artificial Intelligence (AI) in healthcare settings and hospital systems stands as a critical frontier for groundbreaking innovations. As a model underpinned by an extensive database, it can easily make a quick analysis of given symptoms [5] and generate highly accurate information in response to diverse medical queries [6]. Several studies have demonstrated the flexibility of ChatGPT 4.0, showcasing its capacity to not only successfully tackle questions from the United States Medical Licensing Exam but also achieve a high percentile in the Clinical Knowledge section of the Chinese Medical Licensing Examination, which is estimated to be in the top 20% [7, 8]. Furthermore, its utility extends to aiding in clinical decision-making [9], compiling medical documentation [10], and facilitating diagnostic processes [11, 12].

Hospitals, as a critical sector in healthcare, require efficient information processing power and highly accurate and consistent responses regarding medical inquiries. Challenges such as prolonged wait time, complex diagnostic procedures, and fragmented communication channels necessitate a reevaluation of existing workflows of emergency department and outpatient services. Consequently, applying ChatGPT, grounded in ergonomic and human factors engineering principles, to emergency triage and outpatient guidance in hospitals has the potential to swiftly provide judgments, and address the challenges of medical resources shortage and high pressure. A recent study observed a near-perfect concordance between the triage team's decisions and the established gold standard, as well as between ChatGPT-4's recommendations and that gold standard [13]. Another study highlighted ChatGPT-4's proficiency in making patient admission or discharge decisions in cases of metastatic prostate cancer in emergency departments, demonstrating a sensitivity of 95.7% compared to the judgments of emergency physicians [14]. However, as another crucial function in hospitals, outpatient departments have received less research attention regarding the integration of LLMs.

In recent years, the Internet has emerged as a critical health resource. Reports have indicated that up to 80% of users have explored health information online [15], and around 60% of patients reported investigating their symptoms online before or after visiting a doctor [16]. Furthermore, the potential for integrating AI into outpatient services is highlighted by public receptivity to digital assistance, as a previous study suggests most internet users are open to using health chatbots (with an acceptability rate of 67%) [17]. Nevertheless, research concerning the integration of AI into outpatient services are limited. Given this context, the deployment of ChatGPT in outpatient guidance is not only timely but could also substantially enhance operational efficiency across outpatient departments. By utilizing the tendency of patients to engage with digital platforms for health information, ChatGPT can serve as a critical bridge between online health searches and structured medical guidance, potentially optimizing the patient experience and improving outpatient services.

To understand ChatGPT's performance in Chinese outpatient guidance, this study aims to specifically assess the consistency of ChatGPT 3.5 and 4.0's judgment in Chinese outpatient settings through within-version analysis and between-version comparisons. The results are expected to examine the influence of the integration of LLMs in outpatient operations.

2 Methods

2.1 Study Design

This study employed a comparative design to assess the consistency of response generated by ChatGPT-3.5 and ChatGPT-4.0 in the context of Chinese outpatient guidance. We prepared a pre-tested prompt for ChatGPT (both 3.5 and 4.0 versions) to ensure they understood the required information. Fifty-two questions in Chinese encapsulating verbalized symptom descriptions, all of which were randomly collected from Xiaohongshu, a widely used Chinese social media, and Dingxiang Doctor, a Chinese online medical platform. To test the between-version and within-version consistency, each question was respectively inputted into both versions of ChatGPT three times. Considering the memory bias of LLMs, every question was treated as a new chat independently, instead of consecutive entries. The responses were carefully cataloged and recorded, noting the top three recommended outpatient departments ranked by probability, along with the probability of symptom recognition and being cured in each recommended outpatient department.

2.2 Data Collection

A total of 52 questions generated 156 responses, which were each assessed for consistency between the responses for a same question. The ineffective responses (such as 0 or Nan) were excluded to ensure the validity of data. Additionally, when calculating consistency, the order of recommended departments was excluded from consideration. The data collection was conducted between January 2024 and March 2024.

The within-version consistency of responses to individual questions was closely monitored. Each set of three responses, corresponding to the same question and the same GPT version, was evaluated based on the two-tier grading system as Completely inconsistency and Partially consistent.

In addition to the consistency within the three responses, significant attention was dedicated to the consistency of the top recommended department for each question, which is also a key aspect of internal consistency. Two categories (Partially consistent/inconsistent, and Completely consistent) were included.

Additionally, the between-version consistency of the responses from GPT3.5 and GPT4.0 was taken into consideration. A horizontal comparison was conducted using a three-point grading system: (1) 0-point—incoherence, where there are no matching recommended outpatient departments between the two versions' responses. (2) 1-point – partially consistent with only one department is common between the two responses. (3) 2-points – mostly consistent with only one inconsistent department. (4) 3-points – completely consistent.

2.3 Data Analysis

The data analysis was conducted in Python, focusing on examining the differences in within- and between-version response consistency between ChatGPT-3.5 and ChatGPT-4.0. To determine if there are statistically significant differences in responses across the two versions, we employed the Chi-square test. A significance level of $\alpha = 0.05$ was set.

3 Results

3.1 Completeness and Recommendation Probability

Of all the recorded responses, only 6 (1.9%) out of 312 were categorized as invalid or ineffective, lacking critical elements such as recommendations. Seventy-one (22.8%) responses were incomplete, missing elements such as probability, urgency degree, or recommended departments (26 responses from ChatGPT-3.5 and 45 responses from ChatGPT-4.0). The completeness rate of response from ChatGPT-3.5 was statistically significantly higher than that of ChatGPT-4.0 ($p = 0.02$).

The proportion that the top-recommended department has a Recommendation Rate (RR) of higher than 50% is 58.4%, among which 11.2% responses had a RR higher than 80% for the top recommendation. Additionally, the probability that the top-recommended outpatient department can successfully treat the symptom is 61.1% (187 out of 306 responses), among which 11 (11 out of 187 responses, 5.9%) responses had a probability higher than 80% that the symptom would be successfully treated.

3.2 Within-Version Consistency

Here are the results of internal consistency of responses to individual questions. The total number of questions analyzed for both ChatGPT-3.5 and 4.0 was 52. For ChatGPT-3.5, there were 20 (38.5%) completely inconsistent sets of responses among the 52 questions, while ChatGPT-4.0 exhibited only 9 (17.3%) completely inconsistent sets. ChatGPT-4.0 demonstrated higher internal consistency in the response sets for each question ($p = 0.03$).

3.3 Between-Version Consistency

The between-version consistency of the responses between ChatGPT versions 3.5 and 4.0 is presented in a descriptive analysis: after removing the invalid data, 150 paired responses remained. The mean score is 1.43, with 13 pairs (8.7%) scored 0 point, 69 pairs (46%) scored 1 point, 59 pairs (39.3%) scored 2 points, and 9 pairs (6%) scored 3 points. The median score of the entire dataset was 1, indicating that there is a moderate level of match between the responses from versions 3.5 and 4.0.

4 Discussion

This study explored the potential of using ChatGPT in the outpatient triage process. Our findings suggest that ChatGPT could aid in outpatient guidance, with ChatGPT-4.0 showing superior internal consistency, potentially offering stable responses to patient-reported symptoms. The integration streamlines the workflow in outpatient services, reducing wait times, and facilitating more consistent and timely medical recommendations. However, both ChatGPT versions only moderately align in generating consistent top recommendations, highlighting the risk of inaccurate advice in practical applications. Also, the between-version response comparison revealed low consistency, suggesting significant variability in accuracy between ChatGPT-3.5 and ChatGPT-4.0.

In our study, changing prompts led to various responses, highlighting the significance of prompt engineering in LLMs-based chatbots. Effective LLM utilization involves inputting appropriate prompts to obtain accurate responses, highlighting the importance of precise prompts skill for medical professionals [18]. Thus, tailored prompts could direct AI responses more effectively in healthcare, regarding improved accuracy and efficacy. The potential of prompt engineering needs to be explored in future studies.

The memory property of AI should be considered in such evaluations. Meanwhile, differences in response speed between ChatGPT-3.5 and 4.0 were observed, with speed ratios reaching 6:1. Despite 4.0's higher consistency, its slower response may affect operational efficiency, especially under high time pressure scenarios.

The integrity of our consistency analysis depended on question quality. Poorly described symptoms resulted in inconsistent outcomes, emphasizing the importance of detailed, precise symptom information to improve AI's diagnostic accuracy. Future studies may consider description patterns to refine question description methodologies, ensuring that workflow optimization does not come at the expense of comprehensive and personalized patient care. Future studies may consider LLMs specifically tailored for outpatient settings for more comprehensive assessments.

5 Conclusion

This study examined the feasibility of applying ChatGPT in outpatient triage, demonstrating its potential to augment medical decision-making. While indicating the need for further AI refinement, our findings particularly spotlight the varied performance between different versions, suggesting a tailored approach to its application in healthcare. Future research may focus on carefully optimizing LLMs and AI integration in healthcare systems, precisely aligning with the specific needs of effective outpatient triage.

Acknowledgements. This research is partially supported by funding from the 1-3-5 project for disciplines of excellence at West China Hospital, Sichuan University.

References

1. Schulman, J., Zoph, B., Kim, C., Hilton, J., Menick, J., Weng, J., Uribe, J.F.C., Fedus, L., Metz, L., Pokorny, M.: Chatgpt: optimizing language models for dialogue. OpenAI Blog. **2**, 4 (2022)
2. Zarouali, B., Van den Broeck, E., Walrave, M., Poels, K.: Predicting consumer responses to a chatbot on Facebook. Cyberpsychol. Behav. Soc. Netw. **21**, 491–497 (2018)
3. Ghosh, S., Bhatia, S., Bhatia, A.: Quro: facilitating user symptom check using a personalised chatbot-oriented dialogue system. Stud. Health Technol. Inform. **252**, 51–56 (2018)
4. Cooper, A., Ireland, D.: Designing a chat-bot for non-verbal children on the autism spectrum. Stud. Health Technol. Inform. **252**, 63–68 (2018)
5. Obermeyer, Z., Emanuel, E.J.: Predicting the future—big data, machine learning, and clinical medicine. N. Engl. J. Med. **375**, 1216 (2016)

6. Johnson, D., Goodman, R., Patrinely, J., Stone, C., Zimmerman, E., Donald, R., Chang, S., Berkowitz, S., Finn, A., Jahangir, E.: Assessing the accuracy and reliability of AI-generated medical responses: an evaluation of the Chat-GPT model. Res. Sq. (2023)
7. Zhu, Z., Ying, Y., Zhu, J., Wu, H.: ChatGPT's potential role in non-English-speaking outpatient clinic settings. Digit. Health. **9**, 20552076231184092 (2023)
8. Kung, T.H., Cheatham, M., Medenilla, A., Sillos, C., De Leon, L., Elepaño, C., Madriaga, M., Aggabao, R., Diaz-Candido, G., Maningo, J.: Performance of ChatGPT on USMLE: potential for AI-assisted medical education using large language models. PLoS Digit. Health. **2**, e0000198 (2023)
9. Chen, J.H., Dhaliwal, G., Yang, D.: Decoding artificial intelligence to achieve diagnostic excellence: learning from experts, examples, and experience. JAMA. **328**, 709–710 (2022)
10. Patel, S.B., Lam, K.: ChatGPT: the future of discharge summaries? Lancet Digit. Health. **5**, e107–e108 (2023)
11. Bilal, M., Jamil, Y., Rana, D., Shah, H.H.: Enhancing awareness and self-diagnosis of obstructive sleep apnea using AI-powered chatbots: the role of ChatGPT in revolutionizing healthcare. Ann. Biomed. Eng. **52**, 136–138 (2024)
12. Rahsepar, A.A., Tavakoli, N., Kim, G.H.J., Hassani, C., Abtin, F., Bedayat, A.: How AI responds to common lung cancer questions: ChatGPT versus Google Bard. Radiology. **307**, e230922 (2023)
13. Paslı, S., Şahin, A.S., Beşer, M.F., Topçuoğlu, H., Yadigaroğlu, M., İmamoğlu, M.: Assessing the precision of artificial intelligence in emergency department triage decisions: insights from a study with ChatGPT. Am. J. Emerg. Med. **78**, 170–175 (2024)
14. Gebrael, G., Sahu, K.K., Chigarira, B., Tripathi, N., Mathew Thomas, V., Sayegh, N., Maughan, B.L., Agarwal, N., Swami, U., Li, H.: Enhancing triage efficiency and accuracy in emergency rooms for patients with metastatic prostate cancer: a retrospective analysis of artificial intelligence-assisted triage using ChatGPT 4.0. Cancers (Basel). **15**, 3717 (2023)
15. Muse, K., McManus, F., Leung, C., Meghreblian, B., Williams, J.M.G.: Cyberchondriasis: fact or fiction? A preliminary examination of the relationship between health anxiety and searching for health information on the Internet. J. Anxiety Disord. **26**, 189–196 (2012)
16. Stiftung, B.: Gesundheitsinfos. Wer suchet, der findet. Patienten mit Dr. Google zufrieden. In: SPOTLIGHT Gesundheit. Daten, Analysen, Perspektiven, p. 2 (2018)
17. Nadarzynski, T., Miles, O., Cowie, A., Ridge, D.: Acceptability of artificial intelligence (AI)-led chatbot services in healthcare: a mixed-methods study. Digit. Health. **5**, 2055207619871808 (2019)
18. Meskó, B.: Prompt engineering as an important emerging skill for medical professionals: tutorial. J. Med. Internet Res. **25**, e50638 (2023)

Estimating Lumbar Compression Force Using LumboRisk AI Technology

Yordán Rodríguez[1(✉)], Elizabeth Pérez[2], Manuel Martorell-González[3], and Yasser León-Montes de Oca[3]

[1] National School of Public Health, University of Antioquia, Medellín, Colombia
yordan.rodriguez@udea.edu.co
[2] Grupo de Investigación y Desarrollo en Ergonomía, Ergoyes: Comunidad de Ergonomía, Medellín, Colombia
elizabeth.perez@ergoyes.com
[3] Ergoyes: Comunidad de Ergonomía, Medellín, Colombia

Abstract. Lumbar problems are one of the main ailments affecting the health of workers who perform manual lifting activities. One way to measure the risk associated with these activities is by calculating the lumbar compression force using biomechanical models. However, the accuracy of the field measurement of the input variables may be compromised when taken by inexperienced ergonomics professionals, and their measurement may be difficult in difficult-to-access work settings. This study analyzed the accuracy of LumboRisk AI technology for estimating lumbar compression force in lifting tasks from images using the LumboRisk AI technology developed by Ergoyes. LumboRisk AI is based on the Hand Calculated Back Compressive Force v1.2 (HCBCF v1.2) model to estimate lumbar compressive force and integrates computer vision algorithms to obtain HCBCF v1.2 input variables from images. The findings of this study indicate that the LumboRisk IA technology enables the estimation of the lumbar compression force of lifting tasks with good accuracy.

Keywords: Biomechanical Model · Computer Vision · LumboRisk · Lumbar Ergonomic Assessment

1 Introduction

Lumbar problems are one of the main ailments affecting the health of workers who perform manual lifting activities [1, 2]. One way to measure the risk associated with these activities is by calculating the lumbar compression force using biomechanical models [3]. However, the accuracy of the field measurement of the input variables may be compromised when taken by inexperienced ergonomics professionals, and their measurement may be difficult in difficult-to-access work settings.

The Hand Calculated Back Compressive Force v1.2 (HCBCF) biomechanical model [4] is simple, easy to use, and requires few input variables. Nevertheless, the accuracy of field measurements of the input variables (e.g., trunk flexion angle and horizontal

S. Jin et al. (Eds.): IEA 2024, SSDI 39, pp. 239–242, 2025.
https://doi.org/10.1007/978-981-95-0211-0_37

distance from the hands to the lower back) may be compromised when conducted by inexperienced ergonomics professionals, and measuring them can be challenging in hard-to-access work environments.

Artificial intelligence technologies can automate the process of collecting and analyzing data used as input in ergonomic assessments with reasonable levels of accuracy [5]. This reduces the time and effort required to perform ergonomic assessments, allowing ergonomics professionals to focus on implementing ergonomic solutions.

This study analyzed the accuracy of LumboRisk AI technology for estimating lumbar compression force in lifting tasks from images using the LumboRisk AI technology developed by Ergoyes. LumboRisk AI technology is based on the HCBCF v1.2 model to estimate lumbar compressive force and integrates computer vision algorithms to obtain input variables.

2 Methodology

In this study, 14 subjects participated (13 women and one man). Each subject simulated eight lifting postures under laboratory conditions using an empty plastic box weighing 0.1 kg (see Fig. 1). For this purpose, two lifting parameters were established:

- Vertical load height: below the knee, from the knee to the waist, from the waist to the shoulders, and above shoulder height.
- Horizontal distance of the load: close (0 to 30 cm horizontal distance from the center of the ankles to the grip of the load) and far (30 to 60 cm horizontal distance from the center of the ankles to the grip of the load).

Fig. 1. Subject simulating lifting postures.

Each lifting posture was photographed from the lateral view using a fixed camera and tripod placed at a horizontal distance to the person of approximately 180 cm and a height of 108 cm.

The procedure for each posture was as follows: the subject simulated the posture, three persons assisted in measuring the variable horizontal distance from the hands to the lower back, the persons withdrew, and the subject remained static to take a photograph. The anthropometric variables were also measured: height (cm) and weight (kg).

The images taken were processed using LumboRisk AI, which uses the open-source Mediapipe library developed by Google. Mediapipe is based on computer vision techniques and uses convolutional neural network models and other machine learning algorithms to detect and track key points in the human body [6].

The mean absolute deviation (MAD) between the horizontal distance from the hands to the lower back measured in the laboratory and that obtained using LumboRisk AI was calculated. The effect of MAD on the final result of the calculation of lumbar compression force obtained with LumboRisk AI was simulated by setting load weights of 5, 10, 15, 15, 20, and 25 kg in the eight lifting postures. Only the 13 women were included in this simulation.

Finally, the MAD between the results of the lumbar compression force calculated from the data collected in the laboratory and the results obtained with LumboRisk AI, considering the effect of the error, was calculated to load weights of 5, 10, 15, 15, 20, and 25 kg.

3 Results

Subjects data: mean height 162.3 cm (SD = 6.3); mean weight 69.7 kg (SD = 19.3); mean age 33.5 years (SD = 3.7). A total of 112 images were processed and analyzed.

The MAD obtained for the variable horizontal distance from the hands to the lower back measured in the laboratory and obtained using LumboRisk AI was 4.91 cm.

The MAD values between the lumbar compression force calculated from the data collected in the laboratory and LumboRisk AI were 36.25 N for 5 kg, 72.50 N for 10 kg, 108.75 N for 15 kg, 145.00 N for 20 kg, and 181.25 N for 25 kg (see Fig. 2).

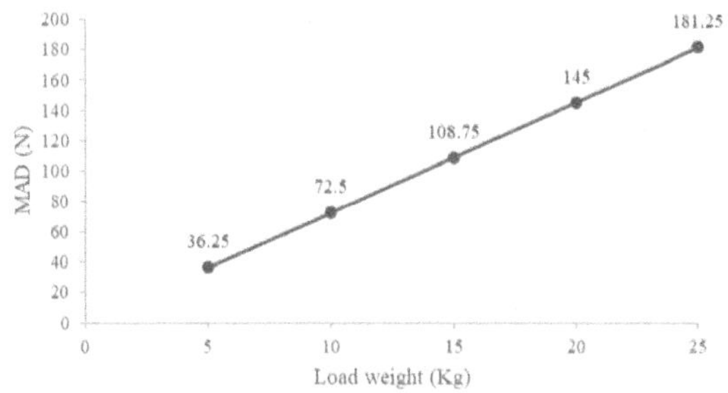

Fig. 2. MAD values for lumbar compression force according to load weight.

4 Discussion

Although the results obtained with LumboRisk AI technology are promising, some aspects may compromise the accuracy achieved and are related to the current limitations of computer vision. For example, the image capture angle, the image's quality, the subjects' clothing, and the presence of objects obstructing the image, among others.

The MAD values obtained for the horizontal distance from the hands to the lower back and the lumbar compression force can be considered low. However, it should be noted that as the load weight increases, the effect of MAD on the lumbar compression force also increases.

In general, the results of the MAD for calculating lumbar compression force (N) are acceptable. It is expected that similar results will be obtained under imaging conditions similar to those described in this study.

A limitation of this study was that the simulation of the effect of the error on the final result of the lumbar compression force calculation was only performed for women. It is important to note that, to date, two experimental studies have been conducted to analyze the accuracy levels of the LumboRisk AI technology for estimating lumbar compression force. In both experiments, the same research protocol was followed.

In this article, only the first experiment's results are reported, in which 13 women and one man participated.

In the second experiment, eight women and six men participated. The report of the results of the second experiment and the integration of the data from both experiments will be included in future publications.

5 Conclusions

The findings of this study indicate that the LumboRisk IA technology enables the estimation of the lumbar compression force of lifting tasks with good accuracy. This technology automates the collection of the input variables: trunk flexion angle and horizontal distance from the hands to the lower back, facilitating the application of the HCBCF model. v1.2.

References

1. Marras, W.S., Cutlip, R.G., Burt, S.E., Waters, T.R.: National occupational research agenda (NORA) future directions in occupational musculoskeletal disorder health research. Appl. Ergon. **40**, 15–22 (2009)
2. Bernard, B.P., Putz-Anderson, V.: Musculoskeletal disorders and workplace factors. In: A Critical Review of Epidemiologic Evidence for Work-Related Musculoskeletal Disorders of the Neck, Upper Extremity, and Low Back (1997). https://doi.org/10.26616/NIOSHPUB97141
3. Weston, E.B., Dufour, J.S., Lu, M.-L., Marras, W.S.: Spinal loading and lift style in confined vertical space. Appl. Ergon. **84**, 103021 (2020)
4. Merryweather, A.S., Loertscher, M.C., Bloswick, D.S.: A revised back compressive force estimation model for ergonomic evaluation of lifting tasks. Work. **34**, 263–272 (2009)
5. Li, L., Martin, T., Xu, X.: A novel vision-based real-time method for evaluating postural risk factors associated with musculoskeletal disorders. Appl. Ergon. **87**, 103138 (2020)
6. Google Pose landmark detection guide | Google AI Edge. In: Google for Developers. https://ai.google.dev/edge/mediapipe/solutions/vision/pose_landmarker. Accessed 31 May 2024

Information Support for Human Error Prevention During Augmented Reality Assisted Manual Assembly

Junfeng Wang[1(✉)], Ting Shi[1], and Hui Xiong[2]

[1] School of Mechanical Science and Engineering, Huazhong University of Science and Technology, Wuhan 430074, China
wangjf@hust.edu.cn

[2] School of Mechanical and Electrical Engineering, Hainan University, Haikou 570228, China

Abstract. Manual assembly is still an important method for complex products. There are various manual assembly errors due to distinct factors under changing production environments. Information assistant is an efficient way for preventing human errors during manual assembly operations. Augmented reality can superimposes the information in front of the users' view to facilitate their work. Offline training and onsite assistant based on augmented reality were research hotspots in academic and industry. In this paper, the human assembly errors in literature were collected and analyzed from human reliability analysis and skill-rule-knowledge behaviour model aspects. The information characteristics of traditional paper manual, electronic file manual, 3D manual and augmented reality manual for assembly assistant were discussed. Augmented reality based information presentation for error prevention was proposed for on-site manual assembly assistant. Seven typical assembly operations were identified and classified to different skill-rule-knowledge levels for on-site workers. The functions and visual elements of augmented reality for error-less assistant were discussed.

Keywords: Manual Assembly Error · Human Reliability Analysis · Skill-rule-knowledge Model · Augmented Reality · Information Assistant

1 Introduction

In Industry 5.0, human-centered manufacturing is one core value of production. Assembly is an important stage in the product development process. Currently, production of high-end and complex products (e.g. automobiles, engines, aerospace equipment) are difficult to be automated and rely on manual operations [1]. Human workers still remain a cost effective way for the flexible production systems with increased product complexity. Under modern society, the assembly work of enterprises is facing two major challenges, the increased complexity of assembly process and the aging of human assemblers.

From the aspect of assembly complexity, the personalization of demand have promoted the rapid upgrading of products. The multi-variety and variable-batch production mode dominates the mainstream of enterprises. The work contents of manual assembly

S. Jin et al. (Eds.): IEA 2024, SSDI 39, pp. 243–249, 2025.
https://doi.org/10.1007/978-981-95-0211-0_38

operations for complex products are constantly changing with required product types, and the cognitive load of workers is increasing [2]. In addition, the assembly of high-performance and high-precision products not only requires simply operation based on standard operation procedure, but also requires more knowledge support. The real time information supply for manual assembly operations is more and more important under ever-changing production situation.

From the aspect of workers, the assembly workload of complex products accounts for an average of about 45% of the product development, and there is a large gap of age appropriate human resources. The world population are gradually aging and the research of aging workers in manufacturing is receiving increased attention [3]. Although elder workers generally have rich experience, they also have significant characteristics such as decreased learning ability, accelerated forgetting, and memory loss. More information assistance must be provided in order to reduce the cognition load and avoid the assembly errors for the aging workers and even young workers.

Augmented reality (AR) can superimposes the information in front of the users' view to facilitate their work, which is a promising technology which delivers right information to right worker at right time and place. The research have shown that the assembly time and assembly errors decreased with the assistant of AR technology in assembly work [4]. In this paper, In order to prevent human errors, the real time AR assisted information reminding, monitoring and warning were discussed.

2 Classification of Human Errors in Manual Assembly

The classification of human assembly errors is the precondition for error prevention based on information requirement. Many different human assembly errors have been identified in literature. Two main methods, i.e. human reliability analysis (HRA) and skill-rule-knowledge (SRK) model, were most usually used to classify the human errors during assembly process.

HRA method has been developed to quantify the probability of human error when performing specified tasks. The main focus of HRA is to identify the sources of human errors, predict and mitigate errors for optimizing safety, reliability and productivity in process industry. Several HRA techniques have been used to identify and assess the human errors possibility in manual assembly and the quality defect of product was predicted. Yaniel et al. [5] used systematic human error reduction and prediction approach to identify human error modes associated with the tasks analyzed. In the case study of mechanical product assembly, about 89 errors were categorized in error taxonomy: action error, retrieval error, checking error and selection error. An improved CREAM (Cognitive Reliability and Error Analysis Method) was proposed to perform the human error analysis in the process of the engine assembly [6]. Four error categories, i.e. negligence, omission, error and illegal, were identified based on the actual process of engine assembly based on eight error modes of CREAM. Riedel et al. [7] identified 70 safety and functionally relevant defect types during a complex tubular lamp assembly. The identified errors were classified into the four categories (omission error, execution error, confusion error and quantitative error).

SRK behaviour model considered that human workers had three kinds of performance levels and associated errors [8] (see Fig. 1). At skill-based performance level, the human behaviour was linked to familiar patterns which he had learned before. Slips and lapses were common skill-based human errors. At rule-based performance level, the human workers applied a stored rule or procedure which he empirically had derived through the previous occasion or instructions. If he did not choose a rule correctly, the intended outcome would not be achieved and the mistakes occurred. At knowledge-based level, the workers faced an unfamiliar environment or situation. The diagnose, decision and plan phase were required before his action. The failures (mistakes) happened when the worker lacked the knowledge and did not know how to formulate a proper plan of performing the task for a given situation.

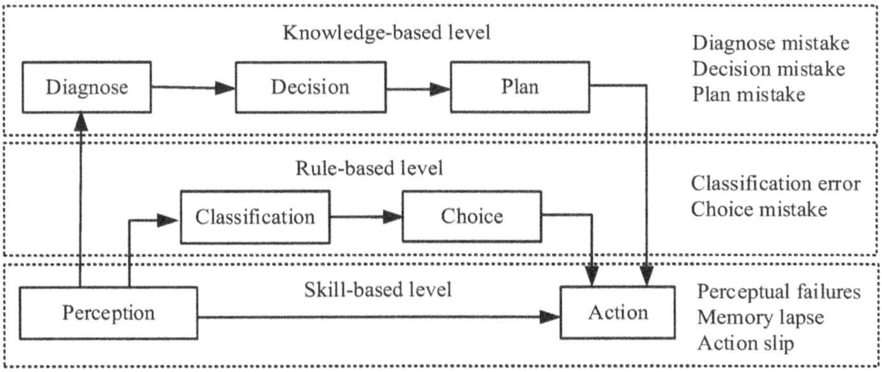

Fig. 1. SRK model and human errors.

For an order picking process at an BMW assembly plant, Murauer et al. [9] assigned the process steps into SRK behaviors levels based on their proposed Rasmussen index. Skill-based tasks and rule-based tasks were identified as the main operations. A framework of identifying and managing the root cause of aircraft snags was proposed based on SRK model in [10]. A study was conducted to discover the possible cause(s) of clip-related snags in the assembly process. The mistakes and slips including description similarity error, capture errors, memory lapse errors, and interruptions were identified at a UK aerospace company.

Other methods were also used for assembly error identification in literature. By selecting "failure to properly install bracket" as the main event, Yaniel et al. [11] analyzed human errors in a complex manual assembly line at an aeronautical manufacturing facility in Canada. They identified 31 factors that caused those errors based on AcciMap and STAMP. Alqahtani et al. [12] identified seven common errors (omission errors, commission errors, transposition errors, timing errors, procedural errors, communication errors and fatigue-related errors) in manual assembly process and determined their affecting factors using Fuzzy Delphi and DEMATEL.

The above related work identified and classified the manual assembly errors from different aspects. The main aim of the research was to predict the possibility of the assembly errors. Few work focused on the reduction of assembly errors from information support aspect [13]. Efficient information supply can be an essential method of preventing human assembly errors.

3 Information Support in Manual Assembly Process for Reducing Human Errors

3.1 From Manual 1.0 to Manual 4.0 for Assembly Work

Assembly process manual (also known as assembly manual or standard operating procedures) is commonly used as operational guidance in production activities. It plays an important role in helping operators to understand assembly process, standardize assembly operations, and ensure assembly quality. With the development of modern information and communications technology, four types of assembly manual are used in industry as follows [14].

Traditional paper-based manuals (manual 1.0) usually include parts lists, operation steps, quality requirements, graphic annotations, product explosion diagrams, etc. (see Fig. 2). With the increasing popularity of electronic screens in assembly shops, assembly process manuals are gradually presented in the form of electronic files (manual 2.0). However, the content has not fundamentally changed, only the display medium has changed from paper to screen. Paper-based and file-based manual have no interactivity, and static elements such as text, images, and annotations are often used for process expression. The manual content also does not have differences for personnel with different experiences and qualifications. All assembly personnel see the same process content. With the emergence of 3D visualization technology, 3D assembly instruction has become an important way due to its intuitive and easy to understand. The 3D virtual manual (manual 3.0) has a full 3D animation mode to express the assembly process and has the advantages of interactivity and 3D display. AR technology with 3D registration, virtual-real integration, and real-time interaction is used to overlay assembly process guidance information on the real assembly scene. AR manual (manual 4.0) can provide personalized and differentiated assembly operation guidance for each worker, improve

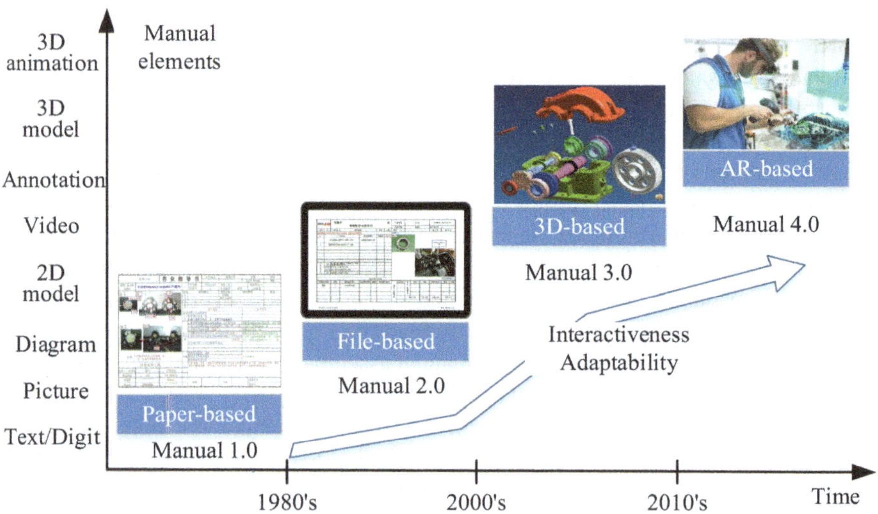

Fig. 2. The development of four types of assembly manual and their characteristics.

cognitive efficiency of operators, and assist them in completing assembly tasks with high quality and speed.

3.2 AR Information Support for Error Prevention in Manual Assembly

The application of AR in assembly field has two aspects, i.e. assembly training and on-site assembly assistant. The aim of the two scenarios is different and the human performance levels in training and on-site work are also distinctive. Throughout the current research, there lack classification of AR information presentation for different purpose. AR is helpful to all SRK behaviour levels for its real time recognition, location and visualization ability, which are important for remaindering the worker.

In assembly training, AR is more used as an instruction tool to tell user how to do the work. The basic assembly skills are learned and the assembly procedure is to be remembered. The training time can be reduced and the performance level of the user changes from knowledge-based level to rule-based and skill-based level. Even if a human is trained for assembly work and his performance level is skill-based level. For a long and ever-changing assembly process, any operators can not remember all the details for time-limited work pace and errors may occur. Therefore, during on-site assembly work, AR is also an indispensable tool for remaindering, monitoring and warning operators whether his performance level is knowledge-rule-skill-based level.

For trained workers, seven typical assembly operations were identified and classified to different SRK levels for on-site assembly support in this paper (Table 1). The function and visual elements of AR were listed for these assembly operations for preventing SRK errors. For complex adjustment operation (e.g. panel alignment in car body assembly [15]), AR combined with digital twin (DT) and artificial intelligence (AI) will be the recommended practices [16].

Table 1. AR functions and elements for error-less assembly assistant.

Assembly activity	SRK level	AR function	AR element
Sequential operation	Skill, Rule	Step by step operation list, preventing omission error.	Text
Selection operation	Skill	Highlighting the object to reminder the user and monitoring the selected object, warning wrong selection.	Model, light, annotation, warning pic.
Quantitative operation	Rule	Reminder the correct quantity and comparing the execution results.	Number

(continued)

Table 1. (*continued*)

Assembly activity	SRK level	AR function	AR element
Placement operation	Skill, Rule	Highlighting position/orientation, checking the matching degree and warning the wrong placement.	Model, animation, warning pic.
Connection operation	Skill	Checking the connection result.	Warning pic
Adjustment operation	Rule, Knowledge	Indicating adjustment object based on DT and AI for correct action.	Text, model, number
Inspection operation	Skill, Rule	Warning the wrong part.	Annotation

4 Conclusion

In this paper, the human assembly errors were analyzed from HRA and SRK model. The four types of manual for assembly information assistant were discussed. For AR based information support, seven typical assembly operations were identified and classified to different skill-rule-knowledge levels for on-site workers. The functions and visual elements of AR for error-less assistant were discussed. Experiments will be conducted to verify our method in the future.

Acknowledgments. The authors acknowledge the support from the National Natural Science Foundation of China (72271100).

References

1. Klages, B., Zaeh, M.: Concept of a data-based approach for the prediction and reduction of human errors in manual assembly. Procedia CIRP. **116**, 209–214 (2023)
2. Giridhar, M.P., Panicker, V.V.: Experimental analysis of cognitive issues impacting manual assembly task. In: 2020 ICSCAN, pp. 1–6. IEEE, Piscataway, NJ (2020)
3. Calzavara, M., Battini, D., Bogataj, D., Sgarbossa, F., Zennaro, I.: Ageing workforce management in manufacturing systems: state of the art and future research agenda. Int. J. Prod. Res. **58**(3), 729–747 (2020)
4. Marino, E., Barbieri, L., Bruno, F., et al.: Assessing user performance in augmented reality assembly guidance for industry 4.0 operators. Comput. Ind. **157**, 104085 (2024)
5. Yaniel, T., Nadea, S., Landau, K.: Classification and quantification of human error in manufacturing a case study in complex manual assembly. Appl. Sci. **11**, 749 (2021)
6. Wang, Y.B., Zhang, T., Xue, Q.: The design and realization of HRA service system for the engine assembly. Appl. Mech. Mater., 1900–1905 (2014)
7. Riedel, A., Gerlach, J., Dietsch, M., et al.: A deep learning-based worker assistance system for error prevention: Case study in a real-world manual assembly. Adv. Prod. Eng. Manag. **16**(4), 393–404 (2021)

8. Reason, J.: Human error: models and management. BMJ. **172**, 393–396 (2000)
9. Murauer, N., Gehrlicher, S.: Evaluation of order picking processes regarding the suitability of smart glasses-based assistance using rasmussen's skills-rules-knowledge framework. In: AHFE 2018, pp. 13–24. Springer, Cham (2019)
10. Alogla, A.A., Alruqi, M.: Aircraft assembly snags: human errors or lack of production design. Aerospace. **8**(12), 391 (2021)
11. Yaniel, T., Nadeau, S., Landau, K.: Applying AcciMap and STAMP to the analysis of human error in complex manual assembly. Hum. Factors Ergonom. Manuf. Serv. Ind. **32**, 462–481 (2022)
12. Alqahtani, F., Noman, M., Alabdulkarim, S., et al.: A new model for determining factors affecting human errors in manual assembly processes using fuzzy Delphi and DEMATEL Methods. Symmetry. **15**(11), 1967 (2023)
13. Qeshmy, D., Makdisi, J., da Silva, E., Angelis, J.: Managing human errors: augmented reality systems as a tool in the quality journey. Procedia Manuf. **28**, 24–30 (2019)
14. Wang, J., Li, W., Fu, Y., Wu, L.: Research progress on human factor adaptability in augmented reality assisted assembly. J. Mech. Eng. **58**, 16–30 (2022)
15. Dalle Mura, M., Dini, G.: An augmented reality approach for supporting panel alignment in car body assembly. J. Manuf. Syst. **59**, 251–260 (2021)
16. Yin, Y., Zheng, P., Li, C., Wang, L.: A state-of-the-art survey on augmented reality-assisted digital twin for futuristic human-centric industry transformation. Robot. Comput. Integr. Manuf. **81**, 102515 (2023)

Real or Virtual? The Effects of Appearance, Voice and VR for AIGC on Learning Performance and Interactive Experience

Qianxi Xiao, Zhe Chen(✉), and Yihang Lv

Beihang University, Beijing 100191, China
zhechen@buaa.edu.cn

Abstract. The rapid development of artificial intelligence has continuously impacted traditional education and gradually changed the traditional education model. In order to cope with the changes brought about by artificial intelligence, this study investigates the impact of AI-instructor's appearance, voice and VR devices on users' learning performance, overall experience and social presence in AI-generated educational videos. This study recruits 36 participants and conduct a 2 (appearance: real-human vs. virtual) $\times$ 2 (voice: real-human vs. virtual) $\times$ 2 (VR device: wear vs. not) experiment with the learning performance, social presence, and overall experience as dependent variables. The results indicate that the AI-instructor's appearance and voice significantly influence learning performance and social presence, while the use of VR devices has a significant effect on overall experience. Instructor with real-human appearance and real-human voice has the best performance, while instructor with virtual appearance and virtual voice has poorer performance.

Keywords: AI-instructor · appearance · voice · virtual reality (VR) · learning performance · social presence

1 Introduction

With the continuous development of Large Language Models, Artificial Intelligence Generated Content (AIGC) and virtual reality device (VR), Artificial Intelligence (AI) is increasingly used in education, and the model of education has also undergone significant changes (Bhutani & Wadhwani 2018). Since they are not constrained by location, time and space, online courses are becoming more and more common (Alfred et al. 2018). AIGC and VR are increasingly used in online education, including some professional and practical education and teaching, which have begun to use VR for teaching (Kaplan et al. 2021). For example, the hospital uses VR to reproduce clinical scenes and provide a practical platform for medical students who have no clinical experience (Scerbo et al. 2006). This not only saves money and space, but also reduces the cost of learning and ensures practical learning results. Educational Robotics originated from the Artificial Intelligence Laboratory established by the Massachusetts Institute of Technology in the

S. Jin et al. (Eds.): IEA 2024, SSDI 39, pp. 250–254, 2025.
https://doi.org/10.1007/978-981-95-0211-0_39

1960s. In the early twenty-first century, Japan and South Korea successively launched humanoid robots for classroom teaching (Edwards et al. 2018). By 2017, professors at Georgia Tech University in the United States were using AI teaching assistants in the classroom. AI teaching assistants were mainly used to answer students' questions after class. At present, most AI-instructors play a supporting role in classroom teaching and have not yet truly assumed the responsibility of lecturers. However, with the increase in the functions of intelligent interactive devices and the diversification of the voices and appearances of AI-instructors, in classrooms led by AI-instructors, can basic learning efficiency be guaranteed? When students use intelligent interactive devices such as VR for online learning, how students' learning performances and interaction perceptions will be affected. In order to test the effect of using AI as a classroom lecturer, an online questionnaire is used to measure the credibility of the AI-instructor, students' perceptions of AI as a lecturer and willingness to participate in the course (Kim et al. 2022). The results show that students do not reject virtual voice instructors. The impact and interactive experience brought by the AI-instructor's appearance and VR equipment are not yet clear, and there is a lack of relevant research attention. As important factors of the instructor, the first thing students see in class is the instructor's appearance, and the first thing they hear is the instructor's voice. Therefore, the appearance and voice of the instructor will have the most direct impact. This article aims to study the impact of voice and appearance of the AI-instructor in online education videos and whether or not to wear a VR device while watching online courses on students' learning performance, social presence and overall experience through filed experiments. And this study will provide suggestions for the design of AI-instructors in AIGC's video content and the improvement of interactive functions of VR devices based on the experimental results.

Specifically, research objectives/questions include:

Determining the impact of a AI-instructor's image (real-human vs. virtual) on students' learning performance, social presence and overall experience.
Examining the impact of a AI-instructor's voice (real-human vs. virtual) on students' learning performance, social presence and overall experience.
Evaluate the impact of using VR devices to watch educational videos on the learning performance, social presence and overall experience.

2 Experiment

2.1 Participants

The experiment involved 36 participants from a university in Beijing, China, consisted of 18 males and 18 females. The average age was 23.42 with a standard deviation of 2.16. All participants were graduate students without prior exposure to law studies. 91.67% of the participants had previous experience with online courses.

2.2 Experiment Design

This study includes three independent variables: AI-instructor's appearance and voice in online educational videos, and whether participants wore VR while watching the online educational videos. The AI-instructor's appearance has two levels: real human and virtual appearance. Similarly, the AI-instructor's voice has two levels: real human and virtual voice. The VR is a between-group variable, with one group of participants wearing VR while watching the course videos and another group not.

To measure participants' learning performance under different levels of AI-instructor's appearance and voice, we measured their scores on post-video tests of law course as an indicator of learning performance. The test consisted of ten multiple-choice questions which were selected from National Law Examination, ensuring the authority of assessing learning performance. A higher score indicates better learning performance. Overall experience is the subjective rating by participants on their viewing experience after watching the course video, with a scale from 0 to 100, where 100 represents "very satisfied" and 0 represents "very dissatisfied". Social presence is measured using a 5-point Likert scale (Gefen, D., and Straub, D. Managing user trust in B2C e-services. e-Service Journal, 2,2 (2003), 7–24), where the Social Presence Scale (SPS) reflects the sense of social presence felt by individuals in computer-supported collaborative learning. Social presence falls under the metacognitive category for learners, highlighting self-awareness and self-reflection in a collaborative learning environment, and the Social Presence Scale is designed to measure this aspect (Kim & Merrill Jr., 2022).

2.3 Experimental Procedure

The experimental procedure mainly includes the following steps: the participants who need to wear VR start watching online course videos after becoming familiar with the basic operation of VR; the participants who do not need to wear VR watch online course videos directly on the computer. Each participant needs to watch four online course videos, including real appearances with real voices, real appearances with virtual voices, virtual appearances with real voices, and virtual appearances with virtual voices.

After watching each course video, the participants first take a test to evaluate the learning performance of the course. After completing the test, the participants fill out a social presence questionnaire and then evaluate the overall experience. After completing all videos, tests, and questionnaires, each participant will receive a brief interview to discuss how the appearance and voice of the instructor affect their experience and learning performance; and the difference between watching course videos using VR and watching course videos on traditional computers.

3 Result

A total of 36 participants are recruited for the experiment, with each participant completing three tasks under four experimental conditions. Therefore, there are a total of $36 \times 4 \times 3 = 432$ data entries.

3.1 Learning Performance

The test score rate after class shows that the appearance and the voice of the instructor in the online course video has a significant impact on the learning performance. And the impact of the instructor's appearance, voice and whether to wear a VR device produce the best learning performance of the participants. Among them, the real-person appearance of the instructor in the online course video produces a better performance. Regarding the instructor's voice, instructors with real voices in online course videos result in a better performance.

3.2 Overall Experience

It is found that wearing a VR device and the appearance of the instructor in the video have a significant impact on the overall experience of course watching. Without wearing a VR device, the best overall experience is obtained when the instructor's appearance in the course video is a real human appearance and the instructor's voice is a real human voice. Among them, for VR devices, the average overall experience score of the participants is higher when they do not wear VR devices. Similarly, when the instructor appearance in the course video is a real human, it results in a higher overall experience.

3.3 Social Presence

Through the analysis of the social presence of course watching, the appearance and voice of the instructors have significant impacts on the participants' social presence. When participants do not wear a VR device, and the appearance of the instructor in the course video you watch is a real person, and the instructor's voice is a real person's voice, it leads to the highest sense of social presence. For the appearance and the voice of the instructor, the participants' social presence score higher when the instructor's appearance or voice is a real human.

4 Discussion

According to the results analysis, when designing the appearance and the voice of instructor for AI-generated education courses, priority should be given consider designing the appearance and the voice of the instructor in the video to be a real human, or making the instructor acts closer to a real human when synthesizing the appearance and the voice. This can bring better learning performance, overall experience and social presence to users. Simultaneously applying virtual reality in the field of education, the appearance and the voice of character should be designed to be more consistent with real human.

VR devices still have problems in optimizing the user's overall experience; combined with the interview analysis after the experiment and the actual problems, when improving VR devices, it should be noted that online course videos are relatively long, which may reach 45 minutes or 60 minutes per class, and users are mostly more focused during the watching process, and their heads maintain a posture for a long time. Therefore, the focus should be on reducing the weight of the equipment or improving the wearing method of the VR device to alleviate the pressure on the head and shoulders when watching videos. Secondly, enrich the interactive functions of the video, and the VR device itself should also add more interactive options to make educational videos more compatible with the multi-channel, multi-modal and multi-functional modes of the VR device, so as to maximize the functions of the VR device, so as to improve user satisfaction.

5 Limitations

Since VR equipment is already worn, it is difficult to measure physiological data such as eye movement and Electroencephalogram (EEG). Subsequent research will introduce more dependent variables to refine the impact of virtual lecturers on students and classes.

The participants mentioned in the interview that there are fewer interactive functions when watching VR. Future experiments will design interactive options in the video to explore whether the increase in interactivity will affect the participants' interactive perception experience.

Future research needs to explore the mechanism by which virtual lecturers and VR interactions affect students, so as to obtain a better interactive experience.

References

Gefen, D., Straub, D.: Managing user trust in B2C e-services. e-Service J. **2**(2), 7–24 (2003)

Kaplan, A.D., Cruit, J., Endsley, M., Beers, S.M., Sawyer, B.D., Hancock, P.A.: The effects of virtual reality, augmented reality, and mixed reality as training enhancement methods: a meta-analysis. Hum. Factors. **63**(4), 706–726 (2021)

Bhutani, A., Wadhwani, P.: AI in Education Market Growth - Global Industry Report 2024. Global Market Insights, Inc (2018)

Kim, J., Merrill Jr., K., Xu, K., Kelly, S.: Perceived credibility of an AI instructor in online education: the role of social presence and voice features. Comput. Hum. Behav. **136**, 107383 (2022)

Edwards, C., Edwards, A., Spence, P.R., Lin, X.: I, teacher: using artificial intelligence (AI) and social robots in communication and instruction. Commun. Educ. **67**(4), 473–480 (2018)

Kim, J., Merrill Jr., K.: Dynamic roles of social presence and individual differences in social TV platforms. Convergence. **28**(1), 291–305 (2022)

Scerbo, M.W., Bliss, J.P., Schmidt, E.A., Thompson, S.N.: The efficacy of a medical virtual reality simulator for training phlebotomy. Hum. Factors. **48**(1), 72–84 (2006)

Alfred, M., Neyens, D.M., Gramopadhye, A.K.: Comparing learning outcomes in physical and simulated learning environments. Int. J. Ind. Ergon. **68**, 110–117 (2018)

Predicting Intensive Care Unit Length of Stay for Inflammatory Bowel Diseases Patients Using Machine Learning

Ke Xu[1,2], Jiayi Nie[1], Yifan Chen[1], Ziqi Ban[1], Ling Liu[3], Kang Li[1,2], Di Liu[1,2(✉)], and Rong Yin[1,2(✉)]

[1] Industrial Engineering, Pittsburgh Institute, Sichuan University, Chengdu, China
{di.liu,rong.yin}@scupi.cn
[2] West China Biomedical Big Data Center, Sichuan University, Chengdu, China
[3] Department of Gastroenterology, West China Hospital, Sichuan University, Chengdu, China

Abstract. This study aimed to predict the Intensive Care Unit (ICU) Length of Stay for individuals with Inflammatory Bowel Disease (IBD) using the XGBoost model. Electronic Health Record (EHR) data from The Medical Information Mart for Intensive Care (MIMIC) - IV (version 2.2) dataset was used in the study. Variables included patients' demographic information, first measurements of basic physical and laboratory tests after ICU admission, and some important comorbidities. After data preprocessing, 652 IBD patients and their first ICU records were selected. With ten-fold cross-validation, the XGBoost model demonstrated strong performances with area under the curve (AUC) (0.787), accuracy (0.768), and sensitivity (0.943). The most significant variables include age, mean corpuscular volume (MCV), red blood cell distribution width (RDW), acute respiratory failure, among others. Our study could serve as a predictive model for the ICU Length of Stay and offer guidance and references for medical organizations in resource allocation, staff assignments, and bed preparation. This, in turn, can improve efficiency and reduce patient mortality rates.

Keywords: ICU Length of Stay · Machine Learning · Medical Resource Allocation

1 Introduction

Inflammatory Bowel Diseases (IBDs) make up a chronic, recurring inflammatory disorder affecting primarily the gastrointestinal tract, consisting mainly of Ulcerative Colitis (UC) and Crohn's disease (CD) [1, 2]. Its progressive and worsening nature makes it a significant health concern, given its current incurability and the high reoccurrence morbidity burden it places on patients [3, 4]. Moreover, the increasing global incidence of IBD signifies an increasing health concern worldwide [5]. The increasing incidence lifts the need for greater medical support and even ICU intervention, thereby placing higher pressure on the demands of medical resources globally. Therefore, to alleviate this problem, predicting the Intensive Care Unit (ICU) Length of Stay (LOS), for example, would be beneficial.

S. Jin et al. (Eds.): IEA 2024, SSDI 39, pp. 255–261, 2025.
https://doi.org/10.1007/978-981-95-0211-0_40

IBD patients need to undergo relevant indicator tests after entering hospitals and ICUs to diagnose the disease and monitor data during the later treatment stage to follow up on the disease activity. Multiple studies have explored various indicators related to IBD. For instance, blood markers and stool markers are commonly used in the diagnosis and treatment of IBD patients and have proven to be effective [6]. In the study of IBD, comorbidities also gained increasing attention, and researchers have found that addressing these comorbidities can significantly aid in IBD diagnosis and treatment [7]. In recent years, Machine Learning (ML) methods have been increasingly used to predict ICU LOS. For example, Saadatmand et al. have used the XGBoost model to predict the ICU LOS for COVID-19 patients [8]; and Iwase et al. have validated high predictive accuracy of ML models in forecasting mortality and LOS for ICU patients [9].

This study aimed to identify the key factors affecting ICU LOS, and to precisely predict the ICU LOS of IBD patients using the XGBoost model. Our objective is to empower healthcare practitioners with the capability to predict the ICU LOS for IBD patients. By doing so, we aim to enable the healthcare industry to devise more personalized treatment strategies, enhancing the overall hospitalization experience for patients. This foresight will facilitate a more efficient allocation of healthcare resources, ensuring that hospitals can optimally meet the hospitalization needs of their patients.

2 Methods

2.1 Study Population and Data Preparation

In this study, 652 IBD patients were gathered from The Medical Information Mart for Intensive Care (MIMIC)-IV dataset, which contains intensive care and routine medical records from Beth Israel Deaconess Medical Center between 2008 and 2019 [10, 11], as illustrated in the data processing flowchart in Fig. 1. Initially, we identified 2417 patients with the International Classification of Diseases version 9 (ICD-9) "555X" and "556X" as IBD cases. Subsequently, utilizing the ICUSTAYS table in the dataset, we differentiated patients based on their ICU history, narrowing down to 683 IBD patients. Following this, variables with more than 5% missing values were removed. Ultimately, we retained 652 ICU IBD patients who had complete diagnostic data.

We categorized the variables into three dimensions. In the demographic dimension, we extracted the patient's age, sex, language, marital status, and insurance information. For the physical test dimension, we included common indicators like heart rate, respiratory rate, hematocrit, red blood cell distribution width (RDW), mean corpuscular volume (MCV), among others. Additionally, we incorporated prevalent comorbidities diagnosed in most IBD patients into the model. The final dataset comprises 652 data samples with 25 features.

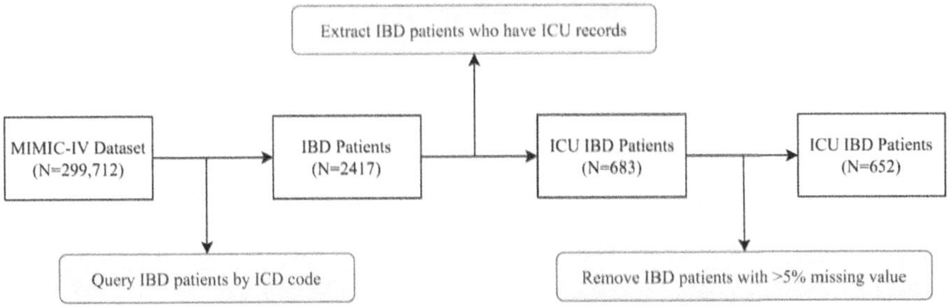

Fig. 1. Flowchart of data processing.

2.2 Model Construction

Before proceeding with the model, we performed various operations on the variables. To minimize confounding, marital status was simplified to a binary variable: "married" and "others". We opted to categorize LOS as a binary dummy variable - values below the average LOS were coded as "0", and those above as "1". To mitigate the influence of varying demographics, we included only the first ICU stay record of each patient. All continuous variables were normalized using Min-Max standardization.

We construct XGBoost models with ten-fold cross-validation in R Software, using the "xgboost" package (version 1.7.7.1) to predict the ICU LOS and assess the significance of predictor variables. AUC ROC, accuracy, sensitivity, and specificity were used to evaluate the model performance. In this study, a two-tailed significance level of alpha = 0.05 was applied to determine statistical significance.

3 Results

3.1 Demographics

Table 1 provides a comprehensive overview of descriptive statistics of the ICU LOS and various other variables. The data is further categorized by the diagnostic records of IBD patients, specifically noting instance of mortality within the ICU. All continuous variables were analyzed by t-test, while the chi-square test was used for binary variables. The results showed that there were significant differences in age ($p < 0.001$), heart rate ($p = 0.0013$), and insurance type - Medicare ($p < 0.001$) between the individuals who died in ICU and who did not.

Table 1. Descriptive statistics.

	Not die in ICU (N = 988)	Died in ICU (N = 139)	P-value
	Means ± SD	Means ± SD	
LOS (days)	3.11 ± 4.20	3.88 ± 5.64	NS[a]
Age (years)	62.95 ± 15.69	67.69 ± 13.78	0.0008
Heart rate (bpm)	87.55 ± 19.51	93.30 ± 21.11	0.0013
Respiratory rate (insp/min)	19.16 ± 5.60	19.91 ± 6.95	NS
Hematocrit (%)	30.20 ± 5.76	30.71 ± 5.39	NS
RDW (%)	16.13 ± 2.57	16.04 ± 2.18	NS
Platelet (K/uL)	247.69 ± 156.37	246.94 ± 152.51	NS
MCV (fL)	90.51 ± 8.55	91.53 ± 8.71	NS
MCH (pg)	29.57 ± 3.17	29.67 ± 3.02	NS
Hemoglobin (g/dL)	9.89 ± 1.95	10.02 ± 1.80	NS
Male (%)	46.66%	38.13%	NS
Married (%)	44.74%	50.36%	NS
Medicare (%)	44.33%	61.87%	0.0002
Race			
Black (%)	9.51%	5.76%	NS
Hispanic/Latino (%)	2.02%	0.72%	NS
White (%)	81.68%	86.33%	NS
Asian (%)	0.72%	0%	NS
Other (%)	6.07%	7.19%	NS

[a]NS: non-significant at alpha = 0.05

3.2 XGBoost Model Results

We successfully built an XGBoost model using hospitalization records of IBD patients to predict ICU LOS. The model achieved an AUC of 0.787, accuracy of 0.768, sensitivity of 0.943, indicating robust performance in predicting ICU LOS. By calculating the importance matrix of the XGBoost model, we identified the most critical factors influencing the prediction of ICU LOS to be age, MCV, RDW and acute respiratory failure (Fig. 2).

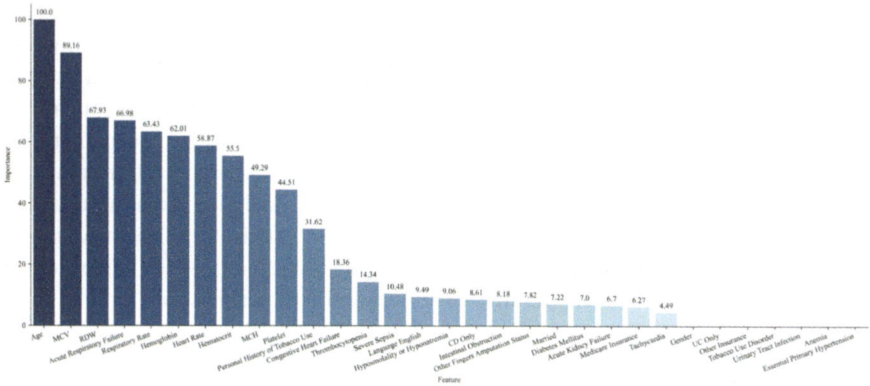

Fig. 2. Importance Matrix of XGBoost model.

4 Discussion

This study highlights the critical impact of specific variables, including test results, demographic information, and comorbidities, in forecasting ICU LOS for IBD patients. Significant differences were found in age, heart rate and insurance type-Medicare for IBD patients who died in the ICU or not. Our results showed a significantly higher average heart rate for patients who died in the ICU. Similarly, previous studies suggest that parasympathetic nervous system activity seems to be lower in people with IBD and irritable bowel syndrome [12] and heart rate recovery was impaired in IBD patients. IBD patients may have a higher economic burden, with almost twice the out-of-pocket costs [13], while the high out-of-pocket costs may discourage IBD patients with Medicare from using specialty IBD medications [14]. According to our results, patients with Medicare had a significantly higher percentage died in the ICU.

Our results found that age, MCV, RDW and Acute Respiratory Failure are the most important factors contributing to predicting ICU LOS. Patients over 80 typically had more complex conditions leading to fewer treatment options than patients aged 65-79 [15], whereas we found patients who died in the ICU were older, which may lead to shorter ICU LOS due to mortality. The release of immature red blood cells into the peripheral circulation during inflammation leads to a higher RDW value in IBD patients during the active disease stage compared to the remission stage. Consequently, the RDW value serves as an indicator of IBD patients' active stage and influences ICU LOS [16]. One cross-sectional study [17] suggested that out of 102 IBD patients, 43 were diagnosed with respiratory diseases, indicating a potential association between IBD and an elevated prevalence of respiratory symptoms. This observation is aligned with our study, as it underscores the significance of Acute Respiratory Failure as a critical variable in predicting ICU LOS in IBD patients. Although our findings underscore the role of MCV as a critical predictor of ICU LOS, limited study examined how MCV influences LOS among the IBD population. Further research is needed to delve into the relationship between MCV and IBD.

Through our study, healthcare providers could have a rough estimation of the ICU LOS of IBD patients during their daily work, providing some guidance for medical resources allocation such as arranging patient beds, assigning staff, and preparing medical resources. In this way, a more effective and efficient working environment may be more acquirable, and also risks may be reduced under reasonable management. For patients who meet some characteristics emphasized in our study, organizations may have in-advance preparations for the possibly severe conditions and give them more tailored healthcare services. The impact of patients' characteristics such as age and heart rate on their ICU LOS were also highlighted, which may provide references for nurses to have correct prospects and thus give preferable medical and humanistic care.

5 Conclusion

We constructed a prediction model for the ICU LOS of IBD patients using the XGBoost model. Using patients' demographics, laboratory tests results, and some comorbidities, the model reached relatively good accuracy and AUC. Important variable impacting the ICU LOS are found and could be used as a reference in medical practice.

Acknowledgements. This research is partially supported by funding from the 1-3-5 project for disciplines of excellence at West China Hospital, Sichuan University.

References

1. Strober, W., Fuss, I., Mannon, P.: The fundamental basis of inflammatory bowel disease. J. Clin. Invest. **117**, 514–521 (2007). https://doi.org/10.1172/JCI30587
2. Yin, R., Neyens, D.M.: Online health resource use by individuals with inflammatory bowel disease: analysis using the National Health Interview Survey. J. Med. Internet Res. **22**, e15352 (2020). https://doi.org/10.2196/15352
3. Fan, Y., Lyu, B.: Research frontier of inflammatory bowel disease. Zhejiang Da Xue Xue Bao Yi Xue Ban. **48**, 334–341 (2019). https://doi.org/10.3785/j.issn.1008-9292.2019.06.15
4. Liu, G.X.H., Day, A.S.: Plant-based diets for inflammatory bowel disease: what is the evidence? Inflamm. Bowel Dis. **30**, 1865 (2023). https://doi.org/10.1093/ibd/izad213
5. Kaplan, G.G., Windsor, J.W.: The four epidemiological stages in the global evolution of inflammatory bowel disease. Nat. Rev. Gastroenterol. Hepatol. **18**, 56–66 (2021)
6. Sands, B.E.: Biomarkers of inflammation in inflammatory bowel disease. Gastroenterology. **149**, 1275–1285.e2 (2015). https://doi.org/10.1053/j.gastro.2015.07.003
7. Argollo, M., Gilardi, D., Peyrin-Biroulet, C., Chabot, J.-F., Peyrin-Biroulet, L., Danese, S.: Comorbidities in inflammatory bowel disease: a call for action. Lancet Gastroenterol. Hepatol. **4**, 643–654 (2019). https://doi.org/10.1016/S2468-1253(19)30173-6
8. Saadatmand, S., Salimifard, K., Mohammadi, R., Kuiper, A., Marzban, M., Farhadi, A.: Using machine learning in prediction of ICU admission, mortality, and length of stay in the early stage of admission of COVID-19 patients. Ann. Oper. Res. **328**, 1043–1071 (2023)
9. Iwase, S., Nakada, T., Shimada, T., Oami, T., Shimazui, T., Takahashi, N., Yamabe, J., Yamao, Y., Kawakami, E.: Prediction algorithm for ICU mortality and length of stay using machine learning. Sci. Rep. **12**, 12912 (2022). https://doi.org/10.1038/s41598-022-17091-5

10. Johnson, A.E.W., Bulgarelli, L., Shen, L., Gayles, A., Shammout, A., Horng, S., Pollard, T.J., Hao, S., Moody, B., Gow, B., Lehman, L.H., Celi, L.A., Mark, R.G.: MIMIC-IV, a freely accessible electronic health record dataset. Sci Data. **10**, 1 (2023)
11. Meng, C., Trinh, L., Xu, N., Enouen, J., Liu, Y.: Interpretability and fairness evaluation of deep learning models on MIMIC-IV dataset. Sci. Rep. **12**, 7166 (2022)
12. Sadowski, A., Dunlap, C., Lacombe, A., Hanes, D.: Alterations in heart rate variability associated with irritable Bowel syndrome or inflammatory bowel disease: a systematic review and meta-analysis. Clin. Transl. Gastroenterol. **12**, e00275 (2021)
13. Park, K.T., Ehrlich, O.G., Allen, J.I., Meadows, P., Szigethy, E.M., Henrichsen, K., Kim, S.C., Lawton, R.C., Murphy, S.M., Regueiro, M., Rubin, D.T., Engel-Nitz, N.M., Heller, C.A.: The cost of inflammatory Bowel disease: an initiative from the Crohn's & Colitis Foundation. Inflamm. Bowel Dis. **26**, 1–10 (2020)
14. Dong, J., Ladonne, M., Feuerstein, J.D.: Medicare patients face high out-of-pocket costs for specialty inflammatory Bowel disease medications. Am. J. Gastroenterol. **118**, 481–484 (2023). https://doi.org/10.14309/ajg.0000000000002057
15. Brandberg, C., Blomqvist, H., Jirwe, M.: What is the importance of age on treatment of the elderly in the intensive care unit? Acta Anaesthesiol. Scand. **57**, 698–703 (2013)
16. Ipek, S., Cekiç, C., Alper, E., Coban, E., Eliacik, E., Arabul, M., Aslan, F., Vatansever, S., Yalcin, H., Unsal, B.: Can red cell distribution width be a marker of disease activity in ulcerative colitis? Int. J. Clin. Exp. Med. **8**, 13848–13853 (2015)
17. Valentin, S., Renel, B., Manneville, F., Caron, B., Choukour, M., Guillaumot, A., Chaouat, A., Poussel, M., Chateau, T., Peyrin-Biroulet, C., Achit, H., Peyrin-Biroulet, L., Chabot, F.: Prevalence of and factors associated with respiratory symptoms among patients with inflammatory bowel disease: a prospective study. Inflamm. Bowel Dis. **29**, 207–216 (2023)

Deep Integration: The Revolutionary Applications and Challenges of Artificial Intelligence in Video Production

Tao Yu, YiHui Chen, and Younghwan Pan(✉)

Department of Smart Experience Design, Kookmin University, Seoul 01706, Republic of Korea
{ytkmu0517,peterpan}@kookmin.ac.kr, swearchan@yeah.net

Abstract. This study investigates the transformative applications and challenges of artificial intelligence (AI) in video content creation. By reviewing literature and conducting qualitative interviews with industry experts, five major pain points of AI in video production were identified: data privacy, ethics and copyright, content quality, technical limitations, and creative limitations. The findings highlight the necessity to enhance AI algorithms, improve the integration of human creativity, establish transparent and fair usage policies, and implement robust data protection measures. Addressing these challenges is crucial for fully leveraging AI's potential in video con-tent creation, ensuring sustainable innovation and fostering development within the media industry. Future research should prioritize these areas to promote effective and ethical use of AI in the field.

Keywords: Artificial Intelligence (AI) · Video Content Creation · Human Creativity Integration · Creative Limitations · Technical Limitations

1 Introduction

The application of AI tools in video content generation encompasses multiple aspects. Firstly, automated video generation tools can analyze user data and preferences to create highly personalized video content. Secondly, AI has demonstrated significant potential in the creative and special effects aspects of video content. By utilizing deep learning algorithms, AI can automatically add visual effects, subtitles, and sound effects, making video content more vivid and engaging. In addition, AI plays a crucial role in optimizing video content. By analyzing real-time playback data and user feedback, AI can continuously improve video content, optimizing playback effects and user experience. For instance, AI can adjust the playback order and recommendation strategies of videos based on data such as viewing duration, click-through rates, and comments to ensure the content is more appealing and interactive.

However, the widespread application of AI tools in video content generation also brings new challenges. Firstly, there are issues related to technical dependence and algorithm transparency. Ensuring the fairness and transparency of AI algorithms and preventing technological monopolies and data misuse are pressing issues that need to

S. Jin et al. (Eds.): IEA 2024, SSDI 39, pp. 262–268, 2025.
https://doi.org/10.1007/978-981-95-0211-0_41

be addressed. Secondly, content quality and copyright protection are also significant challenges. With the proliferation of AI-generated content, ensuring the originality and legality of content and protecting creators' intellectual property rights are critical topics that require thorough exploration. This paper will explore the innovative applications of AI tools in video content generation and analyze their advantages in enhancing content production efficiency and creativity. Additionally, it will discuss the major challenges AI faces in this field and propose corresponding solutions, aiming to provide valuable references for the industry and academia.

2 Literature Review

In recent years, the application of AI in video content generation has garnered widespread attention and gradually become a crucial tool in media content production. Studies have shown that AI technology can significantly lower the barriers to video content production, enhance production efficiency, and free up creators to focus on more creative tasks. AI also demonstrates substantial potential in the analysis and optimization of video content. AI algorithms can effectively filter high-quality content, improving the overall quality of platform content [1].

Additionally, AI provides personalized and interactive viewing experiences during video production and streaming by generating more realistic and creative visual effects through deep content indexing and quality assessment [2]. Chan-Olmsted's comprehensive evaluation of AI applications in the media industry highlights AI's significant potential in content recommendation, user engagement, message optimization, content management, and operational automation. However, balancing AI with human judgment and addressing issues of technological dependency and transparency remain significant challenges [3]. Ghozia et al. proposed a context-aware AI system that enhances the accuracy and efficiency of information extraction by deeply understanding video content through the extraction of emotional, temporal, and spatial data [4]. Sančanin and Penjišević emphasized the importance of responsible and ethical use of AI in high-performance data analysis and media content generation, pointing out that the transparency and standardization of AI product data are key to building trust and managing potential risks [5]. Neri and Carli discussed the application of AI in immersive multimedia content quality assessment, suggesting that AI technology can pro-vide objective evaluation methods to improve user experience [6]. Chen, Zu, and Wang designed an AI-based integrated media platform that achieves efficient production and distribution of media content through the integration of content acquisition, intelligent creation, and multi-channel publishing [7]. Fieiras-Ceide et al. examined the application of AI in European public broadcasting companies and found that although AI shows potential in content recommendation and audience interaction, its high costs and lack of specialized talent limit the widespread use of AI tools [8]. Li explored AI applications in the short video industry, noting that AI can efficiently handle video production, editing, and performance tasks but also emphasized the need for rational thinking to better leverage AI technology for creative empowerment [9]. Adru, Johnson, and Hemalatha investigated an innovative platform combining AI and blockchain technology, exploring the possibilities of content sharing and collaborative interaction driven by non-fungible tokens (NFTs).

They believe this could enhance content creators' creative and revenue-generating capabilities [10]. Despite the enormous potential of AI in video content generation, it faces numerous challenges.

3 Methods

This study explores the application of AI tools in video content generation through case studies and semi-structured interviews. We selected a small media company in China as the case study subject, which recently began using AI tools such as Run-way, Pika, and Lumen5 for scene creation, special effects, content innovation, and video optimization. We documented the settings, operational steps, encountered problems, and solutions during the use of these tools. The generated videos were preliminarily evaluated based on quality, production efficiency, and creativity.

Building on the case study, we conducted semi-structured interviews to gain deeper insights into practitioners' perceptions and experiences with AI tools in video content generation. We selected 10 professionals from the field of video content innovation, including video editors, content creators, and technical support personnel. Each interview lasted approximately 30 min. An interview questionnaire was developed, covering the following questions: 1. What are your specific experiences with using AI tools in projects? 2. What do you perceive as the significant advantages of AI tools in video content generation? 3. What major challenges or problems did you encounter while using AI tools? 4. How do you assess the effectiveness of AI tools in improving video content quality and creativity? 5. What suggestions or expectations do you have for the future development of AI tools? Each interview was recorded and transcribed to ensure the accuracy and completeness of the information. We used content analysis to code and analyze the interview transcripts, summarizing the main viewpoints and conclusions (Fig. 1).

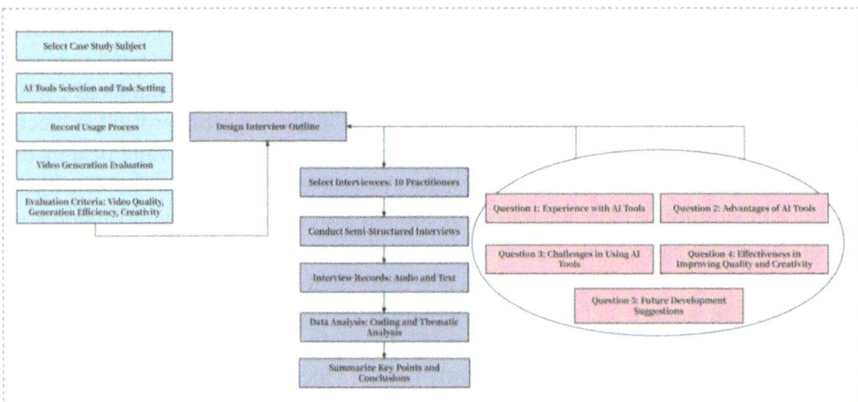

Fig. 1. Flowchart of the study.

4 Results

Through semi-structured interviews with 10 video professionals, this study identified five major pain points of AI tools in video content generation: content quality, creative limitations, technical limitations, ethical and copyright issues, and data privacy concerns.

Respondents acknowledged that while AI tools improve production efficiency, the quality of generated content remains unstable and inconsistent. AI-generated content often lacks creativity and uniqueness, appearing templated and failing to meet the demands of high-creativity projects.

AI tools often struggle with processing high-resolution videos and complex special effects efficiently, leading to slow and unsatisfactory performance.

Ethical and copyright issues arise from unclear ownership and usage rights of AI-generated content, potentially leading to legal disputes and the inclusion of unauthorized material in videos. Data privacy concerns are also significant, as AI tools handle large volumes of user data, raising risks of breaches and privacy violations. There are fears that collected data could be misused, impacting users' privacy rights (Table 1).

5 Discussion

While AI tools significantly improve video generation efficiency, they face notable issues with content quality instability and inconsistency. Respondents highlighted errors in subtitles and poor special effects, indicating that AI technology needs improvement to ensure high quality and precision. Future development should focus on enhancing AI algorithm accuracy and flexibility to reduce manual intervention and improve content quality.

Creativity and uniqueness in AI-generated videos are major challenges. Templated videos fail to meet high-creativity project demands due to AI's reliance on preset patterns and data. Future research should explore ways to enhance AI's creative expression through human feedback and develop algorithms that simulate human creativity.

Technical limitations, such as slow processing speeds and inefficiency with high-resolution and complex special effects, affect the practicality of AI tools. Current AI technologies and computational resources are inadequate for complex tasks. Future development should focus on improving computational efficiency and algorithm optimization to handle large-scale data and complex tasks more effectively.

Ethical and copyright issues are significant, with unclear ownership and usage rights of AI-generated content leading to potential legal disputes. Future research and policy should clarify these rules to protect creators' rights and prevent misuse of AI-generated content.

Data privacy issues are crucial, as AI tools handle large amounts of user data, raising risks of breaches and privacy violations. Future development should establish stricter data protection measures and privacy management mechanisms to ensure data security and user trust.

Table 1. Demonstration of some results of the qualitative content analysis.

Meaning Units	Condensed meaning units	Codes	Categories
"When using Pika, sometimes the ideas generated are not precise enough and require multiple adjustments to achieve satisfactory results"	Pika's ideas are sometimes not accurate, need adjustments	Idea accuracy	Creative limitations
"Hopefully, in the future Pika will be able to further optimise the accuracy of idea generation and reduce the time it takes for users to make adjustments"	Hope Pika improves idea accuracy, reducing adjustment time	Improve idea accuracy, reduce adjustments	
"The biggest challenge is the initial learning cost. Each tool has its own operating logic that takes time to master"	High initial learning cost, needs time to master	Learning cost	Technical limitations
"It is hoped that in the future Lumen5 will further optimise its ability to process Chinese text and reduce recognition errors"	Hope Lumen5 improves Chinese text processing, reducing errors	Optimize Chinese text processing, reduce errors	
"Overall, AI tools have been effective in improving video quality and creativity"	AI tools significantly improve video quality and creativity	Improve video quality, creativity	Content quality
"Runway's scene creation feature is very smart and generates high quality scenes quickly"	Runway's scene creation is smart, generates high-quality scenes	Scene creation, high-quality scenes	

(continued)

Table 1. *(continued)*

Meaning Units	Condensed meaning units	Codes	Categories
"The AI tool automatically identifies if the video footage has copyright issues and can alert the user to make changes"	AI tools automatically identify copyright issues in video materials, alerting users to modify	Automatic copyright identification, alert modifications	Ethics and copyright
"Users are concerned that the copyright of video footage needs to be further clarified when using these AI tools"	Users are concerned about copyright issues in video materials	Copyright issues in video materials	
"AI tools need to be mindful of data privacy and security when processing user data"	AI tools need to pay attention to data privacy and security when handling user data	Data privacy, data security	Data privacy
"Hopefully, future AI tools will provide better privacy protections when processing user data"	Hope AI tools provide better privacy protection measures when handling user data	Provide privacy protection measures	

6 Conclusions

Through literature review and qualitative interviews with industry professionals, this study identifies five pain points of AI in video production: data privacy, ethics and copyright, content quality, technical limitations, and creative limitations.

AI-generated content often lacks stability, necessitating substantial human intervention. The templated nature of AI-generated videos fails to meet high-creativity project demands, highlighting the need for improved creative expression and uniqueness. Technical constraints, the current AI technologies and computational resources are inadequate for complex video generation tasks. Additionally, unclear ownership and usage rights of AI-generated content can lead to legal disputes, and data privacy concerns are significant, raising the risk of data breaches and privacy violations. To address these challenges, improving the accuracy and flexibility of AI algorithms, enhancing AI's creative expression through human feedback, optimizing computational efficiency, and establishing clear ownership and usage rules are essential. Strengthening data protection measures will also help build user trust. While AI tools have immense potential in video content generation, continuous technological optimization and policy improvements are necessary to fully harness their advantages, driving industry development and progress.

References

1. Lu, Z., Nam, I.-Y.: Research on the influence of new media technology on internet short video content production under artificial intelligence background. Complex. **2021**, 8875700 (2021)
2. Jayanthiladevi, A., Raj, A., Narmadha, R., Chandran, S.S., Shaju, S., Prasad, K.K.: AI in video analysis, production and streaming delivery. J. Phys. Conf. Ser. **1712**, 012014 (2020)
3. Chan-Olmsted, S.M.: A review of artificial intelligence adoptions in the media industry. Int. J. Media Manag. **21**(3), 193–215 (2019)
4. Ghozia, A., Attiya, G., Adly, E., El-Fishawy, N.: Intelligence is beyond learning: A context-aware artificial intelligent system for video understanding. Comput. Intell. Neurosci. **2020**, 8813089 (2020)
5. Sančanin, B., Penjišević, A.: Use of artificial intelligence for the generation of media content. Soc. Inform. J. **1**(1), 01–07 (2022)
6. Neri, M., Carli, M.: Artificial Intelligence techniques for quality assessments of immersive multimedia. In: Proceedings of the 2023 ACM International Conference on Interactive Media Experiences (2023)
7. Chen, K., Zu, Y., Wang, D.: Design and implementation of intelligent creation platform based on artificial intelligence technology. J. Comput. Methods Sci. Eng. **20**, 1109–1126 (2020)
8. Fieiras-Ceide, C., Vaz-Álvarez, M., Túñez-López, M.: Artificial Intelligence Strategies in European Public Broadcasters: Uses, Forecasts and Future Challenges. El Profesional de la información (2022)

Anthropometry (I)

The Conundrum of Integrating Manual and Digital Anthropometric Measurement Methods

Robin L. Carufel(✉), Hyegjoo E. Choi-Rokas, Elizabeth D. Perry, Peng Li, and K. Blake Mitchell

U.S. Army Combat Capabilities Development Command Soldier Center, Natick, MA, USA
robin.l.carufel.civ@army.mil

Abstract. Body scanning is a time efficient, precise, and reliable anthropometric data capture method, but digital and manual measurement values often do not align [1-11]. To understand how well a commercial digital measurement extraction software program aligns with current U.S. Army manual anthropometric measurement methods, this study assessed body measurement similarity between 12 manually measured and digitally extracted dimensions from 105 subjects in the U.S. Air Force's Aircrew Sizing Survey 2011 dataset. Descriptive statistics, adjustment percentage, repeated measures analysis of variance, and allowable error comparisons were computed for each measurement method. Findings indicated that digital circumferences were larger than manual circumferences, while manual lengths were larger than digital lengths, with means differing by up to 39 mm. Results demonstrated high levels of similarity between manual and digital Cervicale Height and Calf Circumference means, suggesting digitally measuring these dimensions may maintain quality and save time. Scan occlusion at the crotch caused significant differences between digital and manual Crotch Height and Vertical Trunk Circumference means, suggesting manual measurement is best for these dimensions.

Keywords: digital anthropometry · manual anthropometry · validation

1 Introduction

Body scanning is a time-efficient anthropometric data capture method [1], producing reliable and precise body measurement values [2–5]. However, differing scanner hardware, measurement extraction software, scanning postures, and breathing cycles often cause digital and manual measurement values to not align [3, 6–11]. Thus, anthropometric teams must validate their body scanner systems. To understand how well a recently acquired commercial digital measurement extraction software program aligns with current U.S. Army manual anthropometric measurement methods, this study assessed body measurement similarity between 12 manually measured and digitally extracted dimensions from 105 subjects in the U.S. Air Force's Aircrew Sizing Survey 2011 dataset (ACSS 2011) [12]. This paper shares the major differences encountered between measurement methods and discusses the conundrum of integrating manual and digital anthropometric methods within anthropometric surveys.

S. Jin et al. (Eds.): IEA 2024, SSDI 39, pp. 271–276, 2025.
https://doi.org/10.1007/978-981-95-0211-0_42

2 Method

A stratified random sample of 105 subjects (53f/52m) were selected from ACSS 2011 [12]. Subjects were stratified by sex and level of obesity, represented by body mass index (BMI) [13], ensuring a wide variety of body sizes were included. Frequency rates for each sex/BMI group provided the total number of subjects required to reach overall statistical significance. The extra female is the only subject belonging to the underweight category in the sample. All selected subjects had good quality scans and a complete set of manual data. Twelve dimensions were assessed. These dimensions' definitions aligned on landmarking, posture, and instrument orientation, suggesting their measurement values should equate between methods.

Measurements were collected using three methods: (A) manual (Manual), (B) automated digital extraction (Digital), and (C) researcher adjusted digital extraction (Adjusted Digital). Digital (B) measurements provided a baseline for the commercial software, while Adjusted Digital (C) measurements demonstrated whether the software took measurements from the correct anatomical locations. Software algorithms may incorrectly place measurements (e.g., placing Stature's top-of-head landmark on the highest point of a subject's bun, instead of at the top of the skull); adjusting manually improves measurement accuracy. For Adjusted Digital (C), the lead researcher visually inspected each dimension's location and adjusted its position when deemed incorrect.

Descriptive statistics, adjustment percentage, repeated measures analysis of variance (ANOVA), and allowable error comparisons were computed for each measurement method. Higher adjustment percentages (i.e., number, percent, and type of adjustments made to each dimension) combined with statistically significant mean differences between methods (A–B, B–C, A–C) discovered during the ANOVAs, suggested greater dissimilarity between measurement methods. Allowable error comparisons indicated whether average differences between measurement methods fall within accepted U.S. Army thresholds for measurement reliability. ACSS 2011 did not produce their own allowable errors, therefore the 1988 and 2012 Anthropometric Survey of U.S. Army Personnel (ANSUR I & II) allowable error values were used [12, 14, 15].

3 Results

Among the 12 dimensions, ten dimensions were adjusted for the females, with five of these only adjusted for one person. Six dimensions were adjusted for the males, and all were adjusted for at least three subjects. On average, two adjustments were made per subject, with one female and eight male subjects requiring no adjustments. The largest adjustment was for female Vertical Trunk Circumference (74%), followed by Waist at Natural Indentation (Waist NI) Circumference and Height (60% males, 49% females) (Table 1). For Vertical Trunk Circumference, the Shoulder landmark was moved closer to the body 90% of the time, and the Crotch landmarks were adjusted 23% of the time. When adjusted, the Waist NI location was primarily moved higher up the torso (87% males and 100% females).

Manual (A) and Digital (B) means were significantly different for eight female and 11 male dimensions ($p \leq .05$). Manual (A) and Adjusted Digital (C) means were significantly different for eight female and 11 male dimensions ($p \leq .05$). For both sexes, (i)

Digital/Adjusted Digital (B/C) means were larger than Manual (A) means for five circumferences, and (ii) Manual (A) means were larger than Digital/Adjusted Digital (B/C) means for all six heights. Vertical Trunk Circumference produced the largest differences (31–37 mm females, 38–39 mm males) between Manual (A) and Digital/Adjusted Digital (B/C) methods, while Calf Circumference produced the smallest (1 mm, both sexes). Table 1 summarizes the ANOVA, allowable error, and adjustment percentage results.

Both sexes' Cervicale Height, Buttock and Calf circumferences were within the ANSUR allowable errors for Manual versus Digital (A–B) and Manual versus Adjusted Digital (A–C). Adjusting the Waist NI landmark location shifted the Manual versus Adjusted Digital (A–C) Waist NI Circumference value within the ANSUR allowable error for both sexes. Differences between measurement methods were often larger for heights than circumferences, resulting in heights falling outside allowable errors while circumferences fell within (e.g., Buttock Circumference & Height).

Table 1. Measurement method results organized by sex (mm).

		Females				Males			
Dimensions	A.E.	A-B	B-C	A-C	Adj. %	A-B	B-C	A-C	Adj. %
Bust/Chest Circ.	14	-19 **	-1	-20 ***	2%	-38 ***	0	-38 ***	0%
Buttock Circ.	12	-10 **	0	-10 **	0%	-5 **	2	-3	0%
Buttock Ht.	4	23 ***	2	25 **	0%	7 *	0	7 *	0%
Calf Circ.	4	1	0	1	2%	-1 *	0	-1 *	0%
Cervicale Ht.	7	5	1	6	28%	5	1	6 *	15%
Crotch Ht.	10	15 **	0	14 **	2%	17 ***	0	17 ***	0%
Hip Circ.	-----	-1	-1	-2	2%	-10 ***	3	-8 *	6%
Hip Ht.	-----	39 ***	1	40 ***	2%	24 ***	3	27 ***	6%
Stature	6	10	3	13 **	28%	9 ***	0	9 ***	0%
Vertical Trunk Circ.	24	-37 ***	6 *	-31 ***	74%	-39 ***	1	-38 ***	46%
Waist NI Circ.	11	-27 ***	17 **	-10 **	49%	-17 ***	9 ***	-9 ***	60%
Waist NI Ht.	4	31 ***	-11 *	20 ***	49%	25 ***	-12 ***	13 ***	60%

Note: Alpha level: 0.05; * ≤.05, ** ≤.01, *** ≤.001

Note: Green cells: within allowable error; Red cells: outside allowable error

Note: Red text: ≥50% of subjects were adjusted.

4 Discussion

Overall, digital measurement values (B, C) did not align with manual measurement values (A), differing between 1 mm and 39 mm. Digital circumferences were larger than manual circumferences, while manual lengths were larger than digital lengths. These findings align with previous research [3, 6, 8, 9, 16, 17], which cited posture, scan quality, respiration, and tape tension as sources of variation between measurement methods.

Manual measurements are often taken with the feet together, while digital measurements are taken with the feet apart to improve inner leg and crotch visibility. Standardizing posture between manual and digital methods is a common recommendation in body scanning literature, usually because differences are discovered between manual and digital methods when using differing postures [3, 10, 11]. Moving the feet apart may increase buttock and hip circumferences, while decreasing stature, waist, and hip heights [3, 7]. The ACSS 2011 dataset was chosen because it utilized the same posture for manual measurements and scans, eliminating foot posture discrepancy between measurement methods. Subjects' feet were rotated outwards 33° and placed 10.7 cm apart for both manual measurements and scanning [12].

While minimal differences between Manual and Digital/Adjusted Digital (A–B, A–C) Buttock and Hip circumferences existed, lower torso Digital/Adjusted Digital (B/C) heights were much shorter than Manual (A) heights. Waist NI Height displays a similar trend to the Buttock and Hip heights, but the Waist NI location was regularly moved up the torso to align with subjects' natural indents. This Adjusted Digital (C) Waist NI Height value drew closer to the Manual (A) value but was still shorter by 13–20 mm. A minor contributing factor to the height discrepancy may have been the few millimeters unavoidably removed from some subjects' feet when the platform they stood on was removed during scan preparation. However, height loss due to scan preparation insufficiently explains the large average height differences for these dimensions.

Scan occlusion at the crotch caused significant differences between Manual and Digital/Adjusted Digital (A–B, A–C) Crotch Height and Vertical Trunk Circumference means for both sexes. Digital Crotch Height could not be adjusted, and Vertical Trunk Circumference Crotch landmark adjustment was limited to moving landmarks from the left to the right side of the body, both due to missing data at the crotch which is a noted issue [6, 16]. In this study, the average differences between measurement methods for these dimensions are smaller than those from the literature (Crotch Height: 27–105 mm; Vertical Trunk Circumference: 31–103 mm) [16, 17] but may be partially accounted for by differing manual measurement methods between studies. However, manual measurement will likely produce the most accurate data for these two dimensions.

Even though the commercial software accurately located subjects' Bust/Chest Circumference, large differences were discovered between measurement methods (19-38 mm). Previous literature showed similar average differences (14–46 mm) [17]. Respiration and tape tension may contribute to the differences. During manual measurements, data collectors can choose when in the breathing cycle to capture a measurement (e.g., maximum point of quiet respiration), however the value will be impacted by tape tension variation. Body scanners eliminate tape tension variability but cannot provide the compression required for some dimensions (e.g., Chest Breadth), and choosing which point of the breathing cycle to capture is challenging. When compared to neutral breathing, scans with a subject at maximum exhalation or inhalation may generate differences of 16 mm and 33 mm, respectively [7]. As with manual measurements, digital data collectors must guide subjects through correct respiration during scanning.

Cervicale Height and Calf Circumference barely differed between measurement methods. While Cervicale Height was adjusted 15–28% of the time, the average Digital versus Adjusted Digital (B–C) value was 1 mm, suggesting adjustment was not impactful. It is unclear why Cervicale Height does not follow the same pattern as the Buttock, Hip, and Waist NI heights. The commercial software accurately located Calf Circumference, and the average differences concurred with previous research, which discovered differences of 0–2 mm between measurement methods [17]. These two dimensions may be accurately, reliably, and quickly extracted digitally.

The literature reviewed for this study did not mention adjusting digital measurements as a strategy for improving digital measurement data collection. Previous experience with the commercial software by the primary researcher supported using the digital adjustment method. Not all instances of digital adjustment were impactful (e.g., Cervicale Height, Vertical Trunk Circumference). However, adjusting the Waist NI landmark brought the Manual versus Adjusted Digital (A–C) Waist NI Circumference value within the ANSUR allowable error. Since the Waist NI location was below subjects' natural indents so often, the commercial software's Waist NI location algorithm may require modification.

5 Conclusion

Anthropometric surveys can be made more effective by blending accurate, reliable, and precise manual and digital measurement methods [1, 11]. Even minimally reducing data collectors' labor can save precious time during large-scale surveys. Using the manual measurements as the standard, the results of this survey could not validate this commercial software program's digital body measurement extraction tool for these 12 dimensions. Cervicale Height and Calf Circumference are good candidates for digital measurement as they fall within the ANSUR allowable errors and require no adjustments. Manual measurement is best for highly occluded scan areas (e.g., Crotch Height and Vertical Trunk Circumference) and locations of digital location inconsistency (e.g., Waist NI Circumference).

Limitations included the unavoidable, slight height loss due to data preparation, scan occlusion at the crotch, and not knowing when in the breathing cycle scans were captured for each subject. This study introduced the concept of digital adjustment as a method for improving digital data collection and began determining which dimensions digital adjustment is necessary for. Future research should assess alignment between dimensions whose definitions only partially align or do not align at all, as well as experiment with postural differences to pinpoint why digital heights are so much shorter than manual heights.

References

1. Bye, E., LaBat, K.L., DeLong, M.R.: Analysis of body measurement systems for apparel. Cloth. Text. Res. J. **24**(2), 66–79 (2006)
2. Robinette, K.M., Daanen, H.A.M.: Precision of the CAESAR scan-extracted measurements. Appl. Ergon. **37**, 259–265 (2006)
3. Koepke, N., Zwahlen, M., Wells, J.C., Bender, N., Henneberg, M., Rühli, F.J., Staub, K.: Comparison of 3D laser-based photonic scans and manual anthropometric measurements of body size and shape in a validation study of 123 young Swiss men. PeerJ. **5**, 1–22 (2017)

4. Parker, C.J., Gill, S., Hayes, S.G.: 3D body scanning has suitable reliability: an anthropometric investigation for garment construction. In: Proceedings of 3DBODY.TECH 2017 8th International Conference and Exhibition on 3D Body Scanning and Processing Technologies, Montreal, Canada, pp. 298–305 (2017)
5. Rumbo-Rodríguez, L., Sánchez-SanSegundo, M., Ferrer-Cascales, R., García-D'Urso, N., Hurtado-Sánchez, J.A., Zaragoza-Martí, A.: Comparison of body scanner and manual anthropometric measurements of body shape: a systematic review. Int. J. Environ. Res. Public Health. **18**, 1–17 (2021)
6. Mckinnon, L., Istook, C.: Comparative analysis of the Image Twin system and the 3T6 body scanner. J. Text. Apparel. Technol. Manag. **1**(2), 1–7 (2001)
7. Mckinnon, L., Istook, C.L.: Body scanning: the effects of subject respiration and foot positioning on the data integrity of scanned measurements. J. Fash. Mark. Manag. **6**(2), 103–121 (2002)
8. Wang, J., Gallagher, D., Thornton, J.C., Yu, W., Horlick, M., Pi-Sunyer, F.X.: Validation of a 3-dimensional photonic scanner for the measurement of body volumes, dimensions, and percentage body fat. Am. J. Clin. Nutr. **83**(4), 809–816 (2006)
9. Han, H., Nam, Y., Choi, K.: Comparative analysis of 3D body scan measurements and manual measurements of size Korea adult females. Int. J. Ind. Ergon. **40**, 530–540 (2010)
10. Kuehnapfel, A., Ahnert, P., Loeffler, M., Broda, A., Scholz, M.: Reliability of 3D laser-based anthropometry and comparison with classical anthropometry. Sci. Rep. **6**, 1–11 (2016)
11. Mocini, E., Cammarota, C., Frigerio, F., Muzzioli, L., Piciocchi, C., Lacalaprice, D., Buccolini, F., Donini, L.M., Pinto, A.: Digital anthropometry: a systematic review on precision, reliability and accuracy of most popular existing technologies. Nutrients. **15**, 1–39 (2023)
12. Choi, H., Coate, A., Selby, M., Hudson, J., Whitehead, C., Zehner, G., Fleming, S.: Aircrew Sizing Survey 2011. Human System Integration Directorate, Wright-Patterson Air Force Base (2014)
13. About adult BMI: https://www.cdc.gov/healthyweight/assessing/bmi/adult_bmi/index.html. Accessed 5 Mar 2024
14. Gordon, C.C., Bradtmiller, B., Churchill, T., Clauser, C.E., McConville, J.T., Tebbetts, I., Walker, R.A.: 1988 Anthropometric survey of U.S. Army personnel: methods and summary statistics. U.S. Army Natick Research, Development and Engineering Center, Natick, MA (1989)
15. Gordon, C.C., Blackwell, C.L., Bradtmiller, B., Parham, J.L., Barrientos, P., Paquette, S.P., Corner, B.D., Carson, J.M., Venezia, J.C., Rockwell, B.M., Mucher, M., Kristensen, S.: 2012 Anthropometric Survey of U.S. Army personnel: Methods and Summary Statistics. U.S. Army Natick Soldier Research, Development and Engineering Center (2014)
16. Li, P.: Comparing Human Solutions Anthroscan measurements to ANSUR II manual measurements. U.S. Army CCDC Soldier Center (2019)
17. Mullenger, C.R., Choi-Rokas, J., Bowens, J.: Comparing 3D-extracted anthropometric measurements to traditionally collected measurements [PowerPoint Slides]. (2023)

Chinese Auricular Shape Types for Ear-Related Wearables

Hao Fan[1,2,3,4,5](✉), Mengcheng Wang[2], Jifeng Xu[1], Dedong Zheng[1], Jingyuan Tian[1], Wei Zhou[1], Han Gao[1], Zequan Lin[6], Jinlei Shi[4], Ao Jiang[7], Hao Fang[8], Feng Gan[1,3], and Chunlei Chai[4]

[1] Department of Design, Southeast University, Nanjing, Jiangsu, China
404763257@qq.com
[2] School of Art and Design, Xi'an University of Technology, Xi'an, Shaanxi, China
[3] State Culture and Tourism Industry Think Tank - Chinese Art Evaluation Institute, Southeast University, Nanjing, Jiangsu, China
[4] Institute of Modern Industrial Design, Zhejiang University, Hangzhou, Zhejiang, China
[5] Key Laboratory of Industrial Design and Ergonomics, Ministry of Industry and Information Technology, Northwestern Polytechnical University, Xi'an, Shaanxi, China
[6] Institute of Creativity and Innovation, Xiamen University, Xiamen, Fujian, China
[7] College of Mechanical and Electrical Engineering, Nanjing University of Aeronautics and Astronautics, Nanjing, Jiangsu, China
[8] Department of Industrial Design, Wuhan Institute of Technology, Wuhan, Hubei, China

Abstract. There remains a notable gap in research focusing on the anthropometric classification of human ear shapes among the Chinese population, particularly across diverse age groups and geographical regions using 3D data, a critical aspect for designing ear-related products. In this study, 3D scanning and casting were utilized to collect 18 ear measurements from 1400 participants aged 15 to 79. Based on six key factors, human ear shapes were categorized into five distinct types. A significant correlation was observed between human ear types and age groups, suggesting that ear morphology may evolve with age. A comprehensive understanding of the auricle's complex structure and its shape variations in mainland Chinese populations is vital for developing ergonomic, functional, and user-centric ear-related products.

Keywords: anthropometry · shape characterization · ergonomic design

1 Introduction

The auricle plays a critical role in facial aesthetics and serves as the first structural component in the auditory system's response to sound stimuli [1]. Given its cultural, social, physiological, and psychological significance, human ear morphology has become a key focus for researchers and designers [2]. Ear-related wearable technologies—such as headphones, hearing aids, and earphones—have transformed daily life by facilitating communication, entertainment, and hearing protection [3, 4]. To ensure optimal comfort and functionality, ergonomic design must incorporate anthropometric data, accounting for variations in human ear shape and size [8–11], [12–15].

S. Jin et al. (Eds.): IEA 2024, SSDI 39, pp. 277–282, 2025.
https://doi.org/10.1007/978-981-95-0211-0_43

Ear wearables are typically categorized into three types based on positioning: over-ear, in-ear, and behind-ear [5, 6]. Since the auricle serves as the primary contact point for these devices, its morphology directly impacts fit and usability [7]. Previous studies suggest that human ear dimensions vary significantly by sex, age, and laterality (left/right ear) [8]. Thus, a detailed understanding of these variations is essential for designing natural, functional, and user-friendly wearables [9].

However, limited research has systematically examined the anthropometric shape variations of Chinese auricles across different age groups and geographical regions using 3D data, which hinders the development of tailored ear-related products. This study aims to address this by employing casting and 3D scanning techniques to measure and classify human ear shapes among a diverse Chinese population, providing critical insights for ergonomic wearable design.

2 Methods

2.1 Participants

This study was conducted from 2016 to 2020, involving 1400 Chinese participants (aged 15–79) from 30 provinces across mainland China. Participants were evenly distributed across seven groups: 10 s, 20 s, 30 s, 40 s, 50 s, 60 s and 70 s. Each group consisted of 100 males and 100 females, ensuring balanced demographic representation. Individuals with the following conditions were excluded:

1. Hereditary or congenital ear deformities.
2. Human ear trauma or prior ear surgery.
3. Maxillofacial abnormalities.
4. Significant ear piercings affecting human ear morphology.
5. Additionally, no participants were genetically related, minimizing familial bias in morphological variations.

2.2 Measurements Variables

Based on previous studies [1–3, 5, 8, 10, 11], eighteen human ear measurement variables were defined (Fig. 1). The auricles were bilaterally measured through an indirect 3D scanning method (Fig. 3). A high-precision EinScan HD Scanner (SHINING 3D Inc.) was employed to capture detailed scans of the subjects' heads and ears. For the concha region, ABR impression materials were used to create precise casts, which were then digitized using the 3D scanner. The resulting human ear and conchal scans were merged and processed into a unified 3D mesh model using RapidForm XOR3 software (INUS Technology, Inc., Korea).

2.3 Data Analysis

Statistical analyses were performed using MATLAB with a significance of $\alpha = 0.05$ ($p < .05$ considered significant). To examine human ear shape variations, we first applied factor analysis with varimax orthogonal rotation to extract key morphological factors.

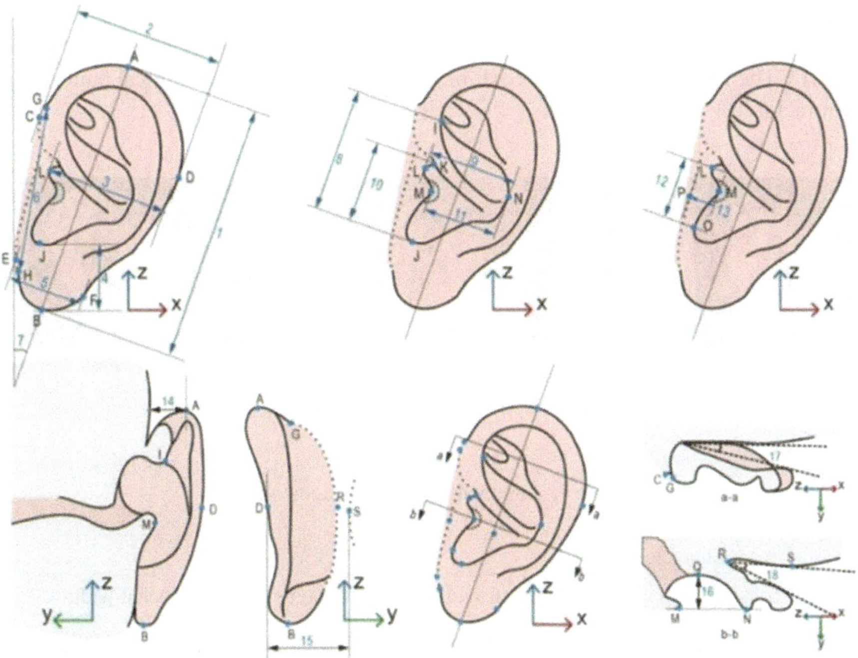

Landmark: (A) superaurale, (B) subaurale, (C) preaurale, (D) postaurale, (E) lobule anterior, (F) lobule posterior, (G) otobasion superius, (H) otobasion inferius, (I) anterior cymba concha, (J) incisura intertragica inferior, (K) superior cavum concha, (L) incisura anterior auris posterior, (M) tragion, (N) posterior concha, (O) lowest point on the lower border of tragus, (P) cardinal point of tragus, (Q) medial concha, (R) otobasion posterius, (S) anterior mastoid. Measurement variables: (1) AL: auricular length, (2) AWP: auricular width at postaurale, (3) AWI: auricular width at the incisura anterior auris posterior, (4) LL: lobular length, (5) LW: lobular width, (6) EML: ear morphologic length, (7) AIA: auricular inclination angle, (8) CL: conchal length, (9) CW: conchal width, (10) CCL: cavum concha length, (11) CCW: cavum concha width, (12) TL: tragal length, (13) TH: tragal height, (14) EPS: ear protrusion at superaurale level, (15) EPT: ear protrusion at tragal level, (16) CD: conchal depth, (17) CAP: concho-mastoid angle at postaurale, (18) CAO: concho-mastoid angle at otobasion posterius.

Fig. 1. Landmarks and measurements.

Subsequently, Hierarchical Cluster Analysis (HCA) was employed, and Euclidean distance were used as the similarity metric and Ward's method for linkage. This approach optimizes cluster cohesion by minimizing within-group variance while maximizing between-group separation. The optimal number of clusters was determined through multiple criteria with the Cubic Clustering Criterion, pseudo-F statistic and pseudo-T-squared values. Finally, Pearson's test (chi-square test) was used to evaluate potential associations between derived ear types and age categories.

3 Results

The factor analysis of eighteen human ear measurements revealed six principal shape variation factors (Fig. 2), with adequate sampling adequacy (KMO = 0.674) and significant sphericity (Bartlett's test, $p < .001$). Cluster analysis determined five distinct human ear types as the optimal solution based on the pseudo-F statistic (n = 5, pseudo-F = 113). A strong association existed between ear types and age groups ($\chi^2 = 583.29$, $p < .001$). The five human ear types exhibited characteristic morphological patterns are shown in Table 1 and Fig. 2.

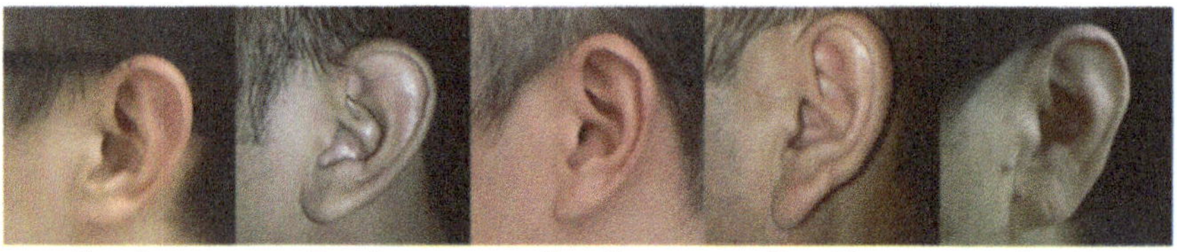

Fig. 2. The human ear shapes.

Table 1. Landmarks and measurements.

Type	Characteristics		
	Overall size	Cavum concha & tragus	Conchal width
Type I	Smallest	Second shortest	Below average
Type II	Above average	Second longest	Below average
Type III	Second smallest	Longest	Below average
Type IV	Second largest	Above average in length	Widest
Type V	Largest	Shortest	Narrowest

4 Discussion

Current ear-related products typically adopt a one-size-fits-all approach, which fails to accommodate the diverse human ear dimensions across different age groups. Unlike clothing or footwear, ear-worn devices require precise fitting across multiple contact points - over, inside, and behind the ear - making conventional S-M-L sizing systems inadequate. To address this limitation, our study employed Hierarchical Cluster Analysis (Ward's method with Euclidean distance) to develop a comprehensive classification system for Chinese human ear morphology. We identified five distinct human ear types based on six key shape variation factors, providing scientifically derived size references for age-specific wearable device design. Key findings revealed significant age-related patterns in human ear morphology:

Prevalence Patterns: Types I and II dominated across both genders; 70% of adolescents (15–19 years) exhibited Type I characteristics; 90% of older adults (60–79 years) displayed either Type IV or Type V morphologies.

Age-Related Trends: Type I prevalence showed an inverse relationship with age; Types IV and V demonstrated positive age correlation; the strong type-age association

($\chi^2 = 583.29$, $p < .001$) suggests potential morphological changes with aging, though longitudinal validation is needed.

Design Recommendations: Hybrid Sizing System: Integrate our typological classification with traditional S-M-L sizing for improved product fit.

Age-Specific References: Primary reference: Type I for adolescent users (15–19 years).

Primary references: Types IV-V for elderly users (60–79 years).

5 Conclusion

Based on anthropometric data from 1400 Chinese participants, this study proposes a five-type human ear classification system to improve the design and fit of ear-related wearables. The analysis revealed that Type I, characterized by a small human ear contour with minimal posterior protrusion, and Type II were the most prevalent forms across both genders. These findings suggest using Type I as the primary reference for 15–19 years and Types IV and V for older adults. The significant association between human ear types and age groups further indicates potential age-related morphological changes in ear structure. This classification framework provides valuable guidance for developing more ergonomic and age-appropriate wearable devices.

Acknowledgments. We express our thanks to the participating individuals for their time and effort.

Funding. This study is supported by the Major Project of the National Social Science Fund (NSSF) of China (Grant No. 21ZD11), and the Fundamental Research Funds for the Central Universities (SEU Grant No. 2242024S30013). Additional support comes from the Southeast University, Xi'an University of Technology, Zhejiang University and Northwestern Polytechnical University.

References

1. Jung, H.S., Jung, H.S.: Surveying the dimensions and characteristics of Korean ears for the ergonomic design of ear-related products. Int. J. Ind. Ergon. **31**(6), 361–373 (2003)
2. Alexander, K.S., Stott, D.J., Sivakumar, B., Kang, N.: A morphometric study of the human ear. J. Plast. Reconstr. Aesthet. Surg. **64**(1), 41–47 (2011)
3. Fan, H., Wang, M., Adamson, C.H., Ren, Y., Chu, J., Yu, S.: Anthropometric analysis of external acoustic meatus for ergonomic design. Proc. Hum. Factors Ergon. Soc. Annu. Meet. **64**(1), 1833–1835 (2020)
4. Wang, M., Fan, H., Harris, C., Yu, S.: Anthropometric characteristics of Chinese auricles for ergonomic design. Proc. Hum. Factors Ergon. Soc. Annu. Meet. **63**(1), 1962–1963 (2019)
5. Lee, W., Jung, H., Bok, I., Kim, C., Kwon, O., Choi, T., You, H.: Measurement and application of 3D ear images for ear-phone design. Proc. Hum. Factors Ergon. Soc. Annu. Meet. **60**(1), 1053–1057 (2016)
6. Fan, H., Yu, S., Chu, J., Wang, M., Chen, D., Zhang, S., Wang, W., et al.: Anthropometric characteristics and product categorization of Chinese auricles for ergonomic design. Int. J. Ind. Ergon. **69**(1), 118–141 (2019)

7. Fan, H., Yu, S., Wang, M., Li, M., Zhao, X., Ren, Y., Zhang, S., et al.: Analysis of the external acoustic meatus for ergonomic design: part II—anthropometric variations of the external acoustic meatus by sex, age and side in Chinese population. Ergonomics. **64**(5), 657–670 (2021)
8. Fan, H., Wang, M., Zhao, X., Ren, Y., Chen, C., Dou, Y., Shi, J., et al.: Effects of variations in the tragus expansion angle on users' comfort for in-ear wearables. Proc. Hum. Factors Ergon. Soc. Annu. Meet. **67**(1), 877–883 (2023)
9. Wang, M., Fan, H., Yu, S., Wang, L., Chu, J., Tang, X., Li, W., et al.: Analysis of the auricles and human ear shape types for ear-related wearables: a study of mainland Chinese sample aged 15–79. Work. **73**(1), 335–352 (2022)
10. Fan, H., Yu, S., Wang, M., Li, M., Chu, J., Yan, Y., Zhang, S., et al.: Analysis of the external acoustic meatus for ergonomic design: part I—measurement of the external acoustic meatus using casting, scanning and rapid estimation approaches. Ergonomics. **64**(5), 640–656 (2021)
11. Wang, M., Fan, H., Yu, S., Zhao, X., Wang, L., Li, W., Wang, L., et al.: Effects of variations in the tragus expansion angle on physical comfort for in-ear wearables. Ergonomics. **65**(10), 1352–1372 (2022)

A Review of Anthropometric Databases for an Inclusive Workforce: Constructing Databases

Ana Maria Rincón Jaramillo[1,2], Marcus Yung[3], Amin Yazdani[3], and Ornwipa Thamsuwan[2](✉)

[1] Universidad de Caldas, Cl. 65 #26-10, Manizales, Caldas, Colombia
[2] École de technologie supérieure, 1100 R. Notre Dame O, Montreal, QC, Canada
ornwipa.thamsuwan@etsmtl.ca
[3] Canadian Institute for Safety, Wellness & Performance, Conestoga College Institute of Technology & Advanced Learning, 25 Reuter Drive, Cambridge, ON, Canada

Abstract. Poor design of products and processes across different industries may contribute to accidents, injuries and productivity losses, but it can be improved with the aid of anthropometric databases. However, many anthropometric databases lack a good representation of the intended work population. Through a literature review, this paper identified the diverse methods in constructing anthropometric databases and best practices for the design of products for an inclusive workforce. It was found that manual measurements are the most commonly-cited method in peer-reviewed literature because of its low cost and long-standing tradition. Meanwhile, 3D scanners have been reported in a few recent studies, but there is a surge of interest in these methods. We recognized a need for increased representation of different segments of the population to better characterize the cultural and ethnic mosaic present in different countries.

Keywords: Anthropometric database · Product design · Workforce · Methodology

1 Introduction

Anthropometry is a branch of biological anthropology and ergonomics, and can be defined as "the measurement of human body dimensions such as lengths, breadths, girths, and skinfolds using surface landmarks for reference" [1]. These anthropometric measurements can be used for different purposes like nutritional assessment [2], identification of the biological profile of individuals in archaeological and forensic contexts [3], design of ergonomic equipment and workspaces [4], fashion and clothing design [5], etc.

In ergonomics, the user-centered approach is used to cater to the specific need of a population regarding the tools they use, their physical work settings, and their cognitive demand [4]. For this, ideally, designs should be based on the data of physical and cognitive characteristics, behavior, and reported experience of the users. In that way,

S. Jin et al. (Eds.): IEA 2024, SSDI 39, pp. 283–290, 2025.
https://doi.org/10.1007/978-981-95-0211-0_44

the equipment and work layout would fit and accommodate as many potential users as possible while still matching the necessities for the task-specific work.

According to Pheasant and Haslegrave [4], to optimize the design of equipment, it is necessary to know the anthropometric characteristics of the user population, i.e., the dimensions of body parts and their statistical distributions. There are different types of anthropometric measurements, but the three most relevant are static, functional or dynamic, and strength measurements.

Static measurements are taken when the body is in a standardized static posture. Postures can be the standard standing posture, where the subject is erect, with the body relaxed, feet set apart, and the head in Frankfurt plane which is the "standard horizontal plane at the level of the left tragion and the left orbitale (infraorbitale) when the midsagittal plane of the head is held vertically" [6], and its variations regarding the position of arms and feet [4, 7, 8]; or the standard sitting posture, in which the subject sits erect on an anthropometric box or a chair, with the upper arms parallel to the body, the forearms in a 90° angle to the upper arms, the thighs horizontal and the lower legs vertical, along with some other postures with changes in the arms position [4, 7, 8]. Static measurements are the most used since they include stature, weight, breadths, circumferences, lengths, and skinfolds of different parts of the body [1, 9].

Functional measurements represent the range of motion; that is, the limits that a segment of the body has in relation to movement. They are usually focused on the distance between certain body parts and an object at the front, top and side of the body [9]. They can be used to design a reach envelope or clearance that allows a person to move while performing their specific tasks without putting them at risk.

Strength measurements are forces that a body part needs to perform an action like pushing or pulling, or an action with an object [9]. This information is used to predict the maximum capacity of a person or a population, or the strength needed to perform repetitive cyclic tasks without fatigue [10].

All these individual measurements, along with the demographic information of a sample are what constitutes an anthropometric database [11]. They usually focus on a targeted group of people which can represent a general or specific population that has the characteristics desired of the research being conducted.

2 Methodology

In this literature review, we tried to identify the anthropometric measurements used for the design of tools, equipment, and workplace, along with the existing databases for working population and how they were created. Even though we did not do a systematic review, we performed searches on PubMed, Scopus, Web of Science and IEEE Xplore with a time limit of existing literature until August of 2023 using keywords related to anthropometry, design and working population, as shown in Table 1. We included peer reviewed research articles and conference proceedings, and some doctoral and master thesis, in which the participants are the working population regardless of age, gender, previous medical conditions or type of job.

Table 1. Search key words.

Main theme	Key words
Exoskeleton	exoskeleton* wearable robot*, exoskeleton robot*, exoskeletal robotic device*, mechatronic device*, assistance exoskeleton*, human-exoskeleton system*, exoskeleton structure*, assistive device*, exoskeleton device*, assistive robot*, assistive wearable exoskeleton*, exoskeletal device*, human-robot interaction*, robotic device*, exoskeleton assistance, anthropometric exoskeleton*, Assistive technolog*, robotic assistance, Human-Robot Cooperation, exoskeleton suit*, exosuit*, personal lift assisting device*, PLAD
Anthropometry	anthropometry-based structural design, anthropometric measure*, user anthropometric*, anthropometric variability, anthropometric data, anthropometrically adjustable, human physical measurement*, standard*, dimension*, dimension measurement*, Size measurement*, Digital anthropometr*, anthropometry-based customization method*, adequate anthropometr*, anthropometric variab*, 3D measurement technolog*, three-dimensional anthropometr*, 3D anthropometric data, 3D anthropometr*, design dimension*, measure*, body composition
Design	design engineering, iterative design process, ergonomic design, equipment design, exoskeleton design*, mechanical design, product design, product development, design optimization, design consideration*, design requirement*, design specification*, design methodolog*, industrial design, user centred design, fabrication process, structure design, ergonomic design, comfort, fit, accommodate

3 Results

3.1 Standards for Anthropometric Measurements

Standardization is an important step for the creation of anthropometric databases, to ensure the replicability of measurements and the potential comparison between populations. There are two institutions that have standards in regards of anthropometric measurements: The International Organization for Standardization's (ISO) and The International Society for the Advancement of Kinanthropometry (ISAK). The former is the one with the most acceptance and use in research thanks to the ISO 7250 for two-dimensional measurements [6] and ISO 20685 for three-dimensional scans [12]. The latter has the Restricted and Full profiles, which use body mass, stature, sitting height, arm span, 8 skinfolds, 2–13 girths, 0–19 lengths and 2–11 breaths [1]. Both the ISO and the ISAK have measurements in common, with the difference that the latter includes skinfolds to do a body fat assessment with the aid of equations for this [13, 14].

3.2 Equipment and Tools

Anthropometric measurements may be taken with two main methods: the traditional or manual method, and with 3D scanners. Both methods require the use of anatomical landmarks, which helps to understand which body parts are taken into account for data collection [6, 8, 12]. These landmarks are marked on the body prior to any measurement, their locations and the instructions on how to locate them can be found on Table 4 of [15].

Traditional methods have been used for the longest time because they are inexpensive, easy to access, simple to use, portable, reliable and accurate [16]. They also need a qualified and experienced person to take measurements and different tools that allow them to collect girths, lengths, breadths, depths, heights, strength, among others. A summary of the different instruments that can be used for this can be seen on Table 5 of [15].

Apart from the traditional method, there is a more advanced technology found on 3D scanners. They allow to collect high-resolution 3D images in a short period of time [7] but have higher costs because three different scanners are needed to conduct a full body assessment with the same reliability and accuracy as manual measurement: a full body scanner, a head scanner, and a hand and feet scanner [8].

As for 4D scanners, they usually capture the body in motion over a period of time [17, 18]. Move 4D is one of the ones available to the market and allows to record a space of 2 m width, 2 m depth and 3 m height [18].

3.3 Anthropometric Databases for Workforce in Different Countries

Many countries have conducted surveys to provide anthropometric measurements of the working population, as well as of children, teenagers and elderly, which were used for the design of equipment for different industries or for healthcare and demographic purposes. Thirty-one countries have conducted surveys to create anthropometric databases as shown in Table 1 of [15].

From these studies, the percentiles fifth, 50th and 95th can be found on Table 2 (male) and Table 3 (female) of [15], which illustrate the measurements from the ISO 7250 [6] and ISAK [1] standards. It was also noted that most studies refer to the ISO 7250 [6] that only uses length, breadth and circumference measurements but leaves out fat percentage data gathered through skinfolds.

Many of the countries have opted to apply a standard term of "Size" followed by the name of the country [5, 19–26]. This could come from national surveys that targeted garment design and started to gain attention with SizeGermany [21, 27]. Many of these databases are not readily available to the public as they are found in conference proceedings, or are behind a paywall.

Apart from the databases of the "Size" model, other researchers have gathered data that compared populations [27–30], focused on a specific population such as farmers [4, 9, 16, 23, 31–42], or did not disclose the demographic information of the population.

4 Discussion

4.1 The Importance of Representativeness to the Diversity of the Population

There are many factors that need to be considered when sampling for an anthropometric database. This is because human variability creates significant differences in size when sex/gender, ethnic background, geographical location, occupation, and social status are taken into account [4, 31, 43, 44]. All species, including humans, have sexual dimorphism which makes females and males have different body composition, for example, women tend to have more fat accumulation in the breasts, hips, and thighs [4], and strength also varies with upper limbs performing differently in both sexes for tasks such as pulling, pushing and lifting [4, 45]. Thus, taking measurements from only men for design purposes or having only a small non-representative sample or women, as it has been done in multiple studies [16, 32–34, 46], would bring discomfort to the female anatomy [45, 47].

An ethnic group can be defined as "a population of individuals who inhabit a specified geographical distribution and who have certain physical characteristics in common which serve, in statistical terms, to distinguish them from other such groups of people" [4]. This is a factor that needs to be taken into account since there is a representation of ethnic minorities for greater than 30% of the population in many countries [4, 19–21, 28], and even when the population is homogenous in ethnicity, the regional differences might also create differences in the body dimensions because of geographical and environmental conditions [4, 5, 16, 19–21, 43, 48].

Another factor that has to be considered in the design of an anthropometric database is the secular trend which are the "alterations in the measurable characteristics of a population of human beings occurring over a period of time" [4], such as an increase in the height, with the influence of the environmental and social factors like migration [49], living conditions and maternal education [50], affecting as well the genetics. This means that the data collected for a database needs to be updated frequently in order to provide the most accurate information for the design. Some authors have recently started to update old databases containing data from the 1990s and early 2000s, suggesting that an update on the information should be made every 10 years [4, 7, 8, 16, 20].

4.2 The Opportunity and Gaps in the Emerging 3D and 4D Scanner Technologies

The main advantage of 3D scanners is that they collect high resolution 3D images and allow the process to be fast, around 15 min per subject, making it less time consuming for the participants, since they don't have to be present during the extraction of the manual reading process, unlike with the traditional anthropometry [5, 7, 8, 19–21, 23–26, 30, 48]. On the other hand, one of the biggest challenges for this technology is the occluded areas of the body, which don't give an accurate representation of body sections like the axilla, making this missing data in the scan [8, 49]. On the same note, three different scanners are needed to conduct a full body assessment since whole body scanners cannot take proper measurements for hands, feet, head and stature [8, 42, 48], and all these equipment as well as its software and storage have a high cost of making this unachievable for most surveys [51].

As for 4D scanners, this device is still new and additional research needs to be done to establish its reliability in comparison to manual measurements and 3D scanners [18].

Last but not least, it should be noted when comparing different databases that same anthropometric parameters obtained from manual measurements and 3D/4D scanners are pooled together; thus, they are subjected to different biases.

5 Conclusions

We identified a need for increased representation of different segments of the population, to better represent the cultural and ethnic mosaic present in different countries. Manual measurements are the most commonly cited method in peer-reviewed literature because of its low cost and longtime tradition; 3D scanners have been reported in few studies, but there is a surge of interest in these methods. There is a necessity to publicly share anthropometric data for better inclusive product design.

Our literature review findings will inform the development of a protocol that considers key factors for the design of products in a variety of industries [52]. This protocol outlines the solutions to the problems that were identified for the stages before, during and after the collection of measurements for databases.

References

1. Norton, K.I.: Standards for anthropometry assessment. In: Norton, K., Eston, R. (eds.) Kinanthropometry and Exercise Physiology, pp. 68–137. Routledge, London (2018)
2. WHO Working Group: Use and interpretation of anthropometric indicators of nutritional status. Bull. World Health Organ. **64**(6), 929 (1986)
3. İşcan, M.Y.: Anthropometry. In: Siegel, J.A. (ed.) Encyclopedia of Forensic Sciences, pp. 284–289. Elsevier, Oxford (2000)
4. Pheasant, S., Haslegrave, C.M.: Bodyspace: Anthropometry, Ergonomics and the Design of Work, 3rd edn. CRC Press, Boca Raton, FL (2006)
5. Almousa, M.: Body measurements with 3D body scanner: the case of female population in Saudi Arabia. RJTA. **25**(4), 380–395 (2021)
6. ISO: ISO 7250-1:2017 Basic Human Body Measurements for Technological Design—Part 1: Body Measurement Definitions and Landmarks. International Standards Organization, Geneva (2017)
7. Bonin, D., Ackermann, A., Radke, D., Peters, M., Wischniewski, S.: Anthropometric dataset for the German working-age population using 3D body scans from a regional epidemiological health study and a weighting algorithm. Ergonomics. **66**(8), 1057–1071 (2023)
8. Keefe, A.A., Angel, H., Mangan, B.: 2012 Canadian Forces Anthropometric Survey (CFAS). In: Defence Research and Development Canada (2015)
9. Stirling, M.: National Anthropometry Survey of Female Firefighter. Designing for Safety, Performance and Comfort (2002)
10. Xiao, G., Lei, L., Dempsey, P.G., Lu, B., Liang, Y.: Isometric muscle strength and anthropometric characteristics of a Chinese sample. Int. J. Ind. Ergon. **35**(7), 674–679 (2005)
11. ISO: ISO 15535:2012 General Requirements for Establishing Anthropometric Databases. International Standards Organization, Geneva (2012)
12. ISO: ISO 20685-2:2015 Ergonomics—3-D Scanning Methodologies for Internationally Compatible Anthropometric Databases—Part 2: Evaluation Protocol of Surface Shape and Repeatability of Relative Landmark Positions. International Standards Organization, Geneva (2015)
13. Durnin, J.V., Womersley, J.: Body fat assessed from total body density and its estimation from skinfold thickness: measurements on 481 men and women aged from 16 to 72 years. Br. J. Nutr. **32**(1), 77–97 (1974)
14. Siri, W.E.: Body composition from fluid spaces and density: analysis of methods. Nutrition. **9**(5), 480–491 (1961)

15. Rincon Jaramillo, A. M., Thamsuwan, O., Yung, M., Yazdani, A.: Human Anthropometric Database: Literature Review and Recommendations (2024)
16. Obi, O.F., Ugwuishiwu, B.O., Adeboye, B.S.: A survey of anthropometry of rural agricultural workers in Enugu State, south-eastern Nigeria. Ergonomics. **58**(6), 1032–1044 (2015)
17. Bartol, K., Bojanić, D., Petković, T., Pribanić, T.: A review of body measurement using 3D scanning. IEEE Access. **9**, 67281–67301 (2021)
18. Parrilla, E., et al.: A methodology to create 3D body models in motion. In: Cassenti, D.N., Scataglini, S., Rajulu, S.L., Wright, J.L. (eds.) Advances in Simulation and Digital Human Modeling, pp. 309–314. Springer, Cham (2021)
19. Bougourd, J., Treleaven, P.: UK National Sizing Survey – SizeUK. In: Proceedings of the 1st International Conference on 3D Body Scanning Technologies, pp. 327–337. Hometrica Consulting, Switzerland (2010)
20. Kim, J.Y., You, J.W., Kim, M.S.: South Korean anthropometric data and survey methodology: "Size Korea" project. Ergonomics. **60**(11), 1586–1596 (2017)
21. Kuebler, T., Luebke, A., Campbell, J., Guenzel, T.: Size North America – The New North American Anthropometric Survey. In: Duffy, V.G. (ed.) Digital Human Modeling and Applications in Health, Safety, Ergonomics and Risk Management. Human Body and Motion, pp. 88–98 (2019)
22. Ball, R.M.: SizeChina: A 3D Anthropometric Survey of the Chinese Head. Doctoral thesis, TU Delft (2011)
23. Kulkarni, D., Chitodkar, V., Gurjar, V., Ghaisas, C.V., Mannikar, A.V.: SIZE INDIA—anthropometric size measurement of indian driving population. In: The SIAT 2011, pp. 1–8 (2011)
24. Stampfli, P.V., Rissiek, A., Trieb, R., Seidl, A.: SizeITALY—The Actual Italian Measurement Survey. In: Proceedings of the 3rd International Conference on 3D Body Scanning Technologies, pp. 261–268. Hometrica Consulting, Switzerland (2012)
25. Xia, S.: Sizing Systems Created Using SizeUSA Data for Three Body Shapes. Master's thesis, North Carolina State University (2013)
26. Charoensiriwath, S., Tanprasert, C.: An overview of 3D body scanning applications in Thailand. In: Proceedings of the 1st International Conference on 3D Body Scanning Technologies, pp. 158–165. Hometrica Consulting, Switzerland (2010)
27. Rissiek, A., Trieb, R.: iSize—Implementation of International Anthropometric Survey Results for Worldwide Sizing and Fit Optimization in the Apparel Industry. In: Proceedings of the 1st International Conference on 3D Body Scanning Technologies, pp. 269–281. Hometrica Consulting, Switzerland (2010)
28. Abd Rahman, N.I., Md Dawal, S.Z., Yusoff, N., Mohd Kamil, N.S.: Anthropometric measurements among four Asian countries in designing sitting and standing workstations. Sādhanā. **43**(1), 10 (2018)
29. Chuan, T.K., Hartono, M., Kumar, D.N.: Anthropometry of the Singaporean and Indonesian populations. Int. J. Ind. Ergon. **40**(6), 757–766 (2010)
30. Trieb, R., et al.: EUROFIT - integration, homogenisation and extension of the scope of large 3D anthropometric data pools for product development. In: Proceedings of the 4th International Conference on 3D Body Scanning Technologies, pp. 19–20. Hometrica Consulting (2013)
31. Bhattacharjya, B.R., Kakoty, S.K.: A survey of the anthropometric data relating to five ethnic groups in Assam considering gender and ethnic diversity: Application of the data in designing an improvised pedal-operated Chaak. Int. J. Ind. Ergon. **76**, 102927 (2020)
32. Gite, L.P., Yadav, B.G.: Anthropometric survey for agricultural machinery design: an Indian case study. Appl. Ergon. **20**(3), 191–196 (1989)
33. Instituto Nacional de Tecnologia: Pesquisa Antropometrica e Biomecacica dos Operarios da Industria Transformmacao - RJ. Institute Nacional De Tecnologia, Rio de Janeiro (1989)

34. Mokdad, M.: Anthropometric study of Algerian farmers. Int. J. Ind. Ergon. **29**(6), 331–341 (2002)
35. Lee, Y.-C., Chen, C.-H., Lee, C.-H.: Body anthropometric measurements of Singapore-an adult and elderly population. Measurement. **148**, 106949 (2019)
36. Batogowska, A., Slowikowski, J.: Anthropometric Atlas of the Polish Adult Population for Designer Use. Instytut Wzornictwa Przemystowego, Warsaw (1974)
37. de la Vega, B.E., Duarte, K.L., Millán, O.L.: Mexican practical anthropometry of automotive industry workers. Proc. Hum. Factors Ergon. Soc. Annu. Meet. **54**(15), 1125–1129 (2010)
38. Del Prado-Lu, J.L.: Anthropometric measurement of Filipino manufacturing workers. Int. J. Ind. Ergon. **37**(6), 497–503 (2007)
39. Kothiyal, K., Tettey, S.: Anthropometric data of elderly people in Australia. Appl. Ergon. **31**(3), 329–332 (2000)
40. Lavender, S.A., Marras, W.S., Sabol, R.J.: A study of female mexican anthropometric measures useful for workstation design in light manufacturing facilities. AIHA J. **63**(3), 300–304 (2002)
41. Rebiffé, R., Guillien, J., Pasquet, P.: Enquête Anthropométrique sur les Conducteurs Françaises. Laboratoire de Physiologie et de Bioméchanique de l'Association Peugeout-Renault, Paris (1983)
42. Min-yang Wang, E., Wang, M.-J., Yeh, W.-Y., Shih, Y.-C., Lin, Y.-C.: Development of anthropometric work environment for Taiwanese workers. Int. J. Ind. Ergon. **23**(1), 3–8 (1999)
43. İşeri, A., Arslan, N.: Estimated anthropometric measurements of Turkish adults and effects of age and geographical regions. Int. J. Ind. Ergon. **39**(5), 860–865 (2009)
44. Sadeghi, F., Mazloumi, A., Kazemi, Z.: An anthropometric data bank for the Iranian working population with ethnic diversity. Appl. Ergon. **48**, 95–103 (2015)
45. Rayssiguie, E., Erden, M.S.: A review of exoskeletons considering nurses. Sensors. **22**(18), 7035 (2022)
46. Hassan, S.N., Yusuff, R., Zein, R.M., Hussain, R., Tamil Selvan, H.K.: Anthropometric data of Malaysian workers. In: New Ergonomics Perspective - Selected Papers of the 10th Pan-Pacific Conference on Ergonomics, pp. 353–360 (2015)
47. Haning, S. L.: Exoskeletons and Women: A Laboratory Study of Usability of Passive Occupational Exoskeletons for Women. Master's thesis, Ohio University (2019)
48. Hanson, L., Sperling, L., Gard, G., Ipsen, S., Olivares Vergara, C.: Swedish anthropometrics for product and workplace design. Appl. Ergon. **40**(4), 797–806 (2009)
49. Malina, R.M., Zavaleta, A.N.: Secular trend in the stature and weight of Mexican-American children in Texas between 1930 and 1970. Am. J. Phys. Anthropol. **52**(4), 453–461 (1980)
50. Ríos, L., Terán, J.M., Varea, C., Bogin, B.: Plasticity in the growth of body segments in relation to height-for-age and maternal education in Guatemala. Am. J. Hum. Biol. **32**(4), e23376 (2020)
51. Daanen, H.A.M., Ter Haar, F.B.: 3D whole body scanners revisited. Displays. **34**(4), 270–275 (2013)
52. Rincón Jaramillo, A.M., Yung, M., Yazdani, A., Thamsuwan, O.: A protocol to create an anthropometric database applicable to any population. In: Proceedings of the IISE Annual Conference, pp. 1–6 (2024). https://doi.org/10.21872/2024IISE_7096

ATWAD (I)

Debating Safety Culture: A Multi-Thematic Definition Open to Divergent Opinions

Mateus Pereira Abraçado[1] (✉), Francisco Lima[2], Raoni Rocha[3], Vitor Pereira[1], Eliel Prueza[1], and Francisco Duarte[1]

[1] Federal University of Rio de Janeiro, Rio de Janeiro, RJ 21941-853, Brazil
mateus.abracado@pep.ufrj.br
[2] Federal University of Minas Gerais, Belo Horizonte, MG 31270-901, Brazil
[3] Federal University of Ouro Preto, Ouro Preto, MG 35400-000, Brazil

Abstract. Safety culture assessments reveal underlying organizational values and assumptions, functioning as a "collective unawareness" still to be developed. However, a set of broad and precise criteria to characterize the different degrees of maturity has yet to be defined. The article suggests a set of orientations and concepts, for undertaking diagnostics on safety culture through a divergent-sensitive analysis. It focuses on refining themes and using quantitative and qualitative methods to determine different maturity levels in safety culture based on existing literature and practices within an oil production company. Through case studies, it demonstrates how thematics like Safety Priority and Operational Experience Feedback influence safety, leading to classifications and definitions. The importance of diversity in driving changes is highlighted, encouraging learning, and addressing issues such as organizational silence. The approach that values divergences proved to be successful in promoting learning within organizations and stimulating discussions. In mature safety cultures, differences foster prevention and uncertainty management, acknowledging provisional consensus.

Keywords: Safety Culture · Multifactor Analysis · Controversy · Feedback

1 Introduction

Safety culture assessments seek to reveal underlying values, beliefs and assumptions within the organization [1], functioning as a "collective unawareness". This culture is created through the sharing of practices. Management must therefore encourage convergence between messages and practices [2].

The body of literature has developed in order to establish levels of maturity of safety culture [1, 3], identifying characteristics of each organization. However, a set of criteria has yet to be defined that is broad enough to characterize the different degrees of maturity. The very idea of "maturity" or "development" clashes with studies on culture, which contest any hierarchy, today seen as a Eurocentric or colonialist ideology [4, 5]. The question is fundamental because advances in the reliability of high-risk systems are attributed to the development of safety engineering and management systems, which

S. Jin et al. (Eds.): IEA 2024, SSDI 39, pp. 293–298, 2025.
https://doi.org/10.1007/978-981-95-0211-0_45

today characterize the "managerial culture" [1], which has overcome the initial stages of these industries where the prevailing principle was production at any cost.

The thematic issues surrounding safety culture are wide-ranging. Duarte et al. [6] have established 5 relevant themes for the diagnosis: Blame, Relevance of Rules, Safety Priority, Safety Bureaucracy and Operational Experience Feedback (OEF), each of which is broken down into sub-themes, which may partially overlap. Analyzing these themes contributes to a more accurate diagnosis of safety culture.

This article aims to show how a quantitative and qualitative approach, based on differences of opinion between groups of organizational actors, can contribute to the identification and development of safety. Based on concepts observed in the literature and interventions carried out in an energy production company, the study proposes a systematization of the levels of maturity in safety culture for the issues of Safety Priority and OEF, showing how this characterization can be used to obtain consistent results in the construction of safety culture diagnoses.

2 Methods

The intervention method was inspired by Rocha et al. [9] and used combined quantitative and qualitative data. In the quantitative stage, homogeneous groups were formed to apply a questionnaire of 80 questions, seeking to assess the safety culture maturity of each group. The answers were classified on the Likert scale, which assigns scores from 0 to 10 to the groups based on their level of agreement.

In the qualitative assessment, discussion groups were held to explore the central issues identified in the previous stage and understand the different perspectives on safety, thereby giving value to the diverse points of view. Charts were produced to illustrate the scenario revealed in the quantitative stage, and the discussions were oriented on the basis of the workers' experiences.

The quantitative and qualitative analysis was based on general descriptions of the five levels of safety culture maturity proposed by Parker et al. (2006) and the IOGP (2010): pathological, reactive, managerial, proactive and resilient. Five themes were explored, conceptualized interactively based on theoretical principles and practical experiences. The results of both stages were presented in radar charts used to show the level of maturity in different areas.

As the safety culture is built on sharing practices and values, the divergences observed in the quantitative phase became opportunities to discuss and build safety. In the discussion groups, viewpoints were explored in depth with statements that exposed values and beliefs, as well as cases that embodied practices and experiences. These situations made it possible to observe contradictions/alignments between discourses and practices, alignments and divergences in values/beliefs between the different groups.

When the discussions showed that the values and beliefs of a group were more aligned with a different level than that observed in the quantitative stage, based on the values indicated by Parker et al. (2006) and the IOGP (2010), consideration was given to that issue. In order to facilitate future analysis, this study presents a table extrapolating the significance of safety culture levels for two issues: Safety Priority and OEF.

In the focus groups, a total of 43 cases were observed involving the different homogeneous groups. In this study, 3 representative cases are presented, in order to show how the analysis of the change in the level of maturity of safety culture was carried out.

3 Results

The cases observed are shown below:

Case A During a work activity, a maintenance worker was observed by three inspectors, one of whom noticed that the worker had picked up a hammer without wearing gloves, considering this a breach of the "golden rule" and liable to punishment. The worker said he was preparing to nail a box, and picked up the hammer without wearing the glove. Although the nailing action was not yet in progress, one of the inspectors immediately reported the "infraction", emphasizing the absence of PPE (personal protective equipment). The infraction was later notified by e-mail, limiting the ability of the worker to explain. In the subsequent DDS (Daily Safety Dialogue), the infraction was discussed, showing the repercussion of the inspection report to higher levels.

Case B During the painting of a pipeline, the painter questioned the distance to the pipeline, which made conditions unsafe. It was agreed to use a tied ladder and a lifeline to reduce the risks. The activity continued throughout the implementation of the solution due to the tight deadlines, despite the obvious risks. The worker emphasized his priority for safety, but attributed his continued activity to fear of reprisals.

Case C The design of the catchment raft, responsible for keeping the pump afloat on the river, underwent improvements suggested by field operators. Initially proposed by the company, the original design was improved based on a suggestion made by a maintenance team foreman.

3.1 Analysis of the Cases

This item shows how cases influenced change in the level of maturity. Other cases and statements were considered in order to ratify these changes, but the relationships set out below show how the analysis is carried out. Figure 1 shows the general results of the safety culture diagnosis in the 5 thematic issues for the Management and Contracted Maintenance groups.

On the topic of Safety Priority, the management group produces a statement, recognizing that this issue still needs to be improved. In this respect, the example of case B shows a critical situation, because even with measures to reduce risks, priority was given to completing the task to the detriment of the safety of the workers. Thus, although a safety-oriented discourse is adopted, situations reported by other teams confirm that this is not the general practice. Consequently, the group's maturity level drops to managerial level. With regard to OEF, the management team mentions that many reports do not reach them through the hierarchy, although they believe that the issues are addressed with the immediate leadership. Case A describes situations in which the inspectors do not communicate directly with the employee, but the punishments and corresponding

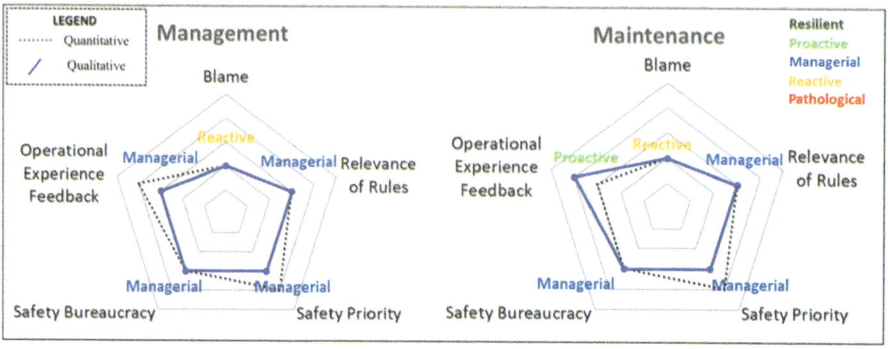

Fig. 1. Appraisal of the Management and Contracted Maintenance groups.

irregularities are already shared with everyone during meetings. In conclusion, although there are exchanges between operational teams, relevant issues do not appear to reach the management, which has firm confidence in its management mechanisms. As a result, the level of this issue is also reduced, and the group seems to be leaning towards a managerial level of maturity.

As for the Maintenance group, concerning the Priority of Safety, the team emphasizes the importance of individual safety, stating that safe alternatives should be sought to perform the task, but as observed in case B, fear of reprisals still favors prioritizing the completion of the activity over a longer and safer route. In this respect, the tendency is for the group to find itself at the Managerial level, reducing the level resulting from the quantitative analysis. As for the OEF, the team highlights its readiness for dialogue with its direct leadership. For example, the group mentions case C, relating to creating a new type of raft for collecting water. Thus, the presence of a robust case in this group creates a trend towards the proactive level.

3.2 Safety Culture Levels by Thematic Topic

Based on the observations, statements and cases presented to the team, it has been possible to develop an insight into the meaning of each level of maturity in the topics studied, as shown in Tables 1 and 2. This conceptualization is an extrapolation of the descriptions proposed by Parker et al. [3] and the IOGP [1], for the two topics selected: Safety Priority and OEF.

The study highlights the importance of a diagnosis that integrates quantitative and qualitative approaches to assessing safety culture. The change in maturity levels between the stages is based on evidence obtained in the focus groups and case analyses, balancing quantitative and qualitative results. Such changes are limited to one level, based on clear and consistent evidence. Finally, it should be noted that the maturity levels of safety culture are only referential. The analytical focus is on the implementation of measures for the continuous development of safety culture, highlighting the importance of periodic evaluations aimed at the progressive development of safety.

Table 1. Levels of safety culture for the topic of Safety Priority.

Resilient	Safety is incorporated by the organization, which discusses it naturally. Local solutions are circulated to spread knowledge throughout the organization. Synergy, trust and equal treatment between workers and hierarchical levels are values that are built up and propagated on a daily basis
Proactive	Safety comes first. Issues are discussed openly and the right of refusal is respected. Decisions are consistent and predictable. Workers from different positions and companies are treated equally on safety issues. Workers feel safe in the unit
Managerial	There are formal areas for discussion, although in practice organizational silence is evident. Protocol speeches in defence of the right of refusal and equality between workers and the prioritization of safety, although in practice there are contradictions. PPE and other work equipment is available
Reactive	Production is sometimes accorded priority over safety. Decisions are hierarchical and inconsistent, with little room for dialogue. When a worker uses the right of refusal, someone else does the work. Unequal treatment is given to people from different positions and companies. Workers feel insecure in the unit
Pathological	Production is given priority over safety. Decisions are monocratic and decontextualized. Workers who exercise their right to refuse are punished, albeit in a veiled manner. Workers who are contractually or hierarchically vulnerable are liable to heavier punishment. The quality of the unit is considered unfavourably

Table 2. Levels of safety culture for the topic of Operational Experience Feedback.

Resilient	Information flows through the organization all the way, from the collection to the feedback. Trust generates commitment on the part of the participants, who get feedback from the organization within a satisfactory timeframe. Actions are disseminated and debated, generating organizational learning
Proactive	People report accidents, incidents and irregularities so that risks can be dealt with. Accidents and irregularities are discussed, and actions are taken to prevent recurrence. Proposals for improvements are encouraged and actively pursued by the workforce. Information circulates freely throughout the organization
Managerial	Protocol speech in defense of feedback tools, although practice shows contradictions. Organizational silence. After an accident, safety processes are activated for treatment. The tools for proposing improvements are available. Information circulates slowly throughout the organization
Reactive	Safety is the responsibility of specialists. Individuals avoid reporting incidents and irregularities for fear of punishment. Proposals for improvement are discouraged and it is difficult to get feedback on the demands submitted. Information circulates with difficulty and intermittently throughout the organization
Pathological	Reporting irregularities and proposing improvements are frowned upon, as they generate costs and can have a negative impact on the indicators. After an accident, the injured person is held up as an example of what not to do. Workers withhold information from each other in order to protect themselves

The idea is that these tables offer a broader conceptual framework, with elements for understanding and assessing safety culture. In this way, a novice analyst would have a more robust tool than traditional general descriptions to assess whether the information obtained in the discussions falls into one level of safety culture or another.

4 Discussion and Conclusion

The concept of culture faces challenges due to the constant change of values and behaviors in modern societies. Cultural diversity reveals differences between hegemonic and emergent rationalities even in seemingly homogeneous groups. This diversity allows for finding prevalent trends and patterns, key elements guiding transformative actions. In this sense, this approach highlights the promotion of learning and overcoming challenges such as organizational silence and blaming as key elements for developing a safety culture. Facing the uncertainty of technologies demands a collective process of co-design and social experimentation, avoiding individual accountability for failures.

The divergence-sensitive approach has proven effective in building a safety culture. The evolution of safety culture is sustained by the capacity of an organization to learn and develop its own safety rules. Resilient cultures value debate and controversy, seeking organizational learning as an open process to deal with uncertainty. Therefore, organizing debates among managers, technical staff, and operational teams becomes essential. In a mature safety culture, differences result in a greater capacity for preventing and managing uncertainties and acknowledging that all consensus is provisional.

Acknowledgments. We thank the support from the Carlos Chagas Filho Research Support Foundation in the state of Rio de Janeiro (FAPERJ) (ref. 210.621/2019) and the National Agency of Petroleum, Natural Gas, and Biofuels (PRH-ANP) (Resolution 50/2015).

References

1. IOGP (International Association of Oil & Gas Producers): A Guide to Selecting Appropriate Tools to Improve HSE Culture. Report 435. London (2010)
2. Daniellou, F., Simard, M., Boissières, I.: Facteurs humains et organisationnels de la sécurité industrielle : un état de l'art Numéro 2010–02 des Cahiers de la Sécurité Industrielle. Institut pour une Culture de Sécurité Industrielle, Toulouse (2010)
3. Parker, D., Lawrie, M., Hudson, P.: A framework for understanding the development of organisational safety culture. Saf. Sci. **44**, 551–562 (2006)
4. Escobar, A.: Designs for the Pluriverse: Radical Interdependence, Autonomy, and the Making of Worlds. Duke University Press, Mexico City (2018)
5. Santos, B. (ed.): O fim do império cognitivo: a afirmação das epistemologias do Sul. Autêntica, Belo Horizonte (2019)
6. Duarte, F., Rocha, R., Lima, F., Fernandes, M., Garotti, L.: Safety culture assessment and transformation of practices. Saf. Manag. Hum. Factors. **105**, 31–41 (2023)
7. Dekker, S.: Just Culture: Balancing Safety and Accountability, 2nd edn. Ashgate, Hampshire (2012)
8. Dekker, S.: The safety anarchist. Routledge, New York (2018)
9. Rocha, R., Duarte, F., Lima, F., Mercado, M., Araujo, A., Garotti, L., Campos, M.: Framework for the assessment of the safety culture in the oil and gas industry. Int. J. Occup. Saf. Ergon. (2023)

Putting the Human Back in the System: A Cybersecurity Activity System Modeling

Ayoub Bourhim[1,2,3](✉), Julie Lassalle[1,3], Laurent Guillet[1,3], and Christine Petr[1,2]

[1] Université Bretagne Sud, Lorient, France
{ayoub.bourhim,julie.lassalle,laurent.guillet}@univ-ubs.fr, christine.petr@univ-us.fr
[2] Laboratoire de Gestion de l'Ouest, Vannes, France
[3] Laboratoire des sciences et techniques de l'information, de la communication et de la connaissance, Lorient, France

Abstract. This study aims to model Cybersecurity by using Engeström's activity system model to challenge the notion of human error as the primary cause of cybersecurity breaches. By emphasizing the influence of organizational constraints, it highlights the need for a cybersecurity approach that integrates human actors.

Keywords: Cybersecurity · Human Approach · Activity Theory · Organization

1 Introduction

1.1 Cybersecurity and the "Human Error" Paradigm

In recent years, cyberattacks against organizations have multiplied. According to IBM (2023), the global average cost of a single data breach of an organization amounts to 4.45 million USD. In this alarming context, the solutions until now have been primarily based on technology, it now appears crucial to propose and develop new solutions by adopting a cybersecurity approach centered on humans.

The effectiveness and prevalence of attacks based on social engineering, like phishing (Hweidi & Eleyan, 2023), have led to a certain stigma regarding individuals within cyber systems. They are often seen more as vulnerabilities than as system actors. Humans are often characterized by cybersecurity experts as the "weakest link" in the cybersecurity chain. Security breaches are frequently attributed to individual factors such as cognitive biases (Hweidi & Eleyan, 2023). To mitigate cyber risks, organizations tend to invest in technical solutions or implement policies aimed at controlling individuals without taking social context and human complexity into account, which yield limited results (Bada et al., 2015; Smith et al., 2020; NCSC, 2019). However, literature suggests that work constraints and organizational factors weigh heavily on individuals and cyber risks, challenging the thesis of the individual as the "weakest link" (De La Garza et al., 2022). Authors highlight the negative impact of factors such as time pressure, lack of individual training and communication within the organization, on cyber risk (Triplett, 2022). This study questions the idea that human error is the main source of security breaches, highlighting the influence of organizational constraints on computer system security.

S. Jin et al. (Eds.): IEA 2024, SSDI 39, pp. 299–304, 2025.
https://doi.org/10.1007/978-981-95-0211-0_46

1.2 The Principles of Engeström's Activity Theory

To understand how organizational constraints impact cybersecurity activity, we have decided to model the cybersecurity activity of an organization by employing cultural-historical activity theory (CHAT) (Engeström, 2015). CHAT is supported by a systemic analysis comprises six components: subjects, objects, tools, rules, division of labor, and community (Engeström, 2001). This model analyzes activity systems as units of analysis and highlights interactions between different components, emphasizing the plurality of voices and cultural and historical elements inherent in the system. Activity systems evolve over time and undergo transformation cycles when the goal or the object of activity are reconceptualized due to changes in the system (Engeström, 2001). In our study we are interested by two of the model's central principles. The first one is multi-voicedness of the system, this key concept highlights the innate multi-voiced nature of activity systems, meaning that an activity system is an ensemble of viewpoints from the different actors of the activity. In complex systems like organizations, multi-voicedness is pertinent because it allows a more nuanced analysis of the activity and in the context of cybersecurity understand the relationship of the actors to the object of the cyberactivity and to each other, thus explaining the emergence of contradictions (Engeström, 2001).

Contradictions, i.e., tensions (dilemmas, conflicts, errors etc.) between different components within the system, are another central principle of Engestrom's model. Four main types of contradictions have been identified, primary contradictions happen within a component of the activity system, secondary contradictions happen between components of the activity system, tertiary contradictions happen when a new form of the activity system is introduced, quaternary contradictions happen between neighboring activity systems. Contradictions are seen a source of change and development (Engeström, 2015: Engeström, 2001).

The objective of our cybersecurity activity modeling is precisely to identify these contradictions to understand how they limit cybersecurity effectiveness and how solutions to these contradictions can be co-constructed with the actors to make the system evolve.

2 Methodology

2.1 Case Study

The present work is based on a case study of an organization, the Université Bretagne Sud. Notable for its cybersecurity research center, it has experienced an increase in attacks, particularly phishing, since the COVID crisis. Our research takes a qualitative approach using the CHAT to capture the complex nature of the interaction a) that makes up the activity system of cybersecurity in the University and the contradictions that emerge from it.

2.2 Data Collection

To gather the necessary information for understanding the system, we conducted eight semi-structured interviews with members of the university's information systems management, the Data Protection Officer and the University's President. Each exchange lasting approximatively one hour. The purpose of these interviews was to identify the mains elements of the organization's cybersecurity activity system and to emphasize the historical changes the system has undergone over the years. The interview guide was designed to highlights components of Engstrom's model, subjects, objects, tools, rules, community, and division of labor, in the system. We also asked questions about the constraints in their activity. We based our methodology on Engestrom's case studies and other authors that based their analysis of activity on this model (Engeström, 2001; Mwanza, 2001; Duignan et al., 2006; Schroder et al., 2020).

Here is a sample of a question from each category (interviews were conducted in French, these questions have been translated to English):

- Object: What is the function of cybersecurity at Université Bretagne Sud?
- Actors/Subject: What are the different profiles of individuals involved in cybersecurity at UBS Université Bretagne Sud?
- Community: How is cybersecurity organized at Université Bretagne Sud?
- Tools: Why were these process chosen to ensure cybersecurity at Université Bretagne Sud?
- Rules: What are the consequences in case of violations?
- Division of labor: How is distributed the responsibility for ensuring cybersecurity at Université Bretagne Sud?
- Constraints: What are the constraints you might encounter in implementing cybersecurity at University Bretagne Sud?

It is important to consider that due to the semi-directive nature of the interviews, these questions represent the basic questions and that conversations may have led to questions not present in the grid.

2.3 Analysis

The interviews were transcribed and imported into NVivo for coding. Relevant statements were coded according to the components of Engestrom's model as well as different types of contradictions. This process helped us understand the complexity of the system, the role of each participant in cybersecurity and the function of cybersecurity in the system. We also identified contradictions.

3 Results

The preliminary findings from the study seems to confirm the complex nature of the university. The university main object is to 'Provide teaching and conduct research". This object is supported by a network of subsystems with their own objectives but sharing this overarching goal. For example, IT service object is the maintenance of the university's technological infrastructure, which includes sub-objects like cybersecurity or the implementation of new software. This structuration really highlights the multivoicedness of the organization. If we place ourselves at the point of view of the organization as a whole, meaning the university as the subject of the activity, cybersecurity is viewed as a tool to maintain the integrity of the university so it can keep carrying on its activity of

"Teaching and Researching". But if we place ourselves as the IT service cybersecurity is one the object of their activity, when for the other components of the organization cybersecurity is mainly categorized as a set of rules to follow.

This multi-voicedness is also visible in the identified contradictions. The nature of the contradictions can change depending of the level we decide to look at them, at the level of the organization contradiction are mainly identified as primary and secondary contradictions, but at the level of the components of the systems they become quaternary contradictions. Several secondary contradictions were identified. For instance, the Ecology department decided to implement a carbon tracking app that was blocked by the IT department due to security concerns and noncompliance with the standards of security. This incident represents multiple contradictions at different levels of the organization, see Fig. 1.

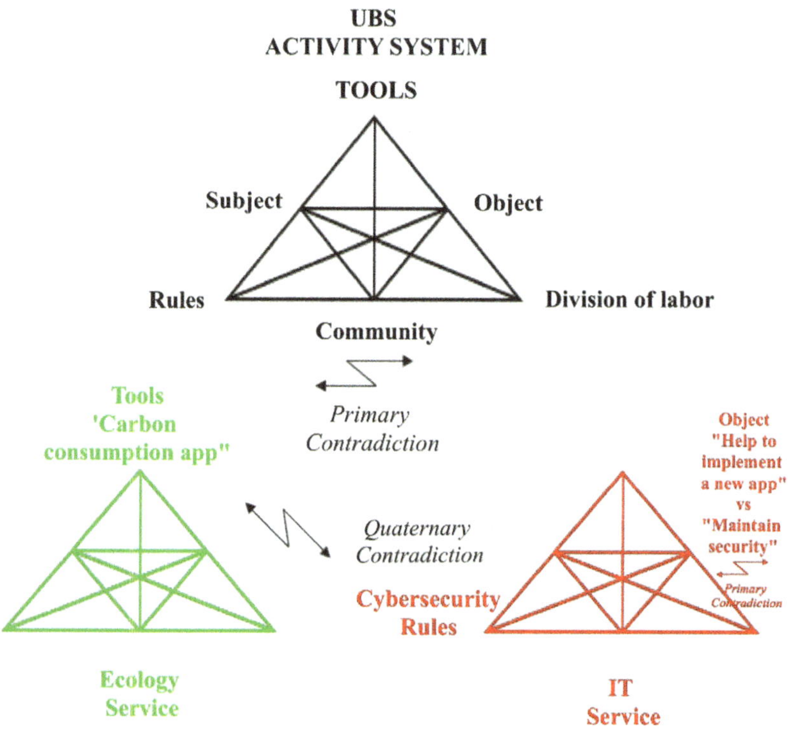

Fig. 1. Representation of Contradictions in UBS Activity System.

Something else that seems to be shown by the results is that the voice of the users is lacking in the system, espicially when it comes to cybersecurity aspects of the system. They are not perceived as subjects of the activity as they are not active contributors to the developpement and achievement of the object (Engestrom, 2015) and they mostly perceive cybersecurity mainly as constraints placed upon them by the organisation, while recognising it's importance.

4 Discussion

Our case study of Université Bretagne Sud's cybersecurity system, seems to demonstrate that organizational systems are characterized by their complexity, multi-voicedness, and it the case of cybersecurity the lack of involvement of users as actors in the system. At the core of this system complexity is the interaction of multiple subsystems, often resulting in inherent contradictions, such as balancing security needs with work activity, innovation or sustainability goals. To make the system evolve and become more resilient it's important to resolve these contradictions. Multivoicedness within the system highlights diverse perspectives among actors. Different components of the system may share an overarching goal; however, they still have distinct priorities and objectives, which may not always align with cybersecurity. Multi-voicedness is a key element to show that cybersecurity doesn't happen in a vacuum and that it's extremely dependent on the cooperation from other components of the system to be effective.

Our study highlights the organizational context's importance, emphasizing that cybersecurity cannot be addressed in isolation. Relationships and communication within the organization are key elements in the success of cybersecurity. Therefore, our approach offers essential insights for adaptable and effective policies, focusing on work activity and systemic contradictions. Integrating these dynamics into cybersecurity efforts enhances resilience and ensures the efficacy of security measures. Future research should focus on the involvement of users in cybersecurity.

5 Limits

The main limitation of this study is the lack of perspective from final users, as focus group data collection is still ongoing. Future analysis will incorporate these insights to provide a more comprehensive understanding of cybersecurity system. This will further validate and refine our activity system model and its implications.

References

Bada, M., Sasse, A.M., Nurse, J.R.C.: Cyber security awareness campaigns: why do they fail to change behaviour? In: International Conference on Cyber Security for Sustainable Society, pp. 118–131 (2015)

De La Garza, C., Stoessel, C., Oufi, N.: Prise en compte des Facteurs Organisationnels Humains en cybersécurité : Aller au-delà de l'erreur humaine. In: 42ème Congrès Lambda Mu de l'IMdR. EDF Lab, Paris Saclay (2022)

Duignan, M., Noble, J., Biddle, R.: Activity theory for design from checklist to interview. In: IFIP International Federation for Information Processing/IFIP, pp. 1–25 (2006). https://doi.org/10.1007/978-0-387-36792-7_1

Engeström, Y.: Expansive learning at work: toward an activity theoretical reconceptualization. J. Educ. Work. **14**(1), 133–156 (2001). https://doi.org/10.1080/13639080020028747

Engeström, Y.: Learning by Expanding. Cambridge University Press, Cambridge (2015)

Hweidi, R.F.A., Eleyan, D.: Social engineering attack concepts, frameworks, and awareness: a systematic literature review. Int. J. Comput. Digit. Syst. **13**(1), 691–700 (2023). https://doi.org/10.12785/ijcds/130155

IBM: Cost of a Data Breach Report 2023 (Par Ponemon institue). IBM. Consulté le 21 février 2024, à l'adresse (2023). https://www.ibm.com/reports/data-breach

Mwanza, D.: Where Theory meets Practice: A Case for an Activity Theory based Methodology to guide Computer System Design. In: Proceedings of INTERACT' 2001: Eighth IFIP TC 13 Conference on Human-Computer Interaction, 9–13 July 2001, Tokyo, Japan (2001)

National Cyber Security Centre (NCSC): Annual Review 2019: Making the UK the safest place to live and work online (2019). https://www.ncsc.gov.uk/annual-review-2019

Schröder, L.U., Wals, A.E.J., Van Koppen, C.S.A.: Analysing the state of student participation in two Eco-Schools using Engeström's Second Generation Activity Systems Model. Environ. Educ. Res. **26**(8), 1088–1111 (2020). https://doi.org/10.1080/13504622.2020.1779186

Smith, Z.M., Lostri, E., Lewis, J.A.: The Hidden Costs of Cybercrime, vol. 38. McAfee (2020)

Triplett, W.J.: Addressing human factors in cybersecurity leadership. J. Cybersecur. Privacy. **2**(3), 573–586 (2022). https://doi.org/10.3390/jcp2030029

In Uncertainty We Trust: The Entrepreneurial Activity in the Favela of Rocinha, An Experience of Design and Control

Aline Brufato[1(✉)] and Roberto Bartholo[1,2]

[1] Production Engineering Program, Federal University of Rio de Janeiro, Rio de Janeiro, RJ, Brazil
aline.brufato@coppe.ufrj.br
[2] Universität Erlangen-Nürnberg, Erlangen, Germany

Abstract. The article examines the multiple rationalities involved in the trajectory of entrepreneurial activity under conditions of radical uncertainty in the favela of Rocinha, Rio de Janeiro. The research is a qualitative analysis of the case of Carteiro Amigo, which can provide valuable insights into how entrepreneurial activity responds to change designing its trajectory through a balance between uncertainty and control. In doing so, we use the lens of effectuation theory combined with a structural feature of near-decomposability from Herbert Simon as an interpretive key to exploit locality and contingency through control strategy. As a result, the article sheds light on understanding what and how sustain the endurance of this entrepreneurial development journey over 20 years in Rocinha.

Keywords: Entrepreneurial Activity · Effectuation · Near-decomposability

1 Introduction

This study delves into the effective management of uncertainty in entrepreneurial decision-making, particularly in Rocinha, one of Rio de Janeiro's largest favelas and the second largest in Brazil. It focuses on a logistics firm rooted in Rocinha and explores how entrepreneur balances uncertainty and control in their decision-making activity to build an enduring firm and a new market.

While uncertainty entails navigating unknown elements, control involves shaping outcomes within this uncertainty. Uncertainty, defined as the inability to accurately predict future outcomes due to incomplete information or the unpredictable nature of the environment (Knight, 1921), poses a significant challenge for entrepreneurs in such contexts. In the entrepreneurial activity, control is the ability to shape and construct the future rather than predict it, aligning with the concept of "entrepreneurship as a science of the artificial" (Sarasvathy and Simon, 2000; Sarasvathy, 2001, 2003). Also, this study emphasizes design-oriented inquiries and the processes underlying entrepreneurial decision-making activity, aligning with Bourmaud's (2015) perspective.

This article aims to answer two research questions as follow: (1) how does entrepreneurial activity create and develop an enduring firm in a favela? and (2) What

S. Jin et al. (Eds.): IEA 2024, SSDI 39, pp. 305–311, 2025.
https://doi.org/10.1007/978-981-95-0211-0_47

decision logic and key heuristics were instrumental in building a feature that underpin the endurance of a firm in a high-uncertainty environment?

To address these research questions, this study adopts an interpretative approach focusing on two key constructs: effectuation logic (Sarasvathy, 2001, 2022) and the principle of near-decomposability (Simon, 1996; Sarasvathy and Simon, 2000). As a result, the study sheds light the logics and heuristics used by the entrepreneur that led to the creation and development of a firm rooted in the Rocinha favela. Analyzes the creation and development journey of of a firm Carteiro Amigo (CA) rooted in the Rocinha covering 24 years in Rocinha. It underscores the effective utilization of control heuristics combined with relational networks as key strategies for managing uncertainty in the decision-making processes of entrepreneurial activity in Rocinha.

The article proposes identifying and demonstrating the relationship between effectuation and near-decomposability, highlighting their roles in creating and developing enduring firms. It then outlines the methodology, examines the case of Carteiro Amigo, and concludes with the findings and implications.

2 Effectuation and Near-Decomposability

Effectuation logic offers a new perspective on entrepreneurship, introducing a fresh rationale to conventional models, moving away from planning, market analysis, and benchmarking. Derived from empirical research mapping the decision-making heuristics of expert entrepreneurs, effectuation presents a set of heuristic principles centered on non-predictive control (Sarasvathy, 2001, 2022). These principles are (1) Bird-in-hand (starting with available means); (2) Affordable-loss (risk assessment based on affordable losses); (3) Crazy-quilt (engagement with self-select stakeholders); (4) Lemonade (exploitation of contingencies); and (5) Pilot-in-the-plane (management of uncertainties through non-predictive control). In essence, "effectuation is a design logic for making things happen in a human-made universe" (Sarasvathy, 2008, p. 149).

Therefore, non-predictive control underpins a decision-making approach that prioritizes control (with low emphasis on prediction), aiming to "transform current means into co-created goals with others who commit to building a possible future" (Wiltbank et al., 2006, p. 983). In contrast, the causation logic also seeks control but through predictive means using the techniques of conventional planning. Sarasvathy (2001) distinguishes between two decision-making reasoning: effectual (non-predictive) and causal (predictive) and the expert entrepreneurs know how and when to use both logics.

The perspective of entrepreneurship as a science of the artificial emerged from the dialogues between Sarasvathy and Simon (2000), highlighting the interplay between the one of design principles from Herbert Simon's Sciences of the Artificial - near-decomposability - as a key principle in the design of enduring artifacts -, and effectuation logic, her empirical research on expertise (Sarasvathy, 2003). In this way, "To study entrepreneurship as an artifactual science, we need to focus on how individuals and firms design their inner and outer environments, especially how new goals, adaptive and negotiated, come to be; how particular strategies shape environments, reformulate individual preferences and reorganize firm structures" (Sarasvathy, 2008, p. 156).

Finally, the near-decomposability as a key principle in the design of enduring artifacts. There is a meeting point in a decision-making process, characterized by a set of interdependent heuristics grounded in entrepreneurial experience, that combined with near-decomposability, within the structure of the business, allowing for the exploitation of "leveraged independence to exploit the same locality and contingency" (Sarasvathy and Simon, 2000, p. 18). In line with Sarasvathy (2008), "The principle of near-decomposability describes the structural aspects of artifacts that are required to satisfy certain stability properties. Effectual entrepreneurship, I shall argue, builds stakeholder networks that implement this principle. Note that the principle is ubiquitous, useful, simple (but non-trivial), often confused with modularity and a relatively neglected idea in entrepreneurship" (p. 156).

These ideas serve as the interpretive key points for analyzing the journey of Carteiro Amigo.

3 Method

This qualitative research study examines the case of Carteiro Amigo (CA), selected from empirical research monitoring of 12 entrepreneurial initiatives in the favela of Rocinha. These initiatives are supported by FAPERJ (Carlos Chagas Filho Foundation for Research Support of the State of Rio de Janeiro) in its first call focused on the favela. To monitor these initiatives, from April 2022 to January 2024, we utilized the Territorial Effectuation Monitoring (TEM) tool. This tool involves collecting data in two distinct perspectives: first, focusing on the entrepreneur and his/her decision-making process, intertwining their life story with the decision to create the business; and second, focusing on the structure of the business model of the firm. The study is coordinated and conducted by the authors of this article, allowing for a comprehensive understanding of the entrepreneurial activity in Rocinha, shedding light on both individual and business dynamics of relational networks (Brufato & Bartholo, 2023).

According to Yin (2018), we chose CA because it exhibits a distinct attribute of above-average endurance over time. This attribute is termed by Sarasvathy (2021) as "middle-class businesses", characterized by modest growth and size yet possessing the ability to endure over time. Depending on the structure of the business model that has been designed, this attribute serves as a meeting point between effectuation and the near-decomposability principle (Sarasvathy and Simon, 2000).

The analysis was based on CA's 24-year journey characterizing its turning points and distinguishing between two types of decision-making reasoning - causal (predictive) and effectual (non-predictive) logics -, and key heuristics used by the entrepreneur that led to the development and endurance attribute of a firm rooted in the Rocinha favela. Thus, depending on the structure of the business model that has been designed, this attribute serves as a meeting point between effectuation and the near-decomposability principle, in line with Sarasvathy and Simon (2000).

4 Carteiro Amigo

The phases of Carteiro Amigo journey following Bartholo & Brufato (2023). The sentences in quotation marks are from the interviews with two of its founders.

In 2000, the Carteiro Amigo emerged to address a common issue in favelas: the difficulty of delivering mail to households, due lack of postal addressing codes (zip code or CEP in Portuguese), absence of street identification and to inadequate physical access. Despite the approval of Senate Law's Project 122/2017, which allows citizens to request the creation of a CEP for their property, many favelas still lack this service.

Phase I - 2000 to 2009 - In October 2000, three members of a family born and raised in Rocinha were employees of a cleaning Comlurb (Municipal Company for Urban Cleaning) program in Rocinha (Community Cleaner) and were doing temporary work in Rocinha as census enumerators for IBGE (Brazilian Institute of Geography and Statistics), and realized that the residents had difficulty receiving letters. Whith out previus experience as entrepreneur, they decided create the Carteiro Amigo with the aim of solve the difficulty of delivering mail in the favela. "*We used the census badge. But we put our brand on top of the census logo and started registering people door-to-door in Rocinha*". Initially operating as a family business, two partners left their jobs to focus entirely on CA. With funds from their layoffs, they rented a small space in Rocinha and developed the mail delivery process. "*We create the whole process of delivering letters in the favela. At first it was all manual, but after a few years we bought computers*". CA offered a 30-day free trial of letter collection, sorting, and delivery, followed by a fixed fee per home. The firm was officially registered in 2001, with all partners dedicating themselves full-time by 2002. In 2004, CA formed a partnership with Correios, which began delivering letters directly to CA's store, averaging 13,000 letters daily.

Phase II - 2010 to 2012 - CA expanded by opening a store in the Rio das Pedras, a favela near to Rocinha. In 2010, it began a training and consulting partnership with SEBRAE (Brazilian Service of Support for Micro and Small Enterprises) and together with them writing a business plan to expand the business to others 11 favelas in Rio via franchise model. "*In business plan process,* SEBRAE *prescribe an ideal entrepreneur. But the ideal entrepreneur was to be entrepreneurial, to be proactive and have money to invest, rather generic things that led to franchisees*". The partnership with SEBRAE also resulted in articles in national newspapers and magazines with CA, the first franchise from favela. To address this advertisement, the entrepreneurs opted to rent a larger store in Rocinha. "*In a few months, we realized the investors in franchise were who didn't live in the favela and/or didn't know anyone in the favela and when we are going to start earning, the president of resident's association wants to earn together and the investors were dissatisfied*". The franchise model failed in a year and a half period. "*We didn't make a loss. Because the investor knew, there is a risk when he invested. In reality, during this period, he had already taken a bit out of his investment. We made mistakes, and this has remained an experience*".

Phase III - 2013 to 2019 - CA concentrated its business in Rocinha and Rio das Pedras. "W*e couldn't have opened all those stores either, so what are we going to do? This month we've paid everyone, but there's so little left for us*". At the same time, in 2016, there was a drop in the number of letters and an increase in e-commerce orders. CA began to deliver goods, and this transformation was the embryo of its evolution into a logistic firm. "*At that time, we hardly had any partnerships outside Rocinha*".

Phase IV - 2020 to 2021 - "*In the pre-pandemic of COVID, we're talking about 10000 letters a day. And during and after the pandemic, we're talking about 500 letters* *a day when letters came in. So, there were days when there were no letters at all".* They shifted focus to a home delivery service, prompted by the impact of new technologies and the COVID-19 pandemic's social isolation measures. CA adapted its business model, transitioning from per-household to individual revenue models and expanding its capacity to deliver various goods. In 2021, a partnership with FAPERJ facilitated seed funding for developing an application and digitalization process, prompting CA to redesign its model and involve the founders' successor in intensifying partnerships beyond the favela.

Phase V - 2022 to date - In 2022, a new partner, an investor and executive from a large franchise retail and logistics company, joined CA from outside the favela. Since then, CA aimed to expand via franchises to other favelas, creating a spin-off called CA Express and establishing partnerships with logistics and retail giants. CA has strengthened its position and developed a new model including a franchise-subsidiary. In the second half of 2023, CA sold 30% of the company on Shark Tank Brazil TV Program for R$one million, attracting six investor partners. They've also consolidated partnerships, invested in technology, and enhanced social media strategies. In January 2024, CA prioritized customer growth in Rocinha and nearby areas, pausing expansion to other favelas. With 36,000 registered users, CA offers various delivery subscription plans.

5 Findings and Conclusion

In CA's first decade, its entrepreneurs primarily use non-predictive effectuation logic, focusing on who they are, what they know, who they know, and affordable loss. CA evolves from addressing mail delivery challenges to adapting to technological shifts and the COVID-19 pandemic's impact on consumer behaviour. A key aspect of CA's strategy is its response to uncertainties, facilitated by control heuristics and relational networks. These mechanisms help CA navigate unpredictability, adapt its business model, and build networks beyond the favela. For instance, the partnership with FAPERJ in 2021 enabled digitalization, enhancing CA's readiness for a new expansion movement after its initial attempt to expand to 11 favelas through a franchise model.

The succession and entry of a new partner in 2022 catalyzed CA's expansion plans, leading to the creation of the spin-off Carteiro Amigo Express. In 2023, CA sold 30% of the firm in exchange for the entry of six more investors from Shark Tank Brazil. This highlighted CA's commitment to scaling operations while maintaining a focus on Rocinha, thereby strengthening its identity and brand. This strategic turning point underscores CA's agility and innovation in seizing expansion opportunities amidst challenges, and in developing new commercial partnerships. Understanding CA's entrepreneurial journey involves two key aspects: firstly, a predominant of effectuation logic of non-predictive decision, and secondly, a pivoltal moment in its relational networks and stakeholder formation. This led to a completely new architecture of CA's business model. The predominant strategy integrates control modes, mainly non-predictive, alongside affordable loss, bird in hand, and crazy quilt principles, forming a triad that guides the business's structural design process. This dynamic reveals the emergence of an architecture of effectual networks that intersects with the new business model architecture, enabling resilience in the face of evolving contingencies and challenges. Within this framework, different types of relational networks complement each other, facilitated by the Simonian concept of near-decomposability, which shapes the firm's new architecture. As evidenced in its evolution, CA's decision-making heavily relies on effectuation logic until mid-2022, transitioning to the establishment of networks beyond the favela, marking a significant shift in its business model architecture. An in-depth and comprehensive analysis of CA's expansion and contraction movements, as well as its decision-making design logics, control modes, and their connection with the principle of near-decomposability, was conducted by Brufato (2024).

The identification of the convergence between effectuation and near-decomposability enables CA's endurance, allowing it to thrive and innovate in dynamic environments. Through the interplay between control heuristics and relational networks, CA navigates uncertainties and forges strategic partnerships, contributing to its endurance and impact. In essence, CA's ability to leverage effectuation and near-decomposability principles creates enduring value in complex socio-economic contexts.

In conclusion, CA's entrepreneurial journey exemplifies the symbiotic relationship between effectuation logic, near-decomposability, and adaptive strategies in navigating uncertainties. By leveraging control heuristics and relational networks, CA not only sustains its operations but also thrives amidst evolving market dynamics. This study offers valuable insights into the nuanced interplay between entrepreneurial decision-making, environmental factors, and strategic adaptation, contributing to a deeper understanding of entrepreneurial activity's intricacies in complex socio-economic contexts.

References

Bartholo, R., Brufato, A.: Activité entrepreneuriale et stratégie de vie dans la favela de Rocinha à Rio de Janeiro. In: Morlet, T. (ed) Développer l'écologie du travail - Ressource indispensable aux nouvelles formes de souveraineté. *Actes du 57ème Congrès de la Société d'Ergonomie de Langue Française* (SELF) (2023)

Brufato, A.W.: Effectuation e seus caminhos na favela e nas artes. In: Tese de Doutorado em Engenharia de Produção na COPPE/UFRJ (2024)

Brufato, A., Bartholo, R.: Desenvolvimento e aplicação da Territorial Effectuation Monitoring (TEM) para identificação de padrões de empreendedorismo na favela da Rocinha no Rio de Janeiro. Multidiscip. Sci. Rep. **3**(3), 1–26 (2023). https://doi.org/10.54038/ms.v3i3

Knight, F.: In: Kelley, A.M. (ed.) Risk, Uncertainty and Profit (1921)

Sarasvathy, S.D.: Causation and effectuation: toward a theoretical shift from economic inevitability to entrepreneurial contingency. Acad. Manag. Rev. **26**(2), 243–263 (2001). https://doi.org/10.5465/AMR.2001.4378020

Sarasvathy, S.D.: Entrepreneurship as a science of the artificial. J. Econ. Psychol. **24**(2), 203–220 (2003)

Sarasvathy, S.D.: Effectuation: Elements of Entrepreneurial Expertise. New Horizons in Entrepreneurship Series. Edward Elgar, Cheltenham (2008)

Sarasvathy, S.D.: The middle class of business: Endurance as a dependent variable in entrepreneurship. Entrep. Theory Pract. **45**(5), 1054–1082 (2021)

Sarasvathy, S.: Effectuation. Elements of Entrepreneurial Expertise, 2nd edn, (2022)

Sarasvathy, S.D., Simon, H.A.: Near-decomposability, effectuation, and the speed of growth of entrepreneurial firms. In: Presented at "The first annual technology entrepreneurship research policy conference", May 19 and 20, 2000. Robert H. Smith School of Business, University of Maryland. www.effectuation.org (2000)

Simon, H.A.: The Sciences of the Artificial. MIT Press, Cambridge, Ma (1996)
Wiltbank, R., Dew, N., Read, S., Sarasvathy, S.D.: What to do next? The case for non-predictive strategy. Strateg. Manag. J. **27**(10), 981–998 (2006). https://doi.org/10.1002/smj.555
Yin, R.K.: Case study research and applications, vol. 6. Sage, Thousand Oaks, CA (2018)

Unraveling the Valves: An Ergonomics Journey to Integrate Operational Experience in Offshore Projects

Sarah Silva Medeiros Correa[1](✉), Camila Pinheiro Marins[1], and João Marcos Bittencourt[2]

[1] Federal University of Rio de Janeiro, Rio de Janeiro, RJ 21941-853, Brazil
sarah.correa@pep.ufrj.br

[2] Federal Fluminense University, Niterói, RJ 24210-240, Brazil

Abstract. The purpose of this study is to explore ergonomic challenges in the design of valves for continuous process industries, focusing on FPSO platforms (Floating Production Storage and Offloading). Regulatory standards for valve positioning and access differ from the actual needs of operators and maintainers. To better align with user requirements, the objective is to evaluate the ergonomic aspects of the valve design process. A qualitative approach is employed in this project, which covers the period of September 2022 to March 2024 through case studies and participatory observation. It outlines valve categorization criteria based on functionality and maintenance frequency, dividing them into critical, non-critical, and rarely used categories. The study emphasizes the importance of integrating ergonomics from the early design stages and involving operators to ensure practical and safe solutions. Key findings include more adaptable and integrated categorization criteria, improved communication and collaboration between design and operational teams, and more effective design review sessions. The results show the impact of ergonomic involvement while identifying areas for refinement to enhance project outcomes and operational efficiency. Based on the findings of this study, it could be possible to design effective offshore platforms by continuously reflecting on and improving the ergonomic integration process.

Keywords: Ergonomics · Project Process · Valves · User participation

1 Problem Statement

In projects involving valves in continuous process industries, there is often a discrepancy between the standards set for valve positioning and access and the practical needs of operators and maintainers.

Ergonomics underscores the importance of a dynamic approach that fosters harmony between regulatory standards, design dynamics, and end-user requirements.

Essentially, the current valve design process does not sufficiently incorporate regulatory considerations with operational insights, leading to notable hurdles in operational efficiency and safety.

S. Jin et al. (Eds.): IEA 2024, SSDI 39, pp. 312–317, 2025.
https://doi.org/10.1007/978-981-95-0211-0_48

2 Objective

This study aims to evaluate the valve design process in FPSO (Floating Production Storage and Offloading) platforms. It will investigate the ergonomic aspects involved in this process, highlighting both the positive points and areas that need improvement for more effective integration of the various actors involved, aiming for a final result that meets the users' needs.

The literature indicates that many projects overlook the impact of working conditions, resulting in negative consequences [7]. The Activity Ergonomics approach, which considers work as the starting point for design, promotes more efficient and safer solutions [3]. Involving users in the design process allows for anticipating problems and better understanding their needs from the outset [4].

Additionally, the National Agency of Petroleum, Natural Gas, and Biofuels (ANP) has adopted a stricter stance regarding ergonomics and human factors in FPSO platforms, intensifying oversight and imposing stricter requirements [2]. These measures have significantly impacted the way projects are conducted.

3 Methodology

This work is part of a research project initiated in 2018, aiming to develop methodologies for incorporating ergonomics into the project of offshore oil platforms. This article discusses the data collected from September 2022 to March 2024. During this period, the researchers followed the basic design and detailing stages of five production units, interacting with designers and workers.

It is a qualitative study, developed from a case study and guided by the method of participant observation and the activity ergonomics approach. The descriptive case study provides a detailed description of the valve categorization process on FPSO platforms, offering a deep understanding of the phenomenon in the project context [10]. Evidence was collected from various sources, as proposed by Yin [10]: (a) documents; (b) file records; (c) interviews; (d) direct observation; and (e) participant observation.

Participant observation allowed the researchers to actively engage in activities, acting as members of the ergonomics team and contributing to decision-making [9]. Activity ergonomics was employed to integrate user knowledge into work situations' designs through constant dialogues with workers and the inclusion of users in design decisions. Specific guidelines were provided to improve working conditions and workers' health without compromising the designers' flexibility and production objectives [5].

4 Results

This study delves into the valve design process in oil and gas extraction platforms such as FPSOs, which encompass activities ranging from exploration and production to refining, energy generation, and marketing. The focus is on the role of the ergonomics team involved in the design process.

It is worth noting that these are the first production units to have ergonomics as an independent discipline involved from the early stages of the [8], leading to many discoveries and adjustments regarding the role of ergonomics as the process unfolds.

4.1 Categorization Criteria

The company has implemented valve categorization to effectively manage and comply with platform regulations. This classification takes into account the criticality, function, and frequency of valve use, as outlined in the "Guidance Notes on the Application of Ergonomics to Marine Systems" [1]. Developed collaboratively, the categorization is divided into three main categories.

Category 1 encompasses valves critical for normal or emergency operations and frequently used in routine maintenance. Examples include block valves for PSVs (Pressure Safety Valves), essential for personnel and process safety, cargo protection, and environmental protection, where failure can cause severe damage.

Category 2 comprises valves that are not crucial for regular or emergency operations and are utilized during maintenance at intervals exceeding six months. This category includes manual valves for standard startup and shutdown, as well as pneumatic and hydraulic valves that require thorough maintenance due to mechanical stress in offshore environments.

Category 3 encompasses valves that are seldom used in specific situations, such as during initial commissioning. These valves only require occasional maintenance and are not essential for continuous operations.

The categorization is outlined in the company's Technical Specifications (TS), which offer guidance to facilitate valve operation and maintenance, enhance safety, and prevent ergonomic issues. The TS is categorized into topside and hull, addressing ergonomic requirements for platform construction, valve location, accessibility, and safe operation parameters. In essence, the TS establishes clear guidelines for categorization, which are crucial for operational efficiency and regulatory compliance, ensuring that all ergonomic requirements are met. The following section will elaborate on how this categorization is put into practice.

4.2 Stages of Categorization in the Project Process

The basic design of the units is internally developed by the company (contractor). At this stage, a preliminary list of unit valves with available information is issued. However, at this stage of the project, the operation and maintenance teams of the future unit are not yet defined, so the list is drawn up by the project team based on normative criteria and with the support of a professional designated to represent the operation. For the topside area, it is the process team, and for the hull, it is the naval projects team.

In the detailing phase, the design is carried out by contracted companies after a bidding process. At this stage, one of the activities of the contractor's ergonomics team is to monitor this design process. A central aspect of this analysis is the consideration of specific principles of valve location and access, as determined in international guidelines and by the documents prepared by the client.

During the detailing phase, the contracted company takes on the responsibility for the detailed elaboration of the valve list, including valves not initially foreseen. This list is then meticulously reviewed by the contracting ergonomics team and validated by the operations team. This process is particularly challenging due to the large number of manual and automatic valves on an FPSO platform, which can reach up to 20,000 valves, requiring a meticulous approach to ensure that each valve is categorized according to the established criteria and that operators can consider real working situations for efficient categorization.

Once the ergonomics team incorporated the obligation of positioning the valves according to the categories into the project's technical specifications, it had an impact on the project activity of the units themselves, as the project teams (especially piping) needed information and validations from the operations team to proceed with the project. This included the circulation of items such as valve lists (with detailed module, height, tag/identification, wheel position, etc.), 3D models, and emails between project teams and future users, mediated by ergonomics.

Throughout this process, cases were identified where the definition of the relationship between category and valve position was not easily resolved, and this was one of the reasons that led to the holding of specific ergonomics events to discuss the valve project, involving designers, operators, and ergonomists.

After adjustments, the contracted company prepares a final ergonomics report, which is required by Brazilian regulatory authorities for the platform's operation release, demonstrating the project's compliance with the established criteria.

5 Discussion

The current projects under observation mark the initial set of company divisions overseen by a dedicated ergonomics team, implementing a specific Technical Specification (TS) for valve design. The validation and design review stages are pivotal in assimilating operational experience into valve design. Active participation by operators ensures that the solutions developed are effective and practical. Nonetheless, time constraints and regulatory issues frequently impede the full integration of workers' experience.

The ergonomics team conducts valve design reviews to deliberate on specific solutions, ensuring that ergonomic criteria are considered from the outset. However, certain aspects necessitate improvement. The criteria for valve categorization require revision for a more comprehensive approach that takes into account all operational variables and contexts. The current protocols are excessively restrictive, limiting the flexibility required to adapt the design to real operational and maintenance conditions. Additionally, interaction with the contracted company must be better coordinated to guarantee effective collaboration and a shared understanding of project objectives. Without clear and efficient communication, aligning expectations and meeting all requirements becomes challenging.

The tools used during categorization also require enhancement to be more meaningful and efficient. Well-designed integration tools aid in identifying and resolving problems before they arise during operation. However, the effectiveness of these tools depends on their suitability to user needs and their integration into the design process. Design Review sessions should be better structured to ensure productivity and operator integration. These sessions are valuable for gathering feedback and adjusting the project as necessary, but this is only possible if they are well-organized and conducted.

Furthermore, the dialogue between operational teams needs to be more cohesive. Each discipline aims to integrate solutions that best meet its specifications within the project. Continuous and unified communication between different company sectors, including operations, maintenance, piping, electrical, and ergonomics, is essential. This not only facilitates problem identification and resolution but also ensures all stakeholders are aligned with project objectives. Effective communication is crucial for collaboration and overall project success.

Among the identified issues are overly restrictive categorization protocols that consider anthropometric factors without factoring in the actual work of the operator. This limits the necessary flexibility to adapt the design to actual operating conditions, leaving little room to maneuver within the process variables, making necessary adjustments and adaptations difficult. Additionally, it is imperative to increase the effective participation of the operations and maintenance teams from the early stages of the project to ensure their specific needs and challenges are considered, resulting in a more effective and efficient design.

Finally, the use of intermediate objects [6], tools, and documents used to facilitate communication and integration between different project phases and all involved actors, needs reevaluation. More effective use of these objects can improve team coordination and ensure that all project aspects are considered in an integrated manner.

6 Conclusions

The project of valves on offshore units has a direct impact on future operational efficiency. This article explores how the ergonomic perspective is incorporated into the platform conception process. The ergonomics team has been actively involved in integrating project parameters that consider real work conditions, in addition to existing normative criteria. Although the initiative is still in its early stages, the results have been promising, particularly in enhancing interaction between designers and future users.

One of the key contributions of ergonomics has been the implementation of specific events (design reviews) to discuss valve design. These events foster discussions, especially between designers and workers, focusing on access solutions based on operational and maintenance needs.

However, as ergonomics is a relatively new discipline in this context, the team must reflect on the outcomes of ongoing projects to improve project processes.

References

1. ABS - American Bureau of Shipping: Guidance Notes on the Application of Ergonomics to Marine Systems (2013). https://ww2.eagle.org/content/dam/eagle/rules-and-guides/current/other/86_applicationsofergonomicstomarinesystems/ergo-gn_e-aug18.pdf. Accessed 18 Nov 2024
2. Agência Nacional Do Petróleo, Gás Natural E Biocombustíveis – ANP: Nota Técnica n° 10/2023/SSO-CSO/SSO/ANP-RJ. In: Assunto: Disseminação de melhores práticas da indústria em Fatores Humanos. ANP, Rio de Janeiro (2024)
3. Bittencourt, J.M., Duarte, F.: Contribuições da simulação em ergonomia para a Engenharia do Trabalho. In: Braatz, D., Rocha, R., Gemma, S. (eds.) Engenharia do trabalho: saúde, segurança, ergonomia e projeto, vol. 1, pp. 463–490 (2021)

4. Daniellou, F.: The French-speaking Ergonomists' approach to work activity: cross-influences of field intervention and conceptual models. Theor. Issues Ergon. Sci. **6**(5), 409–427 (2005)
5. Guérin, F., et al.: Compreender o Trabalho para Transformá-lo: a Prática da Ergonomia. Editora Edgard Blücher, São Paulo (2001)
6. Jeantet, A.: Les objets intermédiaires dans la conception. Éléments pour une sociologie dês processus de conception. Sociol, du travail. **3**, 291–316 (1998)
7. Maline, J.: Simuler le travail: une aide à la conduite de projet. Edições ANACT, Montrouge (1997)
8. Marins, C.P., Leite, P.B., Mercado, M.P., Garotti, L.V., Duarte, F.J.: The practice of ergonomics as a design discipline in the basic design of oil platforms. Work. **73**(s1), S189–S198 (2022)
9. Minayo, M.: Trabalho de campo: contexto de observação, interação e descoberta. In: Minayo, M. (ed.) Pesquisa social: teoria, método e criatividade. Vozes, Petrópolis (2015)
10. Yin, R.K.: Estudo de caso: planejamento e métodos. Bookman, Porto Alegre (2015)

Two Scales of Workplace Flexibility and Their Impact on Activity: Modularity and Versatility

Eva Goulois[1,2,3](✉), Danie Jon[1,2], Nadia Heddad[4], and Pascal Béguin[1,2,5]

[1] Université Lyon 2 Lumière, 4bis Rue de l'Université, 69007 Lyon, France
{e.goulois,danie.jon,pascal.beguin}@univ-lyon2.fr
[2] UMR 5600 EVS-AECTT, Lyon, France
[3] Kardham, 10 Rue du Débarcadère, 75017 Paris, France
[4] Université Paris I Panthéon-Sorbonne, 21 Rue Broca, 75005 Paris, France
nadia.heddad@icloud.com
[5] Institut d'Etudes du Travail de Lyon, 4bis Rue de L'Université, 69007 Lyon, France

Abstract. Flexibility has become a major concern for many organizations today, especially in the service and education sectors. This concept brings about significant changes in the spatial and temporal dimensions of work, although it is not always clearly defined. This paper aims to clarify two key aspects of flexibility regarding its spatial dimension: modularity and versatility, and their impact on work activities.

Keywords: Flexibility · Workspace · Activity-Based Flexible-Office · Education

1 The Socio-Economic Context as an Imperative for Flexibility

The term "flexibility" is polysemic and ambiguous [1]. First, it is "the ability [...] to bend and recover with suppleness, to adapt to change without breaking" [1]. It seems that the concept of flexibility is primarily related to work [2] and is seen as a rational recourse, as "the only credible response to environmental uncertainties". Historically, flexibility has been promoted through two key characteristics [3]: quantitative flexibility, which refers to the adaptability of employment, and functional or qualitative flexibility, which refers to the adaptation of production and work organization based on demand variations. Flexibility could almost be considered a form of "cultural inscription of contemporary capitalism" [2]. Thus, the concept seems to be linked to financial and strategic dimensions. How, then, has it developed in the context of workplaces?

Workspaces are not exempt from the rationalization strategy described above. Technological advances have made possible forms of flexibility at the heart of work organizations. Work no longer depends on a fixed point in space and time, and presence must be justified. Unoccupied or underutilized space is no longer an option. Workspaces must have a new value in the eyes of business leaders and facility managers. The discourse promoting flexible space emerged in the 1990s and continues to evolve today [4]. With the standardization of the creation of "white box" spaces in office buildings - completely empty floors without walls or partitions - coupled with the financialization of corporate

S. Jin et al. (Eds.): IEA 2024, SSDI 39, pp. 318–323, 2025.
https://doi.org/10.1007/978-981-95-0211-0_49

real estate [5], flexible spaces thus contribute to increasing the active value of corporate real estate [4] through the competitive advantage they provide.

2 Thee Need to Define the Term Flexibility

2.1 Problem Statement

The preliminary elements we have just presented position "flexibility" as a multifaceted concept, making it inherently difficult to define. We have observed that the term is often used in contexts that neglect the central issue of work. However, we believe that flexibility is fundamentally based on work activities. In this article, we aim to clarify the unity of "flexibility" by examining its implications both as a source of prescription and as a product of activity. We seek to elucidate the translation of flexibility in workspace projects through the lens of two concepts: modularity and versatility. This will be achieved through an operational decomposition from a work perspective that will guide the design of such spaces.

2.2 Methodology

Our methodology is based on a literature review across disciplinary fields and sectors, as well as analyses of workspace projects that are considered flexible. We conducted thematic content analyses of 93 articles published in peer-reviewed journals and 125 gray literature texts that addressed flexible learning spaces in higher education institutions. In addition, we rely on activity analysis through observations and interviews within a service sector company specializing in corporate real estate, whose offices are designed according to the flex-office model. This model features a diverse range of workspaces without assigned desks [6]. Observations and interviews were also conducted in a university *learning lab.*

3 The Concept of Flexibility Applied to the Workspace

3.1 The Use of the Term "Flexible": Degrees of Flexibility from a Space Design Perspective

Our analyses reveal a diversity of formulations associated with flexibility, with two constants: flexibility is central to spatial design, and all formulations convey a normative character. Flexibility is often discussed in terms of prescriptions that describe desired practices rather than standardizing what the space should be. The space must be able to accommodate a variety of uses and configurations. This translates into particular attention to the technical elements of the built environment, such as furniture and layout, rather than a systemic vision that integrates organizational dimensions. Flexibility seems to be less about physical characteristics and more about the ability to reconfigure and adapt the space according to work activities.

At this point, it is important to distinguish between the concepts of task and activity. A task refers to "what is to be done, a goal to be achieved under certain conditions" [7].

Activity, on the other hand, corresponds to what is done in reality. It includes the adaptations, strategies, adjustments, and improvisations necessary to meet the requirements of the task under often unpredictable or variable conditions. This distinction is crucial to understanding the nuances of flexibility. Similarly, we are interested in Lefebvre's concept of space, both designed and lived [8]. Designed space refers to the space of designers and decision-makers who express the projected needs of workers in the exercise of architectural design and the "decoding-recoding" of reality. Lived space is the space of the individuals who inhabit and use it on a daily basis, which cannot be reduced to a single need or function. From an ergonomic point of view, this distinction is interesting because designed space can be seen as a functional representation of work needs, i.e. the task, while lived space is closer to the actual reality of work, i.e. the activity, which can only be understood from the point of view of those who perform the work.

Looking at flexible spaces through the lens of designed space, it seems possible to interpret different approaches to flexibility along a scale of four degrees: mutualization, modularity, versatility, and permeability. Each of these orientations offers a unique perspective on the relationship between space and activity. Mutualization refers to the pooling of human, material, or immaterial resources within the space and is based on the idea of optimizing spatial resources by diversifying the users who can access the space. Modularity, a principle borrowed from modular architecture, is based on the ability to exchange units that can be assembled, modified, or removed without disrupting the whole. Versatility suggests that the space is designed to serve multiple functions simultaneously. Permeability refers to the openness and fluidity of interactions between the interior and exterior of a space towards a territory.

3.2 Modularity and Versatility: Transformations of Work and Lived-Space

We now propose to illustrate two of these different degrees through the example of educational and tertiary workspaces.

The first example is a university learning lab. This learning lab is designed to facilitate the practical application of knowledge acquired in the classroom and to encourage interaction among a variety of stakeholders. In its design, one of the intentions was to have a space that could accommodate a variety of situations: individual or group student work, pedagogical activities, events, etc. This design relies on spatial configurations that can be rearranged according to the needs of the task. However, this modularity is not without consequences for the work. The adaptation of spatial arrangements to the needs attributed to the situation represents a new task for which responsibility must be clarified. This issue is not neutral, because if the status of this task has not been discussed, the resulting confusion of roles and responsibilities leads to tensions. While the task sometimes falls to teachers and students, it is often the space administrators (sometimes called lab managers) who must take it on at the request of their colleagues. Matching furniture to needs and returning it to a neutral configuration after use adds to the other tasks they perform. In the absence of collective construction around the status of this task, no distribution is made. Lab managers take on this organizational work by managing coordination among stakeholders and task allocation. Modularity is considered in relation to a catalog of spatial configurations designed in relation to the task. These tasks are approached independently and sequentially. However, real work is based on a simultaneous temporal interweaving of all these actions. Therefore, true flexibility is manifested in activity, as it requires constant adaptation to unforeseen situations, variations and dynamics of reality.

In tertiary workspaces, especially in the flex-office model and the spaces designed around it, there are rules of use for which we find three degrees of flexibility. First, mutualization, since employees do not have assigned desks. They are asked to move to different workspaces according to their "activity". Here, "activity" means different task-related communication characteristics that influence movement between different spaces. For example, "concentration" rooms for individual production tasks without interaction, and "project" rooms without reservations for tasks requiring discussion with colleagues. The latter are particularly interesting to illustrate the other two degrees. Firstly, modularity, as these rooms are equipped with furniture that allows the arrangement and restructuring of the open plan workspace. Second, versatility, since these project rooms offer multiple functions thanks to their modularity, which also frees up space. For example, a project room can be transformed on a monthly basis into a "plenary" room where all employees can gather. This is also illustrated by the ability to change the use of different workspaces, such as the radical changes during the Covid-19 pandemic, where spaces were organized into team territories. This flexibility through versatility is made possible by the ability to change the "rules of use and life" according to current needs. These characteristics make the flex office a designed workspace model that allows for flexible and efficient management of corporate space. However, this degree of flexibility can only exist if the employee "plays the game" (verbatim) or makes the effort to change workstations according to their tasks. Searching for a workstation, deciding where to locate it, and actually occupying it could even be considered an activity in itself. This flexibility is less common and difficult to implement. Workers may not move or change workstations within a single workspace. Changing spaces or workstations must be justified in terms of the work and how the space can be a resource for the worker. Similarly, the flex office does not take into account the complexity of the collective dimension of work and its consequences for the way spaces are occupied.

Thus, the flexibility found in so-called flexible spaces, designed to achieve varying degrees of flexibility, ultimately overlooks what this use prescription requires of tertiary workers, students, teachers, lab managers, and many others.

3.3 Designing for Flexibility: A Dialog Between Lived-Space and Conceived-Space

The distinction made by Lefebvre [8] describes a tension between the vision of designers and the realities of the actual use of space. In our findings, this contradiction is particularly pronounced in relation to work issues, with a normative and prescriptive approach to space and organization on the one hand, and the realities of work activity seeking to articulate space and organization on the other. In designed space, flexibility is a means of multifunctionalizing spaces by multiplying configurations and possible uses within the same space. There seems to be a bias that suggests that the characteristics of space dictate its use. In design, needs assessment is done from a "ratio" perspective (number of workstations, area, etc.) that rationalizes the resources designers deem useful for tasks. From a lived space perspective, however, flexibility lies less in the physical characteristics of space than in activity. In fact, it is about articulating spatial resources according to the needs of reality.

If we consider designed space as the result of the work of designers, we must then question how design decisions are made. On the design side, the demand for flexibility is setting new standards. Design criteria have shifted, and the compromises made often prioritize the "communicative" value of space [11] at the expense of the "functional" value. This position is not compatible with the challenges of work activity. However, it is not a question of deciding which should prevail, as both positions have different logics. The challenge of designing such spaces should be to create a common vision from the perspective of shared worlds as defined by Béguin [12]. It is through the "polyphony" [12] created by the participation of a heterogeneity of actors that the resource for such projects is built. However, the "simple" encounter between designers and end users is not enough. In fact, the importance of discussing work in project management has already been documented in the past in ergonomics [12, 13]. The use of intermediary objects in simulation methods has been identified as a useful tool for facilitating exchanges that can position work as a factor for transforming the project and technical choices [14]. Considering these elements, the central question in designing for flexibility is no longer space, but work. By first questioning the work, the spatial solution can then be constructed.

4 Conclusion

We have examined the concept of spatial flexibility in the context of work, focusing on the relationship between designed space and lived space. Through an analysis of different projects of spaces labeled as "flexible," we identified four possible degrees of designed space: mutualization, modularity, versatility, and permeability. Our findings suggest that flexibility lies not only in the physical characteristics of the space, but also in the ability of workers to reconfigure and adapt this space in their work activity. This raises questions about the methods of designing flexible spaces by questioning the object of design. It seems necessary to adopt an approach that integrates both the designer's vision and the user's reality in a perspective of discussing work. An approach to flexibility through work seems to be an opportunity to develop a better understanding of the challenges of designing such spaces.

References

1. Périlleux, T.: Être à l'épreuve dans le travail. In: de Nanteuil-Miribel, M. (ed.) La société flexible, pp. 111–136. Érès (2005)
2. De Nanteuil-Miribel, M.: La flexibilité est-elle un choix rationnel? In: La société flexible, pp. 51–78. Érès (2005)
3. Jetin, B.: La flexibilité du travail en Corée du Sud. Revue Tiers Monde. **1998**, 403–423 (1998)
4. Fillonneau, J.: Les consultant·es workplace & change: La construction d'une identité professionnelle entre espoirs et frustrations. In: 18th Edition of the International Days of Work Sociology, Université d'Évry (2024)
5. Nappi-Choulet, I., Cléret, C.: Quand l'immobilier d'entreprise devient stratégique. Le journal de l'école de Paris du management. **104**(6), 29–36 (2013)

6. Jon, D.: Le Travail De Bureau dans le modèle du Flex-Office, une vision du travail réduite à la tâche. In: Doctoriales ARPEGE 2022 (2022)
7. Leplat, J.: L'analyse psychologique de l'activité en ergonomie: Aperçu sur son évolution, ses modèles et ses méthodes. Octarès Ed. (2000)
8. Lefebvre, H.: The Production of Space. Blackwell (1991)
9. Jon, D., Heddad, N., Béguin, P.: Résister à la dissonance dans le travail en Flex-Office. In: Dissonances dans le travail, interpellations contemporaines de la prescription. Annual Seminar of the Ergonomics Pole, Université Paris 1 Panthéon-Sorbonne (2023)
10. Lai, C.: Le rapport espace/activité au cœur du processus d'appropriation des nouveaux espaces de travail: Du flex-office aux environnements de travail basés sur l'activité (activity-based workspaces). Conservatoire National des Arts et Métiers (2023)
11. Lautier, F.: Ergotopiques: Sur les espaces des lieux de travail. Octarès Ed. (1999)
12. Béguin, P.: Conduite de projet et fabrication collective du travail: Une approche développementale [Habilitation à Diriger des Recherches]. Université Victor Segalen Bordeaux 2 (2010)
13. Daniellou, F.: Le statut de la pratique et des connaissances dans l'intervention ergonomique de conception [Habilitation à Diriger des Recherches]. Laboratory of Ergonomics of Complex Systems, Université Victor Segalen Bordeaux 2, Bordeaux (1992)
14. Oggioni, B.: A simulação como recurso para a participação dos operadores no processo de projeto: O caso do projeto de um centro de operações integradas na indústria do petróleo. Federal University of Rio de Janeiro (2023)

Techno-Solutionism and Sustainable Development: The Activity Analysis as a Way of Reintroducing the Primacy of the "Living" Over Technology

Lassalle Julie[1](✉), Goutille Fabienne[2], and Boudra Leila[3]

[1] LAB-STICC (UMR 6285), Université Bretagne Sud, 4 rue Jean Zay, 56100 Lorient, France
julie.lassalle@univ-ubs.fr

[2] Epicene, Bordeaux Population Health Center, INSERM (U1219), Université de Bordeaux - ISPED Case 11, 146 rue Léo Saignat, 33076 BORDEAUX Cedex, France

[3] Laboratoire Paragraphe (UR 439), Université Paris 8, 2 rue de la Liberté, 93200 Saint-Denis, France
leila.boudra@univ-paris8.fr

Abstract. This contribution challenges the techno-solutionism that dominates public policies for sustainable development. A cross-discussion of two sectors studied in the field of constructive ergonomics provides a better understanding of the - non-automatic - link between technological solutions, appropriation process and the transformation of activities to make them more sustainable.

Keywords: New technologies · activity-centered ergonomics · sustainable development · energy · agriculture

1 Introduction

The current political and regulatory measures envisaged to limit the degradation of the environment and resources caused by human activities are generally technology centered. European strategies for energy efficiency and environmental protection are essentially based on the deployment of new technologies. One of the aims of deploying smart-grid technologies for energy efficiency (combining smart meters, e.g., electrical, and digital interfaces) is to give users better control over their energy consumption, thanks to the information provided by these systems. An objective of deploying precision technologies in the agricultural sector is to make more efficient and productive use of plant protection products. In both cases, these strategies correspond to a public policy action focused on techniques and technology to influence the individual behaviors. Activity analysis provides information on the role of these technologies, which are rarely designed with actual activities in mind, in environmental transitions. It shows how they are or not enough to achieve the results they are designed to achieve. The question of appropriation of these technologies by users and workers is central to meeting today's environmental challenges. This contribution addresses the process of socialization and appropriation of

S. Jin et al. (Eds.): IEA 2024, SSDI 39, pp. 324–329, 2025.
https://doi.org/10.1007/978-981-95-0211-0_50

technologies deployed as part of European policies to support sustainable development. It examines the criteria for the appropriation of these new digital technologies by users and agricultural professionals in their daily lives. By combining the analyses and results of the two research projects, we aim to gain a better understanding of the relationships that people have with the technologies they use, and the way in which these ones are or are not established as a resource for sustainable activities.

2 Method

The theoretical and methodological approaches used for the two studied sectors come from the field of activity-centered ergonomics and activity theories for work and activity analysis. These approaches are based on longitudinal studies based on semi-directive interviews and observations of activity.

Then, to better understand the uses and the appropriation process, the theory of instrumental genesis [1] was mobilized as the framework analysis.

2.1 Technology and Energy Efficiency: The SOLENN Experimental Smart-Grid

The SOLENN project (SOlidarity –Energy- INnovation) was conducted over 3 years (2016-2018) to deploy and test smart-grids systems for measuring electricity consumption in Brittany, to meet European and national regulatory requirements. This research has been supported by the French Environment and Energy Management Agency (ADEME) and was conducted in a 12 partners consortium (academics, manufacturers, representatives of civil society - consumer support associations, local energy agency -, local authorities). 10,000 local households have been fitted with the French "smart" meter (Linky meter), 300 benefited from a specific smart-grid web interface (SGI) to monitor their electricity consumption data. The SOLENN project was an opportunity to study the appropriation of SGI using the theory of instrumental genesis [1] and to understand the conditions of its emergence. Four different SGI were deployed to monitor households' electricity consumption in near real-time. The household sample was divided into four groups corresponding to a specific access to one of the 4 SGI. A total of 36 households participated (voluntary-based). In the longitudinal study, data were collected over three study periods: period 1 (2016, $n = 30$), period 2 (2017, $n = 32$) and period 3 (2018, $n = 15$). Two types of data were collected, processed, and analyzed: discourse (from semi-structured interviews and spontaneous verbalizations collected during SGI use) and data from observations of SGI use. A total of 73 interviews were conducted over the 3 study periods. The data set was encoded using both a deductive (based on the instrumental genesis framework) and an inductive strategy (to integrate emerging themes). Text segments (words, sentences, paragraphs) formed the unit of analysis, grouped together according to a thematic meaning (for more details on the coding method [2]).

2.2 Ergonomic Analysis of Precision Agriculture Technology (PAT) Uses

The ergonomics studies used to discuss the constraints and resources of precision agriculture are based on several research interventions conducted between 2014 and 2024.

These six long studies involved researchers and stakeholders from the Epicene team of INSERM and from various prevention institutes in France and Canada [3–5], mobilized open and then filmed observations of work and individuals in action (N = 29), with and without measurement equipment (heart rate monitors, surface and atmospheric samplers, eye trackers). They are based on semi-directed interviews and self-confrontations (N = 34) supported by various materials constructed with engaged agricultural professionals (Technical specifications of agricultural equipment, maps, photos, testimonies, etc.). The results were also built from data capitalized in workshops (N = 6) bringing together agricultural peers and their professional and non-professional relatives around reflective and prospective activities such as activity simulation.

3 Main Results

3.1 Technology and Energy Efficiency

In all, only 22% of participating households have used and appropriated SGI - i.e. the web interface to monitor electricity consumption -. This profile is characterized by sufficient prior knowledge to read and interpret energy data graphs; a preliminary multi-instrumentalized consumption monitoring activity (excel-type personal monitoring file, power meter, supplier application, invoices) and an intrinsic motivation for electricity consumption and its analysis. The proposed tool does not initiate a new engagement but responds to a pre-existing user need to monitor electricity consumption in greater detail, and/or to a real appetite for energy issues approached from a technological angle. The SGI makes it possible to consult the household's electricity consumption for the purposes of detailed analysis - which requires a high investment of time (requiring the keeping of a household activity log and/or experimentation to better understand consumption curves) - and diagnosis. The SGI is then used as a decision-making tool, mainly to guide the choice of building interventions and equipment purchases. After a period of intense use, technology use stabilized at the end of the project, once the main household transformations had been implemented. Interactions became less frequent, raising the question of how to maintain use over time. The individual's sense of competence and efficiency in relation to his or her environment and autonomy increases, more so as action choices are validated by the evaluation of their effects based on the SGI. This, in turn, stimulates interest in electrical data and electricity consumption management, and even in other areas (consumption of other fluids, food, mobility). The conditions for appropriation could be summed up as follows: having the desire, having access, knowing how to use and experimenting successfully.

In total, 77% of participants have not appropriated the SGI. Either there was non use or use was blocked by usability defects, particularly to understand the electrical data (58%), or use was ephemeral (19%). In this case, the technology was abandoned when the household's usual consumption pattern was observed on the SGI graphs. Consumption is deemed as unavoidable, as a consequence of daily life such as meal preparation, visits or hygiene care, and therefore not modifiable. Overall, appropriation is slowed down or prevented by a lack of energy knowledge (what does the observed peak correspond to? what does 1 kWh represent?) and practical knowledge (how to act to reduce peaks and better control household consumption?). SGIs are "technical", niche systems that cater for "knowledgeable, expert" profiles. These technologies have been developed by companies of different sizes (very small, intermediate-sized and large) and with different objectives (digital companies, electricity distributors, associations). Nevertheless, the strong constraints on usability observed apply to all the SGIs on offer. This reveals the negative consequences of a techno-centric approach in which the end-user is not considered in the design process. But more broadly, these results raise the question of the cost (design, deployment)/benefit (appropriation, energy savings) ratio and the illusion of a positive outcome commensurate with the socio-ecological stakes.

3.2 Precision Agriculture Technology (PAT)

The results reveal how farmers are adopting precision technologies while facing various constraints in their use. Offering opportunities for flexible hours, time savings, reduction of physical strain, work-life balance, and representing an opportunity for farm modernization that could influence the decision of younger generations to enter the profession (attractiveness of the sector), they nonetheless induce detrimental transformations in agricultural work and require significant adjustments from farmers. Precision agriculture technologies (PATs) are not autonomous and can even dehumanize agricultural work, distancing farmers from the living aspects of farming. Farmers often find themselves in the role of reliability operators, monitoring and intervening in case of machinery malfunction. The activity of seeding involves planting seeds, soil preparation, adjusting machinery and precision technologies, as well as necessary checks. With the introduction of PATs, difficulties have been observed, such as programming errors, imprecise alerts, and situations where farmers had to stop their activity to resolve technical issues. The complexity and constant evolution of technologies demand continuous adaptation and adequate training from farmers to fully benefit from them. Despite the contribution of precision technologies, farmers emphasize the importance of their traditional expertise and connection with the land, which remain at the core of their work. They express the need to maintain a deep understanding of the land, beyond what precision technologies can offer. For cow milking, the introduction of milking robots disrupts work organization, offering flexible hours but introducing new tasks and altering the human-animal relationship. The installation of these robots entails a high initial cost, facility rearrangements, and regular maintenance. Farmers also highlight a significant learning curve to adapt to managing the robots and the data they provide. Additionally, the relationship between farmers and their cows may be affected by robotization, with a loss of proximity, observation, and individual inter-knowledge between humans and animals. PATs for crop treatment led to increased maintenance activities managed by farmers. Their adoption often results in increased mental burden and additional physical and organizational constraints. PATs allow for field mapping, automatic opening of spraying arms, and automatic adjustment of ramp height. They enable farmers to reduce control and adjustment activities while operating the sprayer. However, significant difficulties are identified. Firstly, learning and mastering these technologies require a high level of training, which can be problematic for some farmers less familiar with new technologies. Moreover, the unreliability of equipment, despite its potential performance, poses a major obstacle to the reliability of treatment operations, occupational health, and environmental preservation. Incidents such as delays in GPS connection and breakdowns can lead to significant time losses and inefficiency in crop and environmental protection. These reliability issues can also have environmental repercussions. For example, deviations between the tractor and the GPS during the automatic opening and closing of spraying can result in untreated areas or excessive spraying on paths between plots. Additionally, frequent interventions on the equipment due to breakdowns and incidents can lead to situations of pesticide exposure for farmers, as well as for other internal and external workers on the farms, who meet residues of persistent pesticides during application, other equipment uses, or maintenance operations.

4 Discussion and Conclusion

The results of the two sectoral studies determined by increasing demands towards sustainability converge despite the very different timeframes, application frameworks and activities involved. The appropriation of the technologies studied (smart-grids interfaces or precision agriculture technology) depends on various characteristics as artefactual (possibilities and constraints specific to each technology), individual (cognitive and conative) or social and environmental context (work, relationship with the Living). These results show a non-mechanical link between technological deployment and the transition movement. It depends on a complex set of factors that constitute the *sine qua non* condition for the technology's appropriation. The techno-centered design doesn't integrate these conditions set places the user outside the design loop. The technologies produced are therefore poorly adapted to the real-life socio-domestic and professional activities studied. In most cases, at best, the technology is ineffective and leads to an experience of incompetence; at worst, to a deterioration in working conditions and a loss of autonomy. In other sectors concerned by sustainable development as household management and recycling, studies in France and Brazil have shown that technological solutions implemented in material recovery facilities led to work intensity, harsh working conditions, and worsening working conditions [6]. Still dominant in technology design today, the techno-centered approach does not allow us to grasp the complexity of activity and of work situations and the strategies established by individuals into their activity. Worst, it crystallizes often partial and inaccurate representations of human cognitive and social functioning, and of the conditions that make transitions possible. Our results underline that appropriation is a long-term process, embedded in a singular historical, legal and cultural reality and in individual, contextual and situated characteristics. A first challenge, still relevant today, is to propose technologies for transitions which are designed with an anthropo-centered approach that integrates real work and human activity. A second challenge is to overcome a techno-centered approach to a broader *living*-centered approach (i.e. within a symbiotic relationship). The ergonomics of activity offers the possibility of thinking differently about the design of innovations and more broadly solutions for sustainable development. This approach calls for moving away from the illusion of techno-solutionism and focus solutions to be useful, relevant and adapted to support individual, collective and symbiotic transitions. A final challenge concerns the very idea of solutions to support the transition, technological or otherwise, as part of politico-industrial strategies and introduced into society to compensate for the deleterious effects of human activities on natural ecosystems. These solutions are based on a positivist postulate and a deterministic vision of technology on the individual, which these studies call into question. This approach needs to be enriched by requiring of the systemic and historical complexity of usage, behaviour and of the socio-domestic or professional activities as well as the different levels of articulation and interdependency (individual, social, political, etc.). This is the way to co-construct and experiment solutions that aim at appropriation more than performance to achieve the sustainable development goals set by the United Nations.

References

1. Rabardel, P.: From artefact to instrument. Interact. Comput. **15**(5), 641–645 (2003)
2. Lassalle, J., Amelot, A.: Appropriation of technologies for energy transition: Contributions of the instrumental approach to design. Activités. **20**(2) (2023)
3. Garrigou, A., Théry, L., Chassaing, K., Effantin, E., Mercieca, P., Di-Merman, S., et al.: Une approche pluridisciplinaire du processus de construction sociale de la prévention du risque CMR. Béguin, P., Rabardel, P. (eds.) SELF 2015, 476-489. Scand. J. Inf. Syst. **12**(1) (2015)
4. Goutille, F., Albert, M., Fredj, J., Pannetier, J., Garrigou, A., Nascimento, A., Jolly, C.: O Uso de tecnologias de precisão: recursos e limitações no trabalho agrícola. Laboreal. **19**(1) (2023)
5. Goutille, F., Candau, J., Lambert, E.: Exposition aux Pesticides: Ce qu'en disent les sciences humaines et sociales. Octarès, France (2024)
6. Boudra, L., Souza, M., Varella, C., Béguin, P., Lima, F.P.A.: Analyzing the territorial dimensions of work through a comparative study of waste recovery facilities in France and Brazil. Work. **77**(1), 377–389 (2024)

Design Review and Ergonomics: Support and Limitations of Digital Technologies in Oil Platform Projects

Camila Pinheiro Marins[1](✉), Valérie Pueyo[2], and Francisco Duarte[1]

[1] Federal University of Rio de Janeiro, Rio de Janeiro, RJ 21941-853, Brazil
camila.marins@pep.ufrj.br
[2] Lumière Lyon 2 University, Lyon 69007, France

Abstract. This article explores the subject of how new digital technologies can foster ergonomics activities and interactions between designers and operators. As an example, the case of Design Reviews (DR) sessions held in oil platform design processes is presented. The study discusses the participation of researchers as members of the ergonomics team for the detailing project of 5 platforms, whose projects were developed using a 3D model and included several DR events. From the data gathered in these projects, the researchers identified features that had the potential of favoring or limiting participation and discussions about the work to be carried out in the situations under development. These points include aspects related to the establishment of ergonomics as a design team, the characteristics of the 3D model, and the organization of DR events, among others. Furthermore, the research highlights the creation of a specific ergonomics DR event based on the operational experience of the operators, focusing on the positioning of valves and instruments.

Keywords: Ergonomics · Design Review · Design Process · Digital Technologies

1 Introduction

Technological advances related to digital representations and design information-sharing resources are spurring new dynamics in design processes. This is also observed in oil platform projects, where ergonomics pursues ways to use the new resources available to incorporate work-related elements, aiming to provide better future working conditions.

In this sense, the DR sessions represent one of the resources that can be used by ergonomics to promote participation through discussions related to future work. However, for this to happen, ergonomics must take part in the structuring of the project.

This paper aims to discuss how new digital technologies such as 3D modeling have been used in oil platform projects, as well as the opportunities and limitations that these resources represent for ergonomics. This topic will be addressed through the analysis of design review sessions that use the 3D model as the main verification resource.

S. Jin et al. (Eds.): IEA 2024, SSDI 39, pp. 330–335, 2025.
https://doi.org/10.1007/978-981-95-0211-0_51

Design Review sessions correspond to verification events scheduled in the project that bring together representatives from different teams to carry out a shared analysis of the project centered on the 3D model. Since, in design processes, one of the contributions of ergonomics consists in fostering conditions for debate, using as a basis knowledge about real work and simulations of future work [1], it is understood that DR sessions would carry conducive elements to achieving this goal. Nonetheless, for this to occur, ergonomics must organize its participation among other activities and design teams [2].

2 Method

This study is part of a research project developed in cooperation between the university and a company in the energy sector, which allowed the researchers to follow the design process of oil platforms. This qualitative study consists of a case study aligned with the theoretical framework of Activity Ergonomics [3].

For this article, data from May 2021 and February 2024 were analyzed, a period in which the detailed design stages of 5 platforms were in development.

For each unit under development, the contractor establishes that DR sessions must be held when the project reaches 30%, 60%, and 90% completeness. However, due to the complexity of the platforms, the projects are divided into hull and topside areas, where the hull comprises the habitability areas, facilities, and tanks of the unit, while the topside refers to the processing area. Therefore, for each unit, six DR events are carried out: three for the hull and three for the topside.

As will be discussed in subsequent topics, for the aforementioned projects, ergonomics, design, and operation teams also carried out specific DR sessions to address issues related to ergonomics, more specifically the positioning of valves and instruments.

Thus, by December 2023, researchers had participated in more than 20 DR events, comprising the projects of the 5 units in the detailing stage.

Data gathered for analysis consisted of 3D models, blueprints, piping and instrumentation diagrams (P&ID), lists of items to be checked in each DR, reports of DR results, written records of events made by the researcher, and records of meetings held between ergonomists for discussion about the participation in the DR.

3 Results

In the oil platform detailing projects presented in this study, ergonomists' activities included the analysis of reference situations, development of ergonomics recommendations, validation of the proposed recommendations with users, and verification of compliance with the recommendations.

As for the detailing projects themselves, these were carried out entirely in 3D, using software with BIM (Building Information Modeling) resources. In the detailing stage, as previously mentioned, the DR sessions occurred when the projects reached 30%, 60%, and 90% maturity. At these events, representatives from different design teams (ergonomics, operations, structures, architecture, safety, among others) carried out a shared analysis of the 3D model, based on criteria pre-established by each discipline, although predominantly technical or normative.

As most of the platform detailing projects were developed in Asian countries such as Singapore, China, and Malaysia, the DRs were carried out in a hybrid format (with the possibility of presential or remote participation) and in the English language.

Although the event is conducted by representatives of a hired company and follows a pre-defined script, the 3D model is made available to all participants. As defined in the project contract, the 3D model to be analyzed in the DR session should be made available to the contractor one month before the event. This way, the teams (designers, operators, etc.) would have this period to carry out preliminary analyses of the 3D model before the DR.

In the analyzed context, additional DR sessions were created specifically to verify ergonomics requirements, focusing on valve positioning, which is considered a critical issue for work on platforms [4]. The objective of these DR sessions was to bring the work dimension into the project through continuous exchanges between operators, ergonomists, and designers. To this purpose, several meetings were held between the aforementioned groups, to align the parameters established in international standards and the experience of the operators.

4 Discussion

By bringing together designers, ergonomists, and future users around an intermediate object [5] – the 3D model –, and considering the knowledge constituted by ergonomists based on previous analyses and the operational experience of future users, the DR already articulates part of the necessary elements to carry out a simulation of the future work situation.

In other words, DR sessions can be considered as a possibility of shared space for discussions related to the characteristics of production systems under development, putting the work in evidence.

However, to achieve this goal is necessary to organize the event in a way that fosters participation and discussions related to the work to be developed in the future system.

In the projects analyzed, some points were identified that either favored or limited this purpose. Among the points that favored participation and discussions about the work, the following stood out:

- Ergonomics as a design team: the incorporation of ergonomics as a design discipline brought more legitimacy to the actions of the ergonomics team. Also, ergonomics documentation helped to disseminate the discipline's objectives. The contractor's teams, for example, read the ergonomics documents, spoke with the ergonomists, and thus were more aware of what they could "require" concerning ergonomics in the project.
- Characteristics of the 3d model: the 3D model was easy to manipulate and analyze: as previously mentioned, one month before each DR event, the contracted company made the 3D model available for prior analysis by the contractor's teams. The model was available in ".nwd" format and participants used the Navisworks software to analyze it. According to participants' comments and the researchers' experience, the software was considered easy to use, with features that allowed saving viewpoints, carrying out measurements (of valve heights, for example), searching for equipment

by tag, isolating elements, etc. Furthermore, the model was relatively light, allowing for quick loading and navigation;

- Hybrid format (presential and remote): regarding event format, the hybrid configuration allowed the participation of actors who would not otherwise have participated (considering that the detailed projects were developed in Asia, mainly). This enables richer exchanges and the involvement of a greater number of actors, with the possibility of requesting the knowledge of different experts at specific moments. For example: when there is a specific doubt related to the possibility of a valve repositioning in a pipeline, a specialist from the piping or process team can be quickly asked to join the meeting and clarify the issue.
- Ergonomics DR: about the integration of ergonomics and encouraging the participation of the operation team, it is worth highlighting the creation of specific ergonomics DR events. These events were held in the 5 units' projects mainly to verify issues regarding the categorization and positioning of valves based on the operational experience of operators. Preliminary work was carried out which involved: sharing information about the valves (tags, heights, modules, handwheel position, etc.), exchanges between operators and designers, validations, and solution proposals. Based on a list of valves with categories validated by the operators, the designers sought to position the valves in the height ranges applicable to each category. During the DR, cases were discussed in which designers had difficulty positioning the valves in the correct range or in which operators identified problems in the arrangement or access. For these cases, possible solutions were discussed, using work-related demands and restrictions as main premises.

In contrast, other points were identified that could potentially undermine or limit participation and discussions about work:

- DR scope: DR events for hull and topside areas have a pre-established check schedule which leaves little scope for additional checks. However, once the teams (operation, safety, cargo handling, architecture) were familiarized with the ergonomics design requirements, it was noticed that they started making spontaneous checks concerning ergonomics aspects throughout the DR events. For example: pointing out lack of access to a certain area or equipment, questioning the feasibility of cargo handling maneuvers, etc.
- Organization of DR events: for all events (hull, topside, or ergonomic DR) organization is fundamental and guides the smooth running and satisfactory results of the event. In the context analyzed, some aspects that contribute to this objective include:

  Prior selection of points to be checked. For example: in ergonomics DR, this comprises, among other things, a list of items (valves) to be checked and saved viewpoints of the 3D model (to quickly find the location in the model);
  An agenda compatible with the areas and items to be checked. This means structuring an agenda providing for time gaps that allow for an adequate analysis of the project and that allow participants to organize themselves to participate in the review of areas for which they are requested. For example: analyzing the offloading area requires the participation of operators with knowledge of this activity, in the same way that checking the workshop area requires the participation of the maintenance team.

The organization of DR outputs (also called punches). This subject is extremely relevant for the treatment of issues raised during the verification. In addition to information such as the origin of the comment, location, equipment tag (when applicable), snapshot, and disciplines involved, the way comments are written must be succinct, but incorporate the necessary elements to remember and resolve the issue. At the end of a topside DR, for example, more than 500 comments (punches) can be generated, which will need to be dealt with later and not necessarily by the people who participated in the event.

- Language and time: although the hybrid format of the DRs represents a positive feature in the sense of enabling the participation of a wider range of actors, the time difference between countries and the language adopted entails a certain degree of restriction on participation. For contractual reasons, the DR sessions for the projects should be held in the contracted company's time zone. Thus, it was not uncommon for professionals located in Brazil to participate in DR events that took place from 9 p.m. to 6 a.m. (which corresponds to the 8 a.m. to 5 p.m. work shift in Singapore, for example). A similar issue can be observed about language. By contractual determination, all events should be in English. Although this aims to facilitate communication among the teams, the fact that English is not the native language of either the contractor or the contracted sometimes creates difficulties in understanding between the participants.

5 Conclusions

The evolution of design technologies and the growing engagement of ergonomics in platform projects create a propitious context for new approaches to participation. In the context of this study, the DR sessions held to discuss ergonomics requirements are an example of how new resources can be used to promote greater operational participation and carry out a project analysis that goes beyond technical criteria.

Concerning DR activities, all points indicated as support or limitation of the use of the 3D model to verify the project interfere directly or indirectly with the work that will be carried out in the future situation. From discussions with future workers to pre-identify the main points to be checked in each area (which should not be a restrictive list, but should guide the analysis), to the organization of the event and records, all of these are elements that exert influence on the final product of the project: which is the future work situation that operators will have to deal with.

For this reason, based on the cases analyzed, the authors understand that the participation of ergonomics in the project, specifically in moments of DR, contributes to improving the connection and exchanges between designers and operators.

Although several publications can be found focusing on fostering exchanges between designers, ergonomists, and users [6–9], this work specifically explores these exchanges when their central elements are the 3D model and DR events. Particularly in complex projects (due to the number of processes and teams involved) and in a post-pandemic context, virtual resources gained even more prominence, justifying analysis efforts aiming at improving the use of these resources.

Therefore, the topics presented in this work aim to report the positive points and opportunities for improvement identified through the participation of researchers in oil platform design processes, expanding knowledge, and fostering discussion on the topic in similar design situations.

References

1. Daniellou, F.: Participation, représentation, décision dans l'intervention ergonomique. Actes des Journées de Bordeaux sur la Pratique de l'Ergonomie. Editions du Laboratoire d'Ergonomie des Systèmes Complexes de l'Université Victor Segalen Bordeaux 2, Bordeaux (1998)
2. Marins, C., Leite, P., Mercado, M., Garotti, L., Duarte, F.: The practice of ergonomics as a design discipline in the basic design of oil platforms. Work. **73**, 189–198 (2022)
3. Guerin, F., Laville, A., Daniellou, F., Duraffoug, J., Kerguelen, A.: Comprendre le travail pour le transformer: La pratique de l'ergonomie. ANACT (2001)
4. International Association of Oil & Gas Producers: Report 454: Human factors engineering in projects, 2nd edn. Energy Institute, London (2020)
5. Boujut, J., Blanco, E.: Intermediary objects as a mean to foster co-operation in engineering design. Comput. Support. Coop. Work. **12**(2), 205–219 (2003)
6. Béguin, P.: Prendre en compte l'activité de travail pour concevoir. Activités. **4**(2), 107–114 (2007)
7. Broberg, O.: Integrating ergonomics into engineering: empirical evidence and implications for the ergonomists. Hum. Factors Ergon. Manuf. **17**(4), 353–366 (2007)
8. Bittencourt, J., Duarte, F., Béguin, P.: From the past to the future: integrating work experience into the design process. Work. **57**, 379–387 (2017)
9. Conceição, C., Broberg, O., Duarte, F.: A six-step model to transform an ergonomic work analysis into design guidelines for engineering projects. Work. **66**, 699–710 (2020)

Comparative Analysis of Safety Culture Interventions on Four Offshore Platforms

Mariana Toledo Martins[1(✉)], Mateus Pereira Abraçado[1], Lucas Chrisostimo Farah[1], Adriana Nunes Araujo[2], and Raoni Rocha Simões[3]

[1] Federal University of Rio de Janeiro (UFRJ), Rio de Janeiro, RJ 21941-853, Brazil
mariana.martins@pep.ufrj.br
[2] Petrobras, Santos, SP 11010-310, Brazil
[3] Federal University of Ouro Preto (UFOP), Ouro Preto, MG 35400-000, Brazil

Abstract. There is not a standard formula to diagnose an organization's safety culture. Since an organization is a complex system with various interactions, each intervention will possess unique characteristics. This study aimed to present the outcomes of interventions conducted on four offshore production units (identified as A, B, C, and D) owned by a Brazilian oil and gas company. It investigated the influence of research conditions, including local conditions and researchers' practices, on the success or failure of these interventions. To this end, the case study method was employed, combining quantitative and qualitative tools, to comprehend the characteristics of business processes, local work practices, and the environmental context. The study revealed that researchers' practices, alongside unit characteristics and environmental, structural, technical, and organizational factors, guided the development and results of the interventions on the four offshore platforms. Additionally, it demonstrated how an adequate social construction ensured the success of these interventions. In conclusion, acknowledging the influence of the research conditions on the processes and results of the interventions emphasizes the importance of situated approaches. This allows researchers to better understand the circumstances and reflect on their own research practices.

Keywords: Offshore platforms · Safety culture · Human factors · Intervention characteristics

1 Introduction

Every organization is comprised of subgroups, each containing various sets of individuals and groups, values, perceptions, behavior patterns, and other elements [1]. Building a safety culture depends on several factors, such as technological, organizational, and environmental factors [2]. For this reason, there is not a standard formula to diagnose the safety culture of an organization.

This diagnosis does not aim to find a culture that is "more correct" than others but to understand the unique behaviors, values, and interactions of that environment. To properly conduct an intervention, the safety culture of each unit must be examined. Then, actions should be implemented considering the reality of local activities. The

S. Jin et al. (Eds.): IEA 2024, SSDI 39, pp. 336–341, 2025.
https://doi.org/10.1007/978-981-95-0211-0_52

safety culture does not involve a single individual, but a group or an organization as a whole [3]. Furthermore, there is no consensus regarding the different approaches for evaluating safety culture, but several different interpretations and methods [4].

Therefore, this study aims to present the results of the interventions carried out on four offshore production units, demonstrating how the research conditions, including both local conditions and researchers' practices, may influence the outcome of these interventions.

2 Methods

This study investigated four production units belonging to an oil company following the case study method proposed by Yin [5]. The planning stage regarded the case study as appropriate for understanding the impact of the units' local characteristics on safety interventions. The combination of quantitative and qualitative approaches was essential for obtaining the characteristics of the processes and the results of the interventions.

The study design included the identification of theoretical references. Approaches related to the ergonomics and human factors of the activity were selected, particularly the factors that constitute a safety culture: environmental, technological, and organizational factors.

At the preparation stage, a research protocol was developed for each unit following the classification proposed by Rocha et al. [3], which was based on the safety culture literature and prior knowledge of the energy industry. Rocha et al. [3] identified five essential themes related to safety culture: blaming, rule relevance, safety priorities, safety bureaucracy, and return on experience.

A mixed approach was used for collecting evidence, combining quantitative and qualitative methods. At the quantitative stage, homogeneous groups were formed with individuals who performed similar activities and were on the same hierarchical level. Then, customized surveys were carried out using an adapted Likert scale for data analysis. At the qualitative stage, discussion groups were formed to validate and enhance the results, encouraging an exchange of safety-related experiences and values.

Evidence analysis combined both deductive and inductive approaches. The independent variables were identified, and the behavior of these variables was observed in safety culture development projects on offshore platforms according to the standard combination technique. The behavior of three variables was observed in the comparative analysis of safety culture development projects on offshore platforms: environmental factors, organizational factors, and technological/structural factors. The results of this comparison revealed how the local conditions on the units influenced the process and results of the interventions.

The last stage of the case study report is described in the following section, which details the study results.

3 Results

Interventions on four platforms belonging to an oil and gas company were analyzed. The research conditions, influenced by environmental, structural/technological, and organizational factors, guided the development and results of the actions. The differences between the interventions on the four platforms are presented below.

3.1 Characteristics of the Interventions on Each Platform

Platform A is a fixed platform that has been in operation for 13 years. This study on the unit started in 2020. Meetings with leaders were arranged so the research team could be informed of the activities and safety practices on the unit. At the beginning of the quantitative stage of the research project, the safety survey was customized to adjust its language and themes according to the experiences of the workers aboard the unit, resulting in a survey with 79 statements. A total of 16 survey sessions were conducted with the homogeneous groups. The qualitative stage occurred in two steps: a boarding in October 2021 and another in March 2022. A total of 9 discussion sessions were carried out on each boarding. After the cases and oral reports provided at the qualitative stage, the quantitative-qualitative diagnosis of the unit was concluded, and actions were suggested to change certain practices that are typical of reactive safety cultures. The research team and participants jointly decided to prioritize two of the proposed actions: the development of a return on experience system, which could enhance the "power to act" of the operational teams, and the development of an accident analysis method, which could convert an "investigation culture" into a "learning culture" and transform the working conditions. During the action implementation stage, the strong support and commitment of the unit leaders to the research project were essential, along with the assistance of a facilitator who worked as an intermediary with the unit. These factors ensured a solid social construction and, thus, the efficiency of the actions.

Platform B is a 6-year-old floating production, storage, and offloading unit. Research on the unit started in 2020. The quantitative stage consisted of survey customization, which resulted in an 82-statement survey applied in 33 sessions adapted to the homogeneous groups. All sessions were carried out online due to the COVID-19 pandemic. At the qualitative stage, 11 discussion sessions were conducted during a boarding in April 2022. After data collection in the qualitative stage, the quantitative-qualitative diagnosis of the unit was concluded. Based on this diagnosis, potential vulnerabilities in the safety culture of the unit were identified, particularly the predominance of organizational silence. Finally, practices that could enable the development of a resilient culture were suggested. Similarly to platform A, the prioritized actions were the creation of a return on experience system and the development of an accident analysis method. Differently from platform A, the social construction on platform B had issues related to the high turnover of leaders and researchers. In addition, the difficulty of boarding the unit hindered the research process, leading to its interruption until the beginning of 2024.

Platform C is a 6-year-old floating production, storage, and offloading unit. Research on the unit started in 2021. At the quantitative stage, the survey was customized, resulting in 86 statements. Due to the COVID-19 pandemic, the safety technicians were trained on survey application procedures so they could apply the survey with the teams on board. At the qualitative stage, a boarding occurred in September 2022, where 11 discussion sessions were carried out. Based on the data collected at the qualitative stage, the quantitative-qualitative diagnosis was concluded. Some areas for improvement were identified, particularly related to vulnerabilities in the unit's safety culture, organizational silence, and project issues on the unit. Three of the proposed actions were prioritized: the development of an accident analysis method, the creation of an ergonomic assessment report to list recommendations for improving the material conditions on the platform, and the restructuring of the unit's return on experience system. At the action implementation stage, the high turnover of researchers, leaders, and participants resulted in a damaged social construction, leading to a delay in the research on the unit.

Platform D is a 24-year-old semi-submersible platform. Research on the unit started in 2021. At the quantitative stage, the survey customization resulted in 56 statements. The safety technicians were trained on survey application procedures so they could replicate them with the homogeneous groups on the unit. At the qualitative stage, which occurred in June 2023, 8 discussion sessions were carried out. Based on the data collected at the qualitative stage, the quantitative-qualitative diagnosis was concluded. The high turnover of leaders on platform D resulted in a significant delay in this stage. Although the action plan for unit D was still in its conception stage, the diagnosis revealed some areas for improvement, such as degradation of installations due to the platform's age, limited participation of the workforce in the development of solutions, and vulnerability of report and feedback mechanisms.

3.2 Discussion

Based on the details of the research stages on the four platforms, it is possible to identify some similarities and differences in the development of each intervention, as well as factors that influenced the results. The high turnover of unit leaders and researchers had a greater impact on the social construction of the units. Platform D was found to be the most critical case. Since the beginning of the research project, the social construction has been impaired by constant changes in management. Consequently, this platform is at the least advanced stage of the intervention. Additionally, turnover occurred on both platforms B and C during the final stage of the research project. The presence of a facilitator on platform A, consistently working as an intermediary with the unit, had a major role in the development of the intervention. Furthermore, the leaders' commitment to the project's actions and support for implementing the recommendations was another decisive factor for the success of the intervention. Similarities between the safety culture of the four platforms, particularly those related to blaming in accident analyses and insufficient return on experience tools, prompted similar actions on the units. However, the individual characteristics of each platform prompted different recommendations. For example, on platform C, there were project issues, and, on platform D, installations were damaged. The COVID-19 pandemic was an environmental factor that affected the length and completion of the research project stages. Meetings during the quantitative stage, which were intended to occur in person, were conducted online. The estimated time for submission of the quantitative-qualitative diagnosis was also extended due to the increase in the number of disease cases. Decisions made by researchers regarding the reduction in surveys and the adoption of different application methods improved the quantitative analysis. Table 1 below shows a summary of the factors that affected the intervention.

Table 1. Summary of factors that affected the intervention.

	Environmental factors	Organizational factors	Technological/infrastructural factors
Platform A	• COVID-19 pandemic	• Financial support and commitment by unit leaders regarding research actions • Assistance of a facilitator who worked as an intermediary with the unit	*
Platform B	• COVID-19 pandemic	• Difficulties when implementing actions due to several restrictions imposed by the unit • Changes in the research team	*
Platform C	• COVID-19 pandemic	• High turnover of unit's leaders and the research team • Existence of a return on experience program on the unit	• Project issues (especially regarding access to the unit)
Platform D	• COVID-19 pandemic	• High turnover of unit's leaders	• Damaged installations (especially due to corrosion)

4 Conclusion

The integrated approach of quantitative and qualitative analyses was essential for elucidating the complexity of the organizational and cultural dynamics within the production units. Understanding the research conditions as influential in the processes and results of the intervention highlights the importance of situated approaches, which reveal the individual characteristics of each circumstance and promote reflections on the researchers' practices. Study limitations include dependence on the company's internal data, potential biases in the interpretation of results, and the difficulty of generalizing and replicating the results. Future research can complete the transformation actions to assess this approach's effectiveness.

Acknowledgments. This study received support from the Coordination for the Improvement of Higher Education Personnel (CAPES) and the Carlos Chagas Filho Research Support Foundation in the state of Rio de Janeiro (FAPERJ) (ref. 210.621/2019), as well as financial support from the Program for Human Resources Training for the Oil, Natural Gas, and Biofuels Sector (PRH-ANP 15.1), with Research, Development, and Innovation resources, per resolution ANP No. 50/2015. The authors also express their gratitude to the oil and gas company where the research took place.

References

1. Antonsen, S.: Safety culture and the issue of power. Saf. Sci. **47**(2), 183–191 (2009)
2. Wiegmann, D.A., Zhang, H., Von Thaden, T.L., Sharma, G., Gibbons, A.M.: Safety culture: an integrative review. Int. J. Aviat. Psychol. **14**(2), 117–134 (2004)
3. Rocha, R., Duarte, F., Lima, F., Mercado, M., Araujo, A., Garotti, L., Campos, M.: Framework for the assessment of the safety culture in the oil and gas industry. Int. J. Occup. Saf. Ergon. **30**(1), 224–237 (2023)
4. Guldenmund, F.W.: The nature of safety culture: a review of theory and research. Saf. Sci. **34**(1–3), 215–257 (2000)
5. Yin, R.K.: Case Study Research: Design and Methods, vol. 5. Sage, Thousand Oaks, CA (2009)

The Offshore Well Builder: Cross-Sector Cooperation and Building Trust in a High-Risk Industry

Eliel Prueza de Oliveira[1](✉) and Francisco de Paula Antunes Lima[2]

[1] Federal University of Rio de Janeiro, Rio de Janeiro, RJ 21941-853, Brazil
elielprueza@pep.ufrj.br

[2] Federal University of Minas Gerais, Belo Horizonte, MG 31270-901, Brazil

Abstract. Trust is fundamental to safety culture, and its absence reduces cooperation. In high-risk industries, cooperation between different actors is crucial to preventing accidents, which requires relationships of trust between controllers, contractors, and providers. This study examines case studies to determine how the "company man" role affects these relationships of trust, influencing performance, cooperation, and safety in well construction operations. The analysis reveals that mistrust undermines cooperation and is linked to the fear of opportunistic behavior. Contractors have discretionary power in assigning penalties, and there is heterogeneity among company men. Although opportunities for cooperation improve performance and safety, a fragile level of trust prevents progress. The company man's actions affect trust and cooperation between the contractor and the operating company, shaped by organizational issues. These relationships become fragile unless they are reflected upon, jeopardizing operations' efficiency, learning, and safety. This study faces limited access to the field and the scarcity of research in this context.

Keywords: Trust · Cooperation · Team management

1 Introduction

The role of trust in organizational operations has received increasing attention, partly due to the evidence that trust fosters performance in work environments characterized by constant transformation and uncertainty. These transformations have resulted in the rise of increasingly less hierarchical organizational structures and the growing number of temporary and outsourced workers, hallmarks of current times. Despite scholars' growing attention, it is not easy to find consensus on the concept of trust [1]. In this work, we opted for Karsenty's definition [2], who understands trust as "a feeling of serenity that emanates from the relationship with an actor on whom we rely in a given situation, hoping that he or she will take care of our interests," which is based on three general dimensions of trust: affective, cognitive, and relational.

S. Jin et al. (Eds.): IEA 2024, SSDI 39, pp. 342–347, 2025.
https://doi.org/10.1007/978-981-95-0211-0_53

One of the issues observed in studies about trust is its influence on developing cooperative relationships, especially in organizations [3, 4]. Cooperation between organizations refers to coordinated actions taken by partners to achieve desirable results mutually or individually [5]. This cooperation arises from the perception that a given objective cannot be achieved unilaterally. This awareness is a determining factor in cooperative behavior on an individual and organizational level [6]. Such is the case with the offshore well construction industry, a collective activity of high technological complexity, great uncertainty, and high risk in the development of each operation, which depends on cooperation between different parties and specialties.

In recent decades, technological advances have led to significant changes in the oil and gas industry [7]. Naturally, many work activities have undergone significant transformation. In the context of offshore well construction rigs, we find the company man, known in Brazil as the well inspector [8]. The company man is the contractor's representative on-site and a strong vector for relationships of trust on board, which is fundamental for cooperation between the parties and for safety in this high-risk industry [9]. However, with increasingly discretionary contracts, a collegiate decision-making system, and increasing bureaucracy regarding compliance and evidence gathering, the role of this worker, whose demeanor strongly interferes with the dynamics of trust and cooperation on board, is being called into question. Therefore, this study aims to present, based on case studies, how the role of the company man positively or negatively affects the relationships of trust in the day-to-day operations of well construction, considering the uncertainties and conflicts of interest between different teams and companies, thus influencing the performance, cooperation, and safety of operations.

2 Methods

The intervention method employed in this study is based on Rocha [10], and it uses a quantitative and qualitative approach to diagnose the level of maturity of the safety culture and foster its development. For this study, researchers selected the population of an offshore drillship that had been operating as an outsourced contractor in Brazil for more than two years. During the research, the drillship was considered one of the best vessels in terms of overall performance assessment. Data was collected through four boardings between March and December 2023, totaling 18 days on board. In this study, we considered the workers who serve as company men and those who are part of the drillship team. In the quantitative stage, homogeneous groups of workers, distinguished mainly by hierarchical level, were asked to answer a customized questionnaire. A 42-question questionnaire was answered by 223 respondents (95% confidence interval and 2% margin of error). The questionnaire sought to survey the workforce's perception, covering different themes. The study's qualitative assessment involved interviews and focus groups to explore the central issues identified in the previous phase and understand the different perspectives on safety, thus recognizing the diversity of points of view. As a result, charts illustrating the scenario captured in the quantitative phase were presented, and the workers' experiences guided the discussions. A total of 60 drillship workers took part in the focus group stage (divided into 16 sessions). Although the questionnaire and the focus group sessions allowed different issues to be raised, this study's results are limited to the findings concerning the trust and cooperation issue, a critical point for operations. The material presented here is based mainly on data from the Human and Organizational Factors of Industrial Safety research project, an ongoing four-year study in the Brazilian oil industry.

3 Results

We present: 1) a contextualization of the work organization of offshore well construction; 2) a quantitative result as a basis for the discussion on trust and cooperation; and 3) the selection of empirical material (cases) presented in the focus groups and related to the subject of this article.

3.1 Quantitative Results

From the first contacts, it became clear that the relationship with the contractor, mediated by the company man, was a key point for the dynamics that interfere with on-board relationships. Figures 1 and 2 show the results of two questions directly related to the role of these professionals.

28	The Company man is consistent when it comes to safety, as he acts according to what he says.				
GROUP	STRONGLY DISAGREE	DISAGREE MORE THAN AGREE	AGREE MORE THAN DISAGREE	STRONGLY AGREE	GROUP SCORE
Company man team	0	0	8	21	9,08
Drillship Management	1	1	5	1	5,83
Drillship Supervisors	3	9	17	10	6,24
Drillship Operators	12	22	55	48	6,72
EHS team	2	4	3	1	4,33
TOTAL	18	36	88	81	6,80

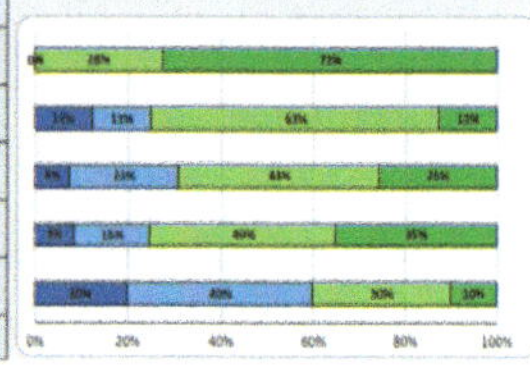

Fig. 1. Item 28 of the customized questionnaire answered by the workforce.

32	The Company men on board work cooperatively with the unit's team.				
GROUP	STRONGLY DISAGREE	DISAGREE MORE THAN AGREE	AGREE MORE THAN DISAGREE	STRONGLY AGREE	GROUP SCORE
Company man team	0	0	5	24	9,43
Drillship Management	1	3	4	0	4,58
Drillship Supervisors	1	8	23	7	6,41
Drillship Operators	9	27	59	42	6,59
EHS team	3	1	4	2	5,00
TOTAL	14	39	95	75	6,79

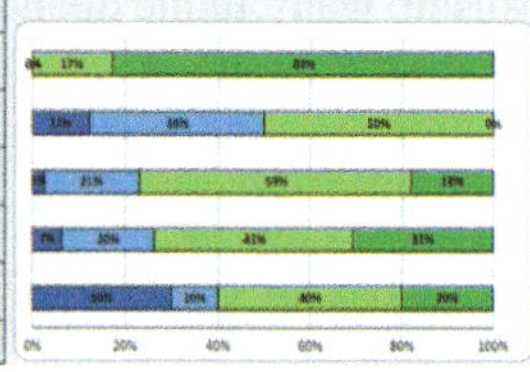

Fig. 2. Item 32 of the customized questionnaire answered by the workforce.

While the first question deals with the professionals' consistency regarding safety, the second deals with the participants' perception of how cooperative these professionals are daily. One point that stands out is that, in both questions, the company men's perception of their attitude is the opposite of that of the workers. They see themselves as highly consistent and cooperative (9.80 indicates strongly agreeing with the statement). At the same time, the workforce indicates a critical perception of their performance (scores ranged between 4 and 6, indicating a divergent perception of this crucial player's attitude). Perception conflicts are related to heterogeneity in professional posture, arbitrary and nebulous contractual sanctions, and pressures in negotiations related to adverse weather conditions, which were constantly mentioned during the research team's contact with workers.

3.2 Qualitative Results

The answers to the questions were presented in the focus groups. The different groups were able to explain their perspectives through verbal statements and cases, which were then explored in greater depth. The analysis of the material collected first reveals the existence of mistrust, which negatively affects cooperation. This mistrust is reciprocal and is part of the feeling that separates "them and us." If, on the one hand, company men do not seem to trust the information provided, especially when it involves stopping the operation, on the other hand, requests or remarks are always received as mistrust or a way of pressuring the operation to resume. Once, the operation was stopped because the wind exceeded the procedural limit. In response, the company man asked a safety professional to take measurements in the area every 30 min. He had to climb a few floors of the facility in the rain to execute this task. This situation was perceived as a way of forcing a resumption or even punishing the workers for the interruption. Those measurements were reported to the onshore team, who pressed the company man to resume operations as soon as possible. However, this information was not widely acknowledged by the workforce. The constant suspicion and punitive behavior (with monetary sanctions for poor performance) are part of the relationship on board. These elements are coupled with the high discretionary power of the contractor in assigning penalties (reduction of per diems or low-performance scores), often without the necessary transparency to restore trust and, consequently, cooperation and timely organizational learning. One case illustrating this difficulty was the event of a damaged hydraulic line as it ran through a pulley, resulting in more than 24 h off the per diem rate. It was unclear whether the responsibility lay with the drillship operating company that assembled the pulley or the specialist company hired to certify the assembly. After the event, the pylons were found to be bent, which could have had something to do with the damage. The issue was "settled" by holding the rig crew responsible without clarifying the event. Considering that the drillship's per diem rate was the highest among the providers, company men and drillship workers stated that these "50/50 balls" always fall on the ship's operating company. A few months later, another pulley from the same company – equally damaged – was boarded on the drillship, indicating that, once the drillship was held responsible, the specialist provider did not review its process. It was noted that opportunities for cooperation beyond contractual terms – when they occur – have resulted in gains in performance and safety. However, fragile trust relationships are obstacles to developing these positive experiences.

4 Discussion

Cooperation can be classified as horizontal, vertical, or transversal when considering the actors' relative position and their heterogeneity: horizontal cooperation is between peers; vertical cooperation is between actors at different hierarchical levels; transversal cooperation is between actors with different functions such as product/customer, producer/maintainer, etc. [11]. A range of asymmetries can cross these configurations: wage labor subordination and antagonistic and agonistic contradictions [12]. Thus, although the company men's presence is an admittedly important measure for prevention, their potential is hampered by the difficulties of building cooperative relationships between people and organizations separated by unequal relationships – in the case of providers and contractors, the latter having the power to supervise and penalize. Whether the contractual clauses are fairly applied according to the parties will depend on how the company man acts in everyday situations that involve assessing and assigning responsibility.

The feeling of unfairness comes from unclear penalties decided at the end of the process by the contract's commercial manager in direct negotiation with the provider's commercial managers. The on-board teams from both sides are not always made aware of the discussions that lead to a decision. However, even within this coercive organizational structure, there is still space for the company man's autonomy. They are constantly called upon—when faced with conflicting situations—to analyze and interpret the actual conditions of poor performance, such as the causes of equipment breakdowns or production stoppages due to adverse conditions, even when the weather parameters are within the contractual limits. This is where the rig team's perception of the difference in behavior between company men becomes more evident. The differences between the company men practices should, therefore, be the subject of more detailed analysis to move forward in building cooperation even in situations where there is a conflict of interests, moving from "antagonistic contradiction", when the actors relate to each other as enemies, to "agonic contradiction" when they cooperate while recognizing the conflicts and interests that separate them [12].

5 Conclusion

The company man's actions can affect trust and cooperation between the contractor (whom he represents) and the rig operator (provider). Different issues shape these actions, and many of them are organizational. Unless this practice is reflected upon, the relationship of trust between the parties tends to weaken, making it impossible to identify opportunities for cooperation, which can be a path to greater efficiency and safety in operations. This study's limitations include the difficulty of accessing the field and the need for studies related to this context.

We would like to thank the support of the Carlos Chagas Filho Research Support Foundation in the state of Rio de Janeiro (FAPERJ) (ref. 210.621/2019) and the financial support from the Human Resources Program of the National Agency of Petroleum, Natural Gas, and Biofuels (PRH-ANP) through R&D&I resources from ANP Resolution 50/2015.

References

1. Kramer, R.: Trust and distrust in organizations. Annu. Rev. Psychol. **50**, 569–598 (1999)
2. Karsenty, L.: Comment appréhender la confiance au travail? In: Karsenty, L. (ed.) La confiance au travail, pp. 13–51. Octarès Editions, Toulouse (2013)
3. Morgan, R.M., Hunt, S.D.: The commitment-trust theory of relationship marketing. J. Mark. **58**(3), 20–38 (1994)
4. Conchie, S.M., Donald, I.J.: The role of distrust in offshore safety performance. Risk Anal. **26**(5), 1151–1159 (2006)
5. Rindfleisch, A.: Organizational trust and interfirm cooperation. Mark. Lett. **11**(1), 81–95 (2000)
6. Udy, S.H.: Organization of work. Human Relations Area Files Press, New Haven (1959)
7. Ramstad, L.S., Halvorsen, K., Holte, E.A.: Implementing integrated planning. In: Rosendahl, T., Hepsø, V. (eds.) Integrated Operations in the Oil and Gas Industry: Sustainability and Capability Development, pp. 171–190 (2013)
8. Rappini, S.G., Neto, F.A.D.: Company man, 1st edn. Synergia editora, Rio de Janeiro (2020)
9. Skarholt, K., Lamvik, G.: Reversing the trend through collaboration in the petroleum industry. In: Haugen, S. (ed.) Safety and Reliability, pp. 279–286. CRC Press, Trondheim (2018)
10. Rocha, R., Duarte, F., Lima, F., Mercado, M., Araujo, A., Garotti, L., Campos, M.: Framework for the assessment of the safety culture in the oil and gas industry. Int. J. Occup. Saf. Ergon. **30**(1), 224–237 (2023)
11. Du Tertre, C.: Économie servicielle et travail. Travailler. **29**(1), 29–64 (2013)
12. Mouffe, C.: Agonistics. Verso, Londres (2013)

Building an Operational Experience Feedback in a Thermal Power Plant

Vitor Fernando S. G. Pereira[1](✉), Mateus Abraçado[1], Raoni Rocha[2], and Adson Resende[3]

[1] Federal University of Rio de Janeiro, Rio de Janeiro, RJ 21941-853, Brazil
vitor.pereira@pep.ufrj.br

[2] Federal University of Ouro Preto (UFOP), Ouro Preto, MG 35.400-000, Brazil

[3] Federal University of Minas Gerais (UFMG), Belo Horizonte, MG 31270-901, Brazil

Abstract. The theme Operational Experience Feedback (OEF) has been discussed in safety literature for decades, and authors have presented studies on how knowledge management allows organizations to understand how they collect, manage, and use the knowledge they develop, and discuss different approaches, such as learning by practice, lessons learned systems, and experience feedback cycles. This study presents the process of an OEF carried out in collaboration with the workforce at a thermal power plant. In this process, discussion spaces, tools and resources already used were identified, and the intervention was to systematize the process, improve existing tools, create new tools and assign responsibilities to ensure the closure of the cycle: input, processing, monitoring, and feedback. A general map was developed, identifying the main limits of this process and a new round of meetings allowed the co-construction of the unit new OEF instrument. Once implemented, it can contribute to a proactive organization, acting preventively in seeking operational continuity, contributing to forming a cohesive and well-trained team.

Keywords: Feedback · Safety · Debate Spaces

1 Introduction

Operational Experience Feedback (OEF) mechanisms are essential for organizational learning, as they identify and propagate relevant information from the field for the purpose of decision-making. In this respect, OEF focuses on analyzing the origins and ramifications of incidents in order to extract lessons and formulate improvement actions [1]. Although there is a wealth of knowledge on the concept of a learning culture, its implementation is considered to be a challenge [2].

Various forms of OEF are mentioned in literature, including the analysis of incidents and accidents, the analysis of day-to-day production difficulties, attention to alerts issued by workers and feedback from staff representative bodies [3]. In this respect, learning from events is fundamental to effective safety management, where retrospective and prospective analysis of events plays a complementary role in identifying and preventing future accidents [4].

S. Jin et al. (Eds.): IEA 2024, SSDI 39, pp. 348–353, 2025.
https://doi.org/10.1007/978-981-95-0211-0_54

Schon [5] highlights the importance of reflection during work, emphasizing the capacity to think and make decisions while in action and facing complex situations. According to Foguem et al. [6], in an industrial context of greater integration and interoperability, organizations face increasing challenges in analyzing and resolving everyday problems. The author also argues that effective management of organizational knowledge is central to the success of OEF, but encounters two central challenges: capitalization and exploitation of knowledge. Capitalization involves reusing stored knowledge to perform new tasks, while exploitation disseminates knowledge to benefit current practices and the development of future professionals. Finally, he explains that existing models in literature are limited by an imprecise vocabulary and a lack of formal tools for a thorough analysis.

Dekker [7] highlights the importance of feedback in promoting safe behaviour and identifying the underlying causes of risky behaviour. In addition, he emphasizes the need to go beyond traditional accident investigation, considering real day-to-day work, near-miss situations and operational success for a more complete understanding of the system. Finally, the author points out that this information is a fundamental resource for creating more robust and flexible processes and monitoring and reviewing risk models. In this way, the organization would have resources to respond to reality, anticipate potential risks and have the capacity to learn from the facts.

The issue of reluctance to report events is discussed by Reason [2] and Sandberg and Albrechtsen [8], who identify reasons such as fear of repercussions and under-reporting of less serious incidents. To encourage participation, it is crucial to create an environment of trust and demonstrate the value of workers' contributions. In this sense, Rocha et al. [10] stress the importance of engaging all levels of the organization in the development of effective OEF systems. They propose discussion spaces as a tool to promote collective reflection on action at work, not only for safety issues, but also for improving workers' performance and well-being.

The aim of this article is therefore to describe the process of jointly constructing an experience feedback device in a thermal power plant, focusing on the main tools used and the forms of interaction with the workforce. In this process, potential spaces for discussion and tools already used as resources for gathering information and feedback have been identified. The idea behind the work was to systematize the process, thereby improving existing tools and assigning responsibilities to guarantee the closing of the cycle: input, processing, follow-up and feedback.

2 Methods

The intervention at the thermoelectric plant was conducted using a safety culture assessment approach inspired by Rocha et al. [9]. This is a hybrid approach, combining quantitative and qualitative data. Initially, homogeneous groups were formed to answer a personalized questionnaire, assessing the maturity of the safety culture. The quantitative analysis generated data on the level of agreement in relation to different questions. At the qualitative stage, on the other hand, discussion groups were conducted to explore deeper insights and perspectives, focusing on the workers' personal experiences and valuing the diversity of points of view.

The results were revealed using radar charts, showing maturity in various areas and highlighting the importance of sharing practices and values in building a safety culture. Based on the data obtained in the analysis and diagnosis, a number of actions were defined for the unit, aimed at developing this safety culture over time.

In this unit in particular, one of the plans prioritized in collaboration between the unit and the research team concerned the construction of a OEF mechanism. In this process, ten specific meetings were held with representatives of each homogeneous group in the unit, which allowed for the construction of perception charts for each group, identifying the current collection, treatment, monitoring and feedback mechanisms that are recognized and used. This dynamic was carried out through face-to-face meetings lasting an average of 2 h, in which the representatives, together with the researchers, set up on a physical pasteboard their representation of the current system using post-its.

A general map of the unit was then drawn up, allowing for identification of the main limits of this process, which was subsequently validated by the unit. Finally, a new round of meetings allowed for the joint construction of the thermoelectric plant's new experience feedback mechanism, formalizing the instruments and assigning responsibilities for collection, processing, follow-up and feedback. The Fig. 1 shows a summary of the steps followed in this methodology.

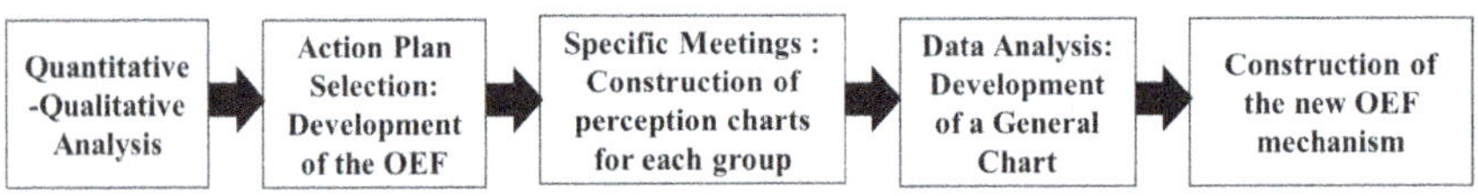

Fig. 1. Methodology.

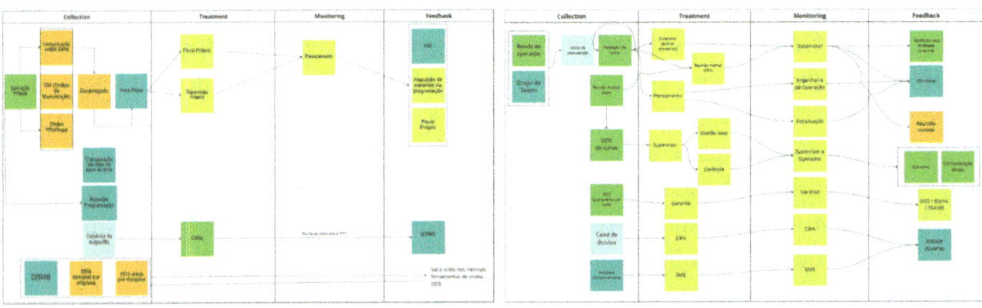

Figs. 2 and 3. OEF table for the groups of maintenance and proximity leadership of the unit.

For the purpose of demonstrating the process of building the OEF mechanism, two homogeneous groups, Maintenance and SMS (Safety Management System), were used as a reference to show how (1) the different points of view were identified and worked on to build the general framework and (2) how this process was able to detail the restrictions on the fluency of the feedback (return on experience) process, from the gathering of information, through to decision-making in the relevant area and back to the operation.

3 Results

3.1 Construction of the OEF Tables

Of the ten tables jointly constructed together with the homogeneous groups, two have been selected for this article. These are the maintenance group (see Figs. 2 and 3) and the proximity leadership group (see Figs. 2 and 3). Looking at the tables, even though the names of the devices have not been translated to avoid identifying the companies, it is clear by contrast that the recognition of OEF devices differs between the groups. In the process of constructing the tables, carried out by the workforce itself, it was possible to observe how the tools are recognized and even constructed in a particular way by each of the groups. This produces a diversity that, on the one hand, isolates the working groups in the unit due to particular solutions that cater only to the group in question and, on the other hand, is caused by the absence of a single tool that can be shared by the entire workforce, which would produce greater scope for exchanging experiences and records across the entire production unit.

3.2 Construction of the General Table

From the tables containing the mechanisms currently used for OEF by each homogeneous group, it was possible to establish the limits of the current return on experience format in which the participating teams show: A) hesitation in using the tools available in the unit, due to lack of confidence attributed mainly to the scarcity of feedback; B) fear of being blamed when reporting situations of accidents or irregularities; C) lack of awareness of the processes for handling and monitoring the data collected; D) accumulation of functions in the same instrument; E) absence of short-term feedback that allows acceleration of the decision-making process in the face of impasses that arise on the performance of tasks.

Based on this data, it was possible to draw up a general table, where the operating and management mechanisms are separated (see Fig. 4), and where again the difference in items existing for operation and management is visible.

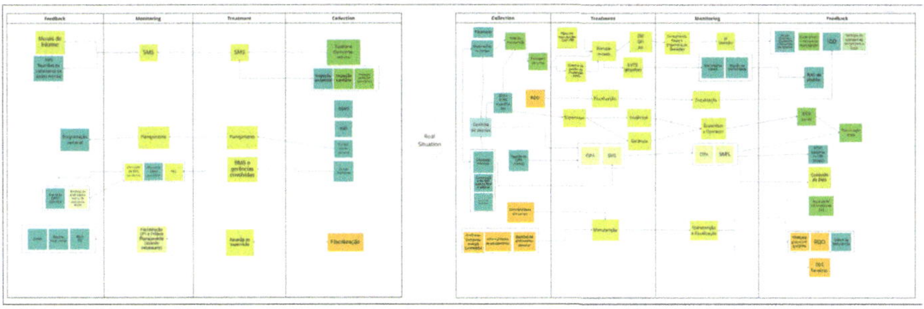

Fig. 4. Unit OEF general table.

3.3 Construction of New OEF Mechanism

It was therefore possible to define a new OEF system structured by hierarchical levels, based on the establishment of responsibilities, periodic evaluation and feedback meetings, control spreadsheets for the different organizational levels, all of these tools aimed at guaranteeing the complete cycle of handling demands from the field.

The hierarchical levels were divided into three tiers: Local Level with the Operational Teams and Supervisors; Intermediate Management Level with the Sector Managers; and Systemic Management Level which includes the Plant Managers together with EHS (Environment, Health and Safety). In addition, a multidisciplinary OEF group was set up, with one representative from EHS, one from Operations and one from Maintenance, with the aim of concentrating the demands received via data collection and carrying out the first stage of filtering and forwarding the demands received.

For this purpose, a form is made available both physically and via QR Code in which workers can report significant events that may be: a situation for improvement or innovation, an alert of an incident or irregularity, or a problem (difficulty, disturbance, failure or doubt). These data are then organized by the multidisciplinary group in an excel spreadsheet, which allows each level to act on their demands, either to resolve them or to forward them to the higher level.

4 Discussion and Conclusions

The tables drawn up together with the workers have made it possible to identify the different points of view on the information processing system underway at the unit. The joint construction of the new system with the workforce has proved to be important in the quest for the tool's effectiveness, as it highlighted the different perceptions and uses of the current instruments among the workforce. This intervention model has been essential for recognizing the current limits of the system and building a single model that recognizes these perspectives, adopts what has been working and promotes conscious intervention via the proposed new OEF tool. In this way, the practice developed aims to go beyond the limits of traditional safety studies, since it promotes learning and overcoming challenges such as organizational silence, creating a space for dialogue and cooperation.

The joint meetings have led to a shared definition of the tools used, thereby increasing commitment and the levels of acceptance of the system by the workforce, which are key to the smooth running of the device and to the unit's progress towards a more mature safety culture. When implemented, the OEF system can contribute to a proactive organization that acts preventively in the search for operational continuity in a more developed and mature safety environment.

We would like to thank the support of the Carlos Chagas Filho Research Support Foundation in the state of Rio de Janeiro (FAPERJ) (ref. 210.621/2019) and the financial support from the Human Resources Program of the National Agency of Petroleum, Natural Gas, and Biofuels (PRH-ANP) through R&D&I resources from ANP Resolution 50/2015.

References

1. Rocha, R., Daniellou, F., Mollo, V.: O Retorno de Experiência e o lugar dos Espaços de Discussão sobre o Trabalho: Uma Construção Possível e Eficaz / The return of experience and the place of the discussion spaces about the work: a possible and effective construction. Trabalho Educação. **23**(1), 61–74 (2014)
2. Reason, J.: Managing the Risks of Organizational Accidents. Routledge, London (1997)
3. Daniellou, F., Simard, M., Boissières, I.: Facteurs humains et organisationnels de la sécurité industrielle : un état de l'art Numéro 2010-02 des Cahiers de la Sécurité Industrielle. Institut pour une Culture de Sécurité Industrielle, Toulouse, France (2010)
4. Lundberg, J., Rollenhagen, C., Hollnagel, E.: What you find is not always what you fix—how other aspects than causes of accidents decide recommendations for remedial actions. Accid. Anal. Prev. **42**(6), 2132–2139 (2010)
5. Schön, D.A.: The Reflective Practitioner: How Professionals Think in Action. Routledge (2017)
6. Foguem, B.K., Coudert, T., Béler, C., Geneste, L.: Knowledge formalization in experience feedback processes: an ontology-based approach. Comput. Ind. **59**(7), 694–710 (2008)
7. Dekker, S.: Foundations of Safety Science: A Century of Understanding Accidents and Disasters. CRC Press, Boca Raton (2019)
8. Sandberg, E., Albrechtsen, E.: A study of experience feedback from reported unwanted occurrences in a construction company. Saf. Sci. **107**, 46–54 (2018)
9. Rocha, R., Duarte, F., Lima, F., Mercado, M., Araujo, A., Garotti, L., Campos, M.: Framework for the assessment of the safety culture in the oil and gas industry. Int. J. Occup. Saf. Ergon. **30**(1), 224–237 (2023)
10. Rocha, R., Mollo, V., Daniellou, F.: Contributions and conditions of structured debates on work on safety construction. Saf. Sci. **113**, 192–199 (2019)

The Contribution of Permits-To-Work for Safety

Vitor Fernando S. G. Pereira[1](✉), Lucas Chrisostimo Farah[1], Mariana Martins[1], Rodrigo Arcuri[2], and Adson Resende[3]

[1] Federal University of Rio de Janeiro (UFRJ), Rio de Janeiro, RJ 21941-853, Brazil
vitor.pereira@pep.ufrj.br
[2] Fluminense Federal University (UFF), Niterói, RJ 24210-240, Brazil
[3] Federal University of Minas Gerais (UFMG), Belo Horizonte, MG 31270-901, Brazil

Abstract. This article describes the role of Permit-to-Work (PTW) as a safety tool, highlighting its limitations based on users' experiences in real work situations. This research was developed within the context of an intervention project conducted using a quantitative-qualitative methodology to assess the level of safety culture in an oil and gas industry, and after a diagnosis promote interventions to increase the safety culture. In this context the specific objective of this article is to explore the different logics of PTW used in those units and develop a critical analysis of its current functioning in two studied units of an oil and gas industry. The effectiveness of the document in promoting safety is questioned when viewed in light of the decisions made in day-to-day work, revealing a delicate balance between quality and quantity in operational routines. Based on the data obtained, it was possible to discuss the key concepts as: partial logic of use, collective strategies to manage the PTW and the bureaucracy involved in preparing and using the tool, in the PTW process, aiming to indicate pathways for effective changes.

Keywords: Permit-to-Work · Safety · Bureaucracy · Blaming

1 Introduction

The Permit-to-Work (PTW) system plays an important role in current industrial safety management systems. It is a regulated and everyday practice in facilities operations and maintenance. The importance of this system has been highlighted over the past decades, during which large-scale accidents have shown the trade-off between production and safety [1]. After the Piper Alpha accident, the Cullen report conducted an extensive investigation and formally criticized the safety management system of the platform operator, highlighting failures in the PTW system [2]. Other accidents, such as BP Grangemouth (UK, 1987), Shell Port Eduoard Herriot Depot (France, 1987), Phillips Chemical Company (USA, 1989), and Motiva Enterprises LLC (USA, 2001), reinforce critical aspects of this system including the importance of drawing greater attention to changes in workplace during the execution of tasks, the essential monitoring performed by safety supervisors and specialists, the failures in the records, the weakness in internal communication, and the shortcomings in the risk assessment procedures [3].

S. Jin et al. (Eds.): IEA 2024, SSDI 39, pp. 354–359, 2025.
https://doi.org/10.1007/978-981-95-0211-0_55

The Health and Safety Executive (HSE) [4], Britain's national workplace health and safety regulator, defines the PTW system as a formal and registered process to control potentially hazardous work. In addition, the PTW system is a means of communication between local managers, supervisors, plant operators, and those performing hazardous work. The PTW system presents some operational challenges to achieve its goals, such as the adaptability of the planned PTW to the reality of the field context, which enables different teams to have the same knowledge about the work, its risks, and the current situation [5]. Other important features include the effective adoption of the document by the executing workers [6] and good decision coordination and information sharing [7]. The work generated by this process is another important issue, and HSE [4] states that the permit issuers need sufficient time to verify the workplace conditions.

The PTW follows the growing demand for modern control in organizations, which has spread through industries and has increased bureaucracy, as pointed out by Dekker [8]. This leads to "super-specified" bureaucratic processes, which are misdirected and generally large, which, in turn, may have lost connection with the actual work to be performed. Makin and Winder [9] highlighted that safety systems are important in risk identification. However, if poorly executed, they can create an environment known as paper-only system. Another issue is the growing accountability of workers for their own safety [10], with increasing importance given to the PTW system and its volume related to blame attribution within the units. In addition, when conducting this study, a persistent dissatisfaction of workers with the PTW system has arisen in the field. In general, PTW is related to bureaucratization, work overload, accountability of workers, and distancing from PTW's main goal of promoting safety.

Thus, this study aims to identify the main characteristics of the current PTW systems in industrial production units and highlight their impact on safety. In order to do so, we apply a cross-sectional research design encompassing a quantitative and qualitative analysis methodology to two operational units in O&G. From findings we discuss possible interventions to transform this practice.

2 Methods

This study was performed within an intervention project that used quantitative and qualitative methods to assess the safety culture in the oil and gas industry, as described by Rocha et al. [11]. This project led to several intervention actions with the participating units, focusing on developing new PTW systems. A case study was conducted following the six stages proposed by Yin [12].

In the planning stage, an exploratory and descriptive case study was designed, and the oil and gas company selected the units participating in the intervention project. In the project stage, a literature review was performed to explore the research topic, and thermoelectric and warehousing were defined as the participating units since the intervention project showed a demand linked to the development of PTW systems. The preparation stage determined that evidence collection would be based on the Ergonomic Work Analysis (EWA), which is suitable since it helps to understand the work and the usage patterns of the PTW document.

In the evidence collection stage, ethnographic fieldwork encompassing direct observations of common work situations and interviews with workers were performed [13].

Data collection was guided by demand and followed three main steps: (1) investigating how the organization works, (2) understanding the PTW system, and (3) observing the systematic activities, followed by open-ended interviews and formulation of analyses and insights. Around 80 virtual meetings with the participating units were conducted between 2021 and 2023. In the qualitative phase, discussion groups were conducted to investigate the experiences faced by workers. We conducted 26 meetings with 182 workers from the warehouse (out of 501) and 14 meetings with 69 workers from the thermoelectric plant (out of 179). In addition, on-site visits were performed to monitor the activities, spanning seven days in the warehouse and 11 days in the thermoelectric plant, with about 10 h each day. In these visits, the activities related to PTW were observed. Then, two cases were selected from the 16 initially studied. The first case corresponded to a round with a production operator responsible for releasing the PTWs in the thermoelectric plant. The second case included the monitoring of an electrical maintenance service in the warehouse. Open-ended interviews complemented these systematic observations to broaden understanding of the challenges and problems workers face in their tasks, using an approach known as self-confrontation [14]. Then, initial evidence was analyzed based on theoretical propositions to deepen the analysis and diagnosis of actual situations by comparing field observations and interviews of workers with the literature. Finally, the report stage listed the results, presented in the next section.

3 Results

First, we present two situations related to the PTW system, one at the thermoelectric plant and the other at the warehouse. Then, some limits and usage patterns were identified in this process.

3.1 Thermoelectric Plant – Operation: Releasing PTWs

In the thermoelectric plant case study, shift operators play a crucial role in the PTW process. They are responsible for starting up the generating units, performing unit rounds, and overseeing the release and completion of the PTW in the field. Most maintenance services occur during the day, and three operators are in the field per-forming these activities in the entire area. Figure 1 presents the log of one of the opera-tors responsible for the water treatment plant and four turbines.

This log allows us to observe several places the operator visited and highlights many interruptions and brief interactions related to service release. According to the operators, there are more than 20 PTWs on some days (approximately one every 36 min). Many of them must be closed, in addition to 20 PTWs that the operator must open. They claimed, "There is no time left for the technical part, just putting out fires. There is a high demand for little workforce in the maintenance and operation services."

3.2 Warehouse – Maintenance: Light Bulb Changing Activity

The studied warehouse stores material to be transported to the oil production platforms. The workforce in the unit is mostly outsourced. In this case study, we observed the

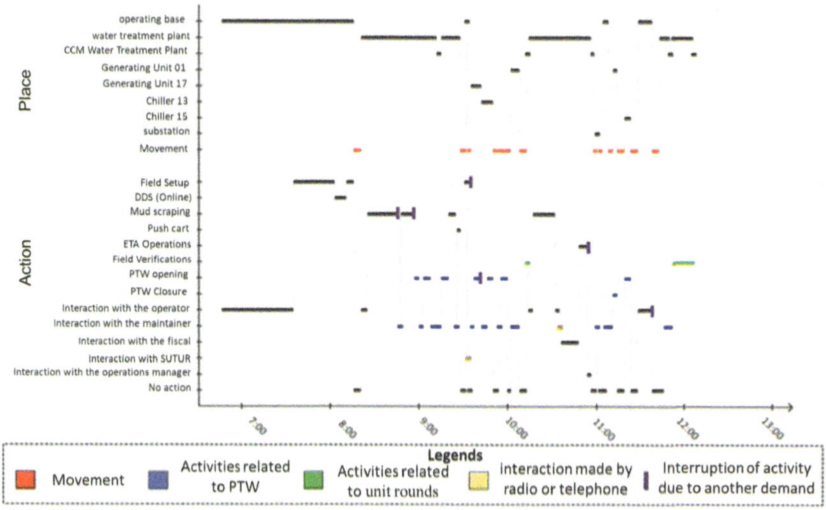

Fig. 1. Operator log – Morning (Pereira, 2022).

process of changing light bulbs in the warehouse since the workers criticized this activity in the group discussion. They claimed, "A simple light bulb change can take up to 3 hours." On the monitoring day, the PTW issuer, along with the PTW and risk assessment, reported that the team was already in the workplace. On arriving at the workplace, the two executors responsible for the activity were waiting for the inspector to sign the documents. The signing process was quick. The executors reviewed and signed the documents with little interaction during the process. When discussing the case, the electrical technician mentioned that the activity was quickly released. However, in analyzing the situation, we can observe one hour and a half between the start of the team shift and the start of service, which was the first of the day. The technician said that this delay is often caused by several interruptions, mainly from the inspectors or Warehouse staff from other areas.

This case study also investigated the electronic system for issuing PTW before the service. Following a filling procedure, we can observe that it is an electronic linear checklist in which the technician fills in the required information. The little integration between documents (e.g., service order, previous service documents), disorganization in the document versions, and difficulty in updating workers' records are some issues found in this filling procedure.

3.3 PTW Limits

Based on the case study and the group discussions with the workers, we can recognize characteristics of how PTW works in the units and identify the development dynamics, PTW issuance and release in the field, and maintenance service completion. Thus, we can identify some limits, such as A) divergences in the perception of the activity risk, B) high bureaucratic demand in the document preparation process, C) dynamic work context contrasting with a document lacking flexibility, D) excessive simultaneous release of activities, and E) perception of document use for accountability of workers. In addition, we can observe some partial usage patterns by the main actors in the PTW dynamics: I) the developer: the PTW electronic system user who inserts the relevant information; II) the executors: the maintenance workers who will first be in contact with the activities through the document, which must contain the required information and allow a discussion with the field technician; and III) the health and safety specialist: those who seek to answer the legal safety requirements in the unit and identify potential risks. These dynamics, to a certain extent, have distortions that affect the tasks of the executors and contribute to the PTW bureaucratization, distorting the original purpose of one of the main tools in the safety system.

4 Discussion and Conclusions

The results presented are from two units selected for additional studies on the subject, however, similar issues were identified in 17 other units participating in the project. Such as: refineries, drill ships, platforms, and others, which will allow us to advance in the generalization of problems and solutions. The PTW and its adjacent systems are part of a complex process, involving the participation of various actors in the organization, and over time have assumed several functions. This convergence of purposes and different patterns employed simultaneously under the same system sometimes increases the complexity of the document, leading to excessive bureaucracy. Each actor decides to add a certain characteristic or content to the process or the PTW itself. This decision is certainly relevant and linked to its interaction with the PTW. However, how this decision affects the activity of other user actors may not be proportional. It may even have a negative impact. In many situations, the workers perceived changes as something negative. The prescriptive nature of the system and information about constant rework due to the current model of issuing and processing PTW consume valuable resources from workers and diminish the relevance of the system as a safety-oriented practice. This way, the identified limits indicate the risks of, in the current format, PTW being a process paper-system only, impacting safety in industrial production units. In addition, using the document for accountability of workers shows a lack of trust within the organizational environment and creates an environment of mistrust around the PTW or its connection to this singular purpose, blame attribution.

PTW document is acknowledged by all who recognize its importance for safety and see it as an opportunity for reflection and prevention of accidents and incidents. However, the current process is performed in a manner that results in a high workload, which does not align with the benefits of PTW usage. The effectiveness of the PTW is questioned when analyzing the decision-making in day-to-day work. It reveals a delicate balance between the quality and quantity of operational routines. Based on the data, we elaborated some proposals for transformations. The overload of various functions in a single document and system is evident; in this case, modularization may reduce irrelevant information at certain times. In addition, the current issuing system may potentially become an action support tool rather than just an electronic linear checklist. Studies of the same nature continue in other units on the use of electronic PT, helping in the modularization and better distribution of document functions.

We would like to thank the support of the Carlos Chagas Filho Research Support Foundation in the state of Rio de Janeiro (FAPERJ) (ref. 210.621/2019) and the financial support from National Agency of Petroleum (PRH-ANP).

References

1. Mearns, K.J.: Safety leadership and human and organisational factors (HOF)—where do we go from here? In: Human and Organisational Factors: Practices and Strategies for a Changing World, pp. 15–23 (2020)
2. Swuste, P., Groeneweg, J., Van Gulijk, C., Zwaard, W., Lemkowitz, S.: Safety management systems from Three Mile Island to Piper Alpha, a review in English and Dutch literature for the period 1979 to 1988. Saf. Sci. **107**, 224–244 (2018)
3. Atherton, J., Gil, F.: Incidents That Define Process Safety. Wiley, Hoboken, NJ (2008)
4. HSE: Guidance on Permit-To-Work Systems: A Guide for Petroleum, Chemical and Allied Industries, 1st edn. Health and Safety Executive (2005)
5. de Andrade, J. G.: O processo de permissão para trabalho: entre a eficiência e a segurança nas plataformas de petróleo. Orientador: Duarte, F. J. C. M. Dissertação (mestrado) - UFRJ/COPPE/ Programa de Engenharia de Produção, Rio de Janeiro (2016)
6. Ramiro, J.S., Aísa, P.B.: Risk reduction in operation and maintenance. In: Risk Analysis and Reduction in the Chemical Process Industry, pp. 283–313 (1998)
7. Karsenty, L., Lacoste, M.: Comunicação e trabalho. In: Falzon, P. (ed.) Ergonomia, pp. 193–206. Blucher, São Paulo (2007)
8. Dekker, S.: Foundations of Safety Science: A Century of Understanding Accidents and Disasters. Routledge, London (2019)
9. Makin, A.M., Winder, C.: A new conceptual framework to improve the application of occupational health and safety management systems. Saf. Sci. **46**(6), 935–948 (2008)
10. Dekker, S.W.: The bureaucratization of safety. Saf. Sci. **70**, 348–357 (2014)
11. Rocha, R., Duarte, F., Lima, F., Mercado, M., Araujo, A., Garotti, L., Campos, M.: Framework for the assessment of the safety culture in the oil and gas industry. Int. J. Occup. Saf. Ergon. **30**(1), 224–237 (2023)
12. Yin, R.K.: Case Study Research: Design and Methods, vol. 5. Sage, Thousand Oaks, CA (2009)
13. Guérin, F., Kerguelen, A., Laville, A.: Compreender o trabalho para transformá-lo: a prática da ergonomia. Editora Blucher (2021)
14. Mollo, V., Falzon, P.: Auto-and allo-confrontation as tools for reflective activities. Appl. Ergon. **35**(6), 531–540 (2004)

Leveraging Activity Theory and Functional Modelling for Implementing Extended Reality in Design Reviews

Francisco Garcia Rivera[1](✉), Francesco Ferrise[2], and Massimo Panarotto[2]

[1] University of Skövde, Högskolevägen 1, 541 28 Skovde, Sweden
francisco.garcia.rivera@his.se
[2] Politecnico di Milano, Via Privata Giuseppe La Masa, 1, 20156 Milan, Italy
francesco.ferrise@polimi.it

Abstract. Effective communication and stakeholder collaboration are vital for successful design reviews. Traditionally reliant on physical mediums, design reviews now predominantly use digital 3D models for their flexibility and cost-effectiveness. Recent advancements in extended reality (XR) technology allow for immersive interactions with 3D models, enhancing spatial understanding. However, research often limits the choice to XR or flat screens, overlooking task-specific needs. This paper proposes a methodology using functional modeling and activity theory to assess XR's suitability for various design review tasks. By categorizing tasks and analyzing functionalities, it guides the optimal use of XR and flat screens, enhancing design review effectiveness. Future research will empirically validate and refine this framework to support hybrid design review protocols, improving collaborative design processes.

Keywords: Design Reviews · Functional Modeling · Activity Theory · Asymmetric Collaboration

1 Introduction

Effective communication and stakeholder collaboration is essential for successful design reviews (DRs) within the product development process (PDP) [1]. Visual support is vital in DRs, allowing participants to articulate their ideas, and discuss and evaluate design proposals [2, 3]. Traditionally, physical mediums like blueprints or physical prototypes were used as visual support in DRs. However, digital mediums involving 3D (often CAD models) models offer advantages in flexibility and cost-effectiveness and have become predominant [4].

Recent advancements in extended reality (XR) technology introduce new possibilities for visual support in DR [5]. XR allows participants to interact with 3D models in an immersive environment, allowing designers and especially non-technical stakeholders to gain an increased spatial understanding of the design proposals comparable to physical prototypes [6]. While research has explored the advantages of XR in DRs [7, 8], it has

S. Jin et al. (Eds.): IEA 2024, SSDI 39, pp. 360–366, 2025.
https://doi.org/10.1007/978-981-95-0211-0_56

often been presented as a choice between XR and flat screens. This creates a limitation, as different tasks within a DR may benefit from different visualization approaches.

The concept of asymmetric collaboration breaks this dichotomy by allowing each individual in the DRs to choose what visual support method may work better for them [9, 10]. However, due to its early stages, asymmetric collaboration still lacks guidelines for implementation in DRs. This paper proposes a methodology based on functional modeling and activity theory (AT) to assess the suitability of XR for various tasks within DRs. This framework guides the selection of visualization methods based on the specific tasks being undertaken within a DRs, and aims to be a decision-support tool for implementing XR in DRs.

2 AT, DRs, and XR

PDPs can be analyzed at various scales, ranging from the entire design process to the individual tasks and actions performed by designers. AT offers a framework for decomposing PDPs into three interrelated levels: activity systems, tasks, and actions [11, 12]. Actions represent the smallest measured unit of work that contributes to achieving immediate goals, for example: taking individual notes on specific design aspects or verbally providing feedback on a design feature. Tasks are collections of logically combined and organized actions aimed at achieving a specific objective. For instance, the task of "documenting a design review meeting" might involve performing a series of actions such as taking notes, capturing screenshots or recordings, and summarizing key discussion points. Activities represent broader goal-oriented various interconnected tasks. In the context of DRs, a complete DR activity could involve several interrelated tasks like presenting the design proposal, facilitating discussions about various aspects, or identifying design flaws or areas for improvement.

Cash et al. [12] expand on activity theory by introducing the concept of macro-scale, meso-scale, and micro-scale processes. Macro-scale processes encompass sequences of activities linked by a broader, overarching goal (e.g., the entire design development phase). Meso-scale processes involve sequences of tasks linked by a common objective within an activity system. Micro-scale processes refer to sequences of actions linked by a specific, immediate goal within a task (e.g., the individual actions involved in taking comprehensive notes during a DR discussion). Figure 1 illustrates this differentiation in the scales of PDP.

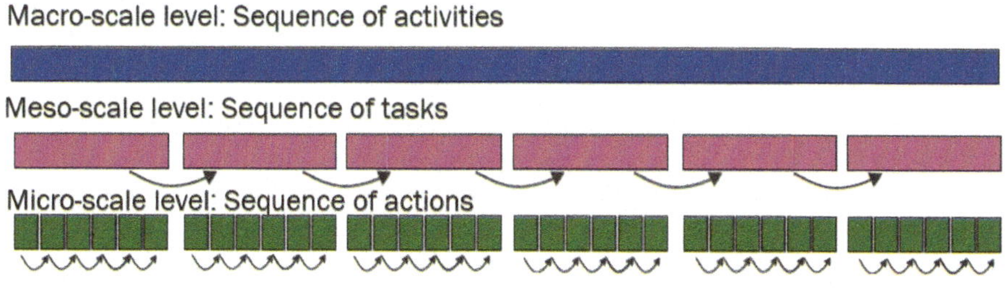

Fig. 1. Macro-scale, meso-scale, and micro-scale levels in PDP

Traditionally, discussions on XR implementation in DRs have often focused on the macro-scale level, examining its overall impact on the review process. However, a more nuanced approach involves analyzing DRs at the meso-scale level. At this level, it is possible to analyze what value XR implementation may bring to individual tasks, thereby allowing people to choose the devices that better fit their tasks. Analyzing the implementation of XR at a meso-scale level involves the use of asymmetric collaboration, as some participants will benefit more than others from the implementation of XR in performing their tasks. This paper will provide an approach that can be used as a decision-support tool, based on previous research on how XR can support different task categories, thereby providing a framework to guide the implementation of XR in DRs.

3 Task Categories in DRs

Although DRs vary from different organizations and products, the common tasks that are carried out to complete DRs can be categorized according to different criteria. One taxonomy that can be especially useful is [13]. One of the ways that process-oriented tasks can be categorized according to this taxonomy is summarized in Table 1.

Table 1. Process-oriented tasks

Task Category	Description	Objective
Descriptive Tasks (This/What/Where/Who/When)	Communications that convey design features or request more information. The goal is to form a common understanding of the design	Form a common understanding on design features
Explanatory Tasks (The Reason/So/Because)	Usually, in response to clarification requests. The goal is to clarify the rationale behind design features and considerations behind design choices	Explain the rationale behind design features and design choices
Requirement/Concern Checking Tasks (Concern/Hazard/Risk; Asking Questions)	Validate the design against requirements and concerns, which can be codes, standards, workflow requirements, or personal requirements. Outcomes can be satisfied, escalated, or unaddressed	Ensure the design meets standards, code, best practices, and usability
Explorative Tasks (How about/What if/Instead/Which/Recommend)	Activities and communications that explore alternatives to the current design solution. Focus on problem-solving and evaluating options	Explore, analyze, and compare alternative solutions to resolve an issue or unsatisfied requirement
Decision-Making Tasks (Select/Choose/Further Investigate)	Usually conclude the previous discussions and follow explorative activities. Make informed decisions by voting on options, prioritizing next steps, and approving or recommending revisions to the design proposal	Conclude discussions by deciding an action plan

Analyzing design review tasks using this taxonomy offers a powerful approach to understanding how XR can bring value to different tasks at a meso-scale level. This classification allows for a more nuanced it is possible to ng down DRs into categories it is possible to identify the functionalities required for each category. This analysis can highlight areas where XR is a better option than flat screens and vice versa.

4 Functional Analysis

Functional analysis is a technique that is often used in PDP. It was introduced by [14] and it consists of abstracting a product into its functions at different abstraction levels, and deciding what technologies or approaches can better solve those functions. By applying this analysis to the various DRs task categories (descriptive, explanatory, requirement/concern checking, exploratory, and decision-making), it is possible to determine which functionalities are needed in the different task categories, and what technologies can better solve those functionalities. In analyzing DRs, the functionalities defined by [15]) for DRs can be used.

In descriptive tasks, flat screens can be sufficient for presenting static information like layout and key features [9, 15–17]. In explanatory tasks, XR might be preferred as it allows walking through 3D models highlighting specific features, and enhancing communication of design rationale. Engineering aspects can be better supported by flat screens [8, 18]. In requirement/concern checking tasks XR can be better as it eases the visualization of spatial information and manipulation of objects, especially by non-technical users [19]. In exploratory tasks, XR offers a powerful environment for exploring design alternatives and facilitates discussions [5, 20–23]. In decision-making tasks, flat screens can be better as they are usually preferred for visualizing data through charts, tables, text, and graphs [24].

A more nuanced analysis involves considering extra factors, such as the objectives of the DR and the roles involved in it. As an example, the DRs studied by [25] of car interiors will be used as an example. These DRs aimed to validate aesthetic, engineering aspects, and ergonomics aspects. e involved roles were: Product Designer: Focuses on the aesthetic elements, ensuring the design meets visual and stylistic goals. The involved roles are designers, ergonomists, engineers, final users, and project managers (Table 2).

This example demonstrates how different roles in an automotive interior design review benefit from specific technologies based on their tasks. XR is particularly effective for tasks requiring immersive spatial understanding, such as those performed by the product designer and ergonomist. Flat screens are more suited for detailed documentation and technical evaluations, tasks typically handled by the engineer and project manager. Mixed technology usage ensures that final users can leverage both XR for interactive assessments and flat screens for detailed analysis and feedback. Functional analysis enables the determination of the most suitable technology for different roles in a design review. This approach enhances the efficiency and effectiveness of the review process, ensuring that each participant can optimally perform their tasks. By applying this method to the example of an automotive interior design review, we demonstrate its practical application and the potential for generalization to other design scenarios.

Table 2. Example of Functional analysis

Role	Primary Task Type	Functionalities	XR/Flat	Rationale
Product Designer	Descriptive/Exploratory	3D model representation, Lighting representation, Dimension representation	XR	Requires immersive interaction to visualize and modify aesthetic elements in real-time [8]
Ergonomist	Descriptive/Requirement Checking	3D model import, Digital human model representation, Dimension representation, Body-track navigation, Object position, Object scale	XR	Needs immersive environments to assess ergonomic factors and user interactions effectively [19]
Engineer	Requirement Checking/Explanatory	3D model import, Simulation and analysis tools, Dimension representation, Clearance/collision representation, Metadata transfer	Flat Screens	Engages in detailed technical evaluations requiring precise data representation and analysis [18]
Final Users/Customers	Descriptive/Exploratory	3D model representation, Document representation, Body-track navigation, Visual communication, Verbal communication	Mixed	XR for immersive experience of the interior and flat screens for documentation [5]
Project Manager	Decision-Making	Document import, Document representation, Report provision, Timeline visualisation, Verbal communication	Flat Screens	Needs to manage and review detailed reports, timelines, and overall project coordination effectively [24]

5 Discussion and Conclusion

This paper proposes a methodology to assess XR's suitability for various DR tasks using functional modeling and AT. By categorizing tasks and analyzing required functionalities, the paper provides a framework for implementing XR in DRs, supporting asymmetric collaboration and optimizing the use of XR and traditional flat screens. Future advances in the XR field will likely increase the suitability of XR to perform tasks related to documentation or management. However, for the foreseeable future, asymmetric collaboration seems to be the most suitable way to leverage the advantages of XR without hindering the design process or replacing established technologies where it is not needed. Future research will focus on finding empirical evidence of what devices are more suitable for different types of tasks through empirical and observational studies. This ongoing research will help refine the framework, ensuring that the use of XR and flat screens in DRs is both practical and beneficial. As technology evolves, the integration of more advanced XR features and standardized hybrid DR protocols will further enhance collaborative design processes across various industries, leading to more streamlined DR processes.

Acknowledgements. This project was funded by Swedish innovation agency Vinnova in the PLENUM project (Grant Number: 2022-01704). The support is gratefully acknowledged.

References

1. Adams, R.S., Cardella, M., Purzer, Ş.: Analyzing design review conversations: connecting design knowing, being and coaching. Des. Stud. **45**, 1–8 (2016). https://doi.org/10.1016/j.destud.2016.03.001
2. Chen, J., Zucco, G., Olechowski, A.: A survey of design reviews: understanding differences by designer-roles and phase of development. Proc. Des. Soc. **1**(1), 2745–2754 (2019). https://doi.org/10.1017/dsi.2019.281
3. Huet, G., Culley, S.J., McMahon, C.A., Fortin, C.: Making sense of engineering design review activities. AI EDAM. **21**(3), 243–266 (2007). https://doi.org/10.1017/S0890060407000261
4. Dominach, R.F.: Design reviews at a distance. IEEE Spectr. **31**(6), 39–40 (1994). https://doi.org/10.1109/6.284789
5. Wolfartsberger, J.: Analyzing the potential of virtual reality for engineering design review. Autom. Constr. **104**, 27–37 (2019). https://doi.org/10.1016/j.autcon.2019.03.018
6. Kent, L., Snider, C., Gopsill, J., Hicks, B.: Mixed reality in design prototyping: a systematic review. Des. Stud. **77**, 101046 (2021). https://doi.org/10.1016/j.destud.2021.101046
7. Horvat, N., Brnčić, M., Perišić, M.M., Martinec, T., Bojčetić, N., Škec, S.: Design reviews in immersive and non-immersive collaborative virtual environments: comparing verbal communication structures. Proc. Des. Soc. **2**, 211–220 (2022). https://doi.org/10.1017/pds.2022.23
8. Horvat, N., Martinec, T., Perišić, M.M., Škec, S.: Comparing design review outcomes in immersive and non-immersive collaborative virtual environments. Procedia CIRP. **109**, 173–178 (2022). https://doi.org/10.1016/j.procir.2022.05.232
9. Burova, A., et al.: Distributed asymmetric virtual reality in industrial context: enhancing the collaboration of geographically dispersed teams in the pipeline of maintenance method development and technical documentation creation. Appl. Sci. **12**(8), Art. no. 8 (2022). https://doi.org/10.3390/app12083728
10. Ouverson, K.M., Scherber, C., Oldham, E., Gilbert, S.B.: What does "asymmetric VR" mean? A directed content analysis of co-located use of VR by users on reddit. Front. Virt. Real. **2** (2021) [Online]. Available: https://www.frontiersin.org/articles/10.3389/frvir.2021.765881. Accessed 25 Sep 2022
11. Bedny, G.Z., Harris, S.R.: The systemic-structural theory of activity: applications to the study of human work. Mind Cult. Act. **12**(2), 128–147 (2005). https://doi.org/10.1207/s15327884mca1202_4
12. Cash, P., Hicks, B., Culley, S.: Activity theory as a means for multi-scale analysis of the engineering design process: a protocol study of design in practice. Des. Stud. **38**, 1–32 (2015). https://doi.org/10.1016/j.destud.2015.02.001
13. Liu, Y.: Evaluating design review meetings and the use of virtual reality for post-occupancy analysis (2017). https://doi.org/10.13140/RG.2.2.16650.11204
14. Pahl, G., Beitz, W., Feldhusen, J., Grote, K.-H.: Engineering Design. Springer, London (2007). https://doi.org/10.1007/978-1-84628-319-2
15. Horvat, N., Kunnen, S., Štorga, M., Nagarajah, A., Škec, S.: Immersive virtual reality applications for design reviews: systematic literature review and classification scheme for functionalities. Adv. Eng. Inform. **54**, 101760 (2022). https://doi.org/10.1016/j.aei.2022.101760

16. Bueckle, A., Buehling, K., Shih, P.C., Börner, K.: 3D virtual reality vs. 2D desktop registration user interface comparison. PLoS One. **16**(10), e0258103 (2021). https://doi.org/10.1371/journal.pone.0258103
17. Huang, J., Sun, M., Qin, J., Gao, B., Qin, G.: Climbing keyboard: a tilt-based selection keyboard entry for virtual reality. Int. J. Hum. Comput. Interact. **40**(5), 1327–1338 (2024). https://doi.org/10.1080/10447318.2022.2144120
18. Liu, Y.: Evaluating the impact of virtual reality on design review meetings. J. Comput. Civ. Eng. **34**, 04019045 (2020). https://doi.org/10.1061/(ASCE)CP.1943-5487.0000856
19. Zhang, Y., Liu, H., Zhao, M., Al-Hussein, M.: User-centered interior finishing material selection: an immersive virtual reality-based interactive approach. Autom. Constr. **106**, 102884 (2019). https://doi.org/10.1016/j.autcon.2019.102884
20. Jetter, H.-C., Rädle, R., Feuchtner, T., Anthes, C., Friedl, J., Klokmose, C.N.: "In VR, everything is possible!": sketching and simulating spatially-aware interactive spaces in virtual reality. In: Proceedings of the 2020 CHI Conference on Human Factors in Computing Systems, in CHI '20, pp. 1–16. Association for Computing Machinery, New York, NY (2020). https://doi.org/10.1145/3313831.3376652
21. Drey, T., Gugenheimer, J., Karlbauer, J., Milo, M., Rukzio, E.: VRSketchIn: exploring the design space of pen and tablet interaction for 3D sketching in virtual reality. In: Proceedings of the 2020 CHI Conference on Human Factors in Computing Systems, in CHI '20, pp. 1–14. Association for Computing Machinery, New York, NY (2020). https://doi.org/10.1145/3313831.3376628
22. Joundi, J., Christiaens, Y., Saldien, J., Conradie, P., Marez, L.D.: An explorative study towards using vr sketching as a tool for ideation and prototyping in product design. Proc. Des. Soc. **1**, 225–234 (2020). https://doi.org/10.1017/dsd.2020.61
23. Lin, M.-H., Chiang, I.-C., Lee, L., Lu, H.-X.: Examining performance of VR sketch modeling tool in personal sketches'. In: DRS Biennial Conference Series (Jun. 2022) [Online]. Available: https://dl.designresearchsociety.org/drs-conference-papers/drs2022/researchpapers/21
24. Beltrán, F., Geng, J.: Building a distributed XR immersive environment for data visualization. In: 2021 ITU Kaleidoscope: Connecting Physical and Virtual Worlds (ITU K), pp. 1–8 (2021). https://doi.org/10.23919/ITUK53220.2021.9662103
25. Bordegoni, M., Caruso, G.: Mixed reality distributed platform for collaborative design review of automotive interiors. Virtual Phys. Prototyp. **7**(4), 243–259 (2012). https://doi.org/10.1080/17452759.2012.721605

Activity-Based Accident Analysis: The Case of Nitrogenous Fertilizer Factory

Raoni Rocha[1](✉), Francisco Lima[2], and Francisco Duarte[3]

[1] Federal University of Ouro Preto, Ouro Preto, Brazil
raoni@ufop.edu.br
[2] Federal University of Minas Gerais, Belo Horizonte, Brazil
[3] Federal University of Rio de Janeiro, Rio de Janeiro, Brazil

Abstract. Based on the analysis of an accident that occurred in the granulation sector of a nitrogen fertilizer factory, this article proposes a method of accident analysis based on work activity. Unlike classical analyses, which focus on the use of tools such as the "Cause Tree" or "Ishikawa Diagram" and assume human and/or technical failures as the stopping point, the analysis presented in this article seeks to bring everyday work performed by workers as the central axis. This work, represented by the activities they perform daily, can help recover or avoid accident-generating situations. For this, we are inspired by models that value both the knowledge of activity elements and historical and organizational aspects. The method of analysis developed and presented in this article was able to answer questions previously unanswered by the official analysis constituted by the company, and more than that, it was able to elucidate the reasons why certain behaviors were adopted by the operator at the time of the accident. From this perspective, removing the blame-focused approach of classical analyses, understanding work activity more accurately reveals the objective and subjective contributing factors of accidents, thus being more effective in achieving the main goal of any analysis: generating learning and advancing prevention.

Keywords: Accident analysis · activity analysis · human factors · risk management · occupational safety

1 Introduction

Classic accident analysis models, based on methods such as the "Cause Tree" or the "Ishikawa Diagram," have limitations that hinder progress towards a deeper understanding of the complex combination of objective (material and organizational) and subjective causes that lead to an undesirable event. Several factors contribute to this.

Firstly, in contemporary organizations, the culture of standardization prevails, prioritizing rules and procedures as the main operational tools, which generates an excess of norms – sometimes conflicting – that can create difficulties for those performing the work.

Secondly, accidents are often analyzed with a retrospective bias, usually concluding with blame attributed to the victim (Dekker and Breakey 2016). In other words, the

S. Jin et al. (Eds.): IEA 2024, SSDI 39, pp. 367–373, 2025.
https://doi.org/10.1007/978-981-95-0211-0_57

accident essentially happened because the frontline operator made a mistake. Analyzing undesirable events after they have occurred induces a "retrospective illusion," where past events are evaluated with present data, eliminating the circumstances at the moment of decision-making and making what was merely possible seem objective and evident. Thus, "human error" remains ubiquitous in both accident theories and analyses.

Finally, a fundamental issue for understanding the accident is ignored: the work activity, including the interactions between the individual(s) and the environment, the relationships between work interfaces, and the influence of the organization on individual behaviors (Rocha et al. 2012). It is only through the analysis of labor activity that we can understand the true reasons for the errors that could not be recovered and led to undesirable events.

Thus, there are three main reasons justifying this research: the overvaluation of rules to the detriment of reality; the omnipresence of human error in accident analyses; and the neglect of actual work activity in these analyses. The hypothesis raised in this article is that to achieve a deep understanding of the accident, analyses must include the study of the daily activity performed around the accident-causing situation and its relationship with the organization and management of work.

To this end, we resort to two theories: the theory of organizational accidents, encompassing historical, transversal, and vertical analyses (Llory and Montmayeul 2014); and the Course of Action Theory, or CAT (Theureau 2004). This leads us to an approach that associates singular elements of specific work situations with organizational issues, aiming to understand, for example, how the activity performed can be an element of organizational development and, conversely, how the organization can influence the behavior of frontline individuals.

The foundation of this hypothesis will be established through a case study conducted in a nitrogen fertilizer production company, related to a burn accident in its production sector. Starting from the official accident analysis conducted by the company using classical methods, we reanalyze the event based on the theory of organizational accidents and the course of action theory. Using a method that integrates these two approaches, called here Activity-Based Accident Analysis (ABAA), we can arrive at significantly different results compared to the official analysis and understand the implication of the organization and work management in the behaviors and possible errors committed by frontline operators.

2 Methodology

A team consisting of three researchers with experience in ergonomics and accident analysis was formed to understand a first-degree burn accident that occurred in a fertilizer industry. This incident happened in the sector known as "Granulation" (where the granulation of liquid urea occurs), with a team of 9 workers, who work in 8-h shifts across three shifts. The operator was hit by hot urea, which overflowed from the containment vessel when the passage valves were opened to start the granulation process. The liquid material hit the operator's arms, back, and helmet, from where it dripped, causing a burn on the neck.

As advocated by the Course of Action Theory, the study began with a preparatory phase, in which the researchers conducted preliminary interviews with the demand formulators and managers of the unit under investigation. This phase aimed to familiarize themselves with the organization's vocabulary, values, and practices, while clarifying the research method to be used. In total, six one-hour interviews were conducted, three with employees of the company's Research Center and three with intermediate managers of the unit under investigation. Subsequently, historical, transversal, and vertical analyses were carried out, supported by activity analysis at the accident site.

In total, about 15 h of activity observation were conducted, both of the victim and other workers, at the accident site and in the upstream and downstream sectors, as well as in the control room. Simultaneously, approximately 15 h of interviews were conducted with various stakeholders in the company directly or indirectly involved in the accident, including the victim, their coworkers, members of the health and safety area (doctors, technicians, and engineers), Human Resources (psychologist and social worker), Production Process (operators, managers), Optimization/Engineering and Maintenance (engineer and boiler supervisor), and Project Engineering (engineers).

3 Results

3.1 Granulation Sector and the Official Accident

The nitrogen fertilizer plant under study began its operations in 1982, producing urea and ammonia. Starting from 2016, it also initiated the production of sulfuric acid. The urea sector comprises 9 operators who divide their work between the control room, the granulation sector, and the pearlization tower. The latter, specifically on its third floor where the accident occurred, houses a urea tank with a filter and 9 pipelines called "distributors," which are intended to release the urea present in the tank.

The accident occurred at 03:30 on March 25, 2014, when the operator was aligning the fifth distributor during the startup of the pearlization operation. At that moment, the worker was struck by hot urea (around 120 °C) in the neck region, resulting in a first-degree burn. Upon feeling the burn, the operator notified the supervisor of the need to halt the process by closing the reservoirs feeding the distribution tank.

3.2 Organizational Analysis: Historical, Transversal, and Horizontal

As part of the Historical Analysis, efforts were made to understand the types of events occurring in the granulation sector and other sectors of the industry, their frequency, and whether they were recorded or addressed. Between 2011 and 2016, a total of 178 anomalies were recorded in the urea and ammonia plants. In addition to accidents, these anomalies were classified by the company as "Non-Conformities" (without direct involvement of people), "Incidents/Non-Conformities" (may or may not involve people directly), "Incidents" (involving people), or "Deviations" (high-potential events). Accidents and anomalies are recorded in documents called "Anomaly Treatment Records" (ATRs). Of the 52 accidents recorded during this period, 30 of them (57.7%) occurred in the urea plant. The majority of non-conformities (65.3%), incidents/non-conformities (100%), incidents (51.8%), and deviations (66.6%) also occurred in the urea plant.

Specifically in the urea plant, these records were divided among the pearlization, granulation, and control room sectors. The pearlization sector leads in almost all indices, with 22 accidents (73.3%), 25 non-conformities (53.2%), 1 incident/non-conformity (33.3%), 9 incidents (64.3%), and 8 deviations (50%). Of the 65 records occurring in the pearlization sector during this period, 18 of them (65%) were related to urea overflow, including 11 accidents (resulting in minor burns from overflow), 2 non-conformities, 1 incident/non-conformity, 3 incidents, and 1 deviation. The remaining records, both accidents and other event classifications, mainly involved falls, cuts, and bruises.

As part of the Transversal Analysis, it was observed that most of the identified causes in the company's official analysis did not lead to any corrective action. For example, issues such as "incompatible flow with distributor alignment and thief" and "lack of protective barrier" at the tank were identified. Additionally, there was also an ATR requesting "thief resizing" due to an incident involving "molten urea overflow from the tank" that occurred about a year before the accident. However, none of these equipment and process-related issues were resolved by the Project Engineering or Maintenance departments, even after being identified in the official analysis and receiving specific recommendations in the ATR.

Moreover, there are several other situations formalized in the company's ATRs that were not adequately addressed or addressed in a timely manner. Among these situations, various improvisations in the production area and clear signs of equipment degradation, such as leaks in steam pipes, can be observed.

As part of the Vertical Analysis, a series of conditions in the ATRs are not addressed by those responsible. On the other hand, it is also evident that there are several risk situations in the area that deliberately remain unrecorded. Many of these situations resemble those mentioned earlier: recurring overflows, other types of improvisations, new blocks of urea falling, or water vapor leaks at new points.

Operators express that "all operators have been burned there at the filter or while cleaning the distributors." At the same time, "the entire line has been leaking for a long time, mainly water vapor leaks, but talking about it doesn't help because it doesn't get resolved." These events are not reported to management or project engineering because, according to the operators themselves, "this has been mentioned many times, but they (the managers) don't solve it" (Production Operator).

These results are summarized in Table 1.

3.3 Activity-Based Accident Analysis

Firstly, according to the operators, three hypotheses can be formulated to identify the causes of the urea projection and overflow: (i) filling of the filter basket due to impurities present in the urea; (ii) reduction in the fluidity of the urea, which, with a melting point of 120 °C, becomes thicker and less fluid if the temperature system drops; and (iii) alteration of the balance between the urea inlet and outlet flow from the tank. The dynamic balance to maintain the situation under control or to cause the urea to overflow depends directly on the operators' experience.

At the same time, it is possible to identify details about the work situation at the time of the accident. Among these, the data recorded on the control system screens stand out. This description was made possible by retrieving these data from the PI (Plant

Table 1. Results of the historical, transversal, and vertical analyses.

Historical Analysis	Transversal Analysis	Horizontal Analysis
– Between 2011 and 2016: 178 anomalies recorded – Anomalies classified as Non-conformities, Incidents/Non-conformities, Incidents, Accidents, or Deviations – Accidents and anomalies recorded in ATRs – Of the 52 accidents recorded during this period, 30 of them (57.7%) occurred in the urea plant – The majority of non-conformities (65.3%), incidents/non-conformities (100%), incidents (51.8%), and deviations (66.6%) also occurred in the urea plant – In the urea plant, the pearlization sector has 22 accidents (73.3%), 25 non-conformities (53.2%), 1 incident/non-conformity (33.3%), 9 incidents (64.3%), and 8 deviations (50%) – Of the 65 records occurring in the pearlization sector, 18 of them (65%) were related to urea overflow, including 11 accidents (resulting in minor burns from overflow), 2 non-conformities, 1 incident/non-conformity, 3 incidents, and 1 deviation	– Most of the causes identified in the company's official analysis (such as "incompatible flow with distributor alignment and thief" and "lack of protective barrier") did not lead to any corrective action – Presence of an ATR requesting "thief resizing" due to an incident involving "molten urea overflow from the tank" that occurred about 1 year before the accident – None of these issues were resolved, even after being identified in the official analysis and receiving specific recommendations in the ATR – Several other situations formalized in the ATRs were not adequately addressed (such as improvisations in the production area and clear signs of equipment degradation, such as leaks in steam pipes)	– Various records in the ATRs not addressed – Several risk situations in the area deliberately remain unrecorded (such as recurring overflows, other types of improvisations, new blocks of urea falling, or water vapor leaks in new points) – Frequent verbalizations: ""all operators have been burned there at the filter or while cleaning the distributors"; "the entire line has been leaking for a long time, mainly water vapor leaks, but talking about it doesn't help because it doesn't get resolved" – Events are not reported because "this has been mentioned many times, but they (the managers) don't solve it"

Information) system and comparing them with both field and panel operators. In this case, the comparison involved the workers directly involved in the accident: the panel operator who was in the control room on the day of the event and a field operator who was at the site when the accident occurred. The most relevant variable indicated that before the filter tank overflowed, the urea volume suddenly reached near maximum, possibly resulting in a jet expulsion at that moment. This fact, confirmed by the accident victim, indicates that the burn occurred before the actual overflow.

4 Discussion

In his theory on accident models, James Reason (1997) draws attention to the latent condition of accidents. Once an accident occurs, what was once latent seems to become obvious in the tools of traditional analyses. The difficulty lies in explaining why the risk situation was not previously identified or why, over time, it ceased to be perceived as a problem. In other words, the challenge is to recognize when a weak signal or deviation has become normalized (Vaughan 1996). How do we enter this field of the normal and make it more questionable or problematized? Our answer necessarily involves the analysis of activity and organization through the analysis model proposed in this research.

The organizational accident theory (Llory and Montmayeul 2014) represents an advancement over classical approaches to accident analysis as it seeks to understand deep organizational causes, incorporating a historical perspective and analyzing interfaces and hierarchies. However, this theory still lacks a thorough study of work activity to understand how these broad historical and contextual causes influence activity execution. It is in this sense that the Course of Action Theory (Theureau 2004) complements the organizational analysis, as it provides theoretical and methodological insights to understand how subjective, material, and organizational aspects intertwine to generate accidents. By privileging the intrinsic perspective of activity, the description of the course of action internalizes the contextual elements that make sense to the operator here and now. Thus, we propose the ABAA model, which integrates these two theories (see Fig. 1).

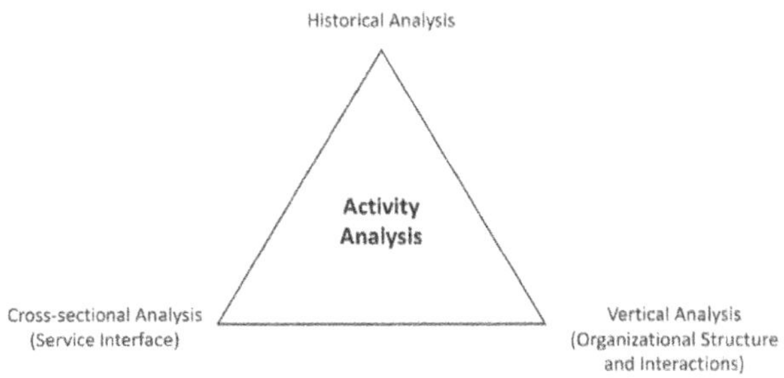

Fig. 1. Accident Analysis Model Based on Activity and Organization.

Therefore, the contributions of this study are clear. From a practical standpoint, it represents a methodological contribution to accident analysis that goes beyond the commonly used approach of human error and retrospective bias. From a theoretical perspective, the study proposes an integration between organizational accident theory and activity theory, thereby advancing accident analysis theories. These advancements represent, above all, the need for the development of participatory approaches in ergonomics (Rodrigues and Rocha 2023), whether in the field of safety, health, or the efficiency of production processes.

5 Conclusion

The ABBA model allows us to move beyond the more common pattern of conclusions drawn from classical analyses, which attribute accidents to human error combined with technical system failures. It is from human error and technical failures that our approach begins. By considering other dimensions, such as the dynamic organization of activity during the action at the time of the accident, collective work, and the relationship with the context (situated action), organizational decisions, and management practices, the analysis of activity enables us to escape the reductionist view inherent in the behavioral approach to accident analysis. We thus contribute to developing a fair safety culture beyond that proposed by Dekker and Breakey (2016) and a solution to the impasse facing accident investigations within a judicial framework.

References

Dekker, S.W.A., Breakey, H.: Just culture: improving safety by achieving substantive, procedural and restorative justice. Saf. Sci. **85**, 187–193 (2016)

Llory, M., Montmayeul, R.: O acidente e a organização. Fabrefactum, Belo Horizonte (2014)

Reason, J.: Managing the Risks of Organizational Accidents. Ashgate, Farnham (1997)

Rocha, R., Daniellou, F., Nascimento, A.: The rotation and collective strategies for health preservation developed by operators at a soft drinks factory. Activités. **9**(2), 1–21 (2012)

Rodrigues, V., Rocha, R.: Participatory ergonomics approaches to design and intervention in workspaces: a literature review. Theor. Issues Ergon. Sci. **24**(4), 413–428 (2023)

Theureau, J.: Le cours d'action: méthode élémentaire. Octares, Toulouse (2004)

Vaughan, D.: The Challenger Launch Decision: Risky Technology, Culture, and Deviance at NASA. University of Chicago Press, Chicago, IL (1996)

"We Aren't a Blank Page Waiting to Be Filled In": The Activity's Viewpoint and Its Contributions to the Design of Future Transport Automation

Daniel Silva[1,2](✉) and Liliana Cunha[1,2]

[1] Faculty of Psychology and Education Sciences of the University of Porto (FPCEUP), Porto, Portugal
danielsilva@fpce.up.pt
[2] Center for Psychology at University of Porto (CPUP), 4200-135 Porto, Portugal

Abstract. Driving automation is expected to improve working conditions, support the present transport workforce to remain on the job longer, safely and healthy, and make the job more "attractive" for the next generation of professional drivers. Yet, is this just a matter of getting technology into vehicles? To pluralize a predominant technocentric outlook on automated driving, our research adopted the work activity's point of view, concretely the bus driving activity, to explore how work experience in urban passenger transport can contribute to the design of future automated buses. The study followed a qualitative approach with a group of bus drivers providing public passenger transport service in a metropolitan area of Portugal. The bus drivers presented a set of conditions that should be considered when discussing future transport systems with automated buses: employment and working conditions, the work organization (bus services timetables) and even the urban environment (road infrastructure). Our findings also reveal the integrative nature of work experience since, in the face of a technological change promising to reconfigure the technical conditions of work, it links the actual ways of working to a possible future work situation with automated buses.

Keywords: Bus drivers · Automated buses · Work experience · Work design

1 Introduction

The road transport industry is commonly said to be at a crossroads today. On the one side, the demanding reality of the work that professional drivers are exposed to day-to-day is related to detrimental impacts on their health [1–3]; on the other side, the automation of driving is presented as the leading solution to this reality that threatens the sustainability of work [4–6], yet without new challenges looming on the horizon, such as the possible displacement of drivers or deskilling [7].

Against this backdrop, the design of future work situations with automated buses (ABs) in urban public passenger transport (UPPT) is receiving increasing attention.

S. Jin et al. (Eds.): IEA 2024, SSDI 39, pp. 374–379, 2025.
https://doi.org/10.1007/978-981-95-0211-0_58

However, research has been devoted to explaining professional drivers' acceptance of automated driving technologies while missing their work and organizational contexts [4, 8]. The most immediate consequence of this is the backseat role generally reserved for bus drivers in the current initiatives and projects towards driving automation. Then, and relatedly, once the technology is designed, bus drivers are asked to accept it, bridging the gap between what was initially idealized for technology operation and the reality of the transit environment that exceeds the functionalities of ABs [4]. What is ultimately at stake is the possibility of bus drivers being taken as the "variable of adjustment" of a new system designed without knowing the complexity of their work and, more insidiously, the specificity of their work experience [2].

Our research seeks to reverse this tendency by making visible the work experience of drivers and exploring its contributions to thinking and designing future work with ABs. This way, we propose to investigate the contours of future activity based on the reality of current work situations [9], in the face of which know-how relating to a particular context is developed. Such know-how, as part of the transpersonal heritage of a professional milieu [10], is also directed towards the future, potentially connecting the past and present work activity to possible and desirable future activity.

2 The Work of Bus Drivers: On the Brink of Unsustainability?

The very demanding conditions to which bus drivers are subject have been consistently documented in the literature. Having to work irregular schedules, remaining in the driving position for long periods, or being exposed to tight deadlines are just a few factors contributing to the work intensification reported by bus drivers [1, 3]. Particularly in UPPT, these constraints are more substantial since bus drivers have to manage higher traffic density, more sources of unexpected events, and situations of tension and hostility with the public (e.g. conflicts related to delays in the bus schedule or fare enforcement) [2, 5]. According to the European Transport Workers' Federation [1], this scenario is made worse due to the low average salaries in the sector. This reality opens the door for pushing workers out of the profession. In fact, today's growing labor shortage is known as the Achilles heel of passenger road transport across Europe [6, 11] and the US [5]. So, this landscape is particularly challenging for the sustainability of work [4].

In this context, ongoing technological change in UPPT is seen as key to improving job quality, though some worries over the disruptive effects on employment remain [6, 7]. The possibility of raising the profession's attractiveness and, thus, remedying the bus driver shortage is a prospect [6], as automation could reduce the physical and psychological demandingness of driving. Besides supporting drivers to remain on the job longer, these shifts are also expected to influence the profession's attractiveness among younger workers, mainly because 32% of European bus drivers are aged 55+ [11].

Two research questions were set: (1) From bus drivers' point of view, what are the conditions for more efficient and sustainable passenger transport? (2) How do bus drivers prospect their activity with ABs, i.e., how does their current operative framework of reference question the probable future activity? It is, therefore, from the present work activity of bus drivers that future work with ABs is thought of. Such an approach is "intrinsic to work" [12, 13], i.e., it opposes exclusively top-down approaches that take work as a residual variable in techno-organizational transitions [2].

3 Method

The study was carried out with a group of bus drivers ($n = 10$) from a company providing public passenger transport service in a metropolitan area of Portugal. Their average age was 47 years, and the average seniority in UPPT was 21.3 years. Even though the bus drivers have not worked with ABs yet, this company participated in a European consortium to deploy ABs pilots in six European cities. To collect the drivers' points of view, we set up three collective sessions as spaces for dialogue and reflection on work (see Fig. 1). These sessions shared the aim of bringing the drivers' past activity to the fore, whose collective discussion defined the stage to prospect the probable future activity [9] with ABs. This strategy can be seen as falling into the methodology of eliciting activity [14]. The sessions took place at the company's facilities between January and February 2023 and lasted 80–120 min. Ethics approval for this study was obtained from the Ethics Committee of the FPCEUP.

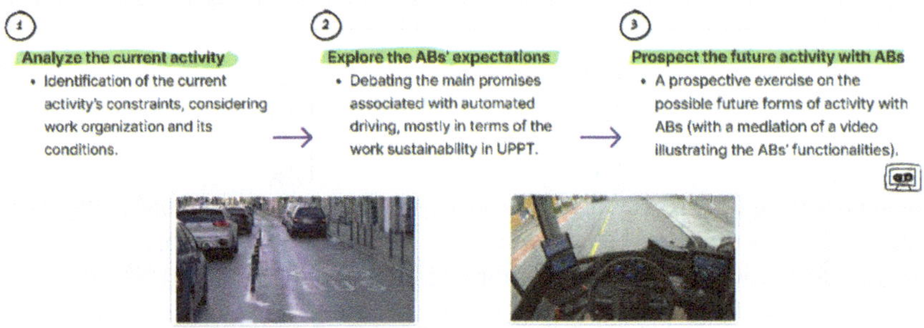

Fig. 1. Summary of the sessions with the bus drivers.

The sessions' transcripts were imported into NVivo to organize and code the data. Then, our analysis followed an inductive thematic approach [15]. First, we carried out a reading dedicated to becoming familiar with the data and generating an initial narrative from each collective session. In the second stage, we surfaced themes that emerged from the codes. Verbatim excerpts are provided in the following section.

4 Results and Discussion

To start with, the workers emphasized that bus driving, mainly in UPPT, is *"a job nobody wants anymore"*, given the working and employment conditions, the intensiveness of the work, the risks they have to face (primarily those related to managing tension with the public), and the deterioration of their health. *"In our case, it's not attractive for anyone to have the pay we have, with the responsibility we have, to be exposed to all kinds of situations, from verbal abuse to not having time to get up for a while between services... Nobody wants that these days"*. Therefore, for the interviewed bus drivers, the design of future UPPT systems is not just about getting technology into the vehicles; instead, it calls for discussing the employment, the work organization and the urban infrastructure.

According to the drivers, the bus driver shortage will not be solved by automation, as a "silver bullet", if the employment conditions are not revised.

Concerning work and its organization, the drivers specifically called attention to the stipulated timetables for bus routes/lines. In doing so, they revealed how the current timetabling is not adjusted to the reality of the city (e.g. the high number of construction zones; or the increase in traffic, especially after the pandemic). *"We have a huge constraint related to road closures and construction, which makes everything chaotic. Some detours take more than 15 min when the original route would be 3 or 4 min, even counting the bus stops"*. By alluding to the need to reroute when facing the city's situational constraints, the bus drivers pointed out their knowledge regarding the specificities of the streets (e.g. road surface conditions; the narrower streets that make cornering angles difficult for buses). This knowledge, referring to a particular city, its roads and points of constraints, is inscribed on a map *"in our head"*. *"I already know it, where the holes in the road are, where there are traffic jams, delays, everything, I mean, our job isn't just to know the routes; it's to know when they cause problems, where we're going to be delayed, what the possible detours are if that road is closed, and what are the alternatives to reroute when a first detour isn't possible. (…) After 24 years of work…, We have all the routes inside us, the city is in our heads"*.

It is worth noting that having "the city in one's head" does not mean that each bus driver has an isolated representation of the city; instead, it is a shared representation, which is fine-tuned according to a "repertoire of successes" over the years, which, in Oddone et al.'s words [10], is indicative of how individual activity is structured in a collective consciousness. Similarly, Akridge et al. [5] also allude to these specific forms of knowledge bus drivers developed that exceed the capacities of automated systems since "rerouting requires more than knowing the quickest way around an area" (p. 6).

The bus drivers insisted on the importance of thinking of the lanes where ABs will operate and, more broadly, the urban infrastructure. They pointed towards the regular obstruction of the bus lanes by other road users, making it impossible to circulate and contributing to the idea that public transport is inefficient. Such a problem could be a significant challenge for ABs. *"I think ABs will work well in streets where there's no abusive parking, streets completely wide and open, where there're no unexpected events, where there's no one suddenly opening doors* [of parked cars], *and the driver has to run to the left. Otherwise, our environment has so many constraints that the driver would always be driving the AB (...). You almost have to build an infrastructure from scratch"*.

Concerning our second research question, the bus drivers raised some questions about the future role they will be given when working with ABs, namely the widespread promise that this role could alleviate the fatigue associated with driving. In fact, at intermediate levels of automated driving, drivers are expected to supervise the system and regain manual control of the vehicle after a takeover request (e.g. in the presence of unexpected events, technical failures, or other conditions exceeding the operational design domain of ABs). However, this supervisory role could be challenging. *"Supervising an AB could be a rest that isn't quite like that. It's taking my hands off the wheel, ok, but I'm alert, it's a rest from a driver who's going beside someone else driving. (…) We're never in a rest position when looking at the road. So, I don't think it's a rest at all, I think stress can even increase"*. This bus driver's account is in tune with some previous contributions in the literature, flagging that automation can intensify work and lead to a possible increased mental workload in the early stages of working with automated driving modes [3, 4, 16]. In concrete, Martelaro et al. [16] highlighted that this "can intensify work as people primarily take over from automation in the most challenging situations" (p. 1).

By prospecting the probable future forms of their activity with ABs, the bus drivers regarded that automation will not put out the specificity of their experience as professional drivers. To sustain their viewpoint, the bus drivers ask, "*who will be the worker in charge of supervising the new machine* [ABs]". "*We could say, 'Well, just put anyone behind the wheel, and if anything happens, they'll react'. But, if that person doesn't know how to brake with a bus full of passengers, on stone flooring, when it's raining... We know how to stop a vehicle of this size without braking hard, for example. So, will that person know how to do the job?*".

"*After all, we're not a blank page waiting to be filled in* (...). *We aren't going to lose our know-how overnight, if so, anyone would be a bus driver*". This way, the bus drivers reveal how their professional experience is oriented towards a possible future situation, which simultaneously illustrates the potential of their contributions to discuss and inform the design of future situations in UPPT with ABs [2].

5 Conclusion

From the bus drivers' operative framework of reference, we sought to identify factors and conditions to be considered when debating the design and deployment of ABs in UPPT. As we addressed, these factors are beyond a purely technological dimension, directing our attention towards employment and working conditions, issues related to work organization and urban infrastructure to accommodate the ABs. Such results also illustrate the ways work never ceases to reveal possible and "desirable" evolutions [12] and how they have the potential to inform projects meant to reconfigure technical and organizational conditions of work.

In line with recent contributions [5, 8], our research reinforces the call for participatory design projects by involving professional drivers since the early stages of designing and setting dialogical spaces meant to debate work. These spaces are opportunities to bring together different actors implied in preemptively thinking UPPT systems of the future [2]: designers, professional drivers, companies, decision-makers in urban planning, and public transit authorities. Still, these dialogical spaces need mediation tools to structure the discussions. On this, our analysis of bus drivers' activity has the potential to contribute to the construction of "intermediary objects" [13, 17], i.e., objects (e.g. maps, mock-ups, diagrams) whose primary goal is to support the co-production of knowledge for action.

Acknowledgements. This work was supported by the FCT – Portuguese Foundation for Science and Technology under Grant SFRH/BD/139135/2018.

References

1. ETF: Driver Fatigue in European Road Transport. ETF, Brussels (2021)
2. Silva, D.: "Entre mim e a máquina": o papel da experiência de trabalho em contextos em mudança pela automação e os seus contributos para pensar o futuro do trabalho. PhD Thesis in Work Psychology, University of Porto – Faculty of Psychology and Education Sciences, Porto (2024). https://hdl.handle.net/10216/158697
3. Cunha, L., Barros, C., Baylina, P., Silva, D.: Work intensification in the road transport industry: an approach to new working scenarios with automated vehicles. Work. **69**(3), 847–857 (2021). https://doi.org/10.3233/WOR-213517
4. Silva, D., Cunha, L.: Aside from deterministic prophecies, what is missing in the contemporary debate on automation and the future of work? The case of automated vehicles. Soc. Sci. **11**(12), 1–29 (2022). https://doi.org/10.3390/socsci11120566
5. Akridge, H., Fan, B., Tang, A., Mehta, C., Martelaro, N., Fox, S.: "The bus is nothing without us": making visible the labor of bus operators amid the ongoing push towards transit automation. In: Proceedings of the CHI Conference on Human Factors in Computing Systems (CHI'24), pp. 1–16, New York, NY (2024). https://doi.org/10.1145/3613904.3642714
6. European Commission: Study on the Social Dimension of the Transition to Automation and Digitalisation in Transport, Focusing on the Labour Force. Directorate-General for Mobility and Transport, Brussels (2021). https://data.europa.eu/doi/10.2832/95224
7. International Transport Forum: Adapting (to) Automation: Transport Workforce in Transition. OECD Publishing, Paris (2023). https://doi.org/10.1787/905fdc2c-en
8. Johansson, M., Ekman, F., Karlsson, M., Stromberg, H., Jonsson, J.: ADAS at work: assessing professional bus drivers' experience and acceptance of a narrow navigation system. Cogn. Technol. Work. **24**, 625–639 (2022). https://doi.org/10.1007/s10111-022-00704-4
9. Daniellou, F.: Simulating future work activity is not only a way of improving workstation design. Activités. **4**(2), 84–90 (2007). https://doi.org/10.4000/activites.1704
10. Oddone, I., Re, A., Briante, G.: Redécouvrir l'expérience ouvrière. Vers une autre psychologie du travail? Problèmes/Éditions sociales, Paris (1981)
11. IRU: Driver Shortage Report 2023: Passenger – Europe. IRU, Geneve (2023)
12. Pueyo, V., Béguin, P.: Supporting professional transitions in innovative projects. In: Bagnara, S., et al. (eds.) Proceedings of the 20th Congress of the International Ergonomics Association (IEA 2018), vol. 824, pp. 1949–1957. Springer (2019). https://doi.org/10.1007/978-3-319-96071-5_204
13. Garrigou, A., Judon, N., Galey, L.: Contributions of ergonomics to the development of prevention projects: the role of intermediate prevention objects. In: Bagnara, S., et al. (eds.) Proceedings of the 20th Congress of the International Ergonomics Association (IEA 2018), vol. 824, pp. 2008–2016. Springer (2019). https://doi.org/10.1007/978-3-319-96071-5_211
14. Van Belleghem, L.: Eliciting activity: a method of analysis at the service of discussion. Le Travail Humain. **79**, 285–305 (2016). https://doi.org/10.3917/th.793.0285
15. Braun, V., Clarke, V.: Conceptual and design thinking for thematic analysis. Qual. Psychol. **9**(1), 3–26 (2022). https://doi.org/10.1037/qup0000196
16. Martelaro, N., Fox, S., Forlizzi, J., Rajkumar, R., Hendrickson, C., Caldwell, S.: How to Make Sense of Bus Transit Automation? Considerations for Policymakers on the Future of Human-Automation Teaming in the Transit Workforce. Carnegie Mellon University (2022)
17. Vinck, D., Jeantet, A., Laureillard, P.: Objects and other intermediaries in the sociotechnical process of product design: an explanatory approach. In: Perrin, J., Vinck, D. (eds.) The Role of Design in the Shaping of Technology, pp. 297–320. European Commission Directorate-General Science, Brussels (1996)

Decisions in Decommissioning Projects: Bringing Health and Safety Closer to Future Work

Laís Bubach Carvalho Simão[1(✉)], Beatriz Bandeira dos Santos[1], Carolina Mathias Esporcatte[1], Tomás Pinho Ferreira[1], Eduardo Ribeiro Nicolosi[2], Claudio Violante Ferreira[2], Marcelo Igor Lourenço de Souza[1], and Francisco José de Castro Moura Duarte[1]

[1] Federal University of Rio de Janeiro, Rio de Janeiro, RJ, Brazil
{lais.bubach,biabandeira,Carolmesporcatte, Tomaspf06}@pep.ufrj.br, migor@lts.coppe.ufrj.br, fjcmduarte@coppe.ufrj.br

[2] Petrobras, Rio de Janeiro, RJ, Brazil
{Nicolosi,cviolante}@petrobras.com.br

Abstract. Decommissioning industrial facilities in Brazil poses challenges for ensuring safe and efficient shutdowns, considering risks like safety and health. Linking decommissioning with operational risk management methods can lead to resource savings, improved worker safety, assessment of future scenarios, and enhanced transparency among stakeholders. This study aims to compare Worker Health and Safety data using a decision analysis method developed by COPPE/UFRJ, to determine optimal decommissioning options for subsea installations. It utilizes data from SAFETEC Report and CNAE to analyze operational risks. In Brazil, worker safety faces unique challenges, and understanding effective decommissioning activities can guide future work and reduce risks for workers in this sector.

Keywords: Decommissioning · Safefy · Work Activity

1 Introduction

Several offshore oil and gas platforms, installed in recent decades to provide global energy, now need to be decommissioned (Gourvenec 2018). Currently, the operational lifespan of these installations is coming to an end, and their decommissioning raises growing concerns about environmental, social, economic, and health impacts on the people involved (Watson et al. 2023).

According to Petrobras (2023), decommissioning is the permanent cessation of operations of a platform and its associated equipment when there are no more opportunities for continued production. This process can be lengthy due to the removal of complex structures, government regulations, and consultation with various stakeholders (Caprace et al. 2023).

S. Jin et al. (Eds.): IEA 2024, SSDI 39, pp. 380–385, 2025.
https://doi.org/10.1007/978-981-95-0211-0_59

The number of offshore oil and gas platform decommissioning projects is increasing, especially in Brazil, where a significant amount is expected in the coming years. The International Association of Oil & Gas Producers (IOGP) estimates that by 2030, around 80 offshore platforms and a large amount of subsea infrastructure will be decommissioned due to aging installations and the need to comply with environmental regulations (IOGP 2023). In Brazil, studies on the topic of decommissioning offshore oil and gas production systems are on the rise due to the completion of many production projects. Given the country's geographical and environmental diversity, it is crucial to analyze each unit individually (Muniz 2020), especially when decommissioning in the South Atlantic waters, which differs from experiences in other locations.

Brazil, with its vast territorial expanse, offers a variety of scenarios for the decommissioning of subsea equipment. This includes everything from shallow waters to ultra-deep waters that can exceed 5000 m. The country also has a diversity of biotas, invasive species, and ecosystems, as well as a wide range of equipment used in oil exploration, such as the large number of flexible pipelines. This context is distinct from that of other countries (Delgado and Michalowski 2021). The decommissioning challenge in Brazil involves the safe and efficient shutdown of installations, taking into account various environmental, economic, technical, and social factors, along with operational risks and worker health considerations. Both onshore and offshore activities associated with each chosen decommissioning method must be evaluated to address these complex requirements effectively.

This study aims to present the results of applying the Multicriteria Analysis Methodology to select the best decommissioning alternatives for subsea equipment of a platform in Brazil. It promotes the discussion on the comparative analysis of Occupational Health and Worker Safety data, using information from the Safetec (Safety and Environmental Technology) report and the CNAE (National Classification of Economic Activities) codes to evaluate operational risks.

1.1 The Decommissioning Process

The Decision Support Methodology for Decommissioning Subsea Oil and Gas Production Systems (MCDA - Multi Criteria Decision Analysis), developed by COPPE/UFRJ, is used in this study for comparative analysis. In the Decommissioning Project, it is essential to characterize each alternative based on six criteria: Environmental, Technical, Waste, Economic, Social, and Health and Safety, the latter being the focus of the study. The variation of operational and local parameters requires a systematic procedure for decommissioning, considering various scenarios (COPPE 2022).

1.2 The Health and Safety Criterion

In the application of the MCDA methodology, Occupational Health and Worker Safety aspects are evaluated through five subcriteria. Three are related to Occupational Health (Exposure to Toxic Materials, Exposure to NORM, and Exposure to Hyperbaric Conditions), while two deal with Worker Safety (Fatal Accidents and Impacts on Other Sea

Users). The scores for each subcriterion are determined based on risk assessment, considering the decommissioning alternatives and their corresponding activities (COPPE 2022).

2 Methodology

This research can be characterized as a case study as described by Yin (2015), with the aim of defining parameters and systematizing results within an existing context. Thus, five stages were followed:

In the first stage of the MCDA Methodology application process, an exploratory and descriptive study was conducted. In this study, each alternative was evaluated for its impact on six criteria, one of which was related to Health and Safety (COPPE 2022). In the second stage of the process (referred to as "Literature Investigation"), a detailed search was conducted to deepen understanding of the topic. The focus of this research was on subsea equipment, especially flexible pipelines of an FPSO vessel. For this study, a comparative simulation was conducted between the Health and Safety data presented in the SAFETEC Report and the data obtained through the CNAE Codes, applied in the calculation methodology of the MCDA method. This specific analysis focused on a section that will be decommissioned for the removal of subsea oil and gas production equipment.

In the third stage of the process (referred to as "Research Protocol"), a detailed plan was developed for data collection. This protocol aimed to gather the following information: the CNAE activity codes related to the decommissioning process; onshore and offshore activities associated with these codes; onshore and offshore activities described in the Safetec Report; and finally, the Fatal Accident Rates (FAR) from the two analyzed methodologies (CNAE Codes and Safetec). In the fourth stage of the process (titled "Assay"), a comparative analysis was conducted in May 2024. This analysis focused on a specific section of the subsea equipment that would be decommissioned on the FPSO vessel. For this comparison, the FAR related to a set of activities linked to the decommissioning process between the Safetec documents and the CNAE Codes were evaluated. In the fifth stage, the process involving the comparison between the two methodologies was analyzed in detail.

2.1 The Decommissioning Project - Case Study

The Z platform analyzed in this study is a Floating Production, Storage, and Offloading (FPSO) unit, which serves two deepwater fields off the Brazilian coast in the Campos Basin. The decommissioning alternatives proposed for this case were: Total Removal via Reverse Coil, Total Removal via Cutting and Lifting, and In Situ Retention.

3 Results and Discussion

In the Brazilian context, there are no detailed records of fatalities in workplace accidents during the decommissioning of offshore oil and gas production equipment. However, the National Institute of Social Security annually releases Mortality Rate indices related to activities categorized in the CNAE registry (AEAT, 2017). These codes are used for health and safety analyses in evaluating decommissioning alternatives. However, these data are not reliable because there is no identification and categorization of decommissioning activities by these codes. On the other hand, the Safetec Report, developed in collaboration by companies such as Shell, BP, and the UK Health and Safety Executive, quantifies risks and workplace accidents during the decommissioning of oil and gas production facilities in the North Sea. This methodology reviews analytical methods associated with serious accident risks and identifies data sources to estimate the FAR (Safetec 2005).

To meet the study objective, activities correlated between the CNAE Codes and the Safetec Report were analyzed. Comparing data from the two methods allows understanding FAR values in different contexts, such as the Brazilian oil and gas industry. Figure 1 presents this comparison in a section of flexible pipelines of the FPSO vessel under study.

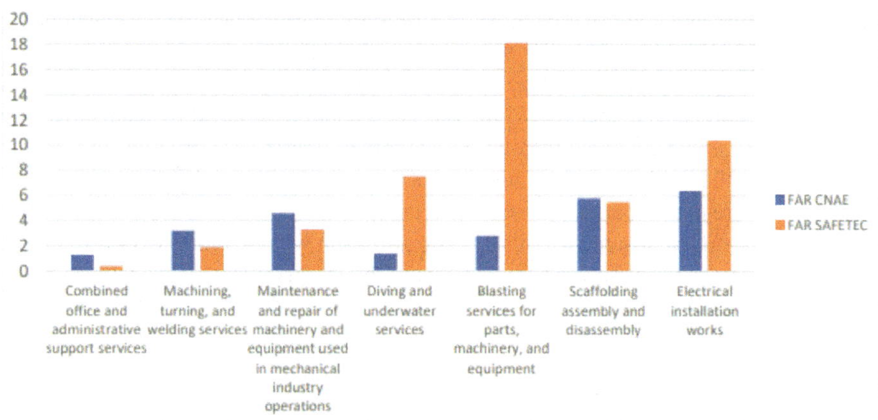

Fig. 1. Comparison of FAR values between the two presented methodologies.

From the graph above, some points can be concluded:

1. The graph shows a significant discrepancy in FAR, especially in the activities of "Diving Services", "Sandblasting Services for Parts, Machinery, and Equipment", and "Electrical Installation Works". These differences in values presented by the CNAE Codes and the Safetec Report may reflect variations in operational processes, specific risks associated with decommissioning, and working conditions in each sector.
2. Limitations of the CNAE Codes: The disparity highlights a gap in considering specific decommissioning activities by the CNAE Codes. Although these codes broadly classify economic activities, they do not specifically focus on decommissioning operations, which involve distinct processes and risks (IBGE 2007). The lack of specific categorization may affect the accuracy of risk estimates and the adequacy of safety measures associated with these operations.
3. Importance of Complementary Sources: Therefore, it is necessary to resort to complementary data sources, such as the Safetec Report, which focuses on decommissioning

operations, allowing for a more accurate assessment of associated risks. By aligning with the reality of offshore work, it is possible to contribute to technological development and enhance Worker Health and Safety, enabling a better understanding of FAR in different decommissioning alternatives (AEAT, 2017; IBGE 2007; Safetec 2005).

Within the understanding of work, resilience engineering emerges as an innovative approach that considers how people react under constant pressure in the workplace, recognizing that under pressure, individuals may act more recklessly, increasing the risks of accidents. In the context of subsea equipment decommissioning, this approach can be applied to understand how productive systems and work teams adapt and recover from unexpected events. However, it is crucial to go beyond resilience engineering and consider human factors more comprehensively, promoting the identification and implementation of conditions that favor a positive contribution from operators and work collectives in industrial safety construction (ICSI, 2010). The concept of human factors, proposed by Daniellou (2001), emphasizes understanding the interactions between workers, tasks, and the work environment. This includes aspects such as skills, training, communication, decision-making, and cognitive load. By incorporating human factors, we can enhance the safety and health of workers during subsea equipment decommissioning.

Transitioning from resilience engineering to considering human factors can allow for a more comprehensive analysis of the risks and challenges faced by teams involved in decommissioning. Understanding the actual work of operators (Daniellou and Béguin 2007), and how they interact with systems, what their capabilities and limitations are, and how decisions are made in critical situations is essential for mitigating accidents and promoting a safe work environment. This holistic approach will enable us to develop more effective strategies to protect workers and ensure the integrity of operations throughout the decommissioning process.

4 Final Considerations

Analyzing the comparative data produced during the simulation proposed in the study highlights the challenges of decommissioning subsea equipment in the Brazilian context to enhance occupational risk management. The disparity in FAR results for certain correlated activities from both documents, the lack of documents with health and safety information about decommissioning activities, underscores the need for complementary data sources, such as the Safetec Report, covering the Brazilian reality. Additionally, the transition from resilience engineering to considering human factors emerges as an essential approach to understanding how workers interact with systems and make decisions in critical situations.

It is necessary to recognize that the research had limits imposed by its temporal historical scope, and proactively considering them will contribute to new simulations and studies seeking to improve the Health and Safety criterion. Thus, this study aims to provide insights for discussion and the development of future research in the field of decommissioning of subsea oil and gas production systems.

Acknowledgments. This study was supported by Coordination for the Improvement of Higher Education Personnel (CAPES) - Brazil and funding from PRH - ANP, through R,D & I resources of ANP Resolution No. 50/2015, and with the support of COPPETEC Foundation - Coordination Foundation for Technological Projects, Research, and Studies. The authors also express their gratitude to the oil and gas company where the work was carried out for the support provided.

References

Caprace, J.D., de Souza, M.I., Ferreira, C. V., Nicolosi, E.R.: A new Multicriteria Decision-Making Tool for Subsea Oil and Gas Asset Decommissioning. Presented Jun, 2023, Melbourne, Australia (2023)

COPPE. Decision Support in Subsea Petroleum Exploration Systems Decommissioning Projects - Health and Safety. Decision Support Guide (2022)

Daniellou, F.: The human factors engineering and ergonomics: a method for the design of work situations. Appl. Ergon. **32**(6), 581–588 (2001)

Daniellou, F., Béguin, P.: Methodology of Ergonomic Action: Approaches to Real Work in Falzon, P. Ergonomics. Edgard Blucher Publisher, SP (2007)

Daniellou, F., Simard, M., Boissières, I.: Human and organizational factors of industrial safety: a state of the art. In: Rocha, R., Duarte, F., Lima, F. (eds.) Industrial Safety Notebooks. ICSI., (n. 2013-07) (2010)

Delgado, F., Michalowski, G. R.: Offshore Decommissioning in Brazil: Decommissioning Handbook. FGV. (2021). Available at: https://www.gov.br/anp/pt-br/centrais-de-conteudo/publicacoes/livros-e-revistas/arquivos/cadernodedescomissionamento.pdf. Accessed 25 June 2024

Gourvenec, S.: Shaping the offshore decommissioning agenda and next-generation design of offshore infrastructure. Proc. Inst. Civ. Eng. Smart Infrastr. Constr. **171**(2), 54–66 (2018). https://doi.org/10.1680/jsmic.18.0000

IBGE: Introduction to the National Classification of Economic Activities—CNAE version 2.0. (2007). Available at: https://concla.ibge.gov.br/images/concla/documentacao/CNAE20_Introducao.pdf. Accessed 1 Nov 2023

International Association of Oil & Gas Producers: Annual Report 2023. IOGP (2023). Retrieved from https://www.iogp.org/bookstore/product/iogp-2023-annual-report/

Muniz, T. J. C.: Multicriteria Decision Support Applied to the Disposal of Offshore Oil and Gas Production Systems in Decommissioning (Professional Master's thesis). Federal Fluminense University, Rio das Ostras (2020)

Oil & Gas UK: Guidelines for Comparative Assessment in Decommissioning Programmes. UK Oil and Gas Industry Association Limited (2015)

Petrobras: Platform Decommissioning. (2023). Available at https://petrobras.com.br/sustentabilidade/descomissionamento-de-plataformas?p_l_back_url=%2Fresultado-da-busca%3Fq%3Ddescomissionamento. Accessed 14 Apr 2024

Safetec: Main Report Risk Analysis of Decommissioning Activities. HSE. (2005). Available at: https://www.hse.gov.uk/search/search-results.htm?query=safetec#gsc.tab=0&gsc.q=safetec&gsc.page=1. Accessed 1 Nov 2023

Ministry of Finance, et al.: Statistical Yearbook of Occupational Accidents: AEAT 2017, vol. 1, p. 996. MF, Brasflia (2017) Annual. ISSN 1676-9694

Yin, R.K.: Case Studies: Planning and Methods, 5th edn. Bookman, Porto Alegre (2015)

Experimental Study to Establish a Psychophysiological Index to Assess the Degree of Self-Determination of Motivation from the Perspective of Organismic Integration Theory

Mayuko Takagi(✉) and Miwa Nakanishi

Keio University, Yokohama, Kanagawa 223-8522, Japan
m_yktkg@skeio.jp

Abstract. Motivation, which is considered to have a significant impact on human behavior, can be arranged along a continuum based on the degree of self-determination, according to the sub-theory of Self-Determination Theory known as Organismic Integration Theory. This continuum includes intrinsic motivation, extrinsic motivation, and other forms, with varying degrees of self-determination. Traditionally, the degree of self-determination has been measured subjectively, often through questionnaires. Therefore, this study aimed to objectively measure the degree of self-determination in motivation by examining the relationship between physio-logical indicators and self-determined motivation. As the experiment, participants engaged in tasks with using a personal computer to search for information and create materials. During these tasks, physiological indicators were measured, and the degree of self-determined motivation was assessed using an existing questionnaire that inquired about the reasons for performing the tasks. Based on the collected data, the study elucidated the correlation between some psychophysiological indices and the degree of self-determined motivation.

Keywords: Self-determination Theory · Motivation · Physiological Index

1 Introduction

1.1 Problem Statement

Motivation has a significant impact on human behavior. It is known to comprise two main concepts: intrinsic motivation and extrinsic motivation. Intrinsic motivation refers to motivation driven by the activity itself, where the act of engaging in the activity is its own reward. On the other hand, extrinsic motivation is driven by the attainment of outcomes that are separate from the activity itself [1]. However, extrinsic motivation is not always aimed at obtaining rewards or avoiding punishments. Even when motivated extrinsically, individuals may internalize the value of the activity, recognizing its importance and engaging in it with a high degree of self-determination. Thus, the way an individual

S. Jin et al. (Eds.): IEA 2024, SSDI 39, pp. 386–392, 2025.
https://doi.org/10.1007/978-981-95-0211-0_60

internalizes the value of the activity can lead to higher self-determination. Furthermore, intrinsic and extrinsic motivations can be placed on a continuum based on the degree of self-determination. This concept aligns with the Organismic Integration Theory (OIT) [2]. We show summary of Organismic Integration Theory in Fig. 1.

Behavior	Non-self-determined → Self-determined					
motivation	Amotivation	Extrinsic motivatin				Intrinsic motivation
Regulatory style	Non-Regulation	Extrinsic Regulation	Introjected Regulation	Identified Regulation	Integrated Regulation	Intrinsic Regulation
Relevant Regulatory Processes	Nonintentional, Nonvaluing, Incompetence, Lack of Control	Compliance, External Rewards and Punishments	Self-Control, Ego-Involvement, Contingent Self-Esteem	Personal Importance, Conscious Valuing	Congruence, Awareness, Synthesis of Identifications	Interest, Enjoyment, Inherent Satisfactio

Fig. 1. Summary of OIT [3]

In Fig. 1, regulatory styles represent the concept of motivation that corresponds to the reasons for engaging in an activity. The content of these reasons is used to determine the extent to which individuals internalize the value of the activity as their own [4].

Traditionally, the degree of self-determination has been evaluated using subjective measures such as questionnaires. However, objective indices for evaluating these aspects have not been thoroughly investigated [4]. Given that the relationship between intrinsic and extrinsic motivation and deep brain regions has already been revealed [5], there is significant potential for finding correlations with other physiological responses as well. It is thus anticipated that the degree of self-determination in motivation can be objectively evaluated using psychophysiological indices.

1.2 Objective

The purpose of this study is to reveal the relationship between psychophysiological indices and the degree of self-determination in order to establish an objective method for assessing the degree of self-determination of motivation at the level of human behavior from the perspective of Organismic Integration Theory.

2 Methodology

An experiment was conducted to measure physiological indices while performing a task and to measure the degree of self-determination to perform that task from an existing questionnaire. The measured physiological indices are cerebral blood flow, heart rate, and respiration rate.

The experiment participants performed the task with creating presentation on three different topics using Microsoft PowerPoint. The three topics were as follows. The first topic was about a Japanese social issue, either "Rising Prices" or the "2030 Problem." The experiment participants chose either of the topics they prefer and created a brief presentation summarizing the specifics of the social issue, potential solutions, and any aspects they found particularly interesting. The second topic was about "Things or Matters You Are Currently Interested In." The experiment participants freely chose and list things or matters they were currently interested in, regard-less of the genre, and created a presentation about them. The third topic was "About Air." They created a presentation summarizing the components and roles of air, along with any other related aspects they found interesting. The order of creating the presentations was randomly assigned to each participant, with a total of six possible sequences. The experiment participants freely searched the internet for the necessary information to create presentations on these topics.

The experiment participants performed multiple tasks believed to vary in the degree of self-determination involved. After completing each task, they responded to a questionnaire asking about their reasons for performing that particular task. The questionnaire used was a Japanese translation of the Situational Motivation Scale (SIMS) developed by Guay, Vallerand, and Blanchard (2000) [6]. SIMS has been reported to be adaptable to experimental induction and is a questionnaire designed to measure situational motivation. From the results of this questionnaire, the Self-Determination Index (SDI) developed by Vallerand & Ratelle (2002) was calculated as an indicator [7]. The interpretation is that the higher the score on this index, the more self-determined the motivation orientation is perceived to be. An analysis was conducted to examine the relationship between this indicator and the results of each physiological index.

3 Analysis Method

3.1 Subjective Evaluation Index

The 16 items of the SIMS questionnaire used in this experiment each pertain to one of four regulatory styles: Non-Regulation, External Regulation, Identified Regulation, and Intrinsic Regulation. The calculation method of the SDI is as follows. First, the average score of the four response scores for each question item is calculated for each adjustment style, and these are used as the scores for each regulatory style. However, to control for variability between participants, standardization was per-formed for each participant's scores of each adjustment style using the following method.

$$z_{ij} = \frac{x_{ij} - \overline{x}}{s_x}$$

$i = 1, 2, 3, 4$ (Kinds of regulatory style)

$j = 1, 2, 3$ (Task number)

$x_{11}, x_{12}, \ldots, x_{43}$:Scores for each regulatory style per task

$\overline{x}$:Average of $x_{11}, x_{12}, \ldots, x_{43}$.

s_x:Standard deviation of $x_{11}, x_{12}, \ldots, x_{43}$

The scores were standardized and adjusted into a standardized-regulatory style, and then used to calculate the SDI for each task using the following formula.

Standardized SDI =(Intrinsic Regulation Score) $\times$ 2 + (Identified Regulation Score)

$$- (\text{Extrinsic Regulation Score}) - (\text{Non} - \text{Regulation Score}) \times 2$$

However, in the above formula, the scores for each regulatory style are all based on standardized scores.

That is to say the higher the score on the SDI, the more self-determined the motivation orientation is perceived to be.

3.2 Psychophysiological Indices

The physiological indices data were analyzed as shown below.

First, for instantaneous heart rate, the average value of instantaneous heart rate during the task and at rest was calculated. Then, the average value during the task was obtained by subtracting the average value at rest from the average value during the task. Additionally, to control for individual variability, standardization was per-formed within each participant. Similarly, the average respiratory rate for each task was calculated using the same procedure for respiratory rate.

Next, the analysis of cerebral blood volume changes was conducted as follows. The OEG-16 used for measuring cerebral blood volume changes in this experiment consists of 16 channels, where ch5, ch8, and ch11 correspond to the Dorsolateral Prefrontal Cortex, ch4, ch7, ch10, and ch13 correspond to the Medial Prefrontal Cortex, ch1, ch2, ch14, and ch16 correspond to the Ventrolateral Prefrontal Cortex, and ch6, ch9, and ch12 correspond to the Orbitofrontal Cortex. The mean changes in oxyhemoglobin (Oxy-Hb) concentration were analyzed for each of these regions. The average changes in Oxy-Hb concentration during the task and at rest were calculated. Additionally, the average value during the task was obtained by subtracting the aver-age value at rest for each participant. Furthermore, to control for individual variability, standardization was performed within each participant.

4 Results

Significant experimental results are shown in order.

First, we show the results about respiration rate. There was a strong negative correlation (correlation coefficient = −0.74) between respiration rate and Self-Determination Index SDI in 7 of the 11 valid data (Fig. 2). That is to say the less self-determined tasks were performed, the higher the respiration rate in these experiment participants. Tasks that are less self-determined, or in other words, tasks that participants felt more compelled to do, likely caused them to experience more stress. It is thought that this stress activated the sympathetic nervous system, resulting in an increased respiration rate. We categorized these participants as Group A. On the other hand, there was a strong positive correlation (correlation coefficient = 0.63) between respiration rate and the Self-Determination Index (SDI) in the data of the remaining four participants (Fig. 3). This suggests that in these participants, as tasks become more self-determined, respiratory rates increase. It is speculated that tasks perceived as more self-determined lead to excitement due to finding interest or enjoyment, resulting in sympathetic nervous system dominance and increased respiratory rates. We categorized these participants as Group B.

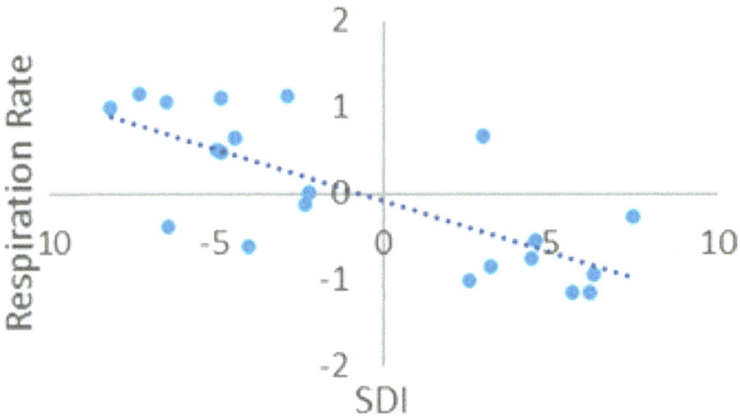

Fig. 2. Relationship between SDI and respiration rate (Group A)

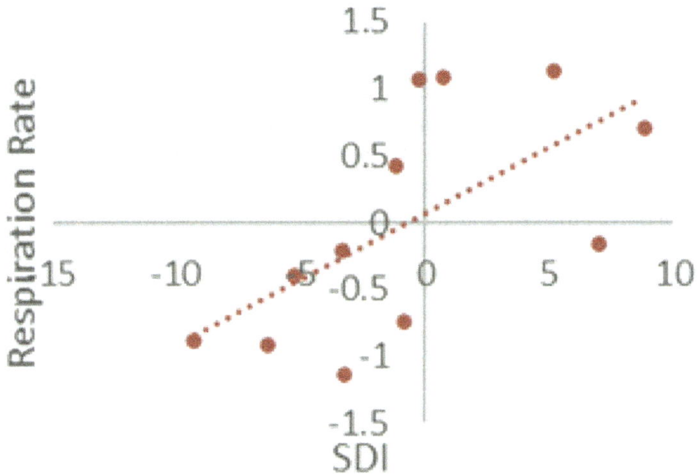

Fig. 3. Relationship between SDI and respiration rate (Group B)

The differences between the two groups were considered from the free-text statements about each task obtained from each experimental participant. Below are examples of the feedback about the tasks with the lowest SDI for each group of experimental participants.

From Table 1, it is suggested that participants in Group A felt bored and distressed during the tasks they perceived as the least self-determined, which corresponds to the lowest SDI. On the other hand, participants in Group B did not feel distressed despite perceiving the tasks as relatively less self-determined.

Table 1. Examples of feedback about tasks with the lowest SDI

Group A	· Upon researching, I found that it was mostly information I already knew, which made it less interesting
	· It was boring because it was all familiar information, leaving no room for new discoveries
Group B	· It has no interest in air but it felt nostalgic as it was a review of what I learned in the past
	· It was relatively easy to summarize and create materials on this topic, so I didn't feel much difficulty

Next, we show the results about cerebral blood volume changes. Since significant results were not obtained from Group B regarding the relationship between cerebral blood volume changes and SDI across the four brain regions, the results are shown only for Group A.

In the data of Group A, there was a relatively strong positive correlation (correlation coefficient = 0.41) between changes in oxyhemoglobin concentration in the Medial Prefrontal Cortex (MPFC) and the Self-Determination Index (SDI). The MPFC is known to be involved in spontaneity and motivation [8]. Therefore, this result suggests that in Group A participants, tasks performed with higher self-determination are associated with increased spontaneity and motivation. Additionally, there was a relatively strong positive correlation (correlation coefficient = 0.47) between changes in oxyhemoglobin concentration in the Orbitofrontal Cortex (OFC) and SDI. Previous studies have reported a negative correlation between the OFC and subjective fatigue [9]. Since the order of tasks was randomly assigned, any sequence effects were neutralized. This suggests that participants in Group A felt more fatigued during tasks that were less self-determined, or in other words, tasks they felt more compelled to do.

Therefore, it is suggested that measures such as respiration rate and the concentration changes of Oxy-Hb in the medial prefrontal cortex and ventrolateral prefrontal cortex could be effective indices for objectively evaluating the degree of self-determination in motivation.

5 Conclusion

This study revealed the relationship between physiological indices and the level of self-determination in order to establish a method for objectively evaluating the degree of self-determination in human behavioral levels from the perspective of Organismic Integration Theory. The results of the experiment suggest a correlation between respiration rate, changes in oxyhemoglobin concentration in the Medial Prefrontal Cortex, changes in oxyhemoglobin concentration in the Ventrolateral Prefrontal Cortex, and SDI.

References

1. Murray, E.J.: Motivation and Emotion. Prentice Hall, Englewood Cliffs, N.J (1964)

2. Ryan, R.M., Deci, E.L.: Self-determination theory and the facilitation of intrinsic motivation, social development, and Well-being. Am. Psychol. **55**(1), 68–78 (2000)
3. Ryan, R.M., Deci, E.L.: Self-determination theory: basic psychological needs in motivation, development, and wellness. The Guilford Press. **193** (2017)
4. Hisashi, U., Osamu, O.: New the Cutting Edge of Motivation Research. Kitaoji Shobo, Kyoto (2019)
5. Lee, W., et al.: Neural differences between intrinsic reasons for doing versus extrinsic reasons for doing: an fMRI study. Neurosci. Res. **73**(1), 68–72 (2012)
6. Guay, F., et al.: On the assessment of situational intrinsic and extrinsic motivation: the situational motivation scale (SIMS). Motiv. Emot. **24**(3), 175–213 (2000)
7. Vallerand, R.J., Ratelle, C.: F.: intrinsic and extrinsic motivation: a hierarchical model. In: Handbook of Self-Determination Research, pp. 37–63. University of Rochester Press, New York (2002)
8. Hiroshi, S., Toshihiro, K.: A change of the blood hemoglobin density in a prefrontal area at the time of attention control task enforcement - examination with "Kanahiroi" multi-cancellation test. Health Sci. **3**, 7–15 (2006)
9. Levy, R., Dubois, B.: Apathy and the functional anatomy of the prefrontal cortex– basal ganglia circuits. Cereb. Cortex. **16**(7), 916–928 (2006)

Aviation (I)

Addressing Complexity Between Controller and Display: Using Discrete and Continuous Concepts

Jaehoo Bae[1], Honghua Lyu[1], Joong Hee Lee[1], and Myung Hwan Yun[1,2](✉)

[1] Department of Industrial Engineering, Seoul National University, Seoul, South Korea
{jetishie,mhy}@snu.ac.kr

[2] Institute for Industrial System Innovation, Seoul National University, Seoul, South Korea

Abstract. Control devices are essential for interacting with displays in various fields. Therefore, effectively designing these controls and displays is crucial to ensure timely task completion and error avoidance. However, the complexity of these interactions has increased as the number of buttons on controllers has decreased while the amount of displayed information has grown. This study addresses usability issues caused by increased complexity. With familiar smart TV remote controls, we experimented with seven participants performing tasks using discrete and continuous controllers over 3 days. We measured task completion time (TCT) and user satisfaction to evaluate performance and learnability. Results showed that continuous controllers performed better for typing tasks, while discrete controllers excelled in content selection tasks. This study clarifies the interaction between tasks on displays and controllers by applying discrete and continuous concepts. Using commercially available remote controls in a familiar environment increases the generalizability of the findings. Further research in different domains and with dimension concepts can help address user discomfort with controllers that have fewer buttons but numerous functions.

Keywords: Human-Computer Interaction (HCI) · Usability · Controller and display · Smart TV · Discrete and continuous

1 Introduction

Control devices have been utilized to interact with displays across various fields, from small household appliances and vehicles to large factories and power plants, to manage situations. Each application possesses unique characteristics, underscoring the significance of designing controllers and displays tailored to specific traits [1]. To ensure that operators can complete tasks on time and avoid errors, controls and displays must be designed to make it easy for them to perform tasks [2].

Nowadays, as in Fig. 1, the complexity between displays and controllers has been increasing as the number of buttons has decreased, but the amount of information displayed has increased. In the automotive industry, introducing large screens has led to

S. Jin et al. (Eds.): IEA 2024, SSDI 39, pp. 395–401, 2025.
https://doi.org/10.1007/978-981-95-0211-0_61

fewer buttons, while the display tasks have become more numerous. Also, in the aviation sector, flight data are shown on digital-based electronic displays, with glass cockpits replacing separate gauges [3, 4]. Many new controllers are being developed and researched to cope with this complexity [5–7]. However, their application to various fields could be improved, often requiring additional learning.

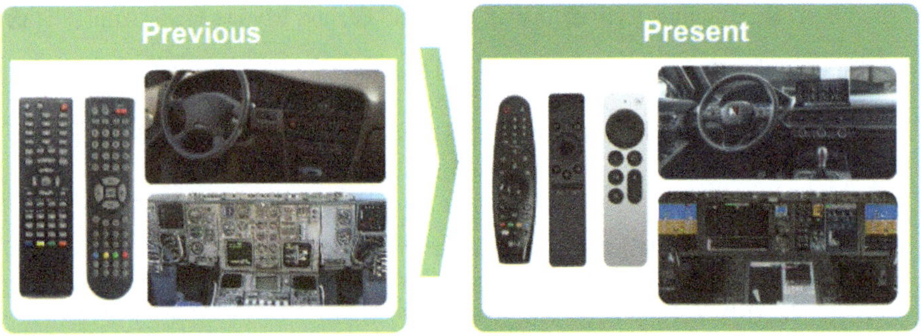

Fig. 1. Compared to the past, more buttons on controllers and more tasks can be done within the display, increasing the complexity between the two. This is the same situation from small home electronics like smart TVs to large automotive and aviation.

Therefore, this study aims to identify the optimal pairs of controllers and task types on display using familiar controllers: smart TVs and their remote controls. Remote controls have long had discomfort caused by several issues. On top of that, with the advent of smart TVs, new problems have emerged. Unlike traditional TV, smart TV offers a more complex interface for accessing a desired channel, necessitating increased interaction [8].

The experiment involved several tasks focused on smart TVs, which were unavailable in traditional TVs, and two types of remote controllers (i.e., discrete or continuous). Seven participants conducted tasks using two types of controllers for 3 days. We measured task completion time (TCT) and user satisfaction; then, performance and learnability were evaluated based on them. As a result, for the typing task, using the continuous controller demonstrated better performance (low TCT and high satisfaction). While for the selection task, the discrete controller performed better.

This study clarifies the interaction between tasks on displays and controllers by applying discrete and continuous concepts. We increased generalizability by using commercially available remote controls rather than specialized controllers in a laboratory setting. Further research in different domain scenarios and adding task dimension concepts could help address users' discomfort with controllers with fewer buttons than the numerous functions on display.

2 Method

Participants The experiment involved seven participants (M:4, F:3), and three had prior experience using smart TVs. All participants subscribed to and used at least one over-the-top (OTT) service through several smart devices.

Apparatus The experiment utilized two types of smart TVs and their corresponding remote controls. The first was a Samsung TV with a remote that only supported button operations (i.e., discrete controller). The second was an LG TV with buttons and an air mouse function (i.e., continuous controller) simultaneously in the remote controller. Each TV was set up considering screen size, participants' physical conditions based on Size Korea's 8th survey data [9], and viewing angles according to ISO 9355-2 standards [10] to ensure appropriate screen height and distance from the participants. We also used the Dikablis Eye-tracker to follow the gaze and analyze the data.

Procedures As in Fig. 2, participants received a brief overview of the experiment and signed a consent form. Afterward, they equipped eye-trackers and performed predetermined tasks. These tasks included finding a specific channel and using an OTT service to search for and play content. While some tasks, like channel selecting, are common to traditional TVs, the tasks primarily focused on those specific to OTT services, such as typing searches and navigating content timelines. The completion time for each task was measured, and after each task, participants provided satisfaction ratings and brief debriefings.

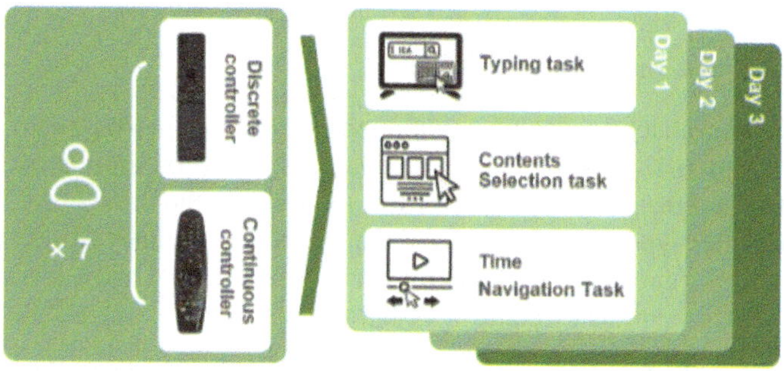

Fig. 2. The experimental process of this study. Seven participants completed tasks related to smart TVs using both discrete and continuous controller types over 3 days.

3 Results

3.1 Discrete Controller

We examined the differences in TCT and satisfaction for three types of tasks using the discrete controller. Due to varying scales across tasks, we normalized the data. The data did not meet parametric test assumptions, so we applied the Kruskal-Wallis H test.

The results showed (see Fig. 3) that while the normalized TCT for the typing task (M = 0.345, SD = 0.300) was the slowest, the difference with other tasks was not statistically significant ($\chi^2(2)=4.825$, $p = 0.090$). In terms of satisfaction, the typing task (M = 4.571, SD = 1.710) had the lowest scores with a statistically significant difference ($\chi^2(2)=7.637$, $p = 0.022^*$).

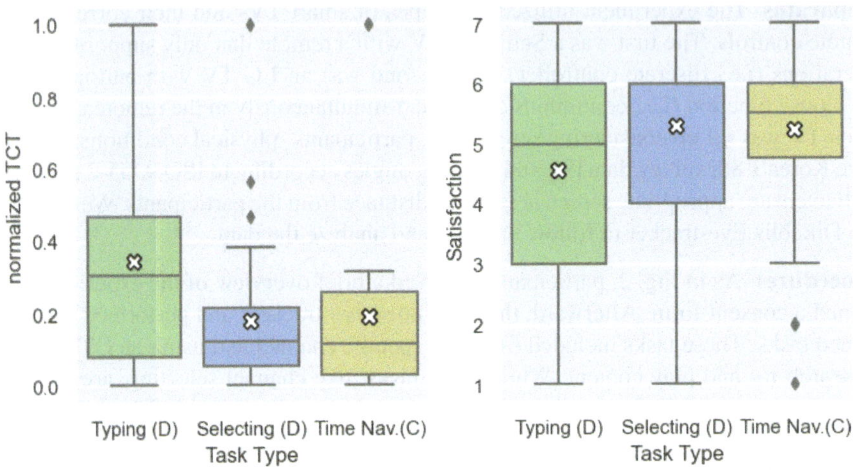

Fig. 3. Comparison of normalized TCT and satisfaction by task type when using a discrete controller. The typing task has the slowest TCT and lowest satisfaction

3.2 Discrete and Continuous Controller

Most data did not satisfy parametric assumptions for analyzing two types of controllers and three types of tasks, leading to two separate analyses. First, similar to the previous approach, we used the Kruskal-Wallis H test to compare the three tasks individually for each controller type. Next, we performed the Mann-Whitney U test to compare the performance of the two controllers for each specific task. Lastly, we analyzed the learnability across the trials by controllers and tasks.

Task Comparison by Controller Type (Fig. 4) For the discrete controller, the Kruskal-Wallis H test results showed that the normalized TCT was slowest for the typing task (M = 0.403, SD = 0.281), and differences were statistically significant ($\chi^2(2)$=26.603, $p < 0.001$***). For the continuous controller, the normalized TCT was slowest for the time navigation task (M = 0.444, SD = 0.382), and differences were statistically significant ($\chi^2(2)$=6.203, p = 0.045*). In terms of satisfaction, the selection task had the highest scores (M = 5.352, SD = 1.481), and differences were also statistically significant ($\chi^2(2)$=12.027, p = 0.002**). For the continuous controller, the selection task had the highest satisfaction (M = 5.067, SD = 1.580), but differences were not statistically significant ($\chi^2(2)$=2.286, p = 0.319).

Controller Comparison with Task Types (Fig. 5) For the typing task, the Mann-Whitney U test indicated that the continuous controller had a slightly faster TCT (U = 264.0, p = 0.255) and higher satisfaction (U = 131.0, p = 0.030*). For the selection task, the discrete controller showed a lower TCT (U = 2116.0, p = 0.007**) and no significant difference in satisfaction (U = 4453.0, p = 0.240). For the time navigation task, the discrete controller had a lower TCT (U = 87.0, p = 0.323) and higher satisfaction (U = 157.0, p = 0.212). However, neither difference was statistically significant.

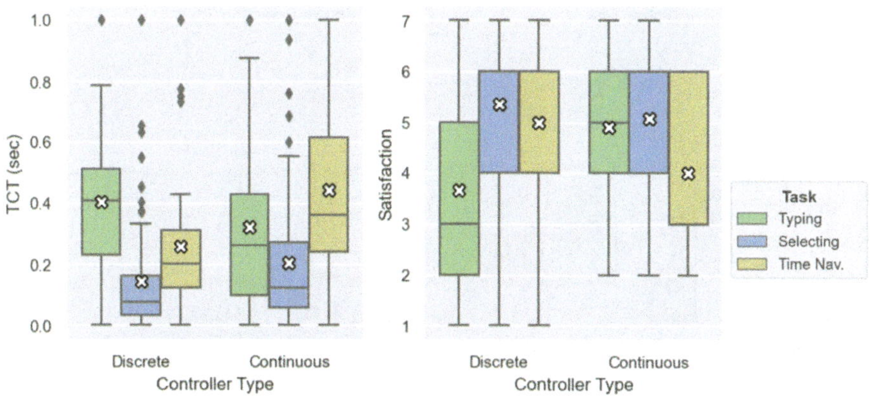

Fig. 4. Comparison of TCT and satisfaction by controller and task types. When performing the typing task with a discrete controller and the time navigation task with a continuous controller, the slowest TCT and lowest satisfaction is seen

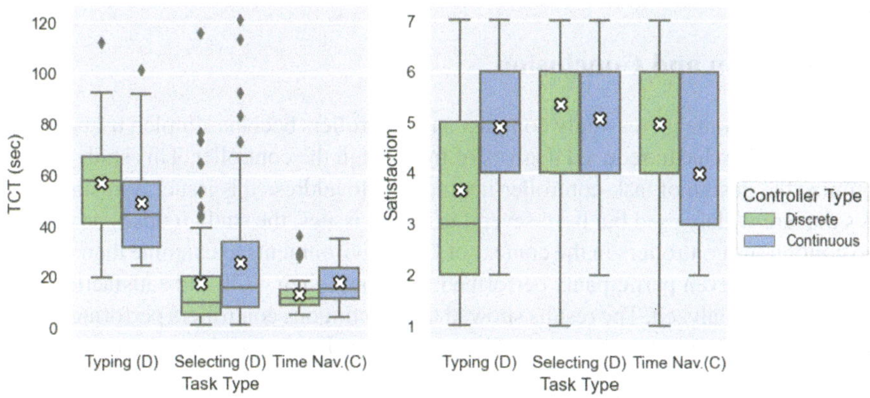

Fig. 5. Comparison of TCT and satisfaction based on task and controller types. The performance of the continuous controller for typing tasks, the discrete controller for selecting tasks, and the discrete controller for time navigation is better

Learnability (Fig. 6) We conducted a Kruskal-Wallis H test on the typing task using two types of controllers. When using the discrete controller (M = 57.000, SD = 26.002), there was a tendency for the TCT to decrease over the three trials. Still, the differences between them were not statistically significant ($\chi^2(2)=4.055$, p = 0.132). For the continuous controller (M = 49.790, SD = 20.464), the results were not statistically significant differences ($\chi^2(2)=0.493$, p = 0.781). For the selection task, when using the discrete controller (M = 17.583, SD = 20.266), the TCT showed no significant differences ($\chi^2(2)=0.778$, p = 0.678). However, when using the continuous controller (M = 25.435, SD = 25.470), there was a tendency for the TCT to increase, and this difference was statistically significant between trials ($\chi^2(2)=8.977$, p = 0.011).

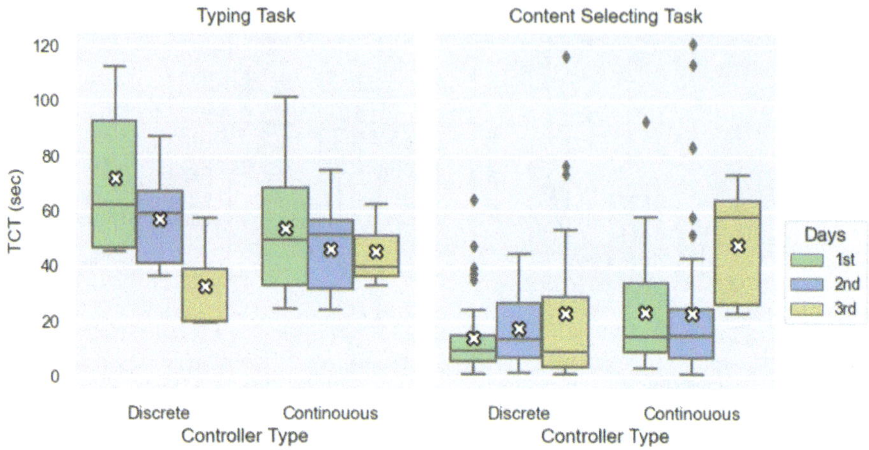

Fig. 6. Comparing learnability with controllers for a typing task and a content selection task across 3 trial days. Discrete controllers perform well on the typing task, but continuous controllers have stable TCTs. On the content selection task, continuous controllers perform poorly.

4 Discussion and Conclusion

As displays become increasingly complex and controllers become simpler, users experience discomfort due to reduced degrees of freedom in the controller. This study aims to optimize the design of task-controller interactions to address this issue. By using smart TVs that are widely used but have several usability issues, the study focuses on discrete and continuous controllers in the context of OTT environments to examine their optimal performance. Seven participants performed tasks, and their TCT and satisfaction were measured and analyzed. The results showed that continuous controllers performed better for typing tasks, while discrete controllers performed better for content selection tasks.

Task Completion Time and Satisfaction The typing task showed the lowest performance when conducted with discrete controllers. This is because typing tasks require frequent and repetitive finger position changes in multiple directions, increasing task complexity and duration. However, the finger position changes were relatively few for content selection and time navigation tasks, which involve pressing a single button multiple times or holding it down. Therefore, even with the same discrete controller, performance varied depending on the task type.

Learnability In typing tasks, the tendency for TCT to decrease indicates that discrete controllers show relatively good learnability. However, the average TCT was faster with continuous controllers, with smaller deviations over successive trials, suggesting a more stable performance. Conversely, continuous controllers showed lower learnability in selection tasks with increasing TCT and poor average TCT. Thus, in terms of learnability, continuous controllers are better suited for typing tasks, while discrete controllers are more suitable for selection tasks.

Previously, many guidelines and research focused on displays and controllers individually [1, 2, 11]. However, this study applied the discrete and continuous concepts traditionally associated with controllers to display tasks and identify their relationship, which was previously somewhat ambiguous. In practice, this study can help users revert to previous remotes with more buttons due to their inability to adapt to the fewer-button layout, and this study suggests possible solutions to this problem. Additionally, the significance of this study lies in its use of commercially available remote controls rather than specialized buttons in a laboratory setting.

Future studies can incorporate the concept of dimensions into the experimental design. In the time-shifting task, despite being a continuous task, participants used discrete controllers, and discrete controllers showed a tendency for better performance, although not statistically significant. This was interpreted as a dimension mismatch when using a 3-dimensional continuous controller (air mouse) for a 1-dimensional continuous task (horizontal movement). While there are commonalities between displays and controllers, different usage environments and scenarios, such as aviation and automotive fields, require additional research and experimentation for broader applicability.

Acknowledgments. This work was supported by the BK21 FOUR Program (Education and Research Center for Industrial Innovation Analytics) funded by the Ministry of Education, Korea.

References

1. Sanders, M.S., McCormick.: Human Factor in Engineering and Design. McGrawHill Book Company, New York, NY (1987)
2. Bhise, V.D.: Ergonom icsin the autom otive design process. CRC Press, Boca Raton, FL (2011)
3. Board, N.T.S.: Introduction of glass cockpit avionics into light aircraft. Safety Study (2010)
4. Thomas, P., Biswas, P., Langdon, P.: State-of-the-art and future concepts for interaction in aircraft cockpits. In: Universal Access in Human-Computer Interaction. Access to Interaction: 9th International Conference, UAHCI 2015, Held as Part of HCI International 2015, Los Angeles, CA, USA, August 2-7, 2015, Proceedings, Part II 9. Springer (2015)
5. Xie, Y., Zhou, R., Qu, J.: Fitts' law on the flight deck: evaluating touchscreens for aircraft tasks in actual flight scenarios. Ergonomics. **66**(4), 506–523 (2023)
6. Kaminani, S.: Human computer interaction issues with touch screen interfaces in the flight deck. In: 2011 IEEE/AIAA 30th Digital Avionics Systems Conference. IEEE (2011)
7. Rouwhorst, W., et al.: Use of touch screen display applications for aircraft flight control. In: 2017 IEEE/AIAA 36th Digital Avionics Systems Conference (DASC). IEEE (2017)
8. Alam, I., Khusro, S., Naeem, M.: A review of smart TV: Past, present, and future. In: 2017 International Conference on Open Source Systems & Technologies (ICOSST). IEEE (2017)
9. SizeKorea: The 8th National Human Body Measurements Survey (2023)
10. Standardization, I.O.f., ISO 9355-2: Ergonomic requirements for the design of displays and control actuators, in Part2: displays (1999)
11. Tsang, P.S., Vidulich, M.A.: Principles and Practice of Aviation Psychology. CRC Press (2002)

A Review of Spatial Disorientation in Flight

Sungho Kim[1(✉)], May Jorella S. Lazaro[2], and Myung Hwan Yun[3]

[1] Republic of Korea Air Force Academy, Cheongju, South Korea
sunghokim1123@gmail.com
[2] CX Insight Team, MX Division, Samsung Electronics, Suwon, South Korea
[3] Seoul National University, Seoul, South Korea

Abstract. Spatial disorientation (SD) is a significant threat in aviation, impairing pilot performance and leading to errors during flight. Despite ongoing research, effective measurement and countermeasures for SD are lacking. This study addresses this gap by conducting a comprehensive review of literature. The articles were collected through a combination of search keywords across databases and evaluated by multiple researchers based on their quality and relevance. Total 71 highly-relevant research papers on SD were selected and reviewed for this study. The selected papers were organized into three thematic areas for a structured analysis: (1) overview of SD, (2) SD countermeasures, and (3) measurements of pilot states during SD episodes. Through this analysis, this study identified promising avenues for future research on SD. This study can be utilized in order to develop and implement more effective strategies to prevent and mitigate SD in pilots. By doing so, it has the potential to significantly enhance SD management and bolster aviation safety.

Keywords: Spatial Disorientation · Countermeasures · Pilot State Measurements

1 Introduction

Spatial disorientation (SD) poses a significant threat to aviation safety. Pilot loss of orientation is a well-documented cause of critical aviation accidents, resulting in substantial casualties and aircraft losses [1]. Studies investigating aviation accidents reveal that SD is a major contributing factor, implicated in 14% of all flight mishaps and 26% of fatal aviation accidents [2]. Furthermore, the mortality rate associated with SD-related accidents is alarmingly high, approaching 100% [3]. Despite the prevalence and severity of SD, the rate of such incidents appears to be stagnant over time. This suggests a potential gap in preventative measures and the implementation of effective counteractive strategies to mitigate SD-induced accidents.

SD significantly hinders a pilot's ability to perform effectively, often leading to critical human errors during flight. These errors can be attributed to a combination of confusion and negative psychophysiological effects, including increased mental stress and heightened workload [4, 5]. Even when pilots recognize SD, successfully mitigating its consequences remains paramount to preventing accidents. Pilots must regain situational

S. Jin et al. (Eds.): IEA 2024, SSDI 39, pp. 402–408, 2025.
https://doi.org/10.1007/978-981-95-0211-0_62

awareness while simultaneously managing the elevated stress levels and increased cognitive demands induced by the disorientation. However, despite ongoing research efforts to understand and mitigate the detrimental effects of SD, a gap exists in our knowledge of truly effective measurements and countermeasures. Therefore, further investigation is crucial to identify and develop robust techniques that equip pilots to manage SD and ensure aviation safety.

While various methods have been explored to measure and counteract SD, re-search on truly effective and practical strategies remains insufficient. The inevitability of SD, often triggered by interactions between human physiology and environ-mental changes [6], underscores the need for immediate and proactive strategies to manage its effects. Fortunately, advancements in science and technology present opportunities to develop more effective SD measurement and countermeasures compared to traditional methods. The implementation of novel, advanced approaches can significantly contribute to preventing SD-related accidents and bolster-ing aviation safety.

This study seeks to contribute to advancements in SD management by conducting a comprehensive review of current literature. More specifically, it aims to solidify the core concepts surrounding SD, to investigate various strategies for effectively counteracting SD, and to explore the psychological and physiological states pilots experience during SD episodes, along with methods for measuring theses states. Through this analysis, the study ultimately aims to identify promising directions for future SD research efforts.

2 Method

2.1 Search Strategy

Acknowledging the potential for variations in keywords and terminologies, the search strategy employed broad and well-established keywords to achieve a comprehensive literature review. The keywords used for the search were "spatial disorientation", with alternate keywords ("SD", "illusion", "vertigo"), "countermeasure", with alternate keywords ("procedure", "engineering", "training"), and "pilot states", with alternate keywords ("psychological state", "physiological response", "measurement"). This approach ensured the search captured not only studies on SD itself but also those investigating potential countermeasures and the physiological and psychological factors influencing pilot states. The primary search utilized established databases including Scopus, Science Direct, Web of Science, and IEEE Xplore. With the aim of identifying a representative sample of research on SD, the search strategy encompassed both peer-reviewed journal articles and conference proceedings from relevant academic databases. To ensure comprehensiveness and capture potentially pertinent literature beyond the primary search, a secondary search strategy was implemented. This secondary approach involved backward referencing through the reference lists of identified review articles, alongside manual searching within Google Scholar.

2.2 Inclusion Criteria

The literature review process targeted a ten-year period (2011–2020) and included peer-reviewed journal articles and conference proceedings identified through selected research databases. The search condition included keywords from titles, abstracts, and author-defined keywords to ensure comprehensiveness. To capture relevant research across multiple disciplines, the search included subject areas related to engineering, psychology, computer science, social sciences, and physiology. Only English-language articles with complete full texts were included. During the initial screening, non-research materials such as workshop notes, editorials, commentaries, theses, dissertations, and incomplete records were excluded. Additionally, articles lacking relevant keywords were removed to ensure thematic focus.

2.3 Eligibility Criteria

Following the initial screening, full-text eligibility screening was conducted on all articles meeting the inclusion criteria. To ensure thematic coherence, articles were included if they satisfied the following criteria: (1) the study investigated SD in pilots specifically within the aerospace and aviation domain, (2) the focus of SD countermeasures was primarily on Human-Machine Interaction (HMI) aspects rather than solely technical solutions, hardware systems, or algorithm development, and (3) the evaluation of pilot states considered human-related factors such as task performance and psychophysiological responses. Additionally, a three-tier quality assessment (high, medium, low) was applied to the shortlisted articles. This assessment ensured thematic relevance by excluding studies deemed "low" quality. The final selection of 71 articles was then categorized into three thematic areas for a structured analysis: (1) overview of SD, (2) SD countermeasures, and (3) pilot state measurements.

3 Results

3.1 Overview of SD

SD refers to the pilots' false perception of the aircraft's position and motion relative to the Earth's surface, encompassing linear and angular movements [7, 8]. According to [9], the types of SD can be classified into three types (unrecognized, recognized, incapacitating) based on the pilot's consciousness and reaction to the flight situation. Type I (unrecognized) SD refers to a type in which pilots are unaware of any sings of disorientation. Type II (recognized) SD refers to a type in which pilots can consciously identify their disoriented state and take corrective actions. Type III (incapacitating) SD refers to a type in which pilots are aware of the disorientation but cannot respond effectively due to the severity of the episode.

Illusions in flight can be further categorized based on the sensory system primarily affected by the misperception [10]. The two main categories are visual and vestibular illusions. According to the features of visual orientation information processing using either focal or ambient vision, visual illusions can include aerial perspective illusion, autokinetic illusion, false horizon illusion, and vection illusion. On the other hand, the specific type of vestibular illusion depends on the combination of motion types (angular, linear) and visual connections (visible, non-visible) involved. This illusion can be classified into the following four categories: somatogyral illusion, oculogyral illusion, somatogravic illusion, and oculogravic illusion. Beyond these sensory-based illusions, other phenomena can contribute to SD, such as fascination, break-off, and flicker vertigo.

3.2 SD Countermeasures

This study examined SD countermeasures through three primary lenses: procedures, technology, and training. Procedural countermeasures encompass various in-flight protocols pilots can implement when experiencing SD. There are various in-flight procedures such as a transfer to instrument flight rules (IFR), maintaining straight-and-level flight, preserving postural stability, handover to co-pilot, and ejection from aircraft. Especially, IFR is a set of regulations that dictate how aircraft are to be operated when the pilot is unable to navigate the aircraft due to poor visual references. This rule is crucial for the pilots since it make them rely on the flight instrumental information as they maneuver the aircraft under disorientation episode.

For technology countermeasures, efforts to address SD problems primarily focus on developing support systems that provide pilots with alternative sensory cues to overcome disorientation including visual, auditory, and tactile senses. For example, external visual cues such as peripheral vision display [11], visual command icon [12], and attitude stabilization display [13] are used to give pilots additional information to control their spatial orientation and recover from an aircraft upset. On the other hand, the use of auditory countermeasures such as three-dimensional auditory displays [14] and acoustic orientation systems [15] have shown potential in helping pilots to improve overall situational awareness and in maintaining aircraft posture during straight-and-level, turning and descending flight phases. Also, the use of tactile stimulation was found to be effective in assisting pilots in recovering from the SD illusion by improving their motion control capability [16].

Three primary training approaches are utilized to address SD: lecture-based, in-flight, and ground-based simulation training. More specifically, lecture-based training helps pilots to understand the theoretical underpinnings of the SD phenomenon through lectures and discourse [17]. In-flight training provides pilots with firsthand experience of SD in an actual flight environment [18]. Ground-based simulation training allows pilots to experience SD similar to an actual flight scenario in a simulator equipped with sophisticated visual and motion cueing systems to induce certain physiological sensations [19].

3.3 Pilot State Measurements

Existing research has explored the various psychological and physiological states experienced by pilots during SD episodes. To give some examples, stress refers to the change in tension levels caused by pressure or demands from internal or external sources [20]. Attention refers to a highly complex concept that encompasses a wide range of cognitive processes such as perception, memory, and action planning [21]. Mental workload refers to the demands placed on the person's mental resources used to carry out different cognitive functions [22]. Situation awareness can be defined as the process of understanding what is going on in the environment and anticipating its implications for the present and future [23].

On the other hand, understanding these psychological and physiological states is crucial. Researchers have developed various methods to measure these states in pilots experiencing SD. More specifically, the performance measures can indirectly assess pilot state by evaluating factors like speed and accuracy in completing tasks. Physiological and behavioral measures provide more robust estimates of pilot state by analyzing bio-signals (e.g., heart rate) and eye-tracking data. Subjective measures have relied on self-reported information obtained through questionnaires.

4 Discussion

This study aimed to provide a comprehensive review of SD in flight through a systematic literature analysis. Papers were rigorously investigated using established procedures, including keyword selection, application of inclusion and eligibility criteria, and evaluation of research relevance. The review identified three key areas where human factors and ergonomics play a critical role in managing SD: understanding the core concept of SD, developing effective countermeasures, and accurately measuring pilot states during SD episodes. By synthesizing existing research on these areas, this review paper contributes to a deeper understanding of SD in flight and offers valuable insights for future research endeavors.

The analysis of research findings in this study has yielded several key considerations for researchers investigating SD. First, researchers are required to continuously explore novel SD types. The continuous emergence of new situations due to evolving environments and advancements in aviation technology necessitates ongoing exploration of potential new types of SD. For example, aerial refueling and unmanned aerial vehicle (UAV) operations may introduce previously unencountered types of disorientation. Next, researchers need to leverage recent technological advancements to develop new solutions and more sophisticated countermeasures against SD. For instance, this includes exploring the potential of virtual reality (VR), augmented reality (AR), and artificial intelligence (AI) in terms of training countermeasures. These technologies could potentially overcome limitations of existing ground-based simulations, maximizing training effectiveness and reducing costs. Last, researchers should find enhanced pilot state measurement techniques. Improving the accuracy and reliability of pilot state measurement remains crucial. Integrating data from flight performance, bio-signals, and eye movements in a non-invasive and real-time manner could provide a more realistic assessment of a pilot's state during SD episodes.

This study highlights the necessity for further investigation into the impact of SD on pilots. A key gap identified in the literature is the lack of research on validating testing protocols to systematically confirm the effects of SD in flight. Empirically testing pilots under various flight conditions and environmental settings is crucial to gain deeper insights into SD. Future research employing empirical studies based on systematic evaluation methods would significantly contribute to a more comprehensive understanding of SD characteristics.

5 Conclusion

This study has provided a comprehensive review of existing research on SD in flight, encompassing the core concept of SD, countermeasure strategies, and pilot state measurement techniques. However, it is evident that significant opportunities exist for further exploration and research to overcome current limitations and advance our understanding of this critical area.

A key recommendation for future research is to address identified gaps in testing protocols for SD. Rigorous validation of these protocols is essential to systematically confirm the effects of SD in flight scenarios. By conducting empirical studies based on robust evaluation methods, researchers can gain deeper insights into the effectiveness of various SD countermeasures. This knowledge would be instrumental in developing and implementing more effective strategies to prevent and mitigate SD in pilots, ultimately enhancing aviation safety.

References

1. Newman, D.G.: An Overview of Spatial Disorientation as a Factor in Aviation Accidents and Incidents (No. B2007/0063). Australian Transport Safety Bureau, Canberra City, Australia (2007)
2. Gibb, R., Ercoline, B., Scharff, L.: Spatial disorientation: decades of pilot fatalities. Aviat. Space Environ. Med. **82**(7), 717–724 (2011)
3. Estrada, A., Adam, G.E., Leduc, P.A.: Use of Simulator Spatial Disorientation Awareness Training Scenarios by the US Army and National Guard (No. RTO-MP-086). NATO RTO HFM Symposium on Spatial Disorientation in Military Vehicles: Causes, Consequences and Cures, La Coruña, Spain (2002)
4. Gresty, M.A., Golding, J.F., Le, H., Nightingale, K.: Cognitive impairment by spatial disorientation. Aviat. Space Environ. Med. **79**(2), 105–111 (2008)
5. Webb, C.M., Estrada III, A., Kelley, A.M.: The effects of spatial disorientation on cognitive processing. Int. J. Aviat. Psychol. **22**(3), 224–241 (2012)
6. Lewkowicz, R., Fudali-Czyż, A., Bałaj, B., Francuz, P.: Change detection flicker task effects on simulator-induced spatial disorientation events. Aerospace Med. Hum. Perform. **89**(10), 863–872 (2018)
7. Gillingham, K.K.: The spatial disorientation problem in the United States air Force. J. Vestib. Res. **2**(4), 297–306 (1992)
8. Martinussen, M., Hunter, D.R.: Aviation Psychology and Human Factors, 2nd edn. CRC Press, Boca Raton, FL (2017)
9. Previc, F.H., Ercoline, W.R.: Spatial Disorientation in Aviation, vol. 203. AIAA, Reston, VA (2004)
10. Stott, J.R., Benson, A.J.: Spatial orientation and disorientation in flight. In: Gradwell, D.P., Rainford, D.J. (eds.) Ernsting's Aviation and Space Medicine, 5th edn, pp. 281–320. CRC Press, Boca Raton, FL (2016)
11. Malcolm, R.: Pilot disorientation and the use of a peripheral vision display. Aviat. Space Environ. Med. **55**(3), 231–238 (1984)
12. Wickens, C.D., Self, B.P., Andre, T.S., Reynolds, T.J., Small, R.L.: Unusual attitude recoveries with a spatial disorientation icon. Int. J. Aviat. Psychol. **17**(2), 153–165 (2007)
13. Poisson, R.J.: Spatial Disorientation: Past, Present, and Future (No. AFIT-ENV-14-M-50). Air Force Institute of Technology Wright-Patterson AFB OH Graduate School of Engineering and Management (2014)
14. Bronkhorst, A.W., Veltman, J.A., Van Breda, L.: Application of a three-dimensional auditory display in a flight task. Hum. Factors. **38**(1), 23–33 (1996)
15. Lyons, T.J., Gillingham, K.K., Teas, D.C., Ercoline, W.R., Oakley, C.A.R.O.L.Y.N.: The effects of acoustic orientation cues on instrument flight performance in a flight simulator. Aviat. Space Environ. Med. **61**(8), 699–706 (1990)

16. Van Erp, J.B., Groen, E.L., Bos, J.E., Van Veen, H.A.: A tactile cockpit instrument supports the control of self-motion during spatial disorientation. Hum. Factors. **48**(2), 219–228 (2006)
17. Kal'avský, P., Ďurčo, S., Rozenberg, R., Antoško, M., Polishchuk, V., Jevčák, J., et al.: Human factors and analysis of methods, forms and didactic means of aviation education of military pilots. In: 2019 New Trends in Aviation Development (NTAD), pp. 77–81, Castle Karlova Koruna, Czech Republic, IEEE (2019, September)
18. Fussell, S., Dattel, A.R., Mullins, K.: Personality types and learning styles of collegiate aviation students. Int. J. Aviat. Aeron. Aerospace. **5**(3), 1 (2018)
19. Szczepanski, C., Skibniewski, W., Gasik, M., Truszczynski, O.: Standard flight simulator as a spatial disorientation training device. In: Modeling and Simulation Technologies Conference, p. 4077. AIAA, Denver, CO (2000)
20. Hancock, P.A., Warm, J.S.: A dynamic model of stress and sustained attention. Hum. Factors. **31**(5), 519–537 (1989)
21. Knudsen, E.I.: Fundamental components of attention. Annu. Rev. Neurosci. **30**, 57–78 (2007)
22. Wickens, C.D.: Multiple resources and performance prediction. Theor. Issues Ergon. Sci. **3**(2), 159–177 (2002)
23. Endsley, M.R.: Toward a theory of situation awareness in dynamic systems. Hum. Factors. **37**(1), 32–64 (1995)

Evaluation of Pilots' Perception While Using Past, Current, and Emerging Aircraft Taxiing Support Technologies

Chang-Geun Oh(✉) and Kyu Wang Kim

Hanseo University, Taean, Republic of Korea
{coh,kimchi1230}@hanseo.ac.kr

Abstract. This study assessed the pilot performance in the human-in-the-loop (HITL) simulation environment with three conditions – the past paper charts, the current electronic 2D maps on the iPad Foreflight app, and the emerging augmented graphics of routing visualized on the windshield. The experimenter asked three groups of pilots to conduct taxiing operations using a medium-fidelity flight simulator in the three conditions. As a mock air traffic controller provided the participants with the simulated taxiing instructions in the airport, participants were asked to mark their current spatial positions on the paper chart to evaluate the situation awareness level. Participants rated their subjective perception of how they identified meaningful spatial objects, other aircraft on taxiing operations, the current spatial position, how they recognized the next taxiing procedures, and how they stayed focused on the ATC's taxiing instructions. The results reveal that the participants felt that referring to the Foreflight and the augmented graphics was better than referring to paper charts. Based on the study implications, a combined interface of augmented routing lines on the airport chart and augmented reality-based egocentric windshield graphics could be a good solution to maximize taxi performance regardless of weather conditions.

Keywords: aircraft taxi operations · augmented reality · electronic flight bag · situation awareness

1 Background

1.1 Aircraft Surface Operation Support Technologies

Aircraft must conduct their taxi operations along specified routes within designated timeframes at major airports, where there is a high volume of surface air traffic. As air traffic increases, any failure to move within the correct space and time can disrupt the flow of aircraft entering and exiting the airports. Pilots rely on airport charts and taxi signs, in conjunction with air traffic controller instructions, to conduct their taxi operations. These charts may be in paper or electronic format. Taxi operations at unfamiliar, busy airports under adverse weather conditions and time pressure can increase pilots' workload and lead to human errors.

S. Jin et al. (Eds.): IEA 2024, SSDI 39, pp. 409–415, 2025.
https://doi.org/10.1007/978-981-95-0211-0_63

To address this, NASA has developed and tested a cockpit display solution to support aircraft surface operations. The Taxiway Navigation and Situation Awareness (T-NASA) system, comprising an electronic moving map (EMM) and a head-up display (HUD), has been shown to enhance pilots' spatial and temporal awareness during taxiing, especially in low visibility conditions [1–3]. The EMM component provides a moving map with a planned taxi route and displays the aircraft's time conformance within the airport [4, 5] developed and tested an augmented reality goggle device—Head-Worn Display (HWD)—as a replacement for the HUD component of the T-NASA system. Simulation tests [1, 6] and actual flight tests [1, 5, 7] have been conducted to evaluate the taxi route function of the T-NASA system. NASA has also discussed the challenges of commercializing T-NASA systems, such as those faced in establishing traffic collision avoidance systems (TCAS) or ground proximity warning systems (GPWS). Identified barriers include traffic surveillance failure, HUD-induced complacency, and mixed equipment fleets [1]. As of 2024, no airlines have adopted the T-NASA system for supporting pilots' safe and efficient surface taxiing operations. This may be due to the system's cost-effectiveness not convincing airlines, unresolved technological limitations, and the increased size of relevant aeronautical data.

Meanwhile, research on aircraft taxi operation support systems has continued. [8] developed an electronic flight bag (EFB) system that displays taxi route lines on a surface map and provides runway incursion alerts. Third-party avionics companies have developed apps that include airport moving maps with augmented taxi route lines. Pilots can now refer to augmented taxi route lines on 2D-based electronic airport charts, such as the ForeFlight app on an iPad. This function helps reduce the cognitive load and effort required for accurate spatial mapping. HUD technologies and AR goggle devices have also become more popular. Additionally, airport facilities have implemented the follow-the-greens (FtG) function, where green surface taxi lights form a single line guiding the taxiing aircraft to their ground destinations (e.g., terminals, hangars, or runways). However, FtG can cause conformance errors [9], and its visibility can be compromised in daylight or heavy snow. Empirical evaluations of these new technologies are necessary to assess their acceptance in the aviation field.

2 Experiment

2.1 Test Objective

This study conducted empirical tests to evaluate past, current, and emerging cockpit technologies that support pilot aircraft taxiing operations, aiming to identify the most promising taxi support methods for the future.

2.2 Research Design

This study utilized a 3×3 within-subject design. The independent variables were the condition of routing reference (Paper Chart, ForeFlight app on iPad tablet, Taxi Ribbon routing graphics of FS2023) and the participant class (student pilot, instructor pilot, and airline captain). The dependent variables were: (1) subjective responses to the post-task questionnaire, (2) SA Accuracy, (3) SA Response Time (RT), and (4) participants' additional feedback.

The post-task questionnaire comprised five questions: Q1 assessed the degree of awareness of terrain, terminals, and guidance equipment; Q2 evaluated the degree of identifying other aircraft on the ground; Q3 measured awareness of the current location; Q4 gauged the recognition of the next taxiing stage; and Q5 examined attentiveness to ATC instructions. Responses were recorded on a 10-point Likert scale. Additionally, the test sheet included a question about any extra mission barriers encountered during the taxiing tasks.

Objective measurements included the response accuracy of marking the current location (queried three times per condition), the RT from the prompt to the marking instance, and the feedback on specific navigation barriers. Experimenters used a stopwatch to measure response times (Fig. 1).

Fig. 1. Experimental Condition: Paper Chart, Foreflight, Taxi Ribbon (from left to right)

2.3 Test Apparatus

This study used a medium-fidelity simulator equipped with a mock ATC station (Fig. 2). The simulator included a yoke, a throttle, a rudder pedal, a pilot sheet, and three 55-in. TVs to display out-the-window scenery. The flight simulation program used was Microsoft Flight Simulator 2020, with the B787 selected as the subject aircraft.

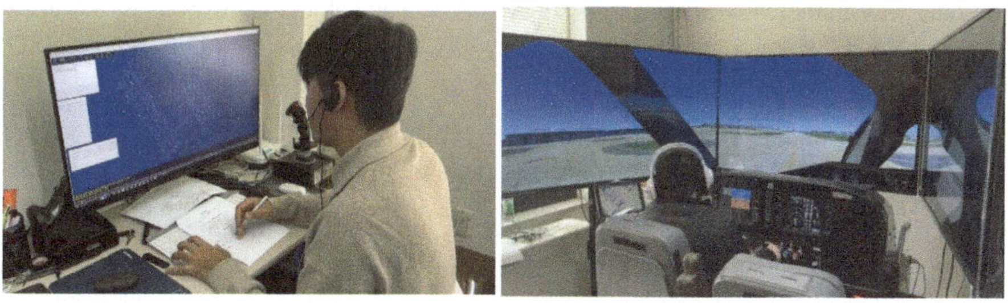

Fig. 2. Mock Air Traffic Controller (left), Flight Simulator for This Study (right)

2.4 Test Procedures

After the informed consent procedure, participants underwent a practice session of simulated taxiing operations in a B787 cockpit setting. In the paper chart condition, participants referred only to the paper chart for their surface navigation. In the ForeFlight condition, participants used the taxi route line on the electronic airport chart. In the taxi ribbon condition, participants focused on the augmented chevron graphics, with the ForeFlight app's current position visible but without the taxi route line. The experimenter counterbalanced the order of the test conditions. By mixing the three prepared taxiing scenarios with the counterbalanced order, the tasks for all 30 participants were heterogeneous.

The scenario did not include take-off and landing. Participants were instructed to maintain a taxiing speed not exceeding 20 knots. They were required to perform realistic taxiing tasks by responding to the mock air traffic controller's instructions. The mock controller instructed participants to hold the aircraft at certain locations and asked them to mark their current location on a given paper chart. The maximum allowed time to mark the position was 12 s. This request was made three times per condition without any cues, and participants' response times were measured.

Upon completion of the tasks in the three conditions, participants were provided with a post-task questionnaire. They responded to rating questions and gave retrospective feedback. The total time to complete all tasks was approximately 100 min.

2.5 Participants

Thirty pilots participated in the experiment, including 10 student pilots, 10 instructor pilots, and 10 airline captains (28 males and 2 females). The student pilots were in training at Hanseo University and held both private pilot and instrument rating licenses. The instructor pilots had accumulated more than 50 flight hours as instructors at Hanseo University. The airline captains were active captains from four different airlines. All participants received monetary compensation. The university's Institutional Review Board (IRB) approved the study.

3 Results

The data was statistically analyzed using ANOVA. The subjective responses, SA accuracy, and SA RT were compared using Tukey's Honestly Significant Difference (HSD) method ($\alpha = 0.05$).

Objective Responses There was no significant difference in SA Accuracy and SA RT among the Paper Chart, ForeFlight, and Taxi Ribbon graphics conditions.

Subjective Responses Figure 3 shows the analyzed results of the interaction between condition and participant class. The indication of "Level" above each bar graph represents the analyzed level of Tukey HSD, where the same letter indicates no significant difference among the conditions. For the instructor and captain groups, the subjective perception of the Paper Chart condition ($M_{Paper\ Chart,\ Instructor} = 5.88$, $M_{Paper\ Chart,\ Captain} = 6.12$) was more difficult than the ForeFlight ($M_{Foreflight,\ Instructor} = 3.44$, $M_{Foreflight,\ Captain} = 3.54$) and Taxi Ribbon ($M_{Taxi\ Ribbon,\ Instructor} = 3.80$, $M_{Taxi\ Ribbon,\ Captain} = 3.24$) conditions. There was no difference between the ForeFlight and Taxi Ribbon conditions in these two classes. In the student group, there was a significant difference between the Paper Chart and ForeFlight conditions ($M_{Paper\ Chart,\ Student} = 4.94$, $M_{Foreflight,\ Student} = 2.88$), but no difference between the Paper Chart and Taxi Ribbon conditions ($M_{Taxi\ Ribbon,\ Student} = 3.76$), or between the ForeFlight and Taxi Ribbon conditions.

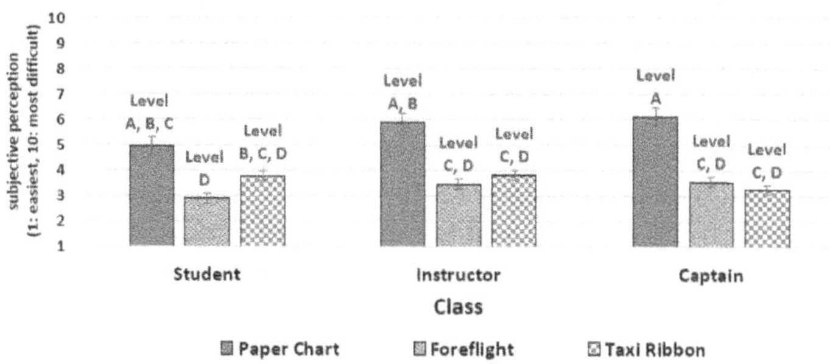

Fig. 3. Subjective Responses in Participant Class and Condition

In terms of the main effects of conditions, the Paper Chart ($M = 5.65$) condition was perceived to be more difficult than the ForeFlight ($M = 3.29$) and Taxi Ribbon ($M = 3.60$) conditions, with no difference between ForeFlight and Taxi Ribbon. Regarding the main effect of the participant class, there was no significant difference among the student ($M = 3.86$), instructor ($M = 4.37$), and captain groups ($M = 4.3$; Fig. 4).

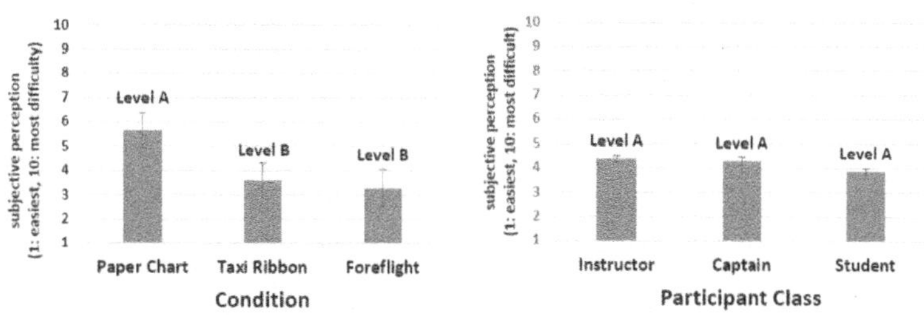

Fig. 4. Main Effects of Condition (Left), Participant Class (Right)

4 Discussions and Conclusions

Pilots felt that using the ForeFlight and Taxi Ribbon technologies supported their taxiing operations similarly and was easier than referring to Paper Charts. This study reflects pilots' perceptions of advanced taxiing support technology as of 2023, compared to the evaluation of SA and subjective responses of the T-NASA system over a decade ago [6, 10]. The ForeFlight (allocentric view display) and Taxi Ribbon (egocentric view display) conditions in this study are equivalent to the T-NASA system's EMM and HUD/HWD components, respectively. The augmented Taxi Ribbon graphics did not outperform ForeFlight, possibly because each function has its advantages as an information source in allocentric and egocentric views [11].

[1] discussed user acceptance of the T-NASA system, which had not been fully embraced by the aviation community at that time. This study evaluated SA and human perceptions using the taxi route indication on the Foreflight app, which represents an advancement of the T-NASA system. Many pilots currently refer to the app for their operations, and the HUD and HWD components of the T-NASA system are now available for implementation.

Recent innovative technologies may offer better options than HUD or HWD. Transportation AI applications could integrate all relevant information for aircraft surface operations to proactively reduce human errors. Transparent display or AR windshield technologies may allow the entire windshield to serve as a display area for augmented taxi routing information, accurately aligning augmented visuals with real objects from the pilot's perspective, similar to the Taxi Ribbon condition in this study. The AR windshield display is currently being seriously considered for surface transportation user interfaces [12].

However, participants' feedback indicated a potential problem: pilots might overly rely on the ForeFlight or Taxi Ribbon functions, which could degrade their operational SA. Without these functions, pilots should mentally set up their navigation maps to avoid taxiing errors.

Acknowledgments. This research was supported by the Basic Science Research Program through the National Research Foundation of Korea (NRF), funded by the Ministry of Education (202201450002).

References

1. Hooey, B.L., Foyle, D.C., Andre, A.D.: A human-centered methodology for the design, evaluation, and integration of cockpit displays. In: Proceedings of the NATO RTO SCI and SET Symposium on Enhanced and Synthetic Vision Systems, NATO (2002)
2. Jones, D.R., et al.: Flight Demonstration of Integrated Airport Surface Technologies for Increased Capacity and Safety. No. NAS 1.15: 206930. (1998)
3. Foyle, D.C., Andre, A.D., Hooey, B.L.: Situation awareness in an augmented reality cockpit: Design, viewpoints and cognitive glue. In: Proceedings of the 11th International Conference on Human Computer Interaction, vol. 1, (2005)
4. Shelton, K.J., et al.: Data-link and surface map traffic intent displays for NextGen 4DT and equivalent visual surface operations. In: Enhanced and Synthetic Vision 2009, vol. 7328. SPIE (2009)
5. Arthur, I.I.I., Jarvis, J., et al.: Design and testing of an unlimited field-of-regard synthetic vision head-worn display for commercial aircraft surface operations. In: Enhanced and Synthetic Vision 2007, vol. 6559. SPIE (2007)

6. Arthur III, JJ., et al. Head-Worn Display Concepts for Surface Operations for Commerical Aircraft. No. L-19449. (2008)
7. Young, S.D., Jones, D.R.: Flight Testing of an Airport Surface Guidance, Navigation, and Control System. ION National Technical Meeting (1998)
8. Theunissen, E., et al.: Evaluation of an electronic flight bag with integrated routing and runway incursion detection functions. In: 24th Digital Avionics Systems Conference, vol. 1. IEEE (2005)
9. Zhang, T., Weiszer, M., Chen, J.: The feasibility of follow-the-greens for 4-dimensional trajectory based airport ground movements. Transport. Res. Part C Emerg. Technol. **116**, 102632 (2020)
10. Prinzel III, L.J., Jones, D.R.: Cockpit technology for the prevention of general aviation runway incursions. In: 2007 International Symposium on Aviation Psychology (2007)
11. Klatzky, R.L.: Allocentric and egocentric spatial representations: Definitions, distinctions, and interconnections. In: Spatial Cognition: An Interdisciplinary Approach to Representing and Processing Spatial Knowledge, pp. 1–17. Springer Berlin Heidelberg, Berlin, Heidelberg (1998)
12. Riegler, A., et al.: Augmented reality windshield displays and their potential to enhance user experience in automated driving. i-com. **18**(2), 127–149 (2019)

Biosignal (I)

Ergonomics Evaluation Modeling of Multi-modal Interaction Technology for Airplane Cockpit and Experimental Validation

Lin Ding[1,2], Minhui Yuan[2], and Ruifeng Yu[2](✉)

[1] AVIC China Aero-Polytechnology Establishment, Beijing, China
[2] Tsinghua University, Beijing, China
yurf@mail.tsinghua.edu.cn

Abstract. With the development of control technologies such as eye movement control, voice control, and gesture control, multi-modal human-computer interaction has become a leading development trend for future aircraft cockpits. However, current research on multi-modal interaction primarily focuses on comparisons between single-modal and multi-modal interaction, and the evaluation models are often conducted for a single-modal method. A com-prehensive ergonomic evaluation method for multi-modal interaction has not yet been developed. This research proposes an evaluation model for multi-modal interaction in aircraft cockpits, incorporating "Task Conflict Evaluation—Channel Conflict Evaluation—Channel Load Evaluation," based on the analysis of pilots' information cognitive processing. The model sequentially evaluates the workload of multi-modal interaction technology in aircraft cockpit scenarios from the perspectives of task level, channel occupancy, and channel resource demand. Validation experiments were conducted using route planning tasks, assessing the workload for tactile interaction modes and multi-modal interaction modes, and comparing them with subjective workload and behavioral performance to confirm the effectiveness of our evaluation model.

Keywords: Multi-modal human-computer interaction technology · Aircraft cockpit · Ergonomics evaluation model

1 Introduction

Multi-modal interaction technology has become a major development trend for future aircraft cockpit. Multi-modal interaction technology mainly utilizes channels such as voice and vision for system control, aiming to free up hands for other tasks and change the traditional cockpit interactions highly rely on tactile inputs. However, irrational design might involve conflicts between tasks and channels, thereby reducing the effectiveness. Therefore, conducting evaluations of Multi-modal interaction technology during the design phase is essential.

S. Jin et al. (Eds.): IEA 2024, SSDI 39, pp. 419–425, 2025.
https://doi.org/10.1007/978-981-95-0211-0_64

Multi-modal interaction technology has been shown to reduce errors, lessen cognitive load, and enhance efficiency compared to single-channel interaction [1]. It also increases user satisfaction in virtual reality environments [2] and compensates for the limitations of single-channel methods [3]. In emergencies, multi-modal responses are quicker and more adaptable, proving their effectiveness across different sensory inputs and urgent conditions [4]. Rakkolainen summarized multi-modal interaction technologies based on human sensory classifications, highlighting the technical feasibility and interactions between various technologies [5]. Current research in multi-modal interaction technology mainly focused on integration methods and application forms, and evaluation methods concentrate on the assessment of single channel. Therefore, a comprehensive ergonomic evaluation method for multi-modal interaction technology remains to be developed.

2 Ergonomics Evaluation Modeling of Multi-Modal Interaction Technology for Airplane Cockpit

2.1 Analysis of Pilot Information Cognitive Processing

Multiple Resource Theory explains resource allocation among multiple tasks and the relationship between load and task difficulty [6], providing a perspective to assess the rationality of multi-channel interaction technology in aircraft cockpits from the resource channel. Based on this theory, pilots' human-machine operation can be decomposed into four channels: Visual, Auditory, Cognitive, and Perception. By analyzing the usage of each channel, the occupancy under multi-channel interaction technology can be evaluated, thus assessing the rationality of multi-channel interaction design or the appropriateness of multi-channel integration.

The pilot information cognitive processing process (Fig. 1) mainly originates from the input of visuals, sound, and somatosensory information, and the output of visual, vocal, gesture, and tactile control. Sound information enters through the ears into the auditory channel, visuals through the eyes into the visual channel, and somatosensory through the haptic into the tactile channel. Human cognitive behavior allows for the selective processing of perceived information, thereby entering working memory [7]. While processing information, working memory updates and mobilizes long-term memory to process information from different perceived channels [7]. Each channel, while processing its own information, can also integrate with other channels to collectively integrate information, such as "visual-auditory integration," "Tactile- auditory integration," and "Tactile-visual integration" [8]. Through the comprehensive integration of information from different channels, the pilot will make decisions and proceed operation, selecting the appropriate control method to manipulate the aircraft. During the process of pilots' operation, there is a possibility that information inputs, outputs or input and output occupy the same channel. Therefore, identifying and analyzing conflicts and including them into the evaluation method will be beneficial for eliminating conflicts both in tasks and channels during the design phase.

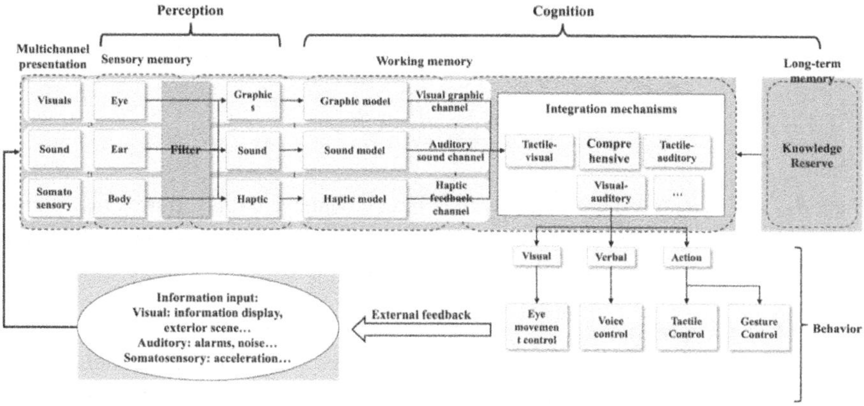

Fig. 1. Pilot information process integrating multi-modal human-machine interaction technology modes

2.2 Comprehensive Ergonomics Evaluation Model for Multi-Modal Interaction Technology

HTA is a method that decomposes complex task systems into sub-tasks and steps, useful for understanding the sequence of task execution and the relationships between steps and sub-tasks. Based on this, this study proposed a "Task Conflict Evaluation—Channel Conflict Evaluation—Channel Load Evaluation" evaluation model.

Task Conflict Evaluation

$\mathrm{N_t}$ represents the number of tasks that the operator needs to handle at time t, evaluated through the decomposition of tasks using HTA.

$$\mathrm{N_t} = \sum_{j=1}^{n} \mathrm{B_{jt}} \tag{1}$$

where $\mathrm{B_{jt}} = 1$ represents the jth task that needs to be completed at time t.

Channel Conflict Evaluation

Channel conflict evaluation assess the occupancy of each channel based on the decomposition of tasks into various channels.

Visual/Auditory. $\mathrm{Nv_t}$ / $\mathrm{Na_t}$ represents the visual/auditory channel conflict of the operator under multi-modal interaction tasks.

$$\mathrm{Nv_t} = \sum_{j=1}^{n} B_{vjt} / \mathrm{Na_t} = \sum_{j=1}^{n} B_{ajt} \tag{2}$$

Where $B_{vjt} = 1/B_{ajt} = 1$ indicates the occupancy of visual/auditory channel at time t during task j.

Behavior Channel. Npt represents the behavior channel conflict of the operator under multi-modal interaction tasks.

$$\mathrm{Np_t} = \sum_{j=1}^{n} \left(B_{sjt} + B_{hjt}\right) \tag{3}$$

Where $B_{sjt} = 1$ indicates the occupancy of behavior channel at time t during task j due to voice control behavior. Similarly, $B_{hjt} = 1$ indicates the occupancy of behavior channel at time t during task j due to hand control behavior.

Channel Load Evaluation

$\mathrm{W_T}$ represents the workload at moment T, constructed based on the channel behavior after task decomposition. It enables the analysis of the changes in channel resource demands of the operator during task [9].

$$W_T = \left[\sum_{\mathrm{i}=1}^{l}\sum_{t=1}^{m} a_{i,\mathrm{t}}\right] + [\sum_{i=1}^{l} c_{i,i}\sum_{t=1}^{m} a_{t,j} + \sum_{\mathrm{i}=1}^{i-1}\sum_{j=i+1}^{l} c_{i,j} \sum_{t=1}^{m-1}\sum_{s=t+1}^{m} \left(\left(a_{t,i} + a_{s,j}\right) + \left(a_{t,j} + a_{s,i}\right)\right)] \tag{4}$$

Where a_{ij} represents the occupancy of channel i in task j, c_{ii} represents intra-channel conflict coefficient, and c_{ij} represents inter-channel conflict coefficient.

3 Model Validation Experiment

The experiment recruited 20 pilots, all of them have extensive flying experience. Participants were required to complete a flight route planning task using both touch interaction and multi-modal interaction modes. The order of interaction modes was randomized. After each task, participants filled out the NASA-TLX scale as subjective workload and recorded the task time.

This study developed a stimulation platform for multi-modal interaction in aircraft cockpit, integrating various control modes such as gesture control, touch control, voice control, and eye movement control. The flight route planning task can be decomposed into eight subtasks: Insert a new waypoint before waypoint 3 (step 1); Set the formation pattern of the new waypoint to Formation 1 (step 2); Set the flight altitude of the new waypoint to 12,000 (step 3); Set the flight speed of the new waypoint to 345 (step 4); Change the geographical location of the new waypoint to enemy target A2 (step 5); Play the simulation process(step 6); Adjust the play speed to five times (step 7); End play(step 8). In the Tactile interaction mode, participants were asked to complete eight subtasks only by haptic channel. In the multi-modal interaction mode, participants' operations are allocated in different channels. For example, step 1 can be decomposed as: Action channel (voice): Long press the voice button and say "Waypoint 3″. Action channel (voice) and Visual channel: After Waypoint 3 is highlighted, gaze at the waypoint list, long press the voice button, and say "Insert".

4 Results and Discussion

Task time ($t(18) = -5.89, P < 0.001$) and subjective workload ($t(16) = -2.11, P = 0.051$) of multi-modal interaction modes($M_{subjective\text{-}workload} = 33.96$, $M_{Tasktime} = 45.13$) were significantly higher than touch interaction modes($M_{subjective\text{-}workload} = 27.79$, $M_{Tasktime} = 41.41$). These findings indicated that tactile interaction mode was found to be more convenient and lower workload, which contradicts previous research [1]. This discrepancy may be due to the high proficiency of our participants with the tactile interaction mode. Consequently, participants required extensive memory and thought in multi-modal interaction mode, leading to cognitive differences, which were confirmed by the subjective workload.

Since the experiment focused on a single task, there was no task conflict. An analysis of channel occupancy for each step of the task is shown in Table 1. The results indicate that channel conflict was low, so the conflict coefficient can be considered as 0. Therefore, the channel load was directly scored by experts referring to the VACP scale [10] (as shown in parentheses in Table 1).

Table 1. Decomposition of Channel Occupancy by Interaction Mode.

Interaction mode	Channel	Step 1	Step 2	Step 3	Step 4	Step 5	Step 6	Step 7	Step 8
Tactile interaction mode	Cognition	Symbol/Signal Recognition (1.2)							
	Action	Discontinuous Response (2.2)		Continuous Adjustment (2.6)			Discontinuous Response (2.2)		
	Visual	Visual Positioning/ Adjustment (4)					Visual Observation/ Inspection (3)		
Multi-modal interaction mode	Cognition	Decoding/Encoding, Recollection (5.3)							
	Action	Simple Language (2)		Continuous Adjustment (2.6)		Simple Language(2)			
	Visual		Visual Observation/ Inspection (3)	Visual Tracking/ Gazing (4.4)		Visual Observation/Inspection (3)			

The comparative analysis of channel workload across various interaction modes at each procedural step is illustrated in Fig. 2(a), highlighting distinct workload discrepancies primarily in cognitive and visual channels. Specifically, the touch interaction mode consistently exhibits a lower cognitive workload compared to the multi-modal mode. In visual channels, certain steps managed by voice command mitigate the need for visual engagement. This aligns with Oviatt's findings, where users prefer unimodal inputs for simple tasks but shift towards multi-modal inputs as task complexity increases [11], possibly due to the cognitive overload and distraction caused by superfluous input channels in straightforward tasks. Figure 2(b) depicts the comparative evaluation of different methodologies, confirming consistent trends across interaction modes, with multi-modal interaction generally incurring higher workload than touch interaction. This aligns with time and subjective workload outcomes, preliminarily validating the efficacy of the Ergonomics evaluation model method.

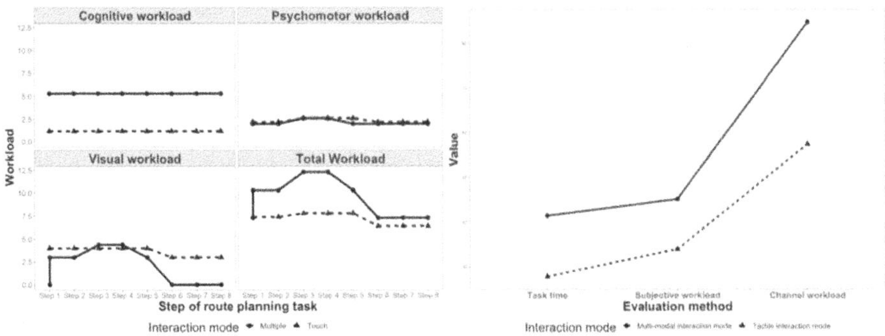

Fig. 2. (a) Comparison of channel workload in each step between different interaction modes (b) Comparison of evaluation method between different interaction modes

5 Conclusion

This study utilizes multiple resource theory to analyze the pilots' information process integrating multi-modal human-machine interaction technology. An ergonomics evaluation model for aircraft cockpit multi-mode interaction technology was developed, incorporating "Task Conflict Assessment-Channel Conflict Assessment-Channel Load Assessment", and preliminarily validated by a flight route planning experiment. The evaluation model helps eliminate irrational designs during the design phase and improves the effectiveness of multi-modal interaction technology.

References

1. LaViola Jr., J.J., Kruijff, E., Mcmahan, P.: 3D User Interfaces: Theory and Practice. Addison-Wesley Professional (2017)
2. Luo, T.: Drxeam-experiment: a MR user Interface with natural multi-channel interaction for virtual experiments. IEEE Trans. Vis. Comput. Graph. **26**(12), 3524–3534 (2020)
3. Oviatt, S.: Mulitmodal interactive maps: designing for human performance. Hum. Comput. Interact. **12**(1–2), 93–129 (1997)
4. Lu, S.: Informing the design of multimodal displays: a meta-analysis of empirical studies comparing auditory and tactile interruptions. Proc. Hum. Fact. Ergon. Soc. Ann. Meet. **55**(1), 1170–1174 (2011)
5. Rakkolainen, I.: Technologies for multimodal interaction in extended reality—a scoping review. Multimodal Technol. Interact. **5**(12), 81 (2021)
6. Wickens, C.D.: Multiple resources and performance prediction. Theor. Issues Ergon. Sci. **3**(2), 159–177 (2002)
7. Baddeley, A.: Exploring Working Memory: Selected Works of Alan Baddeley. Routledge (2017)

8. Alais, D.: Multisensory processing in review: from physiology to behaviour. Seeing Perceiving. **23**(1), 3–38 (2010)
9. Bierbaum, C.R.: Task analysis of the UH-60 mission and decision rules for developing a UH-60 workload prediction model: Summary report: US Army Research Institute for the Behavioral and Social Sciences (1989)
10. Mccracken, J.H.: Analyses of Selected LHX Mission Functions: Implications for Operator Workload and System Automation Goals. Defense Technical Information Center (1984)
11. Oviatt, S., Coulston, R., Lunsford, R.: When do we interact multimodally? cognitive load and multimodal communication patterns. In: Proceedings of the 6th International Conference on Multimodal Interfaces, pp. 129–136 (2024)

Modeling of Human Heat Strain Detection Based on EEG Signals

Yuran Huang[1], Jiangfeng Song[2], Junhui Huang[3], Mengxin Yin[2], Li Ding[1], and Bo Chen[1](✉)

[1] School of Biological Science and Medical Engineering, Beihang University, Beijing, China
chenbo11735@buaa.edu.cn

[2] Wuhan Second Ship Design and Research Institute, Wuhan, China

[3] School of Emergency Management and Safety Engineering, China University of Mining and Technology, Beijing, China

Abstract. The impact of heat strain on pilots' physiological characteristics and operational effectiveness is substantial, necessitating comprehensive assessments using multiple physiological indicators. Although Electroencephalography (EEG) is renowned for its real-time brain function monitoring, its efficacy as a sole indicator for accurately discerning heat strain requires further validation. This study employs a novel three-dimensional single-channel convolutional neural network (3DCNN) to analyze EEG data for detecting heat strain in pilots. Simulated flight experiments conducted under varied temperature and humidity conditions facilitated the extraction of both time-domain and entropy-domain EEG features. These features trained the 3DCNN, using the Composite Index of Heat Stress (CIHS) as the label. Results indicate that the 3DCNN effectively discriminates heat strain using both a single-feature approach based on differential entropy and a multi-feature fusion strategy incorporating time-domain features, differential entropy, and fuzzy entropy, with both methods achieving high accuracy.

Keywords: Electroencephalography · Three-dimensional CNN · Heat Strain

1 Introduction

Heat strain, manifested as conditions like heat stroke and pyrexia, poses risks in high-temperature environments, especially in occupational settings such as tank interiors [1] and aircraft cockpits [2] where limited air circulation and inefficient heat dissipation can lead to substantial heat buildup. This is particularly critical for pilots who may face temperatures exceeding 45 °C, thereby increasing their susceptibility to heat-related illnesses and impairing their performance and safety [3, 4].

Environmental factors such as wind speed significantly affect operations in thermal environments by influencing human heat stress, as evidenced by physiological markers like heart rate, perspiration, and body temperature [5, 6]. Heat strain, involving complex

Y. Huang and J. Song—Contributed equally to this paper and are tied for the first author.

S. Jin et al. (Eds.): IEA 2024, SSDI 39, pp. 426–431, 2025.
https://doi.org/10.1007/978-981-95-0211-0_65

changes across multiple systems, cannot be fully reflected by a single physiological indicator; rather, a comprehensive assessment requires a combination of metrics. The Fighter Index of Thermal Stress (FITS) [7], which accounts for both wet and dry bulb temperatures, helps predict the impact on aircrew performance during missions. Additionally, the Comprehensive Heat Stress Index (CIHS) [8], developed by the Chinese Air Force Institute of Aviation Medicine, classifies heat strain with multiple physiological indicators to assess pilot endurance and apparel suitability in flight conditions.

Electroencephalography (EEG) is valued for its ability to monitor brain function in real time. Research shows that environmental temperature affects power spectral density (PSD), with specific changes in EEG bands reflecting temperature variations [9–11]. Despite these findings, most studies have not integrated time-domain and frequency-domain features effectively, and real-time evaluation methods remain underdeveloped. Machine learning, particularly through deep learning, has proven effective at extracting meaningful information from high-dimensional and noisy EEG data [12]. Convolutional Neural Networks (CNNs), especially useful for their layered processing capability, are predominantly used for detecting brain diseases and assessing cognitive load [13, 14]. While the common two-dimensional CNNs (2DCNN) face challenges in capturing deep temporal features, three-dimensional CNNs (3DCNN) show greater promise, especially in applications like emotion recognition and understanding dynamic interrelations in EEG signals [15].

Considering the existing research and challenges, we propose a three-dimensional single-channel convolutional neural network model for analyzing pilots' heat strain using EEG. This model shows promising predictive accuracy by integrating time domain and entropy domain features.

2 Method

2.1 Data Acquisition Experiment

Thirteen healthy male university students, aged 23–25, averaging 170.9 cm in height and 61.7 kg in weight were recruited. Before the experiment, participants received training in simulated flight and target hitting tasks and were informed about the objectives and risks involved.

The experimental setup utilized a flight simulator displaying cockpit, building, road, and other scenes (Fig. 1). Conditions such as temperature and humidity were controlled using HFW series controllers. Physiological measurements including heart rate was taken using a CMS50D+ oximeter, while skin and axillary temperatures were monitored with iButton sensors from Dallas Semiconductor. Body weight was assessed with Mettler Toledo precision scales. Additionally, EEG signals were captured using Cognionics' Quick-20 wireless dry electrode EEG system.

The experiment was conducted in a fighter jet simulator set to three thermal environments: 21 ± 0.2 °C with 30% relative humidity, 30 ± 0.2 °C with 45% relative humidity, and 38 ± 0.2 °C with 45% relative humidity. Each participant completed three one-hour trials in each environment, each trial comprising three 15-minute tasks. After each task, they rested for 5 min and filled out a thermal comfort scale.

Fig. 1. Scenes from the flight simulator

2.2 Data Processing

EEG preprocessing was performed using EEGLAB, a MATLAB toolbox. This involved band-pass filtering from 0.4 to 40 Hz, unilateral mastoid re-referencing to the A2 electrode, and resampling the data to 250 Hz for efficiency. Artifacts like eye movements and muscle tension were removed with Independent Component Analysis (ICA) to ensure data cleanliness. The processed data were then segmented into 1.5-second windows with a 0.5-s overlap using a sliding window technique.

Besides, sixteen temporal features were extracted from each EEG channel segment, and a genetic algorithm selected the optimal four: rectified mean, skewness, peak factor, and impulse factor. Additionally, EEG frequency bands θ (4–8 Hz), α (8–13 Hz), β (14–30 Hz), and γ (31–40 Hz) were analyzed, from which differential entropy (DE), sample entropy (SE), and fuzzy entropy (FE) were extracted for each band. These processes are illustrated in Fig. 2.

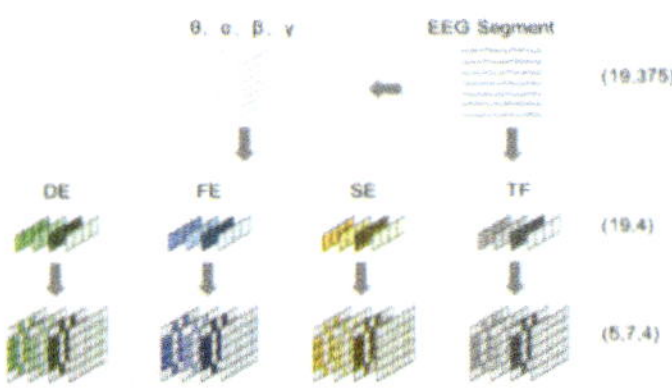

Fig. 2. EEG feature extraction and dataset construction

The Composite Index of Heat Stress (CIHS) was used to assess heat strain in subjects across three thermal environments, serving as the basis for data labeling. The methodology for calculating CIHS is detailed in Reference [8].

2.3 Model Construction

In this paper, we introduce a three-dimensional single-channel convolutional neural network (3DCNN) that integrates time-domain and entropy-domain features. Constructed with three consecutive convolutional layers, this model omits pooling layers to avoid data downsampling and potential information loss, similar to approaches described by Yang [16]. The architecture of the 3DCNN is shown in Fig. 3(b), with comparative 2DCNN architectures presented in Fig. 3(a).

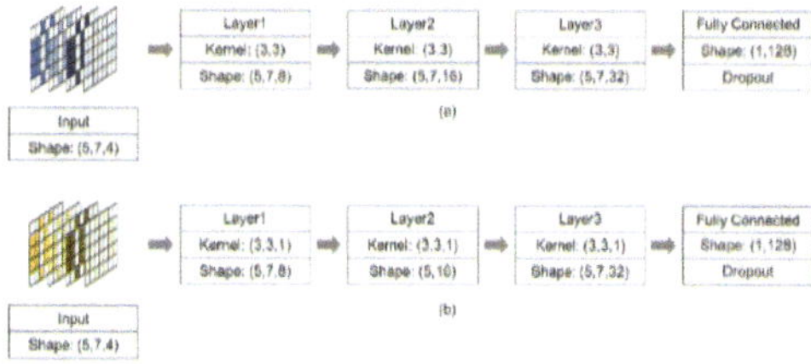

Fig. 3. The structures of 2DCNN and 3DCNN

3 Result and Discussion

3.1 Validity of Labeling Construction

Thermal Sensation Votes (TSVs) recorded and CIHS calculated three times for each working condition were compared using a one-way non-parametric test. The results depicted in Fig. 4 show significant differences in TSVs across different temperature and humidity conditions within the same experimental phase (Fig. 4a) and no significant differences in CIHS values among the conditions during the initial phase (Fig. 4b). This likely results from CIHS integrating multiple physiological indicators, which reduces variability compared to single indicators. Additionally, correlation analysis of the mean TSV (MTSV) and mean CIHS (MCIHS) under identical conditions (Fig. 4c) shows a significant correlation ($R = 0.81$), confirming that CIHS aligns well with subjective perceptions under high temperature and humidity, validating our data labeling approach.

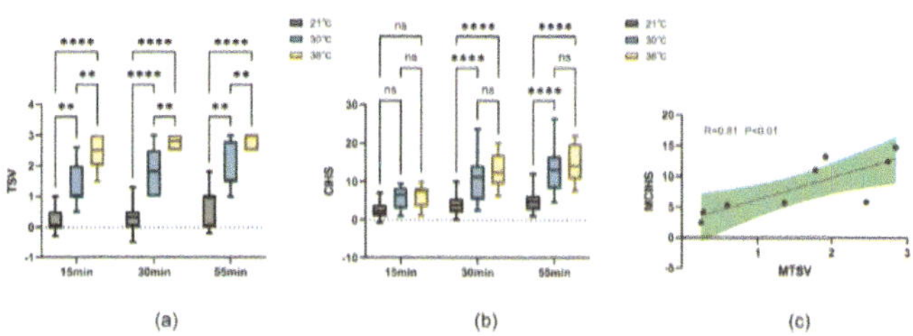

Fig. 4. Non-parametric test results and correlation between CIHS and TSV at different operating conditions and time periods

3.2 Comparison of Feature Domain Results

Figure 5(a) presents the classification accuracy of various entropy and temporal features across different networks at data input. Single-feature use in 3DCNN outperforms multi-feature combinations without hyperparameter adjustments, confirming our hypothesis. Due to its poor performance, SE is excluded from future feature combination training. Two feature integration methods within the same data segment, depicted in Fig. 5(b), were tested: SFFL and FFSL. SFFL stacks features by type following the sequence θ, α, β, and γ, whereas FFSL organizes them by frequency bands. FFSL demonstrated superior performance, as shown by the 3DCNN training results.

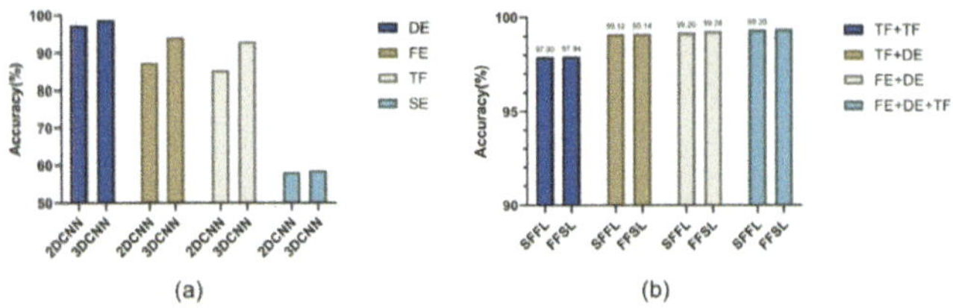

Fig. 5. Classification accuracy of different features and Comparison of feature stacking methods in 3DCNN

3.3 Comparison of Different CNN Structures

We present the results of TF, DE and FE features, along with their combinations, trained on three CNN networks as shown in Table 1. The proposed 3D Convolutional Neural Network (3DCNN) exhibits robust EEG classification accuracy with CIHS as the training label and enhances accuracy while achieving faster convergence due to increased convolution depth from feature stacking.

Table 1. Accuracy of different feature combinations in 2DCNN and. 3DCNN

	TF	DE	FE	TF+FE	TF+DE	FE+DE	FE+DE+TF
2DCNN	85.47%	97.30%	87.44%	92.12%	97.06%	97.68%	97.48%
3DCNN	93.14%	98.80%	94.23%	97.90%	99.12%	99.20%	99.35%

4 Conclusion

In this study, we developed a method to detect human heat strain by transforming multichannel EEG signals into three-dimensional inputs, extracting features, and using the Composite Index of Heat Stress (CIHS) as labels, achieving high accuracy in detection. A key limitation is the infrequent calculation of sweat levels, which results in uniform labels for all EEG segments over 15-minute periods, thereby restricting the analysis of real-time EEG responses. Future research will focus on reducing the interval for label updates by integrating cumulative perspiration estimates, thus refining the temporal sensitivity of EEG responses to heat strain.

References

1. Su, Z., Jiang, Z., Sun, Z.: Study on the heat hazard of deep exploitation in high-temperature mines and its evaluation index. Procedia Earth Planetary Sci. **1**, 414–419 (2009). https://doi.org/10.1016/j.proeps.2009.09.066

2. Singh, A.P., Majumdar, D., Bhatia, M.R., Srivastava, K.K., Selvamurthy, W.: Environmental impact on crew of armoured vehicles: effects of 24 h combat exercise in a hot desert. Int. J. Biometeorol. **39**, 64–68 (1995). https://doi.org/10.1007/BF01212582
3. Froom, P., Kristal-Boneh, E., Ribak, J., Caine, Y.: Predicting increases in skin temperature using heat stress indices and relative humidity in helicopter pilots. Isr. J. Med. Sci. **28**(8–9), 608–610 (1992)
4. Zhou, B., Ding, L., Chen, B., Shi, H., Ao, Y., Xu, R., Li, Y.: Physiological characteristics and operational performance of pilots in the high temperature and humidity fighter cockpit environments. Sensors. **21**, 5798 (2021). https://doi.org/10.3390/s21175798
5. Li, J., Tian, Y., Ding, L., Zou, H., Ren, Z., Shi, L., Feathers, D., Wang, N.: Simulating extreme environments: ergonomic evaluation of Chinese pilot performance and heat stress tolerance. WOR. **51**, 215–222 (2015). https://doi.org/10.3233/WOR-141842
6. Christison, K., Gurney, S., Dumke, C.L.: Effect of vented helmets on heat stress during wildland firefighter simulation. Int. J. Wildland Fire. **30**, 645–651 (2021). https://doi.org/10.1071/WF20182
7. Mac, V.V., Elon, L., Smith, D.J., Tovar-Aguilar, A., Economos, E., Flocks, J., Hertzberg, V., McCauley, L.: A modified physiological strain index for workplace-based assessment of heat strain experienced by agricultural workers. Am. J. Ind. Med. **64**, 258–265 (2021). https://doi.org/10.1002/ajim.23230
8. Stribley, R.F., Nunneley, S.A.: Fighter Index of Thermal Stress: Development of Interim Guidance for Hot-Weather USAF Operations. Presented at the (1978)
9. Ouyang, Y.: Study of heat stress on pilots wearing different complements of protective garments in hot environments. J. People's Liberat. Army Prevent. Med. **9**, 10–16 (1991)
10. Pan, L., Zheng, H., Li, T.: Effects of the indoor environment on EEG and thermal comfort assessment in males. Build. Environ. **228**, 109761 (2023). https://doi.org/10.1016/j.buildenv.2022.109761
11. Son, Y.J., Chun, C.: Research on electroencephalogram to measure thermal pleasure in thermal alliesthesia in temperature step-change environment. Indoor Air. **28**, 916–923 (2018). https://doi.org/10.1111/ina.12491
12. Wu, M., Li, H., Qi, H.: Using electroencephalogram to continuously discriminate feelings of personal thermal comfort between uncomfortably hot and comfortable environments. Indoor Air. **30**, 534–543 (2020). https://doi.org/10.1111/ina.12644
13. Zhou, Y., Huang, S., Xu, Z., Wang, P., Wu, X., Zhang, D.: Cognitive workload recognition using EEG signals and machine learning: a review. IEEE Trans. Cogn. Dev. Syst. **14**, 799–818 (2021). https://doi.org/10.1109/TCDS.2021.3090217
14. Oh, S.L., Vicnesh, J., Ciaccio, E.J., Yuvaraj, R., Acharya, U.R.: Deep convolutional neural network model for automated diagnosis of schizophrenia using EEG signals. Appl. Sci. **9**, 2870 (2019). https://doi.org/10.3390/app9142870
15. Wu, E.Q., Peng, X.Y., Zhang, C.Z., Lin, J.X., Sheng, R.S.F.: Pilots' fatigue status recognition using deep contractive autoencoder network. IEEE Trans. Instrum. Meas. **68**, 3907–3919 (2019). https://doi.org/10.1109/TIM.2018.2885608
16. Liu, S., Wang, X., Zhao, L., Li, B., Hu, W., Yu, J., Zhang, Y.-D.: 3DCANN: a spatio-temporal convolution attention neural network for EEG emotion recognition. IEEE J. Biomed. Health Inform. **26**, 5321–5331 (2021). https://doi.org/10.1109/JBHI.2021.3083525

The Impact of Intelligent Agent Voice Gender and Pitch on Driver Perception in Autonomous Driving

Yonghao Huang and Wei Zhang(✉)

Department of Industrial Engineering, Tsinghua University, Beijing, China
zhangwei@tsinghua.edu.cn

Abstract. With the advancement of artificial intelligence technology, it has become increasingly popular for intelligent agents to perform complex tasks such as fully autonomous driving. However, it remains unclear and needs further investigation whether intelligent agents' voice modes present more assistance or risk to users. By using a within-subjects design, this study examined the effects of voice gender (male, female) and pitch (high, low) of in-vehicle intelligent agents on drivers' likeability and trust in the system. The experiment was conducted remotely via an online platform, where participants viewed four recorded videos as simulated autonomous driving scenarios and completed a questionnaire after watching each video. There were 25 participants in total who participated in the study. The research results indicated that the in-vehicle intelligent agent with a high pitch female voice is most likable and trustworthy among those with low pitch female voice, high pitch male voice, and low pitch male voice. There were no significant differences observed in likeability and trust among last three cases. Moreover, the trust perception of male participants was not influenced by the voice mode of intelligent agents but depended on the characteristics of the autonomous vehicle. The results in the experiment provide some insights of human-computer interaction concerning voice mode for product designers and researchers.

Keywords: Autonomous Driving · In-vehicle Intelligent Agent · Voice Mode · Likeability · Trust Levels

1 Introduction

Intelligent Agents typically refer to computing systems that show some intelligence in assisting humans with specific tasks [1]. In fully autonomous driving scenarios, In-vehicle Intelligent Agents (IVIA) serve as a crucial interface for human-vehicle interaction. They execute drivers' commands and ensure the safety of the driving [2, 3]. Current researches on IVIA mainly focus on both designs related to internal function and external interaction. The design of voice characteristics is particularly critical to an interface of IVIA, including elements such as the voice's gender, pitch, speech style, conversation method, and point of view [4].

S. Jin et al. (Eds.): IEA 2024, SSDI 39, pp. 432–437, 2025.
https://doi.org/10.1007/978-981-95-0211-0_66

Dong et al. found that drivers prefer IVIA with female voices to those with male voices, since male voice agents provided drivers with higher perceived safety scores [5]. However, some other researches also showed that both men and women prefer agents with same voice genders [6, 7]. Additionally, experiments with paired comparisons between high and low pitch voices indicated that the pitch of the sound also affects the user's perceptions and lower-pitched voices are perceived as more trustworthy than higher-pitched voice [8]. However, the application of this finding in autonomous driving scenarios remains unknown. In summary, it is valuable to consider existing researches about the impact of voice gender and pitch of IVIA on driving user's experience and trust under scenarios of fully autonomous driving. This study analyzes how the gender and pitch of IVIA voices affect drivers' likeability and trust, and examines the effects across different genders. The findings provide some insights for vehicle designers in order to enhance the user's experience and acceptance of autonomous vehicles. In addition, it is helpful for the design and application of intelligent agents to understand the impact and mechanisms of IVIA voice modes on user's interaction experiences.

2 Method

2.1 Participants

There were 25 participants (8 females and 17 males) recruited for the study and aged between 18 and 25 years. They all have at least an undergraduate degree, with 84% having practical driving experience. All participants have normal or corrected-to-normal vision and normal hearing. If any participant felt uncomfortable in the study, he/she had the right to withdraw from the experiment at any time.

2.2 Experimental Design

A 2 × 2 within-subjects design was used to evaluate the impact of gender (male, female) and pitch (high, low) on drivers' user experience. The experiment was conducted under four conditions: High Pitch Female Agent (HFA), Low Pitch Female Agent (LFA), High Pitch Male Agent (HMA), and Low Pitch Male Agent (LMA). The dependent variables were likeability and trust of the autonomous vehicle. Likeability was assessed by using the Godspeed III questionnaire, which includes five questions [9]. Trust in the overall autonomous driving system was measured by using a trust questionnaire comprising ten questions [10].

2.3 Experimental Scenario

In order to simulate the state of an autonomous vehicle, the autonomous driving simulation scenarios were created by using SCANeR software (AVSimulation Co.). Each condition included five common events on the highway, with the voice script used for each event as shown in Table 1. The scenarios of four conditions only differed in the IVIA voice mode, in the meantime the events and their corresponding voice texts remained the same. All male and female voices for the agents were synthesized online using Baidu Cloud (https://cloud.baidu.com/). An illustration of simulation scenarios in the experiment is shown in Fig. 1.

Table 1. Driving events and agents' script.

Agent script
Event 1: Overtaking the car ahead
Event 2: A car approaching from the rear side
Event 3: Approaching a curve
Event 4: Construction on the left lane ahead
Event 5: Overtaking the truck ahead

Fig. 1. An illustration of simulation scenarios in the experiment.

2.4 Experimental Procedures

The experiment was conducted online by using the questionnaire platform (https://www.wjx.cn/). The procedure for the experiment is summarized as follows:

Initially, the basic personal information was collected for each participant. Then each participant viewed four videos of a fully autonomous vehicle driving in simulated scenarios with different voice modes agent and completed a questionnaire after each video. Each video lasted approximately 3 min, and a Latin square design was used to eliminate the effects of order. Upon experiment finish, every participant received a reward of 5 RMB.

3 Result

The simulation results about means and standard deviations of the likeability and the trust are shown in Table 2. Two-way repeated-measure analyses of variance (ANOVAs) were conducted on the likeability and the trust, with the factors of agent gender and pitch (Table 2). The results of the evaluation of likeability revealed significant differences between male and female agents, as well as high pitch and low pitch agents among all participants ($F (1,24) = 14.357$, $p < 0.001$, $\eta^2 = 0.374$ for gender; $F(1,24) = 6.204$, $p = 0.020$, $\eta^2 = 0.205$ for pitch). Post-hoc analyses indicated that female voices got higher score in likeability than male voices (Female: $M = 3.50$, $SD = 0.76$; Male: $M = 2.97$, $SD = 0.83$) and high pitch voices got higher score than low pitch voices (High: M

= 3.40, SD = 0.86; Low: M = 3.06, SD = 0.78). The results also showed that there were interaction effects between the gender and pitch of the agent's voice on the dimensions of likeability ($F(1,24) = 5.411$, $p = 0.029$, $\eta^2 = 0.184$) and trust ($F(1,24) = 4.654$, $p = 0.041$, $\eta^2 = 0.162$). Multiple comparisons of different agents (Fig. 2) showed that the HFA was significantly higher than LFA (Likeability: $t(24) = 4.528$, $p < 0.001$; Trust: $t(24) = 2.437$, $p = 0.023$), HMA (Likeability: $t(24) = 4.359$, $p < 0.001$; Trust: $t(24) = 2.982$, $p = 0.006$), and LMA (Likeability: $t(24) = 3.978$, $p = 0.001$; Trust: $t(24) = 2.187$, $p = 0.039$) in both likeability and trust dimensions.

Table 2. Results of descriptive statistics and ANOVAs.

Agent modes		All participants		Male participants		Female participants	
		Likeability	Trust	Likeability	Trust	Likeability	Trust
HFA	M (SD)	3.87 (0.68)	5.07 (1.04)	3.78 (0.79)	4.96 (1.20)	4.08 (0.28)	5.29 (0.55)
LFA	M (SD)	3.13 (0.67)	4.61 (1.19)	3.22 (0.72)	4.73 (1.20)	2.93 (0.51)	4.38 (1.12)
HMA	M (SD)	2.94 (0.78)	4.46 (1.02)	2.95 (0.89)	4.49 (1.11)	2.90 (0.54)	4.40 (0.89)
LMA	M (SD)	3.01 (0.90)	4.71 (1.18)	2.99 (0.82)	4.65 (1.27)	3.05 (1.12)	4.83 (1.03)
Gender	F (p)	14.357 (<0.001***)	3.580 (0.071)	7.552 (0.014*)	2.494 (0.134)	9.926 (0.016*)	0.953 (0.361)
Pitch	F (p)	6.204 (0.020*)	1.188 (0.287)	2.358 (0.142)	0.119 (0.735)	4.730 (0.066)	1.955 (0.205)
Gender× Pitch	F (p)	5.411 (0.029*)	4.654 (0.041*)	1.899 (0.187)	1.365 (0.260)	4.398 (0.074)	3.731 (0.095)

*$p \leq 0.05$, ** $p \leq 0.01$, ***$p \leq 0.001$

Based on further analysis of the relationship between participant gender and agent voice characteristics, differences were revealed in scores between male and female participants. Significant differences in likeability dimension between male and female voice agents were observed both in male ($F(1,16) = 7.552$, $p = 0.014$, $\eta^2 = 0.103$) and female participants ($F(1,7) = 9.926$, $p = 0.016$, $\eta^2 = 0.143$), with no significant differences noted in other dimensions. Multiple comparison results indicated that HFA scored significantly higher in likeability than LFA (Male: $t(16) = 2.654$, $p = 0.017$; Female: $t(7) = 5.487$, $p = 0.001$), HMA (Male: $t(16) = 2.746$, $p = 0.014$; Female: $t(7) = 5.545$, $p = 0.001$), and LMA (Male: $t(16) = 2.837$, $p = 0.012$; Female: $t(7) = 2.900$, $p = 0.023$). However, in the trust dimension, significant differences were only observed among female participants, with HFA scoring significantly higher than LFA ($t(7) = 2.646$, $p = 0.033$) and HMA ($t(7) = 3.425$, $p = 0.011$). No other significant correlations were found.

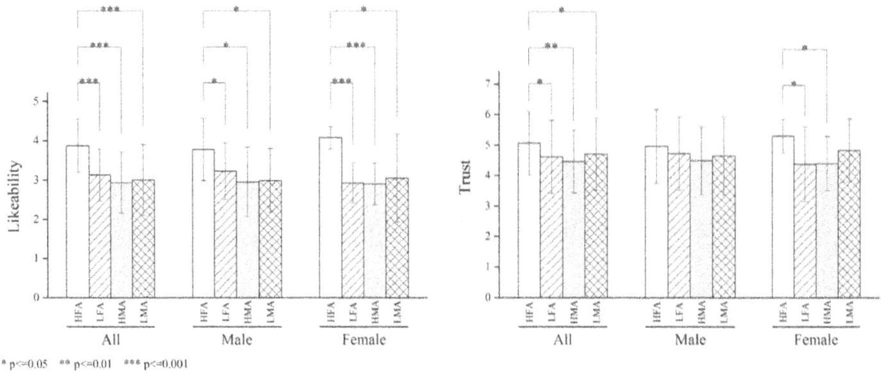

Fig. 2. Multiple comparison results of likeability and trust among different participants.

4 Discussions

The study explored the effect of the gender and pitch of IVIAs' voices on drivers' likeability under fully autonomous driving conditions. The results demonstrated that female voice IVIA received higher scores on the likeability. Participants gave positive comments on female voices, confirming that female voices are more likable than male voices among drivers [5]. However, the multiple comparisons showed that high pitch female voices scored significantly higher than low pitch female voices in both likeability and trust dimensions. Thus, the existing conclusion that lower-pitched voices are perceived as more trustworthy than higher-pitched voices [8], may not apply when selecting voice modes for driving agents. Participants reported that high pitch voices, often associated with youth and energy, provide a more positive experience for drivers.

Further analysis was conducted on how the gender of a participant affects the user experience with different voice modes of IVIA. According to the measure of likeability, both male and female participants preferred high pitch female voices over low pitch female voice and male voices. This contradicts the previous result of studies that drivers prefer voices of the same gender [6]. In the trust dimension, the modes of voice had a more influence on perceptions of trust, with high pitch female voices being trusted more than low-pitched female voices and high-pitched male voices. However, agent voice modes had no significant effect on male participants. Several male participants noted that their trusts in autonomous vehicles were derived from the perceived safety of the control system rather than the agent's vocal modes.

In the study above, participants were recruited from universities, which results in a relatively uniform educational background and limited practical driving experience among the subjects. Additionally, due to objective conditions, the experiment was conducted online, and the conclusions need further investigation and validation in real world driving.

5 Conclusion

The impact of four different IVIA voice modes on the user experience of autonomous vehicle drivers was analyzed by using an online questionnaire in the study. Data analysis revealed that the agent with high pitch female voice was preferred to that with low pitch female voice and male voices agents in terms of likeability and trust. Participants of all genders favored high pitch female voices, but the trust levels of male participants in the automated system were not influenced by the agent voice mode. The findings in the experiment provide valuable insights for designers in enhancing product acceptance and user experience, and lay a foundation for future research on the voice design of an intelligent agent system.

References

1. March, S., Hevner, A., Ram, S.: Research commentary: an agenda for information technology research in heterogeneous and distributed environments. Inf. Syst. Res. **11**(4), 327–341 (2000)
2. Jeon, M., Walker, B.N., Gable, T.M.: The effects of social interactions with in-vehicle agents on a driver's anger level, driving performance, situation awareness, and perceived workload. Appl. Ergon. **50**, 185–199 (2015)
3. Wang, M., Lee, S.C., Kamalesh Sanghavi, H., Eskew, M., Zhou, B., Jeon, M.: In-vehicle intelligent agents in fully autonomous driving: the effects of speech style and embodiment together and separately. In: 13th International Conference on Automotive User Interfaces and Interactive Vehicular Applications, pp. 247–254 (2021)
4. Lee, S.C., Jeon, M.: A systematic review of functions and design features of in-vehicle agents. Int. Journal Hum. Comput. Stud. **165**, 102864 (2022)
5. Dong, J., Lawson, E., Olsen, J., Jeon, M.: Female voice agents in fully autonomous vehicles are not only more likeable and comfortable, but also more competent. Proc. Hum. Fact. Ergon. Soc. Ann. Meet. **64**(1), 1033–1037 (2020)
6. Ji, W., Liu, R., Lee, S.: Do drivers prefer female voice for guidance? An interaction design about information type and speaker gender for autonomous driving car. In: Krömker, H. (ed.) HCI in Mobility, Transport, and Automotive Systems, pp. 208–224. Springer International Publishing (2019)
7. Eyssel, F., Kuchenbrandt, D., Bobinger, S., de Ruiter, L., Hegel, F.: "If you sound like me, you must be more human": On the interplay of robot and user features on human-robot acceptance and anthropomorphism. In: Proceedings of the Seventh Annual ACM/IEEE International Conference on Human-Robot Interaction, pp. 125–126 (2012)
8. Tsantani, M.S., Belin, P., Paterson, H.M., McAleer, P.: Low vocal pitch preference drives first impressions irrespective of context in male voices but not in female voices. Perception. **45**(8), 946–963 (2016)
9. Bartneck, C., Kulić, D., Croft, E., Zoghbi, S.: Measurement instruments for the anthropomorphism, animacy, likeability, perceived intelligence, and perceived safety of robots. Int. J. Soc. Robot. **1**(1), 71–81 (2009)
10. Jian, J.-Y., Bisantz, A.M., Drury, C.G.: Foundations for an empirically determined scale of trust in automated systems. Int. J. Cogn. Ergon. **4**(1), 53–71 (2000)

An Ergonomic Study on the Flicker of Nuclear Symbol Frame Based on Attention Capture

Qian Li[1](✉), Xiaoli Wu[1,2], and Xingcan Yang[3]

[1] Sachool of Design Arts and Media, Nanjing University of Science and Technology, Nanjing, China
wuxlhhu@163.com

[2] Research School of Industrial Internet, Nanjing University of Science and Technology, Nanjing, China

[3] State Key Laboratory of Nuclear Power Safety Technology and Equipment, China Nuclear Power Engineering Co., Ltd., Shenzhen, China

Abstract. The dynamic highlighting of interface elements, represented by flickering, significantly influences the visual cognitive performance of operators. This study focuses on the flickering animation of fault alarms in nuclear power graphical symbols, analyzing the information characteristics of flickering animations in fault alarms of nuclear power control systems. By considering variables such as flicker frequency, flicker duration, and flicker highlighting location, the study investigates the effects of these variables on attention capture effects and highlighting efficiency, employing psychological behavioral response experiments. The results indicate that the three variables are independent of each other, and flicker frequency and flicker highlighting location have a significant impact on highlighting efficiency. At a flicker frequency of 9 Hz, superior attention capture is observed compared to optimal visual search performance. Additionally, flicker highlighting tends to prioritize the middle location, followed by the upper and lower locations. This experiment provides future references and methodological insights for exploring the correlation between dynamic highlighting elements and attention capture effects.

Keywords: Nuclear symbol · Attention capture · Flicker prominence affects · Interaction effect

1 Introduction

With the advancement of computer technology and information theory, the complexity of information systems has increased significantly, particularly in areas like manufacturing, testing, and manipulation. Traditional information systems that focus on acquiring, transmitting, storing, processing, and applying information are gradually evolving into intricate ones [1]. However, operators' visual capacity to process information is limited and highlighting certain features can greatly influence their attention selection [2]. The phenomenon where stimuli with prominent characteristics automatically attract attention

S. Jin et al. (Eds.): IEA 2024, SSDI 39, pp. 438–448, 2025.
https://doi.org/10.1007/978-981-95-0211-0_67

regardless of current task objectives is referred to as attention capture [3]. Assessing the impact of emphasizing complex interface information on operator productivity is crucial for optimal interface design. Effective interfaces enable operators to efficiently discern crucial data, extract relevant tasks, and integrate them to enhance productivity in complex systems.

Scholars, both domestically and internationally, have conducted experiments and research on mechanisms that attract attention and highlight interface information. The impact of sudden changes in local areas and highlighting specific elements on these attention capture mechanisms was explored [4]. Experimental findings further confirmed that abrupt highlighting of interface information was highly effective in capturing attention due to its saliency. Simultaneously, it was observed that static colors only draw attention when they were relevant to the task at hand [5]. The influence of shape features in human-computer interfaces on the ability to capture attention was also investigated. It was believed that shape features played a guiding and restricting role in capturing attention, with experimental evidence suggesting that increasing differences between shape features and their attributes made target shapes easier to notice, leading to improved cognitive performance [6]. The effects of two types of highlighting methods- nuclear power warning lines and pop-up window son operators' visual search performance were examined, resulting in proposed optimization strategies based on experimental results [7].

The use of flickering effects as a dynamic highlighting technique is quite common. Unlike other forms of highlighting, flickering effects have the ability to effectively convey urgent and potentially dangerous information to users [8]. This coding method for warning or signaling can be observed in various fields such as maritime aviation, road transportation, and nuclear power control. The presentation of flickering effects involves factors like flickering frequency, location, duration, color, and deformation, etc. Regardless of the specific encoding form used, all types of flickering effects have been found to capture attention effectively and improve visual cognitive performance in different experiments. Previous research [9–11] conducted experimental studies to investigate the efficacy of flickering effects in enhancing work efficiency. The findings suggested that visual materials with higher flickering frequencies on black and white backgrounds had a greater potential to capture attention, leading to a more pronounced improvement in work efficiency [12]. It was observed that even low frequency flickering could attract attention when time conditions are equal. The ability of flickering frequency to draw visual attention aligned with the attention filter model [13]. The purpose of the study was to examine whether abnormal flicker frequencies in motion perception could capture attention, while also assessing the benefits (target location matching cue) and costs (target different from cue location) of various cue frequencies and durations. The findings indicated that abnormal flicker frequencies can indeed capture attention and exhibit a return inhibition phenomenon [14]. Additionally, a comparison was conducted between the search performance of aircraft radar interfaces with uniform motion at high, medium, and low speeds using flickering motion. The results demonstrated that employing flickering effects at lower speeds significantly enhanced highlighting efficiency by improving participants' search accuracy and reducing reaction time [15].

The presence of flickering effects in interface elements significantly affects the visual search performance of operators in complex information systems. Previous studies conducted by domestic and foreign scholars, have primarily examined the impact of different flickering frequencies using basic geometric shapes or simple characters as experimental materials, with limited research on flickering duration and highlighting position. Recently, there has been a shift in focus from studying attention capture mechanisms to exploring how flickering effects effectively highlight information in complex human-computer interaction interfaces. Expanding on the previous work on single character flickering frequency[12], this study aims to investigate the effectiveness of flickering frequency, duration, and highlighting position for fault alarm flickering effects through monitoring interface symbols within nuclear power plant complex information systems.

2 Analysis of Nuclear Symbol Warning Flicker Prominence

In the context of nuclear power instrumentation and control systems, the present study focuses on the extraction of two prevalent types of symbols from the VDU (Visual Display Unit) display screens. These symbols are crucial for representing the operational status of nuclear power systems, as shown in Fig. 1.

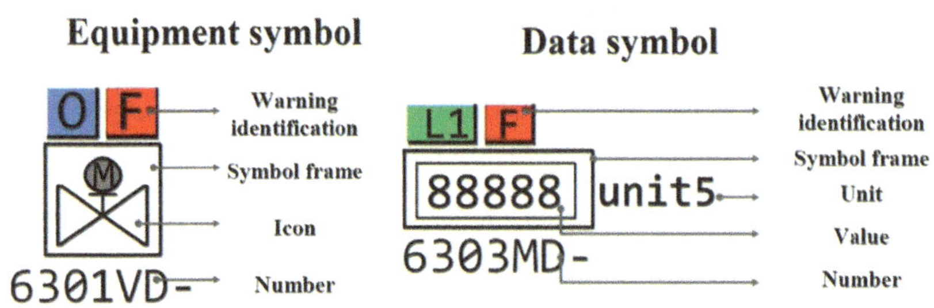

Fig. 1. Splitting the elements of the nuclear power symbol

3 Method

This study examines the influence of flickering animations' frequency, duration, and prominent location on operators' search efficiency and ergonomic performance. Three hypotheses were formulated based on this research background.

H1: The frequency and the prominent location of flickering animations significantly influence attention capture effectiveness. Specifically, higher frequencies of flickering animations lead to superior salience effectiveness. Regarding the location, the upper-left corner exhibits the highest salience effectiveness, followed by the upper-right, lower-left, and finally the lower-right corner.

H2: The duration of flickering animations does not significantly impact attention capture effectiveness.
H3: The interaction among the frequency of flickering animations, the duration of flickering animations, and the prominent location of salience does not produce significant effects.

3.1 Design

Drawing inspiration from the experimental designs of Ge Liezhong and Kong Yan (2000) and Cass et al. (2011), the present study selected three key factors: frequency of flickering animations (3 levels: 3 Hz, 9 Hz, 27 Hz), duration of flickering animations (3 levels: 500 ms, 1000 ms, 2000 ms), and location of flickering animations (9 levels). 4 Through the measurement of participants' reaction times and accuracy rate, this study conducted a rigorous data analysis. Each symbol corresponded to a reaction key (1–9) on a numeric keypad. Participants were instructed to identify the target symbol exhibiting a flickering animation among the nine presented symbols and respond by pressing the corresponding key, as illustrated in Fig. 2.

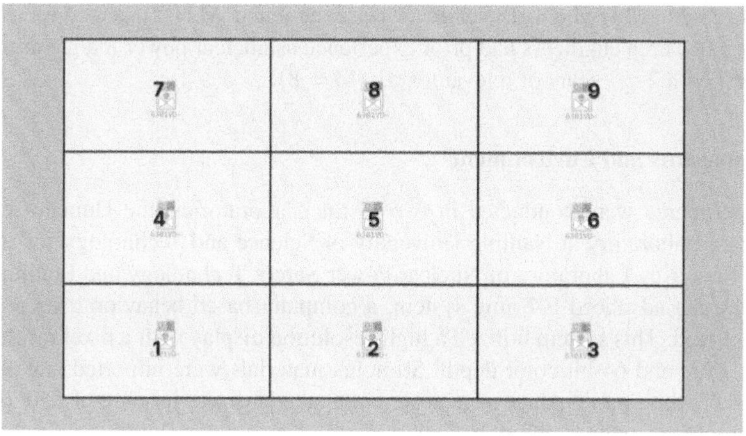

Fig. 2. Symbol abrupt location corresponds to the numeric keypad

3.2 Procedure

Prior to the experiment, the experimenter presented instructions on the computer screen to inform the participants of the specific steps and requirements. After reading the instructions, the participants practiced the tasks before moving on to the formal experiment, following the experimental flowchart outlined in Fig. 3. Post experiment, participants completed a questionnaire that included demographic information. Engineer subjects were asked to rate the visual prominence effect and self-response speed for each flicker frequency.

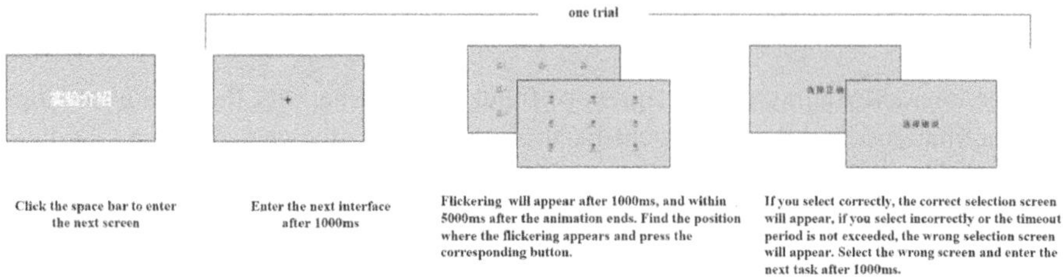

Fig. 3. The progress of trial.

3.3 Participants

This study employed a controlled experiment to investigate visual processing and reaction time differences between two groups: 25 undergraduate engineering students from Nanjing University of Science and Technology (student subjects) and 18 experienced engineers working in nuclear power main control room interface design at China Nuclear Power Engineering Co., Ltd. (engineer subjects). The student subjects ranged from 18 to 24 years old (M = 20) with corrected visual acuity ≥1.0, while the engineers were aged 28–55 (M = 38) with 4–18 years of work experience (M = 10) and corrected visual acuity ≥1.0. Three engineers had prior experience as nuclear power main control room operators, with 2–13 years of relevant work (M = 8).

3.4 Apparatus and Environment

The experiments were conducted in two distinct laboratories: the Human-Computer Interaction Laboratory at Nanjing University of Science and Technology for students, and the State Key Laboratory of Nuclear Power Safety Technology and Equipment for engineers. An advanced E-Prime system, a computer-based behavioral research tool, was employed. This system utilized a high-resolution display with a pixel resolution of 2880 × 1800 and 64-bit color depth. Stimulus materials were imported and precisely configured, while participants were seated at a standardized distance of 550–600 mm from the screen center to maintain consistency.

4 Result and Data Analysis

From a pool of 43 datasets, 38 were deemed valid for further analysis, comprising 24 datasets from student participants and 14 from engineers. Prior to analysis, outliers exceeding three standard deviations from the mean were excluded for each participant, resulting in the elimination of 1.3% of the total data. Reaction time and accuracy rate data from two distinct groups were analyzed using an independent samples t-test in SPSS. Results showed a statistically significant difference in reaction times ($p < 0.01$) despite homoscedasticity violation. Accuracy rate data met homoscedasticity assumptions (Levene's test, $p = 0.083$) but revealed no significant difference between groups ($p = 0.386$). An analysis of Table 1 reveals that students exhibited a significantly faster reaction time (1584.66 ± 174.973 ms) compared to engineers (1733.01 ± 196.636 ms). Both groups achieved accuracy rate above 95% across all reaction conditions. These findings suggest that students performed better in terms of reaction speed while maintaining high accuracy.

Table 1. Reaction time and Accuracy Rate for Student Subjects and Engineer Subjects

	Subject	N	Mean	Std. Deviation	Std. Error Mean
Reaction Time	Students	3866	1584.66	174.973	2.814
	Engineers	2216	1733.01	196.636	4.177
Accuracy Rate	Students	3866	0.99	0.072	0.001
	Engineers	2216	1.00	0.060	0.001

To assess the differential effects of flicker duration, flicker frequency, and flicker salience location on experimental outcomes, a two-way multivariate analysis of variance (MANOVA) was conducted using SPSS. The results, presented in Table 2, indicate significant effects of flicker frequency and flicker salience location on reaction time ($p < 0.05$). Conversely, the duration of flickering had no significant impact on reaction time ($p > 0.05$), aligning with the findings reported by Cass et al.(2011). None of the factors exhibited a significant influence on accuracy rates ($p > 0.05$), and there were no significant interactions among the factors ($p > 0.05$), indicating their independence.

Table 2. Between-subjects effect test for each factor of flicker

Source	Dependent Variable	Type III sums of squares	df	Mean Square	F	Sig.
Corrected Model	Reaction Time	12320050.299[a]	80	154000.629	4.151	0.000
	Accuracy Rate	0.351[b]	80	0.004	0.956	0.591
Intercept	Reaction Time	16333072758.255	1	16333072758.255	440210.018	0.000
	Accuracy Rate	6024.746	1	6024.746	1313732.040	0.000
Duration	Reaction Time	7021.815	2	3510.907	0.095	0.910
	Accuracy Rate	0.017	2	0.008	1.826	0.161
Frequency	Reaction Time	1148839.777	2	574419.889	15.482	0.000

(continued)

Table 2. (*continued*)

Source	Dependent Variable	Type III sums of squares	df	Mean Square	F	Sig.
	Accuracy Rate	0.004	2	0.002	0.463	0.630
Location	Reaction Time	10493495.434	8	1311686.929	35.353	0.000
	Accuracy Rate	0.055	8	0.007	1.494	0.154
Duration * Frequency	Reaction Time	91299.741	4	22824.935	0.615	0.652
	Accuracy Rate	0.012	4	0.003	0.681	0.605
Duration = * Location	Reaction Time	181367.978	16	11335.499	0.306	0.996
	Accuracy Rate	0.101	16	0.006	1.378	0.142
Frequency * Location	Reaction Time	79522.680	16	4970.168	0.134	1.000
	Accuracy Rate	0.052	16	0.003	0.708	0.789
Error	Reaction Time	222654564.078	6001	37102.910		
	Accuracy Rate	27.520	6001	0.005		
Total	Reaction Time	16567397056.000	6082			
	Accuracy Rate	6054.000	6082			
Corrected Total	Reaction Time	234974614.376	6081			
	Accuracy Rate	27.871	6081			

[a] R-Square = 0.052(Adjusted R-Square = 0.040)
[b] R-Square = 0.013(Adjusted R-Square = −0.001)

5 Discussion

5.1 Analysis of Experimental Results on Flicker Frequency

The results of the inter-subject effect test between flicker frequency and participants' reaction time. The results of the one-way ANOVA indicate a statistically significant difference in the effect of flicker frequency on reaction time ($F = 14.780$, $P < 0.001$).This suggests that the frequency of flickering has a significant impact on participants' reaction time.

As shown in Fig. 4, there is a significant difference in reaction times between students and engineers, with the students responding faster (1584.66 ± 174.973 ms) than the engineers (1733.01 ± 196.636 ms).Both groups exhibit a consistent trend of longer reaction times at 3 Hz and shorter times at 9 Hz, with comparable reaction times at 27 Hz. This indicates an initial increase and subsequent stabilization of reaction times with increasing flickering frequency. In contrast, the accuracy rates of the two groups diverge. Engineers show a positive correlation between flickering frequency and accuracy rates, with improved performance at higher frequencies. However, students achieve higher accuracy rates than engineers at 3 Hz and 9 Hz, experiencing a significant decline in performance at 27 Hz. This suggests that the optimal flickering frequency for accuracy may differ between the two groups.

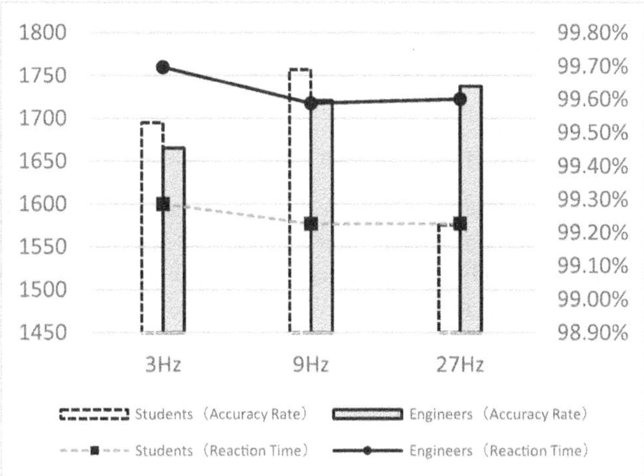

Fig. 4. Reaction time and Accuracy rate for each flicker frequency

The results of the visual salience effect and self-reaction speed ratings of the engineer subjects for each flicker frequency after the experiment are shown in Table 3. The results show that the engineer subjects have higher highlighting effect ratings for the flicker kinetic effect at a frequency of 3 Hz, which may be caused by the fact that higher frequency flicker signals in the fovea vision may be ignored or cause distraction and discomfort to the subjects [16]. At the same time, the subjects' self evaluation of my speed ratings from high to low were 27 Hz, 3 Hz, and 9 Hz. High frequency flickering signals convey semantic signals of danger, uncertainty, and urgency to subjects, which can effectively attract their attention, and drive them to invest more attentional resources to complete the rapid response behaviors in the unconscious state [17].

Flickering as a type of highlighting causes an attention-capturing effect, and the highlighting effect of such flickering is more obvious when the frequency of flickering is higher. In the study of Ge Li zhong and Kong Yan (2000) [12], it was pointed out that the highlighting effect was more obvious when the frequency of flickering display was above 27 Hz, and it was also the more recommended frequency of flickering in the design of computer display. However, the experimental results of this paper show that the flickering frequency has no obvious effect on the correct response rate of the subjects, and the highlighting effect is already very obvious when it is 9 Hz, while higher flickering frequency brings bad user experience for the subjects. Therefore, when coding

Table 3. Engineer Participants' Ratings of Different Flicker Frequency Effects

Frequency Evaluation Dimensions	3 Hz	9 Hz	27 Hz
Visual abrupt effect	4.18	4	4
Self-response speed	4.18	4	4.36

Note: The full score is 5 points, and the higher the score, the better the evaluation.

and designing flickering animations in complex information interfaces, the subjective feelings of users should also be taken into account.

5.2 Analysis of Experimental Results on Flicker Location

Table 4 shows the between-subjects effect test between flicker prominence position and subjects' reaction time, as can be seen from the table. The results of one-way ANOVA showed that the difference between the effect of flicker prominence position on reaction time was statistically significant ($F = 35.437$, $p < 0.001$).

Table 4. Test of between-subjects effects between the location of flicker and Reaction Time

Dependent Variable: Reaction Time					
Source	Type III sums of squares	df	Mean Square	F	Sig.
Corrected Model	10479869.050[a]	8	1309983.631	35.437	0.000
Intercept	16335541551.201	1	16335541551.201	441906.752	0.000
Location	10479869.050	8	1309983.631	35.437	0.000
Error	224494745.326	6073	36966.037		
Total	16567397056.000	6082			
Corrected Total	234974614.376	6081			

[a]R-Square = 0.045(Adjusted R-Square = 0.043)

As depicted in Fig. 5, a significant difference in reaction times is observed between student and engineer participants. Engineers generally respond faster than students. Within the engineer group, the longest reaction time is at location 7 (top left), while the shortest is at location 5 (center). For students, the longest reaction time occurs at location 2 (third column, second location), and the shortest at location 4 (second column, first location). A notable trend emerges: within the same row, reaction times are generally fastest in the center and slower towards the sides, contradicting the assumption of left-upper limit optimality. Engineers exhibit higher accuracy rates than students, achieving

100% accuracy at locations 2, 4, 5, and 8, while students only reach 100% at location 5. The central location of the flickering appears to offer both better efficiency and visual performance.

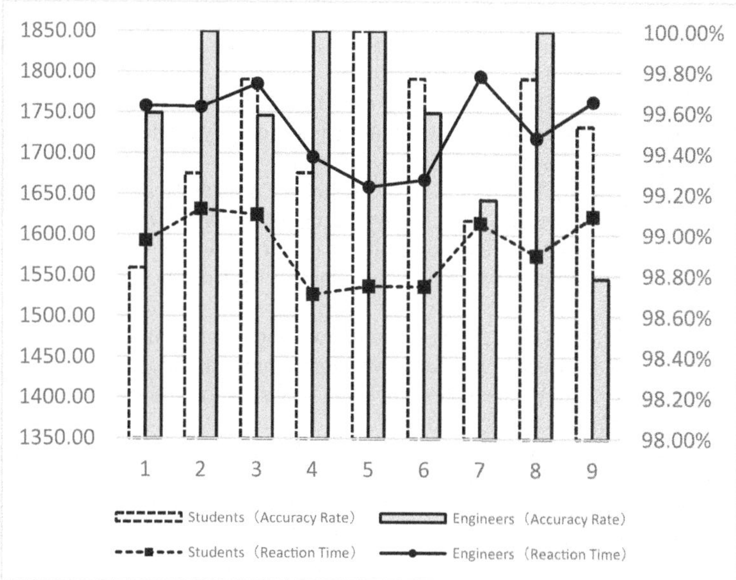

Fig. 5. Reaction time and Accuracy rate for each flicker location

6 Method Conclusion

Attention capture is influenced by the frequency and position of flickering, but the duration of flicker does not significantly enhance attention capture. The factors affecting flickering effects are independent and show no notable interaction. Experimental materials do not impact attention capture effects. Results suggest that as frequency increases, reaction time initially rises then stabilizes, with stable attention capture at 9 Hz, highlighting information efficiently. Highlighting does not follow visual search prioritization rules, with reaction times faster in the middle and slower on the sides within a row. For complex interfaces, such as nuclear power control panels, it is recommended to prioritize central placement of flickering visual effects to enhance highlighted information capture and improve cognitive performance.

Acknowledgments. This work was supported by State Key Laboratory of Nuclear Power Safety Monitoring Technology and Equipment (K-A2021.419), the National Nature Science Foundation of China (52175469), and Jiangsu Province Nature Science Foundation of China (BK20221490).

References

1. Wu, X.L.: Error-Cognition Mechanism of Task Interface Complex Information System. Science Press, Beijing (2017)
2. Ge, L.Z., Hu, F.P.: The ergonomics study on multi-element visual display. Adv. Psychol. Sci. **9**(3), 201–204 (2001)
3. Yantis, S.: Stimulus-driven attentional capture and attentional control settings. J. Exp. Psychol. Hum. Percept. Perform. **19**(3), 676–681 (1993)
4. Owens, C., Spehar, B.: Do sudden onsets need to be perceived as new objects to capture attention? The interplay between sensory transients and display configuration. Atten. Percept. Psychophys. **78**(7), 1916–1925 (2016)
5. Ruthruff, E., Faulks, M., Maxwell, J.W., Gaspelin, N.: Attentional dwelling and capture by color singletons. Atten. Percept. Psychophys. **82**(6), 3048–3064 (2020)
6. Li, J., Yu, S.L., Wu, X.L.: Effects of shape character encodings in the human-computer interface on visual cognitive performance. J. Comput. Aided Des. Comput. Graph. **30**(1), 163–172 (2018)
7. Yu, S.K., Wu, X.L., Feng, H.H.: Research on information highlighting of warning circuit in monitoring display interface of nuclear power plant. China Saf. Sci. J. **31**(12), 106 (2021)
8. Chan, A.H.S., Ng, A.W.Y.: Perceptions of implied hazard for visual and auditory alerting signals. Saf. Sci. **47**(3), 346–352 (2009)
9. Gomberg, B.F Strategic and attentional factors of computer-generated highlighting. MA thesis, New Mexico State University (1985)
10. Fisher, D.L., Coury, B.G., Tengs, T.O.: Optimizing the set of highlighted options on video display terminal menus. Proc. Hum. Soc. Ann. Meet. **29**(7), 650–654 (1985)
11. Van Orden, K.F., Divita, J., Shim, M.J.: Redundant use of luminance and flashing with shape and color as highlighting codes in symbolic displays. Hum. Factors. **35**(2), 195–204 (1993)
12. Ge, L.Z., Kong, Y.: A study of flickering as a type of highlighting in white and black display backgrounds. Psychol. Sci. **23**(1) (2000)
13. Cass, J., Van der Burg, E., Alais, D.: Finding flicker: critical differences in temporal frequency capture attention. Front. Psychol. **2**, 320 (2011)
14. Stolte, M., Ansorge, U.: Automatic capture of attention by flicker. Atten. Percept. Psychophys. **83**(4), 1407–1415 (2021)
15. Tong, M., Chen, S., Niu, Y., Xue, C.: Effects of speed, motion type, and stimulus size on dynamic visual search: a study of radar human–machine interface. Displays. **77**, 102374 (2023)
16. Turner, S., Wylde, J., Langham, M., Morrow, A.: Determining optimum flash patterns for emergency service vehicles: an experimental investigation using high definition film. Appl. Ergon. **45**(5), 1313–1319 (2014)
17. Waldin, N., Waldner, M., Viola, I.: Flicker observer effect: guiding attention through high frequency flicker in images. Comput. Graph. Forum. **36**(2), 467–476 (2017)

Application of Wearable Facial Electromyography Device with Human Metrics Explorer System in Virtual Reality Experiences

Koichi Murata(✉), Akane Kitagawa, Kotaro Ryu, and Masafumi Furuta

Technology Research Laboratory, Shimadzu Corporation, Kyoto, Japan
murata.koichi.9ar@shimadzu.co.jp

Abstract. Virtual reality (VR) systems are widely utilized across diverse scenarios, offering immersive experiences to users. Consequently, the ability to estimate user's emotions via a VR headset is useful during a VR experience. To estimate positive and negative emotions, several systems with facial electromyography (fEMG) sensors embedded in VR headset cushions have been developed. However, these systems are constrained by limited headset compatibility, alongside challenges in aligning with the muscle positions of individual faces. In this study, we confirm that both the developed wearable device, designed to operate independently of VR headsets, and consumer VR headsets can be used, and that fEMG signals can be measured during the VR experience with the human metrics explorer (HuME)™ system. HuME facilitates easy integration, measurement, and synchronous analysis of multiple types of device data. We conducted both a basic performance experiment to assess the compatibility of the developed fEMG device with consumer headsets, and an application experiment to measure fEMG during VR experiences using the device and HuME system. Consequently, both the fEMG device and VR headsets could be mounted without interference, with similar fEMG signals observed with and without headsets. Notably, the fEMG device successfully captured changes in the fEMG signals corresponding to scene changes during VR experiences. In conclusion, our study confirmed that both the developed wearable device and consumer VR headsets can be used, and that fEMG can be measured during the VR experience via the HuME system.

Keywords: Virtual reality · Facial electromyography · Wearable device

1 Introduction

Virtual reality (VR) systems find application in diverse fields such as marketing [1], engineering design [2], and entertainment. To assess user experience, prior studies have employed VR headsets to estimate emotions during VR experiences [3, 4]. Emotions are generally represented by valence and arousal in a dimensional model [5]. Many studies have used facial electromyography (fEMG) and facial-expression-image-based methods [6, 7] to measure emotional valence levels ranging from negative to positive. In fEMG, electrodes are placed on the target muscle to measure muscle activity through electromyography (EMG). Image-based methods involve capturing feature points from facial images via a camera, allowing the detection of muscle-related movements.

S. Jin et al. (Eds.): IEA 2024, SSDI 39, pp. 449–455, 2025.
https://doi.org/10.1007/978-981-95-0211-0_68

The VR headset covers most of the wearer's face, impeding the estimation of emotions using facial expressions. For such cases, fEMG is an effective method. Previous studies have developed systems with fEMG sensors embedded in VR headset cushions [8]. However, the number of compatible headsets is limited, and it is difficult to match the position of the muscles of an individual face. To the best of our knowledge, there are few wearable fEMG devices that can be used simultaneously with various commercial VR headsets and worn independently.

We have developed a wearable device capable of measuring fEMG signals during daily life activities and the human metrics explorer (HuME)™ system. HuME facilitates the integration of various types of measurement devices, simplifies the measurement process, and enables synchronous analysis of multiple-device data using only a graphical user interface (GUI) [9, 10]. In this study, we confirm the specific utilization of both the developed wearable device and consumer VR headset, showcasing the feasibility of measuring fEMG signals during VR experiences using the HuME system.

2 Material and Methods

2.1 HuME System

The HuME system helps integrate various types of measurement devices, including wearable fEMG and electrocardiogram (ECG) devices, enabling easy measurement and synchronous analysis of data from multiple devices and camera footage This synchronization is achieved through two broadcast wireless triggers, one before and one after the synchronization interval, and a synchronization processing software [9, 10].

2.2 Wearable fEMG Device [9, 10]

Our developed wearable fEMG device on the HuME system is a neckband device that records two-channel EMG signals at a sampling frequency of 500 Hz. Two exclusive electrodes were attached to the zygomatic major (ZM) and corrugator supercilia (CS) muscles to estimate the wearer's valence of the emotion. Previous research has established a correlation between fEMG activity of the ZM and CS muscles and emotional valence [11]. A ground electrode was attached to the mastoid process.

2.3 Experiments

2.3.1 Basic Performance Experiment

In the basic performance experiment, we confirmed that the developed fEMG device and commercial VR headset can be worn simultaneously, and that the fEMG signal can be successfully measured using the developed device while wearing the headset. The Oculus Quest 2 (Meta, USA) (hereinafter referred to as "Quest 2"), a standalone-type VR headset without the need for a personal computer (PC), and the HTC VIVE (HTC, Taiwan) (hereinafter referred to as "VIVE") connected to a PC, were chosen for their widespread adoption and availability in the market. There were three participants (2 males and 1 female) aged 25–32 years; all participants provided informed consent.

The task sequence for measuring the fEMG signal is as follows. After 30 s of rest, the muscle contraction task was repeated three times. In the muscle contraction task, the ZM muscle was intentionally maximally contracted for 15 s, followed by a 15 s rest, and then the CS muscle was maximally contracted, followed by another 15 s rest. During the rest interval, the facial muscles were relaxed. The task sequence was performed under three conditions: using only the fEMG device, using both the fEMG device and Quest 2, and using both the fEMG device and VIVE. To assess noise contamination arising from VR headsets, the headset was activated, and a Windows screen saver [12] was displayed as a visual stimulus, chosen to minimize emotional impact. The recorded data were subjected to a 20-Hz high-pass filter (51-coefficient finite impulse response filter) and baseline fluctuation rejection (subtracting the 102 ms moving average), followed by notch filters of 50, 60, 100, 120, 150, 180, 200, and 240 Hz (third sections of the sixth-order infinite impulse response filter). Root mean square (RMS) values were calculated from the filtered fEMG data. The noise levels were determined as the average of the RMS for 10 s following the first 10 s of 30 s rest. The amplitude spectra were generated from the middle 3 s of the first maximal contraction interval using a fast Fourier transform algorithm.

2.3.2 VR Experience Experiment

In the VR experience experiment, the fEMG signals were measured (during the VR experience) while the participant (25-year-old woman who provided informed consent) wore both the developed fEMG device and VIVE headset. To simulate a realistic VR experience, we used a KATWALKCS omnidirectional treadmill (KATVR, China). The VR content used was Nature Trek VR (Greener Games, UK), designed to simulate tropical beaches and discovery of animals. The participant was allowed to walk and explore the VR environment during the experiment. To synchronously capture the fEMG changes, VR experience, and behavior, the participants and display-mirrored VR headset images were recorded using video cameras. Due to individual differences in EMG magnitude depending on the electrode contact condition and muscle size, the EMG signal is commonly normalized using maximum and minimum values. The maximum value is obtained by intentionally activating the muscle completely before the task and updated if exceeded during the task. The RMS values of fEMG in the ZM and CS muscles were normalized by their corresponding maximum value and calculated as positive and negative indices using the same method as that utilized in a previous study [13].

3 Result

3.1 Basic Performance Experiment

Figure 1 depicts the setup with the following wearing configurations: the developed fEMG device alone, both the fEMG device and Quest 2, and both the fEMG device and VIVE. In both the Quest 2 and VIVE cases, there was no interference between the housing of the fEMG device and that of the VR headset. The ear frame and electrodes attached to the facial muscles were held in place by the headset cushion.

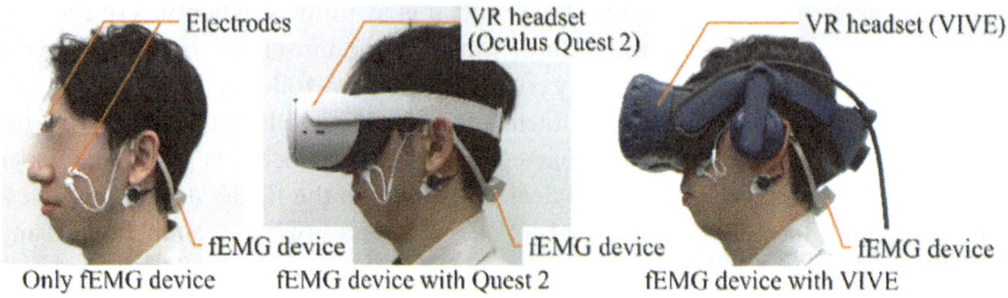

Fig. 1. Participants wearing the fEMG device and VR headset

Figure 2 displays the filtered fEMG signals and the calculated RMS signals of the ZM and CS muscles under three conditions: using only the fEMG device, the device and Quest 2, and the device and VIVE. The grey and red lines represent the raw fEMG and RMS data, respectively. Additionally, the right graph in Fig. 2 illustrates the amplitude spectra of the maximum contraction interval for each condition.

3.2 VR Experience Experiment

Figure 3 presents the results of the synchronous analysis of the VR headset movie, behavior movie, and fEMG signals obtained using the HuME system. Table 1 lists the scene details describing the participants' actions. The positive index calculated from the ZM EMG increased frequently in scene (1) during play involving ball-growing trees and in scene (2) during interactions with the triceratops. Conversely, the negative index calculated from the CS EMG significantly increased with time, as denoted by the blue arrow. However, neither positive nor negative indices substantially changed in scenario (3), involving a field switch.

4 Discussion

The basic performance experiment successfully established that all three participants could wear both the fEMG device and VR headsets concurrently without any interference. Simultaneous attachment is possible as long as the electrode and headset positions do not deviate significantly from those of the participants in this experiment. Moreover, the ZM and CS EMG exhibited no distinctive differences across conditions involving the fEMG device alone, fEMG device with Quest 2, and fEMG device with VIVE. This included aspects such as signal waveform, noise levels during rest intervals, and amplitude spectra during maximum contracting intervals. Because there was no significant difference in the noise levels under the three conditions, the measurement of low EMG activity can be possible with the fEMG device alone. The developed fEMG device, which can be used simultaneously with the Quest 2 and VIVE headsets, both of which have high commercial sales, can be applied in various VR applications.

In the VR experience experiment, the difference in the increase in the positive index between the interactive interval, such as scenes (1) and (2), and the non-interactive interval, such as scene (3), was captured. According to the interviews conducted after the

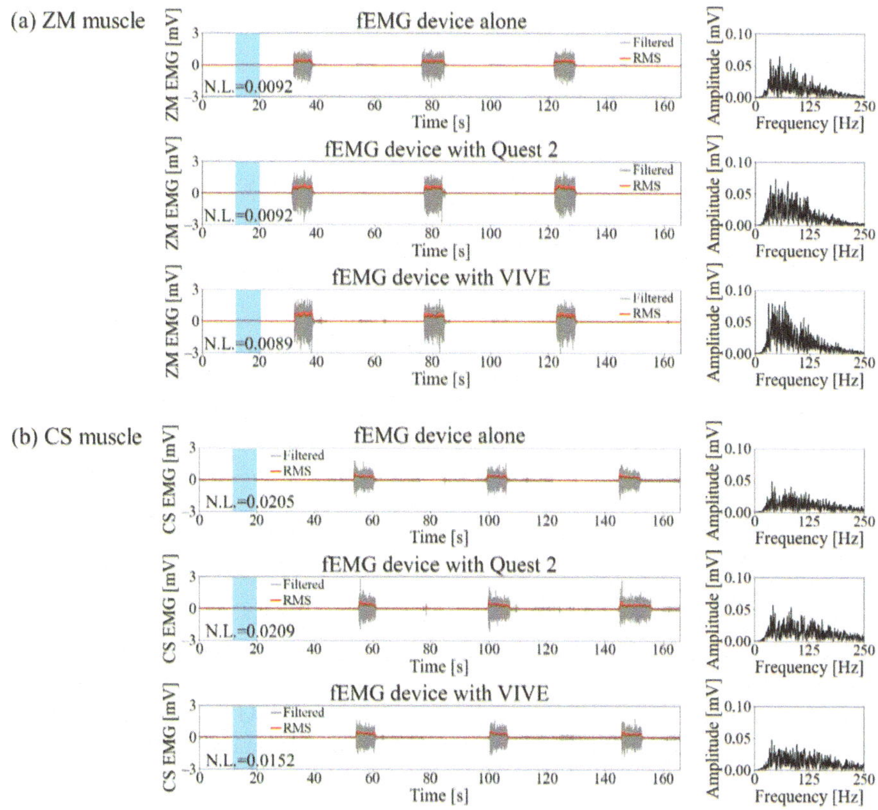

Fig. 2. Filtered fEMG and RMS signals of the (a) ZM and (b) CS muscles with and without the simultaneous use of VR headsets. Amplitude spectra of the intervals each muscle were contracted maximally. N.L. indicates the noise level (10–20 s) for the blue-highlighted interval during the initial rest period.

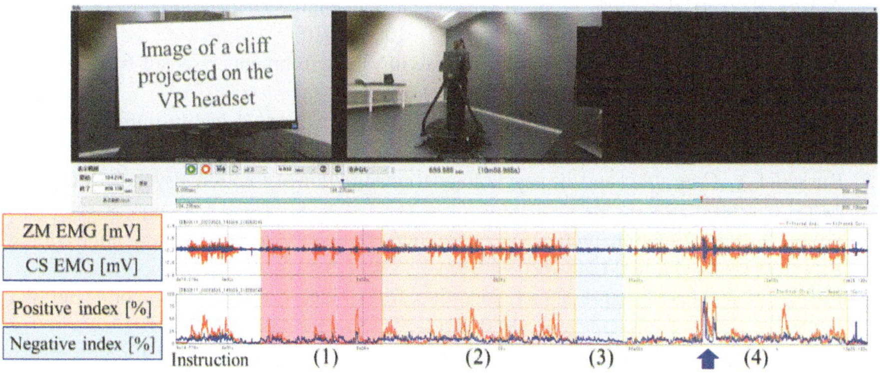

Fig. 3. Result of synchronous analysis using the HuME system

Table 1. Scene details describing participant's activity during the VR experiment.

No.	Scene details
(1)	Throwing action-balls that causes a tree to grow and watching it
(2)	Finding and approaching the triceratops
(3)	Watching screen switching a game field
(4)	Exploring a new field

experiment, a significant increase in the negative index occurred when the participant fell off the cliff and felt afraid. This corroborates previous research findings that CS EMG increases with fear [13]. This suggests that the developed fEMG device can capture fEMG reactions depending on the positive and negative emotions during the VR experience.

5 Conclusion

In this study, we successfully verified the compatibility of both the developed wearable device and consumer VR headsets for measuring fEMG signals during VR experiences using the HuME system.

In the future, we would like to apply the developed fEMG device and HuME system to other practical VR content evaluations, such as equipment usability and spatial experience evaluations within buildings.

References

1. Michel, W., et al.: Virtual and augmented reality: advancing research in consumer marketing. Int. J. Res. Mark. **37**(3), 443–465 (2020)
2. Aurora, B., Yuri, B.: Applications of virtual reality in engineering and product design: why, what, how, when and where. Electronics. **9**(7), 1064 (2020)
3. Jae-Hong, J., et al.: Immersive emotion analysis in VR environments: a sensor-based approach to prevent distortion. Electronics. **13**(8), 1494 (2024)
4. Marzena, M., et al.: Heart rate variability (HRV) during virtual reality immersion. Int. J. Occup. Saf. Ergon. **21**(1), 47–54 (2015)
5. Russell, J.A.: Core affect and the psychological construction of emotion. Psychol. Rev. **110**(1), 145–172 (2003)
6. Lang, P.J., et al.: Emotion, motivation, and anxiety: brain mechanisms and psychophysiology. Biol. Psychiatry. **44**(12), 1248–1263 (1998)
7. Ira, C., et al.: Facial expression recognition from video sequences: temporal and static modeling. Comput. Vis. Image Underst. **91**(1–2), 160–187 (2003)
8. Michal, G., et al.: Emteqpro—fully integrated biometric sensing array for non-invasive biomedical research in virtual reality. Front. Virtual Real. **3**, 781218 (2022)
9. Uraoka, Y., et al.: Development and application of multi-device biometric system "HuME (Human Metrics Explorer)". Shimadzu Rev. **78**(3–4), 245–254 (2021)

10. Kitagawa, A., et al.: Human Metrics Explorer System for multi-device physiological measurements in emotion estimation. In: 2024 IEEE/SICE International Symposium on System Integration, pp. 184–189. IEEE, Piscataway, NJ (2024)
11. Sato, W., et al.: Emotional valence sensing using a wearable facial EMG device. Sci. Rep. **11**(1), 5757 (2021)
12. [16:9 1080p] 3d Pipes Screensaver 10 Hours (no loop, with teapots!), https://www.youtube.com/watch?v=tCpnDTzRAjE. Accessed 30 Nov 2024
13. Ulf, D., et al.: Facial reactions to fear-relevant and fear-irrelevant stimuli. Biol. Psychol. **23**(2), 153–161 (1986)

Short-Term Social Media Abstinence and Self-monitoring Intervention: Higher Life Satisfaction and Positive Affects

Shuo Peng and Ruifeng Yu(✉)

Department of Industrial Engineering, Tsinghua University, Beijing, China
yurf@mail.tsinghua.edu.cn

Abstract. The problematic use of social media has some negative effects on people's lives. Based on Cognitive-behavioral therapy, a short-term social media abstinence intervention combined with self-monitoring was proposed. Unlike total abstinence, this short-term abstinence intervention only required a few hours away from social media each day. This paper conducted a 3×3 experiment under different intervention methods (CG: no intervention; EG1: abstinence; EG2: abstinence combined with self-monitoring) among participants with different procrastination levels (high, medium, low). Results showed subjects with a high procrastination level would have higher life satisfaction and positive affect under abstinence and self-monitoring conditions (EG2). Subjects would have a higher positive affect under the abstinence condition (EG1). This study also analyzed qualitative data and found both positive and negative influences of abstinence, which might originate from feelings and thoughts generated by substitution behaviors during the abstinence period, providing implications for the mechanism of abstinence effect.

Keywords: Social media · Short-term abstinence · Self-monitoring · Life satisfaction · Positive affect · Negative affect · FoMO

1 Introduction

Interpersonal communication has changed a lot due to the development of information technology, with online social media (SM) increasingly interwoven with our everyday lives. Access to SM has reduced the cost of communication, but this could also bring about overuse or misuse of social media, also called social media addiction (SMA). Research has shown that a high level of social media addiction might negatively affect daily life. Many studies on SMA have found that the overuse of SM might cause some problems including lower well-being, more depressive symptoms and poorer academic performance [1]. Many social media users would attempt to abstain from social media for a short time after feeling the negative effect of the overuse of social media [2]. Existing research also explored the effect of abstinence intervention for social media. However, the results were mixed and inconsistent, with both positive effects and negative effects.

For internet addiction, several cognitive-behavioral therapy (CBT) techniques have been recommended for treating and we believed that CBT might be a useful method

S. Jin et al. (Eds.): IEA 2024, SSDI 39, pp. 456–462, 2025.
https://doi.org/10.1007/978-981-95-0211-0_69

for treating social media addiction. Self-monitoring is an important method in CBT which involves the systematic observation and recording of the target [3]. The final goal of abstinence from social media is to help rationally use social media and avoid such negative effects of overuse. Therefore, in this paper, we proposed a short-term abstinence intervention combined with self-monitoring in Cognitive behavior therapy to help people use social media properly. Three questions were focused on in this study: 1) What is the efficacy of short-term abstinence intervention? 2) Would the combination with daily self-monitoring better improve the effects of abstinence intervention? 3) What is the mechanism of the abstinence effect?

2 Methodology

2.1 Participants

30 subjects participated in this program and 26 of them finally completed all processes. Subjects (12 males and 14 females) ranging from 18 to 25 are all undergraduate or graduate students in China. All of them are social media users. They were recruited from social media and would be paid some remuneration after the whole process.

2.2 Experiment Design

This study conducted a 3×3 experiment. 3 groups were divided due to the abstinence intervention (CG: no intervention, EG1: only short-term abstinence, EG2: short-term abstinence combined with daily self-monitoring) and procrastination level was divided into high, medium, and low. The procrastination level was divided using one-third and two-thirds quantile.

2.3 Procedure

All groups attended an introduction session before the experiments (T0, see Fig. 1), where the abstinence requirement was listed. Before experiment (T1), a 2-day preparation was provided and subjects would fill out the pre-survey to collect their baseline data including life satisfaction, Procrastination, FoMO, and Positive/Negative affect.

After the 2-day preparation, the formal experiment was set up, lasting for four days. During the experiment, participants in CG received no intervention, and participants in EG1 and EG2 would be abstinent from social media for 4 hours on 4 consecutive days. They could choose 2 periods from 3 provided periods (9:00–11:00, 14:00–16:00, 19:00–21:00) and not use the APP or network listed in the introduction session. Subjects in EG2 also needed to submit daily questionnaires at the end of each day. Questions would include abstinence outcomes, activities, feelings, reflections, and abstinence difficulty. At the end of the fourth day (T2), participants would fill out a post-survey, including life satisfaction, Procrastination, FoMO, Positive/Negative affect, and other open questions. Participants in EG1 and EG2 would rate abstinence difficulty (5-point Likert Scale), willingness to continue abstinence (5-point Likert Scale), days of abstinence failure, and positive/negative feelings and influences.

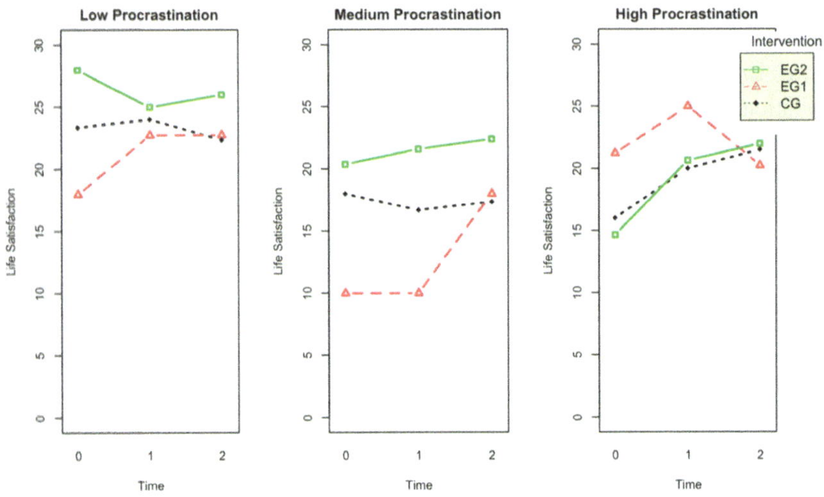

Fig. 1. Timeline of the experiment

7 days later (T3), all participants again would fill out a follow-up survey including life satisfaction, Procrastination, FoMO, and Positive/Negative affect. Participants in EG1 and EG2 would also answer whether they tried abstinence during the past 7 days and their willingness to continue abstinence. After finishing the above process, participants would receive some remuneration and thanks.

2.4 Measurement

The measurement methods of each variable were shown in Table 1. We also provided some open questions in the post-survey. The questions were adapted from studies by Evans et al., including motivation for participating in the program, positive/negative effects of social media abstinence, and other comments [4].

Table 1. Measurement of variables

Variables	Measurement
Procrastination	General Procrastination Scale (GPS) [5]
Life Satisfaction (LS)	Satisfaction with Life Scale (SWLS) [6]
Positive and Negative Affect	Positive and Negative Affect Schedule (PANAS) [7]
Fear of missing out (FoMO)	Fear of Missing Out Scale (FoMOs) [8]

3 Results

3.1 Life Satisfaction, Positive/Negative Affect, and FoMO

Data analysis was performed through SPSS 26.0 software. All scores obeyed Normal distribution, so the repeated analysis of variance (ANOVAs, within-between factor design) was considered in this study to test the effect of abstinence for subjects with different procrastination levels. Simple effect analysis was used to explore the interaction effect. The significant level for this analysis was 0.05.

For LS, results showed that the interaction effect of time, intervention, and procrastination was significant ($F = 2.381$, $p = 0.037$, $\eta^2 = 0.359$). Simple effect analysis showed that only under abstinence and self-monitoring conditions (EG2), subjects with a high procrastination level would have higher life satisfaction scores ($p < 0.05$) on the follow-up day ($M = 22.00 \pm 4.40$) than the baseline score ($M = 14.67 \pm 4.35$). The results were shown in Fig. 2. For Positive affect, results revealed that the interaction effect of time and intervention group was significant ($F = 3.711, p = 0.013, \eta^2 = 0.304$). Simple effect analysis showed that only under abstinence condition (EG1), the positive score at the end day ($M = 30.15 \pm 2.76$) was marginally significantly higher ($p < 0.1$) than the pre-intervention score ($M = 25.33 \pm 2.36$). No significant effect was discovered for Negative affect and FoMO.

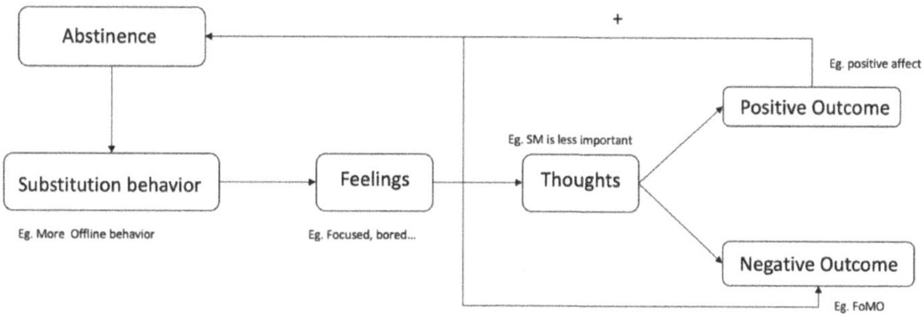

Fig. 2. Interaction Effect of time, intervention, and procrastination on life satisfaction.

3.2 Qualitative Positive/Negative Influences

The qualitative data was analyzed through feelings, activity and influence framework. The 5-point Likert scale about willingness to continue abstinence showed that most subjects would continue abstinence trials after this intervention ($Median_{EG1} = 5, Median_{EG2} = 4$), which implied that the abstinence might bring some positive influence to them so that they wanted to continue. Abstinence from social media helped people focus on other things to compensate for the no-use time of social media. From the daily reflection and post-questionnaire, subjects would benefit from this period in 3 ways. Firstly, most subjects reported that they focused more on offline activities. Secondly, some subjects stated that they felt more focused and efficient and less distracted by the information from social media. And some subjects noted that they felt fuller both in their study and their whole life. Finally, many subjects mentioned their quality of life was improved due to social media abstinence. Apart from that, the thoughts about social media were also changed due to abstinence. For example, *"In the time I controlled myself from playing with my phone, I didn't miss anything important and I found that social media wasn't as important to me"*(Subject 14).

As to the negative influences, 6 subjects (33.3%) noted that they felt no negative influence and the other 66.7% of subjects mentioned some negative feelings and influences. The main negative influence of abstinence could be divided into 4 parts: inconvenience (3), boredom (2), FoMO (2), and anxiety(2) (Table 2).

Table 2. Positive Influence of Abstinence

Positive Influence	Activity & Feelings	Number
Offline activities	Study	11
	Physical exercise	10
	Face-to-face communication	4
	Sleep	2
Efficiency	Increased attention	3
	More efficient	1
	Self-control	3
	Less distracted	1
Life Quality	Health	2
	Life Quality	3
	Meaningful	2
Thoughts about social media	Less important	2

4 Discussion

For the first question, results showed abstinence would bring some improvements in life satisfaction and positive affect, and no significant effect was found for FoMO and negative affect. This proved the efficacy of short-term abstinence of social media, and the effect was delayed, as the follow-up survey one week later showed a higher level of life satisfaction. This might imply that short-term abstinence and self-monitoring would induce a long-term influence on life satisfaction. Radtke et al. pointed out that it was still unclear whether the effects of abstinence were valid only during the abstinence intervention, immediately after the intervention, short-term, or long-term [9]. Our study might give an answer that the effect of abstinence might be long-term, even though it was only a 4-h short-term abstinence during 4 days.

As to the second research question, which is about the role of self-monitoring in the abstinence period, no significant difference between EG1 and EG2 was found. However, we found that only under EG2 condition, people with higher procrastination scores would have higher life satisfaction scores after the intervention. Rozgonjuk et al. pointed out the association between procrastination and problematic smartphone use, so it is of difficulty for those with high procrastination level to find a way to properly use SM [10]. Hou et al. mentioned that self-monitoring could help users identify the link between their thoughts and emotions and would help individuals to recognize their cognitive distortions [3]. Therefore, for people with procrastination problems, this self-reflection session would help them realize the importance and meaning of abstinence and therefore use social media and smartphones properly.

For the last question, we tried to explore the mechanism of abstinence effects from this experiment. Jorge proposed that people would change their behavior and attitudes after new feelings and thoughts [2]. From questionnaire reflection and daily self-monitoring, the effect might be closely related to substitution behaviors during abstinence which generates new feelings and thoughts and then leads to different outcomes, both positive and negative. These outcomes would then influence attitudes toward social media abstinence. The mechanism could be seen in Fig. 3.

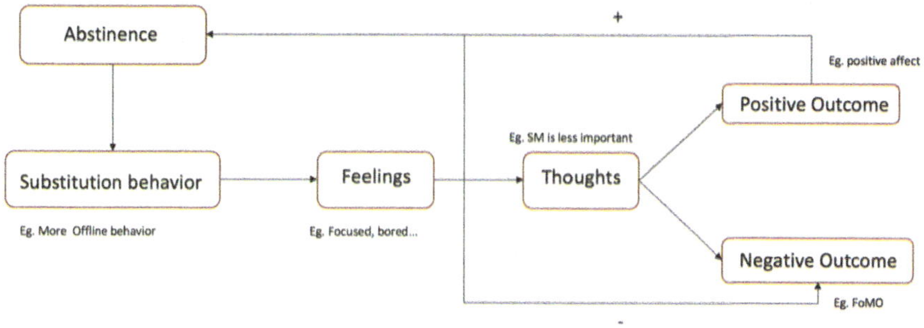

Fig. 3. Mechanism of social media abstinence

5 Conclusion

This study explored the effects of a short-term abstinence intervention from social media and also considered self-monitoring in the intervention program. Unlike existing studies on complete abstinence, this method only required subjects not to use social media for 4 hours and had some positive effects on subjects. Short-term abstinence intervention might improve life satisfaction and positive affect for a long time. Self-monitoring is a good tool for those with high procrastination levels during abstinence. We also found that the effects were mainly through substitution behaviors during abstinence and both negative and positive outcomes might be generated which further influence their attitudes towards abstinence. Further studies could be done on substitution behaviors to deeply study the mechanisms of social media abstinence.

References

1. Kross, E., Verduyn, P., Demiralp, E., et al.: Facebook use predicts declines in subjective well-being in young adults. PLoS One. **8**(8), e69841 (2013)
2. Jorge, A.: Social media, interrupted: users recounting temporary disconnection on Instagram. Social Media+ Soc. **5**(4), 2056305119881691 (2019)
3. Hou, Y., Xiong, D., Jiang, T., Song, L., Wang, Q.: Social media addiction: Its impact, mediation, and intervention. Cyberpsychology. **13**(1) (2019)
4. Evans, C., King, D.L., Delfabbro, P.H.: Effect of brief gaming abstinence on withdrawal in adolescent at-risk daily gamers: a randomized controlled study. Comput. Hum. Behav. **88**, 70–77 (2018)
5. Lay, C.H.: At last, my research article on procrastination. J. Res. Pers. **20**(4), 474–495 (1986)
6. Diener, E., Larsen, R.J., Levine, S., Emmons, R.A.: Intensity and frequency: dimensions underlying positive and negative affect. J. Pers. Soc. Psychol. **48**(5), 1253 (1985)
7. Watson, D., Clark, L.A., Tellegen, A.: Development and validation of brief measures of positive and negative affect: the PANAS scales. J. Pers. Soc. Psychol. **54**(6), 1063 (1988)
8. Przybylski, A.K., Murayama, K., DeHaan, C.R., Gladwell, V.: Motivational, emotional, and behavioral correlates of fear of missing out. Comput. Hum. Behav. **29**(4), 1841–1848 (2013)
9. Radtke, T., Apel, T., Schenkel, K., Keller, J., von Lindern, E.: Digital detox: An effective solution in the smartphone era? A systematic literature review. Mob. Media Commun. **10**(2), 190–215 (2022)
10. Rozgonjuk, D., Kattago, M., Täht, K.: Social media use in lectures mediates the relationship between procrastination and problematic smartphone use. Comput. Hum. Behav. **89**, 191–198 (2018)

Response of Pulmonary Function and Metabolic Rate After Heavy Object Handling at High Altitudes

Chao Sun[1], Shengjun Zhou[2], Jie Chen[2], Li Ding[1], Yiyang Zhao[1](✉), Jiachen Nie[1], and Xiaojuan Bai[3]

[1] Key Laboratory of Biomechanics and Mechanobiology (Beihang University), Ministry of Education; Key Laboratory of Innovation and Transformation of Advanced Medical Devices, Ministry of Industry and Information Technology; National Medical Innovation Platform for Industry-Education Integration in Advanced Medical Devices (Interdiscipline of Medicine and Engineering); School of Biological Science and Medical Engineering, Beihang University, Beijing 100191, China
2986762322@qq.com

[2] Wuhan Second Ship Design and Research Institute, Wuhan, China

[3] Tian Tong Yuan Nan Community Health Service Center, Beijing, China

Abstract. Engaging in heavy physical labor at high altitudes may exacerbate lung injury. The study investigated the changes in pulmonary function and metabolic rate in acclimatized Han individuals in extremely high-altitude environments before and after handling and stacking. Six healthy male volunteers (age 21.7 ± 2.8 years) were recruited to transport five heavy objects (25 kg) for 3 meters and stack them. Pulmonary function parameters were collected by self-developed portable pulmonary function testing machine. Compared to pre-handling, the minute vetilation significantly increased by 8.47 L/min after handling ($p = 0.015$). There were no significant changes observed in tidal volume and breath rate. The $P_{ET}CO_2$ decreased significantly at the end of 15 min of rest after handling ($p = 0.01$). Compared to pre-handling, metabolic rate significantly increased after handling ($p = 0.014$). Engaging in handling activities in high-altitude environments will increase the burden on the lungs and metabolic rate. Results have important implications in reducing lung injury caused by high-altitude heavy physical labor.

Keywords: Handling · Pulmonary function · Metabolic rate

1 Introduction

The Qinghai-Tibet Plateau, with an average elevation exceeding 4000 m, is an extremely high-altitude region [1]. Even after acclimatization to the plateau environment, long-term exposure to low-pressure, low-oxygen environments can lead to many diseases [2] affecting pulmonary function and metabolism. Engaging in manual handling activities at high altitudes may further exacerbate pulmonary burden, leading to changes in pulmonary function, and affecting metabolic rate. Therefore, conducting research on the pulmonary function and metabolic rate of plateau-acclimatized people engaged in heavy handling at extremely high altitudes can prevent lung injuries among high-altitude manual laborers.

S. Jin et al. (Eds.): IEA 2024, SSDI 39, pp. 463–469, 2025.
https://doi.org/10.1007/978-981-95-0211-0_70

Han ethnic residents acclimatized to high-altitude environments experience a decrease in end-tidal carbon dioxide pressure ($P_{ET}CO_2$), increased tidal volume(V_T), similar to Tibetan residents [3]. Han ethnic miners acclimatized to high-altitude environments have higher pulmonary ventilation, breath rates, and oxygen intake than those at sea-level [4]. However, under heavy physical loads, low-altitude acclimatized populations do not possess the same work capacity as native high-altitude residents [5].

Basal metabolic rate (BMR) is the minimum energy expenditure required for individual survival [6]. BMR can be assessed with height, weight, age, and gender, multiplied by activity factors [7]. However, it is still unknown whether model-based assessments of BMR in high-altitude environments are reliable. When lowland individuals first arrive in high-altitude areas, their BMR increases and gradually decreases [8]. Acclimatized Han miners in high-altitude environments do not exhibit significant differences in BMR compared to sea-level miners, but they have higher fat energy consumption [4].

The purpose of this study is to explore the changes in pulmonary function and metabolic rate in acclimatized Han individuals in extremely high-altitude environments before, immediately after, and 15 min after handling and stacking 25 kg of weight, as well as to compare the capabilities and differences in metabolic rate assessment between a self-developed portable metabolic analyzer and classic models.

2 Method

2.1 Participants

This experiment recruited six healthy male volunteers (age 21.7 ± 2.8 years) who had acclimatized to the plateau environment. All subjects received a complete experimental introduction and provided written informed consent before inclusion in this study. This study protocol complied with the Helsinki Declaration and was approved by the Ethics Committee of the School of Biological and Medical Engineering, Beihang University.

2.2 Measurement of Pulmonary Function and Metabolic Rate

2.2.1 Measurement Equipment

To facilitate the measurement of pulmonary function and metabolic rate at extremely high altitudes, a portable pulmonary function testing (PFT) machine was developed by our group. The PFT device consists of two flow sensors, a carbon dioxide (CO_2) sensor, an anesthesia mask, and a microprocessor. The range of the flow sensors is 0 to 100 SLPM with an accuracy of $\pm(0.2 + 0.5FS)\%$. The range of the CO_2 sensor is 0 to 150 mmHg, with an accuracy of ±2 mmHg for 0 to 40 mmHg and ± 5% of reading for 41 to 70 mmHg. The microprocessor collects data and transmits it to PC software for storage.

Before the experiment, the flow sensors were calibrated using a 3 L standard volume syringe. Environmental atmospheric pressure which was used to automatic calibration of CO_2 sensor was measured by an anemometer (WX-QX50, WanXiang™, China).

2.2.2 Calculation of Pulmonary Function Parameters

The breathing rate (BR, bpm) was calculated as the reciprocal of the time difference between adjacent inspiratory onset points:

$$\mathrm{BR} = \frac{60}{T_{n+1} - T_n} \tag{1}$$

where T_n (s) and T_{n+1} (s) are the inspiratory onset point of the preceding and succeeding respiratory cycle, respectively. The expiratory flow data ($Flow_{ex}$, L/min) were integrated, multiplied by the calibration factor α, to calculate the V_T (L) for each respiratory cycle, as in Eq. (2). The minute ventilation (MV, L/min) was calculated by multiplying the V_T by the BR, as in Eq. (3).

$$V_T = \alpha * \int Flow_{ex}\, dt \tag{2}$$

$$\mathrm{MV} = V_T * \mathrm{BR} \tag{3}$$

In the expiratory CO_2 partial pressure curve, the maximum partial pressure of CO_2 at end-expiration was taken as the $P_{ET}CO_2$ parameter.

2.2.3 Calculation of Metabolic Rate Using Pulmonary Function Instrument

Indirect calorimetry is based on the calculation of metabolic rate using oxygen consumption and carbon dioxide production. The calculation formula is the Weir equation, as shown in Eq. (4):

$$\dot{M} = \left(3.941 \times \dot{V}O_2\right) + \left(1.106 \times \dot{V}CO_2\right) - (2.17 \times BUN) \tag{4}$$

where $\dot{M}$ (kcal/min) is the metabolic rate. $\dot{V}O_2$(L/min) and $\dot{V}CO_2$(L/min) are the rates of O_2 consumption and CO_2 production, respectively. BUN(g/day) is the amount of urinary nitrogen excreted.

Respiratory quotient (RQ) can represent the ratio of CO_2 production to O_2 consumption within the same respiratory period. Additionally, the influence of urea nitrogen on metabolic rate was neglected. Thus, the final formula for calculating metabolic rate is:

$$\dot{M} = \left(3.9 \times \frac{\dot{V}O_2}{RQ} + 1.1 \times \dot{V}CO_2\right) \tag{5}$$

where the RQ was set to 0.85. For carbon dioxide production, the amount exhaled per minute was used, as follows:

$$\dot{V}CO_2 = \alpha * \int Flow_{ex} * \frac{P_{CO_2}}{atm} dt * BR \tag{6}$$

where P_{CO_2} (mmHg) is the partial pressure of exhaled carbon dioxide, and atm (mmHg) is the actual atmospheric pressure.

2.2.4 Model-Based Metabolic Rate Calculation

The evaluation model of BMR used in this study is the Mifflin-St Jeor Equation [9]:

$$BMR = 10 * \text{weight(kg)} + 6.25 * \text{height(cm)} + 5 * \text{age(years)} - 161 \quad (7)$$

In this study, metabolic rate at rest and after transportation were calculated using physical activity factors of 1.3 and 1.8 [7], respectively, for the volunteers.

2.3 The Handling and Stacking Tasks

The experiment was conducted indoors in Lhasa, China. The experiment comprised three phases: 1) Pre-handling rest (15 min): Volunteers rested to stabilize physiological parameters. 2) Handling and stacking: Volunteers performed heavy lifting and stacking tasks until they felt exhausted or reached termination criteria based on physiological parameters. 3) Post-handling rest (15 min): Volunteers rested after handling tasks. Portable PFT machine was used to measure respiratory flow and partial pressure of exhaled carbon dioxide signals for 20 breathing cycles at the end of each phase.

Two shelves, 40 cm high, were placed at opposite diagonal ends with a distance of approximately 3 m between them. Five heavy boxes, each weighing 25 kg, were stacked on one shelf. Volunteers transported one set of five objects from one end to the other, stacking them from low to high. After completing each set, volunteers were asked about their fatigue sensation. Volunteers repeated the handling and stacking tasks until their fatigue scores reached 7 (Borg-10), and they were unable to continue handling tasks. The handling process is illustrated in Fig. 1. Handling and stacking tasks were immediately terminated if volunteers experienced the following physiological conditions: 1) Blood oxygen saturation below 75%, 2) Heart rate(HR) above 150 bpm with irregular rhythm, 3) Sudden decrease in HR, 4) Symptoms of pre-syncope such as chest pain, dizziness, or blurred vision.

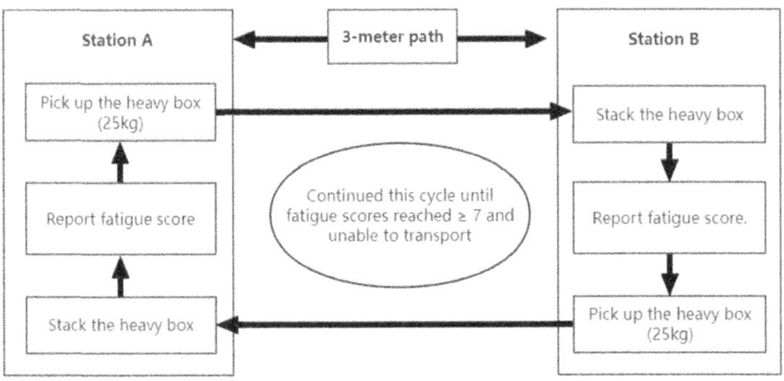

Fig. 1. Handling and stacking tasks.

2.4 Statistical Analysis

Statistical analyses were conducted using SPSS version 25 (IBM Inc., Chicago, IL, USA). Descriptive statistics (mean and standard error) were conducted. One-way repeated-measures ANOVA were employed to examine the differences in pulmonary function and metabolic rate measured at three phases. Post hoc analysis was performed with the Bonferroni adjustment to assess the disparities among three phases. Paired t-tests were utilized to compare the metabolic rate measured by the portable device at the first and second time points with the Mifflin St Jeor Equation calculation results of 1.3 and 1.8 times, respectively. $p \leq 0.05$ was considered statistically significant.

3 Results

The pulmonary function results are shown in Fig. 2. Compared to pre-handling rest, the MV significantly increased by 8.47 L/min after handling ($p = 0.015$). There were no significant changes observed in TV and BR at the three time points. The $P_{ET}CO_2$ decreased by 2.31 mmHg after handling, further declining by 1.14 mmHg after 15 min of rest, significantly lower than the pre-handling resting level ($p = 0.01$).

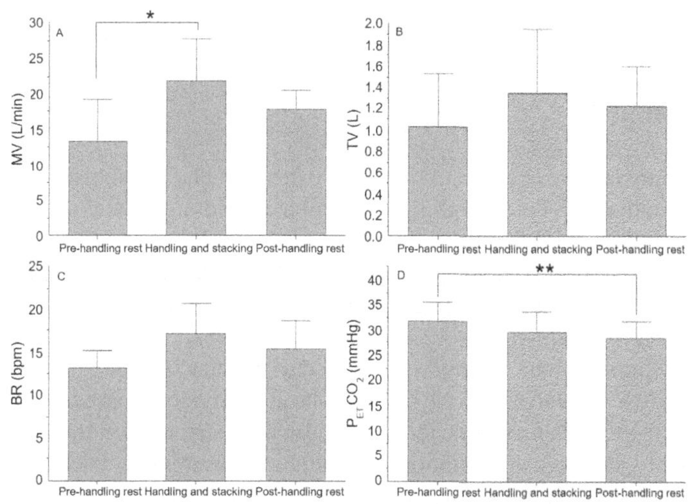

Fig. 2. Pulmonary function results.

Compared to pre-handling rest, the metabolic rate measured by the portable equipment significantly increased after handling ($p = 0.014$) (see Fig. 3).

The metabolic rate measured by the portable machine during the resting phase were significantly higher than the 1.3-fold Mifflin-St Jeor Equation's result ($p = 0.012$). After handling, there was no significant difference between the metabolic rate measured by the portable machine and 1.8-fold model calculations ($p = 0.091$), as shown in Table 1.

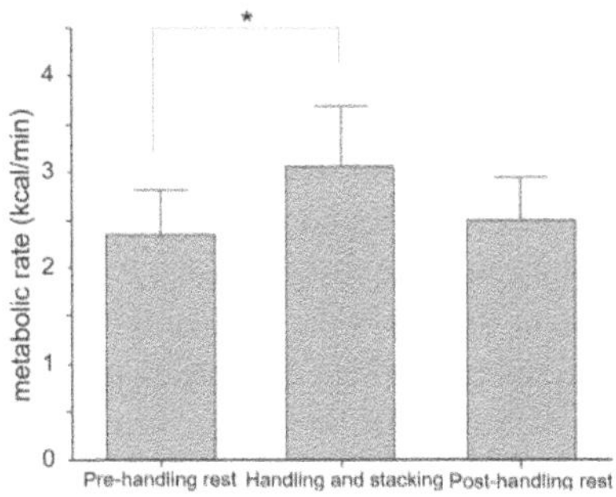

Fig. 3. Metabolic rate result measured by portable machine.

Table 1. Comparison of Metabolic Rate Measured by Portable Pulmonary Function Testing Machine and Calculated by the Mifflin-St Jeor Equation.

	The portable pulmonary function testing device (kcal/min)	1.3 or 1.8 times of Mifflin-St Jeor Equation (kcal/min)	p-value
Pre-handling rest	2.34 ± 0.47	1.79 ± 0.15 (1.3 times)	0.012
Hand and staking	3.05 ± 0.62	2.48 ± 0.21 (1.8 times)	0.091

4 Discussion

This study compares the changes in pulmonary function and metabolic rate in plateau-acclimatized individuals before and after heavy object handling in extremely high altitude environment. Following heavy object handling, the metabolic rate significantly increases, leading to an increase in BR and TV, and exacerbating the burden on the respiratory system. The metabolic rate was significantly higher than that calculated by the model equation at the pre-handling phase.

After acclimatization to high-altitude environments, inhabitants experience increased TV, MV [2], and metabolic rate [8]. The intensity of increased CO_2 production caused by an increase in metabolic rate is lower than the intensity of the increased CO_2 excretion due to an increase in pulmonary ventilation, resulting in a decrease $P_{ET}CO_2$. During the process of handling and stacking, the increase in O_2 consumption and arterial CO_2 pressure, stimulates the chemoreceptors [10], ultimately resulting in a significant increase in MV. As the increase in pulmonary ventilation continues to surpass the body's production of CO_2, resulting in a sustained decrease in $P_{ET}CO_2$ after handling.

Although the BMR of low-altitude individuals does not change significantly after acclimatization to plateau environments, the actual metabolic rate at high altitudes may have changed. When estimating metabolic rate using the same exercise factors as at sea level in plateau environments, there may be significant errors. An adjustment of model is necessary to accurately estimate the actual metabolic rate in plateau environments. There was no significant difference between the results obtained from the portable device and those calculated by the Mifflin-St Jeor Equation at 1.8 times, which does not indicate that the model method can be used to assess metabolic rate during exercise in extremely high-altitude environments. The results for four volunteers measured by the portable device were significantly higher than 1.8 times the model's estimated results, while the other two volunteers' results measured by portable instrument were lower than 1.8 times the model's results. This discrepancy can be explained by individual differences in physical fitness. More data is needed to obtain significant differences.

5 Summary

The results of this study suggest that the MV and metabolic rate significantly increase after heavy object handling, in order to supplement the oxygen consumed and eliminate the generated carbon dioxide during the handling process. The level of MV increase surpasses the level of CO_2 production which leads to a decrease in $P_{ET}CO_2$. The Mifflin-St Jeor Equation for evaluating metabolic rate cannot be used in high-altitude environments and need to be modified.

References

1. Mellor, A., Woods, D.: Physiology studies at high altitude; why and how. J. R. Army Med. Corps. **160**(2), 131–134 (2014)
2. Mallet, R.T., Burtscher, J., Richalet, J.P., et al.: Impact of high altitude on cardiovascular health: current perspectives. Vasc. Health Risk Manag. **17**, 317–335 (2021)
3. Moore, L.G.: Measuring high-altitude adaptation. J. Appl. Physiol. **123**(5), 1371–1385 (2017)
4. Wang, Y., Wang, H., Chen, Y., et al.: Pulmonary capacity, blood composition and metabolism among coal mine workers in high- and low-altitude aboveground and underground workplaces. Int. J. Environ. Res. Public Health. **19**(14), 8295 (2022)
5. Ge, R.L., Chen, Q.H., Wang, L.H., et al.: Higher exercise performance and lower VO2max in Tibetan than Han residents at 4,700 m altitude. J. Appl. Physiol. **77**(2), 684–691 (1994)
6. Westerterp, K.R.: Physical activity and physical activity induced energy expenditure in humans: measurement, determinants, and effects. Front. Physiol. **4** (2013)
7. Alger, A.H.: Nutrition and Physical Fitness
8. Farias, J.G., Jimenez, D., Osorio, J., et al.: Acclimatization to chronic intermittent hypoxia in mine workers: a challenge to mountain medicine in Chile. Biol. Res. **46**(1), 59–67 (2013)
9. Mifflin, M., St Jeor, S., Hill, L., et al.: A new predictive equation for resting energy expenditure in healthy individuals. Am. J. Clin. Nutr. **51**(2), 241–247 (1990)
10. Leacy, J.K., Linares, A.M., Zouboules, S.M., et al.: Cardiorespiratory hysteresis during incremental high-altitude ascent-descent quantifies the magnitude of ventilatory acclimatization. Exp. Physiol. **106**(1), 139–150 (2021)

Impacts of Font Size and Stroke Width of Chinese Characters on the Legibility Under Vibration

Yuzhen Wang, Ruifeng Yu(✉), and Ei Jia

Tsinghua University, Beijing, China
yurf@mail.tsinghua.edu.cn

Abstract. The legibility of characters is a crucial aspect of display design, yet it has been less explored in vibration environments. Using a within-subjects design, this study examined the impacts of different font design parameters (i.e., font size of 12, 14, and 16 pt.; stroke width of 1:6 and 1:10) on the legibility of Chinese characters under vibration. Twenty participants engaged in character-search tasks within pseudo-texts. The total search time and the correct response rate were used to measure the legibility. The results indicated that although font size and stroke width significantly affected the legibility of Chinese characters under vibration, the effects observed differ from those in static conditions. In vibration environments, the legibility of the 14 pt. font size was better than that of the 16 pt. font size, which in turn was better than that of the 12 pt. font size. Besides, characters with thicker stroke width (1:6) were more legible than characters with thinner stroke width (1:10). The combination of the 14 pt. font size and the 1:6 stroke width provided the best legibility. These findings could offer valuable suggestions for the font design of Chinese characters in vibration environments to enhance the legibility.

Keywords: Chinese characters · Legibility · Vibration environment

1 Introduction

The legibility of characters, referring to the ease with which a character can be distinguished from others [1], is an important ergonomics metric for assessing text display quality [2]. Previous studies have demonstrated that various font characteristics, including font size, stroke width, complexity, and line spacing, significantly influence legibility on visual display terminals (VDTs) [3]. The stroke width, in particular, is typically defined as the ratio of the stroke thickness to character height [4]. Research by Liu et al. through character-search experiments revealed that Chinese characters are more legible in font sizes of 12 pt. compared to 16 pt., and a thinner stroke width (1:10) has better legibility than a thicker one (1:6) [5]. Their results also suggested that the combination of the 12 pt. font size and the 1:10 stroke width provides the best legibility for Chinese characters.

S. Jin et al. (Eds.): IEA 2024, SSDI 39, pp. 470–476, 2025.
https://doi.org/10.1007/978-981-95-0211-0_71

Over the last three decades, the widespread use of VDTs has led to increasingly complex operational environments. Vibration has emerged as a common disturbance in the operation of VDTs. Studies have shown that both the presence and intensity of vibration significantly impede the processing of visual information [6]. As a result, font design principles established in static conditions may no longer be applicable in vibration conditions. However, research focusing on the design of Chinese characters for legible display in vibration environments remains scant. Thus, this study aims to investigate the impact of font size and stroke width on the legibility of Chinese characters in vibration environments and to verify whether the optimal legibility combination proposed in static conditions holds true under vibration.

2 Method

2.1 Experimental Design

The experiment conducted character-search tasks in a vibration environment. Participants were required to search for target characters in pseudo-texts (randomly arranged Chinese characters devoid of logical meaning [7]) on a tablet screen and record their results by touching it. A within-subjects design of 3 font sizes (12 pt., 14 pt., 16 pt) x 2 stroke widths (1:6, 1:10) was used, with levels based on Liu et al. [5]. Participants read two content-varied paragraphs under each experimental condition for reliable data. In data processing, the results under each condition were averaged. Each participant completed 12 trials, arranged in a Latin square sequence.

The dependent variable was the legibility, measured by the total search time (TST) and the correct response rate (CRR), as outlined by Lin et al. [8]. The TST referred to the duration from the start to the end of the search within one trial. The CRR was calculated by dividing the number of target characters found (i.e., correct response number) by the total number of target characters within one paragraph (i.e., five).

2.2 Participants

Twenty college students participated in the experiment, with ages ranging from 18 to 25 years. The group included 14 males and 6 females, aligning with the International Maritime Organization's recommendation for the gender ratio of crew members at 7:3. All participants were native Chinese and had normal or corrected-to-normal vision. The study was approved by the Institutional Review Board of Tsinghua University.

2.3 Materials

Software developed by Visual Basic was used to display the experimental interface. The interface displayed the target character and the "Next Page" button at the top, recorded the TST and the correct response number at the upper left corner, and presented the paragraph of pseudo-text in the center with target characters randomly embedded, avoiding the beginning and end positions (Fig. 1). Each paragraph contained the target character five times, which was unknown to participants, and each paragraph featured a different target character. The experiment employed a positive polarity display due to its wider application in VDTs, with dark characters at 4 cd/m^2 luminance and light background at 50 cd/m^2.

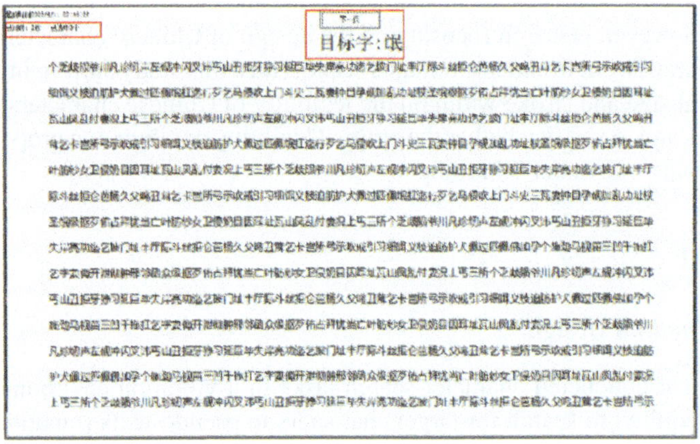

Fig. 1. One sample paragraph displayed with a font size of 12 pt. and a stroke width of 1:6.

All characters were chosen from a pool of 3500 commonly used Simplified Chinese characters, excluding foreign letters, punctuation marks, and special symbols. The font type selected was Songti. To allow precise control over stroke width, FontCreator 6.5 and CorelDRAW X5 were utilized for font design. Each paragraph contained approximately 500 to 600 characters, with text aligned on both ends and a line spacing set to 1.5 times.

2.4 Apparatus and Environment

The vibration environment was facilitated by a simulated cockpit (Fig. 2), with vibration parameters guided by the research of Xue et al. [9]: a vibration frequency of 0.125 Hz and an amplitude of 70 mm in the left-right direction, and frequencies of 0.25 Hz with amplitudes of 70 mm in both the forward-backward and the up-down directions. During the experiment, participants sat in a fixed cockpit seat and interacted with the experimental software by touching a tablet. The tablet was positioned on a table at a height of 70 cm and was tilted at an angle of 105 degrees. Participant's line of sight was aligned perpendicularly to the screen's midpoint, with the viewing distance maintained at 50 cm. The screen boasted a pixel resolution of 2560 × 1600 at a 70 Hz refresh rate and was used under an external illumination of 350 lx.

2.5 Procedure

Before the experiment, participants were briefed on its purpose and tasks, and then signed informed consent forms. They completed two practice trials to get acquainted with the software, using interfaces identical to the formal trials but with different paragraph content. In the formal trials, participants read instructions on the first page, then used

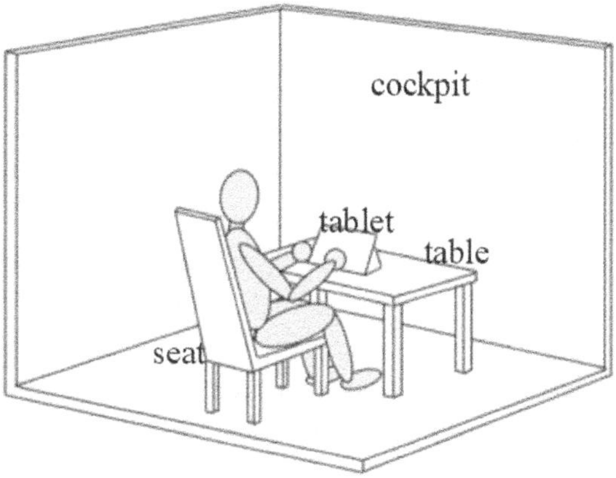

Fig. 2. Design sketch of experimental scene.

the "Next Page" button to progress through the pages. They were required to browse the paragraphs from beginning to end and to find all the target characters and clicked on it, which turned red upon selection. They completed 12 trials, with a 2-min break after the first six to prevent visual fatigue. The experiment concluded when participants clicked an "End" button after the last trial. Participants were then thanked and rewarded.

3 Results

The means and standard deviations of the TST and the CRR are shown in Table 1. Two-way repeated-measure analyses of variance (ANOVAs) were conducted on the TST and the CRR, with the factors of font size and stroke width (Table 2).

Table 1. Results of descriptive statistics.

	1:6 stroke width			1:10 stroke width		
	12 pt	14 pt	16 pt	12 pt	14 pt	16 pt
	M (SD)	*M (SD)*	*M (SD)*	*M (SD)*	*M (SD)*	*M (SD)*
Total search time (s)	66.513 (0.087)	**62.511 (0.110)**	64.485 (0.116)	68.514 (0.098)	64.521 (0.102)	65.489 (0.104)
Correct response rate (%)	29% (0.140)	**71% (0.100)**	47% (0.095)	28% (0.098)	53% (0.097)	33% (0.097)

The main effects of font size on the TST (F = 56.84, p < 0.001) and the CRR (F = 7.32, p < 0.01) were significant. This indicates that font size significantly affects the legibility of Chinese characters. The post-hoc tests showed that the TST for the 14 pt. font size was less than that for the 16 pt. font size (M_{14pt} = 63.516, M_{16pt} = 64.987, p < 0.001), which in turn was less than that for the 12 pt. font size (M_{16pt} = 64.987,

Table 2. Results of ANOVAs.

	Total search time (s)		Correct response rate (%)	
	F	*p-value*	*F*	*p-value*
Font size	56.84	<0.001	7.32	0.007
Stroke width	32.03	<0.001	15.13	<0.001
Font size × Stroke width	74.09	<0.001	27.36	<0.001

$M_{12pt} = 67.180$, $p < 0.001$). Furthermore, the CRR for the 14 pt. font size was higher than for the 16 pt. font size ($M_{14pt} = 61.75\%$, $M_{16pt} = 39.75\%$, $p < 0.001$), which was higher than for the 12 pt. font size ($M_{16pt} = 39.75\%$, $M_{12pt} = 28.67\%$, $p < 0.001$).

The main effects of stroke width on the TST ($F = 32.03$, $p < 0.001$) and the CRR ($F = 15.13$, $p < 0.001$) were significant, indicating that stroke width significantly influences the legibility. Post-hoc test results showed that the TST for the 1:6 stroke width was less than that for the 1:10 stroke width ($M_{1:6} = 64.503$, $M_{1:10} = 65.707$, $p < 0.001$), and the CRR for the 1:6 stroke width was higher than that for the 1:10 stroke width ($M_{1:6} = 48.25\%$, $M_{1:10} = 39.60\%$, $p < 0.01$).

There was a significant interaction effect between font size and stroke width on the TST ($F = 74.09$, $p < 0.001$). Significant differences in the TST were found between stroke widths of 1:6 and 1:10 at 12 pt. ($M_{1:6} = 66.513$, $M_{1:10} = 68.514$, $p < 0.05$) and 14 pt. ($M_{1:6} = 62.511$, $M_{1:10} = 64.521$, $p < 0.05$). However, when the font size was 16 pt., the difference in the TST between the 1:6 and 1:10 stroke widths was not statistically significant ($M_{1:6} = 64.485$, $M_{1:10} = 65.489$, $p > 0.05$). Similarly, there was also a significant interaction effect between font size and stroke width on the CRR ($F = 27.36$, $p < 0.001$). Significant differences in the CRR were found between stroke widths of 1:6 and 1:10 at 14 pt. ($M_{1:6} = 71\%$, $M_{1:10} = 53\%$, $p < 0.05$) and 16 pt. ($M_{1:6} = 47\%$, $M_{1:10} = 33\%$, $p < 0.05$), while no significant difference was observed at 12 pt. ($M_{1:6} = 29\%$, $M_{1:10} = 28\%$, $p > 0.05$). Figure 3 illustrates the interaction effects distinctly.

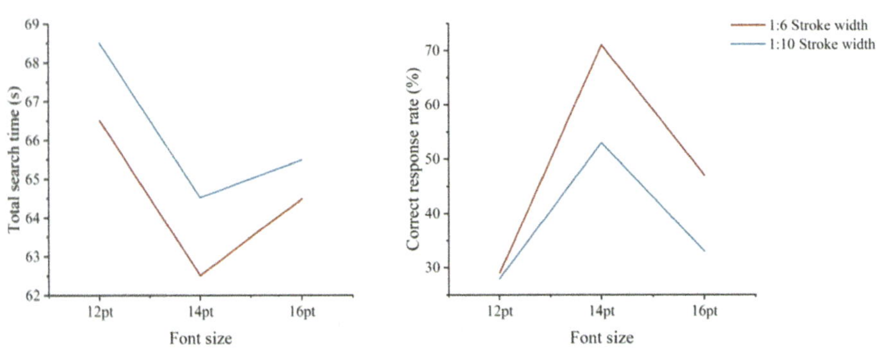

Fig. 3. Total search time and correct response rate of different character under vibration.

4 Discussion and Conclusions

This study was the first to investigate the effects of font size and stroke width on the legibility of Chinese characters under vibration. Mills stated the existence of an optimal font size that maximizes legibility, with variations in either direction (smaller or larger) leading to decreased legibility [1]. This study aligns with their statement, demonstrating that in a vibration environment, a 14 pt. font size proved to be optimal for legibility, outperforming both the larger 16 pt. and the smaller 12 pt. font sizes.

It was revealed that the optimal font size for legibility under vibration conditions is larger than in static conditions, where the 12 pt. font size was found to be most legible [5]. Additionally, a thicker stroke width (1:6) provided better legibility than a thinner stroke width (1:10) under vibration, which contrasts with static conditions where the thinner stroke width (1:10) was more legible. These variations might stem from vibrations impacting individuals' visual stability [10], making it harder to recognize details [11]. Thus, larger fonts and thicker strokes, offering larger visual targets, facilitate quicker recognition and processing. Overall, this study's findings suggest that certain established principles of Chinese character font design in static conditions are inapplicable in vibration conditions. We recommend Chinese character with a 14 pt. font size and a 1:6 stroke width as the optimal combination under vibration.

Despite these findings, our study has limitations. Firstly, we only focused on indicators related to task performance as dependent variables. For follow-up study, incorporating participants' subjective feedback and physiological data (e.g., eye movements) could provide more comprehensive conclusions and explanations. Moreover, the scope of independent variables chosen was relatively narrow. Future research could explore a wider range of font characteristics (e.g., font type, complexity, and line spacing) to delve deeper into this field.

References

1. Mills, C.B., Weldon, L.J.: Reading text from computer screens. ACM Comput Surv. **19**(4), 329–357 (1987)
2. Tan, L., Wang, C., Li, H.: Impact of the size of Chinese characters on the visual search performance under vibration. In: Kurosu, M. (ed.) Human-Computer Interaction. Theories, Methods, and Human Issues, pp. 345–354. Springer International Publishing, Cham (2018)
3. Chan, A.H.S., Ng, A.W.Y.: Effects of display factors on Chinese proofreading performance and preferences. Ergonomics. **55**(11), 1316–1330 (2012)
4. Cai, D., Chi, C.-F., You, M.: The legibility threshold of Chinese characters in three-type styles. Int. J. Ind. Ergon. **27**(1), 9–17 (2001)
5. Liu, N., Yu, R., Zhang, Y.: Effects of font size, stroke width, and character complexity on the legibility of Chinese characters. Hum. Factors Ergon. Manuf. Serv. Ind. **26**(3), 381–392 (2016)
6. Liu, K., Zeng, J., Tao, D.: Assessing touchscreen operations under vibration: effects of vibrational environments, button size, and button spacing on digit- and letter-entry task performance. Univ. Access Inf. Soc. (2022)
7. Lin, Y.-T., Lin, P.-H., Hwang, S.-L., Jeng, S.-C., Liao, C.-C.: Investigation of legibility and visual fatigue for simulated flexible electronic paper under various surface treatments and ambient illumination conditions. Appl. Ergon. **40**(5), 922–928 (2009)

8. Lin, H., Wu, F.-G., Cheng, Y.-Y.: Legibility and visual fatigue affected by text direction, screen size and character size on color LCD e-reader. Displays. **34**(1), 49–58 (2013)
9. Xue, H., Tao, D., Wang, T., Zhang, X.: Visual search in vibration environments: effects of spatial ability, stimulus size and stimulus density. Int. J. Ind. Ergon. **79**, 102988 (2020)
10. Lin, C.J., Liu, C.N., Chao, C.J., Chen, H.J.: The performance of computer input devices in a vibration environment. Ergonomics. **53**(4), 478–490 (2010)
11. Wang, H., Tao, D., Cai, J., Qu, X.: Effects of vibration and target size on the use of varied computer input devices in basic human-computer interaction tasks. Hum. Factors Ergon. Manuf. Serv. Ind. **32**(2), 199–213 (2022)

Moderation Effect of Incentives Between Personality and Intention of Providing High-Quality Reviews (IPHR)

Haiying Wang[1](✉), Siyu Chen[1], Qian Jue[1], Liu Chang[1], and Lin Wang[2](✉)

[1] School of Art Design, Zhejiang A&F University, Hangzhou, China
20190091@zafu.edu.cn

[2] Department of Library and Information Science, Incheon National University, Incheon, South Korea
wanglin@inu.ac.kr

Abstract. A flood of worthless information clouded the judgment of users and vendors about online reviews, and the challenge remains in how to employ effective incentives to motivate users to provide high-quality reviews. The purpose of this paper is to investigate whether the common incentives employed by vendors had a moderating effect on the relationship between personality traits and intention of providing high-quality review. An extended theory of planned behavior and Big-Five personality framework are used in this study. We surveyed 300 participants, including random online participants and offline participants from universities and vendors, by asking them to answer questionnaires. A total of 221 valid questionnaires were analyzed by hierarchical regression analysis method, and the results showed that extraversion, openness, and conscientiousness have a positive relationship with IPHR and Achievement moderates the relationship between neuroticism and IPHR. Vendors can invite more users who score high on extraversion, openness, and conscientiousness to participate in survey without any incentives, and they can encourage users who scored high on neuroticism to post high-quality reviews with achievement incentives.

Keywords: High-quality Review · Personality dimensions · Economy incentives · Achievement incentives · Big Five Model

1 Introduction

Users can share their review information after buying or using products and services in an e-commerce application or downloading an app in app stores. A steady stream of high-quality contributions from the users is critical to the survival of the online review platforms that facilitate interactions between reviewers and readers and eventually affect the product sale and the market structure [1]. The challenge is how to encourage users to volunteer more high-quality reviews through some new incentive schemes that are different from existing ones that have proven effective in increasing the number of online reviews but are not significant in terms of quality [2].

S. Jin et al. (Eds.): IEA 2024, SSDI 39, pp. 477–482, 2025.
https://doi.org/10.1007/978-981-95-0211-0_72

Drawing on the behavioral theory of psychology [3], individual's particular behaviors often can be activated by certain specific goals that can serve as external incentives [4]. The behavior of providing high-quality online reviews is different from the behaviors of providing online reviews in quantity, for that it requires reviewers to spend more time and effort to make the number of words in the reviews more and the text detailed more. As we know that, individuals with different personality traits have different motivations for providing online reviews [5–7].

Therefore, we supposed that the incentives used by vendors are not equally effective in motivating users with different personality traits to provide high-quality reviews. As we know, different individuals, depending on their characteristics, can be significantly motivated by different types of incentive schemes [8]. If it can be shown that users are more willing to provide high-quality reviews when they receive incentives designed for their characteristics, then vendors can tailor incentives to different users to encourage more high-quality reviews.

Some literature has found that achievement incentive and economic incentive are the two most commonly used incentive methods, and both of them can improve the quantity and quality of reviews on online review platforms to a certain extent [2, 9]. Among the related personality traits papers, Big Five Model (BFM), has been recognized by most researchers as the most referenced individual personality model [10]. Some scholars have discussed the different effects of the five different personality dimensions on an individual's intention to provide an online review [5, 11], and investigated the motivations for the behavior of presenting online reviews [5, 7]. But very little attention has been paid to the relationship the BFM and individual's IPHR and why an individual is willing to provide a high-quality online review. Thus, the first objective of this study is to discuss how the five dimensions of BFM influence an individual's IPHR. The second objective of this study is to investigate the moderation effect of the achievement incentive and economic incentive between BFM and IPHR.

2 Theories and Hypotheses

2.1 The Relationship Between Personality Dimensions and IPHR

The BFM implies that personality consists of five relatively independent dimensions that altogether provide a meaningful taxonomy for the study of individual differences [12]. These five dimensions are extraversion, neuroticism, openness, agreeableness, and conscientiousness [10]. In this section, we proposed hypotheses on the relationship between each personality dimension and IPHR based on the analysis of the personality characteristics of each personality dimensions and the relevant motivations for presenting online reviews.

Numerous pieces of evidence have indicated a positive correlation between extroversion and the inclination to present online reviews [13]. Furthermore, related studies have demonstrated that individuals with an extraverted personality trait are more inclined to participate in discussions pertaining to the economy and engage in disclosure behaviors aimed at assisting others [13], as well as exhibit a greater propensity to utilize web services that cater to their needs [7]. Some literature has shown that neuroticism was negatively correlated with online reviews presentation, because users with high scores of neuroticisms were more likely to be emotional, less likely to trust others, and therefore less willing to contribute their reviews [14]. Users with high openness are more abstract in thinking, and like to explore new knowledge, and these variables are highly correlated with online review presentation [6, 15]. **R**elated studies have shown that individuals with high agreeableness are more willing to share information [16]. Individuals high in agreeableness are friendly, helpful, altruistic, modest, trusted, and straightforward [17]. These characteristics are expected to facilitate cooperative behavior [16] (Taggar, 2002). Users with high conscientiousness have a strong will, target and success-oriented structure found that conscientious individuals may be more willing to provide online reviews because they are more cooperative and willing to help others [15, 17]. So, we supposed:

Hypothesis 1: There is a positive relationship between extraversion and IPHR.
Hypothesis 2: There is a negative relationship between neuroticism and IPHR.
Hypothesis 3: There is a positive relationship between openness and IPHR.
Hypothesis 4: There is a positive relationship between agreeableness and IPHR.
Hypothesis 5: There is a positive relationship between conscientiousness and IPHR.

2.2 The Moderation Effect of Achievement and Economy Incentive

Achievement incentives are a means to satisfy the desire for positive recognition from others [17]. Various studies have discussed how individuals with different personality dimensions can be motivated by Achievement incentives [15, 17]. Extroverted individuals have strong desires for social recognition and praise [6, 17], which closely align with achievement incentives [15, 17]. High conscientious individuals demonstrate thoroughness, responsibility, self-discipline, and task-oriented motivation [16, 17]. Neurotic users are motivated by positive self-enhancement tendencies which may be influenced by certain achievement incentives [17]. Some literature has shown a significant correlation between openness and Achievement [14]. The relationship between agreeableness and Achievement has yielded inconsistent results: some studies suggest relevance [3] while others do not [17]; we assume relevance in this paper. Therefore, it is anticipated that Achievement incentives might amplify the effect of personality traits on IPHR.

Based on these findings, the following hypotheses were proposed:

Hypothesis 6: Achievement incentives positively moderate the relationship between extraversion and IPHR.
Hypothesis 7: Achievement incentives positively moderate the relationship between neuroticism and IPHR.
Hypothesis 8: Achievement incentives positively moderate the relationship between openness and IPHR.
Hypothesis 9: Achievement incentives positively moderate the relationship between conscientiousness and IPHR.
Hypothesis 10: Achievement incentives positively moderate the relationship between agreeableness and IPHR.

Economy incentives involve compensating review contributors with rewards such as discounts, free vouchers. This type of incentive is commonly provided by suppliers and has been the subject of numerous studies examining its impact on users' online review behavior. Some researchers identified a significant relationship be-tween economic rewards and users' intention to provide reviews in quantity [22]. Additionally, researchers have found that economy incentives play an important role in eliciting high-quality reviews from readers [2]. Some literature has also explored the connection between personality traits and economy incentives [25], suggesting that these incentives may strengthen the effect of personality traits on IPHR.

Hypothesis 11: Economy incentives positively moderate the relationship between extraversion and IPHR.
Hypothesis 12: Economy incentives positively moderate the relationship between neuroticism and IPHR.
Hypothesis 13: Economy incentives positively moderate the relationship between openness and IPHR.
Hypothesis 14: Economy incentives positively moderate the relationship between conscientiousness and IPHR.
Hypothesis 15: Economy incentives positively moderate the relationship between agreeableness and IPHR.

3 Method

The final sample consisted of 221 respondents from China (54% female), 20–50 years old (M = 25.12, SD = 10.32). 122 participants (55.2%) were undergraduate student, 58 participants (26.2%) were graduate students of Chinese university, 58 participants (26.2%) were graduate students from Chinese university (18.6%) and 41 participants (18.6%) were Employees of Chinese enterprises.

Participants completed self-report questionnaires on personality dimensions, responses to Achievement and Economy incentives, and IPHR. Online questionnaires were shared via a Questionnaire Star link through project team members' WeChat groups. Prior to completing the questionnaire, online participants electronically signed a consent form and received a randomly assigned WeChat Lucky Money reward (ranging from 0 yuan to 5-yuan RMB) upon completion.

We used the 5-point Likert-type Big Five Personality Inventory (CBF-PI-B) developed by Wang et al., 2011 to measure personality traits, with each dimension comprising 8 questions. The data were analyzed using IBM SPSS version 23, including descriptive statistics, correlation analysis, and hierarchical regression analysis to examine relationships between variables and investigate the moderator effect of Achievement incentives and Economy incentives on the relationship between personality traits and IPHR.

4 Results

H2, examining the negative relationship between neuroticism and IPHR, was sup-ported with a significant relationship (−0.226) at a 0.05 error level. Similarly, H3, investigating the positive relationship between openness personality trait and IPHR, was also supported with a significant relationship (0.224) at a 0.05 error level. Additionally, H4 exploring the positive relationship between conscientiousness and IPHR was supported with a significant relationship (0.324) at a 0.01 error level; however, H1 and H5 were not supported as they did not reach significance levels of 0.01 or 0.05.

The study examined the moderator effects of Achievement incentives and Economy incentives on the five personality dimensions and IPHR. Three regression analyses were conducted for each model, with a focus on the significance of independent variables in each step, as well as the meaningfulness of T-values in subsequent regression models. The outcomes are presented in Table 3. Upon review of relevant tables, it was found that Model 1 (H6) and Model 6 (H13) were supported. This indicates that a moderator effect of achievement incentives was observed between open-ness personality traits and IPHR (Model 1), while a moderator effect of economy incentives was identified between extraversion personality traits and IPHR (Model 6). Within this framework, hypotheses H6 and H8 were "accepted", whereas hypotheses H7, H9-H15 were "not accepted".

5 Discussion

We analyzed the relationship between the five personality dimensions of BFM and IPHR using Pearson correlation analysis, finding three constructs to be statistically significant: neuroticism (H2), openness (H3), and conscientiousness (H5). The support for neuroticism is expected due to the potential frustration experienced by neurotic individuals in providing quality reviews, possibly leading to lower IPHR. Additionally, individuals with high levels of openness and conscientiousness are inclined to provide high-quality online reviews, reflecting their consistent intentions to enhance both the quantity and quality of online reviews. In terms of Economy incentives and Achievement incentives as moderator variables in the model, it was found that IPHR is positively associated with Achievement incentives but has no significant relationship with Economy incentives. Notably, there is also no significant relationship between Economy incentives and Achievement incentive. One implication from our study suggests that popular vendor-used incentives such as achievement and economy might not be universally effective for all users. There-fore, different effective incentives should be applied based on users' distinct personality dimensions.

For citations of references, we prefer the use of square brackets and consecutive numbers. Citations using labels or the author/year convention are also acceptable. The following bibliography provides a sample reference list with entries for journal articles [1], an LNCS chapter [2], a book [3], proceedings without editors [4], as well as a URL [5].

References

1. Samiei, P., Tripathi, A.: Exploring reviewers' contributions to online review platforms. In: Workshop of Information Technology and Systems, Milan (2013)
2. Chen, X., Jie, S., Wang, X., Deng, J.: Exploring determinants of attraction and helpfulness of online product review: a consumer behavior perspective. Discret. Dyn. Nat. Soc. **2016**, 1–19 (2016)
3. Berridge, K.C.: Reward learning: reinforcement, incentives, and expectations. Psychol. Learn. Motiv. **40**, 223–278 (2000)
4. Hockenbury, D.H., Hockenbury, S.E.: Psychology, 3rd edn. Worth, New York (2003)
5. Manner, C., Lane, W.: Who posts online customer reviews? The role of socio demographics and personality traits. J. Consum. Satisfact. Dissatisfact. Compl. Behav. **30**(1), 19–42 (2018)

6. Gupta, B.: Role of personality in knowledge sharing and knowledge acquisition behavior. J. Indian Acad. Appl. Psychol. **34**(1) (2008)
7. Amiel, T., Sargent, S.: Individual differences in Internet usage motives. Comput. Hum. Behav. **20**, 711–726 (2004)
8. Mullen, E.: Can Different Incentives Influence Participants' Choice? Carnegie Mellon University (2007)
9. Wang, F., Zhang, J., Wang, S., Li, S., Hou, W.: Analysis of driving behavior based on dynamic changes of personality states. Int. J. Environ. Res. Public Health. **17**, 430 (2020)
10. John, O.P., Srivastava, S.: The big five trait taxonomy: history, measurement, and theoretical perspectives. In: Pervin, L.A., John, O.P. (eds.) Handbook of Personality: Theory and Research, pp. 102–138. Guilford Press (1999)
11. Sergio, P.V., Shih, Y.C., Arlyn, J.M., John, M.P.: Why provide an online review? An extended theory of planned behavior and the role of big-five personality traits. Comput. Hum. Behav. **26**(4), 685–696 (2010)
12. Kuldeep, K., Arti, B., Ekta, R.: Linking the big five personality domains to organizational citizenship behavior. Int. J. Psychol. Stud. **1**(2), 73–81 (2009)
13. Hollenbaugh, E.E., Ferris, A.L.: Facebook self-disclosure: examining the role of traits, social cohesion, and motives. Comput. Hum. Behav. **30**(1), 50–58 (2014)
14. Zhao, J.: The influence of personality traits on knowledge sharing: Organizational trust as a mediating variable [In Chinese]. Inform. Theory Pract. **05**, 34–38 (2013)
15. Cabrera, N., Collins, W.C., Salgado, J.F.: Determinants of individual engagement in knowledge sharing. Int. J. Hum. Resour. Manag. **17**(2), 245–264 (2016)
16. Taggar, S.: Individual creativity and group ability to utilize individual creative resources: a multilevel model. Acad. Manage. J. **45**(2), 315–330 (2002)
17. Costa, P.T., Mccrae, R.R.: Normal personality assessment in clinical practice: the neo personality inventory. Psychol. Assess. **4**(1), 5–13 (1992)

Changes of sEMG Characteristics and Rated Perceived Exertion (RPE) Scale with Weight-Bearing Walking at Acute Hypobaric Hypoxia Environment

Jing Zhang, Jianlin Liu, Chao Sun, Jiachen Nie, Jiayin Li, Wanjing Jia, Xinli Yu, and Li Ding(✉)

Key Laboratory for Biomechanics and Mechanobiology of Ministry of Education, School of Biological Science and Medical Engineering, Beijing Advanced Innovation Center for Biomedical Engineering, Beihang University, Beijing, China
ding1971316@buaa.edu.cn

Abstract. In recent years, the popularity of high-altitude mountain climbing and hiking has soared. To mitigate muscle and bone damage, as well as human errors resulting from physical exhaustion, we investigated the perceived exertion and muscle fatigue during weighted hiking in acute hypobaric hypoxia environments. Eight subjects participated in this study, carrying a 15 kg backpack and walking on a treadmill at 2.5 km/h for 30 min in hypobaric chambers simulating altitudes of 40 m, 3500 m, and 4500 m, at a temperature of 24.2 ± 1.6 °C. Subjects reported their perceived exertion using the modified Borg CR10 RPE scale every 10 min, while surface electromyography (sEMG) data was collected from various muscle groups. Analysis revealed significant increases in RPE scores over time, with marked differences between 40 m and 4500 m, and between 3500 m and 4500 m. At 4500 m, the median frequency (MF) of the erector spinae muscle decreased significantly, while the biceps femoris exhibited initial activation followed by fatigue. Conversely, the biceps brachii and gastrocnemius muscles showed increased activation with exercise duration. This study offers insights into the physiological changes, fatigue progression, and safety considerations for weighted hikers in acute hypoxic environments.

Keywords: Surface EMG · Weight-bearing Walking · Acute Hypobaric Hypoxia · RPE scales

1 Introduction

In recent years, the increasing popularity of high-altitude tourism and outdoor adventures have led to a surge of engagement in hiking at high altitudes. The most significant threat to individuals performing high-intensity exercises at such altitudes is the hypoxia, in which a reduced oxygen partial pressure is inhaled by the human body [1]. During high-intensity exercises, higher physiological stress appears to adapt to the hypoxic conditions, increasing the likelihood of fatigue and subsequent human errors, such as falls and drops, which can lead to bodily injuries or even life-threatening situations.

S. Jin et al. (Eds.): IEA 2024, SSDI 39, pp. 483–488, 2025.
https://doi.org/10.1007/978-981-95-0211-0_73

Extensive research has been conducted on the physiological responses of the human body in acute hypoxic environments. Since the 1960s, high-altitude training for elite athletes has unveiled the effects of hypoxic exposure on the musculoskeletal system. Over the past two decades, researchers have utilized time-frequency domain parameters of heart rate variability to explore the complex cardiovascular regulation during rest and exercise. However, few studies examined fatigue in humans performing tasks in acute hypoxic environments. Nell et al. [2] investigated the effects of hypoxia on deoxygenation and recovery of the flexor digitorum superficialis muscle during submaximal intermittent exercise, revealing that acute exposure to normobaric hypoxia leads to a decrease in SmO2 and a greater degree of muscle fatigue. Research has also shown that muscle fatigue is exacerbated when lowlanders are exposed to severe hypoxia and further aggravated during whole-body exercise. The assessment of muscle fatigue during whole-body exercise often relies on subjective questionnaires and the analysis of surface electromyography (sEMG).

This study aims to study muscle fatigue and investigate the muscle activation patterns under fatigue and non-fatigue conditions in hypoxic environments by recording the sEMG signals of major muscles and Borg-10 Ratings of Perceived Exertion (RPE) scores of participants engaged in a weighted walking task with a 15 kg package for 30 min at three altitudes, including near sea level (40 m), 3500 m, and 4500 m.

2 Methods

2.1 Subjects

Eight healthy male subjects (age: 21.4 ± 1.7 years, height: 177.8 ± 4.2 cm, weight: 69.4 ± 4.9 kg) with regular exercise habits were recruited from fitness clubs for this study. All participants were raised at low altitudes (below 1500 m) and had no history of residing at high altitudes in the past year. This study was ethically approved by the Biomedical Engineering Ethics Committee of the university and adhered to the Declaration of Helsinki, with all participants signing an informed consent form.

2.2 Experimental Procedures

The subjects attended three weight-bearing hiking experiments (at 40 m, 3500 m and 4500 m altitude respectively) in a hypobaric simulation chamber (volume 4 m × 3 m × 3 m, capable of simulating environment of 0–20,000 m and − 40 ~ 50 °C) at the temperature of 24.2 ± 1.6 °C. To mitigate adaptation to the hypobaric environment, an interval exceeding one week was required between trials. This study adopted a single-blind randomized design, ensuring that participants were unaware of the varying altitudes throughout the experiments. The experimental protocol was executed as follows:

Subjects wore attire conducive to electrode placement, with disposable Ag/AgCl electrodes precisely affixed to the biceps brachii, erector spinae, biceps femoris, and gastrocnemius muscles. These electrodes were connected to a wireless EMG system (TeleMyo® 2400DTS, Noraxon Corporation, USA). Additionally, a physiological parameter monitor (Deluxe-70, Shenzhen Creative Industry Co., Ltd., China) was attached to the subjects' fingers. Participants entered the chamber and rested for 10 min. Then, the chamber operator precisely regulated the internal pressure, gradually increasing altitude at 5 m/s, interspersed with 10-min acclimatization periods for every 1000 m rise in altitude, until the desired altitude was attained. For ground-level experiments, the chamber's internal circulation device was activated to generate noise, obscuring the experimental conditions from the subjects. Upon reaching the target altitude, subjects rested for 10 min and provided a self-reported Modified Borg CR10 RPE scores (regarded as the score of start time of hiking). They then carried a backpack and walked on a treadmill at 2.5 km/h. Participants reported their RPE score at the 10th, 20th and 30th min, meanwhile the 40-s sEMG data were recorded. After walking for 30 min, the subject removed their backpack and sat still for 10 min, reporting their RPE score. The experimenter in the control cabin precisely modulates the low-pressure chamber and safely returns it to the ground at a constant rate of 5 m/s. Subjects are instructed to periodically swallow during this process to mitigate any potential ear discomfort.

Throughout the entire process, at least one experimenter accompanied the subject, continually monitored heart rate and SpO_2, and stopped the experiment if the subject's SpO_2 dipped below 75% or heart rate exceeded 180/min. Participants' subjective feelings were prioritized, allowing for experiment termination at any time upon request.

2.3 Data Processing and Statistical Analysis

The raw sEMG data underwent filtering through a fourth-order Butterworth band-pass filter (30–400 Hz) and a 50 Hz notch filter, followed by rectification. Time-frequency domain features (RMS, MF, ZCR) were then extracted using a sliding integration method with a 500 ms window, and the RMS values were normalized based on MVC. The mean and standard deviation of RPE scores of the participants were obtained.

Statistical analysis was performed using IBM SPSS 20.0 (IBM Corp., New York, NY, United States). After testing the normality and homogeneity of variance of the data, two-way ANOVA and Tukey's post-hoc test were employed to RPE scores, and the Mann-Whitney U test was utilized on sEMG characteristics to localize differences, among the three altitudes and walking time moments. The significance level was set at 0.05.

3 Results

3.1 RPE Scores at Different Moments While Hiking at Three Altitudes

The two-way ANOVA showed that there were significant main effects on RPE between altitudes ($F = 29.257, P < 0.001$) and time points ($F = 20.783, P < 0.001$). The interaction was not significant ($F = 0.326, P = 0.955$). Tukey's test revealed significant differences in RPE scores among different altitudes or various time points (Table 1). The RPE scores rose progressively with increasing hiking duration, but declined after 10-min post-rest, and at the same time point, the RPE score was higher at 4500 m than both at 40 m and 3500 m (Fig. 1).

Table 1 The RPE scores for walking and resting at three altitudes

	RPE Score		
	40 m	3500 m	4500 m
walk_0min	1.13 ± 0.99 cB	1.31 ± 1.33 bB	2.94 ± 1.02 cA
walk_10min	2.38 ± 1.06 abcB	3.00 ± 1.41 abB	5.00 ± 1.22 abA
walk_20min	3.94 ± 1.97 abB	4.13 ± 1.25 aB	6.13 ± 1.25 abA
walk_30min	4.13 ± 2.10 aB	4.38 ± 1.51 aAB	6.56 ± 1.59 aA
rest_10min	1.88 ± 0.99 bcB	3.13 ± 1.34 abAB	4.25 ± 1.49 bcA

Note: RPE scores are presented as mean ± standard deviation. Different lowercase letters indicate significant differences ($P < 0.001$) in RPE scores among different time points at the same altitude. Different uppercase letters represent significant differences ($P < 0.05$) in RPE scores between different altitudes at the same time point

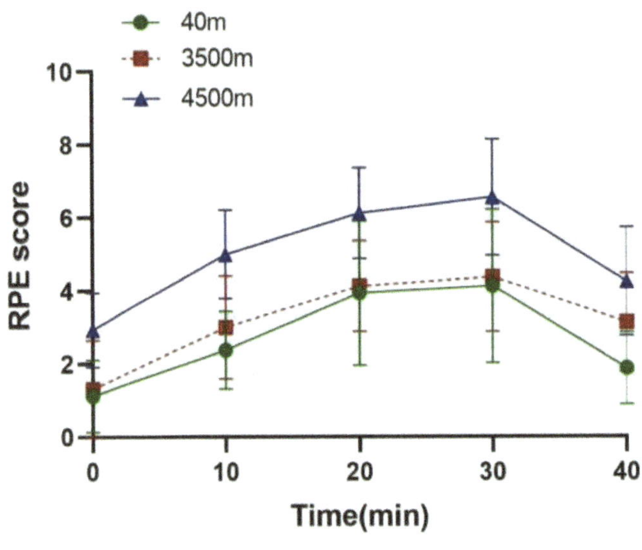

Fig. 1. Changes in RPE scores during hiking and post-rest periods at three altitudes.

3.2 Surface EMG Characteristics at Different Moments While Hiking at Three Altitudes

The normalized RMS, MF reduced proportion (relative to the resting state before hiking), and ZRC values of the biceps brachii, erector spinae, biceps femoris, and gastrocnemius muscles are depicted in Fig. 2. According to the normalized RMS, compared to low-altitude hiking, high-altitude hiking led to increased activation of the erector spinae and biceps brachii, while there was a decrease in the gastrocnemius ($P < 0.05$). Relative to the initial hiking time, the MF reduced proportion of the erector spinae at 4500 m increased significantly with hiking duration, while the biceps femoris exhibited a certain degree of reduction (P < 0.05). At 10 min and 20 min of hiking, the ZRC of the gastrocnemius at 4500 m was significantly lower than that at 40 m (P < 0.05). However, after 30 min of hiking, the ZRC of the erector spinae at 4500 m altitude was significantly higher than that at 40 m (P < 0.05).

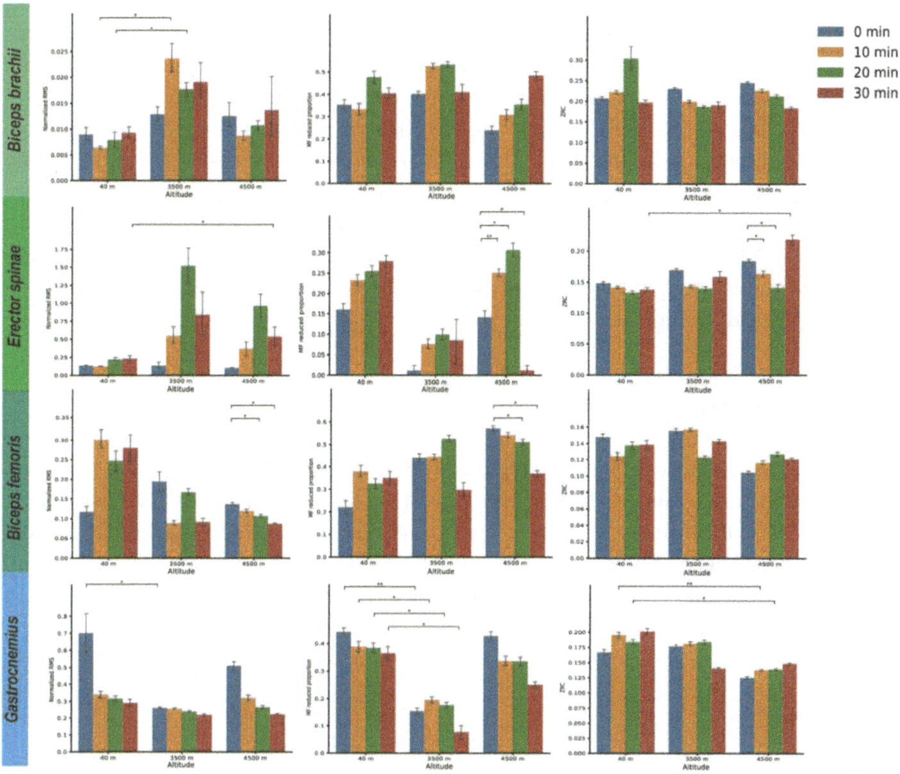

Fig. 2. The sEMG characteristics of muscles during hiking at three altitudes (* *P < 0.05*, ** *P < 0.01*).

4 Discussion

This study delved into the disparities in fatigue levels and sEMG features among humans performing loaded walking under acute hypoxic conditions, in contrast to near sea-level conditions. At a constant altitude, the RPE score escalated with an increment in hiking duration, primarily attributed to the cumulative impact of load duration on the human body. Notably, for a comparable hiking duration, fatigue perception was significantly augmented at 4500 m compared to 40 m and 3500 m, whereas no significant variance in RPE was observed between 40 m and 3500 m. Attributed to the diminished oxygen content at higher altitudes, the respiratory and circulatory systems are initially activated to compensate, elevating heart rate and gas exchange to furnish the body with essential oxygen [3]. At 3500 m, the cardiovascular system's overcompensation is adequate to fulfill oxygen requirements for 30 min of hiking. However, at 4500 m, where oxygen content barely surpasses half of the sea-level concentration, severe hypoxia prevails, rendering the body more susceptible to overall fatigue induced by hypoxia during high-intensity exercise.

Concise EMG alterations substantiate the observations. Compared to sea-level walking, high-altitude hiking induced increased activation in the erector spinae and biceps brachii, while the biceps femoris and gastrocnemius activations remained unchanged. At 4500 m, the erector spinae exhibited a decreased mean frequency (MF) and elevated zero-crossing rate (ZRC), while the gastrocnemius ZRC declined. This indicates that under hypoxic conditions, the cardiovascular system overcompensates to oxygenate skeletal muscles [4]. However, with persistent hypoxia and muscular oxygen depletion, the body recruits additional muscle groups, such as the arms and waist, to assist in hiking movements. While legs primarily bear force at sea level, as altitude rises, force distribution shifts, emphasizing the synergistic role of muscles across the body in coping with physical demands at high altitudes.

5 Conclusion

This study found that at 4500 m, the fatigue level increase noticeably than that of ground and 3500 m, resulting in faster muscle fatigue in the human body. As altitude increases, there is a shift in the primary force-bearing regions, with an elevated activation of arm and waist muscles. This mobilization of the entire body's muscles is a response to cope with the physical demands of the task. The finding is of great significance for understanding the physiological changes during working or exercise in plateau environments.

References

1. Hohenauer, E., et al.: The methodological quality of studies investigating the acute effects of exercise during hypoxia over the past 40 years: a systematic review. Front. Physiol. **13**, 919359 (2022). https://doi.org/10.3389/fphys.2022.919359
2. Yamaguchi, K., Sumi, D., Hayashi, N., Ota, N., Ienaga, K., Goto, K.: Effects of combined hot and hypoxic conditions on muscle blood flow and muscle oxygenation during repeated cycling sprints. Eur. J. Appl. Physiol. **121**(10), 2869–2878 (2021). https://doi.org/10.1007/s00421-021-04738-w
3. Vasquez-Bonilla, A.A., Rojas-Valverde, D., González-Custodio, A., Timón, R., Olcina, G.: Tent versus mask-on acute effects during repeated-sprint training in normobaric hypoxia and normoxia. J. Clin. Med. **10**, 21 (2021). https://doi.org/10.3390/jcm10214879
4. Gronwald, T., Hoos, O., Hottenrott, K.: Effects of acute normobaric hypoxia on non-linear dynamics of cardiac autonomic activity during constant workload cycling exercise. Front. Physiol. **10**, 999 (2019). https://doi.org/10.3389/fphys.2019.00999

Evaluation of Mattress Surface Curves with sEMG and Body Pressure Distribution Analysis Based on Vacuum Mattress

Jing Zhang[1], Ying Gao[1], Mengchen Tang[1], Liwen Bi[1], Chengzhao Zou[1], Fujun Zhang[2], Fanglai Yao[2], and Li Ding[1](✉)

[1] Key Laboratory for Biomechanics and Mechanobiology of Ministry of Education, School of Biological Science and Medical Engineering, Beijing Advanced Innovation Center for Biomedical Engineering, Beihang University, Beijing, China
ding1971316@buaa.edu.cn

[2] Sleep Research Institute, De Rucci Healthy Sleep Co., Ltd, Dongguan, China

Abstract. Sleep is a crucial aspect of human daily life, and the performance of a mattress plays a significant role in sleep comfort. In order to investigate the impact of different mattress curves on muscle activity and contact pressure on the human body, this study utilized three-dimensional scanning techniques on deformable vacuum mattress and obtained four types of mattress curves (no curve, knee elevation, hip subsidence and shoulder elevation) impacting sleep biomechanics comfort during supine sleeping postures. The surface electromyography (sEMG) and pressure distribution measurements were conducted on 12 participants targeting the muscles including the trapezius, erector spinae, gluteus medius, and biceps femoris on four mattress curves. The results indicated that the elevated knee curve and sinking hip curve have a relaxing effect on the erector spinae muscle. Compared to non curved mattresses, the three types of curved mattresses significantly reduce the maximum pressure peak. Through the integration of sEMG and pressure distribution analyses, the sinking hip curve exhibited the highest level of sleep comfort. This study objectively elucidates the impact of positional curves on human sleep comfort and providing guidance for mattress design.

Keywords: Mattress Curve · sEMG · Pressure Distribution · Vacuum Mattress

1 Introduction

Sleep is an integral part of human daily routines. In recent years, people are gradually realizing the importance of sleep quality, and the ergonomic design of bedding such as mattresses is also receiving attention. Studies have shown that uncomfortable mattresses can affect the distribution of spinal loads during sleep, potentially leading to pressure sores, muscle tension, spinal discomfort, and poor blood supply, increasing the risk of musculoskeletal injuries [1]. Appropriate mattress curvature can provide effective body support, reduce musculoskeletal loads, and improve sleep comfort. Designing mattress curvature that conforms to the human sleeping posture and objectively quantifying the

S. Jin et al. (Eds.): IEA 2024, SSDI 39, pp. 489–495, 2025.
https://doi.org/10.1007/978-981-95-0211-0_74

muscle load and body pressure distribution of different mattress curvatures gradually become the focus of mattress manufacturers and ergonomists.

Pressure distribution testing is a commonly used and reliable experimental method in evaluating sleep comfort. In mattress comfort evaluation, pressure distribution can objectively reflect the human-mattress interaction, providing important references for mattress evaluation and zoning design [2]. Muscle activity are also one of the research directions of comfort. Proper mattress performance and sleeping posture will reduce muscle load during sleep, promoting muscle relaxation and benefiting sleep comfort. Surface electromyography (sEMG), as a relatively easy-to-obtain electrophysiological signal, can provide real-time feedback on muscle force, favored by biomechanical researchers [3]. Furthermore, memory vacuum mattress that can deform based on body surface morphology have been widely used in ergonomics and rehabilitation fields, which enable the simulation and measurement of sleep sinkholes and to achieve curve construction on soft mattresses. Compared to commercial ribbed frames and other mechanical adjustment methods, although there is a certain artificial error in curve construction on memory vacuum mattress, it is more convenient and can be further fine-tuned according to the situation of the subjects, "customizing" different surface shapes.

This study investigates the sEMG characteristics of major muscles (trapezius, erector spinae, gluteus medius, and biceps femoris) and body pressure distribution under different mattress curves based on vacuum mattress and 3D scanning technology, determining the effects of different curves on muscle activity and contact pressure on the body, to provide insights for mattress design and optimization.

2 Methods

2.1 Subjects

Twelve healthy subjects (age: 21.8 ± 1.7 years, height: 170.2 ± 11.3 cm, weight: 60.4 ± 9.1 kg) participated in the experiment, which was approved by the Biomedical Engineering Ethics Committee of the University and conducted in accordance with the Helsinki Declaration.

2.2 Experimental Procedures

2.2.1 Extraction of Supine Sleeping Posture Curve on Non-Curved Soft Mattress

To guide the subsequent experiments in curve design, a 3D scanner (Go! SCAN 50, CREAFORMTM, Canada) was used to measure the sleeping posture curves of 12 participants on the positioning mattress. After the experimenter set the positioning mattress (2,991,163/V, Stabilo Grande by AAT, Poland) to a flat, hard and non-deformable state, the participants lay on the vacuum mattress. The experimenter started the mattress pump, deflating the mattress to simulate the softness of a typical soft mattress. During this process, participants remained relaxed, and the mattress collapsed where in contact with the body, forming the sleeping posture curve. After the subject stood up, the experimenter scanned the mattress surface with the handheld 3D scanner and converted it as a 3D model.

2.2.2 Collection of sEMG and Pressure Distribution for Four Mattress Curves

Based on the analysis of the naturally lying posture curves of participants, four support curves were simulated using the memory mattress: no curve, knee elevation, hip subsidence, and shoulder elevation. Firstly, the sEMG sensors were connected to electrodes on the muscles. The vacuum mattress was inflated to prevent deformation and the pressure mat was spread over the mattress. Then, the participant lay flat on their backs with legs shoulder-width apart and arms naturally placed. The experimenter collected the participant's sEMG with 2000 Hz frequency (eego™, ANT Neuro, German) for 40 seconds, and the pressure data of pressure mat (MFD1–007/Smart Pressure Test Mat, DeRUCCI Co. Ltd., China) for 15 seconds. Then, based on the participant's preference, the experimenter set the positioning mattress to knee elevation positions and fine-tuned the curves to align the corresponding body part with the curve. Participants lay on the mattress and the experimenter collected sEMG and pressure distribution.Finally, the participant stood up, and the experimenter reshaped and adjusted the mattress to other two curves for data collection. The trials sequence for four curves is randomly conducted among 12 subjects.

2.3 Data Processing and Statistical Analysis

Matlab 2020b (The MathWorks, Natick, Massachusetts, USA) was used for data processing. The continuous 15 s sEMG signals were filtered using a fourth-order Butterworth bandpass filter with 20–500 Hz and a 50 Hz notch filter, followed by the calculation of integrated electromyographic (iEMG) values. The iEMG of each muscle on a specific curve were normalized relative to the that on a flat mattress. The maximum and average pressures values were calculated for statistical analysis.

Statistical analysis was performed using IBM SPSS 20.0. After confirming that the data conforms to normal distribution and homogeneity of variance, One-way analysis of variance (ANOVA) and LSD multiple comparisons were employed to analyze the the normalized iEMG values, maximum and average pressures under different mattress curves. The significance level is set to 0.05.

3 Results

3.1 Analysis of Mattress Surface After Human Body Supine Sleeping On

The 3D surface image of vacuum mattress after the subject lying supine on top is shown in Fig. 1. By amalgamating the mattress surfaces of 12 participants, the 3D surface of body segments revealed noticeable depressions at the shoulders, buttocks, thighs and shins area. Conversely, there was less pronounced sinking at the knee positions, resulting in a raised knee effect. Starting from the assumption that "mattress curves should closely conform to the human body" mattress curves that elevate the knees, sink the hips, and raise the shoulders may potentially contribute to improving sleep comfort.

Fig. 1. The deformed vacuum mattress and surface 3D scanning image after lying supine on.

3.2 Analysis of sEMG and Pressure Distribution of Four Mattress Curves

The variables including both normalized iEMG and pressure values were found to meet the assumptions of normality and homogeneity of variance. Results revealed that both knee elevation curve and hip subsidence curve have significant differences ($P < 0.01$) from the normalized iEMG value of no curve surface (Fig. 2). However, the results of other tests indicated no significant differences in the iEMG values of other muscles under the three designed mattress curves compared to the no curve mattress.

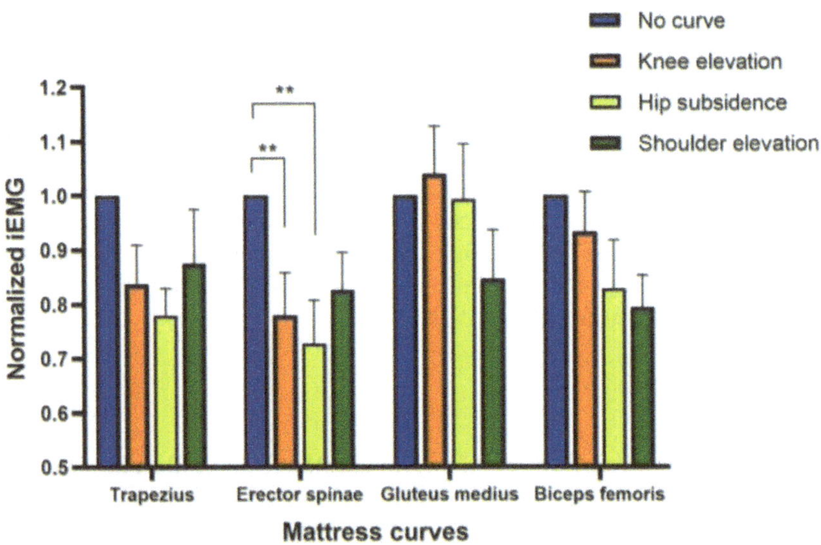

Fig. 2. Normalized iEMG values of muscles under four mattress curves (** $P < 0.01$).

The mean and standard deviation (SD) of maximum and average body pressure values of 12 subjects are shown in Table 1. One-way ANOVA showed that there was a significant difference ($P < 0.05$) in the maximum pressure among mattress curves, while there was no significant difference in the average pressure. The LSD multiple comparison results of maximum pressure revealed that There is no significant difference in the maximum pressure value between the knee raising curve and the shoulder elevation curve, while there are significant differences in the maximum pressure value between any other two mattress curves (see Fig. 3).

Table 1 Maximum and average pressure values of 12 subjects

	Maximum pressure (mmHg)	Average pressure (mmHg)
No curve	69.35 ± 3.00^{a}	12.12 ± 2.85
Knee elevation curve	58.40 ± 8.78^{b}	11.62 ± 2.23
Hip subsidence curve	49.29 ± 9.90^{c}	10.61 ± 2.10
Shoulder elevation curve	60.18 ± 8.17^{b}	11.26 ± 3.08

Note: values are presented as mean ± SD. Use LSD multiple comparisons for maximum pressure values. Labeling with different letters indicates significant differences between groups (P < 0.05)

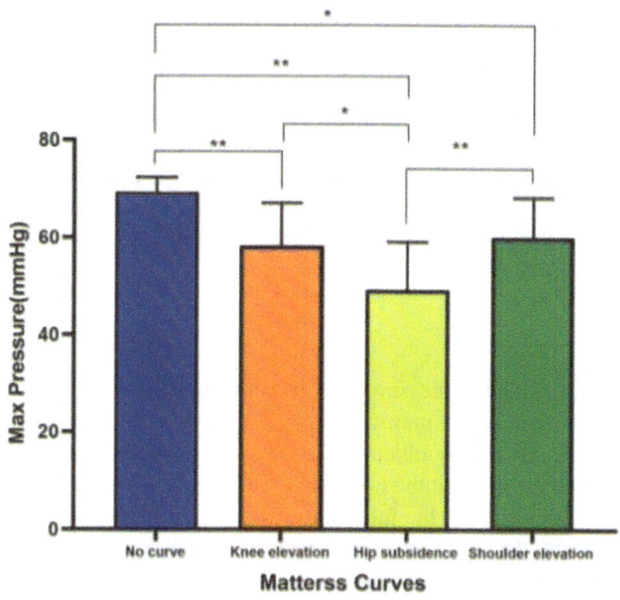

Fig. 3. Maximum pressure of four mattress curves (* $P < 0.05$, ** $P < 0.01$).

4 Discussion

The normalized iEMG values analysis indicates that the mattress with buttock sinking or knee elevation curve have relaxation effect on the lumbar muscles. The supine position with hips sinking contributes to the relaxation of the lumbar region, involving various factors such as the physiological curvature of the spine, muscle stretching, and decompression of inter-vertebral discs. Elevating the knees can assist in decompressing the lumbar nerve roots, reducing the degree of compression on these roots, thereby alleviating lumbar discomfort. Bergholdt et al. [4] conducted interviews with patients suffering from chronic low back pain, and the results indicated that compared to a firm mattress, a certain degree of deformity had a more positive impact on back pain and activities of daily living. When the waist is supported, the pelvis tilts slightly backward, allowing the entire spine to typically maintain its physiological curvature better, thus helping to alleviate pressure on the lumbar spine and pelvic area and reducing the load on these muscles, which eventually reflected in changes of the lumbar muscles sEMG.

From the perspective of pressure distribution, smaller values for maximum pressure indicate higher comfort. Compared with no curve, mattresses with knee elevation, hip subsidence, and shoulder elevation curves can significantly reduce the maximum pressure value, and the values under the hip subsidence curve is significantly lower than the other three curves (Table 1 and Fig. 3). Lee et al. [5], in comparing mattresses defined as comfortable or uncomfortable based on pressure distribution when standing and lying down, concluded that a comfortable mattress needs to support the spine and reduce unnecessary body movement. When lying supine, the pelvic region experiences higher pressure values compared to the thoracic spine area, which might lead to greater improvements in comfort through alterations in the hip curve. Elevating the shoulders and knees can somewhat mitigate the impact of hip support, allowing the lumbar spine to be in a relatively flat position, achieving a similar effect to hip sinking. Overall, the mattress curve design that conforms to the natural concave characteristics of the body in a supine position has a significant effect on relaxing the lumbar muscles and reducing the peak pressure distribution on the human body.

5 Conclusion

The study utilized sEMG and pressure distribution to quantitatively describe body load differences under four different mattress curves. We concluded that a mattress that provides effective support in the shoulders, waist, and knees can effectively reduce the peak pressure distribution throughout the body, and the knee elevation curve and hip sinking curve have a relaxing effect on the lumbar erector spinae. These research findings provide guidance for the design of emerging mattresses and enrich the understanding of mattress curve influences on sleep comfort.

References

1. Wong, D.W.-C., Wang, Y., Lin, J., Tan, Q., Chen, T.L.-W., Zhang, M.: Sleeping mattress determinants and evaluation: a biomechanical review and critique. PeerJ. **7**, e6364 (2019). https://doi.org/10.7717/peerj.6364
2. Shirogane, S., Toyama, S., Hoshino, M., Takashima, A., Tanaka, T.: Quantitative measurement of the pressure and shear stress acting on the body of a wheelchair user using a wearable sheet-type sensor: a preliminary study. Int. J. Environ. Res. Public Health. **19**, 20 (2022). https://doi.org/10.3390/ijerph192013579

3. Radwan, A., et al.: Effect of different mattress designs on promoting sleep quality, pain reduction, and spinal alignment in adults with or without back pain; systematic review of controlled trials. Sleep Health. **1**(4), 257–267 (2015). https://doi.org/10.1016/j.sleh.2015.08.001
4. Bergholdt, K., Fabricius, R.N., Bendix, T.: Better backs by better beds? Spine (Phila Pa 1976). **33**(7), 703–708 (2008). https://doi.org/10.1097/BRS.0b013e3181695d3b
5. Lee, H., Park, S.: Quantitative effects of mattress types (comfortable vs. uncomfortable) on sleep quality through polysomnography and skin temperature. Int. J. Ind. Ergon. **36**(11), 943–949 (2006). https://doi.org/10.1016/j.ergon.2006.07.007

Building and Construction (I)

Urban Morphology, Comfort Conditions and Non-Ionizing Radiation in Home Offices Located on Heat Islands in the City of João Pessoa, Brazil

Flávia Brandão Ramalho de Brito(✉) and Luiz Bueno da Silva

Federal University of Paraíba, João Pessoa, Paraíba, Brazil
flavia_britoo@hotmail.com

Abstract. The SARS-CoV-2 pandemic, responsible for the COVID-19 disease, has led to an increase in the number of people working from home and the amount of time spent on remote work activities. Hence, it becomes imperative to enhance the thermal and environmental comfort, given the heightened frequency of computer screen usage, compounded by the rise in heat sources within the environment. However, over the last few decades, there has been an increase in understanding modern sources of lower frequency radiation in and around building complexes, and their effects on inhabitants and their surroundings. Non-ionizing radiation (NIR) includes a variety of low-frequency electromagnetic radiation that is generated by a variety of sources, such as household appliances, Wi-Fi systems, cell phones, and other electronic devices. Additionally, urban morphology (UM) may also play a role in radiation exposure depending on factors such as population density, building distribution, and communications infrastructure. Thus, this article presents a preliminary study observing and analyzing aspects of the UM (surroundings), thermal characteristics and NIR levels in 13 home offices located in heat islands in the city of João Pessoa, Paraíba, Brazil. The results demonstrate that all home offices presented temperatures and NIR levels above the recommended levels established by current standards and literature. Furthermore, in home offices located in heat islands, the combination of total built density, the roughness and height of tall buildings, and a low sky view factor provides evidence of thermal discomfort and elevated NIR intensity levels in these areas.

Keywords: Indoor comfort · urban morphology · non-ionizing radiation

1 Introduction

Many countries, post-pandemic, have favored and encouraged remote work environments. Consequently, homes have become an extension of companies, but their environments need to meet comfort standards. During the pandemic, a reflection emerged on how we spend all our time in different environments that can be devoid of comfort from an environmental perspective, including thermal and non-ionizing radiation, as well as aspects of urban morphology (UM). Non-ionizing radiation (NIR) is present

S. Jin et al. (Eds.): IEA 2024, SSDI 39, pp. 499–504, 2025.
https://doi.org/10.1007/978-981-95-0211-0_75

in these environments provided with modern technologies, and their surroundings have electrical transformers and morphological characteristics that can intensify them.

Urban morphology is directly related to the quality of life in cities and can affect mobility and environmental comfort. Therefore, building occupants are not isolated from their neighborhood environment. Buildings not only serve to protect occupants from the external environment and harsh weather, but also bring in favorable natural elements such as natural lighting and fresh air. For occupants' work and life, the impact of the neighborhood environment is a key factor that cannot be neglected when studying occupants and their indoor environment [1]. Morphology plays an increasingly important role in changes to the urban microclimate. However, few studies have focused on how such changes are exhibited in indoor environments. Furthermore, due to human activities, cities are experiencing a series of environmental problems, including urban overheating caused by both global warming and the phenomenon of urban heat islands. This excessive urban densification can lead to the formation of heat islands, which are areas with anomalous microclimates caused by the verticalization of buildings and the absence of vegetation, among other factors. This results in increased local temperatures, wind channeling, and unwanted sun exposure, which can lead to greater energy consumption [2].

Therefore, according to [3], even with the relief and end of the pandemic, homes need to be able to answer questions about how to minimize the environmental effect and how to maintain and improve the comfort of people who spend most of their time at home. Thus, the goal of this article is to present an initial study to observe and analyze certain characteristics of urban morphology (surroundings), thermal characteristics and the behavior of non-ionizing radiation levels in 13 home offices located in heat islands in the city of João Pessoa, Paraíba, Brazil.

2 Methodology

Thermal variables – air temperature (t_a); globe temperature (t_g) and mean radiant temperature (t_{mr}) – were measured in 13 home offices over 3 consecutive days using the TGD 400 equipment, as per [4]. The levels of non-ionizing radiation (NIR) at the frequency of 60 Hz were obtained using the Aaronia USA Spectran NF-5035 Spectrum Analyzer. NIR levels $>0.4\mu T$ were considered risk levels for the development of biological alterations in the human body [5–7].

The graphical processing of urban vector data was carried out using the Geographic Information System program QGIS 2.18.2. Based on the vector data, a circular section of the urban network was delimited with a radius of 250 m around each workstation. The methodology used to define and calculate the morphological indicators was developed by [8]. The indicators calculated were total usable built area, built density, land occupation rate, roughness and sky view factor (SVF). After the maps containing information on building height and built and non-built areas were produced in QGIS, the data were stored in Excel software spreadsheets, which were used to calculate the aforementioned indicators.

3 Results and Discussions

3.1 Thermal Variables, Non-ionizing Radiation, and Urban Morphology

Table 1 presents the values of thermal indicators with their respective means and standard deviation (SD), as well as data on non-ionizing radiation, such as maximum value and proportion of records above 0.4 μT for each home office (HO) studied. It also provides the results of morphological indicators in the surroundings of the studied environments. It was found that all home offices exhibited temperatures above what is recommended by international standards [9, 10] for indoor work environments where activities requiring intellectual engagement are performed. It is observed that, in all home offices, the air, globe and average radiant temperatures are very close and high, a minimum of 28 °C and a maximum of 31 °C, during three consecutive days, in a daily period 6 to 8 h of remote activities. And according to [11], working in inadequate thermal environments affects the autonomic nervous system, responsible for maintaining body homeostasis, and severe cases can lead to cardiovascular diseases. These environments can also impair cognitive function, decision-making ability, and work performance.

Table 1. Summary Table - Thermal Indicators, NIR, and Morphological Indicators.

	T_{air} (°C)		T_{globe} (°C)		T_{mr} (°C)		NIR (μT)		maximum value (μT)	proportion of records above 0,4 μT (%)	total constructed useful area (m2)	total built density	Maximum height (m)	average height (m)	occupancy rate	absolute roughness	sky view factor
	mean	S.D.	mean	S.D.	mean	S.D.	mean	S.D.									
HO_1	30,48	0,41	30,6	0,43	30,63	0,43	1,25	0,21	2,76	100%	183827,63	735	36	6,76	237,29	4,20	0,68
HO_2	29,41	0,43	29,68	0,4	29,75	0,39	1,25	0,21	2,16	100%	148135,50	593	24	5,72	255,79	3,10	0,73
HO_3	28,28	0,33	28,43	0,35	28,47	0,36	1,11	0,005	1,32	100%	178141,00	688	81	5,51	288,77	3,34	0,61
HO_4	29,56	0,28	29,55	0,20	29,55	0,19	1,11	0,00	1,6	98,38%	90673,94	362	39	8,89	76,25	4,65	0,9
HO_5	28,9	0	29,7	0	29,97	0	1,2	0,09	1,55	100%	150119,00	601	63	7,83	180,00	1,99	0,82
HO_6	29,4	0,21	29,2	0,2	29,15	0,21	1,46	0,35	2,88	100%	120789,88	483	36	4,97	266,03	2,66	0,8
HO_7	28,45	1	28,55	0,85	28,58	0,79	1,12	0,10	1,55	76%	91136,00	364	12	4,30	228,23	1,87	0,83
HO_8	29,54	0,33	29,81	0,4	29,88	0,43	1,2	0,08	1,55	92,20%	75713,30	303	12	4,10	197,58	1,50	0,83
HO_9	29,75	0,46	29,73	0,45	29,73	0,45	1,2	0,07	1,51	100%	119951,78	480	33	4,60	280,42	2,60	0,97
HO_{10}	31,1	0,32	31,1	0,34	31,1	0,35	1,2	0,00	1,3	100%	255879,08	1023	123	8,97	174,71	4,81	0,95
HO_{11}	30,84	0,77	31,05	0,71	31,1	0,71	1,12	0,00	1,13	100%	112099,33	448	21	11,20	93,17	5,05	0,89
HO_{12}	29,04	0,45	29,51	0,34	29,67	0,36	2,16	0,50	1,4	100%	557651,77	2231	96	16,00	276,93	11,03	0,29
HO_{13}	30,69	0,3	30,71	0,23	30,71	0,22	1,22	0,04	1,48	100%	483644,00	1935	48	11,34	361,91	10,30	0,50

In relation to NIR, it can be seen, according to Table 1, that all home offices presented values higher than those recommended by current research (>0.4μT), on average from 1.1 to 2.1μT, with a 100% proportion record above 0.4μT, which according to [7], this residential exposure for long periods of time can cause epidemiological problems for residents, especially with regard to the problem of childhood leukemia. Sources of non-ionizing electromagnetic radiation may be of clinical importance as a small increase in exposure may cause health risks. However, the maximum NIR level was 2.76μT in HO_1 with Tmr = 30.63 °C, and total density built around 731. This combination of these three variables could lead to multiple adverse factors, with an impact on comfort and worker productivity, in addition to developing possible long-term health problems.

Still according to Table 1, it is observed that home offices 12 and 13 had the highest levels of roughness (11.03 and 10.30, respectively), and the lowest SVF (0.29 and 0.50 respectively), which makes these buildings susceptible to lower intensities of average wind speed. These locations stand out for presenting a wide variation in the height and shape of buildings and a mix of natural and built elements that create a visually complex urban landscape. Furthermore, low SVF combined with high roughness can create a less comfortable thermal environment, due to less natural ventilation and greater heat retention, which is confirmed by the air temperature in these two HOs being around 30 °C. Another point to highlight is that its NIRs exceed 0.4μT, – 2.16 and 1.22 -, respectively, as high roughness can result in variations in occupant exposure.

3.2 UM Indicators on NIR Levels and Thermal Aspects

Table 2 shows a significant moderate association of some thermal indicators with the roughness and average height of buildings around home offices. The relationship between thermal variables and roughness is around $r \approx 0.6$ with p_value < 0.05; and the relationship between thermal variables and average height of buildings is close to $r \approx 0.5$ with p_value < 0.05. These findings warn that, if morphological aspects such as roughness and height of buildings present high values around home offices, it is likely that air temperature, globe temperature, average radiant temperature and thermal radiation exceed thermal comfort levels, resulting in greater discomfort for people while carrying out their activities in each Home Office. Both high roughness and the height of buildings contribute to the phenomenon of urban heat islands. The retention of heat by rough surfaces and the obstruction of natural ventilation by tall buildings intensify this effect, raising temperatures in home offices, given that in the sample collected the minimum average temperature was 28.4 °C in HO_3, and the average temperature maximum was 31.1 °C in HO_{10}, as shown in Table 1.

Table 2. Spearman Correlation Matrix.

Indicators	Maximum height	Average height	Useful area	Built density	Sky view factor	Roughness
Mean T_{air}	0.146	0.505^{a}	0.33	0.33	0.184	$0.599^{a}*$
Mean T_{mr}	0.025	0.522^{a} ·	0.324	0.324	−0.017	$0.577^{a}*$
Mean T_{globe}	0.146	0.505^{a}	0.33	0.33	0.184	$0.599^{a}*$

(*continued*)

Table 2. (*continued*)

Indicators	Maximum height	Average height	Useful area	Built density	Sky view factor	Roughness
T_{globe}- T_{air}	0.025	0.522[a]	0.324	0.324	−0.017	0.577[a]*
Mean NIR	−0.352	−0.28	−0.209	−0.209	−0.204	−0.308
S.D. NIR	−0.091	−0.154	−0.181	−0.181	−0.239	−0.255

[a]Moderate correlations
*Significant correlations at a 0.05 significance level

4 Conclusions

Urban morphology plays an increasingly important role in changes in the urban microclimate. However, few studies have focused on how such changes are exhibited in indoor environments. On the other hand, energy has become an essential part of today's lifestyle, especially for the daily use of household appliances in homes, offices and other built environments.

Although electronic devices have become ubiquitous in modern life, excessive electromagnetic radiation from these devices can cause health effects that affect the performance of their occupants. And in these heat islands there may be unsustainable buildings with remote domestic environments as an extension of companies.

The study carried out highlighted the importance of analyzing comfort in the internal environment but taking into account its surroundings, and raises the hypothesis that in its surroundings there may be factors that intensify levels of discomfort in home remote work environments.

The results presented should be considered as reflections of how areas considered heat islands can contribute to an increase in both internal and external ambient temperatures, which in turn can influence the propagation and intensity of non-ionizing radiation. The additional heat can affect the dispersion of electromagnetic radiation, potentially increasing its intensity in areas affected by these heat islands. And on these islands, tall buildings can block or reflect radiation, while narrow streets can increase radiation exposure by creating "urban canyons" that channel radiation between buildings.

Finally, it is worth noting that the results presented provide support for other more robust studies, given that the data presented in Tables 1 and 2 provide evidence that roughness, density and height of tall buildings can compromise thermal comfort in home offices, especially if they are located in na urban heat island. Another consistent finding in these tables provides preliminary evidence indicating that a high sky view factor may reduce the intensity of non-ionizing radiation levels in home offices.

References

1. Chan, I.Y.S., Liu, A.M.M.: Effects of neighborhood building density, height, greenspace, and cleanliness on indoor environment and health of building occupants. Build. Environ. **145**, 213–222 (2018)

2. Barbosa, G.S., Drach, P.R.C., Corbella, O.D.: Intraurban temperature variations: urban morphologies of the densification process of copacabana neighborhood, Brazil. Climate. **7**, 65 (2019)
3. Tokazhanov, G., Tleuke, A., Guney, M., Turkyilmaz, A., Karaca, F.: How is COVID-19 experience transforming sustainability requirements of residential buildings? A review. Sustainability. **12**, 8732 (2020)
4. ISO 7726: Ergonomics of the Thermal Environment—Instruments for Measuring Physical Quantities. Standard International Organization for Standardization, Geneva, Switzerland (2002)
5. Zaryabova, V., Shalamanova, T., Israel, M.: Pilot study of extremely low frequency magnetic fields emitted by transformers in dwellings. Social aspects. Electromagn. Biol. Med. **32**, 209–217 (2013)
6. Grellier, J., Ravazzani, P., Cardis, E.: Potential health impacts of residential exposures to extremely low frequency magnetic fields in Europe. Environ. Int. **62**, 55–63 (2014)
7. Elwood, M.: Epidemiological studies of low-intensity ELF fields and diseases in humans. In: Wood, A.W., Karipidis, K. (eds.) Non-Ionizing—Radiation Protection, pp. 313–321. Wiley, Hoboken, NJ (2017)
8. Martins, T.A.L., Bonhomme, M., Adolphe, L.: Evaluation of the impact of urban morphology on the estimated energy demand of buildings: a case study in Maceió, Brazil. Ambiente Construído. **13**, 213–233 (2013)
9. ISO 7730: Ergonomics of the Thermal Environment: Analytical Determination and Interpretation of Thermal Comfort Using calculation of the PMV and PPD Indices and Local Thermal Comfort. Standard International Organization for Standardization, Geneva, Switzerland (2005)
10. ISO 9241: Ergonomic Requirements for Office Work with Visual Display Terminals (VDTs) Part 12: Presentation of Information. Standard International Organization for Standardization, Geneva, Switzerland (2012)
11. Shin, Y.-S., Ko, J.-B., Cha, D.-A., Hong, J.-S.: The effect of length of service in a thermal environment on thermal comfort and mental stress. Buildings. **14**, 99 (2024)

Author Index

S. Jin et al. (Eds.): IEA 2024, SSDI 39, pp. 505–508, 2025.
https://doi.org/10.1007/978-981-95-0211-0

The manufacturer's authorised representative in the EU is Springer Nature Customer Service Centre GmbH, Europaplatz 3, 69115 Heidelberg, Germany. If you have any concerns regarding our products, please contact ProductSafety@springernature.com

Printed and bound by CPI Group (UK) Ltd, Croydon, CR0 4YY
30/09/2026
02225300-0017